Taming Uncertainty

Taming Uncertainty

Ralph Hertwig, Timothy J. Pleskac, Thorsten Pachur,
and The Center for Adaptive Rationality

The MIT Press
Cambridge, Massachusetts
London, England

This book was set in Stone Serif by Westchester Publishing Services. Printed and bound in the United States of America.

Library of Congress Cataloging-in-Publication Data

Names: Hertwig, Ralph, author. | Pleskac, Timothy J., author. | Pachur, Thorsten, author.
Title: Taming uncertainty / Ralph Hertwig, Timothy J. Pleskac, and Thorsten Pachur.
Description: Cambridge, MA : MIT Press, [2019] | Includes bibliographical references and index.
Identifiers: LCCN 2018041802 | ISBN 9780262039871 (hardcover : alk. paper)
Subjects: LCSH: Uncertainty. | Decision making--Psychological aspects.
Classification: LCC BF463.U5 H47 2019 | DDC 153.8/3--dc23
LC record available at https://lccn.loc.gov/2018041802

10 9 8 7 6 5 4 3 2 1

Dedicated to all things uncertain including death and taxes.

Contents

Preface   xi

Contributors   xv

I   The Research Agenda

1   Reckoning with Uncertainty: Our Program of Research   3
Ralph Hertwig, Timothy J. Pleskac, and Thorsten Pachur

II   The Heuristic Mind

2   The Robust Beauty of Heuristics in Choice under Uncertainty   29
Ralph Hertwig, Jan K. Woike, Thorsten Pachur, and Eduard Brandstätter

3   Using Risk–Reward Structures to Reckon with Uncertainty   51
Timothy J. Pleskac, Ralph Hertwig, Christina Leuker, and Larissa Conradt

4   Going Round in Circles: How Social Structures Guide and Limit Search   71
Christin Schulze and Thorsten Pachur

5   Strategic Uncertainty and Incomplete Information: The Homo Heuristicus Does Not Fold   89
Leonidas Spiliopoulos and Ralph Hertwig

6   Toward Simple Eating Rules for the Land of Plenty   111
Mattea Dallacker, Jutta Mata, and Ralph Hertwig

III   **The Exploring Mind**

   7   **Adaptive Exploration: What You See Is Up to You**   131
     Dirk U. Wulff, Doug Markant, Timothy J. Pleskac, and Ralph Hertwig

   8   **The Weight of Uncertain Events**   153
     Thorsten Pachur and Ralph Hertwig

   9   **Tomorrow Never Knows: Why and How Uncertainty Matters in Intertemporal Choice**   175
     Junyi Dai, Thorsten Pachur, Timothy J. Pleskac, and Ralph Hertwig

  10   **Experiences and Descriptions of Financial Uncertainty: Are They Equivalent?**   191
     Tomás Lejarraga, Jan K. Woike, and Ralph Hertwig

  11   **Ways to Learn from Experience**   207
     Thorsten Pachur and Dries Trippas

IV   **The Social Mind**

  12   **Rivals in the Dark: Trading Off Strategic and Environmental Uncertainty**   225
     Doug Markant and Ralph Hertwig

  13   **The Ecological Rationality of the Wisdom of Crowds**   245
     Stefan M. Herzog, Aleksandra Litvinova, Kyanoush S. Yahosseini, Alan N. Tump, and Ralf H. J. M. Kurvers

  14   **Crowds on the Move**   263
     Mehdi Moussaïd

V   **The Unfinished Mind**

  15   **Computational Evolution and Ecologically Rational Decision Making**   285
     Peter D. Kvam, Arend Hintze, Timothy J. Pleskac, and David Pietraszewski

  16   **How the Adaptive Adolescent Mind Navigates Uncertainty**   305
     Wouter van den Bos, Corinna Laube, and Ralph Hertwig

  17   **The Life-Span Development of Risk Preference**   325
     Rui Mata and Renato Frey

VI Looking Back to Look Forward

**18 Interpreting Uncertainty: A Brief History of
Not Knowing**   343
Anastasia Kozyreva, Timothy J. Pleskac, Thorsten Pachur,
and Ralph Hertwig

VII Accompanying Material

Glossary of Key Concepts   365
Anastasia Kozyreva and Philipp Gerlach

References   371
Name Index   431
Subject Index   447

Interactive Elements and Supplementary Material:
https://taming-uncertainty.mpib-berlin.mpg.de/

Preface

Almost every decision you make represents a leap into the unknown. You do not know with certainty what the consequences of your actions will be, nor do you know how likely the consequences are or when they will materialize—not to mention whether you and others will like the repercussions of your decisions. Faced with these myriad uncertainties, you may be tempted to throw in the towel. But that is not what people do. In fact, most of the time people are pretty good at navigating the unknown. The mind seems to be equipped with cognitive tools that empower people not only to reduce uncertainties where possible, but also to proceed in light of uncertainties that defy reduction.

In *Taming Uncertainty*, we aim to shed light on the cognitive tools in the mind's adaptive toolbox that help people make the leap into the unknown. For many decades, scholarly work in psychology and economics has understood the human response to uncertainty in terms of an attempt to uncover objective probabilities or, when this proves impossible, to conjure up subjective probabilities. Working with the currency of probabilities, this research has explored how extravagant Bayesian brains might update their estimates. In this book, by contrast, we take a different perspective—one that is rooted in what is known about what real, humble minds can do and resists whittling the human response to uncertainty down to an act of juggling probability quantities. In our view, adaptive intelligence in an uncertain world arises from a variety of simple tools. We focus on three types: first, decision strategies that efficiently permit people to infer and decide based on limited information by cleverly making use of key regularities in the environment; second, flexible search processes that guide where to look for further information and, importantly, when to stop searching and to act; and, third, cognitive tools that help people respond to the opportunities and challenges presented by others. We also trace changes in these cognitive tools brought about by the development of the human mind, both within and across generations. We argue that these tools empower the human mind with what the poet John Keats (1891) called "negative capability"—the ability to survive and thrive in uncertainty.

Ideas and arguments expressed on paper cannot fully replace experience. We have therefore created interactive elements to accompany many chapters. These online companions provide dynamic, hands-on encounters with some of the experimental paradigms, formal theories, and data featured throughout the book. We invite you to explore these elements—which are also referenced individually in the respective chapters—at https://taming-uncertainty.mpib-berlin.mpg.de/.

Taming Uncertainty is not an edited book; it is a joint product of the members of the Center for Adaptive Rationality (ARC), a multidisciplinary team of psychologists, economists, biologists, philosophers, computer scientists, and physicists, that was founded in 2012 at the Max Planck Institute for Human Development in Berlin. We worked on this book as a group in order to reflect and tap into our complementary disciplinary interests, skills, and knowledge; it summarizes our progress so far on our journey to unravel the nature of adaptive rationality in an uncertain world. *Taming Uncertainty* would have been impossible without the generous funding of the Max Planck Society, which has helped create this interdisciplinary group of researchers who are profoundly curious, challenging each other's viewpoints and exploring the mind's toolbox together.

We are also grateful to the colleagues who read drafts of individual chapters and provided their insightful feedback: Joshua Abbott, Ruben Arslan, Florian Artinger, Judith Avrahami, Simon Ciranka, Nadine Fleischhut, Thomas Hills, Ulrich Hoffrage, Sebastian Horn, Anika Josef, Juliane Kämmer, Yaakov Kareev, Robert Lorenz, Lucas Molleman, Shabnam Mousavi, Paul Pedersen, Amnon Rapoport, Samuli Reijula, Job Schepens, Oliver Schürmann, Warren Thorngate, Claus Vögele, Michael Waldmann, Charley Wu, Shuli Yu, and Veronika Zilker. We owe a further debt of gratitude to the scholars whose formidable brains we were able to pick during the production of the book: Bahador Bahrami, Gordon Brown, Jerome R. Busemeyer, Mike DeKay, Adele Diederich, Ido Erev, Craig Fox, Gerd Gigerenzer, Ulrike Hahn, Robin Hogarth, Joachim Krueger, Steve Lewandowsky, Taosheng Liu, John McNamara, Ben R. Newell,

Roger Ratcliff, Lael Schooler, Neil Stewart, Chris Summerfield, Kinneret Teo-dorescu, Peter M. Todd, Peter Wakker, Tom Wallsten, and Greg Wheeler.

Our most heartfelt thanks go to the many people in the Max Planck Institute without whose support this book would not have flourished—to Susannah Goss and Deb Ain for putting their careful eyes and unending patience to work editing the manuscript; to Diana Schieck for managing the references; to Antonio Amaddio and Philip Jakob for leading the development of the interactive elements; to Marianne Hauser for her meticulous work creating the figures; to Katja Münz and Kate Pleskac for keeping the authors and the book organized and running efficiently; and to Valerie Chase for helping us shape chapter 1 and getting us off to a good start. And, of course, our special thanks go to our families for their support and patience when we cruised off into the unknown once again.

This book marks the first step in our exploration of the murky waters of uncertainty. We are looking forward to our future discoveries of the mind's tools and feats. If you want to check on our progress, please visit the ARC website at www.mpib-berlin.mpg.de/en/research/adaptive-rationality.

Ralph Hertwig
Timothy J. Pleskac
Thorsten Pachur

Contributors

Ralph Hertwig   Center for Adaptive Rationality, Max Planck Institute for Human Development, Berlin, Germany (hertwig@mpib-berlin.mpg.de)

Timothy J. Pleskac   Department of Psychology, University of Kansas, USA (pleskac@ku.edu)

Thorsten Pachur   Center for Adaptive Rationality, Max Planck Institute for Human Development, Berlin, Germany (pachur@mpib-berlin.mpg.de)

Eduard Brandstätter   Department of Economic Psychology, Johannes Kepler University, Linz, Austria (eduard.brandstaetter@jku.at)

Larissa Conradt   Center for Adaptive Rationality, Max Planck Institute for Human Development, Berlin, Germany (animcolldec@gmail.com)

Junyi Dai   Department of Psychology and Behavioral Sciences, Zhejiang University, Hangzhou, China (junyidai@zju.edu.cn)

Mattea Dallacker   Center for Adaptive Rationality, Max Planck Institute for Human Development, Berlin, Germany (dallacker@mpib-berlin.mpg.de)

Renato Frey   Center for Cognitive and Decision Sciences, University of Basel, Switzerland (renato.frey@unibas.ch)

Philipp Gerlach   Hochschule Fresenius, University of Applied Sciences, Hamburg, Germany (philipp.gerlach@hs-fresenius.de)

Stefan M. Herzog Center for Adaptive Rationality, Max Planck Institute for Human Development, Berlin, Germany (herzog@mpib-berlin.mpg.de)

Arend Hintze Evolving Artificial Intelligence Laboratory, Michigan State University, USA (hintze@msu.edu)

Anastasia Kozyreva Center for Adaptive Rationality, Max Planck Institute for Human Development, Berlin, Germany (kozyreva@mpib-berlin .mpg.de)

Ralf H. J. M. Kurvers Center for Adaptive Rationality, Max Planck Institute for Human Development, Berlin, Germany (kurvers@mpib-berlin.mpg.de)

Peter D. Kvam Department of Psychology, University of Florida, Gainesville, USA (kvam.peter@gmail.com)

Corinna Laube Center for Lifespan Psychology, Max Planck Institute for Human Development, Berlin, Germany (laube@mpib-berlin.mpg.de)

Tomás Lejarraga Departament d'Economia de l'Empresa, Universitat de les Illes Balears, Spain (tomas.lejarraga@uib.eu)

Christina Leuker Center for Adaptive Rationality, Max Planck Institute for Human Development, Berlin, Germany (leuker@mpib-berlin.mpg.de)

Aleksandra Litvinova Center for Adaptive Rationality, Max Planck Institute for Human Development, Berlin, Germany (litvinova@mpib-berlin .mpg.de)

Doug Markant Department of Psychological Science, University of North Carolina at Charlotte, USA (dmarkant@uncc.edu)

Jutta Mata Health Psychology Lab, University of Mannheim, Germany (mata@uni-mannheim.de)

Rui Mata Center for Cognitive and Decision Sciences, University of Basel, Switzerland (rui.mata@unibas.ch)

Mehdi Moussaïd   Center for Adaptive Rationality, Max Planck Institute for Human Development, Berlin, Germany (moussaid@mpib-berlin.mpg.de)

David Pietraszewski   Center for Adaptive Rationality, Max Planck Institute for Human Development, Berlin, Germany (pietraszewski@mpib-berlin.mpg.de)

Christin Schulze   Center for Adaptive Rationality, Max Planck Institute for Human Development, Berlin, Germany (cschulze@mpib-berlin.mpg.de)

Leonidas Spiliopoulos   Center for Adaptive Rationality, Max Planck Institute for Human Development, Berlin, Germany (spiliopoulos@mpib-berlin.mpg.de)

Dries Trippas   Center for Adaptive Rationality, Max Planck Institute for Human Development, Berlin, Germany (dries.trippas@gmail.com)

Alan N. Tump   Center for Adaptive Rationality, Max Planck Institute for Human Development, Berlin, Germany (tump@mpib-berlin.mpg.de)

Wouter van den Bos   Faculty of Social and Behavioural Sciences, University of Amsterdam, Netherlands (W.vandenBos@uva.nl)

Jan K. Woike   Center for Adaptive Rationality, Max Planck Institute for Human Development, Berlin, Germany (woike@mpib-berlin.mpg.de)

Dirk U. Wulff   Center for Cognitive and Decision Sciences, University of Basel, Switzerland (dirk.wulff@unibas.ch)

Kyanoush S. Yahosseini   Center for Adaptive Rationality, Max Planck Institute for Human Development, Berlin, Germany (yahosseini@mpib-berlin.mpg.de)

I   The Research Agenda

1   Reckoning with Uncertainty: Our Program of Research

Ralph Hertwig, Timothy J. Pleskac, and Thorsten Pachur

1.1   Uncertainty as *the* Human Condition

At a press conference held in East Berlin on the evening of November 9, 1989, Günter Schabowski, a spokesman for the socialist regime of the German Democratic Republic (GDR), read out what seemed like a secondary item on a list of mundane announcements:

> A decision was made today, as far as I know.... A recommendation from the Politburo was taken up that we take a passage from [a draft of] the travel regulation and put it into effect, that, (um)—as it is called, for better or worse—that regulates permanent exit, leaving the Republic. Since we find it (um) unacceptable that this movement is taking place (um) across the territory of an allied state, (um) which is not an easy burden for that country to bear. Therefore (um), we have decided today (um) to implement a regulation that allows every citizen of the German Democratic Republic (um) to (um) leave the GDR through any of the border crossings. (Hertle, 2001, p. 157)

Schabowski continued on, but was interrupted by a reporter with a question that would change the world: "When does it come into effect?" Visibly uncertain, mumbling to his aides and thumbing through his papers, he finally said, "to my knowledge ... immediately, without delay" (Hertle, 2001, p. 158). It is unlikely that he could have imagined the chain of events that these words would set off. Suddenly, the people of the GDR were thrust into their own state of uncertainty: Would the country's armed border guards obey the new travel regulations, granting complete freedom to travel, or would they use force to prevent any border crossing? Would the country's leaders revoke the announcement once its effects became clear, choosing to shed the blood of their people rather than risk a hemorrhaging of their population? Within hours, as joy vied with fear, tens of thousands of East Germans converged on the crossing points to West Berlin chanting "*Tor auf!"* ("Open the gate!"). Stunned, outnumbered, and lacking any information on the new policy or orders from the military leadership, the border guards ad-libbed—and opened the crossings. This division at the heart of Europe, which was literally set in stone, vanished overnight—and with it the certitudes, plans, and projections of millions of people.

Predictions about repercussions varied wildly. The GDR leadership had hoped the travel law would strengthen its regime (Hertle, 2001; Meyer, 2015). French President François Mitterrand, in contrast, believed that the Soviet leadership would never accept this development and that the Germans were unwittingly risking a world war. The very next day, Soviet leader Mikhail Gorbachev warned the leaders of France, the United Kingdom, and the United States of a possible "destabilization of the situation not only in the center of Europe but also beyond" (quoted in Hertle, 2001, p. 138). None of these things came to pass. As the saying often attributed to physicist Niels Bohr goes: Prediction is very difficult, especially about the future.

The quip highlights three more general properties of the human struggle with uncertainty. First, much of what people do—not only in politics but also in ordinary life—is predicated on forecasts of the future. Whether choosing a job, an apartment, or a spouse; whether deciding when to travel the world, have children, or start saving for old age; whether voting in an election or deciding between medical treatments, people base their decisions on predictions about what the future holds. Second, prediction can be difficult because most future events are shrouded in uncertainty—indeed, virtually all the political players in the fall of the Berlin Wall got it wrong (Hertle, 2001). Third, uncertainty and lack of knowledge bedevil not only people's predictions of the future but also their mental constructions of the present and reconstructions of the past (Loftus, 1993; Schacter, 1999; S. M. Stigler, 1980). "Ask any American who brought down the Berlin Wall, and nine of 10 will say Ronald Reagan," said former Secretary of State James Baker, but "we had hardly anything to do with it" (Meyer, 2015, para. 14).

1.2 Our Program of Research: Understanding the Adaptive Toolbox for Taming Uncertainty

If people inhabit "isolated islands of certainty in an ocean of uncertainty" (Arendt, 1958/2013, p. 244), this book is about how people navigate the high seas. Even under daunting conditions—where knowledge is imperfect, complexity is high, and time is short—people make predictions, inferences, and decisions so close to effortlessly that they have been called "masters of prediction" (Clark, 2016), and the accuracy of many of their predictions excels that of the political players in the fall of the Berlin Wall. What are the foundations of this mastery? In this book, we argue that they are a set of tools that the human mind—as an evolved and continuously learning cognitive system—has developed to grapple with uncertainty. And just as a good mechanic has multiple tools, each designed for a specific purpose, the human cognitive system has specific tools for dealing with the different forms of uncertainty it encounters (see chapter 18; Lo & Mueller, 2010).

With this notion of cognition, we challenge the idea that people manage uncertainty as if they were reducing it to risks, that is, as if they could summon at least subjective numerical probabilities for the outcomes of every decision they make (originally proposed by Savage, 1954). If they could, probability would constitute the very currency of human thought. Instead, we argue that people master the myriad types of uncertainty they face, from the inherent unpredictability of their environment (environmental uncertainty) to their limited knowledge and understanding of other people's actions and intentions (strategic uncertainty), by deploying a wide range of cognitive tools, many of which have no or only a rudimentary need to know the probabilities, let alone the utilities, of outcomes. We refer to this repertoire of tools for making predictions, inferences, and decisions as the mind's *adaptive toolbox*.

Guided by this concept, we build on our own and others' work on cognitive tools known as simple heuristics (Gigerenzer, Hertwig, & Pachur, 2011; Gigerenzer, Todd, & the ABC Research Group, 1999; Hertwig & Hoffrage, 2013; J. W. Payne, Bettman, & Johnson, 1993; Todd & Gigerenzer, 2012). Inspired by Herbert Simon and his vision of bounded rationality (1955, 1982, 1990), this work has proposed that much of human (and animal) reasoning, decision making, and behavior can be modeled in terms of such heuristics, which rest on simple principles of information processing and often consider only a subset of the information available. Heuristics are a realistic alternative to more classical approaches to decision making under uncertainty, such as expected utility theory and subjective expected utility theory, which often rest on extravagant implicit requirements and assumptions about the information, processing capacity, and time available (see Simon, 1955, pp. 103–104; see also chapter 2).

Simple heuristics constitute one important class of cognitive tools for reckoning with uncertainty. But a good mechanic's toolbox holds many handy implements in its drawers and trays: calipers for taking measurements; a flashlight to search for information and diagnose the problem so as to select the right tool; wrenches, ratchets, and pliers to fix it. And just as a mechanic can consult with colleagues and friends on tricky problems, people facing uncertainty can deploy social tools. Acknowledging the many facets of the adaptive toolbox, our research program examines two other important sets of cognitive tools, both of which serve to reduce reducible uncertainty or deal with irreducible uncertainty. One set supports search, permitting people to glean information about the future by learning from the environments they encounter. The second set has people teaming up with others and tapping their collective intelligence, that is, a group's ability to sometimes outperform individual decision makers when solving cognitive problems.

Our first goal in this book is to train the spotlight on these three sets of cognitive tools—heuristics, search strategies, and crowd aggregation rules—which we consider indispensable for reckoning with uncertainty. A second goal is to reveal the dynamic nature of the adaptive toolbox. Cognitive tools develop in response to changes inside the mind—for example, when cognitive resources like memory or knowledge grow or decline, or preferences concerning risk change. They also respond to changes outside the mind, such as when environmental demands shift (e.g., from exploring the world and forming alliances to finding a partner and raising children). Such developmental changes influence how the mind reckons with uncertainty and what kind of uncertainty it faces. How cognitive tools such as heuristics or search strategies are selected generally depends on factors such as the person's amount of accumulated knowledge (e.g., what they do and do not recognize), working memory capacity, value processing, and cognitive control, each of which has a distinct developmental trajectory. To understand how the mind handles uncertainty, it is therefore also imperative to understand how the adaptive toolbox is impacted by and develops along with the mind using it, as this book's handful of examples of the toolbox's mutability over the course of developmental change within individuals (ontogenetic change) and across generations of individuals (phylogenetic change) make clear.

Our third goal pertains to the kind of rationality that can arise from the relationship between the adaptive toolbox and the environment. Any cognitive tool will work in some contexts but not in others: its rationality is domain-specific rather than general. Like a lock and key (Barrett, 2005; see also Barrett & Kurzban, 2006), both the architecture of the cognitive tool and the respective environment must be investigated to determine how well they fit together. In this book, we extend this ecological rationality approach beyond the study of heuristics (e.g., Arkes, Gigerenzer, & Hertwig, 2016; Todd, Gigerenzer, & the ABC Research Group, 2012) to search strategies and crowd aggregation rules as well. Like heuristics, search strategies will succeed in some environments but fail in others; the same applies to strategies that harness collective intelligence. The ecological rationality of all these cognitive tools means that there is no master key. The lack of a master key, in turn, implies there are notable costs to using an adaptive toolbox, since the tools that empower the mind to deal with uncertainty are themselves a source of uncertainty. When should a specific tool be deployed? In this book, we seek to identify where tools and environments fit together, and where they do not; in so doing, we advocate a systemic view of uncertainty. This approach locates uncertainty neither solely in the mind (epistemic uncertainty) nor solely in the environment (aleatory uncertainty) but highlights the interactive dynamic of the two (see also chapter 18).

In summary, this book aims to advance the understanding of how the mind deals with uncertainty on three fronts. First, we integrate three important dimensions of human decision making into the concept of the adaptive toolbox: (a) boundedly and ecologically rational heuristics, (b) cognition as a search process, and (c) the tools the mind uses to tap into collective intelligence. Each dimension represents influential visions of human (and animal) cognition that have previously existed apart. Second, we advocate the view that the mind's repertoire of cognitive tools is anything but static— not only the toolbox but also its cognitive foundation and the environment are in constant flux and subject to developmental change. Finally, we demonstrate that each cognitive tool can be analyzed by enlisting the concept of ecological rationality, that is, the fit between specific tools and specific environments. All three goals are informed by the desire to further the understanding of what Arrow (1951) called "realistic" (p. 404) theories of how people make decisions without complete knowledge and, it should be added, where time and computational capacities are limited.

In seeking to capture how real people, alone and in tandem with others, make decisions under uncertainty, we take a decidedly different path than the ones trod by others. Many scholars of the mind see cognition in an uncertain world in terms of a single universal, computationally powerful and optimizing prediction machine—whether Bayesian in nature (Clark, 2016; Griffiths, Chater, Kemp, Perfors, & Tenenbaum, 2010; but see Jones & Love, 2011), resting on neural networks (McClelland et al., 2010; Rumelhart, McClelland, & the PDP Research Group, 1986), or involving a combination of both (e.g., Bayesian deep learning). Others leave the well-worn path of assuming classical information processing properties in favor of alternatives such as quantum information processing (Busemeyer & Bruza, 2012). Each approach has merits and has yielded new insights. For instance, it is useful to understand how the mind might go about implementing an optimal solution (Gershman, Horvitz, & Tenenbaum, 2015), or to what extent the principles of quantum information processing shed light on certain psychological regularities (Kvam, Pleskac, Yu, & Busemeyer, 2015). The adaptive toolbox approach we offer here seeks to understand the mind's amazing machinery for prediction, inference, and decision making as a repertoire of psychologically realistic strategies that fit specific environments. This toolbox promises flexibility and efficiency, thus equipping cognition with the ability to unlock the information that ever-changing environments carry about the uncertain future. We now turn to the conceptual issues that guide our investigations in the four major parts of this book: the heuristic mind, the exploring mind, the social mind, and the unfinished mind.

1.3   The Heuristic Mind

Heuristics are one of the most important types of realistic decision-making tools for coping with uncertainty. Each heuristic's policy represents a wager on the structure of the environment in question; it bets that ignoring some of the (often noisy) available information will enable faster, and potentially even more accurate, decisions (Gigerenzer & Gaissmaier, 2011). Indeed, one of the major discoveries of research on simple heuristics is that they are sometimes more accurate than complex procedures (e.g., Gigerenzer & Goldstein, 1996; Hertwig & Todd, 2003; Pachur, 2010; Pleskac, 2007). This discovery challenges the standard explanation of people's reliance on heuristics, which frames it as a kind of compromise between minimizing cognitive effort and maximizing accuracy (Shah & Oppenheimer, 2008). From this perspective, people rely on heuristics because searching for and processing information is taxing. Heuristics offer relief by trading accuracy for faster and more frugal cognition. This accuracy–effort trade-off—which is sometimes conceptualized as rational (J. W. Payne et al., 1993) and at other times as seriously flawed (leading to "cognitive illusions"; see Gilovich, Griffin, & Kahneman, 2002; Kahneman, Slovic, & Tversky, 1982)—seems to have been accepted as a potentially universal law of cognition.

The world's complexity is unquestionably beyond the grasp of the individual mind, but this David-versus-Goliath imbalance may not be why people rely on heuristics. The fact that simple heuristics can outperform more complex strategies raises a different possibility: the use of heuristics may reflect the power of heuristics rather than the weakness of the mind. Heuristics can be versatile and competitive under at least two conditions: when they are deployed in appropriate environments—that is, when the degree of tool-to-environment fit is high—and equally important, when information about the decision environment is scarce (e.g., Gigerenzer & Brighton, 2009; Katsikopoulos, Schooler, & Hertwig, 2010). This second condition is likely to be the rule rather than the exception in the complex environments that humans inhabit.

Brunswik (1957/2001) likened cognition and the environment to a married couple who have to come to terms with each other through mutual adaptation. The concept of ecological rationality (Todd, Gigerenzer, et al., 2012) highlights the fit between a heuristic—or, as we propose in this book, of any decision-making tool—and an environment. It also raises the following questions:

What structures does the environment offer that a decision-making tool could exploit?

In which environments does a particular decision-making tool succeed?

Which decision-making tools succeed in a particular environment?

How do decision-making tools and environments coevolve?

Cognitive science, psychology, and behavioral economics have often been content to study just one half of the couple: the mind's "software" and capacities. But as any marriage counselor knows, listening to just one side of the story will probably not illuminate why and when a marriage does or does not work. The same holds for cognitive strategies. In research on ecologically rational heuristics, considerable progress has been made toward understanding the intersection between the environment and the mind (Fawcett et al., 2014; Hogarth & Karelaia, 2006; Martignon & Hoffrage, 1999, 2002; Pachur, Hertwig, & Rieskamp, 2013a; Pleskac & Hertwig, 2014; Şimşek, 2001; Şimşek & Buckmann, 2015; Todd, Gigerenzer, et al., 2012). Yet the study of the interplay between the mind and the environment is still in its infancy; important challenges remain. In the second part of this book, titled "The Heuristic Mind," we take on three of these challenges.

1.3.1   How Do Preferential Choice Heuristics Handle Uncertainty?

From the outset, research on ecologically rational heuristics and "Homo heuristicus" (Gigerenzer et al., 2011) has focused on the domain of inference (e.g., which of these paintings is more valuable?) rather than preference (e.g., which of these two paintings would you like to have?). The key reason is that the domain of inference involves external criteria (e.g., the monetary value of a painting) and, therefore, commonly accepted benchmarks for evaluating the performance of inferential heuristics and people's use of them. Since benchmarks for preference are less clear, "accuracy" of choice in this context has been defined in many ways, ranging from adherence to coherence criteria (e.g., transitivity; see Pleskac, Diederich, & Wallsten, 2015) to "gold standards" such as expected value or utility maximization. Examination of choice heuristics in the domain of preference has been limited to the world of risk, where, according to Luce and Raiffa (1957), the outcomes of actions and the probabilities of those outcomes are known (e.g., Brandstätter, Gigerenzer, & Hertwig, 2006; J. W. Payne et al., 1993). In addition, choice heuristics have typically been invoked to explain systematic violations of, for instance, transitivity and axioms such as independence (Katsikopoulos & Gigerenzer, 2008; Tversky, 1969, 1972). But what happens when choice heuristics and strategies of rational choice (e.g., expected value theory) engage in *decision making under uncertainty*, where each action has a set of possible outcomes whose probabilities are not known (Luce & Raiffa, 1957)? Will some heuristics be on a par with, or even more accurate than, computationally more complex strategies in the domain of preference, where the "Olympian" models of rationality (Simon, 1983, p. 19) were originally proposed (e.g., subjective expected utility theory; Savage, 1954)? If so, in which environments can different heuristics be expected to succeed or fail? Chapter 2 addresses these questions.

1.3.2 Which Environmental Structures Are There to Be Exploited?

The second challenge we take on focuses on the environmental half of Brunswik's (1957/2001) married couple. What structures does the environment offer that might enable ecologically rational decisions? In the domain of inference, for instance, recognition has been identified as an important predictive indicator. It builds on the environmental regularity that objects scoring high on a criterion (such as large cities, wealthy people, or successful athletes) are seen and talked about more frequently than objects that score low. This ecological structure is exploited by the recognition heuristic (D. G. Goldstein & Gigerenzer, 2002), which interprets the failure to recognize one object and the recognition of another as a sign that the latter scores higher on a given criterion. But there is also an environmental regularity that binds extreme values and frequency differently: the relationship between risk and reward. Chapter 3 focuses on this structure, which exists in many environments. For instance, the bigger the jackpot one can win in a lottery or casino, the smaller the chances of actually winning it. Being cognizant of this regularity is an ecologically smart way to estimate unknown probabilities, thus reducing uncertainty. Chapter 4 demonstrates that structures in the social world (see also chapter 14), such as spatial clustering of social phenomena and people's hierarchical social network structure, can also be exploited to make accurate and frugal inferences about social statistics such as the frequencies of health hazards in the population.

Like Brunswik (1957/2001), Simon (1990) emphasized the collaboration between cognition and environment and insisted that "to describe, predict and explain the behavior of a system of bounded rationality, we must both construct a theory of the system's processes and *describe the environments* to which it is adapting" (pp. 6–7; emphasis added). The science of bounded rationality has proceeded along these lines by surveying and cataloging choice environments and asking which strategies and solutions would be most effective in each (Marewski & Schooler, 2011; Şimşek & Buckmann, 2015; Todd, Gigerenzer, et al., 2012). One downside to this approach is that one may end up with a different heuristic or set of heuristics for each discernable environment or environmental structure, resulting in a multitude of descriptions of environment–heuristic associations. In order to avoid such "description inflation," let us reframe Simon's goal as follows: In order to explain the behavior of a system of bounded rationality, we must eventually also construct theories of the system's processes as well as *theories of the mechanisms* underlying the emergence of classes of environmental structures. Admittedly, this goal is extremely ambitious, but we have already made modest progress toward it. In chapter 3, we outline a theory that explains and predicts when and why risk–reward structures emerge and, by extension, where a heuristic exploiting this structure can be expected to work well or falter (see Pleskac, Conradt, Leuker, & Hertwig, 2018).

1.3.3   Can Heuristics Succeed under Strategic Complexity?

A third challenge we address is whether the success of heuristics is restricted to static environments that do not require sophisticated strategic responses. There is a firm belief that simple heuristics are destined to fail when employed in "interactions with other intelligent agents, especially competitive agents" (Sterelny, 2003, p. 53). The rationale behind this belief is that social environments populated with other, competitive, agents are much more complex than physical environments (see Hertwig, Hoffrage, & the ABC Research Group, 2013). In competitive environments, strategies face counterstrategies, ostensibly requiring individuals to proactively interpret and forecast the behavior of others. In this view, individuals need to be aware that others will try to get the better of them, whereas nature, in its dispassionate amorality, will not. Is there any way that heuristics can prevail in these competitive interactions, which seem to require that an individual generate a model of the opponents' behavior, as well as a model of the opponents' model of the individual's behavior, and so on? Chapter 5 gives an answer: Heuristics also hold up in worlds invoking strategic interactions (see also Hertwig & Herzog, 2009).

To conclude, perhaps the most important discovery in research on simple heuristics is that they can be as accurate as, and sometimes even more accurate than, strategies that make the greatest possible use of information and computation. We address two important challenges to the generality of this finding: In preferential choice, it appears as if heuristics cannot escape an accuracy–effort trade-off; in strategic interactions with competitive agents, it is commonly assumed that heuristics will crash and burn. We also show that heuristics are not just vehicles for describing how people reckon with uncertainty; they also can be explicitly designed and enlisted to help people make better decisions. Chapter 6 analyzes the many uncertainties of the modern food environment, which cannot easily be reduced to the stock dimensions of outcomes and probabilities, and illustrates how people can use heuristics to safely navigate a world of carefully crafted temptations (see also chapter 14). But heuristics are just one set of indispensable tools for coping with uncertainty; there is another class of cognitive strategy that is equally important. Adaptive cognition is first and foremost about the smart search for information—the focus of the third part of this book, "The Exploring Mind."

1.4   The Exploring Mind

September 30, 1659. I, poor, miserable Robinson Crusoe, being shipwrecked, during a dreadful storm in the offing, came on shore on this dismal unfortunate island, which I called 'the Island of Despair,' all of the ship's company being drowned, and myself dead.

—Daniel Defoe, *Robinson Crusoe*

Can there be a lonelier and more uncertain world than the one described by Robinson Crusoe? What should he expect? Is the island inhabited? Are the locals friendly or hostile? Should he be worried about wild animals? What food sources are there? Is there drinking water? Where can he find shelter? Will anybody come to his rescue? To cope with these and other existential uncertainties, Crusoe recruited what is perhaps the quintessential tool for making decisions: he explored the island to ascertain the lay of the land, his options, and their possible consequences. In fact, search for information—either within the bounds of one's mind or in the external world—is what much of cognition is about.

At least two variants of search strategies can be used to reduce a knowledge gap. One is to simulate and forecast the consequences of one's actions on the basis of past data stored in memory—one's own or others' experiences in similar circumstances (e.g., Dudai & Carruthers, 2005). Of course, relying on past experience to anticipate the future only works if relevant past data are available. Sometimes there are none, as in the case of Crusoe, and sometimes, for whatever reason, the past is a poor predictor of the present or future. In such cases, another search strategy is required, one that permits the individual to explore the world, thus acquiring novel data before deciding. Because the process of sampling information is limited by the decision maker's time and capacity, unbounded search is not an option. But limited search does not necessarily imply poor decision making. On the contrary, mirroring the surprising accuracy of simple heuristics, limited search can yield surprisingly good results—whether it targets the information needed for heuristic inference (e.g., Katsikopoulos et al., 2010; Pachur et al., 2013a) or the properties of options in the context of preferential choice (e.g., Hertwig & Pleskac, 2010; Vul, Goodman, Griffiths, & Tenenbaum, 2014).

Many normative and descriptive theories of choice, including expected utility theory, subjective expected utility theory, and prospect theory (Kahneman & Tversky, 1979; Wakker, 2010), are mute on how people search for and learn from information. This reticence might be taken to suggest that how people search contributes little to comprehending how they handle uncertainty. But nothing could be further from the truth. Like Robinson Crusoe, people survive and even thrive in the ocean of uncertainty by enlisting search processes in external and internal environments: visually searching for targets of interest, looking up information on the Internet, or searching their semantic memory (Hills, Jones, & Todd, 2012). Unless decision scientists comprehend cognition as a search process, they will fail to understand important aspects of human behavior. Consider, by way of illustration, research on risky choice. For at least five decades (E. U. Weber, Shafir, & Blais, 2004), the field has predominantly studied how people make risky choices by asking them to choose between monetary gambles such as the following:

(A) An 80% chance of winning $4, otherwise nothing, and

(B) $3 for sure.

Although the expected value of option A is higher, most people prefer option B. Using choice problems like this, researchers have proposed elegant theories of risky choice that postulate, for instance, how people subjectively represent the objective information given (e.g., subjective functions of probability and outcome information). Yet the process of search is completely missing from these subjective representations and choices; all the necessary information is handed to decision makers on a silver platter. They are thus making *decisions from description*, in what Edwards (1962a) described as "static" decision tasks where, as Busemeyer (1982) highlighted, there is no need to learn from the past: "When a static decision task is used, the decision maker does not have to learn from past experience with the outcomes of previous decisions.... This feature of the static decision task becomes a problem when generalizing results to the many day-to-day decisions that repeatedly confront individuals, since explicit information concerning outcome probabilities is frequently not available and must be learned from previous experience" (p. 176).

Indeed, in everyday life, "it is hard to think of an important natural decision for which probabilities *are* objectively known" (Camerer & Weber, 1992, p. 325). When people decide whether to start a business or ask someone out on a date, there are no actuarial risk tables to consult. Only by considering uncertainty, the opportunity to search, and the process of stopping search in the choice situation can researchers begin to predict and explain how people arrive at *decisions from experience* (Hertwig, Barron, Weber, & Erev, 2004). We and others have studied decisions from experience using the same kind of monetary gambles commonly employed in studies of decisions from description. Systematic comparison of decisions from description with decisions from experience reveals that choices can diverge systematically, an empirical regularity described as the *description–experience gap* (Hertwig & Erev, 2009). Chapters 7 and 8 examine this gap—which could be called a risk–uncertainty gap—and its potential causes. What is increasingly clear is that the major theories developed by decision science to understand decisions from description do not readily apply to decisions from experience. One reason, though not the only one, is that these theories pay no attention to search, the key process through which people pick up on environmental regularities that, in turn, enable them to reduce uncertainty.

1.4.1   How Search and Choice Are Intertwined

Search and learning are at the heart of decisions from experience. Therefore, one path forward is obvious: a computational model of a system that explains decisions from experience must specify (a) the processes that guide sampling, (b) the processes that terminate sampling, and (c) the processes that generate a decision on the basis of the sampled information. Models of decisions from experience have attempted to do this in different ways. Often, however, the models treat search and choice as independent processes—and past and new experience as a record or set of records that can be consulted when making a final choice (e.g., Baron, 2005; Fox & Hadar, 2006; C. Gonzalez & Dutt, 2011; Hau, Pleskac, Kiefer, & Hertwig, 2008; Hertwig, Barron,

Weber, & Erev, 2006; Plonsky, Teodorescu, & Erev, 2015). However, much like Brunswik's married couple of cognition and the environment, search and choice are intertwined. How people search shapes the choices they make. For instance, limited search in decisions from experience results in rare events being underrepresented in people's samples; as a result, they make choices as if they were underweighting rare events (see chapters 7 and 8). At the same time, people also choose how to search. They may make a decision once a predetermined level of preference has been reached—in which case, they often choose the last option examined, especially if that option is favorable. It follows that search and choice form a mutually dependent system for making decisions from experience. Chapter 7 lays out the evidence for the codependency of search and choice and proposes a new modeling framework that accounts for this system (see also chapter 4).

1.4.2 The Significance of Search and Learning Extends beyond Risky Choice

Imperfect knowledge and processes of search and learning are not limited to risky choice. In one of the most important tasks the mind has to perform, it must learn which objects belong together. Equipped with limited knowledge of the world's countless objects, the mind often engages actively in search to test classificatory hypotheses (Erickson & Kruschke, 1998; see also Markant & Gureckis, 2014). Chapter 11 is concerned with how, in judgment and categorization, the mind can develop different types of representations depending on the information encountered during search, and how these representations can be selected in an ecologically rational way to support good decisions. The inherent limits of people's knowledge imply that a description–experience gap may also exist in other areas of choice. If this is the case, the gap could help to explain puzzling discrepancies that can emerge when lines of research accidentally confound description and experience—such as findings that adults are worse in statistical reasoning than children and babies. Indeed, the limited evidence suggests that the description–experience gap is not a fringe phenomenon limited to monetary gambles. It also appears when people have to identify the causes of an effect based on data that are either described or experienced (Rehder & Waldmann, 2017), and when people have to reason in a Bayesian fashion about the positive predictive value of a medical diagnostic test (B. Armstrong & Spaniol, 2017).

Decision making under risk, categorization, causal reasoning, and Bayesian reasoning are among the mind's major cognitive feats. How well or poorly the mind performs these feats has been taken as a benchmark of human rationality. Given that experiential learning and the accompanying search process may be the most important source of adaptation and a building block of intelligence (Hertwig, Hogarth, & Lejarraga, 2018; March, 2010), human rationality should not be reduced to performance in tasks from which search and uncertainty have largely been removed. This is also likely to hold in intertemporal choices, where people are explicitly required to make choices about the future. Chapter 9 reviews the critical role that uncertainty plays when people choose between options whose outcomes materialize at different times (e.g., whether to spend their money now or to invest it in the hope of a future payoff). Again, we find that uncertainty and how people search for information can create a description–experience gap and play a defining role in whether people appear to be patient or impulsive in their choices. Furthermore, as chapter 10 demonstrates, this behavioral gap can also be observed in people's risk preferences when they learn, either by description or through experience, about macroeconomic shocks.

1.5   The Social Mind

While he was struggling to survive on his desert island, a single data point turned Robinson Crusoe's life upside down: a man's footprint on the shore. "Terrible thoughts racked my imagination about their having found my boat, and that there were people here; and that if so, I should certainly have them come again in greater numbers, and devour me; ... destroy all my corn, carry away all my flock of tame goats, and I should perish at last for mere want" (D. Defoe, 1719/1980, p. 155). Crusoe's terror was well founded. Most new arrivals on the island were man-eating adversaries; their presence posed an imminent threat. Yet his alliance with another human being—Friday, who became Crusoe's close companion—ultimately enabled him to fight off the threat of hostile intruders. Conspecifics are often the most significant aspect of an individual's environment. Humans and other animals compete with others for resources such as food, mates, esteem, or affection; these rivals grant the individual little time for deep thought, protracted information search, or complex calculations. At the same time, they wittingly or unwittingly teach the individual how to deal with a fickle world rife with unforeseeable hazards, diseases, and shortages. Social worlds and our knowledge about them present both opportunities and pitfalls (see also chapter 4). In the fourth part of this book, "The Social Mind," we turn to this duality and the challenges it entails.

1.5.1 Search and the Challenges of Competition

Animals and humans are constantly faced with important adaptive problems: what to eat, where to live, which mate to choose. Not infrequently, answers must be found under the threat of competition. Under these circumstances, the mind faces different types of uncertainty (e.g., environmental, strategic) and must learn how to balance their consequences. Take, for instance, hermit crabs, which live in the abandoned shells of other sea creatures—usually snails. Since they require larger shells as they grow, they are always on the lookout for a new mobile home. Since the quality of the available shells in the environment varies, a solitary crab faced with merely this kind of environmental uncertainty will thoroughly inspect any potential new home before moving in. However, if several crabs encounter an empty shell at the same time, each individual crab also faces strategic uncertainty, because it does not know the intentions and strategies of its competitors. Under these conditions, what would otherwise be a meticulous exploration is dramatically curtailed (Rotjan, Chabot, & Lewis, 2010). The crab nearest to the shell will make a split-second decision on whether or not to take it based on a brief visual inspection alone. Once a shell is taken, a chain reaction of shell upgrades may quickly ensue.

This strategic shell game illustrates the challenges and opportunities of sharing the world with others. Exposed to environmental uncertainty alone, the crabs face what is known as the exploration–exploitation trade-off: whether to continue inspecting a shell (exploration) or to move into it (exploitation). In human choice, the exploration–exploitation trade-off in solitary choice situations has been extensively studied, both theoretically (Brezzi & Lai, 2002; Gittins, 1979; Gittins, Glazebrook, & Weber, 2011) and empirically (Cohen, McClure, & Yu, 2007). The presence of competitors creates an even more complex dilemma. For instance, the more time one takes to explore and thereby reduce environmental uncertainty, the higher the risk that a competitor will act first. There is no perfect escape from this dilemma. Hermit crabs solve it by adjusting their exploration strategies and aspiration levels to the situation at hand, acting as meticulous product testers when alone but taking the leap after just a quick peek when faced with fierce competition. Little is known about how people try to come to terms with competition during search. In chapter 12, we examine the extent to which people's search in the external world adapts to the challenges of a competitive environment. Are their search tools as ecologically rational as those of the hermit crab when environmental and strategic uncertainty conspire to create a difficult trade-off?

1.5.2 Complex Collective Behaviors Often Arise from Simple Rules

The presence of others does not always mean competition. In many domains, people are better off cooperating than competing. A fascinating domain in which to examine how large groups of people cooperate is individuals' movement through a shared physical space. The motions of many individuals can combine to create complex collective patterns. Consider pedestrian behavior and other self-organization phenomena in crowds. In many cases, such as when unidirectional lanes form spontaneously as people move, collective behavior can be beneficial. In other cases, such as stop-and-go waves and crowd turbulence, collective behavior can be highly detrimental and potentially disastrous, as when people rush to building exits in an emergency. One modeling approach, inspired by Newtonian mechanics, uses models from fluid dynamics and social force theory to conceptualize crowd dynamics (see Moussaïd, Helbing, & Theraulaz, 2011). This approach treats pedestrians as molecules and their motion as the result of attractive, repulsive, driving, and fluctuating forces, but does not capture the cognitive processes in each mind. Chapter 14 offers an alternative to physics-based models that aims to describe the underlying actual processes: pedestrian heuristics. The view that begins to emerge is that neither strategically demanding interactions (see also chapter 5) nor complex collective behaviors require complex mechanisms (see also Hertwig, Davis, & Sulloway, 2002). Simple heuristics offer a good starting point for explaining both.

1.5.3 The Ecological Rationality of the Wisdom of Crowds

Decision making in humans and animals often occurs in groups. Grouping organisms such as social insects (e.g., ants) must often make rapid decisions about which direction to move in or what action to take in uncertain and dangerous environments. These decisions are rarely solitary. In fact, in swarming ants, schooling fish, and flocking birds, effective distributed decision making occurs across a range of environmental contexts (see Couzin, 2009). Pooling information, votes, and preferences in order to make group decisions can be a powerful way of outwitting both the physical and the social environment (e.g., Krause, Ruxton, & Krause, 2010; Woolley, Chabris, Pentland, Hashmi, & Malone, 2010). But the wisdom of the crowd is not fail-safe. By all means, tapping the wisdom of others and facing environmental uncertainties together can facilitate solutions that go beyond the capacities of the individual, especially when the problem is difficult to solve alone (e.g., catching larger prey). But collective decisions are not invariably better than individual ones (Sunstein & Hastie, 2015). Groups can fail to reach better decisions for a number of reasons: for instance, people do not usually become members of a group at random but are selected for specific reasons; selection processes can produce biased groups. More generally, like other decision-making tools, tools for harnessing the wisdom of the crowd are not good or bad per se; their success depends on the problem and the environment at hand. Again, this set of tools can be understood in terms of ecological rationality, as chapter 13 demonstrates.

1.6   The Unfinished Mind

The mind's adaptive toolbox is a work in progress. It is never completed. In the fifth part of this book, "The Unfinished Mind," we examine how the life-span trajectory of cognitive development shapes the use of the mind's decision-making tools. Admittedly, little is yet known about the intricate dynamics between cognitive development and the adaptive toolbox, but we can hope to gain glimpses into their interplay (see also chapter 4).

One way we have gained traction on uncovering the dynamics involved is by looking for developmental change that is rooted in the change of core cognitive abilities. Take, for instance, the changes during a person's lifetime in "crystallized" cognitive abilities, such as vocabulary and world knowledge, versus "fluid" abilities, such as reasoning, attention, processing speed, and working memory (Li, Lindenberger, & Sikström, 2001). Whereas crystallized abilities increase throughout young adulthood and middle age and then plateau, fluid abilities increase in childhood and adolescence, peak in young adulthood, and decline from middle adulthood through old age. These developmental changes in the mind's cognitive abilities impose age-specific constraints for the processes that draw on them. The coupling of these abilities and decision-making tools—as well as their basic building blocks, such as the abilities to activate, represent, maintain, and process information—can be expected to be particularly strong in childhood, when crystallized abilities are least developed, and in old age, when fluid abilities are in decline. It follows that, depending on the cognitive abilities that make up specific decision-making tools, the degree to which these tools are used efficiently will be higher or lower during some periods of cognitive development than others.

By way of illustration, let us return to the recognition heuristic (D. G. Goldstein & Gigerenzer, 2002). For choices between two alternatives, the recognition heuristic is stated as follows: If one of two objects is recognized and the other is not, then infer that the recognized object has the higher value with respect to the criterion. This heuristic is useful when there is a strong correlation—in either direction—between recognition and the criterion, such as in competitive sports, where successful athletes are more likely to be mentioned in the media and in general conversation than less successful ones and are therefore more likely to be recognized. In contrast, in environments where people or media outlets talk about all objects in question equally often (or equally rarely), recognition is not correlated with the criterion, and the recognition heuristic should therefore not be used to make inferences. For an ecologically rational use of the recognition heuristic, some knowledge of the environment—particularly of the predictive power of recognition for the target in question—is required. Assuming that world knowledge (crystallized intelligence) grows with age, one might therefore expect that young children use the recognition heuristic less discriminately. This is exactly what Horn, Ruggeri, and Pachur (2016) observed when they investigated the use of the recognition heuristic across individuals in three age groups (9, 12, and 17 years old). First, they found that elementary school children already made systematic use of the recognition heuristic; second, 9- and 12-year-olds did not adjust their strategy use between domains in which the recognition heuristic resulted in accurate versus inaccurate inferences; third, older adolescents adaptively adjusted their use of the heuristic between domains. These findings suggest that, when the adaptive use of a heuristic requires crystallized abilities (knowledge and experience) and those abilities are still in the making, the heuristic may be used less adaptively.

The other developmental period during which one may expect a strong connection between cognitive abilities and cognitive tools is old age. During this period, fluid abilities such as working memory are in decline, which can be expected to impact search and learning tools. But what are the consequences? Will aging decision makers explore the world more as their ability to store, extract, and synthesize signals from the sampled data fades? Or will they explore the world less, because their ability to represent, maintain, and process information has declined? These are just a few of the conceptual questions raised by a lifespan perspective on the adaptive toolbox, most of which have barely been investigated. Chapters 16 and 17 report on the progress that we have made in addressing them so far. Chapter 16 deals with the period of adolescence, demonstrating that adolescents respond to uncertainty differently than adults or children and revealing how adolescence is a developmental period fraught with uncertainty. Chapter 17 addresses the development of risk-taking propensity, a major concept in theories of human choice. Two of its main findings are that risk-taking propensity almost universally declines over the adult lifespan and that it is systematically associated not only with the properties and requirements of the decision task but also with environmental conditions such as harsh living conditions.

We also take the analysis of developmental change one step further to include phylogeny. Evolution by natural selection—the longest-running process that produces a fit between environment and behavior—drives developmental change across generations. Chapter 15 demonstrates how computational evolution can be used to examine how natural selection may have shaped the tools in the adaptive toolbox and their ecological rationality.

1.7   A Systemic View of Uncertainty

The discussion of uncertainty has a long and winding history, in which scholars from different disciplines have proposed classificatory dichotomies such as that between measurable and immeasurable uncertainties (Knight, 1921/2002) or between epistemic and aleatory uncertainties (Hacking, 1975/2006). The former dichotomy pertains to whether the calculus of probability theory can be called upon to contain uncertainty by quantifying it. The latter concerns the source and cause of uncertainty, namely, lack of knowledge or the irreducible random variability of natural processes. Chapter 18 concludes the book with a brief history of the conceptual development of uncertainty and outlines our systemic view of uncertainty. As this view is a leitmotif of this book, we briefly elaborate on it here, returning to the notions of ecological rationality and the adaptive toolbox.

No decision-making tool is inherently good or bad; its success always depends on the structure of the environment in which it is used. So how does an ecologically rational mind decide which heuristic to apply to a specific problem in a specific environment (see also chapters 11, 13, and 15)? If the same decision system were applied to every problem across all environments, this question would not arise. Bayesian statistics, expected utility maximization, and neural networks have all been proposed as such all-purpose, domain-general systems. Due to the flexibility of these optimization models, the fit between the mechanism and the environmental structure is of little concern. In fact, their flexibility makes those that maximize expected utility purely a function of the environment and thus independent of decision makers and the mechanisms upon which they rely (Simon, 1990).

But all general-purpose systems have significant limits (Gigerenzer & Brighton, 2009). For instance, in highly complex and multidimensional social and nonsocial decision environments, optimization is either impossible or inflicts an unmanageable computational burden. Moreover, optimizing systems do not generalize as well to new situations as do simpler tools. For these reasons, and because simpler decision-making tools offer a realistic theory of decision making, our vision of the mind is not that of an optimizing prediction machine (Clark, 2016). Rather, we think of the mind and its repertoire of competences much as Wimsatt (2007) thinks of nature and evolutionary change, namely, as a "parts dealer and crafty backwoods mechanic, constantly fixing and redesigning old machines and fashioning new ones out of whatever comes easily to hand" (p. 10). From this perspective, the mind—like a good mechanic—learns to select a tool that can address the problem at hand, repurposes existing tools when necessary, and designs new ones using the available evolved capacities of the human mind, such as recognition, emotions, and perspective taking.

The concept of ecological rationality calls for replacing, or at least complementing, the standard dualistic view of uncertainty, according to which the two main sources of uncertainty are human actors with their limited knowledge and the environment with its inherent randomness. The necessity of a tool–environment fit for reasonably good decisions means that uncertainty cannot be unambiguously attributed to the actor or the environment, but that it is a property arising from the interactive dynamic of the "married couple" introduced in section 1.3. In this systemic view, uncertainty, as experienced by the individual, is the joint product of environmental unpredictability and the actor's epistemic limitations.

Furthermore, ecological rationality is subject to its own distinct source of uncertainty, namely, that associated with selecting the right tool from the adaptive toolbox for the problem and the environment at hand. Depending on where this uncertainty originates—in the actor, in the environment, or in the actor–environment system—it may represent an "in-between" uncertainty. Resolutions to this uncertainty can be found in the mind (e.g., knowledge of the predictive power of recognition, knowledge about the environment; Pachur & Hertwig, 2006), in the environment (e.g., time pressure, an environmental structure that precludes any lexicographic ordering of predictors), or in the actor–environment interplay (see the notion of "cognitive niches"; Marewski & Schooler, 2011). Throughout the chapters of this book, it is this systemic view, implied by the concept of ecological rationality, that guides our investigations.

1.8 Taming Uncertainty

As we emphasized at the start of this chapter, every decision that people make involves a kind of prediction: about how much they like something or someone; about where the road less (or more) traveled is likely to lead; about which choices will make them rich or happy. Little is certain, and time pressure, lack of knowledge, the presence of other individuals, limited computational powers, and simultaneous demands on attention do not make things any easier—remember Günter Schabowski. But there is no reason to throw in the towel. The mind, that crafty backwoods mechanic, can draw on a range of boundedly rational tools. It can greatly benefit from simple heuristics because they are so robust across different kinds of social and nonsocial environments. But it is not just heuristics that empower people to sail the seas of uncertainty successfully. Human cognition is about search—collecting new experiences and thereby reducing uncertainty in adaptive ways. Furthermore, individuals can interface with the minds around them, harvesting the knowledge and wisdom of others. But in decision making, as in life, there is no such thing as a free lunch. Having many tools means having to choose between them, and this choice can go wrong. The adaptive toolbox is thus both the solution to and the source of uncertainty. If we had to make a prediction, our bet would be that the advantages of the former greatly outweigh the disadvantages of the latter.

II   The Heuristic Mind

2 The Robust Beauty of Heuristics in Choice under Uncertainty

Ralph Hertwig, Jan K. Woike, Thorsten Pachur, and Eduard Brandstätter

2.1 Axiomatizing Rational Choice—within Two Hours

> April 14, 1942. Today at Johnny's: axiomatization of measurable utility together with the numbers. It developed slowly, more and more quickly, and at the end, after two hours (!) it was nearly completely finished. It gave me great satisfaction, and moved me so much that afterwards I could not think about anything else....
> (Oskar Morgenstern, cited in Leonard, 1995, p. 753)

The diary writer is the Austrian economist Oskar Morgenstern; Johnny is the Hungarian-born mathematician John von Neumann. The two men first met in the fall of 1938, by which time they had both left Europe for good and were working at Princeton. The culmination of their collaboration, the book *Theory of Games and Economic Behavior* (von Neumann & Morgenstern, 1944/2007), was an intellectual coup that would thoroughly transform a range of fields. One major step on their route to game theory was to formulate—within "two hours (!)"—an axiomatic foundation of Daniel Bernoulli's (1738/1954) path-breaking expected utility theory. According to this theory, a rational decision maker will choose among risky options in such a way as to maximize expected utility. Von Neumann and Morgenstern derived a set of axioms—such as transitivity, completeness, and independence (see Luce & Raiffa, 1957)—that the preferences and choices of a decision maker obeying expected utility theory would have to satisfy. The axiomatized version of utility theory swiftly became a framework for research in areas as diverse as statistical decision theory, management science, operation research, and the theory of the firm. Within a decade, expected utility theory was generalized from "objective" probabilities (or "risk," to use Knight's, 1921/2002, terminology) to "subjective" probabilities (Savage, 1954), giving rise to what is now called Bayesian decision theory. According to the Bayesian approach, a rational person can translate any uncertainty into numbers, that is, subjective probabilities, which must, first and foremost, be consistent—but not necessarily plausible. Diehard Elvis Presley fans who believe he is living among us, now in his early eighties, may estimate this probability to be 99% and assign 1% to him being dead. Largely unconstrained by facts, such beliefs can nevertheless be coherent.

2.2   The Olympian Model and Its Unrealistic Assumptions

Von Neumann and Morgenstern's (1944/2007) axiomatized utility theory also evoked fierce criticism. One challenge was empirical in nature. French economist and later Nobel laureate Maurice Allais (1953) did not mince his words: "Whatever their attraction might be, none of the fundamental postulates leading to the Bernoulli principle as formulated by the American school can withstand analysis. All are based on false evidence" (p. 505). Another challenge was conceptual. Although Herbert Simon respected utility theory's normative appeal (at least for the domains in which its assumptions hold)[1]—he profoundly criticized its unrealistic assumptions. In his article *A Behavioral Model of Rational Choice* (1955), Simon spelled out the "severe demands" of what he later described as an "Olympian model" (Simon, 1983, p. 19)—an ideal that might work for omniscient gods, but was simply out of place in the real world:

> If we examine closely the "classical" concepts of rationality [...], we see immediately what severe demands they make upon the choosing organism. The organism must be able to attach definite pay-offs (or at least a definite range of pay-offs) to each possible outcome. This, of course, involves also the ability to specify the exact nature of outcomes—there is no room in the scheme for "unanticipated consequences." The pay-offs must be completely ordered—it must always be possible to specify, in a consistent way, that one outcome is better than, as good as, or worse than any other. And, if the certainty or probabilistic rules are employed, either the outcomes of particular alternatives must be known with certainty, or at least it must be possible to attach definite probabilities to outcomes. (pp. 103–104)

In actual human choice, such demands are rarely met. Beyond what Savage (1954) called "small worlds"—highly simplified environments such as

---

1. In fact, Simon (1945) wrote a glowing review of *Theory of Games and Economic Behavior*.

monetary gambles, where the consequences (e.g., monetary payoffs) and probabilities of all outcomes are known ("decisions from description"; Hertwig, 2015)—it is impossible for real people to live up to the decision-making ideal of specifying all possible outcomes, assigning them probabilities, and then maximizing the expected payoff. Instead, mere mortals often have access to only some of the information, or are unable to integrate that information in the sophisticated way mandated by expected utility theory, and instead rely on simplifying procedures. What do these constraints mean for the quality of people's choices? Simon (1956) conjectured that real organisms' behavior, although adaptive and satisficing, probably *"falls far short* of the ideal of 'maximizing' as postulated in economic theory" (Simon, 1956, p. 129, emphasis in the original). He further suggested that "the environments to which organisms must adapt possess properties that permit further simplification of its choice mechanisms" (p. 129).

Our goal in this chapter is to examine both of Simon's key theses. First, we investigate the price of simplicity: How far short of the ideal of maximization do simple choice strategies that fail to obey the demands of classical rationality fall? Second, we examine which statistical properties of the environment support or impede the performance of such heuristics. We analyze both questions in the time-honored environment of monetary gambles, that is, the very environment from which the concept of mathematical expectation and the classic notion of rational choice emerged (Hacking, 1975/2006; see also chapter 8). We do not, however, implement the monetary gambles as "small worlds" (Savage, 1954), fully described and with all outcomes and probabilities known; instead, we introduce uncertainty into the simulated environment in the form of imperfect knowledge. Before we describe this paradigm in more detail, let us briefly review two investigations that have inspired our own.

2.3 How Short Do Risky Choice Heuristics Fall of the Ideal of Maximization?

This analysis builds on the foundation of two previous investigations: Thorngate's (1980) strategy tournament and J. W. Payne, Bettman, and Johnson's (1988, 1993) influential research on the adaptive decision maker. Both focused on simple choice strategies and analyzed how short they fall of maximization. They explored this question in the world of risk, in which each choice leads to one of a set of possible specified outcomes, and each outcome occurs with a known probability (Luce & Raiffa, 1957, p. 13)—that is, in a world in which there are no surprises.

2.3.1   Efficient Decision Heuristics and Measures of Success

Since the 1970s, many decision scientists have joined the quest to identify systematic biases originating from people's reliance on heuristics (Kahneman, Slovic, & Tversky, 1982). Ignoring the zeitgeist, Thorngate (1980) instead asked how simple choice strategies can be: How much information can they ignore and still permit successful choices? In one of the early computer simulations in the decision sciences, he orchestrated a computer tournament in which 10 choice heuristics competed against one another. The heuristics were tested in a randomly generated choice environment involving choice problems with two, four, or eight options, with each option offering two, four, or eight outcomes (for details, see Thorngate, 1980). Here, we focus on the performance of the two top-performing heuristics in Thorngate's competition—the equiprobable heuristic and the probable heuristic—and the worst-performing heuristic, the least-likely heuristic. The three heuristics' policies are outlined in box 2.1. Each of the heuristics ignores a different aspect of the available information and thus implements a different variant of cognitive simplification (Gigerenzer & Gaissmaier, 2011). The equiprobable heuristic ignores all probabilities, meaning that it does not multiply (weigh) outcomes by their probabilities. Like Dawes' (1979) "improper linear models," it simply calculates the arithmetic mean of all outcomes per option and chooses the option with the highest mean. It thus acts as if each outcome, no matter how small or large, is as probable as any other outcome. The equiprobable heuristic thus embodies the "principle of indifference," a coinage attributed to Keynes (1921/1973b). It states that whenever there is no evidence favoring one possibility over another, they have the same probability (see also chapter 5). The probable heuristic, in contrast, considers probabilities, but only to classify outcomes into two sets (probable vs. improbable outcomes); it then removes all improbable outcomes from consideration. The least-likely heuristic considers only one kind of outcome per option, namely, the worst possible outcome, and chooses the option with the smallest probability that this worst outcome will occur.

How high is the price that the heuristics pay for straying from the ideal of maximization and ignoring some or much of the available information?

Box 2.1
Heuristics for choices under risk and uncertainty.

We illustrate each heuristic's policy and choice prediction with reference to the following choice problem with four options:

A −50 with a probability of .2 and 250 with a probability of .8.

B −200 with a probability of .4 and 600 with a probability of .6.

C −400 with a probability of .1 and 500 with a probability of .9.

D 100 with a probability of .7 and 400 with a probability of .3.

The *equiprobable heuristic* calculates the arithmetic mean of all outcomes within each option and chooses the option with the highest mean. It chooses option D, because its mean (250) is higher than that of A (100), B (200), or C (50).

The *least-likely heuristic* identifies each option's worst outcome and selects the option with the lowest probability of the worst outcome. It chooses option C, where the probability of the worst outcome (−400) is .1, lower than in A (.2), B (.4), or D (.7).

The *lexicographic heuristic* determines the most likely outcome of each option and selects the option with the highest most likely outcome. If two or more outcomes are equal, it determines the second most likely outcome of each option and selects the option with the highest second most likely outcome. The process is continued until a decision is reached. It chooses option B, because it offers the highest outcome (600) among all options' most likely outcomes.

The *probable heuristic* categorizes each option's outcomes as "probable" (i.e., $p \geq .50$ for a two-outcome option and $p \geq .25$ for a four-outcome option) or "improbable" and ignores all "improbable" outcomes. It then calculates the arithmetic mean of the remaining outcomes and selects the option with the highest average outcome. It chooses option B, because its probable outcome (600) is higher than that of A (250), C (500), or D (100).

The *natural-mean heuristic* calculates the average of all outcomes sampled per option and divides the average by the number of sampled outcomes. It chooses the payoff distribution with the highest average outcome. This choice depends on the sample of experience. For instance, the heuristic may sample five times from each of the four options and encounter the following sequences:

A 250, 250, 250, −50, 250

B 600, 600, −200, −200, 600

C 500, 500, 500, 500, 500

D 100, 100, 400, 100, 400

The heuristic chooses option C, where the average of all outcomes (500) is highest.

Thorngate (1980) used the proportion of times a heuristic selected the option with the highest expected value (henceforth, the "best" option) as benchmark for its performance. Expected value is defined as

$$E(x) = \Sigma p_i x_i, \tag{1}$$

where p_i and x_i are the probability and the amount of money associated with each outcome ($i = 1, \dots, n$) of an option. Measured against this benchmark, all heuristics will, ignoring exceptional circumstances, perform worse than expected value theory. In Thorngate's tournament, all heuristics performed better than chance, but two heuristics stood out: averaged across all variants of the gambling environment, the equiprobable heuristic and the probable heuristic chose the best option in 75.4% and 75.2% of cases, respectively. From this, Thorngate concluded that a "wide variety of decision heuristics will usually produce optimal, or close to optimal, choice and can thus be termed relatively efficient" (p. 223). Given that the best heuristics' performance lagged behind optimal performance (i.e., expected value theory) by a hefty 25 percentage points, this conclusion seems somewhat overstated. Paradoxically, however, due to his choice of performance metric, Thorngate may in fact have underrated the heuristics' efficiency.

To examine this possibility, we replicated Thorngate's (1980) simulation (with 100,000 instead of 200 gambles) but used a different performance metric. Specifically, how costly the failure to choose the best alternative will be depends on the discrepancy between the expected values of the option chosen and the best option. If the difference is small, the costs of deviating from optimality will be minor; if the difference is large, they will be consequential. In our simulation, we expressed performance on the 0%–100% range defined by the sum of the expected values of the worst possible options and the sum of the expected values of the best possible options. On this metric, expected value theory will, by definition, score perfectly (100%), whereas random choice will perform at around 50%. In our replication, the equiprobable heuristic scored 94.1% and the probable heuristic, 94.6%. The performance gap between these heuristics and expected value theory was thus reduced to about 5–6 percentage points. In other words, in this simulation, heuristics evidently tend to err in cases where the consequences are relatively benign. Thorngate's measure therefore underestimated the heuristics' performance (even the worst-performing heuristic, least-likely, jumped from a meager 41.4% on Thorngate's metric to 65.7% on ours).

In sum, although Thorngate (1980) applauded the efficiency of the heuristics, they fell noticeably short of the ideal of expected value maximization on his performance measure (which used the "best" option as a benchmark). In contrast, on a performance measure that gauges how costly it is to fail to choose the best alternative when choosing heuristically, we found that simple choice policies fared substantially better. Furthermore, Thorngate's analysis did not address the role of environmental properties in fostering or impeding the heuristics' performance. For instance, how robust will the top performer, the equiprobable heuristic, prove to be if the environment's probability distribution is skewed, causing high variance in probability information and potentially rendering the assumption of equal weights dangerously inaccurate?

2.3.2   The Adaptive Decision Maker

The interaction between environmental structures and the information-processing architecture of heuristics was a focus of J. W. Payne et al.'s (1993) research program. Its premise was that people can select from a multitude of available strategies. Each strategy combines attractive properties (e.g., simplicity, low cognitive effort, accuracy) with unattractive ones (e.g., higher cognitive effort, lack of accuracy). The impact of these properties varies across choice environments and conditions such as time pressure and cognitive abilities. An adaptive decision maker considering candidate strategies for a task will select the one that affords the best trade-off between anticipated accuracy and effort. The assumption here is that there is an inescapable and law-like *accuracy–effort trade-off*, meaning that the less information, computation, or time a strategy requires and the decision maker invests, the less accurate (rational or optimized) the ensuing behavior will be.

J. W. Payne et al. (1988) used computer simulations to analyze this accuracy–effort trade-off in risky and riskless choice in a range of environments and conditions. We focus on the simulation of risky choice and on a single environmental condition: variance in probabilities. For example, one option may have four possible outcomes, with probabilities of .28, .25, .25, and .22, respectively. In this case, variance in probabilities is low. The outcomes of another option may have probabilities of .7, .2, .08, and .02; in this case, variance in probabilities is high. How did heuristics perform under high and low probability variance? Here, we focus on the equiprobable heuristic (or "equal-weight heuristic," to use the terminology of J. W. Payne et al., 1988), the best performer in the Thorngate (1980) tournament, and the lexicographic heuristic (LEX), the best performer in the J. W. Payne et al. tournament. Like the other heuristics, LEX ignores part of the information (see box 2.1). It is a noncompensatory strategy; note that the environmental cue that in this heuristic overrides all other cues and determines the choice depends on the properties of the choice problem at hand. Details of the simulations are provided in J. W. Payne et al. (1988).

Three key results emerged (J. W. Payne et al., 1988). First, heuristics can be highly competitive in one environment but fail in another. The lexicographic heuristic, for instance, was very successful in the high-variance environment, but its performance dropped by more than 20 percentage points in the low-variance environment. No generalist heuristic emerged that was able to perform consistently well in all environments. Second and relatedly, variance in probabilities affected processing policies differently. Whereas high probability variance fostered the performance of the lexicographic heuristic, it undermined the success of the equiprobable heuristic; low probability variance had the opposite effect. Third, when averaged across all environments, the equiprobable heuristic and the lexicographic heuristic chose the best option in 79% and 56% of cases, respectively (the performance criterion in this simulation was equivalent to the expected value criterion employed by Thorngate, 1980). That is, the two heuristics paid a substantial premium for simplicity, similar in magnitude to that observed in Thorngate's analysis: the top choice performance was more than 20 percentage points below that of the expected value benchmark.

Let us summarize the findings so far. The most successful choice heuristics in Thorngate (1980) and J. W. Payne et al. (1988) represent two very different paths to cognitive simplification (see box 2.1). Whereas the equiprobable heuristic considers all outcomes per option but neglects probabilities altogether, the lexicographic heuristic examines one cue at a time, ignoring all others. Furthermore, low variance in outcome probabilities supports a focus on outcomes, whereas high variance in probabilities is more compatible with a noncompensatory choice policy. These insights were obtained in the world of risk, where the probability and outcome space are known. What will be the trade-off between performance and simplicity—or, to use J. W. Payne et al.'s terminology, accuracy and effort—when knowledge is imperfect and surprises can happen? In other words, how do the heuristics perform in a world of incomplete knowledge and uncertainty? The bias–variance framework, originally developed in machine learning (Geman, Bienenstock, & Doursat, 1992; T. Hastie, Tibshirani, & Friedman, 2001) offers a conceptual approach for understanding the impact of uncertainty on prediction models.

2.4 The Bias–Variance Dilemma

Bounds on people's knowledge about the environment can be hugely consequential, to the extent that limited knowledge intensifies the *bias–variance dilemma* (e.g., Gigerenzer & Brighton, 2009; Katsikopoulos, Schooler, & Hertwig, 2010). To introduce this concept, which is relevant for any kind of prediction model, we offer an example. Bias and variance both contribute to the total error committed by any prediction model. Let us imagine that a prediction model is attempting to learn an underlying (true) function from a sample of (potentially noisy) data that was generated by this function. Averaged across all possible data samples of a given size, the bias of the algorithm is defined as the difference between the underlying function and the mean function computed by the algorithm from these data samples. Consequently, if this mean function is the same as the underlying function, bias will be zero. Variance reflects the sensitivity of the prediction model to different samples drawn from the same environment. High variance implies that the predictions of a model may differ greatly depending on the specific properties of the observed samples. This type of variance increases with model flexibility. For example, the more flexible the model, the more likely it will capture not only the true structure (assuming that there is a true structure and that the models are complex enough to capture it) but also unsystematic patterns, such as noise. Bias and variance both depend on the structure to be predicted (e.g., daily temperature across a year in a specific location; daily stock market fluctuation across a year of a specific index), and at least the variance also depends on how many sampled observations are available for this structure. Therefore, it will not always be adaptive to seek low bias in a prediction model by including as many adjustable components as possible to flexibly capture patterns in the sampled data. Model flexibility can itself become a curse when there is a high risk of increasing error through variance. From this, it follows that a model should be complex enough to avoid excessive bias, but simple enough to avoid overfitting idio-syncratic noise in the limited samples on which the estimates are made (e.g., Pitt, Myung, & Zhang, 2002).

The principles underlying the bias–variance dilemma can be applied to decisions about monetary lotteries under uncertainty—that is, when the task is to predict the value of the lotteries. Let us assume that choice strategies do not enjoy perfect knowledge of outcomes and probabilities but instead gauge them from samples drawn from the environment. Consequently, all strategies face two sources of error—and the possible trade-off between them. One source is error through variance. For illustration, expected value theory assumes that outcomes are weighted (multiplicatively) by their exact prob-abilities and then summed and maximized. Under conditions of imperfect information, other, simpler forms of information integration—for example, additive rather than multiplicative integration (Juslin, Nilsson, & Winman, 2009)—or forgoing integration altogether (e.g., lexicographic heuristic) may be more robust and less likely to suffer from overfitting. Yet simplifica-tions can go too far, causing a substantial bias in the choice strategy and, consequently, prompting performance to deteriorate. How will these two sources of error shape the performance of choice heuristics under uncer-tainty? We examined this question by conducting a new set of simulations.

2.5   What Is the Price of Cognitive Simplicity in Choice under Uncertainty?

The benchmark used in our simulations is the performance of the expected value model under perfect knowledge. We call this model the omniscient expected value model. In addition, we used the same performance metric as in our reanalysis of the Thorngate (1980) competition. On this metric, 100% represents the sum of the expected values across choice problems in the case that a choice strategy always selects the option with the highest expected value (as the omniscient expected value model does); 0% repre-sents the sum of the expected values across choice problems in the case that a strategy always selects the option with the lowest expected value. All heuristics were tested in environments in which the available information on the options' outcomes and probabilities was incomplete. Information was acquired through repeated sampling of monetary outcomes. We define a sample as the draw of a single monetary outcome from each option in a choice problem (with replacement). Each new draw thus offered information about the gambles' possible outcomes and their relative frequency of occurrence (i.e., probability). Furthermore, after each new sample, each heuristic rendered a choice, allowing us to analyze how the heuristics' performance changed as knowledge increased. In this simulated environment, the uncertainty the decision maker faced concerned both the outcome space (i.e., at any given point in time, the decision maker did not know for certain whether they were aware of the full outcome space) and the probabilities (i.e., the decision maker estimated the probabilities from the sequences of the encountered outcomes, meaning that the probabilities of possible outcomes that had not been encountered were unknown and, for known outcomes, the probabilities could only be estimated on the basis of the experienced sample of draws).

2.5.1 Competitors

We tested the equiprobable, the probable, and the lexicographic heuristics—the three top performers in the simulations by Thorngate (1980) and J. W. Payne et al. (1988)—as well as the least-likely heuristic, the worst-performing heuristic in Thorngate's competition. In addition, we tested the natural-mean heuristic (Hertwig & Pleskac, 2008, 2010), whose policy is described in box 2.1. This heuristic has some interesting characteristics. For one, it predicts the same choice as expected value theory if the latter also bases its choices on samples of experience rather than on perfect knowledge. It thus defines the level of accuracy of a sampling-based expected value theory (without Bayesian priors). However, the heuristic rests on a much simpler processing policy than expected value theory. Instead of multiplying each sampled outcome by its inferred (sample-based) probability and summing up the products, the heuristic simply totals up all experienced outcomes per lottery and then divides this sum by the sample size per option. In other words, it replaces the multiplicative core of expected value theory by simple summing and division, thus requiring no explicit representation of probabilities.

2.5.2 Environments

We implemented 20 choice environments, designed by combining five outcome distributions with four ways of constructing the associated probabilities (see also chapter 3). The outcome distributions consisted of a rectangular, a normal, an exponential, a Cauchy, and a lognormal distribution. These distributions permitted us to implement varying degrees of outcome variance. All five outcome distributions were symmetrical (for details, see figure S2.1 and table S2.1 in the online supplement at https://taming-uncer tainty.mpib-berlin.mpg.de/). The four construction mechanisms producing the probabilities (i.e., rectangular, U-shaped, exponential, and skewed), hence-forth *P-generators*, were chosen with the goal of obtaining different degrees of variance among probabilities (see J. W. Payne et al., 1993). As figure S2.2 in the online supplement illustrates, the four P-generators yielded markedly different probability distributions depending on the number of outcomes in the gamble. Table S2.2 in the online supplement quantifies the degrees of probability variance within options, giving a more direct measure of prob-ability variance. Finally, each choice problem consisted of two, four, or eight options, with each option having the same number of outcomes (two, four, or eight). Here, we focus on the condition with two options per choice problem; this resulted in 60 sets of choice problems (i.e., 20 environments consisting of two, four, or eight outcomes).

2.5.3 Learning by Sampling

All heuristics learned about the properties of the choice problem in question by sequentially taking one draw at a time from each of the two options. Based on this information, the heuristics chose what they inferred to be the best option after each sample. The heuristics thus advanced from com-plete ignorance to progressively more knowledge and less uncertainty with each round of sampling. To experience the consequences of this type of sam-pling and heuristic choice for yourself, please visit interactive element 2.1 (at https://taming-uncertainty.mpib-berlin.mpg.de/). In our simulation, learning stopped after 50 rounds (resulting in 50 sampled outcomes for each option and 100 sampled outcomes for each choice problem with two options). For each of the 20 environments, 6,000 choice problems were ran-domly generated (2,000 each for choice problems containing options with two, four, and eight outcomes). Each heuristic therefore made $50 \times 6,000$ choices, amounting to 300,000 choices per environment (when a heuristic was unable to reach a choice, a random choice between the options was implemented). How did uncertainty and the successive reduction of uncer-tainty through learning affect the heuristics' performance? We first turn to how the heuristics fared in the environment that Thorngate (1980) analyzed (i.e., rectangular outcome and probability distributions); we then consider

their performance across all 20 environments and, finally, examine the interaction between the specific simplifying assumptions made by each heuristic
and its performance in specific environmental structures.

2.5.4   How Do Heuristics Fare When Uncertainty Rules?

Figure 2.1 plots the performance of the five competitors as a function of
learning for choice problems involving two options. The figure plots the
average expected value of the option chosen by each heuristic, relative to
chance level (50%) and to the performance of omniscient expected value
theory (100%). Let us highlight four observations. First, there was substantial variability in performance, with the least-likely heuristic again (as in
Thorngate's, 1980, tournament) lagging far behind. Second, in some cases,
performance increased little with learning—or even decreased (e.g., the lexicographic heuristic); in others, it increased substantially (e.g., the probable
heuristic). Third, the natural-mean and the equiprobable heuristics clearly
outperformed the lexicographic heuristic and, by a smaller margin, the probable heuristic. Fourth, when learning samples were small, the equiprobable
heuristic performed as well as or even slightly better than the natural-mean

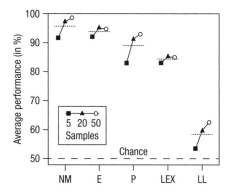

Figure 2.1
Average performance for each of the five heuristics (see box 2.1): the natural-mean
(NM), equiprobable (E), probable (P), lexicographic (LEX), and least-likely (LL) heuristics in the environment that Thorngate (1980) implemented (rectangular outcome
and probability distributions) as a function of learning (5, 20, and 50 samples per
option) for choice problems involving two options (and averaged across two, four
and eight outcomes). The performance benchmark for omniscient expected value
theory is 100%. The dotted line represents the average performance across the three
sample sizes.

heuristic; once more knowledge became available, the latter had the edge. Averaged across the number of outcomes, and with performance expressed relative to the range of best possible to worst possible performance (as in our reanalysis of the Thorngate environment), the equiprobable heuristic scored 92.1% (5 samples), 95.1% (20 samples), 94.8% (50 samples), with a mean of 94.0%; the natural-mean heuristic scored 91.7% (5 samples), 97.3% (20 samples), 98.6% (50 samples), with a mean of 95.9%. The latter represents the performance of expected value theory, assuming it lacks omniscience and has to make do with sampled slices permitting a noisy glimpse of the environment. Thus, the advantage of expected value theory decreases from 5–6 percentage points under conditions of perfect knowledge in our reanalysis of the simulation by Thorngate (1980) to 1.9 percentage points under conditions of imperfect knowledge. Will these findings generalize across environments beyond the specific environment that Thorngate chose for his simulations?

2.5.5 Generalization: Does the Performance Gap Close More Generally?

We next examined the heuristics across all 20 choice environments implemented (see section 2.5.2). We again focused on choice problems involving two options; the results for problems with more options were not qualitatively different. Figure 2.2 plots the heuristics' performance as a function of learning. As before, the natural-mean and the equiprobable heuristics were the frontrunners. Averaged across 5, 20, and 50 samples, the former scored 97.2% and the latter 93.8%—resulting in a difference of 3.4 percentage points, almost half the size of the gap (6 percentage points) found in our reanalysis of Thorngate's (1980) data. In particular, under high uncertainty (5 samples), the performance of the two heuristics was nearly identical: 93.2% vs. 93.9%. The next-best heuristic was again the probable heuristic (average score: 90.7%), followed by LEX (87.4%). These findings show that the equiprobable heuristic, which ignores all probabilities, lagged behind the natural-mean heuristic by just 3.4 percentage points when averaged across all sample sizes; when uncertainty was pronounced, their performance was nearly indistinguishable. As mentioned in section 2.5.1, the latter heuristic is equivalent to expected value theory without the gift of omniscience. In sum, across two simulations, we found that the advantage of expected value theory over simple heuristics shrank substantially, or even reversed slightly,

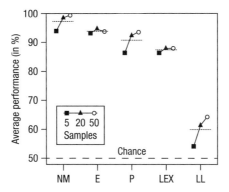

Figure 2.2
Average performance for each of the five heuristics (see box 2.1): the natural-mean (NM), equiprobable (E), probable (P), lexicographic (LEX), and least-likely (LL) heuristics across all 20 environments. The results are plotted as a function of learning (5, 20, and 50 samples per option) and are limited to choice problems with two options (and averaged across two, four and eight outcomes). The dotted lines represent the heuristics' performance averaged across 5, 20, and 50 samples.

when all strategies were tested under realistic assumptions of imperfect knowledge relative to perfect knowledge.

We next turn to Simon's (1956) second proposal: "The environments to which organisms must adapt possess properties that permit further simplification of its choice mechanisms" (p. 129). Taking advantage of the various environments we implemented, we are now, like J. W. Payne et al. (1993), able to examine the impact of distinct environmental structures on the heuristics' performance.

2.5.6   What Are Heuristics' Environmental Allies?
According to J. W. Payne et al.'s (1988) observations, variance in probability information is an environmental ally of the lexicographic heuristic but a foe of the equiprobable heuristic. Our multiple combinations of outcome distributions and probability mechanisms permitted us to systematically analyze the impact of variance (see table S2.2), separately for the dimensions of probability and outcome. In the following analyses, we focus on choice problems with two options and eight possible outcomes per option, making it easier to detect possible dependencies between environmental structures and heuristic policies. Moreover, we limit our analysis to two

heuristics with different policies—lexicographic and equiprobable—and use the natural-mean heuristic as a benchmark; again, the latter is comparable to expected value theory in the context of sampling, where knowledge is limited.

Our first analysis combined the rectangular outcome distribution with the probability distributions obtained from the four P-generators: rectangular, U-shaped, exponential, and skewed (see figure S2.2 and details in the online supplement). Figure 2.3 plots the three heuristics' scores as a

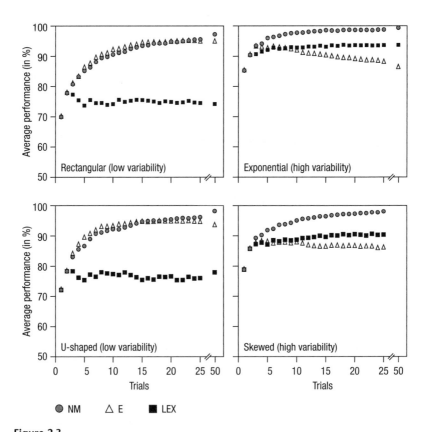

Figure 2.3

Average expected score for the natural-mean (NM), equiprobable (E), and lexicographic (LEX) heuristics as a function of learning ($n = 1 - 50$ samples per option) and of four construction principles for the probability information (rectangular, exponential, U-shaped, and skewed). In each case, the distribution of the outcome information is rectangular. The results refer to choice problems with two options and eight outcomes.

function of learning, by probability distribution. When variance in probabilities was relatively small—as was the case for the rectangular and the U-shaped P-generators—the equiprobable heuristic outpaced the natural-mean heuristic for small to medium sample sizes; in addition, the performance of the lexicographic heuristic did not improve with learning. The reason for this lack of learning is that the "most likely" outcome (LEX's top priority) tends to be experienced early in the learning process; more sampling tends not to yield previously unknown outcomes. When variance in probabilities was high, as was the case for the exponential and skewed P-generators, the natural-mean heuristic clearly outstripped the equiprobable and lexicographic heuristics. Under this condition, the accuracy of the equiprobable heuristic decreased with learning. This phenomenon is explained by the disproportional impact of rare outcomes. Specifically, a heuristic that keeps learning will eventually encounter relatively rare outcomes. This causes a problem for the equiprobable heuristic: no matter how rare an outcome is, the equiprobable heuristic will keep assigning it the same weight as it assigns to much more common outcomes. Consequently, the equiprobable heuristic "overweights" rare outcomes (see chapter 8). The lexicographic heuristic does not fall into the same trap, because its top priority is the most likely outcome.

Variance in probabilities is thus an environmental property that clearly impacts the performance of heuristics. The same does not hold for variance in outcomes. Following the same logic as in the previous simulation, in a second analysis we combined the rectangular P-generator with five outcome distributions: the rectangular, normal, exponential, Cauchy, and lognormal distributions (see figure S2.1 in the online supplement). The equiprobable heuristic outpaced the natural-mean heuristic across all distributions (and degrees of outcome variance) when uncertainty was pronounced (i.e., 20 samples or fewer). It was only after substantial learning that the natural-mean heuristic gained the upper hand. The lexicographic heuristic performed on a much lower level; in addition, it failed to benefit from learning. The reason is that, even in very small samples, LEX settles on the most likely outcome—and the most likely outcome will occur early on, irrespective of how much return it offers. Consequently, rare but (very) large outcomes that are experienced with more sampling are unlikely to lead to a different choice for LEX because they cannot replace the "most likely outcome," to which LEX gives priority.

Taken together, these results help to reveal the relative match (or lack thereof) of choice heuristics to environmental structures: we can thus identify environmental properties that support or hamper the heuristics' performance under uncertainty. First, when variance in probability information is relatively high, boldly ignoring all probabilities—that is, applying the equiprobable heuristic—is detrimental to performance (see figure 2.3). Under these conditions, the equiprobable heuristic risks attaching too much weight to rare events by giving each outcome the same weight. In contrast, noncompensatory heuristics such as the lexicographic heuristic, which shields itself against overweighting low-probability events, learn and perform better than a unit-weight policy. When, however, variance in probability information is relatively low, the equiprobable heuristic, which sums across all outcomes, offers the better simplification policy. For small samples, it even eclipses the natural-mean heuristic. In this environment, the noncompensatory policy of the lexicographic heuristic falls behind. Variance can also occur on the dimension of outcomes. The equiprobable heuristic proves utterly robust against this source of variance. Regardless of whether outcome variance is low or high, the policy of simply summing all (nonweighted) outcomes excels when probability variance is low. In addition, when uncertainty is high to medium (small samples), the equiprobable heuristic even eclipses the natural-mean heuristic.

2.6   Theoretical Realism and Imperfect Knowledge

As Nobel laureate Kenneth Arrow (1951) stressed, incomplete knowledge is the key property and condition of many real-world choices (see chapter 18). People have to choose between actions without being fully aware of the consequences. What theories of choice respect the limits of time, knowledge, and computational power under these ubiquitous environmental and psychological conditions? In Simon's (1956, 1983) view, the classical economic framework makes unrealistic demands on people. Instead, he suggested that most tasks are mastered by "approximate methods" (Simon, 1990, p. 6). However, there are costs to using these methods rather than the optimal model. When Simon first proposed the notion of bounded rationality, he stated that approximate methods are likely to fall far short of the ideal of maximizing as postulated in economic theory (Simon, 1956). He thus appears to have assumed what J. W. Payne et al. (1988, 1993) later portrayed as an accuracy–effort trade-off. The less information, computation, or time a decision maker invests, the less accurate their behavior (choice, inferences, and so on) will be. This appears to be an inescapable and law-like truth about the mind's decision-making machinery. Indeed, both Thorngate (1980) and J. W. Payne et al. (1993) observed evidence in support of this trade-off, notwithstanding the relatively high level of accuracy that some heuristics achieved in their computer tournaments. These tournaments did not, how-ever, implement imperfect knowledge. Instead, the analyses were focused on "small worlds" (Savage, 1954), decisions from descriptions (Hertwig & Erev, 2009), and decisions under risk (as defined by Knight, 1921/2002, and Luce & Raiffa, 1957), where the possible outcomes and their probabilities are pre-cisely known. Without doubt, such choice situations exist, but they may be the exception rather than the rule.

How pronounced is the accuracy–effort trade-off in environments charac-terized by uncertainty, imperfect information, and the need for search? We addressed this question in the context of monetary gambles, that portray decision making in terms of just two basic dimensions: outcomes and prob-abilities. Admittedly, this environment is somewhat odd, divorced as it is from any real content and context. Yet it would be difficult to overstate the role that monetary gambles have played in the development of normative and descriptive theories of choice (e.g., Allais, 1953; Bernoulli, 1738/1954; Kahneman & Tversky, 1979). Moreover, it is the context in which the ideal of rational decision making in terms of weighting and summing all pieces of information was originally conceived. From expected value theory and expected utility theory to the other descriptive neo-Bernoullian choice theo-ries such as cumulative prospect theory (Tversky & Kahneman, 1992)—all suggest, once interpreted as information-processing theories, that people have to weight and sum. Heuristic policies that forgo weighting or summing can lead to surprisingly accurate performance; moreover, our simulation results (see figure 2.2) suggest that—to the extent that an accuracy–effort trade-off exists—it is less severe under incomplete knowledge (uncertainty) than under perfect knowledge (risk).

2.7   The Strategy Selection Problem and Uncertainty

Our results suggest an interesting twist to a key question: How does the mind select a heuristic from the adaptive toolbox? The simulations of choice heuristics by Thorngate (1980) and J. W. Payne et al. (1988), as well as those in this chapter, demonstrate one thing: there is great variability in the performance of heuristics, and choosing the wrong one in a given environment may prove costly. How does the mind figure out which heuristic to select? Selection could be guided by individual reinforcement learning (e.g., Rieskamp & Otto, 2006), by teaching (e.g., physicians, firefighters, and pilots are taught which cues to consult, in which order, and how to process them), by social learning (e.g., when procedures and strategies are copied from peers or other models), or by meta-inductive strategies that consider heuristics' past successes (Schurz & Thorn, 2016). The process might also involve systematic change and adaptation on an evolutionary time scale, as with rules of thumb for predation and mate search in animal species (Hutchinson & Gigerenzer, 2005). There is, however, another answer. The good average performance of the equiprobable heuristic under conditions of highly limited knowledge (see figure 2.2)—a result that held across environmental structures—suggests that some heuristics may offer good fallback options when an informed strategy selection is not possible. In the domain of inference, people have indeed been found to rely more on such unit-weighting strategies under conditions of greater uncertainty (i.e., when the cue hierarchy is unknown) than under conditions of lesser uncertainty (e.g., Pachur & Marinello, 2013).

2.8   Objectives beyond Expected Value Maximization

Our results from the preferential domain of monetary gambles demonstrate that the dynamic of the accuracy–effort trade-off differs, depending on whether performance is tested under "small world" conditions or under realistic conditions of incomplete knowledge and uncertainty. Similar results have been found in the inference domain (Gigerenzer & Brighton, 2009; Gigerenzer, Hertwig, & Pachur, 2011). However, let us emphasize one important point. Simplification in the choice process can go too far. Heuristics with a strong bias (see discussion of the bias–variance dilemma in section 2.4)—for instance, the least-likely heuristic (see figures 2.1 and 2.2)—fall far behind the best-performing heuristics. One could, however, argue that this heuristic achieves a very different objective than expected value theory—namely, it minimizes the risk of ending up with a bad outcome, or even the worst possible outcome. In future analyses, it will therefore be important to evaluate these heuristics against diverse objectives, including risk aversion. Future simulations can also examine the extent to which imperfection in the process of learning outcomes and probabilities, as well as the forgetting of experiences, affects the performance of normative and heuristic models of choice. We suspect that such factors might compromise the more complex normative models to a greater extent than the simpler heuristics, thus bringing them even closer together.

2.9   Do People Use the Simplification Policies Studied?

Models of heuristics are realistic insofar as they respect constraints such as imperfect knowledge, time pressure, and limited computational resources. But do people actually use these heuristics? Relatively little is known about the extent to which people employ the equiprobable, lexicographic, and natural-mean heuristics in choices under uncertainty (e.g., decisions from experience; Hertwig & Erev, 2009; for choices under risk, see Brandstätter, Gigerenzer, & Hertwig, 2006; Glöckner & Pachur, 2012; Pachur, Hertwig, Gigerenzer, & Brandstätter, 2013). However, the equiprobable and lexicographic heuristics have been observed to be used in the domain of inference (e.g., Bröder, 2011; Pachur & Marinello, 2013). Drawing on a meta-analysis of over 45,000 sampling sequences and subsequent decisions from experience (Wulff, Mergenthaler-Canseco, & Hertwig, 2018), Hertwig, Wulff, and Mata (2018) analyzed the ability of various heuristics to predict people's choices. Of the heuristics implemented here, the natural-mean heuristic was best at predicting people's choices, outperforming, for instance, cumulative prospect theory (Tversky & Kahneman, 1992; assuming existing sets of parameter values); on average, it correctly predicted 73.2% of choices (Hau, Pleskac, Kiefer, & Hertwig, 2008). This does not imply that the people in question used this or other heuristics to make those choices. But it suggests that heuristics represent a class of models that should always be taken into account when the aim is to provide a realistic account of how people make choices under uncertainty.

2.10   Revisiting Simon's Expectation

To conclude, the results of the pioneering computer tournaments by Thorngate (1980) and J. W. Payne et al. (1988, 1993) supported Simon's expectation that relying on simple decision strategies necessarily comes at a price: their choices will fall short of the ideal of maximization postulated in economic theory (Simon, 1956). Our simulations substantially qualify both Simon's expectation and the conclusions drawn from the past computer tournaments: in the context of more realistic choices, where the state of knowledge is not perfect, the performance gap between simple choice heuristics and maximization is much smaller than previously thought. It is considerably smaller under uncertainty than under risk, and under some environmental conditions heuristics even take the lead. This is an important result. Heuristics are applied not only because the mind's cognitive resources are inevitably limited when measured against the world's complexity. Equally important, the environment often deprives decision makers of the information required by computationally and informationally more complex strategies. The Olympian models—such as the expected utility theory as proposed by Bernoulli (1738/1954) and axiomatized by von Neumann and Morgenstern (1944/2007)—require perfect knowledge of probabilities. When objective probabilities are unknown or only imprecisely known, the decision maker therefore needs to estimate subjective ones, as in Savage's (1954) subjective expected utility theory. Or—and this is the alternative that emerges from our analyses, as exemplified by the good performance of both the natural-mean heuristic and the equiprobable heuristic—they can do without knowledge of probabilities. In many environments, doing without may be a better bet than running the risk of making consequential errors when estimating subjective probabilities out of thin air.

3 Using Risk–Reward Structures to Reckon with Uncertainty

Timothy J. Pleskac, Ralph Hertwig, Christina Leuker, and Larissa Conradt

3.1 The Risk–Reward Hypothesis

Would you stop to pick up a $1 bill lying on the sidewalk? What about a $100 bill? There is an old story about an economics professor and a keen-eyed student walking across a busy university quad. "Look," says the student, pointing to the ground, "a $100 bill!" As the student stoops to pick it up, the professor mutters, "Don't bother—if it were really a $100 bill, somebody would have picked it up already."

This story is often used to introduce the efficient market hypothesis, which states that share prices on the stock market reflect all available relevant information (Fama, 1965). In other words, it is impossible to beat the market on a consistent basis: investors will not be able to earn above-average returns without taking above-average risks. By the same token, it is unlikely that a real $100 bill will be lying on the street. We contend, however, that the story can also highlight the use of a heuristic. Instead of physically examining the bill to confirm its authenticity, the professor uses its dollar value to estimate the chance of it being real. Because the dollar value of the bill is pretty high, the professor estimates the likelihood of it being real as fairly low. By ignoring other information and using only the bill's value to infer the probability that it is real, the professor is using what we refer to as the *risk–reward heuristic* (Pleskac & Hertwig, 2014).

Our hypothesis is that this heuristic is not something that only economic professors use, but rather a rule of thumb that many people rely on in real situations, such as when estimating the chances of winning a specific amount on the lottery, the likelihood that an insurable event will occur, or even perhaps, as we will see, when a farmer estimates the chances of a successful insemination of a dairy cow from the price of the semen. These situations—when the payoffs or outcomes are known, but the probabilities are not—are typically referred to as *decisions under uncertainty* (Luce & Raiffa, 1957; see also chapter 18). The tricky problem with these decisions is that probabilities have to be estimated. This is where the risk–reward heuristic comes into play. In contexts where payoffs and probabilities are inversely related, the risk–reward heuristic can be used to infer unknown probabilities from observed payoffs. But can this inferential heuristic be accurate? And do people use it accurately?

We address these questions by first summarizing the results of an ecological analysis that identifies conditions under which the risk–reward heuristic can provide accurate estimates of probabilities. This ecological analysis also provides insights into why the relationship occurs. We then review what is known about when people use the heuristic and provide empirical evidence that they use it in adaptive ways. Finally, we illustrate how this ecologically grounded inference can shed light on some basic theoretical problems in the area of judgment and decision making and, more practically, how it can help to evaluate the bets that people might try to sell you. Taken together, we will show that the risk–reward heuristic is a simple tool people use for addressing uncertainty—one that can make good ecological sense to use.

3.2   An Ecological Analysis of the Relationship between Risk and Reward

Time and again, thinkers, writers, and scholars have described the intimate ties between risks and rewards. In considering satisfaction in life, the writer Hunter S. Thompson (1955) stated, "So we shall let the reader answer this question for himself: who is the happier man, he who has braved the storm of life and lived or he who has stayed securely on shore and merely existed?" (p. 5). Similarly, Niccolò Machiavelli, the famous Italian statesmen and political philosopher, once noted that in politics, "Never was anything great achieved without danger." In the area of finance, a casual search of the Internet or self-help books reveals statements like "understanding the relationship between risk and reward is a key piece in building your personal investment philosophy" (Little, 2018). All of these nuggets of wisdom suggest that the key to success is knowing how to trade risk for reward. Yet trade-offs between risk and reward can be made if only there is a systematic relationship between the two.

3.2.1   A Marketplace of Human-Made Gambles

Against this background, Pleskac and Hertwig (2014) conducted an ecological analysis of the risks and rewards inherent in a diverse set of life's gambles. Their goal was twofold. First, they sought to determine whether there are indeed reliable risk–reward structures in various environments. Second, they aimed to shed light on possible causes of this relationship. The first set of environments that they examined were actual monetary gambles. Consider, for instance, the game of roulette. A ball is spun around a wheel with 38 unique pockets, and players bet on where the ball will land. Players have a variety of betting options. For instance, they can bet that the ball will land in pocket number 1 or in a red pocket. In total, there are 155 possible bets; of those, 22 are unique in terms of payout. Figure 3.1 plots the relationship between risks and rewards across those 22 bets. It shows a systematic inverse relationship that we have all come to expect, with increasing payoffs becoming less and less likely to occur.

Figure 3.2a also plots the risk–reward relationship in roulette, but now both payoffs and probabilities are on a log scale. Plotting the risk–reward relationship in this way helps show the same inverse relationship extends to other monetary environments, including the bets offered at a horse track (see figure 3.2b) and the conditions of a life insurance policy (see figure 3.2c).

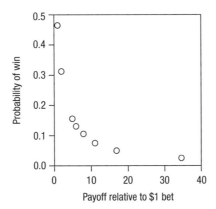

Figure 3.1
Relationship between payoffs and probabilities in the game of roulette (recreated from Pleskac & Hertwig, 2014).

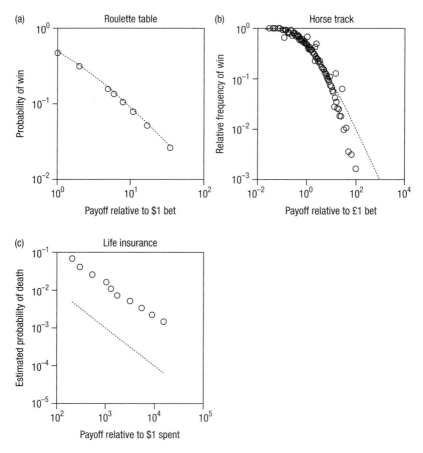

Figure 3.2
Relationship between payoffs and probabilities (plotted in log-log space) in the context of roulette (a), the horse track (b), and life insurance policies (c). The dashed lines in each panel show the fair-bet probabilities p; see text for details (recreated from Pleskac & Hertwig, 2014).

3.2.2 Fair Bets

At this point, you may feel inclined to protest, "Of course there is a risk–reward relationship in these gambles—that is exactly how they were constructed!" This objection is justified, but it also pinpoints the first driver of the risk–reward relationship: the forces of the marketplace. To see how these forces give rise to the risk–reward relationship, let us consider a seller in possession of a gamble that has the prospect of gaining g if an event whose probability is p occurs (e.g., the United States beats Germany at soccer). The seller offers a player this gamble at price c. Naturally, the player desires a high payoff, with the highest of probabilities and at the lowest cost. The seller has the opposite aspiration. These opposing forces push the gambles toward a state in which expected gains correspond to expected losses, such that:

$$p \times g = (1-p) \times c. \tag{1}$$

Reworking this equation shows that under these conditions the probability of winning will be inversely proportional to the total payoff:

$$p = c / (c+g). \tag{2}$$

These fair-bet probabilities—or what we call risk–reward probabilities—are plotted as a dashed line in each panel of figure 3.2 (setting $c=1$). Comparison of actual (roulette) and estimated probabilities (horse track and life insurance) with the risk–reward probabilities shows a close alignment, supporting the intuition that the risk–reward relationship is engendered by market forces.

There are, however, small but systematic deviations (remember that the plots are in log-log space and on different scales). In roulette, the actual probability of winning deviates from p by an average absolute deviation of 0.93 percentage points. In horse racing, the average absolute deviation is 0.74 percentage points; in purchasing life insurance, it is 1.69 percentage points. Casino rule number 1 offers an answer to the question of why there are deviations: the house always wins. That is, there is a bias built into games of chance, as a result of which the risk–reward probabilities in roulette and at the horse track tend to overestimate the true probabilities. The opposite holds for life insurance, where the risk–reward probabilities underestimate the true probabilities. This happens because in insurance the financial risks are spread out across a large number of contributors, thereby offsetting the risk faced by any one contributor.

3.2.3 Beyond Monetary Gambles

In the casino, at the horse track, and when purchasing life insurance, it is hard to escape the fact that one is entering a wager. But to what extent does the relationship between risk and reward also exist outside the marketplace of human-made monetary gambles? Such real-world wagers are more difficult to identify, but consider the three examples plotted in figure 3.3.

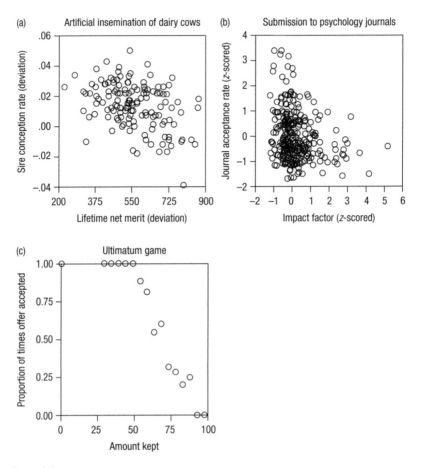

Figure 3.3
Relationship between payoffs and probabilities in farmers' choices of semen for the artificial insemination of dairy cows, scientists' choices of psychology journals when submitting manuscripts, and in the ultimatum game (recreated from Pleskac & Hertwig, 2014).

First, figure 3.3a plots the relationship between risks and rewards for a choice made by dairy farmers on a fairly regular basis: which specimen of bull semen to use to artificially inseminate their cows. To make this choice, farmers typically consult a catalog listing the specimens available from different sires. Various statistics are listed for each specimen, but farmers are generally advised to focus on two factors: (a) the sire conception rate, an estimate of the conception rate of the sire's sperm, and (b) the lifetime net merit of the sample, an estimate of the average improvement in profit that a dairy farmer can expect from the daughters of a specific bull. These factors are essentially proxies for probabilities and payoffs and here, too, there is an inverse relationship between risks and rewards.

Second, scientists weigh up the odds when submitting a manuscript for publication. Should they aim for a high-impact journal that rejects many of the manuscripts submitted, or should they settle for a lower-impact journal that accepts more manuscripts? Figure 3.3b plots this risk–reward relationship in the field of psychology, using a journal's acceptance rate (a proxy for risk, indicating the proportion of manuscripts accepted for publication by a given journal) and impact factor (a proxy for reward, indicating the average number of times an article in that journal is cited).

Even in these environments, market forces can explain the relationship between risk and reward. Dairy farmers would be unwise to buy the sperm of a bull with a low sire conception rate and low lifetime net merit. Scientists would be ill-advised to publish in journals with low acceptance rates and low impact factors. In other words, choosing dominated options is self-defeating. As a result, market forces will remove such dominated options. Companies only sell semen samples that are high on lifetime net merit, sire conception rate, or both, and remove samples that are low on either factor from the reference class. Such filtering is also likely to occur with scientific journals. However, filtering takes time, and not all dominated options are as easily detected as an unfair bet at the roulette table. Moreover, there are sometimes other reasons for picking an option than the potential payoff. All of these factors imply the relationship will be noisy.

But market forces are not the only driver of risk–reward relationships, as indicated by the regularity of the data points in figure 3.3c. These data show the inverse relationship that emerges in the interactions of a pair of players in the ultimatum game, an economic game used to study bargaining. Interestingly, market forces predict—if anything—the absence of a risk–reward relationship in this game. The reason is as follows. In the ultimatum game, one person, the proposer, suggests how to split a fixed monetary pie (in this case, 100 points, with each point worth real money). The split represents a take-it-or-leave-it offer that the other person, the responder, must either accept or reject. If the responder rejects the offer, both players go away empty-handed. From the perspective of a self-interested utility maximizer, this game is devoid of uncertainty: any responder maximizing their self-interest should accept any positive payoff, no matter how small. Thus, the proposer should offer the smallest amount possible to maximize their self-interest, a lick of the spoon so to speak. However, responders rarely accept just a lick of the spoon. Instead, responders are typically willing to forgo any payoff at all so as to punish such violations of fairness (Fehr & Schmidt, 1999; Quervain et al., 2004; Rabin, 1993). But because proposers anticipate this threat of punishment, this exchange turns into an uncertain gamble where the amount of money offered trades off with the risk of being punished, thereby creating a risk–reward relationship.

Our ecological analysis has been inductive in nature, but a more deductive approach is possible. Box 3.1 outlines such a deductive approach, showing how competition for finite resources suffices to create an inverse relationship between risks and rewards. Taken together, these analyses suggest that the risk–reward relationship is not a peripheral phenomenon. Instead, it is a frequent and recurrent ecological structure driven often by market forces and competition over limited resources, but not always. The next question is whether people have learned to exploit this risk–reward structure to reckon with uncertainty.

Box 3.1
How competition for limited resources can create a risk–reward relationship.

The environments in the ecological analysis summarized in figures 3.2 and 3.3 share several factors. One is competition for limited resources, suggesting that competition may be an important ingredient for the development of risk–reward relationships. In fact, we can use a theoretical framework from behavioral ecology, known as ideal free distribution (IFD) theory (Fretwell & Lucas, 1969), to show competition is a sufficient condition for a risk–reward relationship (see Pleskac, Conradt, Leuker, & Hertwig, 2018 for more details).

IFD theory predicts that groups of foraging animals will distribute themselves proportionally to the resources in a patch—in the same way as people distribute themselves among grocery store checkout lines according to the speed at which each line is moving. Formally, IFD theory states that the number of competitors n_y in patch y is proportional to the amount of resources r_y in the patch:

$$n_y \propto r_y. \tag{B1}$$

The IFD assumes that competitors are able to detect the patch with the highest rate of consumption (ideal) and are free to move between patches. These assumptions imply that competitors will move to patches with higher

Box 3.1 (continued)

potential consumption rates and that, over time, the entire system will reach an equilibrium state at which the number of competitors in each patch is proportional to the amount of resources in that patch.

For our purposes, it is useful to consider what a new competitor experiences when entering a landscape with an IFD, namely, a risk–reward relationship. To see this, we can break down the total amount of resources in patch r_y into the number of resource items m_y multiplied by the size of each resource s_y: $r_y = m_y \times s_y$. Thus, the IFD (equation B1) can be formally rewritten as:

$$n_y \propto m_y \times s_y. \tag{B2}$$

We assume that the probability p of an individual competitor successfully obtaining a resource increases with the number of resource items in the patch and decreases with the number of competitors in the patch, such that

$$p_y \propto m_y / n_y. \tag{B3}$$

Substituting equation B3 into equation B2 reveals that the probability of successfully obtaining a resource is inversely proportional to the size of the resource in a patch:

$$p_y \propto 1/s_y. \tag{B4}$$

That is, if there is variation in the size of each resource between patches but not within patches (e.g., because different patches consist of different habitat types), then individual competitors will face a choice between patches that trade off resource size for the probability of obtaining an item. Thus, the probability of obtaining a resource item is inversely proportional to resource item size (i.e., reward size) across landscapes, a risk–reward relationship. It is in these environments that it is ecologically rational to use a heuristic that infers the probabilities of obtaining a resource or reward from the size of the resource itself: the risk–reward heuristic.

One benefit of this framework is that it predicts not only when and why a risk–reward relationship will emerge but also when it will not emerge. By extension, the theory suggests conditions under which inferring probabilities from the magnitudes of rewards will fail. One straightforward answer is that a risk–reward relationship will not be present when the system is not in equilibrium. Thus, all other things being equal, a system that either has not reached or cannot reach equilibrium in terms of the distribution of competitors will not reliably evolve a risk–reward relationship. It follows that reliance on the risk–reward heuristic is not ecologically rational in nascent competitive environments.

3.3   The Risk–Reward Heuristic

Our ecological analysis demonstrates that in many environments the probabilities of an event are inversely related to the magnitude of the associated payoffs. This finding supports our general hypothesis that people can harness the risk–reward relationship as a heuristic to gauge the unknown probability of an event occurring from the payoff associated with that event. Our analysis also provides a precise specification of the risk–reward heuristic for monetary gambles with a pay-to-play structure as follows:

> For gambles that offer a single payoff g, otherwise nothing, infer the unknown probability p of winning a payoff from the ratio of the entry costs of playing the gamble c to the total amount of possible winnings as $p' = c / (c + g)$.
>
> The probability of not winning and forfeiting the price c of the gamble is $1 - p'$.

Many decisions, including the ones in our ecological analyses, have this pay-to-play structure. There are, of course, other types of gambles, including gambles that deal with losses only or with multiple payoffs. In many of these cases, the specification of the heuristic process can be modified to provide precise predictions. For the purposes of this chapter, which seeks to test the general hypothesis that people use the risk–reward heuristic, we focus on gambles with a pay-to-play structure and the chance of winning a single possible payoff. We now review the empirical evidence we have gathered so far on whether and how people use the risk–reward heuristic.

3.4   Do People Use the Risk–Reward Heuristic?

As a first step in examining whether people use the risk–reward heuristic, we offered participants an opportunity to play a gamble for a fixed prize. We were interested in their estimates of the chances of winning and in how these estimates changed with the size of the prize. We have run the study several times (Pleskac & Hertwig, 2014). Here is what we told a recent sample of 455 volunteers in an online study (Pleskac et al., 2018):

> Imagine you have been asked to play the following gamble. The gamble offers the opportunity to win €4, but it costs you €2 to play. If you choose to play you would pay the €2 and, without looking, draw a marble from a basket. In the basket there are 1000 marbles. The marbles are either black or red. If the marble is red you will win €4; otherwise, if the marble is black you will receive nothing. Thus, the

number of red marbles in the basket determines the probability that you will win. You are less likely to win the €4 the lower the number of red marbles in the basket.

Some participants saw the vignette above. Others saw the same vignette, but with a different prize amount. Some had the chance to win €2.5, others €10, others €50, all the way up to €10,000. We asked the volunteers two questions (counterbalanced):

1. How many red, winning marbles do you expect are in the urn?
2. Would you play the bet, yes or no?

Although this is a simple study, there are several competing hypotheses on how people ignorant of the distribution of marbles will respond to the questions. They could employ the risk–reward heuristic, according to which the estimated number of winning marbles will decrease as the value of the payoff increases. Alternatively, they may be influenced by the desirability bias (see Krizan & Windschitl, 2007, for a review) and assess payoffs as more likely to occur as they become more desirable. A final possibility is that they may subscribe to Laplace's *principle of indifference* and treat each outcome as equally likely (Laplace, 1776, quoted in Hacking, 1975/2006, p. 132; Keynes, 1936/1973a; see also the equiprobable heuristic in chapter 2).

As figure 3.4a shows, consistent with the predictions of the risk–reward heuristic, the estimated number of winning marbles in the basket decreased as the size of the reward increased. However, the observed estimates deviated somewhat from the fair-bet probabilities. Estimates were regressive relative to the risk–reward probabilities (dotted line), overshooting them for the high prizes and undershooting them for the low prizes. One possible explanation for this deviation is that decision makers' use of the risk–reward heuristic—like other judgments—is not error-free but perturbed by error from other sources of information (Erev, Wallsten, & Budescu, 1994). This perturbation would be sufficient to produce the regressive effect observed in the estimated number of winning marbles; moreover, it is consistent with the idea that people making decisions about risky prospects from description tend to overweight rare events. In other words, the inferential nature of the risk–reward heuristic can lead to what appears to be nonlinear distortion of probabilities in decision making under uncertainty (see chapter 8; Tversky & Fox, 1995). For another possible explanation related to the makeup of the environment, including the abilities of the other competitors in the environment, see Pleskac et al. (2018).

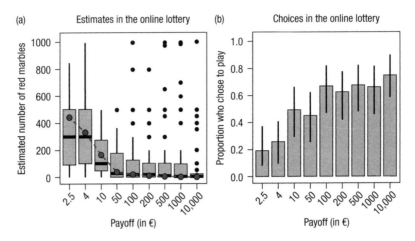

Figure 3.4

(a) Estimated number of red marbles by reward magnitude. Higher rewards were associated with lower estimates. The dashed line depicts the objective number of marbles predicted by the risk–reward heuristic. Each bin contains ~50 responses. (b) Proportion of volunteers who would play the gamble. Those offered higher rewards were more likely to play.

Figure 3.4b shows the proportions of people who said they would pay to play each gamble. Before discussing the choice patterns further, we should emphasize that the risk–reward heuristic is not a choice heuristic but an inferential heuristic. Thus, a choice rule is needed to make predictions about people's choices. It might be that people use the risk–reward heuristic to infer a probability and then use a process akin to prospect theory (Kahneman & Tversky, 1979) to make a choice; alternatively, they may use the estimated probabilities in a heuristic choice process such as a lexicographic rule (see chapter 2).

For the purposes of this chapter, we assume that participants in our study used the estimate from the risk–reward heuristic to calculate the expected value of the gamble and then chose the option with the larger expected value. Strictly speaking then, an expected-value calculator combined with the risk–reward heuristic predicts indifference between paying to play the gamble or not across all prize conditions. As figure 3.4b shows, this was not observed on the aggregate. Instead, as reward magnitudes increased, there was an increasing propensity to choose to play the gamble. This tendency is more consistent with participants exhibiting a desirability bias when they make choices or even relying on the principle of indifference.

However, as figure 3.4a shows, the estimates were regressive relative to the fair-bet probabilities, with the estimates for low payoffs being lower than expected and the estimates for high payoffs being slightly higher. This regressive property actually implies a preference for not playing the gamble at low payoffs, with an increasing propensity to play the gamble as payoffs increase; this is shown in figure 3.4b. Moreover, at the individual level within each condition, people who estimated a higher number of red marbles were more likely to accept the gamble (see also Pleskac & Hertwig, 2014).

In sum, people's estimates and choices reveal the use of a risk–reward heuristic, although the estimates tend to be less extreme relative to fair-bet probabilities. These results imply that the risk–reward relationship found in the world is reflected in people's minds—but how does the relationship enter the mind in the first place?

3.5 Do People Adapt to Different Risk–Reward Environments?

The risk–reward heuristic makes use of a statistical regularity in the environment. To exploit this regularity, the mind must be cognizant that a relationship exists between risk and reward—not least because the nature of that relationship differs across contexts. Whereas we found a near-perfect (though biased) inverse relationship between payoffs and probabilities in monetary gambles in casinos (see figure 3.2), the risk–reward relationship was less reliable in other environments, such as where to submit a scientific manuscript (see figure 3.3), and it may not yet have evolved in still other environments, such as in newly forming markets (see box 3.1). These differences across contexts present a challenge for users of the risk–reward heuristic—especially as people are rarely explicitly informed about the relationship between risk and reward. Nor does it seem that they deliberately set out to learn it. So, do people learn the risk–reward structure, even when it is not their main goal to do so?

To answer this question, Leuker, Pachur, Hertwig, and Pleskac (2018) ran an experiment with three risk–reward environments with monetary gambles: a negatively correlated, a positively correlated, and an uncorrelated environment (see figure 3.5). Each dot in figure 3.5 is a simple gamble of the form "p chance of winning x, otherwise nothing." Participants were assigned to one of the choice environments—without being told which environment they were in or being instructed to learn a risk–reward

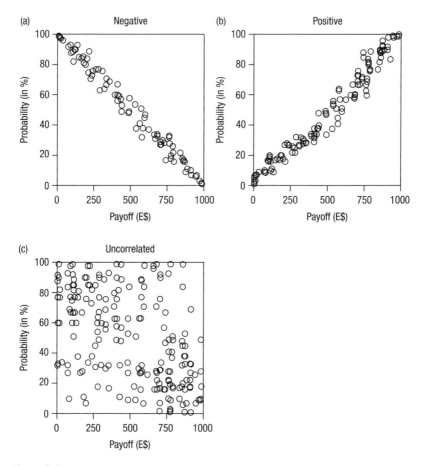

Figure 3.5
The three experimentally manipulated risk–reward relationships. Payoffs were in terms of a laboratory currency E$ to help minimize participants using risk–reward knowledge from other actual currencies (recreated from Leuker et al., 2018).

relationship. Instead, participants were exposed to the environment by evaluating a series of 172 gambles from it. For each gamble, they were asked to imagine they owned the gamble and to state the price at which they would be willing to sell it. To get a feel for how this experiment worked and try your hand at detecting different types of risk–reward environment, please visit interactive element 3.1 (at https://taming-uncertainty.mpib-berlin.mpg.de/).

After a short break, participants completed several more tasks, including the following two. In a probability estimation task, participants were

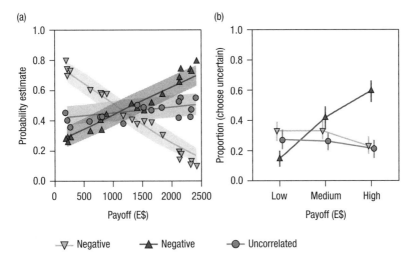

Figure 3.6
(a) Average probability estimates for each of the payoff levels in the probability estimation task. (b) Proportion of times the uncertain option was chosen in the decisions under uncertainty task.

presented with different payoff magnitudes and asked to estimate the chances that they were associated with specific rewards, based on the gambles they had seen earlier. As figure 3.6a shows, the average estimates reflected the risk–reward environment. That is, people learned the risk–reward structure without being given any feedback or having their attention drawn to the relationship.

In order to determine whether, having learned the risk–reward structure, people harness it as a heuristic when making their decisions, participants were asked to make a series of decisions between a gamble that offered a reward with an unknown probability (e.g., E\$100 with $p = ?$) and a sure thing that was half the size (e.g., E\$50 with $p = 1.0$). As figure 3.6b shows, the risk–reward environments to which participants were exposed impacted their choices in a manner consistent with their using the risk–reward heuristic to estimate the odds of the payoffs. Relative to people in the uncorrelated environment, people in the positive risk–reward environment showed an increasing preference for the gamble as the size of the potential reward increased. In the negative risk–reward environment, this pattern was reversed. However, there was less of a difference between the negative and uncorrelated conditions. In particular, participants in the negative condition did not choose the low-payoff gamble as often as was warranted by their probability estimates.

To summarize, people can learn risk–reward structures even when their attention is not drawn to the risk–reward relationship. Moreover, they use those structures to help make decisions under uncertainty. As a result, the risk–reward structures to which people were exposed created environment-dependent preferences. We should emphasize that this change in preferences is not some sort of fallacy, but an ecologically rational bet on the structure of the environment. Next, we review three implications of the risk–reward heuristic that illustrate its ability to help make sense of both old and new problems in the area of decision making.

3.6   Implications of the Risk–Reward Heuristic

3.6.1   Ambiguity Aversion

When people are given a choice between two otherwise equivalent options—one in which the probability information is given and one in which it is missing—they tend to avoid the option with missing probability information. This phenomenon—which has become known as *ambiguity aversion*—was first established by Ellsberg (1961), who used it to distinguish between risk and uncertainty (see also Keynes, 1936/1973a, p. 75). Let us consider, for example, the choice between two gambles:

Gamble A: Win €100 if a red marble is drawn from an urn containing 50 red marbles and 50 black marbles.

Gamble B: Win €100 if a red marble is drawn from an urn containing 100 marbles with an unknown proportion of red to black marbles.

People generally prefer the clear gamble A to the ambiguous gamble B (Camerer & Weber, 1992). However, typically it has been assumed that if you ask people whether a red or a black marble is more likely to be drawn, in either gamble, they would say red and black are equally likely. But observing a preference for gamble A, the clear gamble, seems inconsistent with this assumption. Ellsberg (1961) used this inconsistency to argue that uncertainty cannot simply be reduced to a probability, as subjective expected utility theory would suggest (Savage, 1954).

Yet, as we have seen in this chapter, if you assign one color as the winning marble in gamble B, and ask people how likely it is, they probably would not answer that both colors are equally likely. Instead they may use the risk–reward heuristic and intuit the probabilities from the payoff magnitudes (see figure 3.4a). Thus, it is possible that this so-called ambiguity aversion is actually the result of a reasonable inference based on the structure of the environment. Interestingly enough, this idea was anticipated by Ward Edwards (personal communication cited in Lopes, 1983, p. 141), one of the founders of behavioral decision theory. In considering why people do not adhere to the principles of subjective expected utility theory, but exhibit ambiguity aversion, Edwards observed that "high positive or negative payoffs are typically associated with very low probabilities, while mediocre or zero payoffs are typically associated with high probabilities. This, I assert, is simply a fact about the world in which we live."

To test whether the risk–reward heuristic might help explain ambiguity aversion, Pleskac and Hertwig (2014) created gambles equivalent to gambles A and B and asked two groups of people for their preferences. The first group was told to assume that the payoff for drawing a red marble from either urn was 10 Swiss francs (CHF10). The second group was told to assume that the payoff for drawing a red marble was CHF1,000. Pleskac and Hertwig predicted that, due to the prevalence of an inverse risk–reward relationship in the world, the ambiguous or uncertain option would become increasingly undesirable as the magnitude of the payoff increased. The results support this prediction. In the CHF10 condition, 63% of participants preferred the unambiguous urn (gamble A). In the CHF1,000 condition, by contrast, 81% preferred the unambiguous urn.

The observed increase in ambiguity aversion as the payoff magnitude increased is difficult to explain in terms of the other accounts of ambiguity aversion. The relative variance between the two gambles across the payoff conditions remains constant, meaning that there should be no difference in the comparative ignorance people experience between the two gambles (Fox & Tversky, 1995) or the inclination to avoid variance (Rode, Cosmides, Hell, & Tooby, 1999). Moreover, our ecological analysis of life's gambles suggests the risk–reward account of ambiguity aversion is not an unjustified suspicion (Binmore, 2007; Frisch & Baron, 1988; Kühberger & Perner, 2003; Yates & Zukowsky, 1976). Instead, one can argue that this so-called aversion merely reflects an ecologically grounded belief that high payoffs have a low probability of occurring.

3.6.2 Bets Leak Information

A second implication of the risk–reward heuristic is that the gambles people are offered convey or leak information (see also McKenzie & Nelson, 2003; Sher & McKenzie, 2006)—in particular, information about the beliefs of the person who constructed the gamble. For instance, let us consider a situation where two people—call them Tim and Ralph—are talking about an upcoming soccer match between Germany and the United States. Tim offers Ralph the following bet: for the cost of €1, he will pay Ralph €4 if Germany wins. We might think this is just an ordinary bet between colleagues. But according to the risk–reward heuristic, Tim has also shared some information with Ralph about his own beliefs about the likelihoods of the different outcomes. A challenge for future work is to determine whether and how Ralph will choose to use this information based on what he knows about Tim.

More generally, the idea that gambles can leak information about the seller's beliefs would seem to challenge the conventional approach in the decision sciences, where gambles are treated as stimuli that allow buyers' preferences and beliefs to be gauged (see, e.g., Newell, Lagnado, & Shanks, 2015; Winterfeldt & Edwards, 1986). Indeed, this point resonates with an early concern raised by Frank Ramsey (1926), the mathematician who anticipated subjective expected utility theory, with regard to using bets to identify people's beliefs: "The old-established way of measuring a person's belief is to propose a bet, and see what are the lowest odds which he will accept. This method I regard as fundamentally sound; but it suffers from being insufficiently general, and from being necessarily inexact. [...] Besides, the proposal of a bet may inevitably alter his state of opinion" (p. 68).

In fact, the problem that the bets people are offered may change their opinion is part of the reason that other methods, such as scoring rules, were developed to measure a person's beliefs (De Finetti, 1981). The risk–reward heuristic, with its ecological approach to decision making, can help to make sense of how people use the gambles they are offered to navigate uncertainty.

3.6.3 Making Money with the Risk–Reward Heuristic

A final implication of the risk–reward heuristic is that people can use it to sift through possible bets to find ones to avoid (much like the economics professor deciding not to pick up the $100 bill) and ones to exploit. For instance, Kaunitz, Zhong, and Kreiner (2017) collected the closing odds that online bookmakers placed on soccer games from January 2005 to June

2015. They then calculated the average odds assigned to each game. Following a process exactly akin to the risk–reward heuristic, they then calculated the probabilities that those odds implied. As in the ecological analysis described in section 3.2, these intuited probabilities were good estimates of the probability of the games' outcomes.

Kaunitz et al. (2017) took the analysis one step further, noting that although most of the bookmakers' odds hovered close to the average, some odds appeared to deviate markedly from the average, making them an attractive bet.[1] Having made this observation, the authors developed an algorithm to identify these bets. Specifically, they compared the probabilities estimated from the individual odds via the risk–reward heuristic with the probabilities intuited from the average set of odds. They found that when the estimated probability of a bet was 5 percentage points lower than would be expected from the average odds, a gambler could turn a nice profit by placing a bet with that bookmaker. In fact, when they implemented their strategy with real money, placing 265 $50 bets, they made a profit of $957.50 (a net return of 8.5%). So apart from helping people make accurate inferences about events, the risk–reward heuristic could help people find options that may look too good to be true—but actually are true (see also Leuker, Pachur, Hertwig, & Pleskac, in press).

3.7   Conclusion

Scholars of probability theory have long drawn a connection between common sense and the calculation of probabilities (Daston, 1988/1995). Pierre-Simon Laplace (1814/1902), the father of Bayesian probability theory and the first advocate of the principle of indifference, emphasized the connection when he stated, "the theory of probabilities is at bottom only common sense reduced to calculus; it makes us appreciate with exactitude that which exact minds feel by a sort of instinct without being able ofttimes to give a reason for it" (pp. 196–197).

---

1. Bookmakers may offer odds above fair value either to attract clients from other bookmakers or to maintain a balanced book. For instance, when gamblers bet too much on one outcome, bookmakers might increase the odds of the complementary event to encourage more people to bet on the complementary event and offset the overbooked outcome.

Sometimes, though, calculus fails to provide a means of assigning probabilities to events. In such cases, mathematicians, statisticians, scientists, and laypeople alike fall back on other commonsense rules to finish their calculations, make inferences, and make decisions. The Laplacian principle of indifference, treating each outcome as equally likely, has been one of the rules used to assign probabilities to events in the absence of information (see also chapter 2). Yet, as we have shown, the payoffs associated with the events can carry information about the likelihood of those events, allowing people to estimate the probabilities from the payoffs alone. We have also shown that the risk–reward heuristic is not just an abstract rule divined by armchair psychologists, but a rule that people use and—given enough information and exposure to the environment—adjust to fit the situation. The risk–reward heuristic is a simple tool that people use to navigate uncertainty—a tool that not only makes good common sense, but good ecological sense as well.

4 Going Round in Circles: How Social Structures Guide and Limit Search

Christin Schulze and Thorsten Pachur

4.1 Who You Know Is What You Know

In the months leading up to the 2016 Summer Olympics in Rio de Janeiro, alarming reports of Brazilian babies being born with severe birth defects spread across the globe. The babies' condition was linked to the mosquito-borne Zika virus, which was spreading rapidly in the region, threatening a global pandemic. With an expected 500,000 international spectators and athletes about to travel to the Zika-stricken region, health experts called for the Olympic Games to be postponed or moved (e.g., Attaran, 2016; Sun, 2016). Dismissing these concerns, Eduardo Paes, Rio de Janeiro's mayor at the time, predicted that no harm would come to visitors and that the event should go ahead as planned. "I don't know anyone who's got the Zika virus," he argued, "and I know a lot of people, so this is not a big issue" (Milam, 2016). As it turns out, Paes was right. The thousands of attendees returned to their home countries without a single report of a subsequent Zika infection (M. Payne, 2016).

Like Paes, people often exploit observations sampled from their relatively small social networks to infer an important characteristic of the world at large: the likelihood or frequency of events (see, e.g., Galesic, Olsson, & Rieskamp, 2012; Hertwig, Pachur, & Kurzenhäuser, 2005; Pachur, Hertwig, & Rieskamp, 2013a; Pachur, Hertwig, & Steinmann, 2012; Tversky & Kahneman, 1973). Such instance-based inferences are often made under uncertainty, because relevant statistics are not directly available. Nonetheless, as in the Zika example, instance-based inference can be remarkably accurate; after all, events that are more likely to occur in the population at large are also—all other things being equal—more likely to occur in one's proximate social circles. As such, drawing on information carried by the people one knows personally to make judgments about the social texture of the world at large represents an effective strategy to reduce uncertainty in the many domains of life for which summary tables of objective frequency statistics are lacking—for instance, when predicting the likelihood of a potential threat (Lichtenstein, Slovic, Fischhoff, Layman, & Combs, 1978), forecasting the development of political opinions (Noelle-Neumann, 1974), inferring social norms in unfamiliar situations (Epstein, 2001), or simply assessing the popularity of everyday choices. In these situations, people may act as "intuitive social statisticians," polling information from the internal spheres of their minds and using these samples as windows onto the world—not unlike the "social physics" pioneered by Quetelet (1842/2013). But how does the mind search for relevant instances in memory? How does it determine which search spaces to consider, the order in which to inspect them, and when to terminate the search? Metaphorically put, how does the internal polling firm work?

How to search and when to stop information sampling are questions that people encounter regularly, in both internal and external search (Todd, Hills, & Robbins, 2012). In decisions from experience, for instance, people need to determine how much to sample from the available options before committing to a course of action (see chapter 7). In this chapter, we illustrate how people might exploit structures of the external environment to guide and stop search when sampling social information from memory in order to judge the relative frequency of events in the world.

Wald's sequential analysis offers a normative statistical approach for determining the number of observations taken before an inference is made (see Wald, 1947). According to this approach, data (i.e., instances) are collected and evaluated sequentially, and sampling is terminated as soon as a predefined evidence threshold is reached. That threshold indicates the amount of evidence necessary to support a hypothesis (e.g., that more people in the general population catch chicken pox each year than catch the Zika virus; see chapter 7 for a related sequential sampling approach in the context of decisions from experience). To determine a statistically optimal information threshold, however, a decision maker needs knowledge about the environment (e.g., the effect size of the difference in the events' frequencies). What is more, the threshold may require samples that are considerably larger than typical social networks (see, e.g., Pachur, Hertwig, &

Rieskamp, 2013b, for an analysis in which Wald's rule used an average sample size of over 700 persons).

Rather than computing a statistically optimal threshold, we argue, the mind might exploit structures of the external environment to structure and terminate the search process. Specifically, our key argument is that the search for relevant instances in mnemonic representations of the social environment is guided by the hierarchical structure of social networks, which typically consist of discrete subgroups, such as oneself, one's family, one's friends, and one's acquaintances (e.g., R. A. Hill & Dunbar, 2003; Milardo, 1992). As these subgroups, or "social circles," typically increase in size from central to more peripheral levels of the hierarchy, following them provides a heuristic but principled procedure for sequentially expanding the sample size (see Pachur et al., 2013a). Moreover, this approach gives priority to the people one knows personally, thus implicitly giving more weight to instance-based information that is likely to be more reliable (see Hertwig et al., 2005).

Using the structure of the social environment to guide and stop search may well lead to judgments being based on a fairly small number of instances. Notwithstanding the statistical law of large numbers—according to which more information is better—this limitation may not necessarily be detrimental. After all, small samples of observations sometimes offer surprisingly powerful indicators of properties of the larger population. For instance, "thin slices" of expressive behavior—that is, short excerpts of longer social interactions—have proved to be as predictive of interpersonal outcomes as more extensive observations (Ambady & Rosenthal, 1992). In one study, physicians' first impressions (of how ill a patient looks) were found to be predictive of the morbidity and mortality of patients who presented with nonspecific complaints at emergency departments (Beglinger et al., 2015). Similarly, it has been proposed that reliance on small samples can be beneficial because statistical characteristics—such as the correlation between variables or their mean value differences—are sometimes amplified in small relative to larger samples of information (e.g., Hertwig & Pleskac, 2010; Kareev, 1995).

Instance-based sampling mechanisms are, of course, not the only way to judge event frequencies. Mechanisms that consult other types of information, knowledge, or affective reactions have also been proposed (e.g., Gigerenzer, Todd, & the ABC Research Group, 1999; Pachur et al., 2012;

Pleskac & Hertwig, 2014; Slovic, Finucane, Peters, & MacGregor, 2002). For example, the likelihood of contracting an infectious disease could be judged by using a strategy akin to the risk–reward heuristic (see chapter 3): very harmful (e.g., life-threatening) diseases could be inferred to be rarer than less harmful ones. Additionally, social information may impact likelihood judgments in ways other than the sampling of instances from memory—for instance, through social transmission in direct communication (e.g., Moussaïd, Brighton, & Gaissmaier, 2015), explicit advice taking (Bonaccio & Dalal, 2006), or direct observation of others' behavior (e.g., when selecting an escape route in an emergency situation; see chapter 14). Nevertheless, our main focus in this chapter, which builds on a long and fruitful research tradition (e.g., Dougherty, Gettys, & Ogden, 1999; Fiedler & Armbruster, 1994; Galesic et al., 2012; Hertwig et al., 2005; Pachur et al., 2013a; Tversky & Kahneman, 1973), is on people's use of recalled instances to judge the frequency of events.

Crucially, when people rely on instance knowledge to reduce uncertainty about event probabilities, other uncertainties emerge. People using social sampling strategies may be uncertain about the quality of their instance-based memory (can all instances of relevant encountered events be stored and later recalled?), about whether a person they know indeed represents an instance of a particular event (did my friend's cousin really have the Zika virus or was it something else?), and to what extent the information stored in memory is representative of the distribution in the population (are people in my profession more likely to come into contact with cases of infection than would be typical in the general population?). Different social sampling strategies deal with these uncertainties in different ways. Here, we focus on delineating the ecological conditions under which using social sampling heuristics—and thus reducing one type of uncertainty but accepting others—can be an ecologically rational strategy.

We first describe various cognitive models for social sampling that have been proposed in the literature and discuss how they exploit the structures in a person's social network (see section 4.2). Second, we examine how well these models capture people's frequency judgments; in so doing, we also present evidence for the models' ability to describe children's inferences, thus addressing how instance-based sampling with limited search develops ontogenetically (see section 4.3). Finally, we test to what extent the success of restricting social sampling to proximate social spaces depends on relevant environmental properties; in other words, we investigate the ecological rationality of limited social sampling (see section 4.4).

4.2 Sampling from Social Spaces

How might people use instances sampled from their proximate social environment to make inferences about the frequency of events in the world at large? The social sampling strategies that have been proposed to date differ in their assumptions about the scope of the internal search spaces consulted: Is search exhaustive or limited?

4.2.1 Exhaustive Search in Proximate Social Spaces

The idea that sampling relevant instances from memory could be a useful strategy for judging event frequencies is central to Tversky and Kahneman's (1973) availability heuristic. According to this heuristic, "people assess the frequency of a class or the probability of an event by the ease with which instances or occurrences can be brought to mind" (Tversky & Kahneman, 1974, p. 1127). Numerous studies have investigated the role of availability in people's judgments and decisions (for an overview, see, e.g., Reber, 2017). In the domain of risk perception, for instance, it has been argued that availability explains people's judgments of the frequency of hazardous events (e.g., Lichtenstein et al., 1978; Slovic, Fischhoff, & Lichtenstein, 1982). But it has also been noted that Tversky and Kahneman's (1973) description of the availability heuristic is somewhat vague and consistent with several candidate formalizations (e.g., Sedlmeier, Hertwig, & Gigerenzer, 1998). For instance, Tversky and Kahneman did not specify from which search space instances are retrieved, how a person determines whether search in memory is continued or terminated, and whether it is the number of instances recalled or the ease of retrieval that is decisive (Betsch & Pohl, 2002; Hertwig et al., 2005; Sedlmeier et al., 1998).

The *availability-by-recall* strategy proposed by Hertwig et al. (2005) uses the number of relevant instances in a person's social network to make inferences about unknown frequencies. Availability-by-recall assumes that people attempt to retrieve all available instances from their proximate social network—that is, people they know and interact with personally—and aggregate all the information in this sample. Figure 4.1 illustrates this process. Someone trying to determine which of two sports is more prevalent in the

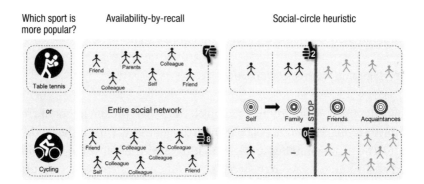

Figure 4.1

Illustration of two social sampling strategies that entail either exhaustive or limited search for instances in memory. Left-hand panel: The inference task is to judge which of two sports is more popular in the overall population, table tennis or cycling. Middle panel: To make this inference, availability-by-recall tallies instances across a person's entire social network and, based on this information, infers that cycling is the more popular sport. Right-hand panel: The social-circle heuristic sequentially considers discrete subgroups of a person's social network and stops the search as soon as a social circle discriminates between the options. In this example, the social circle of family members discriminates between cycling and table tennis, resulting in the correct inference that table tennis is the more popular sport in the German population (based on the total number of active and passive club members in 2010; Statistisches Bundesamt, 2011).

German population—table tennis or cycling—might try to recall everyone they know who belongs to a table tennis or cycling club. (Approximately one German in three is a member of a sports club; Statistisches Bundesamt, 2011.) The sport with the highest number of recalled instances (e.g., eight people in the person's social network are members of a cycling club) is then judged to be more frequent in the overall population. Availability-by-recall thus assumes that the sampling space encompasses a person's entire proximate social network and that search is exhaustive within the bounds of this network. Instances one has learned about from the media, by contrast, are explicitly excluded from the search process. It has been shown that additionally recruiting instance knowledge from the media (e.g., from news, movies, and the Internet) is less predictive of people's judgments than is limiting the search space to the proximate social environment (Pachur et al., 2012). Moreover, constraining the sample space in this way can safeguard against the distorted distribution of events reported in the news (Combs & Slovic, 1979).

The assumption that sampling is focused on proximate social circles is also central to the social sampling model proposed by Galesic et al. (2012; see also Galesic, Olsson, & Rieskamp, 2018). This model assumes that, in order to estimate population statistics, proximate sampling statistics derived from a person's social circles serve as a starting point, which is then extrapolated to the larger population by smoothing extreme values. This model has been shown to accurately predict people's assessments of their life circumstances contingent on the statistical structure of their proximate social environments.

4.2.2 Sequentially Ordered and Limited Search in Social Circles

In principle, exhaustive search strategies give equal weight to all relevant instances stored in memory. However, social memory is known to be structured by the distinct social subgroups to which the stored individuals belong—such as family, friends, and acquaintances (e.g., Bond, Jones, & Weintraub, 1985; Fiske, 1995; Hills & Pachur, 2012). It is therefore possible that search systematically exploits this structure to determine where to start and how to stop. The *social-circle heuristic* (Pachur et al., 2013a) is a model of such a process. It assumes that people search their memory for relevant instances by sequentially probing their social circles and stopping as soon as one circle discriminates between the options (i.e., there are more instances of one option than the other in a circle). In line with the observation that people consider their own behaviors when inferring the relative prevalence of behaviors in the population (Ross, Greene, & House, 1977), the social-circle heuristic first probes information about one's self. If this circle does not discriminate between the options, the search process proceeds following a hierarchy of family (i.e., kin relationships), followed by friends, and finally acquaintances (i.e., nonkin reciprocal relationships).

For example, if you needed to decide whether table tennis or cycling is the more popular sport, you would first consider yourself (see the right-hand panel in figure 4.1). If you regularly engaged in both types of sport, the "self" social circle would not discriminate between the options, so you would continue your search in the next social circle: family members. If your parents played table tennis but did not cycle, your search would stop at this point and you would infer that table tennis is more popular. By relying on this ordering of social circles, you prioritize the sample spaces for which your instance knowledge is likely to be most reliable. In this sense, the social-circle heuristic takes into account the decision maker's uncertainty regarding the quality of instance-based memory and provides an unambiguous blueprint for where and how much to search for instances in memory.

Although the search sequence assumed by the social-circle heuristic may reflect a natural hierarchy of social relations (see, e.g., R. A. Hill & Dunbar, 2003), alternative orders of search for relevant instances are conceivable. One possible alternative order—which has been argued to influence search in cue-based inference (Newell, Rakow, Weston, & Shanks, 2004)—may reflect how frequently a social circle allows people to discriminate between options, thus keeping overall search costs low. For example, the smallest social circle, the self, is unlikely to discriminate between many options (e.g., because most people only belong to one or two sports clubs, if any) and may therefore be inspected later, or not at all. Another possibility is that search is guided by the representativeness of social circles for the domain in question. In some domains, a search might prioritize friends over family or discount the self as an unrepresentative source of information (e.g., when judging the prevalence of one's own family name; see Oppenheimer, 2004). Finally, as people's social circles differ in size and personal proximity, there might be individual differences in the order in which social circles are inspected.

The *social-circle model* (Schulze, Pachur, & Hertwig, 2017) is a generalized model of ordered and limited search in social spaces that allows such differences to be captured. It permits variability in the order in which circles are inspected and acknowledges probabilistic aspects in the search, stopping, and decision stages of inference (Bergert & Nosofsky, 2007; Rieskamp, 2008). Specifically, the social-circle model parameterizes three key components of instance-based inference: the decision maker's search order, an evidence threshold that expresses the amount of evidence required to stop search at a given circle, and response noise (see Schulze et al., 2017, for a detailed model specification). Its parameterization can capture differences between people in these components. The social-circle model thus provides a tool for measuring to what extent and in what way search in social memory may be limited.

4.3   Do People Rely on Social Sampling Strategies?

How well do the social-circle model, the social-circle heuristic, and availability-by-recall describe people's inferences? How do they compare against alternative strategies that rely on other knowledge or on affective signals to make inferences about the frequency of events? Pachur et al. (2013a) conducted two studies in which participants were asked to judge either relative mortality rates from various types of cancer or the relative popularity of various participative sports in Germany. After making these judgments, participants were asked to report any cases of death from cancer or any sports club memberships, respectively, in their own social networks. The studies then examined whether the social-circle heuristic or availability-by-recall was better able to describe individuals' inferences in both domains. Specifically, Pachur et al. (2013a) used people's self-reported occurrences of relevant instances in their social circles to derive the strategies' predicted inferences and then determined the proportion of times that each strategy correctly predicted people's inferences. Additionally, they applied a computational modeling approach to classify each individual as a user of one of the two strategies.

In both studies, participants' frequency judgments were equally well described by availability-by-recall and the social-circle heuristic. In cases where people's reported instance knowledge allowed both strategies to make a prediction, roughly the same proportion of inferences was correctly predicted by each strategy. Furthermore, similar numbers of individuals were classified as users of each strategy. This did not mean that the strategies could not be discriminated, however: the models' diverging predictions regarding the time needed to make an inference were well reflected in the data. Specifically, the social-circle heuristic predicts that response times will be longer when more circles are consulted. In contrast, availability-by-recall assumes that instances are summed across all circles and thus does not predict differences in response time to be contingent on which social circle discriminates between the options. Consistent with these predictions, response times for participants classified as users of the social-circle heuristic increased with the number of circles consulted, whereas response times for participants classified as users of availability-by-recall were not dependent on the discriminating circle (Pachur et al., 2013a).

Testing the two instance-based strategies against alternative mechanisms, such as cue-based strategies (see Gigerenzer et al., 1999) or guessing, further revealed that more than two-thirds of participants applied an instance-based strategy (Pachur et al., 2013a). Similarly, in a study of people's judgments of the likelihood of hazardous events, Pachur et al. (2012) showed that a heuristic exploiting people's direct instance knowledge in their social network was better able to account for their responses than an affect-based mechanism (which predicts that more dreaded hazards are inferred to be more prevalent; see Slovic et al., 2002). Overall, these results suggest that instance-based processes play a key role in people's judgments of event frequencies. In addition, ordered and limited search—as assumed by the social-circle heuristic—seems to be a viable way to conceptualize instance-based inference.

Nevertheless, the social-circle heuristic makes the strong assumption that the order of searching through social circles is deterministic and that everyone applies the same order. This assumption may be unrealistic and thus undermine the evidence for limited search. To address the question of what happens if one allows for individual variability in the search order and acknowledges the probabilistic nature of search and decision processes (aspects that are captured by the social-circle model), we reanalyzed data from Pachur et al. (2013a) with a wider set of candidate models and using a Bayesian hierarchical latent-mixture approach (see, e.g., Bartlema, Lee, Wetzels, & Vanpaemel, 2014).[1] Specifically, we modeled the inferences of participants in Pachur et al.'s (2013a) Study 2 on the popularity of various participative sports in Germany. The candidate models included various generalized models of instance-based inference (e.g., the social-circle model) as well as more constrained models, such as the (deterministic) social-circle heuristic and availability-by-recall. Taking into account differences in model flexibility, we found that the inferences of the large majority of participants were best described by the social-circle model; only a few individuals were classified as users of the exhaustive availability-by-recall strategy. These results further reinforce the idea that limited search plays a key role in instance-based inference. Further, inspection of the distributions

---

1. Hierarchical latent-mixture modeling makes it possible to simultaneously estimate discrete classes of individuals who use categorically different inference strategies and robustly model variation within each group of strategy users, thus combining the advantages of pooling continuous individual differences hierarchically and assuming discrete differences among groups of individuals (see, e.g., Bartlema et al., 2014).

of the social-circle model's individual-level parameters revealed that it is important to take into account individual differences in search, stopping, and decision processes.

In sum, the distribution of instances in a person's social network is an important cue for judging the relative frequencies of events in the world at large—and one that is often preferred over alternatives based on other knowledge or on affective signals. Moreover, people judging event frequencies on the basis of instance knowledge often limit their information search, rather than engaging in exhaustive search. These findings suggest that instance-based inference strategies in general, and sequentially ordered and limited search in particular, are key ingredients in the mind's toolbox for making judgments under uncertainty.

How general is this evidence for limited social sampling? For instance, do children already engage in search that is ordered and limited by social structures? Due to limitations in their ability to selectively focus attention on relevant information, young children may use more exhaustive but unsystematic search strategies (e.g., Davidson, 1991; Mata, von Helversen, & Rieskamp, 2011). To test this possibility, Schulze et al. (2017) gave children (8–11 years) and adults (19–34 years) an inference task: judging the relative frequency of common first names in Germany (e.g., "Which first name occurs more frequently in Germany: Anna or Michael?"). Participants were then asked to recall how many people with each name they knew personally. Perhaps unsurprisingly, adults recalled more instances in their social network than children. Adults' inferences were also more accurate. Schulze et al. used a Bayesian hierarchical latent-mixture approach to model each participant's decisions in the inference task, based on the instances of names recalled from the social network. They assumed three latent subgroups of individuals, each using a different strategy: the social-circle model, which assumes limited search; availability-by-recall, which assumes exhaustive search; and guessing, according to which each name would be selected with probability .50. Although availability-by-recall provided the best account for the judgments of the majority of children, a substantial subset of children was best described by the social-circle model. This finding demonstrates that children aged 8 to 11 years are already able to systematically exploit their instance knowledge in a limited and ordered fashion when making inferences about the frequency of events in the world.

4.4   The Ecological Rationality of Limited Social Sampling

Limiting search to personally experienced instances or even a subset of one's personal social network, as implemented by the social-circle model, runs counter to the common statistical lore that more information is better. But what is the price of limiting search to one's social circles? Might it depend on statistical properties of the environment (see also chapter 2)? In other words, what is the ecological rationality (Todd, Gigerenzer, & the ABC Research Group, 2012) of limited search for instance knowledge? We address this question in two ways here. First, we report results from an analysis aimed at identifying environmental properties that benefit strategies with limited search. Second, we discuss the limitations and possible adaptive functions of attuning one's frequency judgments to the proximate social environment.

4.4.1   Which Environmental Properties Impact the Success of Limited Search?

From a statistical perspective, strategies such as the social-circle heuristic cannot generally outperform exhaustive search when it comes to judging the relative frequency of events in the population. Nevertheless, the loss of accuracy incurred in limited search may be smaller under some conditions than others. Addressing this issue, Pachur et al. (2013a) conducted computer simulations in which the accuracy of the social-circle heuristic and availability-by-recall were tested in environments that varied in two important properties of real-world social environments (see also Pachur et al., 2013b, for a comparison of the two heuristic strategies with the statistical benchmark provided by Wald's rule). The first ecological property was the skewness of the frequency distribution across events. Many environmental quantities in diverse biological, social, and physical systems follow highly skewed distributions in which a select few objects dominate the others (see, e.g., Clauset, Shalizi, & Newman, 2009; Newman, 2005). One example is the distribution of personal wealth in a population. In many countries, a small fraction of people owns a large fraction of the total wealth, and most people have relatively modest assets (Atkinson & Piketty, 2010). Other examples include the population sizes of cities in various countries, the number of times scientific publications are cited, and the magnitudes of earthquakes (Newman, 2005). The second pervasive property of social environments is spatial clustering of instances. People tend to interact and form social ties with others who have similar sociodemographic, behavioral, and attitudinal characteristics, such as ethnicity, religion, or level of education—a phenomenon known as *homophily* (see, e.g., McPherson, Smith-Lovin, & Cook, 2001). Shared characteristics can also arise from people experiencing common environmental factors (such as a major economic crisis, see chapter 10) or mutually influencing one another. Does such clustering foster or hamper the performance of the social-circle heuristic relative to an exhaustive instance-based strategy such as availability-by-recall?

In the Pachur et al. (2013a) simulations, agent populations were represented as two-dimensional grids, with each cell representing an agent and each agent being part of a larger social network. An agent's personal social network was divided into four discrete social circles, as shown in figure 4.2a. Each agent was an instance of at most one event. The task of the sampling strategies (availability-by-recall vs. the social-circle heuristic) was to infer which of two events occurred more frequently in the overall population, given different environmental characteristics. Each environmental condition represented a combination of the type of frequency distribution (flat vs. skewed) and the type of spatial distribution of instances (no, medium, or high clustering).

Figure 4.2b shows that, for both strategies, performance was a function of the combination of skewness and clustering in the environment. With medium and high levels of clustering, the social-circle heuristic performed nearly as well as availability-by-recall, and both strategies performed better in skewed than in flat environments. Importantly, the relatively modest gain in accuracy observed for exhaustive over limited search in skewed and spatially clustered environments came at a high exploration cost: relative to the social-circle heuristic, availability-by-recall consulted between 1.64 and 3.42 times more instances before terminating search. Specifically, whereas the social-circle heuristic probed, on average, between 12 and 25 agents for relevant instances, availability-by-recall always probed all 41 members of an agent's social network. Moreover, in all environments, the social-circle heuristic sampled less information than availability-by-recall (i.e., stopped searching before reaching the last circle) in three-quarters or more of cases.

Another way of studying the influence of environmental structure on the cost of relying on small samples is to examine how inferential accuracy increases as a function of sample size when samples are drawn from the

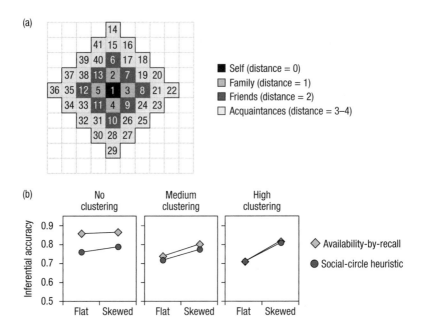

Figure 4.2
Procedure and main results of the simulation study conducted by Pachur et al. (2013a). (a) Illustration of the simulated population (simplified as a 10×10 two-dimensional grid) and the circles of one agent's social network. The circles were defined in terms of the distance to the focal circle, which consisted of the agent. The "family" circle comprised all four agents with distance=1; the "friends" circle, all eight agents with distance=2; and the "acquaintances" circle, all 28 agents with distance=3 or 4. An agent's social network thus consisted of 40 other individuals, allowing the agent to sample up to 41 individuals (including the agent). (b) Inferential accuracy, defined as the proportion of correct inferences excluding cases in which the heuristics made random guesses, of the social-circle heuristic and availability-by-recall in six simulated environments that differed on the type of frequency distribution (flat vs. skewed) and the type of spatial distribution of instances (no, medium, or high clustering).

network at random. In another set of computer simulations, Pachur et al. (2013a) found that although the gain in accuracy from sampling more information was subject to a diminishing return (see also chapter 7 and Hertwig & Pleskac, 2010), the rate of decline in return depended on the environment (to see this for yourself, please access interactive element 4.1 at https://taming -uncertainty.mpib-berlin.mpg.de/). In skewed relative to flat environments, accuracy increased more steeply at small sample sizes and leveled off more quickly with increasing sample size. To illustrate, in both environments, drawing 50 samples (when there was no spatial clustering) increased the chance of making a correct inference from 50% (guessing without drawing any samples) to approximately 84%. In the skewed environment, however, the largest portion of this gain, 6.4 percentage points, was achieved by increasing the sample size from 0 to a single observation. In the flat environment, by contrast, the gain in accuracy achieved by increasing the sample size from 0 to 1 amounted to just 3.7 percentage points. Moreover, in each environment examined, random sampling of a fixed sample size—as implemented in this simulation—fell short of the accuracy achieved by structured sampling that adjusts the size of the sample contingent on the information encountered—as implemented by the social-circle heuristic. This held particularly for environments with no spatial clustering, in which the social-circle heuristic offered the largest benefit over limited random sampling. Specifically, because conditional and ordered sampling potentially ignores redundant information in later social circles, it can achieve higher accuracy than can unconditional random draws of samples of the same size.

Together, these results suggest that it is not inevitable that limited search for instances in memory comes at the price of decreased accuracy. In fact, frugality may even safeguard against drawing erroneous inferences from samples whose representativeness is compromised by a high degree of clustering. These conclusions echo findings on the adaptive value of reliance on small samples in other cognitive domains (e.g., Kareev, 1995). Moreover, the relative affordances of limited search in social memory are a function of the environmental properties and the sustainability of search costs in a given situation. For example, if the cost of further search is high but clustering is low, the structured and limited search policy of the social-circle heuristic may constitute a good middle ground between improving accuracy at the expense of further search and limiting search at a fixed sample size drawn at random.

Let us summarize. Heuristic sampling that starts with a very small sample and sequentially expands search only if that sample does not yield sufficient evidence represents a useful tool for judging event frequencies under conditions that are arguably common in natural environments—when the frequency distribution of the events is skewed and the events occur in spatial clusters. But like any tool, such a mechanism is bound by the structure of the problem at hand—it works well in some environments but not in others.

Exhaustive search strategies also have a place in the mind's toolbox for two reasons. First, sequential expansion of the search space may not always be feasible (e.g., when instance knowledge is low to begin with). Second, it requires the ability to selectively focus attention on some information and ignore other data. The necessary cognitive processes for this selective focus may not be available to decision makers of all ages (see Horn, Ruggeri, & Pachur, 2016; Mata, von Helversen, et al., 2011), and they may incur cognitive costs (see Fechner, Schooler, & Pachur, 2018; Khader et al., 2011).

4.4.2 Limitations and Benefits of Social Sampling from Proximate Environments

We have highlighted the perhaps counterintuitive effectiveness of social sampling in one's local sphere for assessing event frequencies in the global population. This effectiveness is rooted chiefly in people's ability to form accurate impressions of frequency distributions in their proximate social environments (e.g., Galesic et al., 2012; Nisbett & Kunda, 1985)—indeed, a large body of research shows that people automatically encode the frequencies of events encountered in the world (Hasher & Zacks, 1979, 1984; Zacks & Hasher, 2002). Yet it is also important to acknowledge the limits of social sampling. Focusing on a small snapshot sampled from personal experience may prevent people from going beyond the data at hand and taking limitations of the sample or the sampling process into account, causing them to behave as naive intuitive social statisticians (see Fiedler, 2000; Fiedler & Juslin, 2006). This is not to say that people never aim to adjust for potentially unrepresentative information (see, e.g., Oppenheimer, 2004); they just may not always succeed in anticipating precisely when and to what extent to regulate the information experienced.

Consequently, despite its merits, social sampling sometimes leads to inaccurate impressions of the world. For instance, prioritizing the information represented by one's self may create a "false consensus effect," whereby people perceive their own choices and behaviors to be more common in the population than those they do not endorse (Ross et al., 1977). Moreover, because the people in one's social environment tend to be more similar to oneself than to a randomly drawn person, proximate social samples can be unrepresentative (e.g., McPherson et al., 2001). An additional limitation is introduced when social sampling aims to assess the relative frequency of subjective beliefs, values, or attitudes, the observation of which hinges on people's willingness to express them truthfully. For example, in the formation of public opinion, observation of expressed viewpoints in one's proximate social environment—as if operating a "quasi-statistical organ" (Noelle-Neumann, 1974, p. 44)—has been argued to sometimes give rise to a "spiral of silence." Specifically, if people are afraid of being ostracized because their opinions deviate from prevailing views in the population, the upshot may be that the perceived majority opinion is voiced increasingly often—and the perceived minority opinion is eventually silenced. Consequently, assessing popular public opinion is exceedingly difficult and may produce distorted forecasts of people's attitudes and behaviors. Eduardo Paes turned out to be right in dismissing the public's concerns about a Zika pandemic based on his observations of his social network. By contrast, *New Yorker* movie critic Pauline Kael failed to foresee Nixon's landslide victory in the 1972 U.S. presidential election using the same approach. She famously expressed her surprise about the inaccuracy of her personal social sample, saying, "I only know one person who voted for Nixon. Where they are I don't know. They're outside my ken" (Brody, 2011).

But does basing frequency judgments on proximate social samples that deviate from population-wide statistics necessarily result in disadvantageous outcomes? Or are, for example, risk judgments that are well calibrated to the mortality risks of one's own age cohort more relevant than being able to produce accurate population-wide fatality rates (see, e.g., Benjamin & Dougan, 1997)? As Galesic et al. (2012) have shown, although conducting social comparisons by sampling from one's proximate social network can lead to apparent distortions—such as self-enhancement (evaluating oneself as better than others) and self-depreciation (evaluating oneself as worse than others)—the resulting judgments reflect the structure of the immediate social environment that people navigate on a daily basis quite well. These proximate social environments might be a more relevant standard in many situations, and the fact that people are better attuned to their immediate social environments than to the broader population can be considered adaptive: "It is one's social circle, not the 'general population' or an 'average person' that should have the biggest influence on one's happiness and aspirations" (Galesic et al., 2012, p. 1521).

To summarize, we have outlined conditions under which ordered and limited search in proximate social spaces can represent an effective inference strategy, helping to reduce uncertainty about event frequencies in many domains of life. Our aim was not to provide prescriptive guidelines as to when and how information sampled from one's social circles should be used to estimate relative frequencies. Rather, we have identified limits and potential advantages of sampling from proximate social spaces, showing that this approach is not a general-purpose tool and that its effectiveness hinges on environmental conditions (e.g., the skewness and clustering of events) as well as on the objective of the sampling agent (e.g., assessing risks in the proximate vs. general environment).

4.5 Conclusion

In many critical aspects of everyday life, no objective social statistics are available. A remarkably effective tool for forming approximate representations of the world's social texture in such contexts is to take a mental poll of the people one knows personally. But how is such a search structured— where do people begin, how do they navigate through the sampling space, and when do they terminate their search? We have illustrated how natural structures in personal social networks can guide the search for relevant information when people make inferences about the frequency of events in the world at large. The hierarchical structure of personal social networks, whose social circles typically increase in size from central to more peripheral positions in the hierarchy, provides the mind with a heuristic but principled procedure for sequentially expanding the sample size depending on the information obtained from smaller samples. Under common environmental conditions, such an approach incurs only small costs in accuracy relative to exhaustive search. It thus represents one example of how the human mind, by virtue of its ecological rationality, can operate successfully in an uncertain world.

5 Strategic Uncertainty and Incomplete Information: The Homo Heuristicus Does Not Fold

Leonidas Spiliopoulos and Ralph Hertwig

5.1 Strategic and Environmental Uncertainty

In the movie *The Hunt for Red October*, based on the novel by Tom Clancy (1984) and set at the height of the Cold War, Soviet captain Marko Ramius has been given command of a prototype nuclear submarine with a revolutionary stealth propulsion system (Neufeld & McTiernan, 1990). *Red October*'s new technology would allow it to approach the U.S. coast undetected and initiate a first strike with little to no warning. Understanding the consequences of this imbalance between the two superpowers, Captain Ramius plans to defect to the United States, gifting to it the stealth technology and thus eliminating the Soviets' strategic advantage. As Ramius is heading toward U.S. waters, the Soviets learn that he intends to defect and deploy other submarines to stop him. The United States is now in a precarious position. Soviet diplomats tell their U.S. counterparts that Captain Ramius has gone rogue and intends to launch an unauthorized nuclear strike on the United States; they ask for help in capturing him or destroying *Red October*. The U.S. command brings in a CIA analyst, Jack Ryan, to assess the situation. Ryan tries to infer Ramius's motivation, state of mind, and intentions: Is he a rogue captain capable of launching a nuclear attack? Or does he have some other (as yet unknown) motivation? Is he insane or sane? Drawing on prior information about Captain Ramius and interpreting his actions during the rapidly unfolding events, Ryan reaches the correct conclusion: Ramius intends to defect rather than to strike.

Uncertainty about an opponent's characteristics—in terms of preferences, beliefs, or strategies—is termed *strategic uncertainty*. Ramius knows his own intentions and preferences, but they are not common knowledge. If the United States were persuaded by the Soviets' framing of the situation, their best response—given their limited knowledge of the situation—would be to help sink the vessel. In the long run, this would be to their disadvantage, as they would lose access to the game-changing stealth technology. But as the U.S. command is unaware of *Red October*'s new technology, it cannot properly evaluate the consequences of its actions. Thus, not only are the U.S. decision makers exposed to strategic uncertainty about their opponent, but they are also uncertain or ignorant of the payoffs of their actions (*environmental uncertainty*; see also chapter 12). The interaction of strategic uncertainty and incomplete information makes this game a particularly difficult and unpredictable one—not least because it has no historical precedent. In game theory, this "ahistorical" interaction is called a one-shot game—in contrast to a repeated game, where the same game may be played against the same opponent multiple times.

How can people resolve, reduce, or otherwise handle the various kinds of uncertainty involved in strategic one-shot interactions—that is, interactions that do not afford the opportunity for learning? Is this domain one in which *Homo heuristicus*, equipped with computationally modest and informationally frugal decision rules, will thrive or falter? Using computer simulations, we compared the performance of random behavior (a baseline), eight heuristics, and a normative solution (the Nash equilibrium) across environments with different levels of strategic and environmental uncertainty. We refer to these collectively as decision policies. Our focus is on heuristics for two key reasons: First, computation of the normative solution becomes so complex as to be psychologically implausible once strategic and/or environmental uncertainty are entered in the equation. Second, simple heuristics can be as accurate as, and sometimes even more accurate than, decision policies that take all the available information into account, including optimization models (Gigerenzer & Brighton, 2009; see chapter 2). This finding—that simplicity does not necessarily come at the cost of accuracy—has raised a crucial question: In which environments can a simple heuristic outperform optimizing policies, and in which will it lag behind? In discussing the "right" environments for heuristics, the philosopher Sterelny (2003) has suggested that they are likely to succeed only in nonsocial environments, that is, in environments that rarely involve "competitive, interacting, responsive aspects of the environment" (p. 208): "For it is precisely in such situations that simple rules of thumb will go wrong.... Catching a ball is one problem; catching a liar is another" (p. 53).

Our goal is to examine precisely this question: Do heuristics fail in the face of strategic uncertainty and incomplete information? We further explore to what extent heuristics' performance in strategic games is contingent on characteristics of the environment—possibly suggesting a map of bounded rationality that describes relationships between regions (properties) of the environment and properties of heuristics that can either boost or undermine the accuracy of decisions.

5.2   The Unwieldy Normative Solution in Strategic Games

Let us first consider the normative solution. A set of strategies constitutes a Nash equilibrium (see box 5.1 for an example) if no player can gain (increase their payoff) by unilaterally changing their strategy. It is assumed that each player's beliefs about their opponent's action are correct, that players are fully rational—that is, they best respond to their beliefs—and that each player is aware of the other player's strategies (common knowledge assumption). The crucial construct that clears up strategic uncertainty at the equilibrium is the assumption that both players' beliefs about their opponent's behavior are correct.

In games of incomplete information with strategic and environmental uncertainty, a refinement of the standard equilibrium solution, the Bayesian Nash equilibrium (Harsanyi, 1968), assumes correct (probabilistic) beliefs about the possible states of uncertain variables (e.g., payoffs, others' beliefs). In the *Red October* example, Captain Ramius can be modeled as either insane or sane, with the respective state determining his payoffs (assigning high positive or negative utility, respectively, to initiating a nuclear strike). The Bayesian Nash equilibrium requires that people hold consistent beliefs about the probability distribution of their opponent's preferences (e.g., Ramius is insane with $p=0.6$ and sane with $p=0.4$). Similarly, the Bayesian Nash equilibrium requires consistent beliefs about the distribution of the uncertain environmental payoffs (e.g., the payoff is equal to x with $p=0.3$ or to y with $p=0.7$). Uncertainty is resolved through the forced consistency of beliefs at the equilibrium, and the rationality criterion is met by the choice of actions that represent the best responses given those beliefs.

Typically, as illustrated in the example above, beliefs are modeled as exact probability estimates; in other words, the uncertainty associated with the incomplete information is assumed to be reducible to risk (a known probability). But what if it is not possible to assign exact probabilities to the likelihood that Ramius is sane or insane? Extending the Bayesian Nash equilibrium to uncertainty makes it even more complex. In fact, it renders the solution practically intractable, as it would require second-order probability distributions for all the uncertain variables. Note that the indiscriminate application of a Bayesian approach to strategic decision making under uncertainty is widely contested, as are the Bayesian Nash equilibrium's demanding assumptions, even by prominent game theorists (e.g., Binmore, 2007).

Another complication with the normative solution is that multiple Nash equilibria may exist in a single game. Strategic uncertainty cannot be completely resolved in games with multiple equilibria, even under the strict rationality postulates of the Nash equilibrium. Various theories of equilibrium selection address this uncertainty by whittling down the set of Nash equilibria to a single one: payoff- versus risk-dominance equilibrium (Harsanyi & Selten, 1988), trembling-hand equilibrium (Selten, 1975), or evolutionary selection (Kandori, Mailath, & Rob, 1993). However, all of these modifications require ever more complex rationalizations and beliefs about how the opponent selects the equilibrium. They are therefore unlikely to be good, psychologically plausible descriptive models of human behavior—at least in one-shot games.

In repeated games, where players can accumulate experience with the same game and counterpart, it is possible that they inductively learn and converge to the Nash equilibrium (Binmore, Swierzbinski, & Proulx, 2001; Erev & Roth, 1998; Ochs, 1995; Roth & Erev, 1995). But what happens in uncertain environments comprised of one-shot games against different players? In these conditions, it is difficult or impossible to reduce uncertainty by inductive learning. Are players able to deductively solve the Nash equilibrium? The empirical findings suggest that most participants do not play according to the Nash equilibrium. Instead, they appear to employ various boundedly rational decision rules that we refer to as heuristics.

5.3   Why Do People Resort to Simple Heuristics in Strategic Games?

There are at least four answers to this question. First, people are simply unlikely to be able to calculate the Nash equilibrium. The implication here is that they should use the Nash equilibrium (see box 5.1 for an illustration)—but that in reality, as boundedly rational decision makers, they lack the cognitive capacity to do so (Kahneman, 2003b). Second, along with high mental effort, computing the Nash equilibrium exacts high decision costs. A perfectly rational player should take these costs into account and optimize with respect to the time, computation, money, and other resources incurred (e.g., Sargent, 1993). If the decision costs are high enough, it may be rational to save resources—for instance, by resorting to a simpler decision rule. Third, the Nash equilibrium is a rational response only if a player believes that their opponent will also behave rationally. If a rational player comes to believe that their opponent will, for whatever reason, deviate from the Nash equilibrium, they may also switch gears.

Finally, we propose a fourth possibility that is not necessarily incompatible with some of the previous ones. In uncertain environments, heuristics often perform on par with or even better than more complex decision rules. This has been repeatedly demonstrated in games against nature (e.g., Gigerenzer, Todd, & the ABC Research Group, 1999; Hertwig, Hoffrage, & the ABC Research Group, 2013) but less so in games against others. Our goal is to show that what holds for nonsocial environments, in which a person plays against disinterested nature, also holds in environments involving other people. Social environments have often been characterized as more challenging and intellectually demanding than nonsocial ones (see Hertwig & Hoffrage, 2013). Yet, even here—or perhaps particularly here— simple heuristics may be as accurate as, and sometimes even more accurate than, policies that make the greatest possible use of information and computation. We examined how several simple heuristics fare relative to the normative solution in strategic one-shot games. We studied the heuristics' *ecological rationality*, seeking to identify the environmental properties that are conducive to good performance. Our approach parallels investigations into cue-based inference (see Hogarth & Karelaia, 2006). Our aim was to propose a first map of bounded rationality in strategic games, revealing properties of the games being played, and determining the degree of environmental and strategic uncertainty under which heuristics perform well—or fall behind.

Box 5.1
The Nash equilibrium and strategic dominance.

The Nash equilibrium of the game presented in table 5.1 is the combination of player A's Down strategy and player B's Left strategy. It is calculated as follows: for each combination of possible strategies, ask the question whether either player has an incentive to change their strategy (assuming that the opponent's strategy remains the same). If the answer for both players is no, then the combination of strategies constitutes a Nash equilibrium. Let us start in the upper left cell of table 5.1: Up, Left. If player B chooses Left, does player A have an incentive to switch from Up to another strategy? The answer is yes: the payoff for Up is 58 units, but the payoff for Down is 70 units. Does player B have an incentive to switch from Left (with a payoff of 57) to another strategy? Yes, playing Center would give player B a payoff of 89. Therefore, the combination Up, Left is not a Nash equilibrium. The same reasoning can be applied to every combination of strategies. Let us skip directly to the combination Down, Left. Player A achieves a payoff of 70, the maximum available if player B chooses Left. Player B receives a payoff of 74, the maximum available if player A chooses Down. As neither player has an incentive to change, this combination of strategies constitutes a Nash equilibrium.

Table 5.1 also illustrates strategic dominance. We begin with self-dominance. Up dominates Middle for player A, because the payoffs for Up are always larger than those of Middle, whichever strategy player B chooses. If player B chooses Left, player A receives a payoff of 58 for Up relative to 34 for Middle. If player B chooses Center, player A receives 32 for Up relative to 23 for Middle. If player B chooses Right, player A receives 94 for Up and 37 for Middle. Therefore, Middle is a dominated strategy. Analogous comparisons can be performed to determine opponent-dominance.

5.4 Testing Simple Heuristics in Strategic Games

Herbert Simon (1955, 1956) saw bounded rationality in terms of two interlocking components: the limitations of the human mind and the structure of the environment. The implications of this conceptualization are twofold. First, models of simple heuristics need to reflect the mind's actual capacities rather than assume it to have unbounded capabilities. Second, the environmental structure may be the key to a heuristic's performance, to the extent that the heuristic's architecture successfully maps onto the structure of the environment (or parts of it). For this reason, we now describe our computer simulations in terms of the game environment and the competing heuristics.

Table 5.1

An example of a 3×3 normal-form game.

	Player B		
Player A	Left	Center	Right
Up	58, 57	32, 89	94, 41
Middle	34, 46	23, 31	37, 16
Down	70, 74	41, 12	23, 53

5.4.1 The Strategic Games

The games are all one-shot normal-form games with simultaneous moves, meaning that players make their decisions simultaneously—and therefore independently, without first being able to observe the opponent's choice. Table 5.1 gives an example of a normal-form game with two players. Player A can choose one of the strategies in the rows (Up, Middle, Down); player B can choose one of the strategies in the columns (Left, Center, Right). The number of possible actions for each player is denoted by n—we assume that it is the same for both players and refer to this as the *size* of the game. The game in table 5.1 is therefore a 3×3 game, with each player having three strategies at their disposal. The numbers represent the payoffs that each player will receive for every possible combination of strategies. The first number represents player A's payoff; the second, player B's payoff. For example, if player A chooses Up and player B chooses Center, they receive 32 and 89 units, respectively.

The set of strategic games we investigated included, but was not restricted to, widely researched 2×2 games such as the prisoner's dilemma game, the chicken game, and the stag hunt game. In fact, our analysis included all 78 types of 2×2 (ordinal) games taxonomized by Rapoport, Guyer, and Gordon (1976). Similarly, for $n \times n$ games where the size of the game is greater than 2, we did not restrict our attention to a particular type of game. Payoffs for all games were generated by randomly sampling each payoff independently from a normal distribution (with a mean of 0 and a standard deviation of 100); therefore, every possible game has a nonzero probability of being played. We chose the normal distribution, rather than a uniform distribution, to capture the typically negative correlation between magnitudes in payoff (whether negative or positive) and the probability of their occurrence in the real world (Pleskac & Hertwig, 2014; see chapter 3).

5.4.2   The Properties of the Environment

An environment e is defined by the characteristics of the games that nature randomly (or exogenously) determines are to be played. Each environment is characterized by two variables: first, the size of the game, n (the players' action space), and second, the probability that each payoff in the game is missing or unknown to a player (in %). In an environment with m% missing observations, each individual payoff is randomly determined to be unavailable to the players with probability m. In other words, the player's state of knowledge is incomplete, inducing environmental uncertainty. This procedure creates a problem, however. When numerous payoffs are missing, it is unclear how to calculate best-response profiles. To solve this problem, one would have to hypothesize about how a player chooses an action under such circumstances. Because any hypothesis would (at this point) be quite arbitrary, we chose a different solution. Relying on the principle of vicarious functioning (see Brunswik, 1952; Dhami, Hertwig, & Hoffrage, 2004), players can use available cues (here, payoffs) to infer unreliable or unavailable cues (payoffs). For games with missing payoff information, we therefore assumed that the heuristic imputes a value equal to the mean of the player's other payoffs (with small perturbations to avoid complications associated with equal payoffs and ties). In evaluating the heuristics' performance, however, we assumed that the actual payoff a player receives, depending on the heuristic chosen, is based on the true payoff values and not on the thus inferred values. Let us emphasize that a Bayesian Nash equilibrium would require that players impute the whole probability distribution of possible values for the missing payoffs—in other words, they would need to calculate a decision rule repeatedly (a very large number of times) to approximate the distribution of each possible realization of the missing payoffs. Boundedly rational agents would be unlikely to carry out this calculation.

In sum, the set of environments E we investigated consisted of all possible combinations of the sizes of the action space and the likelihood of missing payoff information $\{n,m\}$, where $n \in N = \{2,3,\ldots,19,20\}$ and $m \in M = \{0,5,10,\ldots,70,75,80\%\}$. For example, a single environment $e(n, m)$ consists of a set of $n \times n$ games, sampled using the procedures noted above, with a probability m of payoff values being missing. Using this implementation, we could examine the performance of the heuristics as a function of the size of the game and the degree of missing knowledge (environmental uncertainty). For every environment, we simulated play for 10,000 randomly drawn games, thereby fully covering the game space. An extended analysis of a larger set of environments including different degrees of conflict or common interest between the players can be found in Spiliopoulos and Hertwig (2018).

5.4.3 The Competing Decision Policies

Our analysis compared 10 decision policies: a set of eight heuristics that have been identified as commonly employed by actual players in laboratory settings (Costa-Gomes, Crawford, & Broseta, 2001; Costa-Gomes & Weizsäcker, 2008; Devetag, Di Guida, & Polonio, 2016; Polonio & Coricelli, 2015; Spiliopoulos, Ortmann, & Zhang, 2018; Stahl & Wilson, 1994, 1995), the (normative) Nash equilibrium, and a baseline random policy. The decision policies are defined in table 5.2; more detailed examples of how to compute them will be presented shortly. To play games against simulated opponents using these decision policies, please visit interactive element 5.1 (at https://taming-uncertainty.mpib-berlin.mpg.de/).

We investigated the performance of level-k heuristics as well as somewhat naive heuristic solutions, such as choosing the action with the highest payoff. Level-k heuristics and cognitive hierarchy theory have been particularly successful in modeling boundedly rational behavior (e.g., Camerer, Ho, & Chong, 2004; Chong, Ho, & Camerer, 2016; Costa-Gomes et al., 2001; Nagel, 1995; Stahl, 1996; Stahl & Wilson, 1995). Each of the policies studied, with the exception of the (pure-strategy) Nash equilibrium, always suggests a unique action for any normal-form game (with unique payoffs). In order to resolve the coordination problem in the case of multiple Nash equilibria, we assumed that players choose the equilibrium maximizing the joint payoffs to both players. Some games may not have a pure-strategy Nash equilibrium;[1] we assumed that in such cases the Nash equilibrium strategy chooses an action randomly.

---

1. Although all finite-player, finite-action games—such as the ones we study in this chapter—are guaranteed to have at least one Nash equilibrium, for some games this will be an equilibrium in mixed strategies, not pure strategies. We focused solely on pure-strategy Nash equilibria because the calculation of a mixed-strategy Nash equilibrium is extremely computationally demanding.

Table 5.2

The set of simulated decision policies (excluding the random baseline): Eight heuristics and the Nash equilibrium.

Decision policy	Abbreviation	OwnP	EQW	NW	Dominance Self/Opp.	Description
Maximax	MaxMax	Y	–	Y	Y	Choose the action(s) offering the highest payoff for the player
Maximin	MaxMin	Y	–	Y	Y	Choose the action(s) offering the highest worst-case payoff for the player
Level-1	L1	Y	Y	–	Y	Choose the action(s) offering the best response to the assumption that an opponent is choosing randomly
Social maximum	SocMax	–	–	–	–	Choose the action(s) maximizing the sum of the player's own payoff and the opponent's payoff
Equality	Eq	–	–	–	–	Choose the action(s) minimizing the difference between the player's own payoff and the opponent's payoff
Dominance-1	D1	–	Y	–	Y	Choose the action(s) offering the best response to the assumption that an opponent is choosing randomly over their nondominated actions
Level-2	L2	–	–	–	Y	Choose the action(s) offering the best response to the assumption that an opponent is applying L1
Level-3	L3	–	–	–	Y	Choose the action(s) offering the best response to the assumption that an opponent is applying L2
Nash equilibrium	NE	–	–	–	Y	Choose the action(s) consistent with the Nash equilibrium

Note. OwnP: the heuristic considers only the player's own payoffs and ignores the opponent's payoff; EQW: equal weighting of the opponent's payoff; NW: no weighting. Dominance Self/Opp.: obeys the principle of strategic self-/opponent-dominance (see box 5.1). Y: policy has the property; –: policy does not have the property.

The following examples illustrate how to compute each decision policy from the perspective of player A in the game presented in table 5.1.

Maximax (MaxMax). Identify the action offering you the highest possible payoff in the matrix (94). On this basis, choose action Up.

Maximin (MaxMin). Find the lowest payoff in each row—these are 32, 23, and 23 in the first, second, and third rows, respectively. Identify the maximum of these lowest payoffs (32). On this basis, choose action Up, thereby guaranteeing a payoff of at least 32.

Level-1 (L1). Sum your own possible payoffs in each row—these are 184, 94, and 134 for the first, second, and third rows, respectively. Identify the row with the largest sum (184). On this basis, choose action Up.

Social maximum (SocMax). For each cell, calculate the collective sum of payoffs to both players (e.g., $58+57=115$ for the upper-left outcome). Identify the maximum total payoff (lower-left outcome, 144). On this basis, choose action Down.

Equality (Eq). For each cell, calculate the absolute difference in the players' payoffs (e.g., $94-41=53$ for the upper-right outcome). Identify the minimum absolute difference (upper-left outcome, 1). On this basis, choose action Up.

Dominance-1 (D1). Examine whether your opponent has any dominated actions. Player B's Left action dominates their Right action: regardless of your actions, player B will always have a higher payoff from the former than the latter. Eliminate the dominated strategy (Right) from consideration and perform an L1 calculation on the remaining strategies (Left and Center). The possible payoffs are $58+32=90$ for Up, $34+23=57$ for Middle, and $70+41=111$ for Down. Therefore, choose Down, which yields the highest mean payoff over player B's nondominated actions.

Level-2 (L2). Sum player B's payoffs for each action—these are 177, 132, and 110 for the first, second, and third columns, respectively. Assume that player B uses L1 and will choose the action with the highest sum, Left.

Identify your highest possible payoff in that column (70) and choose the corresponding action, Down.

Level-3 (L3). Assume that player B is an L2 player. By definition, an L2 player assumes that their opponent uses L1. Apply the L1 strategy to your own payoffs—as described above, this will result in the choice of action Up. As an L2 player, player B will respond by searching for their highest possible payoff in the row corresponding to Up, and will play Center. Choose the best response to this action by identifying your maximum possible payoff in the column associated with Center. The corresponding action is Down (41).

Nash equilibrium (NE). Identify the maximum payoff in each row (i.e., the best response to the assumption that player B has played each column). These are 70, 41, and 94 for actions Left, Center, and Right, respectively. The corresponding best response actions are Down, Down, and Up, respectively. Perform the same operations for player B's payoffs when you play each row. The corresponding best responses are Center, Left, and Left for your actions Up, Middle, and Down, respectively. Determine for which actions these two best responses coincide. In this case, this occurs for the combination Down, Left. Therefore, you would choose Down and player B would choose Left.

5.4.4 Classification of Heuristics' Paths to Simplification

Of the policies we simulated, the Nash equilibrium is the most complex computationally. The heuristics implemented represent different paths to reduce computational complexity: by reducing the amount of information required, by rendering the process of integrating information less complex, or by simplifying the assumptions made about an opponent or their beliefs. Spiliopoulos et al. (2018) measured the complexity of the eight heuristics examined in terms of the number of elementary information processing units required to execute each heuristic (see J. W. Payne, Bettmann, & Johnson, 1993; for an alternative approach to measuring complexity, using a cognitive architecture, see Fechner, Schooler, & Pachur, 2018). The paths taken to reduce complexity can be broadly categorized as payoff-based or probability-based simplification.

Payoff-based simplification. A heuristic can choose to completely ignore the opponent's payoffs and thus act as if the game were a nonstrategic task. The heuristics that do so are MaxMax, MaxMin, and L1 (see table 5.2; similar heuristics, applied to games against nature, are also discussed in chapter 8). All other heuristics in table 5.2 require information about both the player's own payoffs and the opponent's payoffs.

Probability-based simplification. Another path to simplification involves the beliefs held by a player about the probability with which the opponent will play each of the actions (see table 5.1). One simple assumption is that the probabilities of each action are equal, resulting in an equal weighting of the player's own payoffs—this can be viewed as a strategic variant of the equal-weighting principle proposed for prediction (Dawes, 1979). The heuristics that make this assumption are L1 and D1. The latter first removes the opponent's dominated actions, and only then assigns equal weights to the remaining actions. The L1 heuristic is of particular interest because it is known to be frequently recruited by real players in strategic games (see Costa-Gomes et al., 2001; Costa-Gomes & Weizsäcker, 2008; Devetag et al., 2016; Polonio & Coricelli, 2015; Spiliopoulos et al., 2018; Stahl & Wilson, 1994). It both ignores the opponent's payoff and assumes that the opponent randomizes over their actions with probability $1/n$. Alternatively, a heuristic can forgo beliefs about the opponent's behavior and focus solely on payoff information. This applies to SocMax and Eq. These two heuristics do not weight payoffs according to the likelihood of the relevant outcomes being obtained. Instead they involve either the addition or subtraction, respectively, of the player's own payoff and the opponent's payoff for every possible outcome, and then perform ordinal comparisons only. Finally, an even more Spartan process is not integrating the player's own payoffs with the opponent's payoffs but instead making a choice based on a single payoff. This approach avoids both weighting and adding and completely forgoes any belief formation. MaxMax and MaxMin belong to this computationally simplest class of heuristics. MaxMax chooses the action with the highest payoff for the player; MaxMin, the action with the highest payoff for the player in the worst-case scenario. Both heuristics involve only ordinal comparisons among the player's own payoffs based on max and min operations.

5.4.5   The Role of Strategic Dominance

The heuristics differ on another important dimension—namely, their adherence (or lack thereof) to the principle of *strategic dominance*—and their assumptions about whether or not the opponent adheres to this principle. If one of a player's (pure) strategies is better than another strategy—independent of the strategy chosen by the opponent—then that strategy *dominates* the other strategy (the latter is the *dominated* strategy). If a strategy dominates all other strategies in a game, it is referred to as a *dominant* strategy. We use the term *self-dominance* to describe the relationship between the player's strategies and *opponent-dominance* to describe the relationship between the opponent's strategies. Box 5.1 gives examples of the comparisons necessary to determine dominance in the game outlined in table 5.1. It is always beneficial to avoid a self-dominated strategy, regardless of any strategic uncertainty about the opponent's behavior, because a dominated strategy is, by definition, inferior to a dominant strategy for all possible actions available to the opponent. Of the heuristics in table 5.1, L1 and MaxMax adhere to the principle of self-dominance but do not assume that the opponent will do so. D1, L2, L3, and NE adhere to both strategic dominance principles. Whether the assumption of opponent-dominance is realistic depends on the heuristic employed by the opponent. It is not realistic if opponents use SocMax or Eq, neither of which systematically adheres to self-dominance.

Whether or not it is advantageous to adhere to the principle of dominance in a particular environment also depends on the probability that dominated actions exist in each of the environment's games. The proportion of games that have at least one dominated action quickly approaches zero as the size of the game increases from three onwards.[2] Therefore, the importance of recognizing dominance can be expected to decrease with larger games. For example, because L1 and D1 differ only in the first-step dominance check performed by D1, they will converge in their recommended actions as the number of actions increases (and the probability of a dominated action decreases).[3] However, in terms of processes and

---

2. The probability for $n = 2$, 3, 4, 5, 10, and 20 is 0.5, 0.53, 0.48, 0.4, 0.08, and 0.0004, respectively.
3. Inspecting a game for the existence (or lack thereof) of dominated or dominant strategies can reveal further relationships between strategies. As observed by

information needs, D1 would still require more steps to arrive at the same recommendation than L1.

5.4.6 Measuring the Competing Decision Policies' Performance

We measured the success of each decision policy against a performance criterion that we refer to as the *Indifference criterion*. Before we describe this criterion, let us briefly outline the reasoning that informed its choice. In the simulations, we matched each of the competing policies (see table 5.1) as opponents in 10,000 randomly drawn games (for each environment) to approximate the performance of pairs of competitors within an environment. Each policy also played against itself. Imagine each player choosing in advance which decision policy to use across all games in a specific environment. Now consider how strategic uncertainty affects the choice of policy. If a player knows the opponent's policy, they can easily figure out the policy offering the best response. If they do not know the opponent's policy, they may form beliefs about the distribution of decision policies in the population and, at least in theory, calculate the expected payoffs for each policy conditional on those beliefs. This is a probabilistic quantity: it requires weighting the expected payoff against each decision policy by the probability of being matched with a player using that particular policy. However, as we argued before, it will be very difficult to learn this distribution. Consequently, players face strategic uncertainty—that is, they are unable to assign probabilities to the distribution of policies in the population. Luce and Raiffa (1957) argued that decisions in such large worlds (Savage, 1954) may be enabled by the principle of indifference (also known as the principle of insufficient reasoning). This principle informs our performance criterion.

According to the principle of indifference, each decision policy is equally likely to be used by the opponent (see also chapter 2 on the role of this assumption in individual choice). A player's expected payoff over the whole

---

Costa-Gomes et al. (2001), a level-k heuristic's proposed action is identical to that of the Nash equilibrium for games that are solvable by k rounds of iterated dominance (in pure or mixed strategies). Dk heuristics are identical to the Nash equilibrium in games that can be solved by $k+1$ rounds of pure strategy dominance. In many 2×2 games, there is significant overlap between strategies, enabling many simpler heuristics to emulate the Nash equilibrium.

set of games in an environment is then simply an average of the expected payoffs against each decision policy. We define this as the Indifference criterion.[4] It is the expected payoff a decision policy will achieve if (a) the policy plays against a population of policies that are uniformly distributed in the player population, or (b) it plays against a single decision policy, but is unaware which one it is, and believes that the policy is drawn with equal probability from the set of 10 decision policies.

More formally, let the action space A (A') of a player (opponent) denote the set of actions a_n (a'_n) available. The number of actions for each player (or size of the action space) is denoted by N and N'. We assume that this is the same for both players and therefore refer to the common value N as the size of a game. A normal-form game g is defined by a mapping from the action spaces of both players to payoff functions $\pi_g(a_n, a'_n)$ and $\pi'_g(a_n, a'_n)$. That is, the combination of actions (a_n, a'_n) determines the payoffs of both players. Let the decision policy space D (D') of a player (opponent) denote the set of policies d (d') available.

The first number in each cell of a normal-form game, as presented in table 5.1, represents player A's payoff; the second, player B's payoff. For example, if player A chooses a_1 and player B chooses a'_2, then the former receives a payoff of 32 and the latter 89. According to the Indifference criterion, denoted by $\bar{\pi}(d|e)$, the performance of a decision rule d in an environment e consisting of a set of games G_e is given by:

$$\bar{\pi}(d|e) = \frac{1}{|D'|} \sum_{d \in D'} E_{G_e}[\pi_g(a(d), a(d'))]. \tag{1}$$

As mentioned in section 5.4.5, the L1 and D1 policies make identical choices for games without dominated strategies. Consequently, the L2 policy is the best response to both of these policies in such games, giving it an unfair advantage over other policies (which at most are best responses to only one other policy; e.g., NE is the best response to NE, L3 to L2, L1 to Random). We leveled the playing field by assigning half the weight to L1 and D1 when calculating the Indifference criterion. Including both with

---

4. A larger set of performance criteria, including one based on Wald's (1945) maximin model and another examining the robustness of policies to different (nonuniform) distributions of policies in the player population, can be found in Spiliopoulos and Hertwig (2018).

full weight does not alter our findings significantly, although as expected it does give L2 a small boost in performance.

In a nutshell, the Indifference criterion captures policies' average performance against the whole set of possible opponent policies, assuming each is equally likely. We now turn to the results of the competition to examine how well or poorly the heuristics fared when facing both strategic and environmental uncertainty.

5.5 Decision Policies' Performance as Measured by the Indifference Criterion

Figure 5.1 shows the performance of the competing policies across the set of environments, measured in terms of the Indifference criterion. The size of the action space (or game) n is shown along the y-axis; the percentage of missing information, along the x-axis. Each heatmap depicts the performance of one policy. As a benchmark, the two top-left panels show the performance of random choice and the Nash equilibrium. The darker the shading, the better the performance. The robustness of a policy is a function of how large the area of dark shading is: the larger the area, the more robust the policy's performance over a range of game sizes and degree of payoff uncertainty. In general, the findings presented in figure 5.1 suggest that some heuristics exhibit consistently good performance over the whole set of environments and can even outperform the Nash equilibrium. Other heuristics perform well only in specific regions. We now move on to summarize the key results. Recall that performance when operationalized in terms of the Indifference criterion (figure 5.1) assumes that each opponent policy is equally likely. The effects of changing the distribution of decision policies in the population can be viewed in interactive element 5.2.

The first result is that assuming equal weighting pays off. The L1 and D1 heuristics, both of which assume equal weighting of the player's own payoffs, are the best performers on average across all the environments, and show robustness to limited payoff knowledge regardless of the size of the game. The next best policies (averaged across all the environments) are the SocMax and L2 heuristics. Note that the former outperforms the L1 and D1 heuristics in niche environments comprised of large games and high payoff uncertainty.

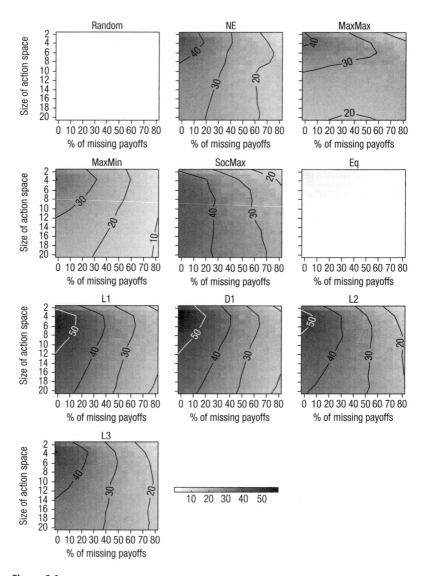

Figure 5.1

Results of the competition among policies, with performance operationalized in terms of the Indifference criterion. The average percentage of missing payoffs ranges from 0% to 80%; the size of the action space ranges from 2 to 20. The darker the shading, the better the performance.

The second result is that there is such a thing as too much simplification. Two of the computationally simplest heuristics, MaxMax and MaxMin, do not perform well. They achieve moderately high mean payoffs in just a small subset of environments, namely, games involving few actions (2–5) and low payoff uncertainty. The extreme simplification embodied in these heuristics seems to overshoot the mark, leading to poor performance.

The third result is that assuming higher rationality in the other player leads to poorer performance. The L1 and D1 heuristics are the most robust policies, achieving excellent performance across the environments. Their performance decreases only when knowledge about payoffs is extremely limited—however, all policies' performance declines under this condition. Increasing the level of rationality attributed to the opponent leads to a further decrease in performance. Although the L2 and L3 decision rules still perform reasonably well, they are less robust than L1 and D1, especially as game size increases. Similarly, the Nash equilibrium policy, which makes the strongest assumptions about the opponent's rationality, performs worse than the L2, L3, and L1 and D1 heuristics (which attribute a lower level of rationality to the opponent). Importantly, the Nash equilibrium achieves relatively high payoffs only in very small games with low payoff uncertainty.

The final result is that the top-performing policies obey the self-dominance principle. According to the Indifference criterion, the best performing heuristics are L1 and D1, in terms of robustness to both limited knowledge and game size. Both heuristics obey the self-dominance principle; D1 also assumes the opponent obeys the dominance principle. Note that the L2 heuristic, which also performs well, obeys both self- and opponent-dominance.

5.6   The Robust Beauty of Simplicity

We investigated the performance of a variety of policies in the face of strategic and environmental uncertainty. All alternatives to the normative Nash equilibrium policy simplify the decision process. Some, such as L1 and MaxMax, make strong simplifying assumptions and, for instance, take no account of the opponent's strategic concerns (see table 5.1); others, such as D1 and L2, take those concerns into account, albeit in a somewhat simplified manner, by making weaker assumptions about an opponent's rationality or common knowledge of rationality. We also investigated the heuristics' performance as a function of environmental uncertainty, that is, the degree of knowledge about the player's own payoffs and the opponent's payoffs. Finally, we varied the games' complexity, that is, the number of actions available to each player.

How did the heuristics fare? Consistent with findings on inferential as well as preferential choice (Gigerenzer, Hertwig, & Pachur, 2011; see chapter 2), simplicity was more robust to strategic and environmental uncertainty than was complexity. The normative Nash equilibrium policy was only relatively competitive for precisely the kind of games typically used in experimental investigations of strategic behavior: complete knowledge of payoff information and game sizes of roughly 2–5 actions. Furthermore, making specific assumptions about an opponent's behavior (e.g., predicting, as an L3 player, that the opponent will behave as an L2 player) may risk misrepresenting actual heterogeneity among players. By contrast, the equal-weighting L1 and D1 heuristics, both of which attach the same likelihood to each of an opponent's possible actions (the latter after removing dominated actions), were the best performers, followed closely by L2 and SocMax.

The L1 heuristic is particularly adapted to environments in which knowledge about payoffs is severely limited. It performs very well, despite turning a strategic task into a nonstrategic one by completely ignoring the opponent's payoffs. Echoing results in games against nature, there is also a "robust beauty" (Dawes, 1979, p. 571) to this improper decision policy in strategic games.

5.7   Sterelny's Error

Sterelny (2003) argued that simple rules of thumb are likely to fail in competitive interactions. Yet we found that even in environments marked by both strategic and environmental uncertainty, heuristics that abandon normative axioms and Bayesian principles need not buckle. In fact, it was typically sufficient that a heuristic obeyed the self-dominance principle, which even the simple L1 heuristic does, and refrained from making precise assumptions about an opponent's behavior. Two simplifications were particularly successful: equal weighting and ignoring an opponent's payoff (or, equivalently, the strategic component of the game). But let us also emphasize the limits of oversimplification. Decision policies that base decisions on a single piece of information without weighting, such as MaxMax and

MaxMin, typically performed worse than other heuristics in terms of the Indifference criterion. Apart from oversimplification, being overly confident in the ability to predict how an opponent is likely to play also represents a risk. For instance, precise assumptions or beliefs about what other players will do often came at a high price. The L3 heuristic and the Nash equilibrium are cases in point.

If anything, our analysis may have underestimated the performance of simple heuristics relative to more complex processes in strategic interactions. First, we assumed that each policy was perfectly executed. Yet the more complex a policy is, the more difficult it will be for it to achieve perfect execution. Consequently, the Nash equilibrium and the relatively complex high level-k heuristics are more susceptible to execution errors. If these errors were random, the performance of policies prone to execution errors would be a linear combination of their performance assuming perfect execution and the performance of the random choice rule (worst competitor). Thus, execution errors would further attenuate the performance of more complex policies relative to simpler ones such as L1. Second, a policy's complexity is likely to be positively correlated with its execution time. Therefore, a decision maker using a heuristic would have more time available to play more games. In other words, if performance were normalized per execution time, the performance of simpler policies would increase relative to that of more complex policies.

5.8 Conclusion

Experimental studies of strategic interactions have found evidence for the frequent use of heuristics (see Spiliopoulos & Hertwig, 2018). Our results cast new light on this finding. The established narrative attributes it to humans' inability to reason according to the complex Nash equilibrium. Alternatively, it has been argued that people still optimize their choice of policy but do so subject to a constraint based on the decision costs, leading to the use of simpler policies. This argument is based on the accuracy–effort (speed) trade-off, often seen as a general law of cognition (see chapter 2): those who invest less mental effort will pay a price in terms of lower accuracy (performance). From this perspective, heuristics are, by definition, always second best; people use them because they take a rational approach to their cognitive limitations. Were resources unlimited, more computation and more time would, from this perspective, always be better. Our analyses show that the accuracy–effort trade-off is not ubiquitous. Simpler solutions such as level-k heuristics—in particular, L1 and D1—do not inevitably sacrifice performance relative to the Nash equilibrium policy. In fact, they can achieve high performance and robustness in the face of substantial environmental and strategic uncertainty. This does not mean, however, that there are no limits to the benefits of simplicity. As we have also observed, simplifying assumptions can be too naive and too minimal.

It has often been argued that "choice in social interaction harbors a level of complexity that makes it unique among natural decision-making problems, because outcome probabilities depend on the unobservable internal state of the other individual" (Seymour & Dolan, 2008, p. 667). We agree that social environments are different from physical ones to the extent that the presence of others along with their strategic intentions and counterstrategies represent additional and important sources of uncertainty. Yet our results challenge the common wisdom that social complexity necessitates cognitive complexity (e.g., Humphrey, 1976, 1988; Whiten & Byrne, 1988). Even in environments fraught with environmental and strategic uncertainty, simple heuristics can reach surprisingly accurate decisions and prevent people from making overly bold, demanding, and specific assumptions about others.

6   Toward Simple Eating Rules for the Land of Plenty

Mattea Dallacker, Jutta Mata, and Ralph Hertwig

Don't eat anything your great-grandmother wouldn't recognize as food.
—Michael Pollan, *Food Rules: An Eater's Manual*

6.1   The Taste of Uncertainty

People eat to live. Food provides the energy that human bodies need for everyday activities. It powers that most energy-hungry organ, the brain. But food is more than just functional. It can be a source of intense pleasure—or of grave harm. In the modern food environment, this harm can take the form of excessive calories, insufficient nutrients, or even ethical challenges. People who do not grow their own ingredients or prepare their own food are often unsure of exactly what they are eating and to what extent their food may have detrimental long-term consequences. Around the world, much food is now produced on an industrial scale, making it abundant and affordable. Yet although the availability and accessibility of food is, for many, no longer uncertain, a high degree of uncertainty remains in the modern food environment: the findings of nutrition research are sometimes weak or unreliable, the food industry not infrequently works with murky marketing strategies and vague health claims, and policy makers fail to sufficiently regulate the foods available to consumers.

What can policy makers and consumers do to reduce or manage these uncertainties and instead promote healthy food decisions? We focus here on individuals' decision-making competences—and on how simple, evidence-based heuristics can be used to boost them. The concise eating rules proposed by author and journalist Michael Pollan (2009) are one example of simple heuristics that aim to facilitate healthy decisions in the complex modern food environment. Heuristic rules are mental tools that help people make smart, fast inferences and decisions when information, time, and computational power are limited (see chapter 1). They can also help people to engineer their environments in ways that foster good decisions in uncertain situations. In this chapter, we describe the heuristics people may use to engineer an important everyday choice domain: decisions on what to eat. We first identify different kinds of food-related uncertainties, and then describe how a repertoire of simple, evidence-based heuristics can help people master these highly uncertain food environments.

6.2   The Obesogenic and Complex Food Environment

Throughout most of human history, the biggest uncertainties about food were how to procure it, whether there would be enough of it, and whether eating it would result in illness or even death. Happily, the modern food environment has largely eliminated these ancestral uncertainties and risks. The products offered in supermarkets are rarely toxic or contaminated by dangerous pathogens. Most contemporary humans have enough food—eight in nine people have enough to eat (World Food Programme, 2016)—and that food is denser in calories, more readily available, and less expensive than during any other period of human evolution. German fables of *Schlaraffenland* tell of a land of plenty where the rivers flow with milk, raindrops are made of honey, and roasted birds fly into the mouths of the sedentary. Once a fantasy depicted by artists and novelists, the land of plenty has in a way become reality: for many people, there is more than enough of everything. And therein lies the rub. Obesity has become a global endemic that affects people of all ages and income groups and carries serious consequences for individual and global health (Finucane et al., 2011). Over 1.9 billion people worldwide are obese; obesity in adults has tripled globally in the last four decades (World Health Organization, 2018); and there has been a tenfold increase in obesity rates among children and adolescents (Abarca-Gómez et al., 2017). Obesity is a major risk factor for noncommunicable diseases such as cardiovascular diseases and diabetes. It is the cause of around 90%–95% of all cases of type 2 diabetes (American Diabetes Association, 2009); as obesity rates have grown, so has the worldwide prevalence of diabetes, which has quadrupled since 1980 (NCD Risk Factor Collaboration, 2016). Expanding waistlines shrink quality of life and probably reduce longevity. In 2005, a study in the *New England Journal of Medicine* predicted that "life expectancy at birth and at older ages could level off or even decline within the first half of this century" in the United States (Olshansky et al., 2005). Recent preliminary data from the Centers for Disease Control and Prevention suggest that this tipping point may now have been reached (Ludwig, 2016).

Today's food decisions are made in an obesogenic environment where unhealthy food is available anywhere, anytime, and at relatively low costs. In the United States, the average share of per capita income spent on food fell from 17.5% in 1960 to 9.9% in 2013 (Barclay, 2015). Food is not only abundant, it is also perfectly designed to exploit our ancestral food preferences. The modern cultural food context has thus pushed back some of what Charles Darwin (1859) called the "hostile forces of nature," only to replace them with the no less formidable forces of the food industry. Despite or possibly because of the extent to which modern consumer culture and food technologies have made foods reliably available, appealing, and safe, uncertainty in food choice has not become extinct. Instead, new uncertainties have entered the choice environment. Today's uncertainties include health-related concerns ("Does this food contain a high level of sugar?"), uncertainty about the energy value of foodstuffs ("Will I gain weight if I eat this food?"), and questions around food's chemical composition ("Are there pesticides in my food?"), as well as ethical concerns about issues such as animal welfare, fair trade, and ecological footprints. We now turn to three sources of uncertainty in the food choice environment: nutritional science, the food industry, and public policy.

6.3 Sources and Producers of Food-Related Uncertainty

6.3.1 Nutritional Science as a Producer of Uncertainty

Several methodological constraints make it challenging for the nutritional sciences to produce strong evidence for policy makers and the public. It is impossible to conduct double-blind studies that assess the long-term effects of foods. For one thing, because people see, taste, and smell their food, they cannot be blind to the foods they are eating (and the experimental condition in which this food is provided). For another, their food intake would need to be strictly controlled over many years, which is unrealistic. Other experimental approaches cannot be realized due to ethical considerations;

for instance, it would be unethical to compare a long-term high dose of sugar with a low sugar dosage in children. While it is common to rely on questionnaires to measure long-term food or nutrient intake, the majority of respondents give implausible reports. As a prime example, participants in the National Health and Nutrition Examination Survey reported too few calories to be able to maintain their body weight (Archer, Hand, & Blair, 2013). Furthermore, many of these studies are underpowered due to small sample sizes or have inadequate control groups (Ioannidis, 2013).

The effects of almost every imaginable nutrient on health outcomes have been reported in peer-reviewed articles—with almost every imaginable outcome. Results indicating, for example, that the risk of a major disease can be reduced or even halved by consuming a small amount of a single food or nutrient, such as five nuts a day, are rife in peer-reviewed journals (Schoenfeld & Ioannidis, 2013). It is highly unlikely that any single nutrient or food has more than a trivial effect on mortality. However, there is stronger evidence for the general health effects of certain food groups. Fruits and vegetables offer more health benefits than highly processed fatty and sugary foods (Slavin & Lloyd, 2012). More recent comparisons of dietary patterns (e.g., Mediterranean versus Western diets) are promising, but they often rely on risk populations or small samples, making it difficult to generalize findings to the public at large (Sofi, Macchi, Abbate, Gensini, & Casini, 2014).

Scientific research programs sponsored by the food industry are another source of uncertainty; the ensuing conflicts of interest render findings unreliable. For example, it is now known that the sugar industry systematically sponsored a decades-long research program to cast doubt on the negative consequences of sugar while endorsing fat as a key factor in coronary heart disease (Kearns, Schmidt, & Glantz, 2016). As we will show next, this is not the only way that the industry brings uncertainty into food choices.

6.3.2 Food Labeling as a Source of Ambiguity and Uncertainty

Understanding the ingredients of processed foods—and thus whether those foods are healthy or not—is another challenge in today's uncertain food environment. Take the example of ready-to-eat breakfast cereals. Cereals enjoy the reputation of being healthy, and wholegrain cereals without added sugars or other additives are indeed nutritious. But highly processed sugary cereals, which lack fiber and protein and cause blood sugar to spike, are more suitable as a sweet treat than as a balanced breakfast. In this kind of environment, consumers cannot rely on either a categorical judgment ("cereal is healthy") or reasonable intuitions about ingredients—many processed foods defy common sense.

Like any industry, the food industry's objective is to sell its product at a profit. To achieve this end, many companies produce highly engineered processed foods that pleasure and delight the taste buds (Cross & Proctor, 2014). One symptom of this development is high sugar consumption. Added sugar was a rare pleasure prior to modern industrialism and marketing. In 1822, the American annual per capita intake was about 3 kg; by the end of the 20th century, it hovered around 50 kg (Cross & Proctor, 2014). This increase was made possible by turning foods—even products that do not appear particularly unhealthy—into sugar bombs. One of America's favorite condiments, ketchup—a seemingly innocuous tomato-based sauce—can now contain as much as 6 g of added sugar per serving of approximately 30 g. Consumers' intuitions about food have not kept up with these radical transformations of food products. We recently tested intuitive knowledge about the sugar content of common foods and beverages in a survey of 305 parents (Dallacker, Hertwig, & Mata, 2018c). To try this yourself, please visit interactive element 6.1 (at https://taming-uncertainty.mpib-berlin.mpg.de/). Parents tended to massively underestimate the sugar content of most foods and beverages, especially those that are perceived as healthy. For instance, over 90% of parents underestimated the sugar content of a 250 g container of fruit yogurt (which was actually 39 g), with the average estimate falling short by 21 g—the equivalent of seven sugar cubes. Children whose parents underestimated the amount of sugar in foods were at twice the risk of being overweight or obese.

One important aspect of food regulation and, at least in theory, an important way to inform consumers and reduce their lack of knowledge and uncertainty is food labeling. But how effective is it? Clearly, simply providing access to a list of ingredients is not effective. Many consumers have problems understanding and interpreting food labels (Grunert, Wills, & Fernandez-Celemin, 2010). This is not surprising. The serving sizes displayed on packages vary by brand and product, and ingredient names are often far from transparent. Even the most diligent consumer could easily overlook several of the 50 names for sugar that are used on food labels (Shulman & Lustig, 2013).

It has been estimated that improved food labeling could decrease health costs in the United States by $4.2 billion over 20 years (Hawkes, 2004).

Ongoing efforts are therefore being made to help consumers understand what they are eating. In the United States, for example, food labels now state the amount of added sugars. But nutrition labels compete for attention with many other health claims, such as "reduced cholesterol," "100% natural," "antioxidant plus," or "immune support." These claims are often independent of a product's nutritional value, instead advertising other (alleged) health benefits of the product. Even if consumers do not actually understand them, such claims make the product seem more attractive or healthy (van Trijp, 2009). The information structure of today's food packages also makes it difficult to think about the ingredients and healthfulness of a product: the amount of nutrition information displayed is high; the daily guided amount of nutrients is often presented in reference to arbitrary, nonstandardized portion sizes; and no criteria are provided to allow consumers to evaluate whether a product is comparably high or low in nutrients such as sugar relative to similar products. The food industry has a record of fighting efforts to develop transparent food-labeling systems. Although its attempt to prevent the Nutrition Labeling and Education Act of 1990 failed, its lobbying met with more success in 2010, when the European Parliament voted down an attempt to introduce a traffic-light system to food labeling.

6.3.3   Policy Makers and Regulators as Producers of Uncertainty

The challenges of producing reliable evidence in the nutritional sciences have implications for policy makers, regulators, and agencies that issue nutritional recommendations. Littered with constantly changing evidence that is often weak and even conflicting, nutritional recommendations for the general public vary over time and across countries. The German food pyramid, for example, recommended foods high in carbohydrates as the basis of daily nutrition until 2005. It now suggests a diet dominated by fruit and vegetables. Within a period of just two decades, the United States Department of Agriculture (USDA) presented no fewer than three recommendations for healthy nutrition: two pyramids and, most recently, MyPlate (United States Department of Agriculture, 2015; see figure 6.1).

The most striking difference between the two pyramids was the switch from grains as the main component to an equal distribution of grains, fruits, and vegetables. The later version no longer included sweets but added a reference to physical activity. The third approach, MyPlate, divides a plate

| 1992: The Food Guide Pyramid | 2005: MyPyramid Food Guidance System | 2011: MyPlate |

Figure 6.1

History of USDA food pyramids illustrating changes in American dietary guidelines within two decades.

in four sections of varying sizes: one each for vegetables, fruits, grains, and proteins, plus a portion of dairy. This most recent concept is itself likely to be replaced eventually as well. MyPlate has already faced criticism for not offering a complete picture: it omits some basic dietary advice such as distinguishing between potatoes and other vegetables (Harvard School of Public Health, 2018), and fails to represent the specific nutrition needs of large and growing groups such as vegetarians and vegans.

Many other attempts to offer definitive nutrition guidelines are likewise blighted by weak evidence. For example, the Austrian food pyramid suggests limiting egg consumption to three eggs per week. Yet two recent meta-analyses found no evidence that a higher consumption of eggs (up to seven per week) is related to a higher risk of cardiovascular diseases (Rong et al., 2013). On a grander scale, the European Prospective Investigation into Cancer and Nutrition study of almost half a million Europeans over 8.7 years showed that an increased fruit and vegetable intake, as suggested by most nutrition guidelines, decreased the incidence of cancer by such a small magnitude that the results must be interpreted with caution (Buchner et al., 2010). Other large-scale studies have likewise found that increased fruit and vegetable consumption has only very small effects on the reduction of cancer, heart disease, and other chronic diseases, particularly in women (Hung et al., 2004; Joshipura et al., 2001). However, studies considering more components of healthy eating (e.g., Harvard University's Alternative Healthy Eating Index) have found that more healthy eating is linked to a higher overall decreased risk of developing these diseases (Akbaraly et al., 2011).

A further difficulty for consumers is in deciding which of the countless guidelines to actually follow. In Europe alone, more than two dozen organizations have issued their own recommendations for healthy nutrition. These stand alongside those offered by the World Health Organization, the USDA, and many other public authorities. To date there is no single independent agency that provides solely evidence-based recommendations for healthy nutrition to the general public. The modern food environment is uncertain beyond the classic dimensions of probabilities and outcomes—there is no clear, normative, evidence-based benchmark for the nutritional content of individual food items. It is no surprise that consumers are inundated by a media avalanche of conflicting claims about what to eat and what to avoid.

6.4   How to Help People Dealing with a Complex Food Environment

The unfolding obesity epidemic is contributing to plummeting health levels and skyrocketing health costs (Biener, Cawley, & Meyerhoefer, 2017), prompting scientists, public health organizations, and policy makers to develop and implement measures to prevent and treat obesity. Policy makers can draw from an expanding toolbox of interventions, including more traditional measures such as bans or restrictions on advertisements for junk food aimed at children or on unhealthy food options (e.g., snack vending machines on school campuses), fiscal measures (e.g., a sugar tax), and measures informed by recent behavioral science evidence. This last-mentioned class of intervention can be divided into two approaches: *nudges* and *boosts*.

6.4.1   Nudging: Steering Good Decisions
Governments and organizations around the globe, such as the World Bank (2015), the European Commission (Lourenso, Ciriolo, Almeida, & Troussard, 2016), and the Organisation for Economic Co-operation and Development (2017) have begun to appreciate the role behavioral science evidence can play in designing effective and efficient public policies to address a wide range of public health and societal problems. This development is the lasting achievement of the nudge approach, presented prominently in Thaler and Sunstein (2008). Nudges are nonregulatory, nonmonetary interventions that steer people in a direction that is deemed good for them

while preserving their freedom of choice (Alemanno & Sibony, 2015; Halpern, 2015). The idea at the core of nudging is that cognitive and motivational deficiencies (e.g., loss aversion, inertia, present bias) that normally lead individuals to make choices detrimental to their health, wealth, and happiness can be used to steer, or nudge, individuals to behave in ways that are consistent with their goals or preferences—and thus produce better outcomes (Rebonato, 2012; Thaler & Sunstein, 2008). Take, for illustration, default rules as a paradigmatic nudge. Default rules establish what will automatically happen if a person does nothing—and "nothing is what many people will do" (Sunstein, 2015, p. 9). Betting on this inertia, a policy maker can put a default in place that brings people closer to a desired behavioral outcome. For example, organ donation rates are much higher in countries where all adults are organ donors by default (Beshears, Choi, Laibson, & Madrian, 2010).

Nudge policies have also become popular in the attempt to help people make healthier food choices (e.g., Hollands et al., 2013). These nudge interventions include changing the placement of food, thereby making options easier or harder to reach (Thorndike, Bright, Dimond, Fishman, & Levy, 2017); altering the properties of food options (e.g., changing the size of plates, bowls, glasses, or the product itself); and raising awareness through nonpersonalized information (e.g., providing information about the nutritional content of food). Due to the relative lack of evidence and also definitional and conceptual issues (Hollands et al., 2013), it is still difficult to fully evaluate the efficacy of different types of nudging interventions and their short- and long-term effects on a healthy diet.

6.4.2 Boosting: Empowering Good Decisions

Across his writings, the founding father and third president of the United States, Thomas Jefferson, repeatedly emphasized that liberty and a functioning democracy depend on an informed and educated electorate (e.g., Jefferson to George Washington, in Jefferson & Johnston, 1903). Similarly, a functioning population of eaters requires information and education. Although people do not always make good decisions—as the domain of food choices readily illustrates—decision making is not as egregiously irrational as the nudge approach may suggest. Based on a short conceptual history of psychological theorizing and evidence on how people reason and make decisions, Hertwig and Grüne-Yanoff (2017; see also Grüne-Yanoff & Hertwig, 2016) have argued that the nudge approach's portrayal of the human decision maker as systematically imperfect is not the only legitimate model of people's decision-making behavior. Evidence from behavioral science supports other, less disquieting, conceptions of human decision-making competences. We therefore believe that there is a compelling alternative to nudging: Hertwig and Grüne-Yanoff (2017) have referred to it as boosting. The objective of boosts is to improve people's decisional and motivational competence, thus enabling them to make their own choices. Boosts are interventions that foster people's existing competences or instill new ones, thus making it easier for them to exercise their own agency (see Hertwig & Grüne-Yanoff's taxonomy of boosts).

Our objective is not to champion one policy approach over the other. Both boosts and nudges have important target domains (Hertwig, 2017). We believe, however, that it is vital to acknowledge and examine different views and findings if behavioral science insights into how people make decisions are to inform public policy—particularly as these different approaches may suggest different types of policy interventions. Applied to the domain of nutritional health, boosts—unlike nudges—do not reduce people to "somewhat mindless, passive decision makers" (Thaler & Sunstein, 2008, p. 73), whose decisions are steered by the way a choice architect places foods. Rather, the objective of boosts is to promote healthy food choices by building relevant competences. As we will show, this can be achieved by interventions such as helping parents develop the skills they need to make family meals more conducive to their children's good health. In addition, children, teenagers, and adults can be provided with simple, actionable heuristics that help them make healthy food choices in commercially designed food environments that aim to hijack their senses and cravings. Boosts offer behaviors that last longer and are more generalizable across a wider range of conditions, including conditions that are much harder to reach by nudges (e.g., the family dinner table; Dallacker, Hertwig, & Mata, 2018b). Furthermore, people can take advantage of their boosted capacities whether the choice architecture supports or thwarts the choices they desire to make. Next, we describe the first steps toward a boost that helps people make healthy dietary choices. Its starting point is where the foundation of people's food preferences is laid: at the family dinner table.

6.5   Boosting Parents' Competence as Choice Architects of the Family Meal

Obesity is a complex phenomenon. There is no silver bullet solution that will end the obesity epidemic. Most weight-loss interventions are not effective over the long term (Jeffery et al., 2000; Wing & Phelan, 2005); in fact, the chance of an overweight man reaching a normal weight within a year is just 1:210 (Fildes et al., 2015). Thus, the most compelling treatment of overweight and obesity is to prevent them from occurring in the first place. Instead of searching for a single factor that can stop obesity, the focus must instead be on effective entry points for *preventing* obesity. Prevention measures starting in childhood promise to be a particularly powerful lever for fighting obesity because food preferences are established early in life. Childhood is a sensitive period for the formation of healthy eating habits. Furthermore, adults make their daily food choices in an obesogenic environment plagued with uncertainty, but children, especially in their younger years, are often not directly exposed to this environment. Instead, parents are usually the nutritional gatekeepers who design their children's food choice architecture: two-thirds of a child's daily calories stem from food prepared at home (Poti & Popkin, 2011) and most of the 10,000 or so meals children have experienced by the age of 10 were in a family context. Consequently, the family environment can be seen as "the cradle of eating behavior": it is the most critical learning environment, and the main source of influence on young people's eating behavior (Pinard et al., 2012).

In a recent meta-analysis, we found that family meals are a key entry point for influencing nutritional health. The results showed that frequent family meals are significantly associated with a lower risk of being overweight, as well as with better diet quality in children (Dallacker et al., 2018b). Sharing food is prevalent across cultures and history, with communal meals serving as an important medium for sharing knowledge, expressing fellowship, and forming eating habits (Salali et al., 2016). However, in the wake of technological, economic, and social changes such as television, digital technologies, eating on the go, and dual-earner families, the family meal as a social institution is in flux (Breaugh, 2008; S. E. Chen, Moeser, & Nayga, 2015). Modern eating culture is increasingly marked by "grazing" or the snackification of meals. Eating happens anywhere and anytime, often throughout the day (Nielsen & Popkin, 2002) and even while per-forming another task ("secondary eating"; Zick & Stevens, 2011). Parents, as their children's nutritional gatekeepers, therefore face new challenges when designing the architecture of family mealtimes. How can parents be empowered in their roles as choice architects? Specifically, are there sim-ple *building blocks* that parents can use to construct a healthy family meal environment?

Various aspects of family meals and their relation to children's average dietary quality and risk for obesity have been investigated. We conducted a meta-analysis in which we identified, categorized, and systematically reviewed these studies (Dallacker, Hertwig, & Mata, 2018a). Our aim was to identify environmental, behavioral, and social attributes of family meals with the potential to positively influence children's eating behavior. In other words, the goal was to determine evidence-based building blocks of healthy family meals. In our meta-analysis, we summarized over 40 studies, 50 effect sizes, and 40,000 participants and identified six frequently investigated build-ing blocks of family meals that are related to better diet quality and lower body weight in children (see figure 6.2). Let us emphasize that the effect sizes obtained are relatively small; however, this is commonly the case in observa-tional studies (as analyzed in Dallacker et al., 2018b) that preserve the causal texture of natural environments.

The first building block is to *turn off the television* during meals. Watching television while eating is distracting. Experimental studies have shown that people eating in front of the television are less able to monitor their food intake and require more salt and fat to be satisfied than people who are not watching television while eating (Bellisle & Slama, 2004; Blass, Kirkorian, Pempek, Price, & Koleini, 2006). Another potent way in which television can thwart healthy eating is through food advertising. It is estimated that children view around 20,000 to 40,000 commercials each year and that 50% of those commercials promote unhealthy food products (Story & French, 2004). Children's exposure to television food advertising has been shown to influence snack choices and dietary behavior (Gorn & Goldberg, 1982; Harris, Brownell, & Bargh, 2009).

The second and perhaps most intuitive building block is to *serve healthy foods during family meals*. The repeated experience of eating and being exposed to healthy foods has been found to make children more likely to accept and enjoy them (Birch, 1989). Serving homemade, unprocessed foods can help

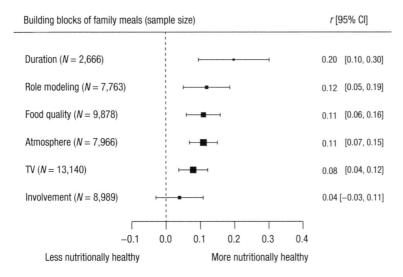

Figure 6.2
The pooled effect size *r* for each of the six building blocks of healthy family meals identified (adapted from Dallacker et al., 2018a). Each of the building blocks rests on data from a substantial number of studies and participants (see sample size in parentheses).

children accept and enjoy healthier foods and, consequently, improve their nutritional health.

The third building block is for parents to *model healthy eating*. Children are more likely to try a novel food if an adult eats it (Addessi, Galloway, Visalberghi, & Birch, 2005). Parents who are aware that their behavior sets an example can promote the consumption of healthy food during family meals by eating it themselves. They can also model positive behavior in applying the fourth building block, which is to *create a positive mealtime atmosphere*. Stressful mealtime situations such as arguments across the dinner table can increase a dysfunctional form of eating known as emotional eating, which is the attempt to regulate negative emotions by consuming foods that are high in energy and fat. It is therefore also a risk factor for overweight (Singh, 2014). Furthermore, the context or atmosphere in which new food is presented is important for a child's food preferences. Children are more likely to like foods presented in a positive context (Aldridge, Dovey, & Halford, 2009).

The fifth building block we identified is to *involve children in meal preparation*. Participating in the preparation process is not significantly associated with better nutritional health in general (see figure 6.2). However, our analysis revealed a significant association with better diet quality ($r = .08$, 95% CI [.04, .11]). People like objects they created themselves (Norton, Mochon, & Ariely, 2012). This "IKEA effect" could explain why children who help to prepare vegetables are more likely to eat them, leading to better overall diet quality. At the same time, there is evidence that children with a high body mass index (BMI) show more interest in food and food preparation (L. Hill, Casswell, Maskill, Jones, & Wyllie, 1998). A higher interest in food and greater involvement in food preparation could be related to higher food intake in general, which could in turn explain why the involvement of children in meal preparation is associated with better diet quality, but not with a lower BMI.

The final—perhaps counterintuitive—building block is to *spend more time on meals*. Spending more time at the family table is actually beneficial for children's nutritional health. One potential explanation of this finding is that people who take more time at the table eat at a slower rate, allowing a sense of satiety to kick in before they have finished (Andrade, Kresge, Teixeira, Baptista, & Melanson, 2012; Berkowitz et al., 2010). Paradoxically, they consume fewer calories even though the meal takes longer. It is also possible that longer mealtimes result in longer periods of satiety between meals, meaning that fewer unhealthy snacks are consumed throughout the day.

In short, informed by the meta-analytical findings on the building blocks of family meals summarized in figure 6.2, one can abstract three simple rules, or heuristics, for how parents can engineer the architecture of the family meal: turn the television off, strive for a positive mealtime atmosphere, and spend more time at the table together. Another two rules inform parents' own behavior: model the desired behavior and involve children in the preparation of the food you want them to eat. The final rule pertains to the food content itself: offer healthy foods at the family table. Clearly, more experimental tests are needed before causality can be claimed between the rules and desirable health outcomes, but the results of the first few experimental studies are promising. For instance, a recent study by Fiese, Jones, and Jarick (2015) investigated family mealtime dynamics within a randomized control setting. One group of families experienced the distracting noise of a vacuum cleaner during the family meal; another group of families were able to eat in peace. Noise and distraction increased both unhealthy eating in children and negative communication patterns in adults. To the extent that these findings can be generalized to the sound of a television set, they explain why both television and a negative atmosphere create a fertile ground for the development of unhealthy eating patterns in children.

Equipping parents with the six simple rules we identified is likely to turn them into competent choice architects of a key social institution within the family, thus enabling them to create a family meal environment that is conducive to healthy food choices. The rules are concrete, relatively intuitive, and actionable; and once practiced, they may become natural routines. The anticipated effects of each individual rule are small (see the results presented in figure 6.2). Yet their combined effect is likely to be larger (although the combination is certainly not additive). Some readers may object that this particular social institution is at best quaint, and at worst almost obsolete. In light of sociocultural changes such as the rising number of dual-earner families, organizing family meals is increasingly challenging. But a family meal does not have to be a traditional dinner with the whole family coming together to sit around a nicely laid table. Our results suggest enormous flexibility in when, how often, and with whom family meals can take place. For instance, family meals seem to be beneficial independent of whether the family shares dinner or breakfast. It also makes no difference to nutritional health whether the whole family eats together or merely some family members take part (Dallacker et al., 2018b). Crucially, the relationship between the frequency of family meals per se and nutritional health is weaker than the relationships between specific mealtime *building blocks* and children's nutritional health (Dallacker et al., 2018a).

The building blocks of healthy family meals that we identified suggest another fruitful area of future research: the architecture of mealtimes in kindergartens and schools. The mealtime architectures of such institutional contexts are particularly important for children whose families are less likely to come together at the dinner table, such as families from lower socioeconomic backgrounds, families with dual-earner parents, or families with busy schedules. The results of a few initial studies suggest that the building blocks we identified may also have positive effects in institutionalized settings such as schools. For example, one study found that when teachers ate fruits and vegetables during school lunches, it was more likely that children would eat these foods as well (Hendy & Raudenbush, 2000).

6.6   Beyond Simple Heuristic Rules for the Family Meal Architecture

Family meal rules are just one example of simple evidence-based eating rules. As children get older, their parents' roles as nutritional gatekeepers fade, leaving children to interact more directly with the modern obesogenic food environment and its many sources of food-related uncertainty. This means that both children and adults need the competencies to deal with this peculiar environment. In our view, one dimension of this competence is a toolbox of simple heuristics for selecting food in an obesogenic environment in which a revolution in food technology has produced a colossal shift in human consumption and sensual experience (Cross & Proctor, 2014), with ever more deliciously manufactured sugar-filled, high-fat foods and sugary beverages unleashing new and intense pleasures—and health problems.

Simple heuristics can offer a first line of defense against attempts to hijack deeply entrenched biological desires that evolved in a world of scarcity and are now miscalibrated in today's land of plenty. In his book *Food Rules: An Eater's Manual*, Pollan (2009) outlined a set of 64 simple, memorable rules for eating healthily, such as *sweeten and salt your food yourself*. Indeed, many people eat more sugar than they realize, and approximately 16% of children's total energy intake is from added sugar (Ervin, Kit, Carroll, & Ogden, 2012). Most of this added sugar is not added by the eater; rather, it is found in processed foods such as sodas or cereals, which contain more sugar than one would usually add oneself. For example, an average frozen pizza contains 18 g of sugar, the equivalent of six sugar cubes. When baking from scratch, one would be hard-pressed to find a recipe that recommends adding six sugar cubes to the pizza dough, sauce, or toppings. The same principle applies to fruit yogurt, lemonade, pasta sauce, and many other mass-manufactured foods. Thus, a person consistently employing the simple rule of *sweeten and salt your food yourself* is likely to significantly reduce the amount of sugar and salt they consume. Another of Pollan's rules that could help people reduce their sugar intake is *don't eat breakfast cereals that change the color of your milk*. Cereals that discolor milk are highly processed and sugary, and thus likely to be full of refined carbohydrates.

Although Pollan's rules are intuitive, they are not yet evidence based. Research is needed to test and quantify their effects on people's nutritional health. If the evidence supports their intuitive logic then they can be added to a toolbox of simple heuristics, joining the evidence-based rules for designing the family meal environment. The toolbox would endow children, teenagers, and adults with the competence to make healthy and autonomous food choices even when facing a barrage of advertising, branding, sponsored social media, and highly engineered, easily accessible pleasures.

6.7 Nutritional Health and the Uncertainties of the Modern Obesogenic Environment: Final Remarks

What a paradoxical world we live in! In large parts of the Western globalized world, the ancestral sources of uncertainty around food no longer exist. Food is always available (there are exceptions—e.g., food insecurity in rich countries such as the United States; Mata, Dallacker, & Hertwig, 2017; Nettle, Andrews, & Bateson, 2017) and relatively safe. However, this seemingly blissful consumer environment—the land of plenty—coincides with an obesity epidemic which is now a major threat to public health. New sources of food-related uncertainties have emerged, such as sponsored research geared more toward obfuscation than discovery, frequently changing recommendations, and highly processed foods with contents that defy normal expectations.

We believe in the need for a proactive policy that prevents obesity in childhood, alongside programs that address existing obesity. There is no silver bullet for prevention; such a policy will have to include a wide range of measures. Some interventions would be regulatory, such as banning vending machines at schools, taxing high-sugar foods, and eliminating advertisements for unhealthy foods that target children (Grigsby-Toussaint, Moise, & Geiger, 2011). But any policy mix must also include measures that take control of commercially constructed choice architectures in public spaces and institutions (e.g., school cafeterias) and redesign those environments with the well-being of children in mind (Downs, Loewenstein, & Wisdom, 2009). Last but not least, healthy food choices necessitate competences. We have proposed simple food choice rules and rules for designing protective family meal environments that can boost parents' competences. Leaving people without those competences risks leaving them defenseless in the many food environments in which there is no benevolent choice architect to curb the temptations of the land of plenty.

III   The Exploring Mind

7 Adaptive Exploration: What You See Is Up to You

Dirk U. Wulff, Doug Markant, Timothy J. Pleskac, and Ralph Hertwig

7.1 The Adaptive Explorer Hypothesis

What you see is all there is. According to psychologist and Nobel Prize winner Daniel Kahneman (2011), this principle is the key to understanding how people make decisions. It captures how the human mind tends to construct a belief or a preference from only the information that is seen or available at the time, even when that information is sparse and unreliable. In other words, the mind jumps to conclusions based on the limited information in front of it. Kahneman's principle would seem to help explain why people ignore base rates (Kahneman & Tversky, 1973), use irrelevant anchors (Tversky & Kahneman, 1974) and, in the case of risky decisions, construct a preference from the described gamble in front of them without regard to the norms of expected utility theory (Kahneman & Tversky, 1979).

Indeed, this principle may help to reveal how people make decisions when they can consult convenient descriptions to learn about their options: when a patient checks a pamphlet from the doctor's office to decide whether to take a certain treatment, a commuter scans the morning weather report to determine whether to bring a jacket, or a consumer inspects the safety rating of a vehicle they are thinking of buying. Yet most of the decisions people face do not come with thorough, close-at-hand descriptions. Instead, whether choosing what to order for dinner or hiring a new employee, the possible outcomes of the decision and the probabilities of those outcomes occurring are not known. As a result, people have to search their memory for prior experiences with the options or generate new experiences with them on the fly. They have to explore the options and learn from experience before making a decision. These types of decisions are what we call *decisions from experience.*

These two different types of decisions—decisions from description and decisions from experience—have important consequences for the decisions people make and how they make them. For instance, consider the choice between an 80% chance of winning €4 (vs. a 20% chance of winning nothing) and a guaranteed €3. This type of decision has been well studied in the behavioral laboratories of psychologists (see E. U. Weber, Shafir, & Blais, 2004). It is here that Kahneman's (2011) principle seems to hold: people make decisions based on the information before them—nothing more, nothing less. They take the outcomes and probabilities and use that information, or merely subsets of it, to make a decision (see, e.g., chapter 8).

However, when people make a decision from experience, there is much more to know than meets the eye; they have to explore the options and learn from experience before deciding. In order to understand how these decisions are made, it is crucial to understand how people explore. In this chapter, we show how people actively seek out experiences to inform their decisions, and we suggest a new principle to help make sense of these decisions: what you see is up to you.[1] People control both the source and the extent of their experiences and adjust their search based on their goals, their cognitive abilities, their past experience, and even their evolving preferences. They are, we propose, adaptive explorers.

To support our claim, we first review some of the empirical evidence for people being adaptive explorers. We then present a model called *Choice from Accumulated Samples of Experience* (CHASE), which formally describes search and choice in the process of adaptive exploration. A key aspect of the model is that search and choice in decisions from experience are an integrated system where experiences are accumulated over time to form a preference. This preference, in turn, helps determine how people search and when they stop searching. In the final section, we show how CHASE helps capture some of the properties of adaptive search, and how it provides new insights into the ways people make decisions from experience.

---

1. Note that Kahneman's (2011) "what you see is all there is" principle is written as a guide for an observer of a decision maker (e.g., a scientist) to help make sense of decisions. Our principle, "what you see is up to you," is written from the perspective of an individual making decisions from experience.

7.2   The Sampling Paradigm

One way researchers study how people make decisions from experience is by taking the monetary gambles often used to study decisions from description and turning them into experience generators (Barron & Erev, 2003; Busemeyer, 1982; Edwards, 1956; Hertwig, Barron, Weber, & Erev, 2004; E. U. Weber et al., 2004). For example, when researchers ask people to make decisions from description they present them with gambles like the one discussed in section 7.1: a choice between an 80% chance of winning €4 or a guaranteed €3. Each gamble produces payoffs with different probabilities. People are then asked to choose the one they prefer (see figure 7.1). When researchers ask people to make decisions from experience they show them the same set of gambles, but without the descriptions. Instead, people have to learn about the distribution of payoffs by sampling from them (Hertwig & Erev, 2009; Wulff, Mergenthaler-Canseco, & Hertwig, 2018).

There are, however, many different ways people can learn from experience. Box 7.1 describes some of the laboratory paradigms that have been developed to study decisions from experience. Here we focus on an implementation

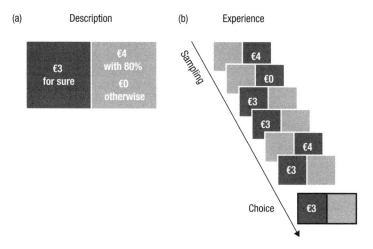

Figure 7.1
The sampling paradigm in (a) decisions from description and (b) decisions from experience. In decisions from experience, people sample one of the possible options (gambles; represented here in light and dark gray), and experience an outcome as a function of the possible outcomes' probability.

Box 7.1
A taxonomy of dynamic decision making.

Decisions from experience can be understood as a special case of dynamic decision making, a class of decision situations that has been studied since the dawn of behavioral decision science (Busemeyer & Pleskac, 2009; Edwards, 1954, 1961; Rapoport, 1964). Edwards (1962b) proposed a taxonomy of dynamic decision making with three dimensions: (a) the nature of the options—whether options remain constant or change over time (stationary/nonstationary); (b) the source of information—whether information is freely available or acquired only through feedback on options chosen (search/feedback); and (c) the nature of the interaction between individuals and options—whether the individual's choice affects the properties of the available options or not (interactive/passive). As illustrated in table 7.B1, current research on dynamic decision making covers all cells of Edwards's (1962b) taxonomy. Notably, however, separate disciplines are involved. For instance, interactive decisions from feedback are commonly studied by neuroscientists interested in the neural representation of model-free versus model-based decision making (e.g., Gershman &

Table 7.B1
A taxonomy of dynamic decision making.

	Search		Feedback	
	Passive	Interactive	Passive	Interactive
Stationary	Sampling paradigm (Hertwig et al., 2004; Wulff et al., 2018)	—	Repeated choice paradigm (Barron & Erev, 2003; Gershman & Daw, 2017)	—
Nonstationary	Observe-or-bet task (Navarro, Newell, & Schulze, 2016; Tversky & Edwards, 1966; chapter 10)	Rivals-in-the-dark game (Markant, Phillips, Kareev, Avrahami, & Hertwig, 2018; Phillips, Hertwig, Kareev, & Avrahami, 2014; chapter 12)	Repeated choice paradigm (Estes, 1959; Plonsky, Teodorescu, & Erev, 2015)	Reinforcement learning (Gershman & Daw, 2017) Foraging tasks (e.g., Mata & von Helversen, 2015)

Note. Interactive contradicts stationary. Hence, cells with both of these features necessarily remain empty.

Box 7.1 (continued)

Daw, 2017), but less so by behavioral decision researchers. Another dimension that has emerged in the literature is the rate of sampling (e.g., Pleskac, Yu, Hopwood, & Liu, 2019; Tsetsos, Chater, & Usher, 2012; Zeigenfuse, Pleskac, & Yu, 2014). Here, participants are shown a sampled outcome anywhere from every 0.05 s to every 0.5 s. The aim is both to understand how decisions are made when information is presented rapidly (e.g., by a stock ticker) and to test some basic assumptions of the sequential sampling models that have been applied to model preferential choice (see Pleskac et al., 2019).

known as the *sampling paradigm*. In it, people can freely explore the options (at no cost) by sampling possible outcomes (typically by pressing a button; see figure 7.1 for an example or visit interactive element 7.1 at https://taming -uncertainty.mpib-berlin.mpg.de/). For each sample, a single outcome is drawn (with replacement) from the option's distribution. People are instructed to sample until they feel confident enough to choose an option for a final draw involving real monetary payoffs. Once they finish sampling, they indicate their preferred option.

Comparing the choices people make from experience to those they make from description has revealed systematic differences between the two, known as the *description–experience gap* (Hertwig & Erev, 2009). The description–experience gap, described next, highlights that decisions from description and decisions from experience are two different animals.

7.3 The Description–Experience Gap

In terms of monetary gambles, the description–experience gap corresponds to a systematic difference between decisions from description and experience in terms of deviances from choosing the option with the greatest expected value (Barron & Erev, 2003; Hertwig et al., 2004; E. U. Weber et al., 2004; see also Hertwig & Pleskac, 2018; Regenwetter & Robinson, 2017). This difference is perhaps best exemplified with reference to what has been called the fourfold pattern of risk attitudes (see Hertwig, 2012a; Tversky & Fox, 1995; Tversky & Kahneman, 1992). This pattern is shown in table 7.1, which summarizes people's preferences from Wulff et al.'s (2018) meta-analysis for four different choices between a risky gamble and a safe option. Focusing first on decisions from description, in the "gain" domain (top two

Table 7.1

The original and reversed fourfold pattern, information search, and predictions of CHASE.

		Gamble options		Percentage preferred risky option		Sample size
Problem	Domain	Risky	Safe	Description	Experience	
1	Gain	4, .8*	3, 1.0	34	**70 (63)**	19 (20)
2	Gain	32, .1*	3, 1.0	58	14 (18)	22 (17)
3	Loss	–4, .8	–3, 1.0*	69	45 (38)	22 (20)
4	Loss	–32, .1	–3, 1.0*	55	**83 (82)**	24 (17)

Note. The gambles are simple gambles of the format x with a probability p otherwise 0 and are noted as x, p. The higher expected value option is denoted by *. Boldface indicates proportions for which the fourfold pattern and its reversal predict a modal preference for the risky option. Sample sizes are average. Predicted choice proportions and sample sizes in parentheses come from fitting the CHASE model to the same aggregated dataset. Observed data are from Wulff et al. (2018), aggregating the data across studies of the description–experience gap.

rows of table 7.1), people were risk averse, preferring the safe option when the probability of winning was high (.8). However, when the gamble had the same expected value but the probability of winning was low (.1), people reversed their preference and chose the risky option. The fourfold aspect to this pattern emerged when people were presented with the same choices but with outcomes in the loss domain; in this case, preferences flipped. This is shown in the bottom two rows of table 7.1. Relatively speaking, people were risk-averse when the stated probability of losing was low but risk-seeking when it was high. Looking at the gambles and choice proportions in table 7.1 can also help reveal the source of this fourfold pattern. In particular, in description-based choices people appear to choose as if they overweight rare events (e.g., overweighting the probability of .2 of obtaining a 0 in problems 1 and 3), which results in the fourfold pattern (Tversky & Kahneman, 1992; van de Kuilen & Wakker, 2011).

Now consider what happens when people make decisions from experience with these same options (see table 7.1). The fourfold pattern reverses, suggesting that people make decisions from experience as if they underweight rare events. Wulff et al.'s (2018) meta-analysis synthesizing 27 datasets has shown that the choice proportions for the option consistent with underweighting the rare event differ by on average 9.7 percentage points between description and experience, with the magnitude of the gap varying considerably across problem types. In choices between safe and risky gambles—the problem type often used to measure people's risk preferences— the difference amounts to about 20 percentage points. In choices between two risky gambles, in contrast, it is about 6 percentage points. To experience this gap yourself or explore the large collection of data from Wulff et al., visit interactive elements 7.1 and 7.2 online.

The largest contributor to the description–experience gap in terms of the impact of rare events in decisions from experience is frugal exploration (e.g., Fox & Hadar, 2006; Hau, Pleskac, Kiefer, & Hertwig, 2008; Hertwig & Erev, 2009; Rakow & Newell, 2010). As table 7.1 shows, people took about 20 samples per problem, implying a sample size of about 10 samples per option. Frugal exploration has two important consequences. First, it means that many individuals will not experience the rare event. For instance, if people take 10 samples from an option offering $4 with a probability of .8 and $0 with a probability of .2, 11% of them will never experience the rare event ($0). Second, the majority of people, including those who do experience the rare event, will see it less often than expected given its objective probability. In the example above, the expected number of experiences of the rare event in 10 samples is two, with 30% of individuals expected to see the rare event exactly twice and 32% to see it more often. But a larger proportion of individuals—38%—are expected to experience the rare event only once or not at all. This is because the binomial distribution of samples is right-skewed for events with a probability smaller than .5, implying more mass below the expected value than above. Due to this statistical regularity, frugal search can result in decisions made from experience appearing as if rare events are underweighted.

Sample size, however, is not the only driver of the description–experience gap when it comes to rare events. This gap, while smaller, persists when sampling error has been accounted for (Camilleri & Newell, 2011a; Hau, Pleskac, & Hertwig, 2010; Hau et al., 2008; Kellen, Pachur, & Hertwig, 2016; Rakow, Demes, & Newell, 2008; Ungemach, Chater, & Stewart, 2009; for an overview, see Wulff et al., 2018). Other potential contributors discussed in the literature include the tendency to place more weight on recent than on earlier experience (Hertwig, Barron, Weber, & Erev, 2006); tallying strategies, which compare the options for small subsets of experiences and choose the option that wins most often (Hills & Hertwig, 2010); and differential probability weighting for stated probabilities and experienced relative frequencies (Abdellaoui, l'Haridon, & Paraschiv, 2011; chapter 8).

Notwithstanding these other drivers of the description–experience gap, the finding that sample sizes is key to the description–experience gap highlights the important role that search plays in decisions from experience. In contrast to decisions from description, where what you see is all there is, decisions from experience afford people the freedom to gather information and terminate their search whenever they see fit. This freedom impacts the information available and as a result, what you see is up to you. But which factors affect how people explore and when they decide to terminate search? Put differently, what are the mechanisms behind adaptive exploration?

7.4 Adaptive Exploration

7.4.1 Small Samples Can Be Smart

Never observing a rare event or observing it less often than expected can have profound consequences on how people evaluate the attractiveness of different options. Why then do people tend to break off their search so soon, forgoing the opportunity to gain a more accurate picture of the available options? For one, it is difficult, if not impossible, for individuals to know when their accumulated experience suffices to afford them a veridical picture of their options. Moreover, the incremental value of further search often diminishes drastically over time, and after a certain point increasing sample size will only marginally improve the understanding of a given option (see also chapter 4). To illustrate this point, we calculated the likelihood of picking the option with the higher expected value as a function of the number of samples drawn in the four problems presented in table 7.1. We assumed that the option with the higher experienced sample mean was chosen. Drawing 40 to 50 samples per option in problem 1 (and its reversal, problem 3) resulted in a mean chance of selecting the higher expected value option of 81.2%. But drawing only 10 to 20 samples per option resulted in a mean chance of 70.7% (see also Hertwig & Pleskac, 2010). Thus, in this case, drawing about one-third of the samples produced two-thirds of the gains in accuracy. In problem 2 (and its reversal, problem 4), the situation was even more extreme. Here, drawing 40 to 50 samples per option resulted in an improvement of 4.7 percentage points over drawing 10 to 20 samples per option and just 2.8 percentage points over chance. Considering that exploration is commonly associated with opportunity costs and, at the very least, processing costs, relying on small samples is thus often the smart thing to do (Hertwig & Pleskac, 2010; Ostwald, Starke, & Hertwig, 2015; Vul, Goodman, Griffiths, & Tenenbaum, 2014).

7.4.2 Moderators of Exploration

Relying on small samples can be smart. Nonetheless, it is often beneficial to adapt exploratory effort to the resources available and the peculiarities of the environment. Research using the sampling paradigm has shown that decision makers indeed adapt their exploration systematically. Table 7.2 summarizes the factors known to affect how much people explore. The table features environmental factors (which pertain more to the choice environment) at the top, contextual factors (which are more related to the choice context) in the middle, and individual factors (which have more to do with the decision maker) at the bottom. For instance, people draw larger samples in the presence of potential losses (Lejarraga, Hertwig, & Gonzalez, 2012), in the affective state of fear (Frey, Hertwig, & Rieskamp, 2014), or when faced with many options (Hills, Noguchi, & Gibbert, 2013; Noguchi & Hills, 2016).

The strongest effects result from manipulating the potential upside of a choice or the downside of exploration. For instance, sample size has been shown to increase when payoffs are increased by an order of magnitude (Hau et al., 2008) or when decision makers are incentivized to maximize the long-term rather than the short-term return (Wulff et al., 2015a). Conversely, the risk of being beaten to the punch by a competitor can slash exploration efforts to just a single draw (Phillips et al., 2014; see also chapters 12 and 15). These results suggest that individuals evaluate whether to terminate or continue sampling as a function of the benefits (or costs) associated with the available options and, more generally, their goals.

7.4.3 Routes to Terminating Search

There are many ways in which people can determine when they will stop searching. In the sampling paradigm and the situations it embodies, perhaps the two most straightforward routes to terminating exploration are a *planned stopping rule* and an *optional stopping rule*. With a planned stopping

Table 7.2
Moderators of search and their potential representation in CHASE.

| Moderator | Manipulation | Sample Size | | CHASE |
		Treatment	Control	
Environmental				
Complexity[a]	32 vs. 2 options	34	5	Unknown
	32 vs. 2 options	51/38	6/4	Unknown
	8 vs. 2 options	113	41	Unknown
Domain[b]	Loss vs. gain	11	9	Possible increase in thresholds for losses
Problem order[c]	1st vs. 30th problem	25.5	9.1	Increased familiarity reduces variability in preference accumulation OR later problems result in lower thresholds
Variance[b]	Variance experienced	16	11	Increased payoff variance leads to a decrease in rate of change in preference
Contextual				
Affect[d]	Fearful vs. happy	45/45	28/6	Fear leads to higher thresholds and greater attention to extreme outcomes (see section 7.6.4)
Competition[e]	Social competition (yes or no)	1	18	Competition leads to a lower decrease in the threshold for making a choice
Health[f]	Medical vs. monetary	17	22	Health domain should increase thresholds, but may change attention to outcomes
Incentives[g]	Incentives×10	33	11	Increased incentives lead to higher thresholds
Social context[h]	Ultimatum game vs. standard paradigm	8	24	Unknown

Table 7.2 (continued)

Moderator	Manipulation	Sample Size		CHASE
		Treatment	Control	
Individual				
Age[i]	Younger vs. older adults	46	58	Unknown
Aspirations[j]	Long vs. short run	34	23	Long-run aspirations result in higher thresholds
Numeracy[k]	High vs. low	23	15	Unknown
Rational ability[k]	High vs. low	22	18	Unknown
Moderator	Predictor	Correlation		CHASE
Fluid intelligence[l]	DSST & 2 options	< .1		Unknown
	DSST & 8 options	~.2 to .4		Unknown
Working memory[m]	Digit span	.38		Unknown
	Operation span	.04		Unknown
	Operation span	−.19/.13/19		Unknown

Note. DSST: Digit–symbol substitution task. a: Frey, Mata, & Hertwig (2015), Hills et al. (2013), Noguchi & Hills (2016). b: Lejarraga et al. (2012). c: Lejarraga et al. (2012). d: Frey et al. (2014). e: Phillips et al. (2014). f: Lejarraga, Woike, & Hertwig (2016). g: Hau et al. (2008). h: Fleischhut, Artinger, Olschewski, Volz, & Hertwig (2014). i: Frey et al. (2015). j: Wulff, Hills, & Hertwig (2015a). k: Lejarraga (2010). l: Frey et al. (2014), Frey et al. (2015). m: Rakow et al. (2008), Wulff, Hills, & Hertwig (2015b), Wulff et al. (2015a). Table adapted from Wulff et al. (2018).

rule, people decide beforehand how many samples to take; with an optional stopping rule, they choose to stop on the basis of incoming information and its significance for their current goals. Evidence suggests that people take both routes. For instance, ongoing analyses of the Wulff et al. (2018) data show that samples in multiples of 10 occur much more frequently than would be expected by chance, suggesting that many people plan to terminate their search at a round number.

Findings of a phenomenon analogous to the gaze cascade effect in the sampling paradigm suggest that people also use an optional stopping rule (Wulff et al., 2018). The term *gaze cascade effect* comes from eye-tracking studies, which have shown that when people make a choice their gaze gradually shifts to the option eventually chosen before the choice is made (Shimojo, Simion, Shimojo, & Scheier, 2003). A similar effect can be seen in decisions from experience, where people sample more often from the chosen option toward the end of a sampling sequence (see figure 7.2) and switch to a different option when they experience negative outcomes (see figure 7.4).

The gaze cascade effect has been taken as evidence that "gaze is actively involved in preference formation" (Shimojo et al., 2003, p. 1317). But it is also indicative of an optional stopping rule where people sample information until their preference reaches a threshold (Mullett & Stewart, 2016). The logic behind this claim is this: if a person employs an optional stopping process, the last sample of information they encountered will be consistent with the choice they make because their preference has reached the threshold required to choose that option. This pattern is more likely to happen when a person is looking at the option (so long as the information they sample from the option they are looking at is favorable). The strength or valence of the second-to-last sample does not have to obey quite the same logic, but it likely will (otherwise, the preference state would not be close to the threshold). The third-to-last will, on average, point to the chosen option but less so, and so on, giving rise to a gaze cascade effect. Thus, the gaze cascade effect is indicative of a link between search and choice, a property that is reflected in our integrated model of decisions from experience, CHASE, to which we return in section 7.6. Corroborating this interpretation, this phenomenon analogous to the gaze cascade effect only occurs in self-terminated sampling and not in environments where sample size is predetermined by the experimenter (see figure 7.2).

In sum, when decision makers are actively involved in exploration, search and choice are intimately connected. People do not just passively tally experiences as they stream past, particularly when afforded the freedom to control the process of exploration (Wulff & Pachur, 2016). By adapting information search to the internal and external characteristics of the situation, people shape the environment they observe and, as a consequence, their final decision (see also Denrell, 2005; Denrell, 2007; March, 1996; Pleskac, 2015). The evidence for adaptive exploration described in the previous section shows that the degree to which description and experience diverge depends on a number of factors. Aside from driving the

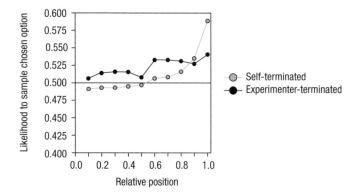

Figure 7.2
Likelihood of sampling from the option eventually chosen over the course of the sampling sequence in self-terminated versus experimenter-terminated sampling. Based on the combined data of Wulff et al. (2018).

description–experience gap, active exploration in decisions from experience presents a thorny problem for many current models of decision making that act according to Kahneman's (2011) "what you see is all there is" principle. Specifically, it implies that models can only successfully describe, predict, and explain decisions from experience if they account for how people learn from experience and make choices from what they have learned.

7.5 Modeling Search and Choice in Decisions from Experience

The link between exploration and choice has been noticeably absent from previous attempts to model decisions from experience in the sampling paradigm. Nearly all models treat experience as a given—like a memory bank that passively records sampled outcomes and is called upon only to make a final choice. In two-stage prospect theory, for instance, the observed relative frequencies of outcomes are merely used as proxies for their objective probabilities (Fox & Hadar, 2006; Tversky & Fox, 1995; see also chapter 8). These subjective frequencies are then entered into prospect theory's probability weighting function to determine the value of the option. Thus, the same model that is used for stated probabilities in decisions from description is recruited to account for choices involving experienced relative frequencies. This approach has frequently been used to understand final choices and the probability weighting pattern in the sampling paradigm (e.g., Fox & Hadar,

2006; Glöckner, Hilbig, Henninger, & Fiedler, 2016; Kellen et al., 2016). However, it offers no account of how people explore in the context of experience-based choice, including when they decide to stop sampling. This limitation is also present in various forms in other models. For instance, reinforcement learning models do not have a stopping rule (Sutton & Barto, 1998), and instance-based memory models treat choice and search as independent processes (C. Gonzalez & Dutt, 2011; Hawkins, Camilleri, Heathcote, Newell, & Brown, 2014). We now present a model that was designed to address this limitation and examine its predictions for decisions from experience.

7.6   Choice from Accumulated Samples of Experience (CHASE)

CHASE models decisions from experience as a sequential sampling process in which experiences are accumulated over time to form a preference (Busemeyer & Townsend, 1993; Laming, 1968; Ratcliff & Smith, 2004; Wald, 1947). As such, it provides a new window onto the process of active exploration and choice in decisions from experience. Full details of the model can be found in the online supplement to this chapter (at https://taming-uncer tainty.mpib-berlin.mpg.de/; see also Markant, Pleskac, Diederich, Pachur, & Hertwig, 2015). In brief, outcomes are generated from gambles depending on how a person searches (the frequency and order with which they sample each option). Each observed outcome could, in principle, contribute to the accumulated preference in direct proportion to the payoff amount. However, previous work has suggested that outcomes may be weighted differently in decisions from experience depending on how they compare with other possible outcomes (see also Ludvig, Madan, & Spetch, 2014; Pleskac et al., 2019; Zeigenfuse et al., 2014). To account for this possibility, CHASE models each outcome's impact, referred to as its *subjective valence*, based on its likelihood and its desirability relative to the other possible outcomes. Over the course of search, subjective valences are accumulated to form a preference for one option over the other, creating a random walk across preference states as depicted in figure 7.3. Under an optional stopping rule, preference at some point reaches one of two thresholds. The final choice is determined by the threshold reached, and the sample size is determined by the number of steps taken to reach it (see figure 7.3).

One important property of the accumulation of subjective valences is that preference is relative. Experiencing an attractive outcome for one

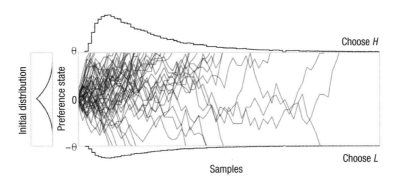

Figure 7.3
Preference accumulation for a choice between options H and L with higher and lower expected values, respectively. Each trajectory represents a different trial, with preference moving up or down after each draw based on the subjective valence of the observed outcome. The initial distribution captures the variability between trials at the starting point. The distributions at the top and bottom edges represent the probability that search ends as a function of sample size, conditional on either a higher expected value choice (H, top) or a lower expected value choice (L, bottom).

option will shift preference toward that option and away from the other. This property is consistent with an empirical result observed in the sampling paradigm. In particular, in self-terminated search in the sampling paradigm, experiencing negative outcomes for one option increases the chance of choosing the other option (see figure 7.4). Note also that, like other sequential sampling models with optional stopping, CHASE predicts a gaze cascade effect like that shown in figure 7.2.[2] Finally, as we will show, CHASE accounts for some key properties of adaptive exploration, such as adapting to costs and benefits and adapting to environmental uncertainty.

7.6.1 Adapting to Costs and Benefits
Under optional stopping, CHASE assumes that people may adjust their decision threshold depending on their goals or the presence of any implicit or explicit costs. Control over the decision threshold is a common feature

---

2. The use of an optional stopping rule is not necessary in self-terminated sampling conditions: A person could, as we discussed in section 7.4.3, decide on a sample size before beginning to search. Such planned stopping can also be modeled with CHASE.

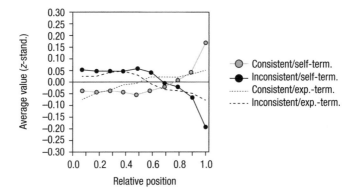

Figure 7.4
Average observed outcome value (z standardized within trial) over the course of the
sampling sequence as a function of whether or not the last sampled option was
consistent with the chosen option for self-terminated and experimenter-terminated
sampling. Based on the combined data of Wulff et al. (2018).

of sequential sampling models of decision making. If, for example, errors in
a perceptual decision are associated with high costs, people would adopt a
high threshold, leading to the accumulation of more evidence and, in turn,
a higher proportion of correct responses. But demanding more evidence
also means that it will take longer to reach a decision. Consequently, the
decision threshold helps control the speed–accuracy trade-off in perceptual decisions (Bogacz, Brown, Moehlis, Holmes, & Cohen, 2006; Ratcliff &
Smith, 2004).

CHASE predicts the same sort of trade-off between sample size and the
proportion of choices that maximize expected value. In this case, higher
thresholds lead to larger sample sizes and more choices that maximize
expected value. Consistent with this prediction, Hau et al. (2008) showed
that increasing the magnitude of rewards by a factor of 10 was associated
with larger sample sizes and more choices that maximize expected value
(and a decrease in the description–experience gap; we will return to this
point shortly). Adjustments in the decision threshold may underlie how people adapt their exploration to a wide array of variables (see table 7.2), including monetary (dis)incentives, opportunity costs (J. W. Payne, Bettman, &
Luce, 1996), the effort involved in gathering information (Fu & Gray, 2006),
competition (Phillips et al., 2014), or even motivational and emotional factors (Frey et al., 2014).

7.6.2   Adapting to Environmental Uncertainty

Another reason for adopting an optional stopping rule is uncertainty about how much experience is needed to reach a conclusion (Edwards, 1965). CHASE predicts that both choice and sample size depend on the degree of uncertainty in the environment. If outcomes unambiguously favor one option over the other, preference will quickly reach the corresponding decision threshold. If outcomes sometimes favor one option and sometimes the other, preference will tend to ebb and flow, and sample sizes will increase. This implies that larger outcome variance will cause both larger sample sizes and a lower proportion of choices of the higher expected value option. Indeed, people making decisions from experience tend to sample for a longer period of time when they experience high variance in outcomes (Lejarraga et al., 2012; Pachur & Scheibehenne, 2012).

This prediction depends on variance actually being experienced. High-variance options (as calculated based on their objective description) do not per se lead to more information search (see Wulff et al., 2018). Options with rare outcomes that are never experienced may in fact be associated with low experienced variance and thus with smaller sample sizes. An unlucky decision maker may happen to experience outcomes that unambiguously favor an option without knowing that a disastrous (but rare) outcome is just around the corner. This brings us back to the description–experience gap and how CHASE accounts for it.

7.6.3   Using CHASE to Explain the Description–Experience Gap

The decision threshold in CHASE is one mechanism that offers a (partial) explanation for the description–experience gap. To see this, we used CHASE to simulate choices for choice problems 1 and 2 in table 7.1 over a range of decision thresholds (the results for the corresponding loss problems are in this case symmetrical). As figure 7.5 shows, the probability of choosing the higher expected value option (i.e., the risky option) increases with the magnitude of the threshold. This is because sample sizes are smaller at lower thresholds, resulting in greater sampling error. At lower thresholds, a majority of individuals will experience the rare event less often than expected, leading to choices consistent with underweighting of the rare outcome and the reversed fourfold pattern of risk attitudes. At higher thresholds, the impact of sampling error is lessened, rare outcomes are more likely to be encountered and thus contribute to the accumulated preference, and

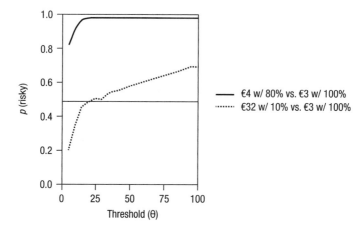

Figure 7.5
The predicted probability of choosing the risky option as a function of decision threshold θ, for the two choice problems in the gain domain used to illustrate the fourfold pattern of risk attitudes in table 7.1 (the results for the loss domain are symmetrical). Assuming an indifferent starting point, equal probability of sampling each option, linear weighting, and no internal noise in the accumulation process, a low threshold is sufficient to result in choices that appear to underweight rare events.

there is a higher likelihood of choosing the higher expected value option for both problems. Thus, CHASE provides a mechanistic understanding of how uncertainty in the environment and the decision threshold interact to drive exploration and choice—one consequence of which is the description–experience gap.

7.6.4 Understanding the Weight of Experience through CHASE
The decision threshold is an important lever for adapting exploration, but other mechanisms can also affect how people explore and choose in decisions from experience. One of them is the weight people award to each sampled outcome. According to CHASE, sampled outcomes do not necessarily get equal attentional weight. Instead, the attention people pay to each outcome depends on its likelihood and desirability relative to the other possible outcomes. This is implemented by making the weight a function of the probability of obtaining a particular outcome or a larger one (i.e., the decumulative rank in the gamble). For instance, rarer outcomes might be down-weighted relative to other outcomes, with the consequence that more frequent outcomes would receive more weight in the

accumulated preference. This subjective weighting of outcomes can also drive the accumulation of preference, which in turn impacts which threshold is reached and when. It is possible to disentangle the influence of the decision threshold from the subjective weighting of outcomes by fitting CHASE to observed data.

To illustrate this point, consider Frey et al.'s (2014) manipulation of affective states during decisions from experience. Figures 7.6a and 7.6b display the choice and sample size data. Four of the choice problems are the same as were used to demonstrate the reversal of the fourfold risk pattern of attitudes (see table 7.1). In general, the reversed fourfold pattern holds (note that this figure plots the probability of choosing the higher expected value option). In the fearful condition, however, sample size was increased and choice proportions were shifted more toward maximizing expected value. In other words, the strength of the reversed fourfold pattern was weaker in the fearful condition. Is this weakened pattern solely the result of people setting a higher decision threshold in the fearful condition?

To answer this question and better understand the effects of affective states at the process level, we fit CHASE to the data from each condition. As figure 7.6 shows, the model accounts quite well for both the choice (7.6a) and sample size distributions (7.6b). The model indicates that participants in the fear condition indeed adopted a higher decision threshold ($\theta = 21.4$) than did happy participants ($\theta = 12.6$). However, fearful participants also appear to have given more attentional weight to the large (but less frequent) gains and losses (see figure 7.6c, left). This differential weight to different sampled outcomes has an important consequence: as sample sizes increase (i.e., thresholds increase), choices from CHASE mimic choices from rank-dependent expected utility models like prospect theory (see Pleskac et al., 2019). Figure 7.6d shows what the inferred decision weights would be for the two conditions (i.e., if people set very high choice thresholds and made choices then these would be the rank-dependent decision weights one would observe if prospect theory were fit to the choices).[3] The results illustrate that fearful emotional states would result in decision weights that give too much weight to rare events. Thus, according to CHASE, two factors

---

3. We emphasize that CHASE does not assume that people explicitly represent probabilities. Rather they make choices as if they do.

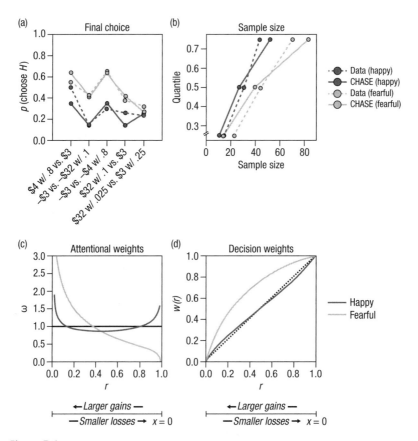

Figure 7.6
Results from fitting CHASE to data from Frey et al. (2014; Study 2, fearful and happy conditions only). (a) Observed and predicted proportion of *H* choices. (b) Quantiles of sample size distribution. (c) In addition to adopting a higher decision threshold, fearful participants weighted higher magnitude outcomes more heavily. The attentional weight is a function of the rank *r* of the outcome in the gamble. In gains, the rank is the decumulative rank such that outcomes decrease in magnitude with increasing rank *r*; in losses, the rank is the cumulative rank such that they also decrease in magnitude. (d) This weighting of extreme outcomes in the preference accumulation process can give rise to choices that appear to have an elevated probability weighting function.

are responsible for the weakened reversed fourfold pattern in the fear condition: people's higher thresholds and greater attentional weight to large (but less frequent) gains and losses. In fact, according to CHASE, all else being equal, if people in the fear condition had set higher thresholds then a fourfold risk pattern akin to what is seen in decisions from description would have been observed. Although more work is needed to understand the conditions that impact how people weigh each sample of experience, these results illustrate the importance of modeling search and choice together in order to distinguish alternative processes involved in preference formation.

To summarize, CHASE provides a framework for modeling search and choice together in decisions from experience, through the lens of a single evidence accumulation process. CHASE makes it possible to explain and predict a number of factors that reflect adaptive exploration during decisions from experience. We should note that, as listed in table 7.2, there are many other factors that impact search during decisions from experience. For some factors, like payoff domain (gain or loss) or familiarity with the problems, CHASE makes some straightforward predictions about how these factors impact search and choice. However, it is unclear if and how CHASE may account for other factors. We do not necessarily see this as a limitation of the model; instead, these unknowns are exciting areas to further explore in order to better understand adaptive exploration during decisions from experience.

7.7 Adaptive Exploration Helps Distinguish Decisions under Uncertainty from Decisions under Risk

By far the most common approach to understanding how people make decisions when the consequences of their choices are uncertain reduces uncertainty to risk—for example, by having people decide between descriptions of monetary gambles. Within this paradigm, the often cited distinction between risk and uncertainty is more semantic than real. To quote Lopes (1983), "this distinction made its way into the psychological literature a long time ago via Edwards' (1954) seminal article in *Psychological Bulletin* on decision theory, but it has since languished for want of empirical relevance" (p. 137). In our view, research on decisions from experience demonstrates the empirical reality of this distinction. People are constantly making decisions without the aid of actuarial tables, or even an awareness of the full set of potential outcomes. Instead they rely on direct experience. When their past experience is not enough, they take action to reduce uncertainty in a way that is adaptive. The wealth of data gathered on decisions from experience over the past 15 years has established that there is a gap between decisions from experience and decisions from description. This gap goes beyond the choices people make and, by extension, beyond their preferences. People making decisions from experience are adaptive explorers, tuning their search to the properties of the environment, their goals and abilities, and their experiences. In other words, in decisions from experience, what you see is up to you.

This empirical reality calls for models of adaptive exploration. CHASE is one such model, describing the interaction between preference and exploration in decisions from experience. It represents a significant step forward from models that have focused on final choices while treating exploration as a given (Erev et al., 2010; C. Gonzalez & Dutt, 2011). Yet it is just a first step. At present, the framework does not capture a number of factors that affect exploration in decisions from experience, including choices between more than two options, learning effects across trials, and individual differences in search and choice (see table 7.1). Nevertheless, CHASE offers a new approach to understanding how people both generate and exploit experience to make decisions in the midst of uncertainty.

8 The Weight of Uncertain Events

Thorsten Pachur and Ralph Hertwig

8.1 The St. Petersburg Paradox

Probably no decision problem has shaped the world of ideas as much as the St. Petersburg game. Originally conceived by Swiss mathematician Nicolas Bernoulli in the early 18th century, it was one of five problems he submitted to Pierre Rémond de Montmort, a French mathematician and man of letters who corresponded with eminent scholars such as Leibniz. Nicolas Bernoulli's cousin Daniel Bernoulli described the St. Petersburg game as follows:

> Peter tosses a coin and continues to do so until it should land "heads" when it comes to the ground. He agrees to give Paul one ducat if he gets "heads" on the very first throw, two ducats if he gets it on the second, four if on the third, eight if on the fourth, and so on, so that with each additional throw the number of ducats he pays is doubled. Suppose we seek to determine the value of Paul's expectation. (Bernoulli, 1738/1954, p. 31)

The puzzling aspect of this seemingly straightforward problem resides in the gap between the "rationally" determined value of the game (i.e., Paul's "expectation") and people's valuations of it (i.e., the price at which they would sell the chance to play the game). According to expected value theory,[1] which was the accepted method of calculating the expectation at the time, the St. Petersburg game gives Paul the opportunity to win an infinite amount of money. Theoretically, he should therefore demand a very high price for it. In reality, "any fairly reasonable man would sell his chance, with great

---

1. As explained by Daniel Bernoulli, "[e]xpected values are computed by multiplying each possible gain by the number of ways in which it can occur, and then dividing the sum of these products by the total number of possible cases" (Bernoulli, 1738/1954, p. 23).

pleasure, for twenty ducats" (Bernoulli, 1738/1954, p. 31). This gap between theory and reality constitutes the St. Petersburg paradox.

Why is the expected value of the St. Petersburg game infinitely large? Expected value theory evaluates a risky option in terms of the sum of all the possible payoffs, each multiplied by the probability of its occurrence. The probability of Peter throwing heads the first time is .5; in this case, Paul would receive 1 ducat, thus contributing $1 \times .5$ to his expectation. The probability of Peter throwing tails on his first attempt and heads on his second one is .25, thus contributing $2 \times .25$ to Paul's expectation. More generally, the overall expectation of the game (in which, in theory, the coin could be tossed an infinite number of times) is

$$\sum_{n=1}^{N} \left(\frac{1}{2}^{n} 2^{n-1} \right) = N \frac{1}{2}. \tag{1}$$

From this it follows that, given an infinite number of throws, Paul's expectation is infinite (Menger, 1934). As mentioned above, however, typical valuations of the game are rather modest, often in the range of twice the amount of money one would win if the game were to end with the first throw (e.g., Hayden & Platt, 2009). How is it possible to explain the St. Petersburg paradox—and to reconcile theoretical expectations with people's actual behavior?

Nicolas and Daniel Bernoulli came from one of the most illustrious families in the history of mathematics and science; it produced half a dozen outstanding mathematicians in just a couple of generations. Daniel Bernoulli was intrigued by the St. Petersburg paradox and offered an explanation that was to become the most influential theory of individual decision making under risk—today known as *expected utility theory* (he referred to "moral expectation"; Bernoulli, 1738/1954, p. 24). Specifically, he retained the core of expected value theory—the multiplication and maximization components—but suggested replacing objective monetary amounts with subjective utilities. He argued that the pleasure, or utility, of money does not increase linearly with the monetary amount (as assumed in expected value theory); instead, the increases in utility diminish, with the result that the expected utility of the St. Petersburg game becomes finite (and can become rather small). A century later, the notion of diminishing sensitivity implied by the marginally decreasing utility entered psychophysics in the form of the Weber–Fechner function, and economics in the concept of diminishing returns.

But Daniel Bernoulli's proposal was not the only possible solution to the St. Petersburg paradox raised at the time (for overviews, see Hayden & Platt, 2009; Jorland, 1987; Menger, 1934). Another began with the observation that for all practical purposes, the very rare possibility of the coin landing heads up only after very many tosses, which would lead to a large gain, can be disregarded. Originally suggested by Nicolas Bernoulli himself (see van der Waerden, 1975), this idea was further developed by French naturalist Buffon (1777). In one of the first scientific simulations (see S. M. Stigler, 1991), Buffon had a child perform a series of 2,048 sets of coin tosses; each time the set continued until the coin landed heads up. On the basis of the resulting statistics, he concluded that the value of the game was about 5 ducats, irrespective of its theoretically infinite expected value. Taking this value as an anchor, one may argue that small probabilities in the St. Petersburg game—specifically, probabilities smaller than 3% (i.e., throwing at least five tails in a row)—can, will, or even should receive less weight than their objective magnitude. In the extreme, they may be completely disregarded (there is some debate about the exact threshold below which a probability is disregarded; see Dutka, 1988).

Building on Buffon's account and emphasizing the role of probabilities, Menger (1934) proposed a subjective function across the entire probability range and argued that "chances are undervalued both where the probabilities are very small (that is, close to 0) and where the probabilities are very high (that is, close to 1). Only chances with medium probabilities are valued in a way which begins to correspond to mathematical expectation" (p. 269). Although this explanation of the St. Petersburg paradox focusing on the probability dimension received less attention than Daniel Bernoulli's account, which focused on the monetary dimension, it planted the idea that people do not perceive or treat probabilities linearly when making risky decisions. In the guise of probability weighting, it later became one of the cornerstones of modern descriptive models of decision making under risk (e.g., Birnbaum & Chavez, 1997; Edwards, 1962b; Kahneman & Tversky, 1979; Lopes & Oden, 1999; Luce, 2000; Prelec, 1998; Savage, 1954; Tversky & Fox, 1995; Tversky & Kahneman, 1992).

Probability weighting also came to be used as a framework for conceptualizing and measuring how people respond to uncertainty. For instance, it has been used to characterize decisions from experience, an important type of decision under uncertainty, and to explain how they differ from decisions from description (see chapter 7). In decisions from experience, there is always at least residual uncertainty about the actual probabilities of the events experienced. Several analyses have suggested that one key difference between decisions from experience and decisions from description consists in their different probability weighting patterns (e.g., Glöckner, Hilbig, Henninger, & Fiedler, 2016; Hertwig, Barron, Weber, & Erev, 2004; Kellen, Pachur, & Hertwig, 2016; Regenwetter & Robinson, 2017)—that is, in how much weight people give to the possible outcomes of an option as a function of their probability of occurrence.

Our goal in this chapter is to illustrate that the concept of probability weighting—although rooted in Daniel Bernoulli's utility framework, which Herbert Simon (1955, 1983) criticized for making unrealistic assumptions about the decision maker (see chapter 2)—can help characterize and measure how an adaptive and boundedly rational individual responds to uncertainty. We start by sketching the historical roots of probability weighting (see section 8.2) and reviewing studies that have compared patterns of probability weighting in experience-based and description-based choice (see section 8.3). Some analyses have concluded that people making decisions from experience choose as if they underweight rare events; others have found that rare events are overweighted, even more strongly than in decisions from description. We clarify these divergent conclusions and explain how, although seemingly contradictory, they can in fact coexist. Second, we discuss how a pattern of probability weighting that overweights small probabilities and underweights large probabilities can constitute an adaptive response to uncertainty (see section 8.4). Third, we highlight how heuristics that can be used to tackle uncertainty result in distinct shapes of the probability weighting function (see section 8.5). In other words, we identify which "footprints" specific choice heuristics leave when a probability weighting function is estimated for the choices that they generate.

8.2   A Brief History of Probability Weighting

Buffon's (1777) simulation was probably the first investigation into the role of (small) probabilities in decisions under risk. Probabilities again became an explicit target of interest in the 20th century. Preston and Baratta (1948) pioneered attempts to measure how people treat probabilities when making decisions under risk. Their participants were presented with lotteries offering the chance of winning a number of points with some probability (e.g.,

250 points with a probability of 5%) and asked to make a bid for each lottery. By comparing these bids with the lotteries' expected values—determined by multiplying the number of points by the probability of winning—Preston and Baratta sought to establish the "psychological probability" (p. 189) of outcomes. Not surprisingly, participants indicated higher bids for lotteries offering a particular payoff with a higher probability than for lotteries offering the same payoff with a lower probability. However, participants did not seem to weight the possible payoffs according to their probabilities, as expected value theory would predict. Instead, as shown in figure 8.1a, "the mean winning bid exceeds the mathematical expectation for small values of the probability and is less than the mathematical expectation for large values of the probability" (p. 186). In other words, low probabilities seemed to be overweighted in people's bids relative to their objective probability, and high probabilities seemed underweighted. This distortion of objective probabilities in the decision weights that people attach to events seemed to reflect their preferences to engage in risk when making a decision.

Edwards (1955) investigated choices between lotteries and likewise concluded that probabilities, like monetary outcomes, are not taken at face value but are subjectively represented in a distorted fashion (see also Edwards, 1962b; Tversky, 1967). He even went so far as to conclude, more than 200 years after Daniel Bernoulli (1738/1954), that subjective representations of probabilities are much more important than utilities (Edwards, 1955, p. 214).

Several theories have since introduced mathematical functions to describe the transformation of objective probabilities into subjective decision weights (e.g., Birnbaum & Chavez, 1997; Lopes & Oden, 1999). Kahneman and Tversky (1979) coined the term *probability weighting function* for these formal descriptions.[2] Arguably the most prominent theory postulating a probability weighting function is cumulative prospect theory

---

2. In some cases, the weighting function applies directly to the objective probability of an outcome; in others, it applies to the rank-dependent, cumulative probability distribution (e.g., Quiggin, 1982). For example, when deriving decision weights, π, from cumulative probabilities for a lottery offering €20, €30, or €40 with probabilities of 55%, 30%, and 15%, respectively, the decision weight for the outcome €30 would follow from the (transformed) probability of obtaining €30 or more, which is $w(.30+.15)=w(.45)$, minus the (transformed) probability of obtaining exactly €30, which is $w(.30)$. The function $w(p)$ formalizes the transformation of the probability (see box 8.1 for details).

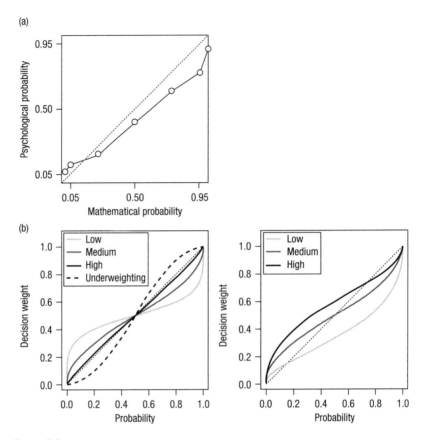

Figure 8.1

(a) Relationship between the objective probability of winning and the weight people seem to attach to the possibility of winning, as derived from bids made in Preston and Baratta (1948). (b) Cumulative prospect theory's weighting function. The left panel shows functions with varying values of the curvature parameter γ (with $\gamma < 1$ yielding overweighting, reflecting low, medium, and high probability sensitivity, and $\gamma > 1$ yielding underweighting). The right panel shows functions with varying values of the elevation parameter δ (with low, medium, and high levels of optimism and pessimism in the gain and loss domain, respectively; see box 8.1 for details).

(Tversky & Kahneman, 1992). Figure 8.1b illustrates cumulative prospect theory's probability weighting function. The function is parameterized, allowing it to assume different types of curvature. Consistent with earlier empirical observations (e.g., Edwards, 1955; Preston & Baratta, 1948; Wu & Gonzalez, 1996; see figure 8.1a), the typically assumed curvature is inverse S-shaped, indicating that small probabilities are overweighted relative to their objective counterparts, and that intermediate and large probabilities are underweighted. The parameterization also allows for different degrees of over- and underweighting (see figure 8.1b). An inverse S-shaped curvature of the weighting function can account for several notable violations of expected value and expected utility theory, such as the fourfold pattern (Tversky & Kahneman, 1992) and the Allais paradox (for an overview, see Camerer & Ho, 1994). Ironically, an inverse S-shaped curvature cannot explain the St. Petersburg paradox, the context from which the concept of probability weighting emerged (Blavatskyy, 2005).

Two main characteristics of cumulative prospect theory's weighting function, which are governed by separate parameters and by which the function can vary gradually, are its curvature and its elevation (see box 8.1 for a formal description or explore the shape of the probability weighting function yourself in interactive element 8.1 at https://taming-uncertainty.mpib-berlin.mpg.de/). As the left panel of figure 8.1b illustrates, the curvature reflects how sensitive a decision maker is to differences in probability; with a more pronounced curvature, the difference between, say, 30% and 50% is less strongly reflected in differences in decision weights than with a less pronounced curvature. As the right panel of figure 8.1b illustrates, the elevation governs the absolute magnitude of the decision weights. For risky gains, a higher elevation implies more optimistic (and thus more risk-seeking) choices than a lower elevation; for instance, a person with a higher elevation would be more willing to take a 10% chance of winning €1,000 (otherwise nothing). For risky losses, a higher elevation implies more pessimistic (and thus more risk-averse) choices. As is also shown in the left panel of figure 8.1b, the parameterization of the probability weighting function also allows it to take an S-shaped form (specifically, when the curvature parameter $\gamma > 1$; see box 8.1), such that small probabilities are underweighted, whereas intermediate and large probabilities are overweighted. This form would be consistent with the solution to the St. Petersburg paradox proposed by Nicolas Bernoulli (see van der Waerden, 1975), Buffon (1777), and Menger (1934).

Box 8.1

Formal description of cumulative prospect theory's weighting function.

To account for choices between options, each having outcomes $x_m > \ldots > x_1 \geq 0$ $> y_1 > \ldots > y_n$ and corresponding probabilities $p_m \ldots p_1$ and $q_1 \ldots q_n$, cumulative prospect theory assumes a rank-dependent transformation of the outcomes' probabilities into decision weights. More specifically, the weight π^+ (π^-) given to a positive (or negative) outcome is the difference between the probability of receiving an outcome at least as good (or bad) as x (or y) and the probability of receiving an outcome better (or worse) than x (or y):

$$\pi_m^+ = w^+(p_m)$$
$$\pi_n^- = w^-(q_n)$$
$$\pi_i^+ = w^+(p_i + \cdots + p_m) - w^+(p_{i+1} + \cdots + p_m) \quad for\ 1 \leq i < m$$
$$\pi_j^- = w^-(q_j + \cdots + q_n) - w^-(q_{j+1} + \cdots + q_n) \quad for\ 1 \leq j < n. \tag{B1}$$

The probability weighting functions for gains and losses—w^+ and w^-, respectively—are typically assumed to have an inverse S-shaped curvature, embodying the overweighting of rare events and the underweighting of common events. Different types of weighting functions have been proposed (e.g., Prelec, 1998; Tversky & Kahneman, 1992; for an overview, see Stott, 2006). One of the most common versions features two parameters that separate the curvature of the weighting function from its elevation (e.g., W. M. Goldstein & Einhorn, 1987; R. Gonzalez & Wu, 1999):

$$w^+ = \frac{\delta^+ p^{\gamma^+}}{\delta^+ p^{\gamma^+} + (1-p)^{\gamma^+}}$$
$$w^- = \frac{\delta^- q^{\gamma^-}}{\delta^- q^{\gamma^-} + (1-q)^{\gamma^-}}. \tag{B2}$$

The parameters γ^+ and γ^- (both > 0) govern the function's curvature in the gain and loss domains, respectively, and indicate how sensitive choices are to differences in probability (with smaller values of γ reflecting lower sensitivity). With $\gamma < 1$ the function has an inverse S-shaped form (indicating overweighting of rare events); with $\gamma > 1$ the function has an S-shaped form (indicating underweighting of rare events). The elevation of the weighting function is controlled by the parameters δ^+ and δ^- (both > 0), respectively. As highlighted by R. Gonzalez and Wu (1999), the elevation reflects the degree of risk aversion (traditionally assumed to be captured by the curvature of the value function; but see Lopes, 1995; Wakker, 2010), with a lower (or higher) elevation in the gain (or loss) domain indicating higher risk aversion (or pessimism).

In sum, people's decisions under risk indicate that more probable events receive more subjective weight than less probable events, but that rare events are overweighted relative to their probabilities, whereas common events are underweighted. The most prominent weighting function formally characterizing the relationship between probabilities and subjective decision weights was proposed in the context of cumulative prospect theory. It can assume both an inverse S-shaped form (implying overweighting of rare events) and an S-shaped form (implying underweighting of rare events). It also permits different degrees of over- and underweighting. As we discuss next, the concept of probability weighting has also been used to conceptualize and measure differences between decisions under risk, where probabilities of outcomes are explicitly stated, and decisions under uncertainty, where probabilities are only vaguely known or unknown.

8.3 Probability Weighting in Decisions under Uncertainty

What determines the shape of the probability weighting function—that is, how sensitive people's decisions are to differences in probability (expressed in the curvature of the function) and how optimistic they are (expressed in its elevation)? Kahneman and Tversky (1979) speculated that the uncertainty of an outcome could play a role. For example, imagine you are offered the chance of winning €200 as a function of the probability of an epistemic event, such as the probability that the maximum daytime temperature in downtown San Francisco on April 1 next year is between 65 °F and 80 °F. How do you weight the possibility of winning €200 in this option relative to an option where the probability of winning is explicitly stated (e.g., 20%)? Tversky and Fox (1995) developed a formal account of probability weighting for the first kind of option, in which probabilities are uncertain (see also Tversky & Wakker, 1995). A crucial assumption is that before making a choice, decision makers first estimate the probability of an outcome (e.g., that the temperature will be between 65 °F and 80 °F) in such a situation. The decision weights are then inferred from their choices.

To illustrate how uncertainty impacts probability weighting, let us consider a study by Tversky and Fox (1995). Participants chose between options that could lead to different outcomes. In the risk condition, the probabilities of the outcomes were precisely described (e.g., "Receive $75 if the number on a single poker chip drawn from an urn containing 100 chips numbered consecutively from 1 to 100 is between 1 and 25."). In the uncertainty condition, the probabilities were not explicitly stated but participants could consult their memory of the past to estimate them (e.g., "Receive $75 if the maximum daytime temperature in downtown San Francisco on April next year is between 65 °F and 80 °F."). Tversky and Fox compared the weighting functions obtained from participants' choices in the two conditions with regard to their subadditivity, a robust property of empirical decision weights.[3] The greater the subadditivity, the lower the probability sensitivity; in other words, subadditivity implies reduced sensitivity to probabilities. Subadditivity of decision weights was found to be larger under uncertainty than under risk—people's decisions were less attuned to differences in probabilities when the probability information was fraught with uncertainty.

In Tversky and Fox's (1995) study, the probabilities were uncertain because they were expressed in terms of epistemic events (e.g., the temperature at a particular location on a particular day), where people's beliefs were informed by their knowledge stored in memory. We next turn to research that has studied probability weighting when probabilities are initially unknown and people could learn about them by sampling from the environment.

8.3.1 "As-If" Inferences about the Weighting of Objectively Rare Events in Decisions from Experience

The goal of the initial studies on the distinction between decisions from description and decisions from experience was to understand when and why people's choices deviate from expected value maximization—and to examine how this deviation differs between description and experience (Barron & Erev, 2003; Hertwig et al., 2004; E. U. Weber, Shafir, & Blais, 2004). Evidence from this and subsequent research (e.g., Erev, Ert, Plonsky, Cohen, & Cohen, 2017; Wulff, Mergenthaler-Canseco, & Hertwig, 2018) suggests that experience- and description-based choices differ systematically in how they deviate from expected value maximization. Wulff et al. (2018) conducted a meta-analysis of 33 datasets examining the difference

---

3. More precisely, a weighting function is subadditive when the decision weight for the sum of probabilities of various individual events is smaller than the sum of the decision weights for the probabilities of the individual events.

between description and experience in the average proportion of choices maximizing expected value. When choice problems involved a risky and a safe option—the type of problem commonly used to infer risk preference in economics and psychology—the size of the gap was rather large (on average, about 20 percentage points). Note that this gap in choice is not premised on any particular theory of choice (e.g., one that assumes probability weighting).

Another perspective on the description–experience gap was prompted by the way Hertwig et al. (2004), Barron and Erev (2003), and E. U. Weber et al. (2004) summarized their findings. These authors used an as-if probability-weighting terminology stating, for instance, that "observed choices indicated not overweighting of small-probability outcomes (henceforth, *rare events*), but rather the opposite: people made choices as if they underweighted rare events; that is, rare events received less weight than their objective probability of occurrence warranted" (Hertwig et al., 2004, p. 535). This and similar statements have invited the interpretation that the description–experience gap consists mainly of a reversal of the probability-weighting pattern. Consequently, numerous investigations have compared probability weighting in experience and description (e.g., Abdellaoui, L'Haridon, & Paraschiv, 2011; Glöckner et al., 2016; Hau, Pleskac, Kiefer, & Hertwig, 2008; Kellen et al., 2016; Lejarraga, Pachur, Frey, & Hertwig, 2016; Ungemach, Chater, & Stewart, 2009).

Like Kahneman and Tversky (1979), both Hertwig et al. (2004) and Barron and Erev (2003) made inferences about people's probability weighting directly from the observed choices. They did not formally estimate a weighting function, nor were their analyses conditioned on people's actual experience. In Hertwig et al. (2004), for instance, lottery problems were selected such that systematically different patterns of choices would result if rare events were accorded less weight in experience than in description. As a consequence, the weighting was meant in an as-if sense (i.e., people behaved as if rare events had less impact than they deserved). Further, the as-if weights referred to the objective probabilities of the outcome distributions—that is, the probabilities that governed the options' payoff distributions—not to the relative frequencies of the events that people had actually experienced.

To date, Regenwetter and Robinson (2017) have conducted the most systematic comparison of the weighting of objective probabilities in description and experience. After accounting for individual heterogeneity in preferences (their paramount concern), they found strong evidence for a description–experience gap in probability weighting and a choice pattern consistent with the original conclusion that, relative to the objective probabilities, rare events are overweighted in description and underweighted in experience (for more details, see table 1 in Hertwig & Pleskac, 2018).

8.3.2 Weighting of Rarely Experienced Events

However, researchers soon began, for good reasons, to measure probability weighting in decisions from experience based on people's actual samples of outcomes, rather than the objective probabilities. Is the shape of a probability weighting function estimated on the basis of the relative frequency with which events were actually experienced still different from that estimated for decisions from description? Are rare events still underweighted? Such underweighting could occur due to factors such as recency effects in memory (Ashby & Rakow, 2014; Wulff & Pachur, 2016). It is important to note that even if description-based and experience-based decision weights did not differ, choices in a given lottery problem could still systematically diverge: relative experienced frequencies (or the perception thereof) can deviate systematically from objective probabilities due to sampling error, recency, and other factors.

Table 8.1 (adapted from Wulff et al., 2018) shows the results of studies that have estimated probability weighting functions for decisions from experience. As can be seen, there is considerable heterogeneity, with some studies finding probability weighting functions consistent with the underweighting of rare events and others finding evidence for overweighting. However, several of these analyses have methodological limitations. Take, for instance, the study by Ungemach et al. (2009), who obtained evidence for underweighting. In their analyses, parameters were estimated based on a set of only six choice problems, and data from all participants were aggregated for the estimation. Both aspects are likely to compromise the robustness of the results (e.g., Broomell & Bhatia, 2014; Estes & Maddox, 2005; Regenwetter & Robinson, 2017).

In a more rigorous analysis, Kellen et al. (2016) asked each participant to make both experience-based and description-based decisions on a total of 114 choice problems from the gain, loss, and mixed domains. Each individual's decisions were modeled with cumulative prospect theory, separately

Table 8.1
Summary of parameter estimates on experience-based probability weighting in decisions from experience (adapted from Wulff et al., 2018).

Study	Description	Experience	Inferred weighting of rare events
Sampling paradigm			
Hau et al. (2008)		$\gamma = 0.99$	Linear weighting
Ungemach et al. (2009)	—	$\gamma^+ > 1$ $\gamma^- > 1$	Underweighting
	—	$\gamma^+ = [0, 2]$ $\gamma^- = [0, 2]$	—
	—	$\gamma^+ > 1^a$ $\gamma^- > 1$	Underweighting
	—	$\gamma^+ > 1^a$ $\gamma^- > 1$	Underweighting
Camilleri & Newell (2011b)	—	$\gamma = [0, 2]$	—
Camilleri & Newell (2013)	$\gamma = [0, 2]$	$\gamma > 1$	Underweighting
	$\gamma = [0, 2]$	$\gamma > 1$	Underweighting
Frey, Mata, & Hertwig (2015)	—	$\gamma^+ = 1.3$ $(\delta^+ = 1)$ $\gamma^- = 1.35$ $(\delta^- = 1)$	Underweighting
	—	$\gamma^+ = 1.03$ $(\delta^+ = 1)$ $\gamma^- = 1.05$ $(\delta^- = 1)$	Underweighting
Lejarraga et al. (2016)	$\gamma = 0.89$ $(\delta = 0.96)$	$\gamma = 0.81$ $(\delta = 0.87)$	Overweighting
	$\gamma = 0.20$ $(\delta = 4.33)$	$\gamma = 0.53$ $(\delta = 3.82)$	Overweighting
Glöckner et al. (2016)	$\gamma = 0.73$ $(\delta = 0.55)$	$\gamma = 0.56$ $(\delta = 0.55)$	Overweighting
	$\gamma = 0.73$ $(\delta = 0.32)$	$\gamma = 0.55$ $(\delta = 0.39)$	Overweighting
	$\gamma = 0.96$ $(\delta = 0.70)$	$\gamma = 0.55$ $(\delta = 0.48)$	Overweighting
	$\gamma = 0.65$ $(\delta = 0.80)$	$\gamma = 0.42$ $(\delta = 0.79)$	Overweighting
	$\gamma = 0.59$ $(\delta = 0.96)$	$\gamma = 0.91$ $(\delta = 1.04)$	Overweighting, but less pronounced relative to description

(continued)

Table 8.1 (continued)

Study	Description	Experience	Inferred weighting of rare events
Kellen et al. (2016)	$\gamma = 0.66$ ($\delta^+ = 0.81$, $\delta^- = 1.53$)	$\gamma = 0.53$ ($\delta^+ = 0.71$, $\delta^- = 1.66$)	Overweighting
Markant, Pleskac, Diederich, Pachur, & Hertwig (2015)	—	$\gamma = 1.41$ ($\delta = 1$)	Underweighting
	—	$\gamma = 1.15$ ($\delta = 1.61$)	Underweighting
	—	$\gamma = 0.92$ ($\delta = 1.3$)	Overweighting
Variants of the sampling paradigm			
Abdellaoui et al. (2011)	$\gamma^+ = 0.65$ ($\delta^+ = 0.70$) $\gamma^- = 0.73$ ($\delta^- = 0.78$)	$\gamma^+ = 0.66$ ($\delta^+ = 0.59$) $\gamma^- = 0.74$ ($\delta^- = 0.67$)	Overweighting, but less pronounced relative to description
	(Nonparametric estimation)		Overweighting, but less pronounced relative to description
Camilleri & Newell (2011b)	—	$\gamma > 1$	Underweighting
	—	$\gamma > 1$	Underweighting
Jarvstad, Hahn, Rushton, & Warren (2013)	(Qualitative evaluation; experienced frequencies)		Underweighting
	(Qualitative evaluation; experienced frequencies)		Overweighting
Zeigenfuse, Pleskac, & Liu (2014)	—	$\gamma = 0.7$ ($\delta = 0.3$)	Overweighting
Kemel & Travers (2016)	—	$\gamma = 0.68$ ($\delta = 0.68$)	Overweighting
	—	$\gamma = 0.59$ ($\delta = 0.78$)	Overweighting
	—	$\gamma = 0.74$ ($\delta = 0.66$)	Overweighting
	—	$\gamma = 0.63$ ($\delta = 0.83$)	Overweighting

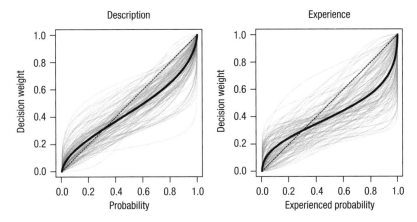

Figure 8.2
Individual-level probability-weighting functions (in gray), separately for decisions from description and decisions from experience in Kellen et al. (2016). The results are shown for the gain domain (differences between description and experience in the loss domain were similar). The black lines show the functions based on the group-level parameters.

for each learning mode. For experience-based decisions, the authors used the outcomes that each participant had actually experienced and, as probabilities, the relative frequencies of those outcomes in each participant's samples (thus taking sampling error into account). As figure 8.2 shows, the resulting probability weighting function for decisions from experience was inverse S-shaped, suggesting overweighting of rare events—the qualitatively same pattern observed for decisions from description. Importantly, however, the curvature was even more pronounced in experience than in description. This finding indicates, consistent with Tversky and Fox's (1995) analyses of decisions under uncertainty, reduced sensitivity to probabilities in decisions from experience (see also Glöckner et al., 2016; Lejarraga et al., 2016). At the same time, Kellen et al. (2016; see their table 1) obtained a choice pattern (on the respective choice problems) that was similar to the one that led Hertwig et al. (2004) to conclude that rare events are underweighted. Thus, although decision weights expressed relative to the objective probabilities suggest underweighting of rare events in decisions from experience—as in Hertwig et al.'s (2004) conclusions (see also Regenwetter & Robinson, 2017)—decision weights estimated using the probability information that people have actually experienced suggest overweighting.

Both patterns, over- and underweighting of rare events, can be obtained, depending on how probability weighting is estimated.

Another important factor that seems to systematically affect the type of probability weighting in decisions from experience is the type of choice problem. For choice problems containing two risky options (making up the large share of problems in Kellen et al., 2016), there is rather consistent evidence for a stronger overweighting of rare events in experience than in description. For problems containing a safe and a risky option, by contrast, the probability weighting function seems to be more linear in experience than in description (Glöckner et al., 2016; see figure 10 in Wulff et al., 2018). These differences between problem types suggest that the pattern of probability weighting is sensitive to the variability of the outcomes that people encounter during information search (see chapter 7)—and is therefore not easily generalizable. In sum, in investigations where probabilities are uncertain and people could reduce the uncertainty by sampling from memory, there is a regressive pattern. In addition, in investigations where probabilities are uncertain and people could reduce the uncertainty by sampling from the environment, there also seems to be a regressive pattern when both options are risky. Next, we discuss a possible explanation for this pattern in probability weighting—namely, that it represents a reasonable response to uncertainty.

8.4   Nonlinear Probability Weighting as a Rational Response to Uncertainty

From the perspective of expected value theory, that people's decision weights show a regressive, nonlinear distortion of the probabilities represents a clear violation of how a rational mind should respond to risk. So should nonlinear probability weighting be considered irrational? Fennell and Baddeley (2012) demonstrated that, far from being irrational, regressive probability weighting can reflect a rational response to uncertainty. They argued that people may internally "correct" probability information by integrating it with relevant background knowledge consistent with a rational Bayesian updating mechanism. Specifically, the stated probability of an event is viewed against the previously experienced probability distribution of similar events ("inference priors") as well as the expected probability distribution assuming a complete lack of knowledge about the class of events ("ignorance priors"). If the stated probability is compatible with the previous experience, the inference prior is used to correct the stated probability; otherwise the ignorance prior is used. Fennell and Baddeley showed that this approach leads to "corrected" probabilities that are regressed relative to the original probability information—in line with an inverse S-shaped weighting function.

To illustrate this point, Fennell and Baddeley (2012) demonstrated how probabilities for two classes of events—namely, positive events (e.g., birthdays, weddings) and negative events (e.g., earthquakes, house fires)—should be revised in light of one's knowledge about the frequency distribution of positive and negative events in the real world. In a first step, the authors analyzed Internet blogs to estimate the ecological distribution of the probability of these events occurring. This ecological analysis showed that in the blogs, both positive and negative events had an average (across different types of events) probability of occurring of less than 50%. Moreover, positive events were more likely than negative events, and the spread of the distribution for positive events was wider. In a second step, the authors used the Bayesian approach sketched earlier in this section as well as the results from their ecological analysis to derive, for different probability levels, posterior (i.e., "corrected") probability assessments. In other words, they determined how a Bayesian mind would assess probability information about positive and negative events against the background of the respective probability distributions in the world at large. When the original probabilities were mapped against the resulting posterior probabilities, the functions showed a regressive trend, with the probability assessments for lower probabilities being pushed upwards toward 50%, and the probability assessments for higher probabilities being pushed downwards. In addition, the regressive trend was more pronounced for positive than for negative events, reflecting the greater uncertainty associated with the former (i.e., the wider spread of the probability distribution).

The key insight from Fennell and Baddeley's (2012) results is that nonlinear weighting of probabilities is not necessarily a sign of irrationality. Instead, a regressive, inverse S-shaped probability weighting pattern is consistent with how a Bayesian mind would rationally respond to uncertainty (leaving aside the question of how exactly the mind may implement or approximate a Bayesian updating process). The amount of uncertainty is evidently higher in decisions from experience than in decisions from description. One interpretation of the regressive probability weighting pattern obtained by, for instance, Kellen et al. (2016) is thus that it represents a rational response to the uncertainty in decisions from experience.

8.5 Probability Weights as Reflections of Heuristics

Up to now, we have discussed several reasons why people might weight events differently than the probability of those events would imply. For instance, they may ignore events with small or very small probabilities because their experience tells them that they barely matter. Fennell and Baddeley (2012) demonstrated that a regressed, nonlinear probability weighting pattern is the natural consequence of a Bayesian mind dealing with uncertainty. Let us add another possible reason for the emergence of nonlinear probability weighting. It reconciles probability weighting—a notion rooted in the Bernoullian utility framework of decision making—with the Homo heuristicus (see chapter 1; Gigerenzer, Hertwig, & Pachur, 2011). Specifically, different kinds of nonlinear probability weighting may arise when decision makers rely on different boundedly rational heuristics.

Let us first turn to a heuristic that was proposed as a decision tool to be used in the face of uncertainty. Savage (1954) suggested that one way to deal with situations in which probabilities are unknown is to expect that the worst possible outcomes occur and to decide accordingly. The minimax heuristic, which implements this notion in games against a dispassionate nature, chooses the option whose worst outcome is more attractive. Importantly, probabilities play no role at all in the minimax heuristic. What form does cumulative prospect theory's probability weighting function take when decision makers apply this and, by extension, other heuristics? To answer this question, Pachur, Suter, and Hertwig (2017; see also Suter, Pachur, & Hertwig, 2016) fitted cumulative prospect theory to choices produced by five heuristics in the context of a computer simulation. The heuristics represent distinct policies in the face of risk and uncertainty: the minimax heuristic, the maximax heuristic, the priority heuristic (a lexicographic strategy), the least-likely heuristic, and the most-likely heuristic. Box 8.2 describes their policies in detail. The procedure was as follows: first, Pachur, Suter, and Hertwig determined the choices of each of the five heuristics for various types of choice problems (in the gain, loss, and mixed domain); second, they

Box 8.2

Definitions of the five heuristics tested in Pachur, Suter, and Hertwig (2017).

We illustrate each heuristic's policy and choice prediction with reference to the following choice problem with two options:

A   500 with a probability of .4 and 2000 with a probability of .6.

B   450 with a probability of .7 and 3500 with a probability of .3.

The *minimax heuristic* identifies the worst outcome of each option and selects the option with the more attractive worst outcome. If the options' worst outcomes are identical, minimax chooses randomly. It never considers probability information. Minimax chooses option *A*, because its worst outcome is higher than that of option *B* (500 vs. 450).

The *maximax heuristic* identifies the best outcome of each option and selects the option with the more attractive best outcome. If the options' worst outcomes are identical, maximax chooses randomly. It never considers probability information. Maximax chooses option *B*, because its best outcome is higher than that of option *A* (3500 vs. 2000).

The *priority heuristic* goes through the attributes in the following order: minimum gain, probability of minimum gain, and maximum gain. It stops examination if the minimum gains differ by 1/10 (or more) of the maximum gain; otherwise, it stops examination if the probabilities differ by 1/10 (or more) of the probability scale. The heuristic selects the option with the more attractive gain (probability). For options with more than two outcomes, the search rule is identical, apart from the addition of a fourth attribute: probability of maximum gain. For loss options, the heuristic remains the same except that "gains" are replaced by "losses." For mixed options, the heuristic remains the same except that "gains" are replaced by "outcomes." The priority heuristic sometimes considers probability information, depending on whether the minimum outcomes differ or not. In the example, the priority heuristic chooses option *A*, because the option has a lower probability than option *B* of leading to the minimum gain (.4 vs. .7).

The *least-likely heuristic* identifies each option's worst outcome and selects the option with the lowest probability of the worst outcome. It always considers probability information. Least-likely chooses option *A*, where the probability of the worst outcome (500) is .4, lower than in option *B* (.7).

The *most-likely heuristic* identifies each option's most likely outcome and selects the option with the more attractive most likely outcome. It always considers probability information. Most-likely chooses option *A*, where the most likely outcome is 2000, higher than in option *B* (450).

estimated the parameters of cumulative prospect theory for the set of choices produced by each heuristic.

As figure 8.3 shows, the heuristics produced distinctly shaped curves. For instance, the weighting functions estimated for the choices produced by minimax and maximax showed a strongly inverse S-shaped curvature, indicating low probability sensitivity. This finding echoes the previous result that people display lower sensitivity to probability information under uncertainty than under risk. Moreover, low probability sensitivity is consistent with the information processing architecture of the minimax and maximax heuristics, which are blind to probabilities. For the priority heuristic, the curvature was less pronounced, indicating somewhat higher probability sensitivity. Again, the shape of the weighting function is meaningfully related to the heuristic's policy: this heuristic sometimes relies on probabilities to make a choice—namely, when the options' worst possible outcomes are similar—but it sometimes ignores probabilities, depending on the characteristics of the choice problem (see box 8.2). For the most-likely and the least-likely heuristics, the weighting function was least strongly curved, reflecting that these heuristics always take probabilities into account when making a choice.

Furthermore, the elevations of the resulting weighting functions point to differences between the heuristics in the degree of "optimism" (i.e., risk attitude) they embody. For instance, whereas in the gain domain minimax resulted in a weighting function with a very low elevation, indicating highly pessimistic decision weights (and thus risk aversion), maximax produced a weighting function with a very high elevation, indicating highly optimistic decision weights (and thus risk-seeking). In the loss domain, this pattern was reversed. These results thus reveal another property of the heuristics' policies—namely, their risk attitude (see also Lopes, 1995). Whereas minimax aims to protect against the worst possible outcomes, maximax reaches for the stars and aims to maximize the best outcomes.

In summary, probability weighting as assumed, for instance, in cumulative prospect theory is agnostic with regard to the cognitive processes that shape the probability weighting function (but see Bordalo, Gennaioli, & Shleifer, 2012; Hogarth & Einhorn, 1990; Johnson & Busemeyer, 2016). Surprisingly, however, the probability weighting function is a construct at which theories of boundedly rational choice heuristics (see chapters 1 and 2) and neo-Bernoullian theories of choice can meet. Moving toward

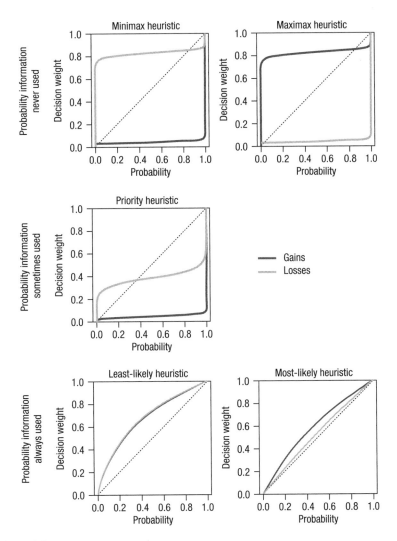

Figure 8.3
Cumulative prospect theory's weighting function estimated for the choices of five heuristics that differ in their consideration of probability information (from Pachur, Suter, & Hertwig, 2017). The functions show the relationship between the objective probability, p, and the transformed probability, $w(p)$, separately for gains (dark gray) and losses (light gray).

integration of theories for decisions under risk and uncertainty, Pachur, Suter, and Hertwig (2017) demonstrated that heuristics with distinct information-processing policies result in distinct shapes of the probability weighting function. In terms of their suggested probability sensitivity and optimism, these shapes are meaningfully related to differences in the heuristics' information processing policies. One practical implication of this finding is that analyses of probability weighting can be employed to track the operations of the Homo heuristicus as well as the underlying cognitive processes (e.g., Pachur, Schulte-Mecklenbeck, Murphy, & Hertwig, 2018; Suter et al., 2016).

8.6   Probability Weighting: A Window onto Uncertainty

Scholars' attempts to explain how the mind weighs risky or uncertain events date back to at least the 18th century and to perhaps the most influential game in the history of economics and psychology: the St. Petersburg game. Our historical account of work motivated by this game prompts an interesting thought experiment: What kinds of theories of choice would have evolved had Nicolas Bernoulli's (see van der Waerden, 1975) and Buffon's (1777) explanations of the St. Petersburg paradox won the day? Perhaps even more would be known about the causes and (adaptive) logic behind different kinds of nonlinear probability weighting in the face of risk and uncertainty. Yet what we have nevertheless begun to discern is that probability weighting offers a window onto how much uncertainty people perceive in the environment—and possibly onto the kind of simple strategies they recruit to deal with it.

9 Tomorrow Never Knows: Why and How Uncertainty Matters in Intertemporal Choice

Junyi Dai, Thorsten Pachur, Timothy J. Pleskac, and Ralph Hertwig

9.1 The Pervasiveness of Uncertainty in Intertemporal Choice

In the 1960s, Walter Mischel and his graduate students looked for a way to measure the development of self-control among preschoolers. In the now famous Marshmallow Test, they offered children a choice of either eating a single treat straight away or waiting until the experimenter returned from a brief errand and then being rewarded with a second treat (Mischel, 2014). This is perhaps the best-known example of an *intertemporal choice*—a decision between options whose outcomes materialize at different times. What is not widely appreciated is that some of Mischel's experiments contained an element of uncertainty: children did not always know how long they would have to wait. The experimenter simply said, "you know, sometimes, I'm gone a long time" (Mischel & Ebbesen, 1970, p. 332).

Uncertainty is an inherent property of intertemporal choice in many real-world situations (Frederick, Loewenstein, & O'Donoghue, 2002). Imagine you have a lump sum of money that you can either spend immediately or invest in the stock market in the hope of reaping benefits later. You face *outcome uncertainty* about whether an investment will turn out to be profitable and about how much profit will be made, and *temporal uncertainty* regarding the length of time it will take to reap the benefits. Or imagine you are considering changing your eating habits. You will have to make the decision without knowing when you can expect to notice results, and without being sure that the results will be worth the effort. Despite the important role that uncertainty plays in many intertemporal choices, most experimental studies of these decisions try to factor it out. Often this is done by asking people to assume that the outcomes of any chosen option would be sure to materialize (for a review, see Frederick et al., 2002; Urminsky & Zauberman, 2015). For instance, a person might be asked to choose between receiving €100 now and receiving €200 in a year, with both outcomes guaranteed. Relative to the extent of the work on intertemporal choice in both economics and psychology over the past century, discussions of the possible role of uncertainty in these decisions have been quite rare. There are, of course, exceptions (see, e.g., Benzion, Rapoport, & Yagil, 1989; Kagel, Green, & Caraco, 1986; Keren & Roelofsma, 1995; Mischel & Grusec, 1967; Stevenson, 1986; B. J. Weber & Chapman, 2007). Yet, of the 10 most cited articles on intertemporal choice on Google Scholar as of July 2017, the majority do not mention the issue of uncertainty at all, and the others either treat it only tangentially or list it as one of many possible factors that might influence people's decisions (e.g., Frederick et al., 2002).

Our goal in this chapter is to zoom in on the role that uncertainty might play in intertemporal choice and to show that uncertainty could be a key factor shaping people's behavior in these choices. To do so, we highlight the various ways in which uncertainty is relevant in intertemporal choice. Table 9.1 provides an overview of the different types of uncertainty we consider; the first three types are specific cases of outcome uncertainty, whereas the last relates to temporal uncertainty. One important insight is that key regularities in intertemporal choice could be understood as adaptive responses to uncertainty. Taking uncertainty into consideration could thus impact how many well-known findings are interpreted. Moreover, we suggest that

Table 9.1

Types of uncertainty in intertemporal choice with examples.

Type of uncertainty	Examples for the choice "Should I start exercising now to be healthier in the future?"
Uncertainty in the materialization of the future outcome	Will the decision definitely lead to better health? If not, how likely is it that I will end up healthier?
Uncertainty in the size of the future outcome	How much healthier will I be if I start exercising?
Uncertainty in the subjective value of the future outcome (i.e., utility uncertainty)	How much benefit will I have from better health?
Uncertainty in the delay until the future outcome materializes	When will I actually attain better health?

decisions from experience, which have been employed to study the impact of uncertainty in risky choice (see chapters 7 and 8), can provide a helpful methodological framework for understanding intertemporal choice under uncertainty. We conclude the chapter with such an illustration.

9.2   The Many Shades of Uncertainty in Intertemporal Choice

Three of the most prominent findings in the literature on intertemporal choice are as follows: (a) people choose between payoffs that materialize at different times as though the values of delayed payoffs were discounted (Fisher, 1930); (b) the degree of discounting per unit of time tends to decrease as delays get longer (Benzion et al., 1989; Chapman, 1996; Thaler, 1981); and (c) over time, people's preference between one option with a smaller-but-sooner reward and another option with a larger-but-later reward may reverse, from preferring the latter to preferring the former (e.g., Ainslie, 1975; Green, Fristoe, & Myerson, 1994).

A common approach to accounting for these three findings is to assume a mathematical function that describes how the utility of an outcome decreases as the delay to its realization increases. These functions are often referred to as *discount functions*. One discount function that is particularly effective at capturing people's intertemporal choices is the hyperbolic function (Mazur, 1987). Figure 9.1 shows such a function and how it produces the preference reversal mentioned above. As we will show, this and other behavioral regularities captured by a hyperbolic discount function may be related to the uncertainty inherent in the prospect of future outcomes.

9.2.1   Will the Future Outcome Materialize? And How Likely Is It?

As indicated in table 9.1, one important source of uncertainty in intertemporal choice is that it is unclear whether the anticipated consequence will actually materialize. In 1965, when French lawyer André-François Raffrey was 47 years old, he offered a 90-year-old widow a deal: he would pay her 2,500 francs every month until her death, at which point he would inherit her beautiful apartment. She accepted—and went on to live another 32 years. She outlasted her unlucky beneficiary, who died after 30 years, having paid approximately 920,000 francs for an apartment he never got to live in ("A 120-year lease", 1995; Coatney, 1997). In the same vein, when the dot-com bubble burst in 2000, washing out 52% of dot-com companies

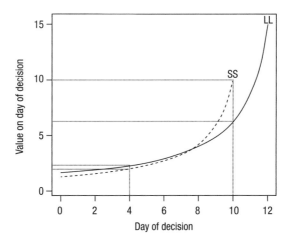

Figure 9.1
The value of two options on different days according to a hyperbolic discount function. In this example, a choice is offered between a smaller-but-sooner (SS) option that is obtained on day 10, and a larger-but-later (LL) option, where a larger payoff is obtained on day 12. Note that the SS option is not available after day 10, so it has no value on subsequent days. The figure shows how a preference reversal can occur. For example, if the choice between the SS and LL options is made on day 4, then the LL option has a greater value, but if the choice is on day 10, then the value of the SS option is greater.

by 2004 and severely affecting many of those that remained (Berlin, 2008), many stockholders lost almost all of what initially seemed to be a profitable investment.

These examples raise the question of what role uncertainty about the materialization of future outcomes might play in the intertemporal choices that people make. One answer is that outcome uncertainty might be an important reason for *delay discounting*—the apparent discounting of the value of future payoffs. In work dealing with animals, researchers have highlighted the possibility that a delayed reward may become unavailable before it is ready for collection (collection risk; Houston, Kacelnik, & McNamara, 1982). Food, for instance, may have already been consumed by a competitor by the time an animal returns to it (see also chapters 12 and 15). Similarly, the anticipated outcome of harvesting and consuming a reward might not actually be realized (e.g., because a planned retrieval is interrupted by a dangerous predator, or because the animal dies before it can return). These and other risks associated with a delayed reward might make it reasonable to find a delayed reward less attractive than an immediate reward of the same—or even smaller—magnitude (e.g., Green & Myerson, 1996; Stephens, 2002; Stevens, 2010). In other words, delay discounting could represent an adaptive response to the inherent uncertainty about whether or not a delayed option will actually materialize (see also Wendt & Czaczkes, 2017).

The degree of delay discounting may be directly related to the degree of outcome uncertainty in the environment. M. Wilson and Daly (1997) compared 77 Chicago neighborhoods—including both poor, crime-ridden communities and wealthy, safe areas—in terms of life expectancy at birth and homicide rate. In estimating life expectancy in each community, the authors removed the contribution of deaths due to homicide. Although the direct effect of homicide on mortality was thus controlled for, the adjusted life expectancy was still strongly correlated with the homicide rate across communities. The authors proposed that low life expectancy in a neighborhood may create high uncertainty about surviving long enough to reap future benefits; this uncertainty might have led to stronger delay discounting and, in turn, more risk taking in social competition, sometimes resulting in loss of life.

Empirical support for the effect of outcome uncertainty experienced in the environment on intertemporal choices has been found in the lab. For instance, Kidd, Palmeri, and Aslin (2013) examined the role of outcome uncertainty in the Marshmallow Test. Before running the test, the experimenters presented their young participants with an art project task in which the promised art supplies or stickers were either provided or not, thus creating different degrees of uncertainty about the materialization of promised rewards. In the subsequent Marshmallow Test, children who had not obtained the promised objects in the art project (unreliable and thus uncertain environment) task were less willing to wait to get more marshmallows than were children who had obtained the promised objects (reliable and thus more certain environment).

A subtler form of outcome uncertainty is that decision makers might be uncertain not only about whether an anticipated outcome will materialize, but also about the likelihood that it will materialize. This type of uncertainty provides an interesting perspective on the enduring debate on the shape of the delay discount function in intertemporal choice (figure 9.1).

Recall that this function describes how the subjective valuation of an outcome changes as a function of the length of the delay. In figure 9.1, the discount rate per unit of time declines over time. Therefore, a person choosing between a smaller-but-sooner (SS) option and a larger-but-later (LL) option on day 10 would prefer the SS option, but the same person choosing on day 4 (and thus experiencing a longer delay before receiving either option) would prefer the LL option (see also box 9.1).

Yet the discount rate per unit of time is often assumed to be constant—that is, not dependent on the length of the delay. This assumption is formalized in the exponential discount function, which has been proposed in the context of the discounted utility model (Samuelson, 1937). Building on this model, Strotz (1955) showed that an exponential discount function can be normatively defensible if (a) a delayed option could become unavailable before the due date; (b) the probability (per unit of time) of this happening given that it has not occurred yet—also known as *hazard rate*—is constant over time; and (c) the hazard rate is known to the decision maker at the time a choice is made. Like other features of the environment, however, the hazard rate is typically unknown to the decision maker. For instance, there is usually no way for a foraging animal to assess the exact number of competitors present in the same area, or the chance of being devoured in the coming hours. The animal might therefore continuously update its belief about the hazard rate, depending on whether a food option remains available. If, as time passes, a delayed option remains available, the objective hazard rate might be rather low. Consequently, it is reasonable for the animal to update its belief such that a relatively low hazard rate is perceived as increasingly more likely. Sozou (1998) offered a formal explanation of this phenomenon, showing that when the initial (subjective) belief about the hazard rate can be expressed by an exponential distribution and this belief is updated using Bayes' rule, the uncertainty in the hazard rate naturally leads to a hyperbolic discount function, where the discount rate per unit of time declines with longer delays (e.g., Green, Fry, & Myerson, 1994; Mazur, 1987; Rachlin, 2006; see box 9.1).

Sozou (1998) showed that a hyperbolic discount function is also normatively defensible in an environment where the hazard rate is exponentially distributed and if one assumes that the overall discount function results from averaging across all possible hazard rates. Under these conditions, it may be appropriate to discount outcomes according to a hyperbolic discount

Box 9.1

Delay discounting: Exponential or hyperbolic?

Research on intertemporal choice has been strongly influenced by the concept of delay discounting, according to which the subjective valuation (or utility) of a payoff x declines as it is delayed into the future. This concept has set the foundation for various delay discounting models on intertemporal decisions, including the discounted utility model, which economists have long held to be the normative model. According to the discounted utility model, the subjective valuation of a payoff declines as a function of delay duration at a constant rate. This relationship can be captured by an exponential discount function:

$$D(t) = \exp(-kt), \tag{B1}$$

where t represents the delay duration and k is a parameter for the constant discount rate. The current subjective valuation of a payoff is then:

$$V = D(t) \times u(x), \tag{B2}$$

where $u(x)$ is the utility of the payoff.

Psychologists, however, have found that a hyperbolic discount function can provide a better description of the empirical data than the exponential

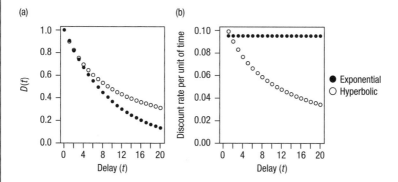

Figure 9.B1

Examples of (a) exponential and hyperbolic discount functions and (b) the corresponding discount rate per unit of time. Although the two functions shown here have similar discount rates per unit of time for shorter delays, the discount rate per unit of time decreases according to the hyperbolic discount function but stays constant according to the exponential discount function. As a result, as delay gets longer, the hyperbolic discount function entails a lower overall discount rate than the exponential discount function does.

(continued)

Box 9.1 (continued)

function (for both humans and animals). This function suggests a decreasing discount rate per unit of time as the delay gets longer. In other words, post-poning an immediate payoff by a certain period of time has a larger impact on its subjective valuation than postponing it further into the future by the same period of time. A number of hyperbolic discount functions have been proposed to capture this property; the simplest and presumably most com-monly used one is

$$D(t) = \frac{1}{1+kt}, \tag{B3}$$

where t again represents the delay duration and k is a discount rate parameter (Mazur, 1987). Figure 9.B1 shows an example of both discount functions and the corresponding discount rate per unit of time as the delay gets longer.

function. This result, which holds if the actual hazard rate is uncertain, is fundamentally different from the normative solution under certainty (i.e., if the hazard rate is fixed and known), where an exponential discount function with a constant discount rate per unit of time is more appropriate. Such a function guarantees consistent preferences between options at dif-ferent time points as time elapses (i.e., no preference reversals).

In sum, the behavioral regularities that are captured by a hyperbolic dis-count function may be due to uncertainty. If there is uncertainty about the materialization of outcomes, hyperbolic discounting is more appropriate, but under conditions of certainty, exponential discounting is more suitable.

9.2.2   How Large Is the Future Outcome?

Another source of uncertainty in intertemporal choice relates to how *much* the decision maker will benefit from a delayed option. MBA students at the start of their program will find it difficult to accurately predict the salaries they will be offered after graduating (especially if their studies span an eco-nomic crisis). The impact of such uncertainty might be manifested in one of two ways. On the one hand, if people are averse to uncertainty about the magnitude of future outcomes (as they are to ambiguity in the odds of obtaining a virtually immediate outcome; Ellsberg, 1961), that uncertainty may make a delayed option less attractive. On the other hand, delay could encourage people to take an optimistic view of uncertain magnitudes, thereby making an uncertain future outcome appear more attractive (e.g., Onay, La-Ornual, & Öncüler, 2013). There may also be individual differences in how delay impacts the level of optimism toward an uncertain outcome, with optimists expecting an uncertain future outcome to turn out well, and pessimists expecting it to turn out badly. Such individual differences could give rise to opposing preferences among delayed outcomes.

9.2.3   What Will It Be Worth to Me?

Even if the magnitude of a future outcome is known, people making an intertemporal choice might still face *utility uncertainty*—that is, uncertainty about how much utility, or personal pleasure, they will derive from the outcome (Loomes, Orr, & Sudgen, 2009). For example, an immediate reward of €100 can mean an enjoyable lunch for two at that new farm-to-table restaurant or a happy afternoon with the family at a local music festival— but years of inflation could reduce the same €100 to the value of a mediocre buffet meal or a pair of movie tickets. A person's social and economic status may also change over time, turning an exciting outcome such as an annual salary of €100,000 into something less impressive several years later. On an emotional level, most people would find it painful to have to wait for a desirable future outcome, but only a rare few could anticipate precisely how painful the waiting process will actually be; people may also overestimate the emotional impact of a future outcome (error in affective forecasting; e.g., T. D. Wilson & Gilbert, 2003) or wrongly estimate its experienced utility (e.g., Kahneman & Thaler, 2006). All these factors make it difficult to evaluate a future outcome, and might thus influence an intertemporal decision. An important topic for future research will be to test whether adaptive responses to utility uncertainty are actually at the root of behaviors such as the failure to delay gratification.

9.2.4   How Long Will I Have to Wait?

All the types of uncertainty we have considered so far refer to the future outcome of an option. But the length of delay until an expected outcome is realized can also be uncertain. As a result, people do not generally know *when* future outcomes will materialize (McGuire & Kable, 2013). This type of uncertainty is usually referred to as temporal uncertainty (as opposed to outcome uncertainty). One way of dealing with temporal uncertainty is to update one's beliefs about the possible delays as time passes without

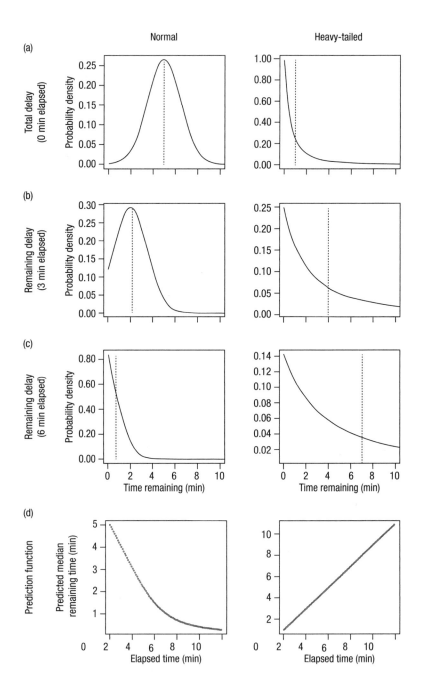

the anticipated outcome materializing (instead of one's beliefs about the hazard rate under outcome uncertainty). This updating process might lead an individual to switch from preferring a larger payoff with an uncertain delay to preferring a smaller payoff that has been available all along (McGuire & Kable, 2012, 2013). This possibility provides a new perspective on Mischel's Marshmallow Test, where, as we highlighted above, the actual delay of the later reward is usually unknown to the decision maker. If the children decide whether to eat their treat based on their beliefs about possible delays, individual differences in how long they are willing to wait could be due to differences in these beliefs. For example, if an initial belief about possible delays follows a normal distribution, the predicted median remaining waiting time will decrease as time passes (see left column of figure 9.2). As a consequence, the larger-but-later option becomes even more attractive than the immediately available option, making it quite reasonable for the decision maker to continue waiting. In comparison, if an initial belief about possible delays follows a heavy-tailed distribution (e.g., a generalized Pareto distribution; see right column of figure 9.2), where long delays are probable, the updated median waiting time increases as time passes. In this case, the preference should shift toward the always-available option, even though this entails revoking the initial decision. To experience these different types of delays firsthand, see interactive element 9.1 (at https://taming-uncertainty .mpib-berlin.mpg.de/). The type of adjustment people actually rely on might thus depend on the features of the environment and what people know about these features.

These insights about ways to deal with temporal uncertainty suggest yet another interpretation of behavior in the Marshmallow Test. Whereas the finding that children often prefer the single, immediate marshmallow is

Figure 9.2
Updating the predicted remaining delay assuming an initial belief with normally distributed total delays (left column) and a heavy-tailed distribution of total delays (right column). (a) The initial belief distribution (normal distribution with a mean of 5 minutes and a standard deviation of 1.5 minutes). (b, c) The distributions of remaining time after 3 and 6 minutes have passed. The dashed lines in (a), (b), and (c) show the median remaining times when 0, 3, and 6 minutes, respectively, have elapsed. (d) The prediction function, expressing the relationship between elapsed time and median remaining time. As time passes, the median predicted remaining time decreases when assuming an initial belief with normally distributed total delays, and increases when assuming a heavy-tailed distribution of total delays.

often attributed to their limited self-control, it may in fact reflect an adaptive response to temporal uncertainty (McGuire & Kable, 2012, 2013). It is possible that children who have waited for a while in vain for the experimenter to come back make the reasonable inference that it will be a very long time until they get the larger reward. By extension, rather than reflecting a developing capacity of self-control, children's increased willingness to wait may be due to them accumulating experience and developing increasingly certain beliefs about possible delay lengths in the world (see also chapter 16).

9.3   Intertemporal Decisions under Temporal Uncertainty: A Description–Experience Gap?

Even in situations where the delay of an intertemporal option cannot be predicted with certainty, it is rarely the case that nothing at all is known about the delay. For instance, the probabilities of different possible, mutually exclusive delays may be—at least approximately—known. This situation is known as *timing risk*. In a study on intertemporal choice under timing risk, Onay and Öncüler (2007) asked participants to choose between a *timing lottery* with two possible delays whose probabilities were known (e.g., receiving 160 Turkish lira either in one month with a probability of .2, or in 11 months with a probability of .8) and a *sure-timing* option, where the timescale was set (e.g., receiving 160 Turkish lira in nine months). Both options offered the same hypothetical payoff, and the expected delay of the timing lottery (i.e., the average delay, with each delay being weighted by its probability) was equal to the delay of the sure-timing option. Most delay discounting models, including the discounted utility model and the hyperbolic discounting model, assume a convex discount function, leading them to predict that the discounted expected utility of the timing lottery is generally higher than that of the sure-timing option and that the timing lottery should therefore be chosen.

Onay and Öncüler (2007) found that actual choices deviated systematically from this prediction. People tended to choose the timing lottery when the shorter delay in the lottery option was less probable than the longer delay (thus suggesting risk seeking). When the shorter delay was more probable than the longer delay, however, people tended to choose the sure-timing option (thus suggesting risk aversion). One way to account for this choice pattern is to assume that the probabilities of the delays are not treated at face value but instead impact the evaluation of an option in a nonlinear fashion—specifically, consistent with an inverse S-shaped weighting function (which is typically also found in risky choice with stated probabilities; e.g., Tversky & Kahneman, 1992). This function implies that rare delays are overweighted—they have more psychological impact than they deserve given their objective probabilities (see chapter 8).

In the Onay and Öncüler (2007) study and other studies on timing risk, the possible delays and the probabilities of those delays occurring were clearly described. Outside the lab, however, such convenient descriptions are rare. As we have mentioned in the previous section, one possible recourse is for people to draw on their own beliefs about the possible delays. Another possibility is to draw on past experience with the options. This raises the question of whether a description–experience gap like that observed in risky choice also arises in intertemporal choice (see chapters 7 and 8). If so, do factors similar to those that play a role in risky choice, such as sampling error, also operate in this context? To investigate this question, we compared intertemporal choices with timing risk, in which each possible delay and its probability of occurrence is provided as a description, with intertemporal choices with *timing uncertainty*, in which possible delays and/or their probabilities of occurrence must be learned from experience and are thus at best vaguely known (Dai, Pachur, Pleskac, & Hertwig, 2018). The design of our study was similar to that in Onay and Öncüler, but with an added experience-based condition. In this condition, people learned about the possible delays of the outcomes as well as their probabilities from sequential experiential sampling—as in research on risky choice using the sampling paradigm (e.g., Hertwig & Erev, 2009; see chapter 7). The sure-timing option always entailed the same delay (e.g., 6 months), whereas the delays in the timing lottery could vary from sample to sample (e.g., 1 vs. 11 months), depending on their probability.

Figure 9.3 shows the proportion of choices of the sure-timing option, separated according to whether the rare delay was longer (i.e., unattractive) or shorter (i.e., attractive), and according to whether the condition was experience-based (timing uncertainty) or description-based (timing risk). As can be seen, there was indeed a gap between the timing risk and timing uncertainty conditions. When a rare delay was relatively long (i.e., 11 months with a probability of .1), people preferred the sure-timing option over the

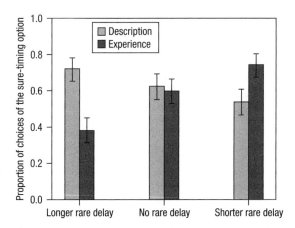

Figure 9.3

A description–experience gap in intertemporal choice. Bars show the observed choice proportions and error bars indicate 95% confidence intervals (recreated from Dai et al., 2018).

timing lottery more frequently in description than in experience. When a rare delay was relatively short (i.e., 1 month with a probability of .2), people instead preferred the sure-timing option more frequently in experience than in description. When the possible delays in the timing lottery were equally probable (and there was thus no rare event), there was no difference between the two conditions in the probability of choosing the sure-timing option. Further analyses suggested that sampling error in the experience-based condition contributed to the gap, but that difference in probability weighting (based on the experienced probabilities) also made a contribution.

9.4   Does Experiencing a Delay Always Reduce Uncertainty?

In our study (Dai et al., 2018), we implemented an experiential mode of learning to induce uncertainty about the options and to contrast this situation to a situation involving risk. Experience can, however, also decrease uncertainty. For instance, a customer deciding whether to order items using an online store's regular delivery service or to opt in for the premium, express service (at a surcharge) could order a few items with the regular service and experience how unpleasant it actually is to wait for three days (rather than just one). In this case, it is the delay length itself that is experienced. People may have a vague idea of how painful it will be to wait for a desirable outcome when the delay information is merely described, but actually experiencing the waiting period might result in a more accurate understanding of the pain involved. This in turn would render the underlying preference more consistent than in cases where the delay has not been experienced (for an initial study on how these experiences impact intertemporal choice, see Jimura, Myerson, Hilgard, Braver, & Green, 2009). The same principle applies to experiencing the actual outcome—having encountered an outcome firsthand, an individual may be able to make a more confident decision. On the other hand, experiencing a delay instead of learning it from description may also introduce perceptual uncertainty, because the objective delay length can only be estimated from experience. There are thus many ways in which experience might impact intertemporal choice, and exploring and disentangling the various influences will be an illuminating task for future research.

9.5 Conclusion

In an uncertain world, decisions about the future are inherently characterized by a lack of foreseeability—in terms of whether the expected outcome will ever actually materialize, how attractive that outcome really is, and how dreadful the waiting time will be. Nevertheless, empirical studies and theoretical work on intertemporal choice have only just begun to recognize the potentially critical role that uncertainty plays in shaping people's choices about future outcomes. Adopting such a perspective may lead to a very different interpretation of the hallmarks of intertemporal choice: what may appear irrational in a fully foreseeable and reliable world could actually represent adaptive behavior under uncertainty. This possibility calls for a shift in the science of intertemporal decision making, one that embraces the uncertainty inherent in the intertemporal choices people make. Such a paradigmatic reorientation may not yield all the answers immediately, but those answers may well be worth waiting for.

10 Experiences and Descriptions of Financial Uncertainty: Are They Equivalent?

Tomás Lejarraga, Jan K. Woike, and Ralph Hertwig

No one can possibly have lived through the Great Depression without being scarred by it.... No "Depression baby" can ever be a yuppie. No amount of experience since the Depression can convince someone who has lived through it that the world is safe economically. One constantly waits for banks to close, for factories to shut down, for the pink slip of discharge.

—Isaac Asimov, *I, Asimov: A Memoir*

10.1 Once Bitten, Twice Shy

In his memoir, science fiction writer Isaac Asimov described the hardships of growing up in Brooklyn during the Great Depression of the 1930s: the uncertainty, the fear, the pessimism. The effects of the crisis were devastating. Unemployment almost tripled in just three years, from 8.7% in 1930 to 25% in 1933. Half of the nation's banks failed due to customers defaulting on their obligations and withdrawing their savings in frantic bank runs. Many households lost everything. Countless families were forced to migrate to regions with better prospects, such as California, in an exodus unprecedented in the history of the United States. The Great Depression left an indelible mark on a generation of Americans that would become visible only decades later, as the economy recovered. Many, like Asimov, believe that growing up in economic hardship produces "Depression babies," who are pessimistic about the vagaries of the economy and unwilling to take economic risks. And their intuitions have recently gained scientific support. Using data spanning almost five decades from the Survey of Consumer Finances, Malmendier and Nagel (2011) found that people who have experienced economic shocks such as the Great Depression are indeed more averse to uncertainty. They are less likely to invest in the stock market and, if they do, they invest a lower proportion of their assets in stocks, favoring safer options. The more recent the experience of a shock, the more averse they are to uncertainty.

Financial concerns profoundly influence many important life decisions: the choice of career, place of residence, and even life partner are, to some extent, influenced by how people cope with financial uncertainty. How does experiencing a financial shock influence the perception of financial uncertainty? Is it possible to teach people about living with financial uncertainty before they are forced to learn from experience? In 2008, the world suffered the worst economic shock since the Great Depression. Again, major investment and savings banks went bankrupt and people around the globe lost their life savings. In the United States alone, households are estimated to have lost 11 trillion dollars, and 5.5 million people lost their jobs. Will this recession have a similar impact on millennials' risk taking as the Great Depression had on that of Depression babies? Although it is too early to draw definitive conclusions, financial analysts are already seeing signs that young adults who began investing in the last decade have much in common with Depression babies: "Millennials are really risk averse" (Russolillo, 2014).

Massive economic shocks are arguably exceptions to the normal functioning of the markets. Ignoring these rare events allows financial theorists to work with parsimonious and—some would argue—dangerously simplistic models of the markets (e.g., Taleb, 2007) and their actors. Traditional financial theory assumes that investors have stable risk attitudes and that they update their beliefs rationally (see also chapter 17). From this perspective, as long as wealth and income are kept constant, personally experiencing financial outcomes should be no different from learning about them from any other source of information, such as a newspaper. These assumptions, reasonable in stable markets, cannot accommodate the changes in risk attitudes that result from experiencing a financial shock. But experts are starting to believe that financial crises have become more frequent (Elliott & Milner, 2001), and acknowledging their impact is currently one of the key concerns for financial economists.

10.2 Does a Description of a Financial Shock "Burn" as Severely as the Experience of It?

Mark Twain's (1894/2004) fictional character Pudd'nhead Wilson recounts the story of a cat sitting on a hot stove, getting burned, and never sitting on a stove again. The story teaches an important lesson about coping with uncertainty: by avoiding all stoves, the cat never got burned again. But it forever forfeited the comfort of a warm stove on a cold winter morning. Much like Depression babies, who avoid the stock market after getting "burned," humans and other animals exhibit the "hot stove effect" (Denrell & March, 2001): after an unexpected negative experience, they avoid the source of the uncertainty altogether.

Humans are practically alone in their ability to learn by means other than experience. Barely any aspect of modern life—from science, commerce, and the World Wide Web to fiction and poetry—would be conceivable without the human ability to produce and interpret symbolic descriptions (Schmandt-Besserat, 1996). Individuals are able to communicate and transmit their experiences to others through descriptions such as statistics, graphs, and texts. For example, later generations can learn about the Great Depression through tables of statistics, graphical representations of dramatic slumps in stock prices, or literary accounts that recreate the experiences of those who suffered. In John Steinbeck's (1939/2014) novel *The Grapes of Wrath*, a family of farmworkers migrates from Oklahoma to California—only to find that the conditions there are even worse than those they left behind. *The Grapes of Wrath* describes what Depression babies lived through in narrative form. But do descriptions of a crisis teach the same lessons about financial uncertainty as does actually experiencing a crisis?

To address this question, we (Lejarraga, Woike, & Hertwig, 2016) created a financial crisis in the laboratory and observed how people reacted to it. Clearly, unlike the Great Depression, our "experimental crisis" did not impact every dimension of investors' lives—but it potentially slashed the value of their portfolio by more than half. Our investors were given an experimental portfolio of €100 and asked to split this amount between a risky and a safe option across a number of monthly periods. The safe option was a cash deposit account offering a 0.25% rate of return each month (i.e., a 3% annual rate of return). The risky option was the Spanish stock market index, IBEX 35, offering the actual monthly rates of return obtained from

July 1999 to September 2013. Between 1999 and 2013, the IBEX 35 experienced two shocks—the first from 1999 to 2002 (resulting in a 57% drop in stock price); the second, from late 2007 to 2009 (resulting in a 52% drop in stock price). At the end of the experiment, investors earned an amount corresponding to the value of their respective portfolios.

For each monthly period, investors stipulated the proportion of their portfolio to be invested in stocks (i.e., the index fund); the rest was invested in a safe cash deposit account. The return on their investment was added to (or subtracted from) their current portfolio balance. Feedback on returns was given in a table (amounts earned from stocks and from the cash deposit account) and in three graphs. One graph showed the current and historical prices of the index fund during the experimental investment period. A second graph showed past and present rates of return on the index fund, the cash deposit account, and the portfolio. A third graph showed the development of the portfolio. The three graphs were updated after each investment.

The central feature of our investigation was that some investors "lived through a crisis," namely, they started making virtual investments before the 2000 dot-com crisis, whereas others learned about a crisis from descriptions. Our descriptions were not narratives like *The Grapes of Wrath*. Rather, investors learned about a past crisis by inspecting a graph—that is, they were informed in the same way as real-world investors are typically informed by banks, financial consultants, or online services. Another set of investors entered the investment game after the first crisis and without knowledge of it; here again, some investors learned from description and others from experience. Figure 10.1a describes the four conditions, overlaid on the evolution of the IBEX 35: solid lines indicate periods of investment and dotted lines indicate periods in which investors learned from descriptive sources (graphs and table). Box 10.1 gives the details of the experimental design. To experience being an investor in the market, please access interactive elements 10.1 and 10.2 (at https://taming-uncertainty.mpib-berlin.mpg.de/).

10.3 Do Descriptions and Experience Steer Investors toward the Same Investment Behavior?

We evaluated investors' behavior during a long evaluation window (72 investments, see figure 10.1). To this end, we defined the measure of risk taking R as the proportion of a person's assets invested in stocks (vs. in

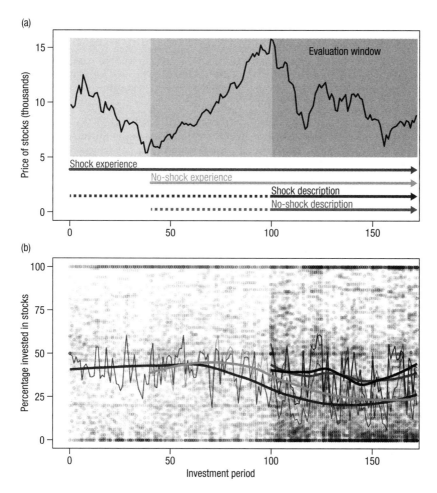

Figure 10.1

(a) Experimental conditions and price of stocks in thousands of euros (i.e., index fund) across 172 monthly periods. Solid arrow segments indicate periods of investment. Dotted arrow segments indicate periods of learning from descriptive sources. The four conditions were compared over the evaluation window from period 100 to period 172. (b) Percentage invested in stocks by condition. Dots indicate individuals' allocations. The thin lines show the mean percentages; the thicker lines show the data smoothed by local polynomial regression fitting. (Based on Lejarraga et al., 2016)

Box 10.1

Experimental market and investment decisions.

Two hundred investors (40% male, mean age 25 years, $SD = 3.5$ years) were randomly assigned to one of four conditions that varied with respect to the length of historical data available and the mode of learning (see figure 10.1a for a summary of the four conditions). The 50 investors in the *shock experience* condition made investments in all 172 periods of the experiment (i.e., the 172 months between July 1999 and September 2013). These investors experienced a stock market that initially fell until about period 40. The 50 investors in the *no-shock experience* condition entered the market in period 40 and made decisions in 133 periods. These investors experienced a market that initially rose for around 60 periods; they were unaware of the previous downward trend.

The remaining 100 investors entered the market in period 100 and made 73 investment decisions. Of these investors, the 50 in the *shock description* condition were shown a graph plotting the price of the index fund since period 1. These investors thus learned from the graph what investors in the shock experience condition learned from experience (i.e., the development of the index fund across periods 1–99). The 50 investors in the *no-shock description* condition were shown a graph plotting the price of the index fund since period 40. Like their counterparts in the no-shock experience condition, they remained unaware of the market's initial downward trend, but they learned about the later upward trend—in this case, from the graph. Investors were not told in advance how many decisions they would make. They were paid according to the value of their portfolio at the end of the investment task.

Interactive element 10.1 allows you to experiment with a simplified version of the interface used by investors. Investors made their investment decisions by manipulating sliders in the upper right of the screen. Graphs and a table in the bottom panel provided information on the development of the stock index, the period-by-period return on each amount invested in stocks and in cash deposit, as well as the return on the whole portfolio. Investors first read the instructions on the computer screen and completed 10 periods as practice trials. They were informed that the return data in the practice trials were randomly generated. They were also given a printed booklet of instructions (including definitions of all concepts involved in the investment task) that they could consult at any time. The return data in the experimental trials reflected the actual returns on the IBEX 35, but the dates were shifted 25 years into the future to prevent investors from using historical knowledge to predict stock movements.

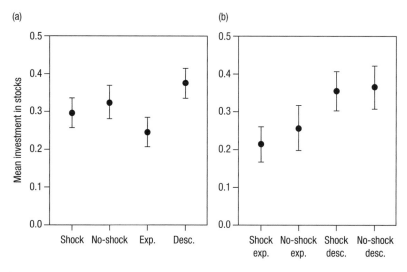

Figure 10.2
Mean investment in stocks (a) by mode of learning (experience, description) and by the experience of a shock or lack thereof; and (b) for the resulting four conditions (shock experience, no-shock experience, shock description, no-shock description). Error bars indicate the 95% confidence interval (CI). Means and confidence intervals were calculated by averaging risk taking for each individual across periods and computing the mean across individuals (i.e., means and CIs reflect independent observations).

the cash deposit account). Lower values of R indicate avoidance of financial uncertainty. Figure 10.1b shows the average trends for each condition; figure 10.2 shows the average R (collapsed across periods). Descriptions and experience were very clearly not equivalent forms of learning about a shock. Investors who experienced the shock (shock experience condition, $R_{se}=22\%$) were much more uncertainty-avoidant than those who learned about it from a graph (shock description condition, $R_{sd}=37\%$), taking 15% less risk. These results indicate that experiencing a market shock indeed makes people shy away from financial uncertainty in a way that exposure to a graphical description of that same shock does not. This result represents an experimental demonstration of the Depression baby effect (Malmendier & Nagel, 2011).

The asymmetry between learning from experience and learning from description goes beyond financial shocks. In fact, a description–experience gap emerged even without experience of a shock. Investors who experienced a shock-free market (no-shock experience, $R_{nse} = 27\%$) were also more uncertainty-avoidant than those who learned about the same market from a graph (no-shock description, $R_{nsd} = 38\%$), taking 11% less risk. Averaged across the shock and no-shock conditions, investors who learned from a graph took 13% more risk ($R_d = 38\%$) than did investors who experienced the market firsthand ($R_e = 25\%$). Moreover, those who learned about past market performance from a graph proved practically insensitive to the type of market history observed.

10.4   Do Recent Experiences Have More Influence on Uncertainty Avoidance than Less Recent Ones?

As figure 10.1b shows, the percentage invested in stocks in the four conditions (i.e., the thin lines) was highly volatile across periods. To determine the extent to which investors reacted to the most recent change in stock prices in each period, we calculated the individual-specific correlation between the change in price of the index fund (stock price$_t$/stock price$_{t-1}$) and the change in investment in the following period (proportion in stock$_{t+1}$ − proportion in stock$_t$). This measure of reactivity is likely to underestimate the strength of the relationship, because the proportion invested in the index fund is bounded between 0 and 1, and an investor who is fully invested in stocks cannot increase the level of risk taking following an increase in stock prices. Across all investors, the mean correlation was 0.29, with little variation across conditions. Our analysis thus shows reactivity to recent changes in both description and experience, consistent with previous findings (Funk, Rapoport, & Jones, 1979; Gordon, Paradis, & Rorke, 1972; Kroll, Levy, & Rapoport, 1988; Rapoport, 1984) suggesting that people react to price changes in an attempt to capture the momentum of the market. Although the experimental design presented here compares the behavior of investors with different levels of wealth (investors who enter the market after the shock start with $100, whereas the endowments of those who experience it reflect the effects of the shock), a subsequent experiment (see study 3 in Lejarraga et al., 2016) showed that the effects described here persisted when wealth was set to be equal across conditions.

10.5   How Do People Navigate Financial Uncertainty?

Uncertainty comes in many shades. Just one of the many ways in which uncertain situations vary is in the degree to which they defy predictability. Take a train's time of arrival at a station. Although the exact time of arrival is unknown, it generally falls within a certain range. Commuters who catch the train every day will have a good idea of its punctuality and should be able to plan ahead. There is some predictability in this sort of uncertainty. On the other hand, there are singular, rare events that cannot be quantified easily. Take, for example, the deadly hurricane-strength winds of Storm Friederike that ripped through northern Europe in January 2018, causing the German rail operator Deutsche Bahn to suspend all long-distance trains nationwide for the first time since 2007. Trains were not late—they simply never left the station. This kind of uncertainty is extremely hard to plan for; it is difficult even to have a sense of the class of events that could arise. There is no predictability in this sort of uncertainty.[1]

Financial markets involve both types of uncertainty, yet financial "storms" tend to be ignored in standard theories of portfolio choice. The prime example is Markowitz's (1952) mean-variance optimization model which, like other optimization models, assumes a world of uncertainty with predictable bounds. This is an important limitation, inasmuch as it can make simple rules better suited for making investment decisions than complicated calculations of mean variance. DeMiguel, Garlappi, and Uppal (2009) studied perhaps the simplest heuristic for dealing with financial uncertainty. The $1/N$ heuristic, also known as "naive diversification," consists of dividing one's budget equally across all investment options (Benartzi & Thaler, 2001). They took a normative approach, examining how well this heuristic performed against several complex instantiations of the mean-variance model and other asset allocation models of optimization. The simple and complex allocation strategies were evaluated, among other

---

1. Makridakis, Hogarth, and Gaba (2009) have referred to these two types of uncertainty as "subway" and "coconut" uncertainty, respectively. The former relates to uncertain but predictable events such as the arrival time of a subway train at the station; the latter refers to singular, unpredictable events, such as a coconut falling on one's head. Similarly, in *Fooled by Randomness*, Taleb (2007) refers to rare events of extreme impact as "black swans" and emphasizes their unpredictability.

benchmarks, in terms of their performance on the Sharpe ratio, a measure of return adjusted for risk, across six datasets. For example, in the S&P 500 dataset, the simple 1/*N* heuristic had the highest Sharpe ratio across all strategies, substantially higher than the mean-variance model. In fact, the mean-variance model did not significantly outperform the 1/*N* heuristic in any of the datasets. Other research has corroborated this finding (Jacobs, Müller, & Weber, 2014; Tu & Zhou, 2011).

Whether heuristics represent good investment strategies is one question; whether people actually use them is another. Although there has been some work on the first question, little is known about the second. Our experimental design provides some answers. We first looked closely at individual investment paths; figure 10.3 gives an idea of the dramatic individual variation we found. We next defined nine simple investment strategies and examined their prevalence in our experiment (see section 10.5.1 and table 10.1

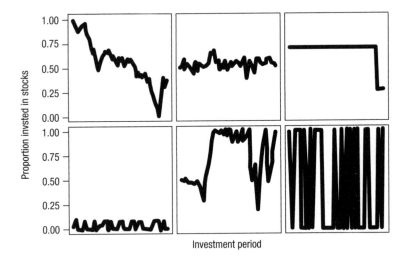

Figure 10.3
Proportion invested in stocks by six individuals in each trial of the evaluation window. These investment paths illustrate the individual variation in the data collected, and helped us to infer the strategies that people used. For example, the investor in the upper right panel was unreactive to price changes in most periods. The investor in the lower left panel took low to no risk throughout, and showed little to no reaction to the market. The investor in the lower right panel did not diversify their portfolio, as the proportion invested in stocks fluctuated from 0 to 1, possibly in response to price changes.

Table 10.1
Definition of investment strategies according to four criteria.

	Mean	*SD*	Trend	Correlation
*Strategies **unreactive** to stock price fluctuations*				
Naive diversification (1/*N*)	[0.4, 0.6]	<0.1	[0.1, −0.1]	ns
Constant risky	>0.8	<0.1	[0.1, −0.1]	ns
Constant safe	<0.2	<0.1	[0.1, −0.1]	ns
Nondiversified		>0.4		ns
*Strategies **reactive** to stock price fluctuations*				
Momentum				
Nondiversified		>0.4		s (+)
Diversified	[0.2, 0.8]	<0.4		s (+)
Risky	>0.8			s (+)
Safe	<0.2			s (+)
Contrarian				s (−)

Note: ns denotes nonsignificant correlations (with *N*=73, *r*<.31), s (+) denotes significant positive correlations, and s (−) denotes significant negative correlations.

for a definition of each strategy). Some of these strategies have been studied previously (e.g., naive diversification, momentum, and contrarian strategies); others we inferred from the investment paths observed in our data. We classified the strategies as either reactive or unreactive to changes in stock prices.

10.5.1   Strategies Unreactive to Fluctuations in Stock Price
Naive diversification (1/*N* heuristic). Investors using the naive diversification strategy divide their budget evenly among the *N* options available (Benartzi & Thaler, 2001). This strategy does not depend on the attractiveness of the options; it is not susceptible to the fluctuations of the market. In our setup, naive diversification means consistently investing 50% of one's budget in stocks.

    Constant-target strategy. Investors using the constant-target strategy select a target level of risk taking in the first investment period (in our experiment, measured in terms of a specific proportion invested in the index fund, e.g., 30% or 80%) and maintain this target throughout. We distinguish two types of the constant-target strategy, depending on the level of risk taken: constant risky (>80%) and constant safe (<20%).

Nondiversified strategy. Investors using this strategy put all of their eggs in one basket—in our experiment, either the "risk" basket (100% index fund) or the "safe" basket (100% cash deposit account).

10.5.2 Strategies Reactive to Fluctuations in Stock Price

Momentum strategies. Investors using momentum strategies continuously adjust their allocations as a function of market changes. Specifically, in period t they increase allocations in the options that increased in price in period $t-1$ (Grinblatt, Titman, & Wermers, 1995). In our setup, momentum strategies imply increasing the investment in stocks after an increase in stock prices, and decreasing the investment after a decrease in price. We distinguish four types of momentum strategies: Using *momentum-nondiversified* strategies means putting the total budget in stocks following a rise in prices and moving the total budget out of stocks following a drop. *Momentum-diversified* strategies are more moderate, and follow stock fluctuations in a proportional manner. *Momentum-risky* and *momentum-safe* strategies respond to changes in stock prices, but adopt different levels of risk: momentum risky entails that more than 80% of the portfolio is invested in the index fund across all periods, and momentum safe denotes that less than 20% of the portfolio is invested in the index fund.

Contrarian strategies. Investors using contrarian strategies reduce their investment in stocks in period t after a price increase in period $t-1$, and increase their investment in stocks after a price drop (Gregory, Harris, & Michou, 2001).

Participants were classified as using a strategy only if all conditions in table 10.1 were met. About 31% of investors were left unclassified. As reported in table 10.2, a substantial proportion of investors (61%) were identified as using momentum strategies—that is, they increased the proportion invested in stocks after a price rise and reduced it after a drop. Two types of momentum strategies were predominant: investors who tracked the stock price while taking generally low risks (27%, momentum safe), and investors who followed stock fluctuations in a proportional manner (27%, momentum diversified). A minority of investors seemed to be unreactive to changes in the stock price, with 2% using naive diversification (roughly a 50/50 split) and 4% using constant-safe strategies. Our classification suggests that the investment strategies used appear not to depend on the mode of learning. Importantly, however, the mode of learning can shift

Table 10.2
Number of investors classified to each investment strategy.

	N	Percentage
*Strategies **unreactive** to stock price fluctuations*	16	8
Naive diversification ($1/N$)	4	2
Constant risky	1	1
Constant safe	8	4
Nondiversified	3	2
*Strategies **reactive** to stock price fluctuations*	122	61
Momentum		
Nondiversified	13	7
Diversified	54	27
Risky	2	1
Safe	53	27
Contrarian	0	0
Unclassified	62	31
Total	200	100

users of a strategy toward more or less risk seeking. For instance, a large proportion of investors relied on momentum strategies, whether they learned from experience or from description. However, more investors employed a momentum-safe strategy (with a lower level of risk) in the experience condition than in the description condition, again indicating that investors who learn from experience prefer less exposure to risk. The levels of risk taking following a shock also differed: more investors adopted safe strategies (constant-safe strategy and momentum strategy) in the shock than in the no-shock condition.

10.6 Can Experience Be Harnessed to Help People Navigate Financial Uncertainty?

Our results show that there is no substitute for experience. But if descriptions are not an adequate tool for warning investors about the possibility of future crises, one possibility is to "create" experiences. Kaufmann, Weber, and Haisley (2013) allowed experimental investors to "try out" as many allocations as they wanted before deciding on a final allocation. Investors were provided with immediate feedback on the risk–return profile of each simulation (try the simulation tool yourself by accessing interactive element 10.2). Kaufmann et al. found that people felt more knowledgeable and better informed when they were allowed to experience the allocations they were considering. As a result, they took more financial risk and their investments were closer to what would be expected on the basis of an optimal investment model. On the face of it, these results seem to contradict our findings—which indicate that experience leads to less risk taking. But Kaufmann et al. had a different goal. Their intention was to devise a way to make investors aware of the various possible outcomes of their investments. Simulating experience of a wide range of outcomes allows investors to evaluate their investments prospectively and at no cost. This approach seems to boost investors' knowledge and confidence in their choices, resulting in more risk taking. In our study, investors did not have the luxury of simulated experience of potential investments; they had to experience the full consequences of their investments to learn—retrospectively—about the market. Bradbury, Hens, and Zeisberger (2014) also found that simulated experience helps people to understand financial uncertainty better, to improve their decisions, and to avoid regret.

The power of simulated experience is enormous (see Hertwig, Hogarth, & Lejarraga, 2018, for a conceptual discussion of experience). Professionals learning to deal with complex situations also use simulations when real experience is costly and dangerous. Training aircraft pilots, for example, relies heavily on simulation. Some universities use simulated hospitals to teach medical students about the surgical procedures to be followed in operations or to teach them how to break bad news. Mistakes made in the context of piloting airplanes or performing heart surgery can clearly be costly. But so can mistakes made by those investing under financial uncertainty. Whereas simulations for pilots and surgeons help them to acquire motor and procedural skills, the crucial factor in the investment case is the simulation of uncertainty: investors need to experience the range of possible outcomes and the potential frequencies of their occurrence. When events are frequent, they need to experience that frequency; when events are rare, their scarcity must be felt. Financial simulations can also recreate collapsing markets for those "Boom babies" who fail to acknowledge the risks lurking in the fog of financial uncertainty.

Research is beginning to reveal some of the many practical implications of simulating financial uncertainty. The European Council Directive 2004/39/EC on markets in financial instruments (European Parliament and European Council, 2004) requires banks and other financial institutions to assess the degree of uncertainty that their clients are willing to accept. Our experimental results suggest that the willingness to be exposed to financial uncertainty differs dramatically depending on whether investors have learned about the uncertainty from description or from experience. Moreover, it is highly dependent on the outcomes experienced (e.g., booms or busts). Financial institutions currently use Likert scales to assess their customers' risk attitudes using a simple description-based approach. The benefits of providing customers with simulated experience of the financial markets and only then assessing their risk attitude could be enormous for them and society. Isaac Asimov described the crippling effects of traumatic experience—it is time to explore its empowering effects.

11 Ways to Learn from Experience

Thorsten Pachur and Dries Trippas

11.1 Traces of Experience: Rules and Exemplars

On June 14, 2017, a fire ripped through Grenfell Tower in North Kensington, London, killing 59 people. In a later interview (Khomami, 2017), Pat Goulbourne, one of the chief firefighters at the scene, said: "As I was approaching it, I just knew we had probably the job of our lives on the go because already I could see fire from the lower floors and I couldn't believe I was looking at fire to the top floor. I've never seen anything like that, ever. The fire was changing, it was moving rapidly." Despite the severity of the fire, the firefighters managed to save 255 people from the flames. It was a daunting task. The stakes were high, every minute counted, and the situation was fraught with uncertainty. Not only was the fire different from anything the firefighters had encountered during their training or in previous incidents, they originally had little information about the situation—the origin of the fire, the stability of the building structure, and the number of people in it.

How do firefighters—and decision makers faced with novel situations more generally—make decisions under uncertainty? Although history never repeats itself perfectly, previous experience in other relevant situations is one way of reducing uncertainty. As we highlight in this chapter, there are qualitatively different ways in which experience—such as knowledge of previous fires, their characteristics, and outcomes—can be used to inform subsequent decisions. Let us consider the following fictional firefighter scenario (inspired by Klein, 1999). Arriving at the scene of a house on fire, the chief firefighter needs to decide whether the crew should attempt to extinguish the fire or let it burn out, focusing instead on evacuating the building. One way to make this decision would be to consider the features of the situation—indications that people are trapped in the building, the distance to other buildings, and when the building was built, for example—and to apply a decision rule that combines these features. For instance, the chief firefighter might know from experience that fires in taller buildings tend to be more difficult to extinguish and that fires in dense areas are more likely to spread, but also that the age of a building is less predictive of the outcome. Using a rule that combines these indicators, the chief might decide to order the crew to extinguish a fire in a one-story building with no neighboring properties, but to let a fire in a tall building in a built-up area burn out. Another, quite different, way of making a decision would be to retrieve specific previous incidents from memory. For instance, the present situation might remind the chief of an incident that resulted in a catastrophic explosion. Based on this and other similar memories, the chief might decide to order to extinguish a fire in a tall building in a built-up area.

These two approaches to making a decision, which differ in how they make use of previous experience, illustrate two classes of strategies that have been shown to be important mental tools in decision making under uncertainty. In *rule-based* strategies (e.g., Hammond, 1955; Smedslund, 1955), previous experience is used to abstract general relationships between cues (e.g., the size of a burning building, the color of the flames) and the relevant criterion (e.g., the difficulty of extinguishing a fire). Based on these abstracted relationships, a rule is derived specifying how to weight and combine the cues. In the second approach, known as *exemplar-based* strategies (Medin & Schaffer, 1978; Nosofsky, 1984), previously experienced episodes serve as exemplars. These episodes and their outcomes directly inform the decision (rather than being summarized in the form of an abstracted relationship, as in rule-based strategies), with more weight being given to the outcomes of episodes that are more similar to the current scenario than to less similar ones.[1]

---

1. In their analyses of firefighters' decision-making strategies, Klein and colleagues (e.g., Klein, Calderwood, & Clinton-Cirocco, 2010) found that many decisions were made by matching the current situation to a prototype that "summarizes the general features of situations along with some specific details where relevant" (p. 203). Overall, the prototype approach described by Klein has many similarities to a rule-based strategy: both abstract general features across individual episodes. The prototype approach may also be formally identical to a rule-based strategy (e.g., H. Olsson & Poom, 2005).

We highlight the distinction between rule-based and exemplar-based strategies as two ways an adaptive mind can exploit experience to deal with uncertainty. We point to the ecological rationality of these mechanisms, explaining how each is best suited to different ecological structures. As a consequence, good decision making requires *adaptive strategy selection*, where the strategy used is matched to the structure of the environment. Reliance on rule-based versus exemplar-based strategies has been shown to be sensitive to properties of the decision task in which previous experience about the environment has been gathered. This opens up the possibility for decision architects to design learning tasks in ways that boost adaptive strategy selection. In the following, we first give an overview of research on rule-based and exemplar-based strategies and illustrate the strategies' ecological rationality. We then discuss the extent to which people's reliance on rules or exemplars is adaptive, and which factors might constrain adaptive strategy selection. After establishing that strategy selection is sensitive to subtle features of the tasks encountered during learning, we then examine how adaptive strategy selection can be boosted by tailoring the design of the learning task to the appropriate decision strategy. Finally, we discuss the relevance of the distinction between rule-based and exemplar-based task representations for decisions under risk and uncertainty.

11.2 The Ecological Rationality of Rule-Based and Exemplar-Based Strategies

An experiment by Juslin, Olsson, and Olsson (2003) illustrates how rule-based and exemplar-based strategies are studied in the lab. In an initial learning phase, participants were presented with descriptions of fictional "death bugs," each characterized by four features, such as head size and back color. The participants' task was to figure out how toxic the bugs were. Toxicity was thus the unknown *criterion*; it could be inferred from the described characteristics of the bugs (the *cues*). What participants did not initially know is that a bug's toxicity was a function of the number of indicators (i.e., positive cue values) present. Bugs with a higher number of indicators were more toxic than bugs with fewer indicators. In addition, the indicators differed in their power to predict the criterion. After each decision in the learning phase, participants were given feedback on whether or not their decision was correct and on the toxicity level of the bug. This feedback allowed participants to learn over time about the association between the bugs' characteristics and their toxicity. In a subsequent test phase, participants completed the same task, with the difference that several new bugs were now presented and feedback was no longer provided. In other words, decision makers made decisions under uncertainty but could recruit their experience from the learning phase to reduce this uncertainty. Participants' decisions on the new bugs provided insights into their ability to generalize beyond the learning material.

To investigate which strategy participants had used to make their decisions in the test phase, Juslin et al. (2003) applied several models representing rule-based and exemplar-based strategies to participants' decisions. A rule-based strategy judges the toxicity level by adding up the cue values, with each cue being weighted according to how predictive it was of a bug's toxicity level during the learning phase. An exemplar-based strategy, by contrast, compares a given target bug with the bugs encountered in the learning phase (and stored in memory), and estimates the toxicity level of the target bug to be the average toxicity level of these bugs, each weighted by its similarity to the given bug. A formal description of the respective model specifications is provided in box 11.1. Juslin et al. (2003) then determined

Box 11.1

Formal description of rule-based and exemplar-based models.

Studies investigating rule-based and exemplar-based strategies usually involve an initial learning phase, followed by a test phase. In the learning phase, participants learn to predict a criterion on the basis of a number of cues. To determine which strategy a participant used, the researchers then model the test phase data by applying a number of formal models. Measures of the models' statistical fit are compared to determine which model describes the data best while taking differences in complexity into account.

The cue-abstraction model exemplifies a common rule-based decision-making strategy (Juslin et al., 2003). The model assumes that, for a given trial and stimulus, the participant integrates the cues in a linear manner by assigning a certain weight to each and summing them up as follows:

$$y = .5\left(1 - \sum_{i=1}^{n} w_i\right) + \sum_{i=1}^{n} w_i c_i, \tag{B1}$$

where y is the estimated criterion value for the current object, w_i is the weight assigned to each of the n cues, and c_i is the value of each cue (e.g., present = 1

Box 11.1 (continued)

and absent = 0, in the case of binary cues). In the common situation where a binary response is required, this estimated criterion value y is translated into a probability of responding positively (e.g., to the question of whether or not the bug is deadly):

$$P(A) = \frac{e^y}{1+e^y}, \tag{B2}$$

where $p(A)$ is a value between 0 and 1. Finally, to apply the model to actual binary data, a Bernoulli likelihood function is assumed.

A common exemplar-based strategy is the generalized context model (Nosofsky, 1984). The model assumes that, for a given trial and object, the decision maker bases their response on the similarity, s_{pq}, between the target object p and the exemplars stored in memory, q:

$$s_{pq} = e^{-hd_{pq}}, \tag{B3}$$

where h is the generalization gradient and d_{pq} is the city-block distance between the target object p and an exemplar q, such that:

$$d_{pq} = \sum_{i=1}^{n} w_i \left| c_{pi} - c_{qi} \right|. \tag{B4}$$

The distance is a function of the absolute value of the difference between the cue values of the exemplars p and q weighted by the attention weights, w_i, assigned to each cue dimension i. The probability of a positive response is defined as:

$$P(A) = \frac{\sum_{a=1}^{A} s_{pa}}{\sum_{a=1}^{A} s_{pa} + \sum_{b=1}^{B} s_{pb}}, \tag{B5}$$

where $P(A)$ is a value between 0 and 1, the numerator is the summed similarity of the target object p to all of the memorized exemplars in category A (e.g., the deadly bugs), and the second part of the denominator is the summed similarity of the target object p to all of the memorized exemplars belonging to category B (e.g., the nondeadly bugs). As before, to fit the model to the data, a Bernoulli likelihood function is assumed.

which model described each participant's decisions best. As it turned out, there were considerable individual differences in strategy use. Critically, these differences in strategy use were associated with differences in task performance during the test phase. In particular, users of a rule-based strategy were better able to generalize—that is, they were better equipped to judge the toxicity of new bugs than were users of an exemplar-based strategy.

This was the case because rule-based and exemplar-based strategies work best in different decision environments—in other words, their ecological rationality differs. The key distinction here is between *linear* and *nonlinear* environments (which we describe in more detail shortly). Juslin et al. (2003) used a linear environment, in which rule-based strategies work best; had they used a nonlinear environment, an exemplar-based strategy would have been preferable. To illustrate this point, let us return to the example of firefighters. Indicators for the severity of a house fire include the color of the smoke, the color of the flames, and the sponginess of the roof (Klein, Calderwood, & Clinton-Cirocco, 2010). In a linear environment, a fire with only white smoke and few visible flames in a building with a solid roof is likely to be much easier to extinguish than a fire with thick black smoke and bright orange flames in a building with a spongy roof: the difficulty of extinguishing the fire follows an additive linear function of the number of indicators present. This is not the case in a nonlinear environment. For example, Klein et al. (2010) described an incident where a firefighter led his crew into a room in a burning house that seemed to be the seat of the fire. They trained their hoses on the visible flames. To gauge the danger of the situation, the firefighters assessed the number of visible flames, the change in heat in the room as they began to target the flames, and the sound of the fire. Taken individually, a reduction in each of these indicators points to an improvement in the situation: fewer flames are better than more flames, a cooling room is better than a hot one, and a quiet fire is safer than one that can be heard devouring the building. As the firefighters pumped water onto the fire, the flames disappeared and the room became quiet. But the heat was unabated; in fact, it got even worse. The commanding officer immediately ordered his crew to leave the house—just before the floor collapsed. In this example, the indicators (i.e., the cues) were linked to the level of danger (i.e., the criterion) in a nonlinear fashion, such that a quiet and cool room with no flames was the safest; a noisy and warm room with some flames was dangerous; but a hot, quiet room with no flames indicated the highest level of danger—namely, that the seat of the fire was elsewhere. In this case, it was in the basement.

Figure 11.1 illustrates linear and nonlinear environments. In a linear environment (see figure 11.1a), the criterion value increases proportionally to the number of indicators present; in a nonlinear environment (see figure 11.1b),

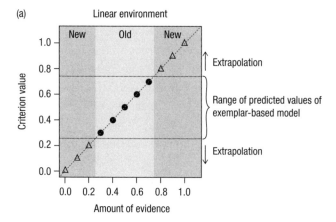

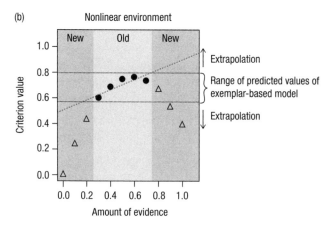

Figure 11.1

Illustration of how a linear rule (indicated by the dotted line) abstracted from a sample of "old" objects encountered during the learning phase (filled circles) is able to capture both those objects and "new" ones encountered in the test phase (open triangles) objects in two decision environments. In a linear decision environment (a), it is able to capture both types of object; in a nonlinear decision environment (b), it only approximates objects encountered in the learning phase and fails to capture new ones. To accurately judge objects that have criterion values beyond the range of criterion values of the previously encountered objects, it is necessary to be able to extrapolate. Exemplar-based models, however, are constrained to generate estimated criterion values within the range of the criterion values of the objects that have been encountered—they cannot extrapolate.

by contrast, the criterion value first increases with the number of indicators, but only up to a certain point, after which it decreases again.[2]

Rule-based and exemplar-based strategies differ in their performance in linear and nonlinear environments. A rule-based strategy simply adds up the number of indicators present and weights them by their respective predictive power. In a linear environment, this approach enables the decision maker to judge the criterion value of new objects accurately, even if they have criterion values that are more extreme (i.e., higher or lower) than those encountered during training. In other words, using a rule-based strategy allows the decision maker to *extrapolate* (DeLosh, Busemeyer, & McDaniel, 1997). This is illustrated in figure 11.1a: the linear rule (dotted line) abstracted on the basis of the objects experienced during the learning phase (the black dots) produces accurate estimates of the criterion value of new objects (the white triangles), even if it is outside the learning range. By contrast, the ability of an exemplar-based strategy to extrapolate is constrained. To understand why, consider how it generates an estimate for an object: an exemplar-based strategy retrieves previously encountered objects from memory and averages their criterion values, giving more weight to objects that are more similar to the target object than to less similar ones (Erickson & Kruschke, 1998). By mathematical necessity, an exemplar-based strategy can thus only produce estimates that are within the range of the criterion values of the previously encountered objects (see figure 11.1); it cannot extrapolate to new, more extreme objects. The underlying mathematical logic is illustrated by the example that, irrespective of how two numbers—say 3 and 5—are weighted, their average will never be lower than 3 or higher than 5.

In nonlinear environments such as the one shown in figure 11.1b, the situation is different. Let us again start with the rule-based strategy. It has been shown that people have great difficulty learning nonlinear rules (e.g., Brehmer, 1980); from this, it has been concluded that the rule-based strategies applied by the human mind are constrained to be linear additive rules (Juslin, Karlsson, & Olsson, 2008). Because a (linear) rule-based strategy predicts higher criterion values whenever the amount of evidence increases, it

---

2. Nonlinear environments are all those in which an increase in one variable (e.g., amount of evidence) is not associated with a proportional increase in the other variable; nonlinear environments therefore also include, for instance, exponential functions.

can only roughly approximate the nonmonotonic pattern in the learning phase in the nonlinear environment of figure 11.1b. Even more pronounced is the failure of the rule-based strategy to capture new objects encountered in the test phase that, despite an increasing amount of evidence, have decreasing criterion values. Exemplar-based strategies fare better in a nonlinear environment: because they do not abstract from the objects encountered during the learning phase (instead, they store all individual objects), exemplar-based strategies can perfectly represent any statistical structure encountered during learning, including the nonlinear function in figure 11.1b. Although the exemplar-based strategy cannot extrapolate and thus cannot capture the objects with a low amount of evidence criterion values in figure 11.1, the lack of extrapolation is actually a blessing for the objects encountered in the test phase that have a very high amount of evidence: these objects are captured more accurately than by the rule-based strategy. You can explore how rule-based and exemplar-based strategies extrapolate in linear and non-linear environments in interactive element 11.1 (at https://taming-uncertainty.mpib-berlin.mpg.de/).

In summary, a rule-based strategy enables good performance in a linear environment; due to the human mind's constraints in terms of representing linear additive rules, however, it will fail in a nonlinear environment. An exemplar-based strategy, in contrast, can capture objects in a nonlinear environment, but is unable to extrapolate and will therefore fail in linear environments when objects with extreme criterion values have not been encountered during training. That a rule-based strategy is best suited to a linear environment and an exemplar-based strategy to a nonlinear environment raises two questions. First, to what extent do people adaptively switch between strategies as a function of whether they are in a linear or a nonlinear environment? Second, if strategy selection proves not (or not fully) to be adaptive, how might people's selection of an appropriate strategy in a given environment be fostered?

11.3   Limitations in the Adaptive Selection of Rule-Based and Exemplar-Based Strategies

On the one hand, people's selection of rule-based and exemplar-based strategies indeed seems to follow the structure of the environment in an adaptive fashion. For example, Juslin et al. (2008) had participants perform the death bug task described in section 11.2, but in two different environments. In one environment, the bugs' features were related to their toxicity in an additive-linear fashion; in the other, the relationship was nonlinear. Analyses of the mechanisms underlying participants' decisions in a test phase following the learning phase indicated much higher reliance on an exemplar-based strategy in the nonlinear condition than in the linear condition. However, despite this evidence for adaptive strategy selection on the aggregate level, not all people decide adaptively in all circumstances. For example, Karlsson, Juslin, and Olsson (2007) asked participants to judge the effectivity of different herbs as a medical treatment for a virus. The herbs were described in terms of four features (e.g., number of weeks in bloom, amount of water emitted per leaf area). In one condition, the herb's effectiveness (expressed in terms of the amount of a fictitious chemical substance that can be extracted from it) was determined by a linear additive function of the features—an environment in which a rule-based strategy is more appropriate than an exemplar-based strategy. Although more than 80% of the participants were classified as using a rule-based strategy, around one-fifth relied on an exemplar-based strategy (see also Hoffmann, von Helversen, & Rieskamp, 2016). Conversely, A. C. Olsson, Enkvist, and Juslin (2006) presented their participants with a nonlinear, quadratic environment (similar to the one shown in figure 11.1b). Although such an environment calls for an exemplar-based strategy, most participants seemed to stubbornly rely on a (linear) rule-based strategy, even if they performed rather poorly as a result.

One reason for such limitations in the adaptive selection of rule-based and exemplar-based strategies may be that adaptivity comes at a cost to the decision maker. For instance, Bröder (2000) found that decision makers with higher intelligence scores were considerably more likely to select a strategy that matched the structure of the environment than were their counterparts with lower intelligence scores. The implementation of rule-based and exemplar-based strategies also requires specific cognitive resources. In addition to strategy use in a judgment task, Hoffmann, von Helversen, and Rieskamp (2014) measured the episodic memory and working memory capacity of participants. Their results suggest that use of an exemplar-based strategy is linked to episodic memory abilities, whereas use of a rule-based strategy hinges on working memory (see also Juslin et al., 2008). For instance, people with higher episodic memory capacity were more likely to select an exemplar-based strategy than were people with lower episodic memory capacity. Finally, adaptive strategy selection is constrained if the mental resources available in a situation are limited due to cognitive load. In studies that induced cognitive load by asking people to perform a secondary task while making decisions, participants relied less on rule-based strategies and instead shifted to exemplar-based strategies, even in environments where a rule-based strategy was more appropriate (Hoffmann, von Helversen, & Rieskamp, 2013; Juslin et al., 2008). In other words, these findings indicate that adaptive strategy selection may be limited in precisely those situations in which important decisions are made—namely, under high cognitive strain. (Just think of the firefighters!)

In sum, although in decisions under uncertainty people's use of rule-based and exemplar-based strategies generally seems to be sensitive to the structure of the environment, several factors can hamper adaptive strategy selection. First, cognitive abilities are necessary to understand which strategy matches a given environment. Second, the execution of rule-based and exemplar-based strategies taps into working memory and episodic memory, respectively. In the next section, we discuss how these limitations in adaptive strategy selection might be overcome with an unobtrusive but powerful way to steer the selection of rule-based and exemplar-based strategies. Decision architects could harness this approach to foster strategy selection in an adaptive direction.

11.4   How to Influence Strategy Selection through the Design of the Learning Task

Pachur and Olsson (2012) have identified a subtle but systematic methodological difference between studies finding that people rely predominantly on rule-based strategies (e.g., Nosofsky & Bergert, 2007) and those finding more support for the use of exemplar-based strategies (e.g., Juslin et al., 2003). In the former, participants are typically trained through *learning by comparison*. At each trial in the learning phase, they are presented with two objects and have to judge which of the two scores higher on a continuous criterion. They then receive feedback on whether the decision is correct. In studies finding that people rely predominantly on exemplar-based strategies, in contrast, participants are typically trained through *direct criterion learning*. Here, one object is presented at a time and participants have to categorize it; category membership depends on the object's criterion value. They then receive feedback on both the accuracy of the decision and the continuous criterion value of the object.

To test whether these differences in the type of learning task impacted strategy selection in the subsequent test phase, Pachur and Olsson (2012) used a "death bug" task similar to that applied by Juslin et al. (2003). Half of the participants were trained through learning by comparison, the other half through direct criterion learning. The results showed that in the test phase, people trained through learning by comparison indeed relied more on rule-based strategies than did people trained through direct criterion learning. These results demonstrate that the mere design of the task by which objects are presented in the learning phase can influence subsequent reliance on rule-based versus exemplar-based strategies.

In a series of experiments, we (Trippas & Pachur, in press) isolated the specific properties of learning by comparison and direct criterion learning that are responsible for these learning task effects. The study examined three possibilities: Are the observed differences in strategy selection attributable to the fact that two objects can be directly compared along their cue profiles in learning by comparison, but not in direct criterion learning? Or is the provision of an object's continuous criterion value during feedback in direct criterion learning the crucial factor driving strategy selection? What is the significance of the fact that relative feedback (i.e., feedback that is not absolute but in relation to another object) about an object's criterion value is provided in learning by comparison, but not in direct criterion learning? To find out, we varied three conditions: whether a second object, to which the target objects could be compared, was available at each trial in direct criterion learning; whether the cue profile of just one object was shown in learning by comparison; and whether feedback was given on an object's continuous criterion value. Findings suggested that the most important factor was the relative nature of the feedback, which increased reliance on rule-based strategies. Specifically, reliance on rule-based strategies predominated even when a cue profile was shown for just one bug in learning by comparison. The provision of continuous criterion values also had an effect, increasing reliance on exemplar-based strategies, but this effect was smaller in size. The opportunity to compare to objects directly during training, by contrast, had no effect on strategy selection: merely presenting two objects at each trial did not affect the use of a rule-based strategy.

11.5 Boosting Adaptive Strategy Selection

Thus far, we have highlighted three major points. First, rule-based strategies work best in linear decision environments (see figure 11.1), whereas exemplar-based strategies are the better fit in nonlinear decision environments. Second, although people select rule-based and exemplar-based strategies in ways that are sensitive to the statistical structure of the environment, several factors can impair adaptive strategy selection. Third, subtle changes to the learning task can have a sizable impact on the strategies people recruit. Next, we elaborate on how these insights could be used to steer strategy selection under uncertainty in an adaptive fashion. To this end, we assume that the conditions under which people learn to make decisions in a given environment are under the control of an external "decision architect." In the context of medical decision making, for instance, trainee doctors are given learning material that is supposed to help them develop the skills to make correct diagnoses based on sets of symptoms. How do such materials need to be designed to ensure that they foster appropriate strategy selection in a given environment? To the best of our knowledge, it is not current practice to match the way in which professional decision makers are trained to the statistical structure of the relevant domain. Here, we argue for a more systematic approach, which takes into account the ecological rationality of rule-based and exemplar-based strategies, as well as the documented effects of learning tasks on strategy selection.

11.5.1 Step 1: Determine the Statistical Structure of the Decision Environment

The first task of the decision architect is to analyze the statistical structure of the environment, examining how the relevant cues are related to the criterion. Let us return to our firefighters. The incidents that firefighters face vary on a range of features, such as building size, construction material (e.g., the combustible cladding used on Grenfell Tower) and distance between buildings (the cues), and on how difficult the fire turns out to be (the criterion). Are the cues linearly related to the criterion, such that a fire in a tall building surrounded by other buildings is more difficult to extinguish than a fire in a small building with several surrounding buildings, which in turn is more difficult than a fire in a small, isolated building? Or do the cues interact in predicting the criterion, yielding a nonlinear structure? For instance, although it may be more difficult to fight a fire in a high- than in a low-density neighborhood, this relationship may hold only for tall buildings. Surrounding buildings (if they are high enough) might in fact be helpful when fighting a fire in a small building, as crews can use them to fight the fire from above.

11.5.2   Step 2: Identify the Strategy That Matches the Decision Environment

Once the statistical structure of the environment has been determined, the next step is to select the strategy appropriate for that environment. If the relationship between cues and criterion is (approximately) described by a linear function, the aim should be to foster the use of a rule-based strategy, which will enable decision makers to correctly judge objects that are more extreme—that is, have lower or higher criterion values—than objects encountered during training. If the relationship between cues and criterion follows a nonlinear function, the aim should be to foster the use of an exemplar-based strategy.

11.5.3   Step 3: Design the Training Conditions to Foster the Target Strategy

The crucial idea now is to foster adaptive strategy selection by exploiting the differential impact of direct criterion learning and learning by comparison on use of exemplar-based and rule-based strategies—with some help from the decision architect. Based on the results from Pachur and Olsson (2012) and our findings (Trippas & Pachur, in press), the logic would be as follows. In a linear environment, a learning task that involves a relative judgment and withholds continuous criterion information as feedback will promote the use of a rule-based strategy. In a nonlinear environment, a learning task that requires an absolute judgment (either classification or estimation) and provides feedback on the continuous criterion value of an object will promote the use of an exemplar-based strategy.

11.6   Rule-Based and Exemplar-Based Strategies in Decisions under Risk

We have discussed rule-based and exemplar-based strategies and their ecological rationality in the context of research on classification and judgment—the domains in which these strategies have thus far been studied most intensely.

As we highlight next, mechanisms rely on rule- or exemplar-based task representations in at least two ways for decisions under risk and uncertainty, the focus of several other chapters in this book (see chapters 2, 3, 7, 8). First, the distinction between rule-based and exemplar-based strategies can be mapped onto descriptive models of preference construction under risk. The most traditional models in this domain, expectation models (see chapter 8), can be viewed as rule-based strategies in the sense that they assume that the attributes (i.e., outcomes and probabilities) of each option are combined using an algorithm that is blind to the previously encountered gambles. Recently, however, strategies have been proposed that, like exemplar-based models, make decisions by comparing the attributes of a given option with those of previously encountered options. One such strategy, proposed by Plonsky, Teodorescu, and Erev (2015), applies to choices between an experienced payoff distribution that can lead to either a gain or a loss, on the one hand, or nothing, on the other. The idea is that people compare the most recent experienced sequence of outcomes drawn from a payoff distribution with other experienced sequences, and base their choice on how the most recent sequence continued in these previous sequences. As in an exemplar-based strategy, the similarity between the previous pattern of experiences and the current situation plays a key role.

Second, the distinction between rule-based and exemplar-based strategies—and the decision task representations they tap into—is relevant for mechanisms of decision making under risk and uncertainty that exploit the link between risks and rewards (see chapter 3). The relationship between risks and rewards in a gamble environment can be represented in terms of either an abstract rule (e.g., a linear function) or storage of individual gambles (Leuker, Pachur, Hertwig, & Pleskac, 2018). Given the learning task effects described in section 11.4 (Pachur & Olsson, 2012; Trippas & Pachur, in press), it is possible that people's reliance on these two representations is sensitive to how gambles are presented during learning—either individually (e.g., in a pricing task) or in pairs (e.g., in a choice task). Further, whether reliance on one or the other of these two representations leads to better decisions may depend on how exactly risks and rewards are related. For instance, there may be environments in which the relationship follows a nonlinear function (e.g., a power function; Pleskac & Hertwig, 2014); as people have difficulty learning nonlinear rules (e.g., Juslin et al., 2008; Pachur & Olsson, 2012), it may be easier to learn about these structures when the gambles are encountered individually. In environments in which the relationship between risks and rewards is linear, by contrast, it may help if the gambles are encountered in pairs. In other words, depending on which risk–reward environment the decision maker encounters during learning, it may also be possible here to boost adaptive strategy selection through the design of the learning task.

11.7 Conclusion

In new situations fraught with uncertainty, experience can be an important asset. We have described two qualitatively different types of strategies for turning experience into action—rule-based and exemplar-based strategies—and explored their separate habitats. As we have shown, strategy selection is sensitive to subtle properties of the learning task. Decision architects should harness the potential of the learning environment to foster appropriate strategy selection—and ultimately better decisions.

IV The Social Mind

12 Rivals in the Dark: Trading Off Strategic and Environmental Uncertainty

Doug Markant and Ralph Hertwig

12.1 From Environmental to Strategic Uncertainty

Choosing a home is one of the most important decisions an animal can face—it warrants careful inspection of any potential habitat. At the same time, the desire to make a well-informed choice is often eclipsed by the need to act before competitors. Unsurprisingly, many species have evolved habitat selection strategies that adapt to competitive pressure. Take hermit crabs, which must repeatedly find new shells as their bodies grow. Upon discovering an empty shell, a lone hermit crab may diligently inspect it, decide it is a good fit, vacate its previous shell, and inhabit the new one. But empty shells of the right size are not always easy to come by. In fact, the surest way to secure the right shell before competitors is simply to clamber in the moment it is discarded by another crab. So groups of house-hunting hermit crabs sometimes self-organize into queues ordered by size, with each crab perched on the back of a slightly larger (but still occupied) shell. When the largest crab at the head of the queue moves into a new shell, it sets off a chain reaction: each crab quickly occupies the shell vacated by the next-largest neighbor before any competitors can muscle their way in (Rotjan, Chabot, & Lewis, 2010).

Honey bees provide another example of adapting the search for a new home when facing competition. In contrast to the unilateral selection made by each hermit crab, honey bees collectively decide where to build a new hive by relying on scouts that explore and "vote" on potential nest sites (Seeley, Visscher, & Passino, 2006), a process that would seem to prioritize consensus-building over speed. Yet honey bees are also sensitive to the cost of losing a high-quality location to competitors. If an attractive site is under inspection by members of a rival colony, scouts will fight to prevent it from being explored until their own colony has reached a decision (Rangel, Griffin, & Seeley, 2010).

Most humans no longer resort to physical conflict over real estate, but they are nonetheless keenly attuned to the need to act before competitors. The mere suggestion that others are considering the same house can push people to make an offer more quickly than they would otherwise—a fact that is well known not just to real estate agents but to all salespeople. Why is this sales technique so effective? It is not simply due to people being impulsive or suggestible. Assuming the threat of competition is credible, acting quickly to claim a resource—even one of uncertain value—can be a rational response. Decision strategies that might be rewarding in a solitary world, such as a meticulous search for the perfect home, are less effective in a social world where there is a risk that others will swoop in to claim attractive options for themselves.

Indeed, an inherent challenge of competition is that one rarely knows for certain how competitors will behave, as they are typically loath to reveal their intentions before they act. People thus commonly face two sources of uncertainty when making decisions under competition: *environmental uncertainty* about the value of choice options and *strategic uncertainty* about how others will act (Brandenburger, 1996). Environmental uncertainty is present when the payoff from choosing an option (e.g., a potential home) is not fully known to the decision maker (see chapters 2, 3, 7, and 8). Strategic uncertainty arises in any interactive setting with other agents who might adopt one of many decision-making strategies (see chapters 5 and 14). Nonsocial decisions, which can be conceptualized as "games against nature" (Hertwig, Hoffrage, & the ABC Research Group, 2013), can involve environmental uncertainty but are typically free from strategic uncertainty. The risks involved in playing roulette depend only on the structure of the roulette wheel, which does not change to anticipate or outwit gamblers. In social settings, however, other people's behavior has consequences for one's own decisions, and uncertainty about how they will act makes it difficult to identify the best strategy for oneself.

12.1.1   The Need to Know vs. the Need for Speed

Searching for a home is just one example of a common conflict between environmental and strategic uncertainty: people must balance the benefits of exploration—an important means for resolving environmental uncertainty—against the potential costs of being preempted by rivals. This conflict exists in many competitive situations, from the momentous to the mundane, but is perhaps most salient when uncertainty is high. Consider the relatively routine task of booking a hotel room in an unfamiliar tourist destination (an example not unlike that of house-hunting, but with considerably lower stakes). How much time should be spent researching different hotels given that other tourists are exploring the same options? How long are those competitors likely to bide their time before claiming the more attractive options for themselves? The same questions could be asked of any resource that is in demand but of uncertain value. In this chapter, we examine how individuals navigate the fundamental trade-off between exploration and the drive to claim resources before competitors do so.

One motivation of this research is to understand whether this trade-off is distinct from other *exploration–exploitation trade-offs* seen in solitary contexts (see chapter 7). Is the cost of losing out to a competitor interchangeable with other costs, such as opportunity costs or costs of acquiring information? Is strategic uncertainty substantively different from environmental uncertainty, or is it just a label for a class of environments that involve social agents? We think there are at least two reasons to expect that strategic uncertainty is more than a label, both of which we explore further here. First, people can mitigate strategic uncertainty to some extent by drawing on social knowledge to predict others' behavior. Even when competing with strangers, knowledge about social norms and past experiences in similar social situations can provide good guesses as to what other people will do. Second, competing with other agents may invoke strategies that are matched to the structure of social interactions and are robust to uncertainty about others' goals or strategies (Hertwig et al., 2013). For example, reasoning about the intentions of others can involve complex chains of perspective-taking ("I think that they think that I think that they will…"), but this process may quickly outstrip the capacity or time available to a human decision maker. Adapting to strategic uncertainty may depend on simpler strategies which exploit regularities that are unique to social, competitive environments (see also chapter 5).

In the following, we use two threads of research to draw out the tension between environmental and strategic uncertainty. We begin with an example from behavioral game theory of how people respond to strategic uncertainty when the costs of being preempted by competitors are fully transparent (i.e., in the absence of environmental uncertainty). We then step beyond the standard confines of game theory by considering the intersection of strategic and environmental uncertainty, where the imperative to act before competitors is in conflict with the drive to learn about choice options. Finally, we argue for an ecological understanding of how people adapt their decision strategies in a heterogenous, competitive world in which the "rules of the game" may themselves be uncertain.

12.2 Strategic Uncertainty: How Will Competitors Act?

How *should* people act when faced with strategic uncertainty? The most prominent theoretical tool for answering this question is *game theory* (see also chapter 5). In game theory, individuals are conceptualized as "players" in a game that reflects the structure of a real-world interaction and which affords multiple courses of action, referred to as "strategies." Game theory aims to explain how the value of a strategy depends on the strategies adopted by other players. As a normative framework founded on the principles of expected utility theory (Luce & Raiffa, 1957; von Neumann & Morgenstern, 1944/2007), it builds on the assumptions that first, all players act to maximize their own utility, and second, they believe their opponents will do the same. A common goal of game theoretic analysis is to identify *equilibria* for a given interaction. An equilibrium occurs when each player selects a best strategy (i.e., the course of action that maximizes their expected utility) given uncertainty about their opponents' strategies. When a set of competitors are at an equilibrium, no individual has an incentive to unilaterally change their strategy. Equilibria are useful normative guideposts for how people (or more generally, companies, countries, or any other kind of agent) should act in strategic interactions, but in practice they often provide a poor description of behavior. Throughout the history of game theory, behavioral researchers have sought to understand why the gap between predicted equilibria and actual behavior exists and what it reveals about the way that people respond to strategic uncertainty (Camerer, 2003; Gächter, 2004).

12.2.1 The Centipede Game: Competing for Known Rewards
Consider a classic problem involving competition for limited resources referred to as the *centipede game* (see figure 12.1; McKelvey & Palfrey, 1992; Rapoport, 2003; Rosenthal, 1981). Imagine that two players are seated

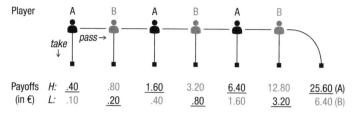

Player	A	B	A	B	A	B

Payoffs *H:* __.40__   .80   __1.60__   3.20   __6.40__   12.80   __25.60__ (A)
(in €) *L:* .10   __.20__   .40   __.80__   1.60   __3.20__   6.40 (B)

Figure 12.1
Depiction of the 6-move centipede game from McKelvey and Palfrey (1992). Player A
and player B take turns deciding whether to take the higher value option H (vertical
lines) or pass to the other player (horizontal lines). Each pass causes both payoffs to
double. The payoffs earned by player A following each take decision are underlined.
If neither player decides to take at any point, the game terminates with player A
receiving the H option (€25.60) and player B receiving the L option (€6.40).

across a table, with two piles of money lying between them (a high-value
pile *H* and a low-value pile *L*). The players are informed that the amount of
money in each pile will double with each passing round of the game, up to
a known maximum number of rounds. For example, the game might start
with pile *H* containing €0.40 and pile *L* containing €0.10. After six turns the
amounts in each pile will have increased to $H=€12.80$ and $L=€3.20$. The
gameplay is simple: players take turns deciding whether to take the *H* pile,
thereby ending the game and forcing the other player to receive the *L* pile,
or to pass and give the other player the chance to decide.

The centipede game is free of environmental uncertainty about the
choice options. Players know the precise payoffs they will receive should
they choose to stop and take an option, and they know how those payoffs will change over future rounds. It also provides perfect information
about the game state: players observe the choices made by opponents and
know that their opponents have the same knowledge of the game structure.
This simple, transparent game nevertheless generates a powerful conflict of
interests. On the one hand, the increase in payoffs across rounds incentiv-
izes players to allow the game to continue as long as possible, as both piles
will double in value after every round. On the other hand, the disparity
between the *H* and *L* options produces a strong preemption motive, in
that there is a clear cost to *not* being the first person to stop and take the
H option. As figure 12.1 shows, whenever a player's opponent decides to take *H*,

the player's own payoff is half of what it would have been if they had stopped on the previous round.

This conflict is fueled by strategic uncertainty. If an opponent's strategy was known in advance (e.g., that the opponent plans to stop on the third round), the best response would be to stop one round earlier, thereby securing the largest possible payoff. What should a player do, however, if they do not know how long an opponent will wait before claiming the H option? Imagine that the game progresses to player B's final choice of whether to *take* or *pass* (see figure 12.1). The payoff for passing (€6.40) is half that of taking (€12.80), so a payoff-maximizing player would be expected to take. Now consider player A's immediately preceding choice. Predicting that player B will take at their next opportunity, player A's payoff from passing (€3.20) is less than that of taking (€6.40), similarly leading to the decision to take. The same logic applies backwards up to the first round of the game; any decision to pass leads to a worse payoff under the assumption that the opponent will take at their next opportunity. This reasoning process, known as *backwards induction*, creates a "race to the bottom" that converges on the first round, such that the equilibrium strategy in this game is to pounce on the H pile at the very first opportunity (Rapoport, 2003; Rosenthal, 1981).

Several behavioral studies on the centipede game have shown that people act quite differently from this equilibrium strategy (Bornstein, Kugler, & Ziegelmeyer, 2004; Fey, McKelvey, & Palfrey, 1996; Krockow, Pulford, & Colman, 2015; McKelvey & Palfrey, 1992; Nagel & Tang, 1998; Parco, Rapoport, & Stein, 2002; Rapoport, Stein, Parco, & Nicholas, 2003). People neither allow the game to continue for the maximum number of rounds, which might be expected if they only paid attention to the overall magnitude of the payoffs, nor do they typically stop on the first round. The most common stopping points fall somewhere in between; the modal choice is to claim the H option when approximately half the number of possible rounds have passed (Krockow et al., 2015; McKelvey & Palfrey, 1992; Nagel & Tang, 1998). Subtle changes in the payoff structure of the game can lead to earlier stopping points, including when larger incentives are at stake (Parco et al., 2002; Rapoport et al., 2003), when the magnitude of the payoffs does not increase across rounds (i.e., constant-sum centipede games; Fey et al., 1996), or when both players receive nothing at the final node (Krockow et al., 2015; Rapoport et al., 2003). On the whole, however, the equilibrium strategy of taking the *H* option at the first opportunity is relatively uncommon in experimental studies of the centipede game.

What explains this stark difference between the game-theoretic prediction and human behavior? In the following, we describe behavioral studies which suggest that people make choices based on their beliefs about how opponents will act—beliefs which may depart in significant ways from the standard assumptions of game theory. In short, strategic uncertainty may be moderated by prior knowledge about other people's competence or preferences, and it may be reduced as a result of learning through experience.

12.2.1.1 Prior beliefs about competitors People may not view opponents as the self-interested, rational actors presumed by game theory. For example, players may be more willing to pass in the centipede game if they believe that competitors are somewhat altruistic (i.e., care about the payoffs received by the other player; McKelvey & Palfrey, 1992) or are likely to make errors (Fey et al., 1996). Such beliefs imply that nonequilibrium strategies are more likely among opponents, leading to a different best response. According to this account, players are more willing to bide their time before claiming the *H* option because they perceive less competitive pressure than assumed by the game-theoretic equilibrium.

In an experimental test of this idea, Palacios-Huerta and Volij (2009) argued that players were more likely to adopt the equilibrium strategy when they had reason to believe their opponent would. The authors examined the behavior of both college students and expert chess players in the centipede game. In games between two chess players, the most common strategy was to stop on the first round in accordance with the equilibrium strategy (and in games between the most skilled grandmaster players, the equilibrium strategy was used 100% of the time). In games between students, behavior was similar to that observed in previous studies, with the majority of pairs reaching half the number of possible rounds. However, when students were informed that they were playing against chess players, they were more likely to stop on early rounds. Thus, given a hint that opponents may be strategically adept, naive players appeared to adjust their own strategy to preempt them.

12.2.1.2 Learning through repeated interaction A number of studies suggest that this kind of adaptation can also emerge as a result of experience in the centipede game (Fey et al., 1996; Rapoport et al., 2003), consistent with evidence from other strategic games that learning supports convergence toward equilibria (Fudenberg & Levine, 2016; Roth & Erev, 1995). Although Palacios-Huerta and Volij (2009) focused on players' knowledge of their opponents' abilities, their results also suggest that naive players converged toward the equilibrium more quickly across multiple games when they competed against chess players than when they faced other students. Being told that an opponent is strategically sophisticated may not be as powerful as actually experiencing competition with them and being forced to adapt.

An even more striking example of this convergence is provided by Rapoport et al. (2003). This study used a three-person variant of the centipede game in which college students played a series of 60 games against randomly matched opponents. The experiment involved considerably higher stakes than in previous studies, with the payoffs received after nine turns equivalent to [$1,280, $128, $128] (versus [$5, $0.50, $0.50] on the first round). Despite this strong incentive to prolong the games, most ended within the first three rounds. Moreover, over the course of repeated competition, players strongly converged toward the equilibrium of stopping on the first turn. This adaptation was best described by a simple learning model in which players' beliefs about when the next game would terminate were updated following each game. On the whole, these students' behavior did not resemble the backwards induction strategy (in contrast to that of the expert chess players from Palacios-Huerta and Volij, 2009), but rather relied on incremental learning from competitive experience.

To conclude, the centipede game provides an elegant example of adaptation to strategic uncertainty in a competitive environment, and illustrates the divide between human behavior and the normative strategies predicted by game theory. It is not the case that people are not motivated to earn larger payoffs for themselves or that they do not understand the need to claim better options before an opponent. Rather, their choices appear to be mediated by their uncertainty about how others will act—uncertainty that can be lessened by additional knowledge about opponents or direct experience. This adaptation takes the form of faster decisions to secure a higher payoff before competitors swoop in, even if it means sacrificing greater rewards in future rounds. Of course, being offered an ever-increasing stack of money is a rare occurrence—usually people compete for resources that are themselves uncertain. What if, in addition to strategic uncertainty imposed by competition, people lack perfect knowledge about the values of available options? How does their response to competitive pressure change when the stakes can only be gleaned through exploration? Next, we examine this interplay between strategic and environmental uncertainty.

12.3   Combining Strategic and Environmental Uncertainty

Unlike the transparent, guaranteed returns of the centipede game, competitors must often contend with environmental uncertainty about available options in addition to strategic uncertainty. To return to the real estate example: Can house hunters be sure a property is really their dream home, or are there lurking risks like a leaky roof or encroaching development? If they are in a hot market, can they devote time to learn more about a home before someone else makes an offer? Exploration is key to making effective choices in the face of environmental uncertainty, whether people are selecting a home, an investment, or an employee. Research on the *sampling paradigm* (Hertwig, Barron, Weber, & Erev, 2004; see chapter 7) has examined how people explore uncertain options prior to making a choice between them. In the sampling paradigm, an individual is faced with a set of choice options of unknown value, each associated with an underlying distribution of outcomes with different probabilities. The individual learns about each option through exploration, generating new experiences one by one, until ready to make a final choice that leads to a consequential payoff. In contrast to the payoff structure of the centipede game, in which players know that options' values increase by a fixed factor over time, what changes in the sampling paradigm is not options' underlying values but the decision maker's uncertainty about them. With increasing experience, people can more accurately choose the option with a greater value; the sampling paradigm thus entails an incentive to explore in order to reduce environmental uncertainty.

As we have seen, however, competition may not afford the luxury of such well-informed decisions. Spending time learning about available options carries the risk that others will swoop in first and claim the best ones for themselves. The value of reducing environmental uncertainty through exploration must therefore be weighed against the possibility that others will act first. In highly competitive settings, it may be necessary to act fast based on relatively little information in order to choose before competitors. Are people able to manage this trade-off effectively?

12.3.1 Rivals in the Dark: Competing for Uncertain Rewards

Phillips, Hertwig, Kareev, and Avrahami (2014) investigated the effects of competitive pressure on exploration using a variant of the sampling paradigm referred to as the rivals-in-the-dark game (or "rivals" game). In this game, two players choose from a number of options of uncertain value—in this case, urns on a computer screen (see figure 12.2). The urns are filled with virtual balls, each labeled with a number representing its value. The urn's value is the average of the values of the balls it contains. As in the sampling paradigm, each option is associated with a set of outcomes—here, the virtual balls—that occur with different probabilities. In each round, players simultaneously draw from an urn of their choice, seeing only the

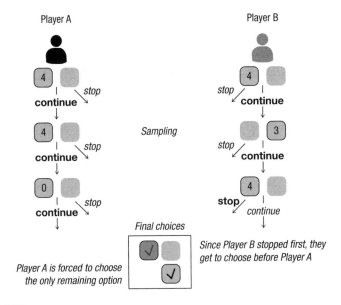

Figure 12.2
In this example of the rivals-in-the-dark game, two players are faced with the same set of two choice options. As in the sampling paradigm, the players can learn about each option through exploration. For example, player A experiences three outcomes from the option on the left (4, 4, and 0), corresponding to potential payoffs if that option is chosen at the end. After every simultaneous draw, each player decides whether to continue learning or to stop and choose one of the two options. In this example, player B is the first person to stop. As a result, sampling ends for both players and player B is able to make the first choice. The other player is then forced to take whichever option remains. If both players simultaneously decide to stop exploring, the first person to choose an option is determined with a coin flip.

results of their own selection. They then each decide whether to continue learning (i.e., voting to allow the game to proceed to the next round) or to stop and claim an option that will produce a consequential payoff. In contrast to the typical, solitary gameplay of the sampling paradigm, in the rivals game one player's decision to choose an option removes it from the pool of available options for the other player. As a result, deciding to continue exploring the options through repeated sampling is associated with the risk that the other player will stop and choose the better option first. You can play the rivals game yourself by accessing interactive element 12.1 (at https://taming-uncertainty.mpib-berlin.mpg.de/).

Phillips et al. (2014) found that—unlike solitary players, who typically experience 10–20 outcomes in the sampling paradigm—competitors in the rivals task drastically curtailed exploration prior to making a choice: their median sample size was just one draw, the minimum allowed. In a large proportion of games, players made decisions without observing at least a single outcome from both options. Is this meager exploration an overreaction to competitive pressure, or is it an effective strategy? Although the rivals game differs from the centipede game in a number of respects,[1] the same game-theoretic analysis based on backwards induction can be applied here. If an opponent's strategy was known beforehand (e.g., that they will stop and choose after 10 draws), the best response would be to stop one round earlier and claim the option that appears to have a higher value based on the observed outcomes up to that point. A rational opponent would be expected to respond similarly. As a result, applying the same logic backwards over decreasing sample sizes, the equilibrium strategy in the rivals game—much like that of the centipede game—is to stop exploring after the first draw. Observing even a single outcome conveys information about the relative value of the options, giving players a slight edge if they are able to make the first choice.

Minimal exploration, such as that observed by Phillips et al. (2014), may therefore be an effective response to competitive pressure in settings that

---

1. The centipede game is a *sequential move* game with *perfect information* (i.e., all players have full knowledge of the game structure and all events that occur during the game). In contrast, the rivals game described here is a *simultaneous move* game (players make decisions concurrently on each round) involving *private information* (e.g., the outcomes experienced by one player are not known to the other player).

are high in environmental uncertainty. It amounts to a bet on the value of choosing first while ignoring any potential downsides of choosing based on little information. To the extent that small samples of experience are correlated with the value of an option, people can benefit by pouncing on an option that appears favorable based on their initial experiences. The results of Phillips et al. suggest that players in the rivals game relied on such a strategy. Experiencing an attractive (positive) outcome on the first draw frequently caused them to immediately stop exploring and to choose that option; experiencing an unattractive (negative) outcome was typically associated with continued exploration. Although they often made decisions based on only very small samples of experience, players who stopped first were nevertheless more likely to obtain the *H* option than their opponents. Like other examples of simple heuristics that curtail information search by exploiting environmental structures (Gigerenzer, Hertwig, & Pachur, 2011; Todd & Gigerenzer, 2012), acting on minimal information can be advantageous in competitive settings, even when the level of uncertainty about the options' relative quality is high.

12.3.2 Adapting Exploration to Competitive Pressure

Should people always make such fast decisions when competing for uncertain options? A cost–benefit analysis would suggest that, when deciding whether to continue exploring, people should weigh the perceived competitive pressure (i.e., the costs of not choosing first) against the benefits of additional experience in the environment in question. Following such a strategy is particularly important when the risks of competition vary from situation to situation. The intensity of competitive pressure can change considerably as a function of resource type (e.g., plentiful vs. scarce goods), social structures (e.g., dominance hierarchies), or even time (e.g., seasonal demand). Although prioritizing fast decisions increases the chance of choosing before competitors, such a strategy may forgo rewards when competitive pressure is actually low (e.g., when there are few competitors relative to the number of available options). Using computer simulations, Phillips et al. (2014) examined how the payoffs from different sample sizes in the rivals game depend on competitive pressure. When the ratio of competitors to options is high (e.g., two players competing for two options, as in their behavioral study) and competitors are expected to make fast decisions, the minimal exploration strategy is most effective. If there are more options than competitors or competitors are expected to make slow decisions, however, larger sample sizes lead to higher payoffs.

Just as the costs of competition may change from situation to situation, the value of exploration can vary based on the structure of a given choice environment, including the distribution of potential outcomes and their respective probabilities. To take an extreme case, if the decision maker knows that the first draw from an option is a perfectly valid indicator of its value (a "sure thing" that always generates the same outcome), no information is gained from sampling it more than once. In contrast, if small samples are misleading with respect to option value (e.g., when the variance in outcomes is high or when the distribution of outcomes is strongly skewed, with infrequent extreme outcomes), exploration is more worthwhile even under intense competition. Of course, the critical question is whether people *know* that continued exploration is beneficial. Although it is difficult to make direct comparisons between choices in the rivals game and the centipede game, one reason that naive participants in the Phillips et al. (2014) study may have come closer to following the equilibrium strategy is their uncertainty about the value of further exploration (unlike the certain increase in payoffs that is common knowledge in the centipede game). After all, if the gains from exploration are unknown, why not focus on beating the other player to the punch?

In another set of experiments, Markant, Phillips, Kareev, Avrahami, and Hertwig (2018) tested whether people adapt their search based on these situational trade-offs between competitive pressure and the value of exploration. The choice environment involved options that tended to have skewed outcome distributions and in which the importance of learning about rare outcomes through repeated sampling was transparent. Each outcome was associated with a low-magnitude common outcome ($p = .8$) and a potentially high-magnitude rare outcome ($p = .2$) that could have a large impact on the quality of an option (see figure 12.3a). Participants were informed about this structure, including the number of possible outcomes and their probabilities, but had to learn the values of each outcome through exploration. In this environment, exploring until at least one of the rare outcomes is experienced improves the chances of identifying the H option by more than 20% on average.

Competitors in this version of the game consistently explored far less than solitary counterparts, just as they did in the environment in the

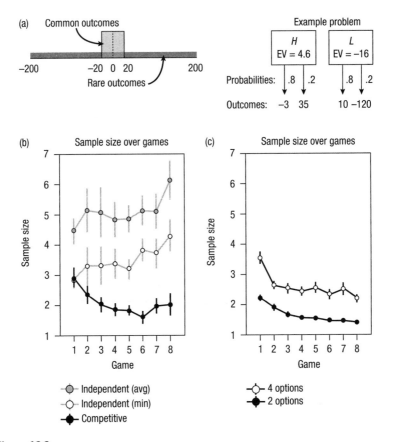

Figure 12.3

Design of choice environment in Markant et al. (2018). (a) Each option was associated with a common outcome that occurred with probability p=.8 and was drawn from a uniform distribution over the interval [–20, 20], and a rare outcome that occurred with probability p=.2 and was drawn from a much wider distribution over the interval [–200, 200]. (b) In this version of the task, sample sizes were higher among independent (solitary) pairs of players than among competitive pairs, and sample sizes changed in different directions as a function of experience. (c) Although competitive pairs tended to sample relatively little, sample sizes were higher when more options were available (4 vs. 2).

Phillips et al. (2014) study (see figure 12.3b). In addition, players stopped exploring prior to experiencing any rare outcomes in more than half of all games. This truncated search is especially notable to the extent that players were aware of the potential for rare, extreme outcomes that could have an outsize impact on the value of the options. However, truncated search was only part of the story. Players also adjusted their exploration in ways consistent with the behavior and simulation results of Phillips et al. When two players were competing for four options rather than two, they collected roughly double the number of samples (see figure 12.3c). In addition, players were more likely to explore when options with negative value (losses) were more common in the environment than when they were rare. Finally, even when the intensity of competition was high (e.g., when two players competed over two options), sample size declined over the course of repeated play, indicating a short-term convergence toward the equilibrium strategy that was driven by repeated experience in the game. Taken together, these results suggest that people adapt their exploration to the current choice context, including the perceived intensity of competition and the potential value of further sampling.

How do people manage this trade-off between exploring options and beating their competitor to the punch? Markant et al. (2018) developed a model in which the expected benefits of further exploration (given previously observed outcomes) are weighed against the expected cost of losing out to an opponent if they decide to stop. If a player believes that the opponent is likely to stop on the current round, the expected benefit of exploring further is outweighed by the cost of being the second person to choose an option. On the other hand, if the risk of an opponent stopping seems to be low, it may be better to continue exploring in order to reduce uncertainty about the options' relative values. This model provided a good account of behavior in the task, including the link between players' beliefs about opponents (i.e., the probability that they will stop) and the reduction in exploration over repeated play. As players gained more experience playing against the same opponent, they learned how likely the opponent was to stop on every trial and adapted their own strategy accordingly. These findings echo the behavior seen in the repeated centipede game (Rapoport et al., 2003), in that naive players appear to incrementally adapt to their competitors rather than relying on more complex forms of reasoning like backwards induction.

12.3.3   Know Thine Enemy: Social Norms and Learning

To date, studies involving the rivals game have focused on an extreme form of competition, with relative anonymity, minimal interaction, and little reason to care about the payoffs received by other players. Although this may resemble some especially cutthroat environments (e.g., investment trading), many competitions take place in the context of richer social interactions that change the way people perceive and respond to uncertainty. We briefly consider two examples here.

Many interactions invoke social norms that may conflict with the self-interested focus seen in extreme competition. Those norms may reduce strategic uncertainty by providing background knowledge about how people will act. For example, Fleischhut, Artinger, Olschewski, Volz, and Hertwig (2018) examined exploration in a version of the sampling paradigm where individuals had to decide how, or whether, to share a payoff. In this *mini-ultimatum game*, a player could suggest one of two ways of sharing a sum of money with their partner. The offer could then be either accepted by the partner, in which case both players received the designated amounts, or rejected, in which case both earned nothing. The choice of offers (e.g., 50:50 or 80:20 split) varied with each new game. Players were able to learn about the kinds of offers that would be accepted or rejected by other players through repeated sampling. Relative to a solitary setting with the same environmental uncertainty, people explored much less in the social framing of the mini-ultimatum game. They appeared to rely on knowledge of social norms to infer the probability of different offers being accepted, reducing the need to gain experience through exploration. For example, lopsided offers that appeared greedy were more likely to be rejected than others due to norms of fairness. Social norms, including aversion to inequitable outcomes, may operate in what seem to be purely competitive settings, especially when there is an opportunity for players to punish unfair play (Fehr & Fischbacher, 2004).

In addition to knowledge of social norms, real-world competition often affords people more opportunity to reduce strategic uncertainty by learning about competitors' goals or preferences. Whereas players in the rivals game were given little to no information about opponents' identities and observed very little of their behavior (only their final choices), observing how competitors explore might provide a clearer picture of the true competitive pressure. Taking note of how others explore can also facilitate learning about the environment. Research on behavioral ecology has examined the use of *public information*, defined as observations of competitors' choices that are used to assess the quality of a resource (Danchin, Giraldeau, Valone, & Wagner, 2004). For instance, one advantage of foraging in a group (rather than alone) is that the individual can learn about the distribution of resources by observing other group members' sampling behavior. Although patches of resources are depleted more quickly due to exploitation by a larger number of competitors, groups of foragers can use public information about others' successes to better discern when a patch is exhausted and it is time to explore further afield (Valone & Templeton, 2002). The foraging behavior of competitors can signal the quality of chosen options even when the actual outcomes are not observed (Goldstone, Ashpole, & Roberts, 2005). Extending this idea to the rivals game, if an opponent samples an option once and immediately switches to a different option, one might infer that they experienced an unambiguously negative outcome and are unlikely to claim that option. This opportunity to glean information from competitors' exploration leads to further reductions in both strategic and environmental uncertainty that would not be possible under minimal exploration. We examine the benefits of information sharing in noncompetitive social settings in further detail in chapter 13.

12.4   Learning to Compete: Toward an Ecological Perspective

Strategic uncertainty poses a qualitatively distinct challenge from environmental uncertainty. For all its vagaries and dynamism, nature is, like a roulette wheel, oblivious to the plans of its inhabitants and does not intentionally act to thwart them. In contrast, competitors are often aware of their opponents and can attempt to reason through how interactions will unfold. Yet whereas sophisticated strategic reasoning is often considered a pinnacle of human cognition (as exemplified by master chess or Go players), the experimental findings discussed above (see sections 12.2.1.2 and 12.3.2) suggest that people rely on incremental, experiential learning to compete in new interactive settings. In both the centipede game and the rivals game, players appear to incrementally update their beliefs about how competitors will act and adjust their strategies accordingly with repeated experience. In both tasks, learning to compete entails acting more or less quickly in response to the competitive pressure experienced.

Of course, as any chess grandmaster knows, competing effectively may at times require more sophisticated or complex strategies in order to outplay opponents. Some researchers have argued that strategic interaction is an important evolutionary driver of cognitive ability (Dunbar, 1998; Whiten & Byrne, 1997). As we have illustrated in section 12.3.1, however, competition itself does not necessitate a sophisticated response (Hertwig & Hoffrage, 2013), particularly when it is a stable property of the social environment. An ecological perspective would suggest that people adopt more complex strategies for dealing with strategic and environmental uncertainty only when compelled to do so by the trade-offs in their natural environment.

Using evolutionary simulations, Hintze, Phillips, and Hertwig (2015) have provided an example of this process in environments similar to the rivals game, each with a different level of competitive pressure, and with a focus on evolutionary adaptation (see chapter 15). Under *direct* competition, two agents could explore to learn about the value of a common option. They could then either choose that option or a private reserve option of known value (which could not be taken by the opponent). In comparison, an *extreme* competition condition, similar to the game used by Phillips et al. (2014), involved two agents who learned about two options and could claim either one, with no private options to fall back on. The strategy that evolved under direct competition was one of adaptive exploration: agents frequently sampled more than once, and the likelihood of continued exploration increased with the variance of the options' outcomes (i.e., when environmental uncertainty was higher). In contrast, the strategy that evolved under extreme competition was to choose after a single draw, regardless of the degree of environmental uncertainty. Thus, a minimal exploration strategy (i.e., one that is insensitive to environmental uncertainty) emerges when extreme competition is a stable property of the social environment, whereas adaptive exploration persists only under less stringent competitive conditions.

Understanding the range of competitive pressures faced by individuals may help to explain how they respond to strategic uncertainty. Does their willingness to explore depend on the intensity of competition they have experienced? Do different life histories influence the ability to adapt to new strategic circumstances? Recent work has suggested that other examples of seemingly impulsive decision making may in fact reflect adaptation to stressful or unreliable social environments (Frankenhuis, Panchanathan, &

Nettle, 2016; Griskevicius et al., 2013; Kidd, Palmeri, & Aslin, 2013). Just as "Depression babies," who have endured periods of financial hardship, may be less likely to take financial risks (Malmendier & Nagel, 2011; see also chapter 10), people who have experienced intense competition for resources (e.g., due to their socioeconomic background or experience in a highly competitive industry) might tend to explore less, even when competitive pressure is low. Experiencing a wide range of strategic situations, on the other hand, may foster the ability to balance the value of exploration against the current risks of competition (as in Markant et al., 2018) or to seek out social information to reduce strategic uncertainty about opponents. If the "rules of the game" are themselves uncertain, competing successfully may require that people adapt quickly based on their early experiences in a new domain.

12.5 Conclusion

Traditional approaches to studying decision making under uncertainty often cast the decision maker as a lone explorer on uncharted seas, buffeted by forces beyond their influence or affinity. The rivals-in-the-dark game highlights that it is necessary not only to examine "games against nature," but also to understand how behavior changes when people's landscape is populated with others. The consequences of a choice often depend on the social context, including how other people anticipate, judge, and respond to one's actions. We have examined how strategic uncertainty arises in competitive settings and interacts with environmental uncertainty in driving decision making. We have also stressed the need for an ecological approach that considers the kinds of competition experienced in different environments, including the information channels through which people can learn about others.

13   The Ecological Rationality of the Wisdom of Crowds

Stefan M. Herzog, Aleksandra Litvinova, Kyanoush S. Yahosseini,
Alan N. Tump, and Ralf H. J. M. Kurvers

13.1   The Wisdom of Crowds

A radiologist looks at an image of a mammogram, searching for visual cues indicating the presence or absence of breast cancer. After inspecting the X-ray, the radiologist decides on a cancer diagnosis. Diagnosing breast cancer based on a mammogram is an example of a broad class of judgment tasks where people need to infer an uncertain criterion, such as whether breast cancer is present, from a set of *cues*, such as the presence or absence of a suspicious mass, that are only probabilistically related to that criterion (Brunswik, 1952; see also chapter 11). Other examples include predicting the future violence of psychiatric patients, forecasting next year's inflation rate, or estimating the probability that a politician will be elected president. In all these scenarios, the decision maker faces uncertainty about a criterion, which needs to be inferred from fallible cues (*inference*), and would like to reduce that uncertainty (e.g., by improving the diagnostic accuracy of mammogram readings) to make better choices.

This chapter shows how relying on the judgments of more than one individual is a powerful way to reduce uncertainty by boosting accuracy, *the wisdom-of-the-crowd effect* (see box 13.1; e.g., Bang & Frith, 2017; Laan, Madirolas, & De Polavieja, 2017; Larrick, Mannes, & Soll, 2012; Malone & Bernstein, 2015; Page, 2007a; Surowiecki, 2004). We focus on situations where multiple individuals (the "crowd") make independent judgments and a person (the "decision maker"), who is not part of that crowd, wants to harness its wisdom to either make better decisions (e.g., diagnosing breast cancer) or improve continuous estimates (e.g., forecasting next year's inflation rate). Let us return to the mammography example and consider two

Box 13.1

Boosting medical diagnostics by combining diagnosticians' decisions.

Recent work demonstrates that combining the independent decisions of diagnosticians can substantially boost diagnostic accuracy in a variety of medical domains, including mammography (Wolf, Krause, Carney, Bogart, & Kurvers, 2015), dermatology (Kurvers, Krause, Argenziano, Zalaudek, & Wolf, 2015), and low back pain (Kurvers, de Zoete, Bachman, Algra, & Ostelo, 2018; see figure 13.B1). Combining as few as three independent judgments with a majority rule outperformed the average individual accuracy, illustrating that even small groups and a simple crowd rule can boost accuracy. Combining independent decisions can be a simple yet powerful tool for boosting decisions in real-world domains (Hertwig, 2017; Hertwig & Grüne-Yanoff, 2017).

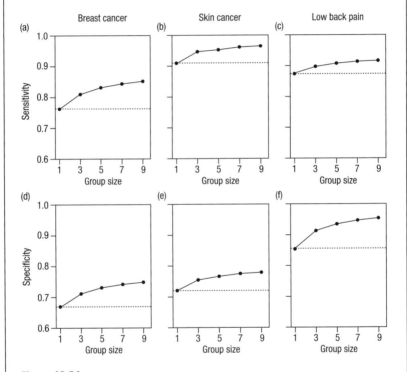

Figure 13.B1

Boosting medical diagnostics. Improvements in (a–c) sensitivity and (d–f) specificity when using a majority rule to combine independent diagnostic decisions of (a, b) radiologists reading mammograms (based on data from Carney et al., 2012); (c, d) dermatologists reading images of skin lesions (Zalaudek et al., 2006); and (e, f) chiropractors/radiologists reading lumbosacral radiographs (de Zoete et al., 2002). Horizontal lines depict the average individual performance. In all domains, both sensitivity and specificity increase as the number of independent diagnostic decisions increases.

more radiologists who examined the same mammogram. The second radiologist, like the first, diagnosed cancer. The third radiologist, however, very confidently reached the opposite diagnosis of no cancer. Two out of three radiologists—the majority—made a cancer diagnosis, but the most confident radiologist interpreted the same X-ray differently. How should a decision maker integrate these conflicting judgments? By weighing all judgments equally and selecting the majority vote ("cancer") or by selecting the most confident vote ("no cancer"; Kurvers et al., 2016)? This example illustrates that there are different ways of combining multiple judgments and that these different methods can result in conflicting recommendations. Thus, using multiple judgments to reduce uncertainty about a judgment task introduces uncertainty on a higher level: how best to harness the *wisdom of crowds*.

The first part of this chapter reviews the *ecological rationality* of several well-known crowd rules (Galton, 1907; Grofman, Owen, & Feld, 1983; Koriat, 2015; Mannes, Soll, & Larrick, 2014; Yetton & Bottger, 1982), that is, when and why a particular crowd rule performs well or poorly. We show that no single crowd rule always outperforms the rest. Rather, crowd rules are more or less suitable depending on the statistical environment. Decision makers, however, rarely enjoy an omniscient insight into the statistical environment they are in; usually, they have no more than partial knowledge about the environment and have to select a crowd rule without being certain of how well it will perform. Therefore, the second part of this chapter focuses on this problem of selecting the best crowd rule in the absence of complete knowledge about the environment.

13.2   Where Do Particular Crowd Rules Excel?

We introduce four key crowd rules, each of which turns multiple judgments into one final judgment: the majority/averaging rule, which blends the judgments of the whole crowd; the best-member rule, which relies on the best individual; the select-crowd rule, which blends the judgments of select members of the whole crowd; and the confidence rule, which relies, for each judgment case, on the most confident individual (see table 13.1). These rules represent four important and conceptually distinct, prototypical approaches to harnessing the wisdom of crowds. Together they encompass a large part of the conceptual space of all previously studied crowd rules (for

Table 13.1
The ecological rationality of crowd rules.

Crowd rule	Works best when ...
For blending discrete judgments: **Majority (plurality) rule** (Grofman et al., 1983)	– Average individual accuracy above 0.5 (see figure 13.1) – Diverse errors (see figure 13.2)
For blending continuous judgments: **Averaging rule** (e.g., Davis-Stober et al., 2014)	– Diverse errors ("bracketing"; see figure 13.3 and box 13.2)
Best-member rule (Yetton & Bottger, 1982)	– Large dispersion in individual accuracy (i.e., best member is substantially better than the others) – Valid cue to identify best member
Select-crowd rule (e.g., Mannes et al., 2014)	– Large dispersion in individual accuracy (i.e., a subset of individuals perform substantially better than others) – Diverse errors – Valid cue to identify high-performing individuals
Confidence rule (e.g., Koriat, 2012b)	– Kind environment: Positive relationship between confidence and accuracy across people (i.e., expressed confidence means the same for every crowd member)

reviews and more crowd rules, see, e.g., Grofman et al., 1983; Laan et al., 2017; Prelec, Seung, & McCoy, 2017; Steyvers & Miller, 2015).[1] The performance of each rule critically depends on the statistical properties of the environment. Here we discuss how average individual accuracy, diversity of errors, dispersion of individual accuracies, and validity of confidence affect the performance of these rules.

---

1. The literature on the wisdom of crowds is vast and includes human (e.g., Larrick et al., 2012; Malone & Bernstein, 2015; Page, 2007b; Surowiecki, 2004) and algorithm crowds (e.g., Kuncheva, 2004; Rokach, 2010, 2016). The wider topic of collective intelligence has been investigated in many domains, such as group decision making (Baron, 2005; Davis, 1973; "groupthink"; Janis, 1972; Kerr & Tindale, 2004), collective pedestrian behavior (see chapter 14), cultural evolution (Boyd & Richerson, 1988; Derex & Boyd, 2015), and swarm intelligence (Krause, Ruxton, & Krause, 2010). Many more aspects of collective decision making have also been investigated (e.g., speed, frugality, shared accountability, cost efficiency, and procedural fairness).

13.2.1 Blending the Judgments of the Whole Crowd

The most straightforward way of aggregating multiple judgments is to weigh all judgments equally; that is, to use the whole crowd. For decision tasks, the *majority (plurality) rule* can be used, which chooses the option that received the most votes. One of the earliest demonstrations of the power of the majority rule was given by Marquis de Condorcet (Condorcet, 1785). According to what is now known as *Condorcet's jury theorem*, increasing the number of independent judgments increases the performance of the majority rule for binary decision tasks as long as the individual accuracy (of independent and identically skilled voters) is higher than 0.5 (Boland, 1989; Grofman, Feld, & Owen, 1984; Grofman et al., 1983; R. Hastie & Kameda, 2005; Sumpter & Pratt, 2009)—in other words, if the task is "kind" (Hertwig, 2012b). However, if individual accuracy is lower than 0.5 (i.e., in "wicked" tasks), adding more judgments will decrease the performance of the majority rule.[2] The accuracy of the average individual is thus a key boundary condition of the majority rule (see figures 13.1 and 13.2), which simply amplifies—for better or worse—the opinion of the typical individual in a group.

A second boundary condition for the emergence of the wisdom-of-crowds effect is the correlation between the members' judgments (Batchelor & Dua, 1995; Davis-Stober, Budescu, Dana, & Broomell, 2014; Herzog & Hertwig, 2009; Laan et al., 2017; Ladha, 1992, 1995; Larrick & Soll, 2006; Page, 2007b). This correlation can be positive, when members' judgments are more similar than expected by chance; absent, when members' judgments are independent; or negative, when members' judgments are less similar than expected by chance. If average individual accuracy is above 0.5 in binary decision tasks, the benefits of the majority rule are largest when members' judgments are negatively correlated: decision makers make different errors, which cancel each other out at the collective level (Ladha, 1992, 1995). If decision makers make exactly the same judgments, and thus the same errors (i.e., there is a perfect positive correlation), applying the majority rule will not improve decision accuracy. However, when average individual

---

2. This use of the terms "kind" and "wicked" differs from Hogarth's (Hogarth, Lejarraga, & Soyer, 2015) distinction between "kind" and "wicked" learning environments. In Hogarth's approach, the focus is on whether there is a match ("kind") or mismatch ("wicked") between the learning and the target environment.

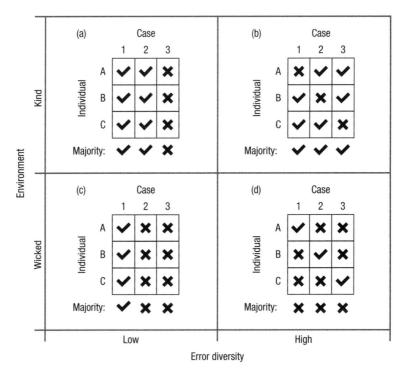

Figure 13.1
Majority voting and the role of error diversity. Four possible scenarios for three individuals A, B, and C (rows) deciding on three cases 1, 2, and 3 (columns); scenarios
depict kind (a, b) and wicked (c, d) environments, and low (a, c) and high (b, d)
error diversity. A check mark/cross indicates that a decision is correct/wrong. (a, c) If
all individuals make the same error, majority voting does not change performance,
regardless of whether cases are kind (i.e., the majority is right) or wicked (i.e., the
majority is wrong). (b) Majority voting improves decisions only if individuals make
different errors across the three kind cases. In this panel, individuals are right in only
two of three cases, but the majority is correct for all three because every question is
incorrectly answered by only one individual. (d) In wicked environments, high error
diversity decreases the already poor performance even further. See also figure 13.2.

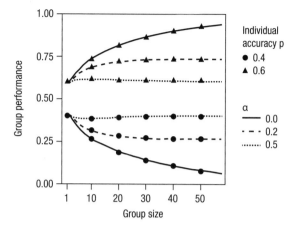

Figure 13.2
Illustration of the effect of group size, individual accuracy, and error diversity on the accuracy of the majority rule. The performance of a group using a majority rule (y-axis) as a function of group size N (x-axis) and individual accuracy p. α indicates the proportion of members voting identically to an opinion leader (i.e., a randomly selected group member with individual accuracy p identical to that of everyone else; see Grofman et al., 1983); $\alpha=0$ implies independent decisions and $\alpha=1$ implies maximally dependent decisions (i.e., everybody makes the same decisions, and thus errors, as the opinion leader). The effect of α on the group performance depends on the wickedness of the case. For kind cases (e.g., p=0.6), the lower the level of α (i.e., high error diversity), the higher the benefits of increasing group size. In contrast, for wicked cases (e.g., p=0.4), the lower the level of α, the worse decisions become with increasing group size (see figure 13.1 for an illustration).

accuracy is below 0.5, these predictions reverse and a negative correlation of members' judgments *reduces* the below-chance performance of the majority rule even further (see figures 13.1 and 13.2).

For continuous estimation tasks, such as predicting next year's inflation rate, judgments can be aggregated using *averaging rules* (e.g., arithmetic mean or median). One of the earliest examples of the success of averaging comes from Sir Francis Galton (Galton, 1907), who collected estimates of the weight of an ox from around 800 visitors to a livestock fair. The median of all these estimates turned out to be less than 1% off from the true weight of the ox, despite many inaccurate estimates. Simple averaging has been shown to generally outperform the average individual (Larrick et al., 2012) in instances such as general knowledge questions (Gigone & Hastie, 1997),

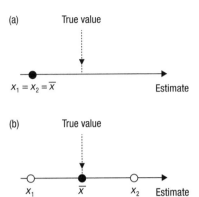

Figure 13.3
The effects of bracketing on error cancellation in estimation tasks. (a) No bracketing, hence no error cancellation: estimates x_1 and x_2 have the same error (here they underestimate the truth by the same amount); therefore, the average $\bar{x}$ is the same as the two estimates and also has the same absolute error (i.e., the absolute distance to the true value). (b) Bracketing, hence error cancellation: estimates x_1 and x_2 have different, but same-sized errors (i.e., they under- and overestimate the truth by the same amount; Larrick & Soll, 2006), so the errors cancel each other out. In this particular case, they cancel out perfectly and $\bar{x}$ has zero error.

management and forecasting (J. S. Armstrong, 2001; Clemen, 1989), and geopolitical forecasting (Steyvers, Wallsten, Merkle, & Turner, 2014). Averaging works particularly well when errors are diverse—when some estimates are too high but others are too low (i.e., estimates "bracket" the true value; Larrick & Soll, 2006; see figure 13.3). In such instances, averaging can at least partially cancel out individuals' errors. Box 13.2 discusses the statistical conditions for error cancellation in more detail. The effect of diversity in errors on the wisdom of crowds has received ample theoretical attention (Ladha, 1992, 1995; Sorkin, Hays, & West, 2001). However, the cognitive processes that underlie this diversity are largely unknown and provide an interesting avenue for future research (see, e.g., Juni & Eckstein, 2017; Tump, Wolf, Krause, & Kurvers, 2018). Interactive element 13.1 (at https://taming-uncertainty.mpib-berlin .mpg.de/) allows you to discover the wisdom of crowds at first hand.

13.2.2 Relying on the Best Individual
Another approach to harnessing the wisdom of crowds is to rely solely on the judgments of the best group member (Yetton & Bottger, 1982). For example, to predict next year's inflation rate, a decision maker may check

Box 13.2
Why and when diverse errors cancel each other out in estimation tasks.

Diverse errors improve accuracy in estimation tasks through error cancellation, as illustrated by the concept of bracketing (Larrick & Soll, 2006; see figure 13.3). Errors are most likely to be diverse when two conditions are met (Soll, 1999). The first is that crowd members' biases are diverse. Even if all members are biased (i.e., they all systematically misestimate the true quantities), as long as their biases are diverse (i.e., some members systematically overestimate, whereas others systematically underestimate), bracketing and thus error cancellation will occur.

The second condition is a low correlation among members' random errors. Even if all members are totally unbiased—that is, they do not systematically over- or underestimate the true quantities—their estimates will usually still scatter around the correct answers (i.e., there will be random error). To illustrate, imagine stepping several times on an unbiased, but imperfect, bathroom scale. Even though the scale does not systematically over- or underestimate your weight across many measurements, it may over- or underestimate your weight each time you step on the scale. Now imagine stepping on a second, equally unbiased yet also imperfect, bathroom scale. If the random errors of both scales are uncorrelated, their measurements will both err in the same direction half the time you step on them. In contrast, if their random errors are highly correlated, their measurements will frequently err in the same direction, reducing the scope for error cancellation (i.e., rarely producing bracketing). If their random errors are perfectly negatively correlated, the scales will always make opposite errors (i.e., always produce bracketing). Such negatively correlated errors are rarely observed in human judgments, however.

In sum, the degree to which bias is shared and the degree to which random errors are correlated in a population both determine how much error cancellation occurs and thus how well averaging performs (Davis-Stober, Budescu, & Broomell, 2015; Soll, 1999). In contrast to the majority rule, which can perform worse than the average individual (see figures 13.1 and 13.2), averaging cannot perform worse than the average individual in estimation tasks, even if all judgments are either over- or underestimates, as long as the error function escalates at least linearly with the distance from the truth.

which macroeconomic expert forecasted last year's inflation rate most accurately and rely exclusively on that expert's forecast for next year. But under which conditions does a best-member rule outperform a whole-crowd rule? For both decision and estimation tasks, similarity in accuracy is a key condition for determining whether it is better to rely on the best member or the whole crowd. When group members have a similar individual accuracy (i.e., there is little dispersion in individual accuracy), combining their decisions using a majority rule or their estimates using the averaging rule generally outperforms the best-member rule (Grofman et al., 1983; Kurvers et al., 2016; Mannes et al., 2014). For example, if the individual errors of a group of macroeconomic forecasters are similar in size, the best forecaster is not much more accurate than the others. Relying on the best individual can bring at most small gains in accuracy relative to the whole-crowd rule. In fact, it is more likely that the whole-crowd rule will outperform the best-member rule because the former can profit from error cancellation. As such, one should only consider relying on the best member when forecasters differ substantially in performance.

13.2.3   Using Select Crowds

Picture an analyst at a central bank preparing strategies for fiscal policy. The analyst consults the inflation rate forecasts of several experts. Unsurprisingly, they disagree. Suspecting that not all experts are equally skilled, the analyst fears that simply averaging all forecasts will impair the performance of the averaging rule because some poor forecasts may be included. The analyst also suspects that, among the top forecasters, there will be little difference in skills. Relying solely on the best individual would therefore mean missing out on the averaging gains from error cancellation. Luckily, there is a third way that lies between relying on the whole crowd and relying on the best member, and that is to rely on a select crowd of high-performing individuals—identified using a valid cue for individuals' future performance. The analyst could, for example, rank the forecasters according to their performance in the last year and average the forecasts of the best, say, five forecasters (i.e., a select crowd following a top-k approach; Mannes et al., 2014).

To understand the conditions under which a select-crowd rule performs well, Mannes et al. (2014) studied how both dispersion in expertise and bracketing (see figure 13.3) jointly affected the performance of the best-member, whole-crowd, and select-crowd rules in estimation tasks. When there was low dispersion in expertise (i.e., no strong interindividual differences in performance) and high error diversity (i.e., estimates often bracketed the truth), the averaging rule performed best. When there was high dispersion in expertise and low error diversity, the best-member rule won. In the other two combinations (high dispersion in expertise coupled with high error diversity and low dispersion in expertise coupled with low error diversity), the select-crowd rule triumphed. Crucially, even when the select-crowd rule did not perform best in an environment, it usually performed almost as well as whichever other crowd rule was the ideal approach. In contrast, in environments where the select-rule performed best, the other two rules performed markedly worse. The select-crowd rule's performance is thus more stable across different statistical environments and therefore less risky. The potential of select crowds has recently been demonstrated in several forecasting domains (E. Chen, Budescu, Lakshmikanth, Mellers, & Tetlock, 2016; Budescu & Chen, 2014; D. G. Goldstein, McAfee, & Suri, 2014; Mannes et al., 2014; H. Olsson & Loveday, 2015).

13.2.4 Relying on the Most Confident Individual

In numerous areas, such as intelligence services (Betts, 1978; Mellers et al., 2014), witness reports (Wixted & Wells, 2017), and medical diagnostics (Berner & Graber, 2008), experts report and act upon the confidence they have in the accuracy of their decisions. Thus, when not only multiple individual judgments but also the associated confidence judgments are available, confidence can be exploited in harnessing the wisdom of crowds. One prominent approach is to employ the confidence rule and select, for each case, the answer of the most confident person (Bang et al., 2014; Kämmer, Hautz, Herzog, Kunina-Habenicht, & Kurvers, 2017; Koriat, 2012b; Kurvers et al., 2016). In decision tasks, this can be done by adopting the decision of the person with the highest confidence judgment; in estimation tasks, it can be achieved by adopting the estimate with the smallest subjective confidence interval (Yaniv, 1997; Yaniv & Foster, 1997). The confidence rule can thus adopt the answers of different people across cases—in contrast to the other crowd rules discussed, which use all individuals, one individual, or a group of selected individuals for all cases.

A key boundary condition for the confidence rule is a positive relationship between confidence and accuracy across people. Which environmental conditions give rise to this positive relationship? Many cognitive models (e.g., the self-consistency model; Koriat, 2012a) assume that individuals sample cues (from memory or the environment) and choose the option more strongly favored by the cues. The more univocally the cues favor the chosen option, the more confident an individual becomes in their decision. Assuming that people use at least some of the same cues for their decisions, it follows that whenever most cues point to the correct option (i.e., in kind cases), the majority of people will make the correct decision. The more clearly the cues point to the correct option, the stronger the majority will be, and the more confident people will be in their decision. In such cases, a positive relationship between confidence and accuracy is expected. In contrast, in wicked cases, where the majority of cues point to the wrong option (e.g., a mammogram from a woman with breast cancer that shows no visible abnormalities), the majority of people will make the wrong decision— and, when the cues clearly point to the wrong option, they will do so with high confidence. In wicked cases, higher confidence implies lower accuracy. The overall validity of confidence in a domain therefore depends on the distribution of kind and wicked cases: the fewer wicked cases there are, the more positive the relationship between confidence and accuracy will be. The confidence rule, like the majority rule, will generally increase accuracy if most cases are kind, but will decrease accuracy if most cases are wicked.

The strength with which confidence predicts the accuracy of decisions across people depends not only on the distribution of kind and wicked cases in the task environment, but also on how closely people's confidence is aligned with their accuracy (Arkes, 2001; Griffin & Brenner, 2004; Murphy, 1973; H. Olsson, 2014; Pleskac & Busemeyer, 2010; Yates, 1990). The confidence rule works best when confidence tracks accuracy (i.e., in kind environments) and people's expressed confidence means the same for everybody (e.g., whenever anybody says "I'm 60% sure," it means that in 6 out of 10 such cases, the decision will be correct). In such a situation, the confidence rule will rely on the person who is most likely to be correct for any particular case. The potential of the confidence rule has recently been demonstrated in breast and skin cancer diagnostics (Kurvers et al., 2016) and in simulated emergency room decision making (Kämmer et al., 2017).

Our ecological analysis has shown that the performance of any crowd rule depends on the statistical structure of the environment (Davis-Stober et al., 2015; Davis-Stober et al., 2014; Herzog & von Helversen, 2018; Kurvers et al., 2016; Luan, Katsikopoulos, & Reimer, 2012; Mannes et al., 2014) and that no crowd rule dominates all other rules across environments (see table 13.1). The emerging research on the "wisdom of the inner crowd," where individuals simulate the wisdom of crowds within their own minds (Herzog & Hertwig, 2014a; Vul & Pashler, 2008), has produced corresponding insights into how to create and benefit from different judgments within a single mind (see box 13.3).

Up to now, we have assumed that the decision maker has complete knowledge about the statistical structure of the environment, making it relatively easy to select the best-performing crowd rule. In practice, however, decision makers rarely enjoy the luxury of omniscience. Instead, they face uncertainty about the environment, which results in uncertainty about which crowd rule will work best. Section 13.3 focuses on these situations, where decision makers face the problem of *strategy selection* (Marewski & Link, 2014; J. W. Payne, Bettman, & Johnson, 1993; Rieskamp & Otto, 2006) when choosing among crowd rules.

13.3 Selecting a Crowd Rule without the Benefit of Omniscience

The previous section introduced four aspects of the statistical structure of the environment that govern the performance of crowd rules: the accuracy of the average individual, the diversity of errors, the dispersion of individual accuracies, and the validity of confidence. These aspects, however, are not usually completely known, which leads to uncertainty about how well the crowd rules will perform in practice. Furthermore, the crowd rules differ in their applicability because they vary in their requirements. The whole-crowd rule is the least demanding rule, as it requires only the judgments. The confidence rule also necessitates confidence judgments for each judgment. The best-member and select-crowd rules are the most demanding: they need additional knowledge to predict individuals' accuracy, or at least the knowledge to rank the members according to their expected accuracy.

13.3.1 Estimating Individual Accuracy and the Bias–Variance Dilemma

To understand why harnessing individual differences in accuracy can be challenging, let us consider the process of estimating different people's accuracy in detail. A common way to estimate people's accuracy is to evaluate a sample of past judgments from each crowd member. However, if this

Box 13.3

The wisdom of the inner crowd.

When there is no crowd available (e.g., when the decision maker has no access to suitable experts or no time to elicit their opinions), a single individual can simulate the wisdom of crowds within their own mind (Herzog & Hertwig, 2014a; Stroop, 1932; van Dolder & van den Assem, 2018; Vul & Pashler, 2008). Stroop first illustrated the power of such an "inner crowd" in a ranking task, where participants repeatedly sorted identical-looking objects according to their weight. He found that averaging ever more rankings within participants increased the correlation between the judged and actual rank of the objects. Impressively, the correlation increased at the same pace as when averaging rankings from the same number of different participants. Because the objects looked identical and individuals could thus not be influenced by their previous rankings, repeated rankings from the same participant were as diverse as rankings from different participants, showing that inner crowds can be as powerful as regular crowds. As is the case with real crowds, the success of aggregation strategies for inner crowds depends on the similarity of the accuracy of initial and later estimates, diversity of errors, and the ability to identify the better estimates.

Several studies (reviewed in Herzog & Hertwig, 2014a) have demonstrated that averaging a person's repeated estimates can improve their accuracy. However, averaging estimates of different individuals usually results in higher gains because error diversity between different individuals' estimates is higher. This raises the question of how error diversity within an individual's judgments can be increased. As illustrated by Stroop (1932), if one can completely blind people to their previous judgments, eliciting more judgments from the same person can be as effective as recruiting different people. It is, however, not always feasible to clear the slate in this way. Herzog and Hertwig (2009) proposed *dialectical bootstrapping* as a general framework for eliciting nonredundant estimates with diverse errors from a single person. They have demonstrated that asking people to "consider the opposite" when generating a new estimate is one possible approach to elicit such nonredundant estimates.

Consulting the inner crowd also poses the problem of strategy selection; here, too, the statistical structure of the environment—which is usually not known—determines how well rules perform. Paralleling the insights for real crowds, it has been shown that similar levels of accuracy, diversity of errors, and a lack of valid cues to identify better estimates favor averaging over choosing single estimates stemming from one mind (Fraundorf & Benjamin, 2014; Herzog & Hertwig, 2014b; Herzog & von Helversen, 2018).

training sample is small, estimates of individual accuracy may be noticeably different from the individual's actual accuracy. As a result, strategies that depend strongly on correct estimates of individual accuracy may overfit to the training cases and thereby generalize poorly to future cases. Consider a scenario where the best member should, from an omniscient perspective, outperform the whole crowd (i.e., high dispersion in expertise and low error diversity). If the training sample is too small to reliably estimate individual accuracy, the best-member rule may nevertheless be outperformed by the whole-crowd rule because the "best" individual selected is not actually the best member in the test set. In this case and others, the "wrong" biased strategy (i.e., the whole-crowd rule in a domain with high dispersion in expertise and low error diversity) can outperform the "correct" unbiased strategy (i.e., the best-member rule).

The insight that biased strategies can outperform unbiased strategies is formalized in the *bias–variance dilemma* (see chapter 2; Brighton & Gigerenzer, 2015; Geman, Bienenstock, & Doursat, 1992). It shows that a biased, less flexible learning mechanism (e.g., putting equal weight on informational cues to predict a criterion, while only learning the direction of the cues) can be more accurate than a less biased, more flexible learning mechanism (e.g., multiple linear regression, which estimates a weight for each cue) because the latter's parameter estimates fluctuate more across different sets of training data. Such fluctuations are especially pronounced for small samples (Dana & Dawes, 2004; Davis-Stober, Dana, & Budescu, 2010; Dawes, 1979; Lichtenberg & Şimşek, 2017). Reducing bias will often increase variance, but the total error depends on both—hence the dilemma. Minimizing total error therefore means finding a good balance between bias and variance. Crowd rules that depend on training data (e.g., the best-member and select-crowd rules) face a similar bias–variance dilemma (Analytis, Barkoczi, & Herzog, 2018; Brown, Wyatt, Harris, & Yao, 2005; Davis-Stober et al., 2015). In contrast, crowd rules that do not use any training data (e.g., the whole-crowd rule) have no variance because their performance cannot fluctuate across different samples of training data (Analytis et al., 2018). Further developing such parallels between crowd rules and judgment strategies (see chapter 11; Gigerenzer, Todd, & the ABC Research Group, 1999; Todd, Gigerenzer, & the ABC Research Group, 2012) is a promising avenue for both research domains (Analytis et al., 2018).

13.3.2 Selecting a Crowd Rule in Practice

Given the challenge of harnessing individual differences in accuracy, how then should a decision maker select a crowd rule? To begin, let us consider the simplest case, where the decision maker knows nothing about the crowd members. In this situation, the whole-crowd rule generally outperforms the other rules. To appreciate why, imagine choosing between a best-member or an averaging rule for a continuous estimation task. Trying to choose a best member without any prior knowledge amounts to selecting a random individual from the crowd. And because choosing the estimates of a randomly selected member cannot perform better than averaging the estimates of all members (when averaging using the arithmetic mean and for all escalating loss functions, such as mean squared error; this follows from Jensen's inequality, see, e.g., Davis-Stober et al., 2014), the best-member rule cannot outperform the whole-crowd rule in this case.

The best-member (or select-crowd) rule comes into play only once the decision maker has gained some experience with the domain and can start to meaningfully rank the crowd members according to their accuracy. However, as we have previously established, a minimum amount of experience is required to reliably outperform the whole crowd—even if the environment is, in theory, best suited for the best-member rule. This raises the question of how much experience is enough. If time and resources allow and if relevant data are available, the problem of strategy selection among crowd rules can, in principle, always be addressed by computational approaches. In machine learning, computational experiments are routinely conducted to train and choose among different predictive algorithms (T. Hastie, Tibshirani, & Friedman, 2009; Kuhn & Johnson, 2013). By calculating the generalization performance of different crowd rules as a function of the number of experiences ("learning curves"; Perlich, Provost, & Simonoff, 2003), a data analyst can select the most promising crowd rule. In the absence of such time, resources, and relevant data, a decision maker can rely on two principles.

13.3.3 Two Principles for Selecting a Crowd Rule without the Benefit of Omniscience

The first principle for mere mortals who need to choose a crowd rule is: *when in doubt, aggregate more rather than fewer judgments*. The rationale behind this principle is twofold. First, more aggregation is less risky than less or no aggregation because aggregation avoids the worst-case scenario of picking the worst individual—or, at least, avoids putting a lot of weight on the worst individuals (Davis-Stober, 2011; Davis-Stober, Dana, & Budescu, 2010; Hibon & Evgeniou, 2005). Aggregating multiple judgments is akin to an "error portfolio" (Timmermann, 2006): compared with hedging the risk by investing in an index fund, betting everything one has on a single stock is a highly risky strategy. Likewise, betting on a single crowd member is risky, and one can hedge that risk by aggregating multiple judgments. The second reason for aggregating more rather than fewer judgments is that it typically works. Empirical studies of human judges and forecasters (e.g., J. S. Armstrong, 2001; Mannes et al., 2014) and machine learning algorithms (Fernández-Delgado, Cernadas, Barro, & Amorim, 2014; Kuncheva, 2004; Rokach, 2010) suggest that aggregation usually leads to good performance—or, at the very least, can substantially reduce the worst-case error (Hibon & Evgeniou, 2005). In the absence of prior knowledge, it is reasonable to expect that aggregation will be beneficial.

The second principle is: *instead of trying to understand the environment, use experience to adapt to it.* Building on the first principle, a decision maker should start out with an aggregation-heavy crowd rule (e.g., the whole crowd) and monitor its success, as well as that of plausible contender strategies, such as the best-member, confidence, or select-crowd rule. As feedback starts to come in, a decision maker will either be reinforced in their approach of relying on the whole crowd or encouraged to gravitate toward one of the more selective approaches. The top-k approach of creating select crowds is particularly useful in this regard (i.e., averaging the judgments of the k most promising individuals; Mannes et al., 2014), as one can start out with the whole crowd (i.e., $k = N$) before gradually relying on fewer and fewer individuals (i.e., reducing k) as long as feedback justifies doing so. Decreasing the size of the select crowd k amounts to moving along the bias–variance continuum from zero variance but likely bias (simple average: $k = N$), suitable for environments where the decision maker has little experience, to possible variance but no bias (best-member: $k = 1$), suitable for environments where the best-member rule performs best.

We have addressed what decision makers can do when they lack complete knowledge of the statistical environment, and we have proposed two principles to guide their choice of crowd rule: (a) *when in doubt, aggregate more rather than fewer judgments*; and (b) *instead of trying to understand the environment, use experience to adapt to it—and become more selective if the environment calls for it.* Such a conservative approach to strategy selection has the advantage that, should the environment change (e.g., should financial markets break down or continuing education improve radiologists' individual accuracy), the choice of crowd rule will adapt accordingly over time.

The problem of selecting a crowd rule in the absence of complete knowledge of the environment highlights an important point for adaptive decision making that transcends the topic of the wisdom of crowds (Analytis et al., 2018; Gigerenzer & Brighton, 2009; see also chapters 2, 5, 11, and 12): the strategy that would work best in principle is not necessarily the one that will work best in practice. To the extent that a strategy needs to learn from experience, it may only start unfolding its true potential once the decision maker has acquired sufficient experience.

14 Crowds on the Move

Mehdi Moussaïd

14.1 Walking Together

It may look simple. It may feel simple. But walking in a crowded place is a challenging cognitive task—not least because uncertainties abound. A pedestrian in the middle of a dense crowd is bombarded with a constant flow of rapidly changing information about the movement of dozens of people. The pedestrian's field of vision is overwhelmed by bodies moving in different directions, approaching at different speeds, or suddenly appearing from behind. In this highly nonstationary environment, avoiding collisions is just one objective. A pedestrian must also keep track of where they need to go while constantly revising their path to the destination, scanning the surrounding physical space, and paying attention to signs and physical obstructions. Anyone who doubts the complexities of walking in a crowd should spend a few moments imagining the challenges involved in getting robots do just that (Trautman & Krause, 2010).

Against this background, it is fascinating to observe the ease with which pedestrians actually walk through a crowd—generally without mishap or body contact, and sometimes while talking to friends or sending text messages. But what is even more fascinating is the behavior of a whole crowd of pedestrians. Seen from a bird's-eye perspective, a crowd often seems to act as a coherent entity that adapts smoothly and smartly to its physical environment. Striking collective patterns of movement emerge, as if everyone were working together to ensure that each individual reaches their destination comfortably. Sometimes, however, this perfectly orchestrated machinery breaks down. Under specific conditions, pedestrians' behavior can produce collective patterns that may, ultimately, lead to deadly crowd disasters.

How do pedestrians manage the many unknowns in crowds? And why do crowds and the single players in them appear so efficient most of the time—but mad at other times? This chapter focuses on the heuristics that pedestrians use to navigate crowded places and describes how these processes trigger amplification mechanisms that create large-scale collective patterns. It will show that the heuristics that help pedestrians deal with the inherent uncertainty of the crowd can produce either advantageous or disadvantageous collective patterns. The pattern that emerges depends on one unique crucial environmental parameter: the level of density. This parameter distinguishes situations in which a crowd behaves wisely from those in which it appears to go berserk.

14.1.1   How Pedestrians Navigate

Pedestrians face two sources of uncertainty when moving in a crowd. The first resides in the social environment: the behavior of other pedestrians can never be completely known or perfectly predictable. For instance, someone trying to avoid a collision with an oncoming person can never be sure how that person will move in the next few seconds. In addition, visibility is often reduced in crowded areas, making pedestrians uncertain about whether somebody else is approaching them or not. Uncertainty about others' behavior is analogous to *strategic uncertainty*, which arises when one does not know how others will act in a competitive environment (see chapters 5 and 12), except that the interactions need not be competitive; they may also be cooperative. The second source of uncertainty resides in an unfamiliar physical environment and emerges when pedestrians have to decide where they want to go and how to get there. A museum visitor may, for instance, need to find out where the bathroom is and how to get there quickly. If a fire alarm sounds, the visitor will need to decide whether or not to leave the building, locate the emergency exits and the routes to them, and evaluate whether or not the recommended route is safe or blocked by obstacles such as smoke or fire. All these decisions need to be taken despite uncertainty about the nature of the danger or the topology of the building.

Despite the gaps in their knowledge, interdependencies of their decisions, and fast pace, pedestrians manage to navigate crowded places efficiently. The key mental tools for achieving this feat are simple navigation heuristics (see box 14.1 for a historical perspective on crowd modeling). In the same way as the gaze heuristic enables both rugby players and moths

Box 14.1
A historical perspective on crowd modeling.

The behavior of pedestrians has not always been described in terms of simple heuristics. In fact, invoking heuristics is a recent development in crowd research. Since the 1960s, the behavior of pedestrians has primarily been described by means of analogies with physical systems—that is, using "as if" models that do not aim to describe the cognitive processes producing pedestrian behavior. The first models of crowd dynamics were proposed by physicists inspired by fluid mechanics, who suggested that a crowd moving along a street might be comparable to a fluid flowing along a pipeline (Henderson, 1974). The most influential physics-based model was proposed in the 1990s by Helbing and Molnár (1995): the *social force model*, which assumes that the behavior of a pedestrian in a crowd is comparable to the movement of a particle in a gas. This analogy made it possible to transfer tools and theories from Newtonian mechanics to the study of pedestrian behavior. In this model, pedestrians are subject to a set of attraction and repulsion forces that "push" them in a certain direction. For instance, pedestrians can be attracted by their destination point and, at the same time, repulsed by the other pedestrians. In the same way, the imitation of others' behavior can be described by a new set of forces that attract people in the same direction as their neighbors (see box 14.2 for a formal description of the model). The high flexibility of the model, coupled with its ability to produce nontrivial collective patterns, contributed to its success. The social force model remains the most commonly used framework in crowd research.

to catch moving objects (Hamlin, 2017), pedestrians are assumed to use a variety of navigation heuristics to weave their way through a crowd and avoid collisions.[1] The crucial property that navigation heuristics have in common with all other heuristics is the smart omission of information (see chapter 1). Pedestrians navigating an environment ignore most of the available information and do not try to optimize every step of their path toward a goal. Rather, they rely on simple heuristics that exploit merely a fraction of the available information to produce solutions that are good enough (Simon, 1955, 1956). For instance, they may follow others when uncertain about where to go, rely on default behaviors when they do not know what

---

1. Individuals relying on the gaze heuristic can catch a target moving through the air by running such that the object remains at a constant angle. This simple rule will lead them to the point where the target will land.

Box 14.2
Physics-based and heuristic-based crowd modeling.

There exist two trends in crowd modeling: the physics-based approach outlined in box 14.1 and illustrated by the *social force model*, and the more recent heuristic-based approach. This box describes more formally how the two modeling frameworks are implemented. In both models, the position $\vec{x}_i$ of a pedestrian i changes according to the vector $\vec{v}_i$ describing their walking speed and direction:

$$\frac{d\vec{x}_i}{dt} = \vec{v}_i. \tag{B1}$$

In the social force model, the movement $\vec{v}_i$ is assumed to result from a set of forces that attract the pedestrian toward their destination and, at the same time, push the pedestrian away from walls, obstacles, and other pedestrians:

$$\frac{d\vec{v}_i}{dt} = \vec{D}_i + \Sigma \vec{F}_{ij} + \Sigma \vec{F}_{iw}. \tag{B2}$$

Here, $\vec{D}_i$ is the "driving force" pushing the pedestrian toward their goal, whereas $\vec{F}_{ij}$ is a repulsive force originating from another individual j, and $\vec{F}_{iw}$ is a repulsive force originating from a wall or other static obstacle w. Repulsive forces are typically expressed as exponentially decreasing functions of the distance d_{ij} between the focal individual and the place where the force originates, using an equation such as the following:

$$\vec{F}_{ij} = Ae^{-d_{ij}/B}, \tag{B3}$$

where A and B are model parameters corresponding to the strength and the range, respectively, of the repulsive force. Hence, the resulting motion sums up the pedestrian's desire to move toward their destination, the repulsion effects of all the other individuals in the crowd, and the repulsion effects of all obstacles in the environment. The time resolution dt indicates how often this calculation is undertaken and is typically set to $dt < 0.1$ seconds.

In contrast, the heuristic-based approach suggests that the pedestrian actively chooses a walking direction α and a walking speed v, based on the available visual information. For instance, the following two rules have been proposed (Moussaïd, Helbing, & Theraulaz, 2011):

Rule 1: The chosen walking direction α is the one that minimizes the walking distance to the destination point.

Rule 2: The chosen walking speed v is the one that limits the time to collision with the nearest obstacle to a minimum of τ seconds, where τ is the individual's reaction time.

Box 14.2 (continued)

The movement vector $\vec{v}$ is the vector pointing in the direction α with norm v. Although the model is easy to describe, its implementation is challenging: deriving the values of α and v requires a representation of the pedestrian's field of vision, which is a difficult programming task. Pedestrians are able to estimate distances and time to collisions with moving objects sufficiently well by relying on evolved abilities (see Gigerenzer, Todd, & the ABC Research Group, 1999). In other words, they can take advantage of the two aforementioned rules with no need to deliberately undertake complex calculations.

Empirical situations that allow for discrimination between the two models are difficult to find. The reason is that both models are robust and flexible. The social force model can easily accommodate a new observation by adding a force component to the framework. For instance, imitation can be described by means of a new attraction force that pushes the pedestrian in the direction of the surrounding flow. Analogously, the heuristics-based model can accommodate a new class of observations by adding a new heuristic to the pedestrian toolbox. For instance, a sidestep heuristic has been suggested to correct for the blockages that occur when two pedestrians face each other at a narrow bottleneck. One conceptual difference may allow for discrimination between the two approaches, however. The social force model treats interactions with multiple people as a superposition of pair interactions. That is, when individual A faces three other individuals, B, C, and D, the force-based model typically assumes that A sums up the repulsion effects that B, C, and D would have separately in the absence of the two others. In other words, repulsive forces cumulate, and the trajectory of a pedestrian avoiding a group of individuals will consequently change depending on the number of people in the group. In contrast, the heuristics-based approach treats all other individuals as an integrated visual pattern, irrespective of their number. The trajectory of a pedestrian avoiding a group is independent of the number of people in the group, as long as the shape of the group remains unchanged. An experiment with this design, if it were conducted, could help to evaluate the predictive accuracy of the two frameworks.

others are going to do, seek empty spaces in their field of vision, or adapt their steps to those of their close neighbors.

14.1.2 The Emergence of Collective Patterns

The *collective* dynamics of the crowd emerge when a specific behavior starts to propagate from one pedestrian to another (Schelling, 1978). In a dense crowd, for instance, a pedestrian who suddenly stops to avoid colliding with the person in front unintentionally forces the people behind to stop as well. The same dynamic replicates to the people behind them, thus making stopping behavior contagious throughout the crowd. Propagation dynamics also emerge when people imitate the exit choice of others during an evacuation. In doing so, they unintentionally amplify the visibility of the choice they are imitating (Boyd & Richerson, 1988; Cavalli-Sforza & Feldman, 1981), thus increasing the likelihood that the choice will, in turn, be imitated by others. More generally, when performing a given action increases the likelihood that others will perform the same action, the large numbers and the spatial proximity of people in moving crowds can create conditions conducive to the emergence of collective patterns. In some cases, such as the spontaneous collective organization of pedestrian flows, collective patterns can be beneficial to pedestrians. But high levels of density often also give rise to *social dilemmas*—that is, tensions between the individual's goals and interests and the collective good. These tensions are typically at the root of detrimental and dangerous collective patterns in crowd behavior. As will become clear in the cases described next, when very high density changes the rules of the collective game, individual concerns often prevail over collective concerns.

14.2   Uncertainty about the Behavior of Others

14.2.1   The Side Preference Heuristic and the Formation of Adaptive Crowd Patterns

Using suitable navigation heuristics can make complex avoidance situations simple. Imagine, for instance, two pedestrians heading toward each other in a narrow walkway. If they continue to walk straight on, they will collide. The solution in this case is clear: the two pedestrians have to dodge each other by moving to the side. The challenge is that both have to move to the same side from their respective perspectives for this to work. Choosing left or right works equally well, as long as both pedestrians make the same choice. This situation is equivalent to a simple coordination game: two individuals have two options to choose from and succeed if they choose the same option but fail if they make different choices (see chapter 5 for examples of similar social games). Both individuals are complete strangers, cannot communicate, and have to make their decision within a few seconds. A random choice thus seems to be the only available strategy, resulting in a fifty-fifty chance of colliding. But pedestrians have found a better solution: they employ a heuristic that takes advantage of the default option. Specifically, if there is no clear sign indicating the side that the other person will choose, they will select the default option (Moussaïd et al., 2009). This simple heuristic works well because the default option turns out to be the same for most pedestrians within a culture. In most countries, it is the right-hand side, though in countries such as Japan the left-hand side has emerged as the default (Helbing, Buzna, Johansson, & Werner, 2005). Interestingly, the default passing side is not officially regulated in any culture. Rather, numerical simulations show that it is likely to have emerged through social learning (Helbing, 1991; Helbing, Molnár, Farkas, & Bolay, 2001).

These simulations assume a population of pedestrians who initially choose their passing side at random. That is, each pedestrian starts out with a 50% chance of choosing the left-hand side and a 50% chance of choosing the right-hand side. In every simulation round, random pairs of pedestrians are formed to then try to avoid each other. With every success (i.e., when both pedestrians choose the same side), the probability of choosing the same side again in the future increases. With every failure (i.e., when the two choose different sides), the probability of choosing that side decreases. In the first few rounds of the simulation, pedestrians oscillate between left- and right-hand avoidance. But as soon as a slight majority of people randomly start to prefer the same side, that preference rapidly begins to spread to the rest of the population. After some time, a global preference emerges; in other words, the entire population ends up going to the same side. Since both sides are equivalent to begin with, the simulations predict that different preferences will emerge in different populations, as can indeed be observed around the world.

This *side preference* heuristic (see table 14.1) enables individual pedestrians to avoid bumping into others when walking in crowded places. But it also has benefits for the collective of pedestrians. In many tourist destinations—say, Barcelona, Budapest, or Berlin—pedestrians have to avoid a steady flow of people walking in the opposite direction. They will tend to move to the right-hand side of the oncoming individuals, and every new encounter will "push" the pedestrian further to the right of the walkway. Similarly, when two flows of people are moving in opposite directions, repeated avoidances between individuals will produce a separation of the flows. After a short time, pedestrians walking in one direction will occupy one half of the available width, and those walking in the opposite direction

Table 14.1

Summary of pedestrian heuristics described in this chapter and elsewhere.

Heuristic	Description
Pedestrian heuristics described in this chapter	
Side preference	Choose the default avoidance side when avoiding a pedestrian moving in the opposite direction.
Speed adaptation	Reduce your speed such that the expected collision time is greater than your own reaction time.
Follow the flow	If you do not know where to go, follow the largest flow of neighboring individuals.
Pedestrian heuristics reported elsewhere	
Seek empty spaces	Walk in the direction of the deepest sight lines in your field of vision (Moussaïd et al., 2011; Turner & Penn, 2002).
Step or wait	Stop moving if the next step will lead to a collision (Johansson, 2009; Seitz, Bode, & Köster, 2016).
Tangential evasion	Move tangentially if the next step will lead to a collision (Seitz et al., 2016).
Sidestep	Sidestep if the next step will lead to a collision (Seitz et al., 2016).
Follow the leader	Choose and follow another person walking in the same direction (Seitz et al., 2016).

will occupy the other half. This collective pattern is called "highway formation" or "lane formation" and it emerges spontaneously from individual pedestrians' systematic avoidance behavior (Helbing et al., 2005; see figure 14.1a). Highway formation strongly enhances the traffic flow. Individuals moving in spatially segregated flows can walk straight ahead with no need to undertake further avoidance maneuvers—like cars driving faster in strictly separated lanes. Furthermore, this collective pattern is flexible and adaptive. Whenever the two opposing flows are not equally balanced—that is, when more people are walking in one direction than the other—the bigger flows will "push" the smaller one more powerfully, resulting in a greater portion of the walkway being allocated to the bigger flow. It is as if an invisible hand were ruling the crowd, preventing congestion and making sure that each flow receives a share of the walkway proportional to its needs. In *The Wealth of Nations*, Adam Smith (1776/2008) used the metaphor of an invisible hand to describe the collective benefits emerging from the actions of a multitude of self-interested individuals. In moving crowds, this hand

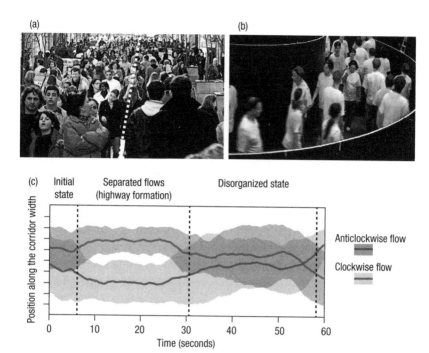

Figure 14.1

Adaptive highway formation. (a) Highway formation observed in the field, in Rue Sainte-Catherine, Bordeaux, France. The dashed line shows the boundary between the two flows. (b) The same phenomenon observed in the laboratory. In this experiment, 60 participants were randomly positioned in a ring-shaped corridor. Half of them were instructed to walk clockwise; the other half, anticlockwise. This snapshot was taken 15 seconds after the start signal. The two flows are clearly separated. (c) Average position of the pedestrians in each flow along the corridor width in the first 60 seconds of the experiment. Highway formation emerges naturally about 10 seconds after the starting signal, but breaks down 20 seconds later. The experiment demonstrated that the collective organization was disrupted by a minority of fast walkers who tried to walk through the opposite flow (Moussaïd et al., 2012).

has a cognitive foundation: large-scale structures like pedestrian highways are side effects of the heuristics that pedestrians use to avoid one another.

As the density of people increases, pedestrian highways become increasingly visible and well structured—until, at some point, they suddenly break down. An experimental study of this breaking point found that the collective pattern tends to become unstable and eventually collapse when too many pedestrians enter the flows; that is, when the density level becomes too high (Moussaïd et al., 2012; see figure 14.1b–c). But which behavioral mechanisms cause this collective breakdown? In structured highways, the speed of the flow constrains each individual's walking speed. This speed decreases gradually as the number of people increases. Crucially, pedestrians dislike walking slower than their desired walking speed—and the slower the flow, the greater their frustration. At a certain level of frustration, some fast walkers will start to overtake those in front of them. In so doing, they meet the opposite flow head-on and pass through it, creating a complex chain reaction and causing the collective organization to unravel. Ironically, the ensuing disorganized state will reduce everybody's walking speed. Pedestrians determined to walk faster can do so only at a cost to all the other individuals in the crowd—a manifestation of the tragedy of the commons (Hardin, 1968). An important lesson from this scenario, and one that holds more generally, is that pedestrians tend to form adaptive, beneficial

Box 14.3
Crowds, flocks, and swarms.

The collective behaviors of human crowds bear similarities to those of social animal species such as ants, fish, and birds. Like pedestrians, fish and birds form herding patterns (Moussaïd et al., 2009), and some species of ants form lanes in their bidirectional foraging trails (Couzin & Franks, 2003). In fact, human crowds and animal swarms belong to the same large family of self-organized biological systems (Couzin, 2009; Moussaïd et al., 2009; Sumpter, 2006). In these systems, collective patterns of movement emerge spontaneously as a result of multiple interactions taking place between individuals on a local scale (Camazine, 2003). Interestingly, qualitatively similar collective patterns can be observed between species, but each species has its own unique abilities and behaviors. For instance, colonies of *Eciton burchellii* army ants going back and forth between their nest and a food source tend to form lanes along their foraging trail—a pattern similar to human highway formation. But whereas human traffic is commonly organized in two lanes, army ants use a three-lane system, with the individuals carrying food back to the nest occupying the center of the trail and those leaving the nest occupying the margins. This pattern develops because ants returning to the nest are heavily loaded with food and have reduced turning capabilities, forcing the opposite flow to the sides. In contrast, human pedestrian lanes are shaped by the side preference—a different mechanism (see Table 14.1).

collective patterns at moderate densities. When there are too many people, however, tensions between individual and collective benefits undermine the collective organization, often triggering new but maladaptive collective patterns.

14.2.2 Slowing Down, Pushing, and the Mechanics of Crowd Disasters

Pedestrians have more tricks up their sleeves to avoid collisions. Beyond moving to the side, they can also adapt their speed. Here again, people cope with uncertainty about others' behavior in a simple and adaptive way. The human brain effortlessly gauges whether a collision with a moving object is likely to occur and, if so, when (Gibson, 1958). Pedestrians exploit this cognitive ability to avoid collisions by applying a *speed adaptation* heuristic (see table 14.1). Specifically, they adapt their walking speed to ensure that the estimated collision time is always greater than their own reaction time (Johansson, 2009; Moussaïd et al., 2011). For instance, if someone needs half a second to stop moving, they will adjust their walking speed such that all obstacles are more than half a second away, making collisions impossible. This heuristic functions well to the extent that all pedestrians adjust their speed to their reaction time. People who need more time to react—because they are carrying a heavy load, for example, or due to their physical condition—will simply start slowing down sooner than others who can react faster.

Although the speed adaptation heuristic gives pedestrians an individual navigation benefit, it may also be involved in the emergence of maladaptive collective patterns. In a unidirectional flow of pedestrians, an increase in the density level reduces the empty space between people. By extension, greater density reduces the expected collision time. As a consequence, the more people there are in a flow, the slower they will walk. This relationship between density and walking speed is a highly predictable collective feature of crowds, and is represented by the *fundamental diagram* of traffic flow (Seyfried, Steffen, Klingsch, & Boltes, 2005; see figure 14.2). Increasing density is necessarily associated with a reduction in walking speed. When density reaches a critical threshold of around 2.5 people per square meter, a new collective phenomenon emerges: stop-and-go waves (Helbing, Johansson, Mathiesen, Jensen, & Hansen, 2006). Stop-and-go waves are characterized by a discontinuity of the flow as people alternate between movement and standstill—a highly uncomfortable walking mode. The mechanism

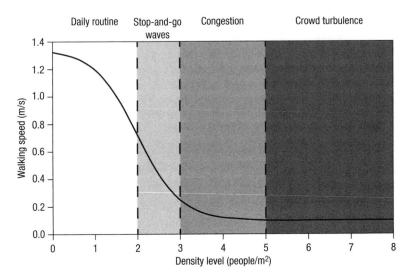

Figure 14.2
Fundamental diagram of traffic flow: changes in pedestrians' average walking speed as a function of the density level, measured in terms of the number of people per square meter. Change in a sole environmental condition, density, produces a variety of collective patterns, without there being any change in the navigation strategies used by pedestrians. The shape of the speed curve may vary with external factors.

underlying this pattern is that when distances between individuals become very small, some people temporarily need to stop moving to avoid collisions, creating a chain reaction of others stopping behind them. When the first individual starts moving again, restart delays create a gap in the crowd that propagates backward in the flow. This pattern sets in solely as a result of an increase in density; it does not involve a change in the individual heuristics that pedestrians use.

As density increases further, the crowd reaches a complete congestion point at which nobody can move any further. Above a threshold located somewhere in the range of five to seven people per square meter, things get bad. Apart from not being able to move, pedestrians cannot help but touch each other. The natural reaction in this uncomfortable situation is to push one's neighbors to create some empty space around oneself. Although this behavior helps the individual, it jams the space for the neighbors even further—which, in turn, prompts them to do some pushing of their own, again easing their own physical pressure but burdening others with more.

Analyses of video surveillance datasets recorded in extremely crowded places reveal that multiple waves of pushing behaviors can travel simultaneously through the crowd, a dangerous phenomenon called *crowd turbulence* (Helbing, Johansson, & Al-Abideen, 2007). When a pushing wave reaches a physical obstacle such as a wall, it "bounces" off it and travels back in the opposite direction, often injuring the people closest to the wall. When two or more waves cross each other, people located at the junction can lose their footing and fall, prompting dangerous crowd stampedes. The phenomenon of crowd turbulence has been shown to be the main cause of crowd disasters such as the Love Parade tragedy in Duisburg in 2010 and the stampede in Mecca in 2006 (Helbing et al., 2014; Helbing & Mukerji, 2012; Moussaïd et al., 2011). Conceptually, crowd turbulence is another manifestation of the tension between individual and collective benefits in dense crowds. Individually, each person reaps an immediate benefit from pushing their neighbors but collectively everybody would be safer if nobody pushed. In such extreme situations, individual concerns often prevail over the collective good, leading to unavoidable mass accidents.

14.3 Uncertainty about the Physical Environment

From the previous section it may appear that, to quote Jean-Paul Sartre, "hell is other people" (Sartre, 1944, p. 61). Indeed, the uncertainty arising from the behavior of other pedestrians raises multiple navigation challenges that would not exist if one could wander empty streets alone. At the same time, other people can also turn out to be useful. They can provide efficient solutions to another source of uncertainty for travelers—namely, uncertainty about the physical environment. But again, in dense crowds, individual and collective benefits are not always compatible. In addition to being able to weave their way through the crowd, pedestrians need to know where to go and how to get there. But people do not always know how to reach their destination, especially when the physical environment is unknown or rapidly changing. Consider the case of a train traveler arriving at a city's vast main station for the first time and looking for the main exit, where they assume they will find a cab stand or the entrance to the subway system. The traveler does not know how many exits there are, where they are located, or which one is the main exit. The available navigation systems are of little help. In principle, a reasonable solution would be to scan the environment for signs, imagine the paths to different exits, and evaluate which is the best alternative. Of course, most pedestrians rarely evaluate the situation so comprehensively. Instead, they rely, at least in part, on a simple heuristic: they look around and walk in the same direction as the dominant flow of surrounding people. This *follow-the-flow* heuristic (see table 14.1), like other heuristics, ignores most of the available information and thus saves travelers the time that searching for and processing routing indications would require. The heuristic's power lies in the structure of the environment. Although pedestrians have different destinations, the topology of a train station is often centralized around transportation hubs that offer good options for reaching most destination points. Because most people, irrespective of their destination, travel through these hubs, following others often constitutes a good strategy for reaching one's own destination—or at least an intermediate point. The exact nature of this follow-the-flow heuristic remains unknown, however. Do pedestrians choose to follow the majority of their neighbors? Or do they use a quorum rule according to which a threshold number of people walking in a given direction suffices for them to adopt the same direction? But then, how do people sample their neighbors? And when do they stop sampling and choose a direction? Might pedestrians also target a specific person in the crowd and follow that individual? In which case, how is this "leader" chosen?

Similar to the other pedestrian heuristics discussed previously, the efficiency of the follow-the-flow heuristic has limits. Suppose a large group of commuters exits the train and heads toward a lower level of the station with the goal of catching a local train rather than leaving the station. A traveler who joins this flow of people and starts walking in the same direction will unintentionally contribute to the growth and the visibility of that flow. Other "lost" pedestrians may, in turn, perceive the movement of our traveler and interpret it as a relevant directional cue, even though the traveler knows nothing about the train station. A snowball effect sets in: as further uninformed people start walking with the flow, the signal emitted becomes stronger, increasing the likelihood that other, equally uninformed, travelers will join it. An excessive number of people may eventually end up walking in the same direction, not because it is the one with the highest benefits but simply due to amplification effects. The practical implications of this phenomenon are that it often results in congestion and unbalanced use of exits (see, e.g., Bode & Codling, 2013). If exit A is, for some reason, more desirable than exit B, amplification effects may attract an excessive number of pedestrians toward it, thereby resulting in congestion, blockages, or even pushing. Exit B will eventually become more advantageous because it is free of congestion, and yet it will remain underused and ignored by most people. You can experience the conditions under which imitation can lead to herding by visiting interactive element 14.1 (at https://taming-uncertainty .mpib-berlin.mpg.de/). To conclude, the follow-the-flow heuristic offers an individual benefit to the lost traveler who is guided toward the exit by the behavior of others. If the imitator erroneously latches onto a group of people whose behavior is not aligned with their goals, however, that person may not only get lost, but also amplify the signal, causing others to follow suit. Too many people relying on the same strategy can produce collective patterns (e.g., jammed exit A) that undermine these individual benefits (see table 14.1 for a summary of the pedestrian heuristics described in the literature).

14.4   Uncertainty in Times of Adversity

The individual gain and the collective loss incurred by imitation can become critical in emergency evacuations. For a long time, the dynamics of emergency situations constituted the blind spot of crowd research. How do people behave when their lives are in danger? Which collective patterns characterize emergency evacuations? The main obstacle to answering these questions was the scarcity of empirical data. Laboratory experiments are an ill-suited methodology for studying emergency situations for obvious safety and ethical reasons. Furthermore, real-world observations of crowd panics are rare and difficult to evaluate. Capitalizing on recent developments in technological tools and virtual reality, Moussaïd et al. (2016) studied the emergency evacuation behavior of pedestrians in a series of controlled experiments conducted in a virtual environment. Specifically, we immersed a crowd of people in a three-dimensional virtual world. Each individual sat in front of a computer screen and controlled an avatar in the virtual environment. They had a realistic first-person perspective on the virtual environment and were free to look around, navigate, and interact with the avatars controlled by other people in real time (see figure 14.3).

Two situations were compared. In the first condition (*normality*), people had to find their way out of a building. They were given plenty of time and received a monetary reward if they succeeded. In the second condition

Figure 14.3
Snapshot of the virtual environment during a simple evacuation procedure. Each avatar was controlled by a real person who had a first-person view of the surrounding environment.

(*emergency*), the virtual building was burning, the time limit was tight, and participants were penalized with a substantial loss of money if they failed (but they were not rewarded for success). The study revealed striking differences in the dynamics of the crowd (see figure 14.4a–b). Whereas people in the first condition searched for the exit in a quiet and disciplined manner, the second condition resulted in mass herding, pushing, and overcrowding. Consistent with traditional views on crowd behavior (e.g., Lebon, 2007) it initially seemed that psychological and monetary pressure had transformed the participants into selfish and unreasonable beings.

However, deeper analyses invalidated this interpretation. The behavior of individuals remained almost unchanged across the two conditions. The apparent disorganized collective behavior of the crowd during emergencies actually emerged from a density effect. For example, to explain the herding patterns observed in the emergency condition, we measured the extent to which people followed each other during the evacuation and compared their imitation curve with that exhibited in the normality condition. The imitation curves were identical, and individuals tended to follow their neighbors equally often under the emergency and normality conditions (see figure 14.4c). Similarly, most behavioral indicators did not differ

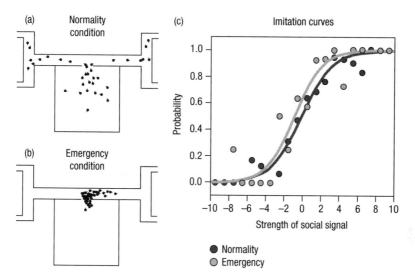

Figure 14.4

Snapshots of an evacuation in the virtual environment under (a) the normality condition and (b) the emergency condition. The dots represent the position of the participants in the building a few seconds after the starting signal. Each participant is trying to find an exit door out of the building. In the absence of time and monetary pressure (i.e., under the normality condition), participants kept a certain distance from one another and tended to explore all parts of the building. Under the emergency condition, participants herded in the same direction. (c) The imitation curves represent the individual probability of choosing one branch (y-axis) as a function of the number of visible others who previously chose that branch (x-axis). The two imitation curves are identical, indicating that people did not change their imitation strategy between the two conditions. However, the social signals in the emergency condition were stronger because the number of neighbors an individual could see was larger as a result of the reduced interindividual distances. In sum, herding emerged not because of an increase in the propensity to imitate, but due to an increase in density.

between the two conditions, and individuals did not change their behavior in response to the emergency. How then could detrimental collective behaviors develop in the emergency condition, given that people used the same navigation strategies? Only one seemingly minor behavioral aspect changed: under time pressure, people tended to walk closer to one another, leaving less empty space between them. This behavioral change implied an increase in density which, in turn, caused a chain reaction that prompted all the detrimental effects observed: herding, pushing, and overcrowding. Because the crowd was denser, individuals were aware of a larger number of other people. Instead of seeing one or two others in their surroundings, they could now see up to 10 people. When an individual arrived at a junction, the stronger social signal sent by the others increased the probability of that person following the flow of preceding people, giving rise to the observed herding patterns. Put differently, pedestrians had a higher propensity to follow their neighbors simply because the neighboring individuals were more numerous due to the increased density level. Because most of them followed the same path, density was further increased relative to the normality condition, creating congestion, body contact, and pushing.

In the end, the seeming madness of the crowd did not result from individual irrationality. People relied on the same set of heuristics as under normal conditions, but tended to walk closer to their neighbors in order to get out a little faster under time pressure. By trying to reap a small individual benefit, people unwittingly created density conditions under which detrimental collective patterns set in. Another interesting aspect of behavior that was not tested is the impact of the speed of movement. Safety professionals propagate the rule to "walk calmly, do not run." Indeed, there is ample evidence that a crowd of people running through a narrow doorway will be slower getting out than the same crowd walking calmly through that doorway, due to coordination issues and physical friction between bodies (Mintz, 1951; Schadschneider et al., 2009). This effect, known as the *faster-is-slower* effect, is a purely physical fact that can also be observed when pouring rice through a funnel (blockages occur when one pours too fast). Yet, for pedestrians, a social dilemma again emerges: if everybody else continues to walk calmly, there is a strong benefit to be gained from running. But once everybody starts running, the group pays the price. In times of adversity such as emergency evacuations, the tension between individual and collective benefits is doomed to be amplified.

14.5   The Ecological Rationality of Pedestrian Heuristics

14.5.1   The Wisdom and Madness of Crowds

When looking at the crowd from a global perspective, a naive observer is equally likely to arrive at either of two diametrically opposing conclusions about the nature of crowds. Some collective patterns, like the formation of pedestrian highways, make the crowd appear wise; others, like crowd turbulence, suggest the opposite. However, what determines the nature of the collective patterns is not the behavior of individuals. The same set of navigation heuristics can lead to either beneficial or detrimental collective behaviors. Rather, the crucial parameter in the environment is density: a given heuristic can produce advantageous collective patterns at moderate density levels but disadvantageous ones at higher densities.

Why do pedestrians continue to use the same heuristics at high densities, despite the risk of harming themselves and producing detrimental collective patterns? It is first important to note that pedestrians almost only ever experience low and moderate density levels. High levels of density at which detrimental patterns emerge are rare. Thus, one answer is that people may not have experienced high-density situations frequently enough to have developed new strategies that are more adaptive in these extreme situations. Another, more subtle explanation is that pedestrians fail to perceive the causality between their microbehavior and the resulting collective patterns. In fact, even under high-density situations, pedestrian heuristics are associated with an immediate individual reward; the harmful collective pattern is an unintended and delayed side effect. When a fast walker tries to overtake a slow walker in a dense crowd, the fast walker does eventually manage to speed up. Fast walkers may not notice the chain reaction they trigger that worsens many other people's walking conditions. Likewise, it is not immediately evident that imitating one's neighbors' exit choices could create large-scale congestion. The only proximate consequence is the immediate reward garnered by the imitator who has, in fact, succeeded in finding an exit.

14.5.2   Simple Rules for Safer Crowds

Having considered how pedestrians move in crowds and explored the conditions under which the simple heuristics guiding their behaviors produce detrimental results, the next step is to think about how to improve this heuristics–environment interaction. Interventions can target pedestrians, policy makers, or both. Pedestrians can be taught to use the right navigation heuristics at the right moment—for instance, when safety officers urge people to *stay calm* and to *walk, not run, toward the exit* during evacuation exercises. Similarly, traffic conditions could be enhanced by simple instructions disseminated in crowded urban areas such as *do not overtake the person in front of you in dense crowds* or *keep as much distance as you can from your neighbors*. The latter recommendation has the double effect of reducing both the density level and the frequency of body contacts. The high level of uncertainty characterizing crowds constitutes an enormous challenge for event organizers, urban planners, and crowd managers. During mass events, organizers may need to anticipate the next move of thousands of people and often improvise routing solutions under time pressure (Helbing et al., 2007; Helbing & Mukerji, 2012; Johansson, Helbing, Al-Abideen, & Al-Bosta, 2008).

Complex approaches such as computer simulations, live video monitoring, and sophisticated procedures informed by expert consultations constitute a principled way of anticipating the causes of accidents. However, policy makers can also benefit from simple strategies that reduce the risks of systemic failures. For example, crowd managers need to pay special attention to areas where the density level is likely to increase—but local density is hard to measure without a proper monitoring system, which is often missing in mass events. Simple rules can help managers to pick up warning signals and anticipate dangerous levels of density (Helbing et al., 2014). For instance, they could *scan the frequency of body contacts* in the crowd. Frequent body contacts typically indicate that density is about to reach critical levels. Likewise, crowd managers should *pay attention to the emergence of stop-and-go waves*. Although not intrinsically dangerous, they represent a very uncomfortable mode of walking. As they are easy to observe with the naked eye, crowd managers could use stop-and-go waves as a signal that the density level has reached a first critical threshold of about 2 persons per square meter. Another rule would be to *remove any bottlenecks in the environment*, as even a small flow of people can create congestion in narrow spots. Ambulances, police cars, people on the ground, and temporary fences can all create unexpected bottlenecks. The final simple rule for crowd managers is to *avoid long waiting times*: impatient visitors often weave their way through the crowd, which further increases the pressure in the critical zone.

The notion of ecological rationality sees the success of a heuristic as dependent on how well it matches the structure of the environment (see chapter 1). In the case of crowd behavior, the structure of the environment is characterized by at least one important dimension: crowd density. Under low and moderate densities, pedestrian heuristics function well and have both individual and collective benefits. In extremely crowded environments, in contrast, the same heuristics no longer work well, but become the source of maladaptive phenomena. Like all heuristics, navigation heuristics work in some or even many circumstances—but not in all. The key is to know when to use them.

V The Unfinished Mind

15 Computational Evolution and Ecologically Rational Decision Making

Peter D. Kvam, Arend Hintze, Timothy J. Pleskac, and David Pietraszewski

15.1 Evolution Is Central to Ecological Rationality

Humans and other organisms navigate uncertain worlds by adapting their behaviors to the environments they encounter, both social and non-social. The problem organisms face is that there are countless ways to do the wrong thing in a given situation, or even to do the right thing at the wrong time or in the wrong place. Yet the number of ways to even approximate a response that fits the environment is vanishingly small—it is a balancing act on a knife's edge. Several chapters have discussed how the fit between cognition and environment occurs via individual or collective learning. But learning is only part of the story. The capacities for individual and collective learning have emerged through evolution by natural selection—the longest-running process that produces a fit between environment and behavior. Natural selection reaches this fit by "picking" different behavioral responses or strategies that arise from the variations of organisms and their experienced outcomes. Given that evolution by natural selection has had a few billion years to tinker with the fit between environment and behavior, a thorough account of adaptive rationality ought to also explore this process and its effects.

A long history of research has explored how evolution shapes humans and other organisms, including their decision strategies and behavior. Such topics are studied under the umbrella of evolutionary biological sciences and evolutionary social sciences (e.g., Barkow, Cosmides, & Tooby, 1995; Buss & Conroy-Beam, 2016; Davies, Krebs, & West, 2012; E. A. Smith & Winterhalder, 1992; see also chapter 16). These methodologically diverse fields employ behavioral observation and experimentation to examine the evolutionary process, using tools like evolutionary game theory (Hammerstein & Selten, 1994), computer models of evolution in action (Buss & Conroy-Beam, 2016; McElreath & Boyd, 2008), observational studies of the consequences of natural selection in the wild (Endler, 1986) and experimental manipulation of evolution (in short-lived nonhuman animals; Dunlap & Stephens, 2014; Lenski, 2017).

Both game theory and computer simulations inform the understanding of the evolutionary process from a modeling approach, in part because studying the real process of evolution in action is difficult. Researchers face stumbling blocks imposed, for instance, by the long intergeneration times of most organisms and the practical challenges of manipulating and observing evolutionary trajectories. One solution to this problem is to study evolution in action using artificial organisms. With continuing advances in computation, artificial intelligence has made it possible to study evolution with increasingly greater fidelity to biological systems. This approach, called computational evolution (outlined in box 15.1), is adopted throughout this chapter.

Computational evolution makes it possible to explore factors that influence evolutionary outcomes by precisely manipulating the characteristics of the environments that agents must navigate. Whereas factors like population size or mutation rate are general to evolutionary dynamics themselves, others are specific to the task under selection, such as risks or rewards for specific behaviors, time limits on decisions, and whether and how organisms can communicate. The resulting strategies can be described either by looking directly at the structure of the agents (the rules they use to process information) or by analyzing the input information and the choice data that the agents produce. Such analyses offer insights into what sorts of information-processing architectures evolve depending on how task environments are manipulated. In other words, computational evolution provides the means to examine how behaviors and environments, admittedly simplified microenvironments, causally interact over time, producing ecologically rational tools for dealing with uncertainty over generations.

Computational evolution complements approaches like rational analysis, an approach from the cognitive sciences which seeks to find optimal solutions to problems so as to better understand the structure of an adapted mind (Anderson, 1990; Griffiths, Chater, Kemp, Perfors, & Tenenbaum, 2010; Oaksford & Chater, 2007). Rational analysis and other such

Box 15.1

What is computational evolution?

Computational evolution is a method for studying the evolutionary process via the life, death, and reproduction of artificial (virtual) organisms. This is done by implementing mechanisms that generate *variation* among organisms, *selection* of these organisms based on their interaction with the environment, and *inheritance* from generation to generation (Pennock, 2007). Computational evolution capitalizes on the fact that evolution is *substrate neutral*—artificial agents evolve just as apes, bacteria, or any other organisms would (Adami & Hintze, 2013; Dennett, 1995). Thus, computational evolution generates data about the evolutionary process and its effects without the long wait times required to observe generation after generation of real organisms.

In the computational evolution studies presented here, each agent's behavior is determined by its genetic code. The code consists of a string or combination of numbers that specify what an agent should do when it receives information input. The input is typically mapped via a series of transformations onto an output, allowing agents to process information and use it to perform different behaviors. These behaviors are then graded relative to some task criterion, such as decision accuracy or stochastic rewards and punishments. In turn, an agent's task performance over the course of its lifetime gives it an overall fitness that determines its ability to reproduce to the next generation.

An agent reproduces to the next generation by generating a copy of its genetic code that can contain some mutations (places where the code has been randomly altered). However, its reproductive success is affected both by its own fitness and by the fitness of other agents in its population, the group of agents with which it interacts and competes. Agents that are better able to perform the criterion task are more likely to reproduce. This process is iterated over many generations, usually such that the resulting pool of agents is capable of performing the task of interest.

Interactive element 15.1 (at https://taming-uncertainty.mpib-berlin.mpg .de/) provides an interface for exploring a computational evolutionary process. You can manipulate mutation rates, task demands, and other variables and watch as the population of string-producing agents evolves to solve the task.

approaches explicitly or implicitly invoke evolutionary processes as one potential generator of optimal or adaptive decision strategies. Computational evolution provides a means to check which solutions might arise via these evolutionary processes. But evolution will not necessary produce the optimal solution. Instead, as we will see, it produces solutions reflecting a fit between the specific environment and the individual's cognition. Next, we illustrate a few ways in which we have applied this approach to inference and decision-making processes. Each of the case studies we feature sheds light on which adaptive strategies may have evolved given specific environmental circumstances. At the same time, the studies illustrate key themes from evolutionary science that can inform, challenge, and ultimately enrich the scientific understanding of how people make decisions in the face of uncertainty.

15.2   How Preferential Decision Processes Can Be Tuned to the Environment

Preferential decisions are scenarios in which an agent must select a choice option based on the agent's own internal states and desires—that is, when there is no objectively correct response for all agents. Despite the subjective nature of preferences, a number of normative or "rational" theories posit sets of rules that individuals should obey in order to maximize their expected rewards. These theories first define a task function that connects behaviors to subjective rewards, then derive an optimal solution to that function (e.g., Dayan & Daw, 2008; Edwards, 1954). In these cases, the "optimal" strategy is the mechanism that a computationally unbounded agent would use to maximize its expected earnings given a specific quantitative utility for each possible choice outcome and an infinite number of iterations of the decision. For example, in risky decisions, the normatively optimal strategy is one which maximizes the average expected utility that an individual can expect to achieve (Savage, 1954; von Neumann & Morgenstern, 1944/2007). An individual can apply this strategy by multiplying the size of the subjective utility of the potential payoffs for each outcome of a choice option by the (subjective) probabilities of obtaining those payoffs, then choosing the choice option that has the highest sum of these products.

This normative approach is a domain-general one that is applicable, in principle, to any choice environment. However, there are several reasons why evolution would not generate these normative strategies but rather produce distinct strategies that are tuned to specific environments. A general principle of adaptive cognition is that practical constraints imposed by the environment and an individual's own abilities lead agents to use domain-specific cognitive processes that exploit particular structures of the environment (Barkow et al., 1995; Brunswik, 1955; Gibson, 1979; Marr, 1982; Shepard, 1987; Simon, 1955). Moreover, an individual's computational architecture (e.g., memory space, motor capacities, vulnerability to mutation) and actual experience (as opposed to expectations) may make implementing normative strategies impossible. Even if normatively optimal strategies can be implemented, the evolutionary process itself may also settle on local rather than global performance maxima (Geisler & Diehl, 2003), with the result that strategies that are "good enough" or sufficiently better than other realistic strategies outcompete them, even though they are not the best strategies theoretically possible. Finally, organisms also trade off mutational robustness against fitness (Wilke, 2001). Instead of staying on the highest peak (best task performance) of the fitness landscape, agents can ultimately produce greater long-term viability by remaining at a lower performance level that is more stable in the face of genetic mutations.

One illustration of the environmental specificity of decision strategies comes from a study that looked at the conditions under which risk aversion evolved. Hintze, Olson, Adami, and Hertwig (2015) examined the evolution of artificial agents in an environment where their fitness was determined by the outcome of a single risky gamble. The gamble was essentially a life-or-death decision (win and reproduce or lose and fail to reproduce) that offered the agents a chance χ ($0 < \chi \leq 1$) of winning a payoff; if they did not win the gamble, they received nothing. The amount that an agent could win was inversely proportional to the chance of winning, such that an agent could win amount $1/\chi$ by wagering on odds χ. Each agent had its own value of χ representing its fitness-determining strategy. For example, a value of $\chi = .01$ would be a very risky strategy that could result in a large payoff of 100 fitness points, while a value of $\chi = 1$ would be a highly risk-averse strategy that ensured a certain payoff of a single fitness point.

The question of interest was how the values of χ in the population would shift over generations based on manipulations of population size (total number of agents) or group size (when the population was divided into smaller groups with migration between them). In other words, how does a key environmental factor like population size impact risk taking? This was a different perspective to that generally taken by theories of decision making, which often take risk aversion as a given (e.g., Friedman, Isaac, James, & Sunder, 2014; von Neumann & Morgenstern, 1944/2007). Here the question was which environmental factors might give rise to risk aversion. It turned out that the size of the population of agents played a substantial role in the strategies that evolved. As figure 15.1 shows, smaller populations tended to show an increased propensity to implement risk averse strategies (higher χ).

Let us illustrate this finding with a more intuitive example: imagine you can choose between either a 100% chance of having one child, or a 25% chance of having four and a 75% chance of having none. Your children (should you have them) are likely to inherit a propensity to choose the same option, but some will randomly mutate such that they choose the other option. This inheritable propensity means that over time, many of those selecting the "risky" option (a 25% chance of four children and a 75% chance of none) will not have children and the gene for the risky selection will eventually disappear from the lineage. With a smaller number of people in the population, the chance of all the risk-taker lineages dying out

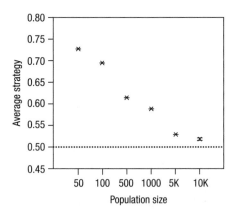

Figure 15.1
Proportion of agents in an evolved population (950 generations) that chose a sure payoff over a risky gamble ("Average strategy") as a function of the number of agents in each generation in the population in which they evolved. Error bars (miniscule for most conditions except the 10,000-agent populations) indicate one unit of standard error (recreated from Hintze, Olson, et al., 2015).

will increase. The same principle applies to the artificial agents: taking risks may yield a successful lineage, but unless enough risk takers exist they may randomly die off due to a string of bad luck.

This increased propensity to avoid risk in smaller populations is an instance of a more general principle in evolutionary biology: events must be frequent and recurrent enough over multiple generations to be "spotted" by natural selection. If a chance event (in this case, receiving the large reward when choosing the risky option) does not meet a minimal level of frequency, it will tend not to have a sufficient impact on fitness to be selected, even if the expected payoffs would be the same or greater if an agent selected the choice option with a rare outcome. In this instance, a factor like population or group size can impact the decision behavior of a population, keeping it from approaching the behavior that maximizes expected value or utility. This suggests that particular bottlenecks in population size or typical group size—such as those experienced by humans (Aiello & Dunbar, 1993; A. Walker & Smith, 1987)—could lead to the evolution of behaviors or structures that promote risk aversion. These bottleneck events could therefore serve as partial explanations for why certain risk-averse behaviors are frequently observed in present-day organisms.

15.3   How Cognitive Constraints and Competition Can Result in Frugal Sampling

Whereas the previous section illustrated how population dynamics can shape risk preferences, research on human decision making often suggests that people construct their preferences from the information around them. One way they do this is by sampling information to form an impression of their possible options, such as when determining whether or not a plant is poisonous, or choosing where to forage for food. Experimental studies of how humans sample information have often found that they tend to rely on small samples of information to make their decisions (e.g., chapter 7; Hertwig & Pleskac, 2010; Kareev, 1995; Vul, Goodman, Griffiths, & Tenenbaum, 2014; Wulff, Mergenthaler-Canseco, & Hertwig, 2018). So is there an evolutionary reason for people limiting the information they consider? A common explanation for such frugal use of information is that the cognitive constraints of the mind limit the amount of information people can sample. Yet why would evolution favor constraints on the mind in this way?

This question seems especially pertinent in inferential decisions—such as determining whether a plant is poisonous (Wertz & Wynn, 2014a, 2014b)—where agents making objectively incorrect inferences by misdiagnosing the state of their environment can experience dire consequences. In these cases, any nonoptimal strategy is strictly dominated by optimal ones in terms of maximizing payoffs from the task.

Kvam, Cesario, Schossau, Eisthen, and Hintze (2015) investigated this question using Markov brain agents, a special type of neural network designed to mimic relevant characteristics of biological organisms, such as inheritable genetic codes and the ability to scale the number of neural connections. A description of these brains is given in box 15.2. In this computational evolution study, agents were tasked with classifying a target stimulus as coming from source A or source B (e.g., poisonous or not). To this end, they sequentially received up to 100 different binary cues and could use each piece of information to update their beliefs. The binary cues were generated from a source that varied in validity across conditions (e.g., 55% to 90% correct information) such that the task could be fairly easy (all cues had high validity) or more difficult (all cues had low validity). Correct decisions yielded greater reproductive fitness, and incorrect ones yielded worse reproductive fitness. The optimal strategy in this case was to take all 100 pieces of information, count the number that favored A, compare it against the number that favored B, and choose whichever one was greater (an "evidence accumulation" strategy similar to the one described in chapter 7). However, mechanisms supporting such optimal behavior did not evolve. Instead, agents used only a few pieces of information to make their decisions, frequently gathering only one or two pieces in the easiest conditions. Their performance hardly suffered, however—agents in these conditions achieved essentially perfect performance despite their relatively simple decision strategies.

Why were agents able to perform so well with such simple strategies? In this study, the complexity of strategies was limited by a combination of three practical factors. First, agents did not need to integrate much information to perform well; two pieces of information were enough to guarantee near-perfect performance in many conditions. Thus, the strategies that used just two pieces of information were frequently good enough to achieve high fitness. Second, the optimal strategy of using all 100 cues was difficult to implement: for a

Box 15.2
Markov brains.

Although evolution can be studied in any sort of artificial agent, one type of agent commonly used in the studies presented here is called a Markov brain. A technical report on how these brains work can be found in Hintze et al. (2017). These brains consist of a series of binary nodes for gathering and storing information as well as actuator nodes for performing behaviors. A typical brain might have 16 binary nodes, where one subset of these nodes is reserved for information inputs (based on the task) and another subset for motor outputs. This structure allows the agents to make decisions. As the output nodes are used to indicate the responses on which agents are graded, mapping from input information to outputs either directly or indirectly is critical to the agents' reproductive success.

Markov brains perform this mapping by using logic gates that map information from one set of nodes to another. The precise rules can vary. For example, one gate could take a [1] from node 3 and map it onto a [1] on node 4 and a [0] on node 7, or it could take input from nodes 1, 2, and 5 and map it onto a [0] or [1] on node 11. The exact rules for mapping between nodes is given by an underlying 4-base-pair genome, where sequences of base pairs code the start of a coding sequence and elements of its information-processing structure, such as the number of inputs, outputs, or mapping rules of a logic gate. This genome allows researchers to directly examine the brains by looking at the structure of the neural network the genome generates and how that network behaves (even allowing agents to be cloned and tested in other conditions).

Between generations, the genomes—and therefore the rules governing information processing—are subject to mutations. Typically, this includes insertion, deletion, and point mutations of individual base pairs of the genome. Mutations render possible variation in the population from generation to generation and permit agents to explore new information-processing rules that could improve their fitness.

16-bit Markov brain, 200 bits of information (two bits per piece) are nearly impossible to integrate. This example illustrates the important role cognitive constraints can play in the evolution of information-processing structures. The third factor that limited the complexity of strategies is a naturally occurring constraint of biological systems: mutation. More complex information-processing structures (required to implement the optimal strategy, which uses all 100 cues) are more vulnerable to mutations over generations. The Markov brains' genetic code was subject to random mutation. Because more complex information-processing architectures require longer genetic codes, a random change was more likely to affect part of a large information-processing architecture than it was to affect a smaller one. This vulnerability is referred to as *mutation load*, which can place a long-term penalty on a complex genome in terms of risking fatal mutations in future offspring. Thus, low mutation load is another advantage for simple cognitive processes, and one that is quite different than the statistical and cognitive advantages that are frequently discussed in the decision-making literature (see, for example, chapter 1; Gigerenzer & Brighton, 2009).

In addition to the pressures individuals face while acting on their own, social pressures like competition can lead to frugal sampling. Competition is a fundamental part of all of the studies we examine here, as the likelihood of an agent reproducing to the next generation is determined by its fitness relative to others in the population. In this sense, competition can help individuals in each successive generation of a population achieve greater fitness. But the dynamics between agents are not always so simple. Interactions between agents competing for common resources, or between predators and prey, are governed by complex systems characterized by extreme interdependence between populations (see the Lotka-Volterra equations; Lotka, 1932; Volterra, 1928). For example, predators thrive in the face of abundant but poorly adapted prey, yet they suffer when these prey species die out or become better adapted.

In some cases, competition can even be detrimental to all of the agents in a population. Hintze, Phillips, and Hertwig (2015) isolated instances where competition pushes agents to "cut corners," as well as extreme cases where competition becomes a destructive factor for evolving sophisticated cognitive processes. The work entailed the computational evolution of a population of agents whose fitness depended on their performance in a task similar to the rivals-in-the dark game investigated in chapter 12. During the game, agents had two urns that they could either sample from or select. Sampling from an urn would show the agent a random draw from that urn, giving the agent an impression of the reward they might be able to receive by selecting it. Selecting an urn would allow an agent to both claim the payoff from the urn and make the urn unavailable to other agents. The payoffs from the urns determined the fitness of each individual agent, which in turn determined how likely it was that the agent's strategy was passed on to the next generation.

This investigation involved three environments that had agents interacting under varying degrees of competition. The first, an "indirect competition" scenario, had agents make a choice between an urn with a known value and an urn with an unknown value. As in our other evolutionary scenarios, the agents' likelihood of reproducing depended on other agents in the population, but their choices otherwise did not directly affect the fitness of others. The second scenario was a "direct competition" scenario where two agents competed over a common unknown urn. In this scenario, each agent knew the value of an urn to which they alone had access (known urn), and could either sample from the unknown urn, choose the known urn, or choose the unknown urn at each step of the game. As soon as one of the agents selected the unknown urn, they received a payoff from that urn and the other agent was forced to take a payoff from its own, known urn. Thus, in this direct competition environment, one agent's decision directly impacted the other's choice environment and, by extension, fitness. Finally, the third scenario was an "extreme competition" scenario. Agents again had their own known urn, but they could choose between keeping their urn (known value) or giving up their urn to steal another agent's urn (unknown value). At each step, agents could guard their urn, steal the other agent's urn, or sample from the other agent's urn. In this extreme competition, agents not only competed over resources but could actively decrease their opponent's fitness by taking their resources.

The results of this study are shown in figure 15.2. When the degree of competition between agents increased, agents took fewer samples from the unknown urn before making their selection. In the most extreme condition, they gathered only one sample before selecting an urn, yielding only slightly above-chance accuracy but ensuring that the other agent could not take the better urn. This strategy not only ensures that both agents get the same reward on average, it also prevents either agent from evolving better sampling strategies. The accuracy of the sampling depends not only on the number of samples, but also on the cognitive ability of the agent to make sense of the samples obtained. If agents pick immediately, they prevent the opponent from taking advantage of a potentially better cognitive ability. As a consequence, under these conditions, overly competitive environments did not drive the evolution of cognitive abilities but prevented it. In fact, this investigation showed that the extreme competition scenario resulted in evolved strategies that were no better than a random strategy that does not respond to the environment at all.

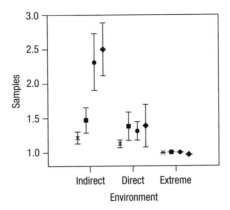

Figure 15.2
The number of samples agents took from the unknown/"sample" urn (y-axis) before making their selection based on the degree of interagent competition (x-axis). The shapes indicate the amount of variance in the new urn (low to high, from left to right) (recreated from Hintze, Phillips, & Hertwig, 2015).

From an evolutionary perspective, the frugal sampling phenomenon (see, e.g., chapters 4, 7, and 12) can be driven by the computational constraints of the agents' cognitive systems, as well as by external factors such as competition with other agents. In both cases—where sampling is bounded by mutation load and where it is bounded by competition—information gathering plays a critical role in choice outcomes. It is also heavily impacted by the context in which a decision unfolds. The result of evolution is then an approach that balances task rewards with the demands of computation and competition. But how can these sorts of simplified strategies be characterized? With computationally evolved agents, the genome of the agents gives an exact description of what each one will do in response to any given input. The information-processing architectures the genome specifies can in turn be described as a set of rules that correspond to heuristics or to (approximately) optimal algorithms. The particular rules they implement arise as evolutionary trade-offs between task performance and the uncertainty arising from mutation, task demands, and computational constraints. It is then possible to compare these evolved rules against those proposed in decision theory, examining if and when task environments give rise to the strategies that have been proposed to explain human behavioral data.

15.4   How Heuristics Exploit the Information Structure of Task Environments

With many agents apparently evolving relatively simple but still successful decision strategies, a natural question to ask is which strategies they implement instead. One proposal is that they use ecologically rational heuristics (Gigerenzer, Todd, & the ABC Research Group, 1999) that ignore some information in order to achieve faster, more accurate, or more efficient decisions. These heuristics often structure the cues they use based on the cues' validity, or the number of times a cue successfully discriminates between choice alternatives relative to the number of times it can be used. They are closely related to "rules of thumb" in biology, where simple decision strategies can provide accounts of how and why organisms integrate different cues (Hutchinson & Gigerenzer, 2005). Perhaps the best-known heuristic in the ecological rationality research program is take-the-best (Gigerenzer & Goldstein, 1996), which is specified for inferential tasks involving a choice between two alternatives (e.g., which city is larger: Hamburg or Cologne?). To make this choice, the decision maker searches one-by-one through cues ordered in terms of their cue validity until the first cue is found that discriminates between the alternatives, then picks the alternative favored by that cue.

Take-the-best corresponds to just one point in a vast space of potential decision strategies, the overwhelming majority of which could be classified as heuristics. What sorts of trajectories does computational evolution take as mutation and selection drive it across the strategy landscape over generations? Do agents tend toward strategies embodying the take-the-best policy? And are take-the-best and other heuristics stable strategies into which evolved agents might settle? If so, this could suggest an evolutionary basis for this heuristic process, or at least provide insight into its adaptive nature. And if not, this would indicate that there might be other aspects responsible for the adaptive properties of the heuristic (e.g., perhaps heuristics like take-the-best benefit from the computational ease with which the agent can implement it). Moreover, the computationally evolved strategies that do emerge can point to strategies—or at least general properties of strategies—that might be more successful.

We explored what sorts of decision architectures evolved in a task environment where different cues could be used as information to discriminate

Table 15.1

Cues, ecological validities, discrimination rates, and mutual information for the German city environment.

Cue	Ecological validity	Discrimination rate	Mutual information
National capital	1.00	.02	.024
Exposition site	**.91**	**.28**	**.160**
Soccer team	**.87**	**.30**	**.136**
Intercity train line	**.78**	**.38**	**.090**
State capital	.77	.30	.064
License plate	.75	.34	.067
Home to a university	.71	.51	.069
In the industrial belt	.56	.30	.004
In the former East Germany	.51	.27	.000

Note: The cues in **bold** type are the ones the evolved heuristics tended to use.

between two choice alternatives. This environment was fashioned after the city problem used by Gigerenzer and Goldstein (1996), where the task was to identify which of two German cities had the larger population. The cities were restricted to those that had a population of more than 100,000 in 1993 and have become a standard dataset in the literature on simple heuristics (Gigerenzer et al., 1999; Todd, Gigerenzer, & the ABC Research Group, 2012). Nine cues were made available for each decision. These cues varied in their validity as well as in how often they could be used to identify the city with the larger population (see table 15.1). Gigerenzer and Goldstein (see also Gigerenzer & Brighton, 2009) showed that take-the-best performed well in this environment, yielding a level of accuracy that under some circumstances (e.g., imperfect knowledge) was higher than that of sophisticated compensatory strategies which used all the cue information. For example, take-the-best outperformed a tallying heuristic in which each option's positive cues are tallied and the option with the largest total is chosen.

To investigate how evolution would solve the German city problem, we created a population of Markov brain agents whose fitness depended on their success at identifying which of two German cities had the larger population for all possible pairs of cities in the dataset (3,916 pairs). These agents had all the necessary components to use any of the nine cues in any possible permutation or combination, including the optimal solution (the solution that uses all nine cues to maximize chance of a correct answer across all 3,916 pairs of cities). The agents did not start with the optimal solution (nor did they appear to end with it). Instead, a set of randomly specified agents were compared against ones that were initialized to execute take-the-best or tallying heuristics. This set-up ensured that both heuristics could in principle be implemented in the particular Markov brain architecture, and it tested the evolutionary stability of these strategies in the city task environment. If tallying and take-the-best were stable strategies located at (local) performance peaks, the agents would stick with tallying or take-the-best when evolutionary processes were applied. If not, evolution would guide them on a path away from these heuristics in favor of more successful ones.

Figure 15.3 maps out the evolutionary trajectories of the decision strategies that evolved. It plots the strategies in a space defined by the deviation

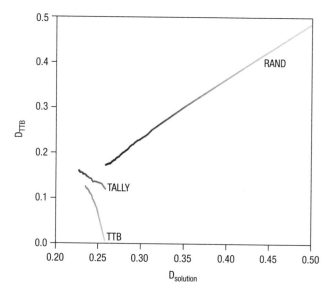

Figure 15.3

Map of the evolved strategies in the German city environment. Each strategy is plotted as a function of the deviation from the proportion of correct answers resulting from the optimal solution ($D_{solution}$) and the deviation from the proportion of correct answers resulting from take-the-best, using the ecological cue validities to order the cues (D_{TTB}). The top line shows the average trajectory of the agents that began with a random connection (RAND). The dark gray line in the middle indicates the average trajectory of agents that began implementing the tallying strategy (TALLY). The lightest gray line on the bottom represents the average trajectory of agents that began by implementing take-the-best (TTB). Denser lines indicate later generations.

from the proportion of correct answers resulting from the optimal solution and the deviation from the proportion of correct answers resulting from take-the-best (assuming it orders the cues by the ecological cue validities). The topmost black line shows the average trajectory of the agents that began with random Markov brains. Over the generations, their performance improved steadily, moving toward take-the-best but driven primarily in the direction of ideal performance. The bottom light gray line displays the lineage of agents that began with take-the-best, and the middle dark gray line shows the lineage of agents that started with tallying. In both cases, they moved away from the take-the-best strategy and converged toward a common solution, which we will describe shortly. We should note that this analysis forced each generation of Markov brains to make all 3,916 possible inferences between pairs of cities. Similar results occurred when agents in each generation were graded on a subset of the cities and later made inferences on a second, hold-out set of questions (cross-validation).

These findings illustrate a point that may be obvious in hindsight but that is easily overlooked: implemented heuristics may not be as clean and simple as heuristic algorithms like take-the-best. Yet in this experiment, evolved heuristics did tend to develop along consistent paths. Two properties of the evolved strategies set them apart from other heuristics. First, the agents combined a small set of cues (e.g., soccer team and intercity train line together) rather than using them separately in sequence. Second, cue validity was not the only factor determining the most-used cues. For example, the evolved heuristics stopped using the national capital cue over the generations, even though it had the highest validity. Instead, they moved toward cues with the greatest *mutual information* (Cover & Thomas, 2012; Shannon & Weaver, 1949). Specifically, most agents grew to use the three cues with the highest mutual information (exposition site, soccer team, and intercity train line; see bolded cues in table 15.1). Mutual information measures how much one random variable (e.g., a cue) tells decision makers about another (e.g., a criterion). It comes from information theory and can be understood as the reduction in uncertainty about one random variable given knowledge of another. The national capital cue is less informative than whether a city was an exposition site because the national capital cue can only be used when that particular city (Berlin) is in the choice set. Relying on cues based on mutual information also appears to correspond to how people search through cues to make a decision in some situations.

Specifically, Newell, Rakow, Weston, & Shanks (2004) found that success rate (the product of cue validity and discrimination rate, which is linearly related to mutual information) is a key determinant in how people search through cues to make a decision (see also Martignon & Hoffrage, 1999, 2002). One open issue is how and to what extent uncertainty about the cue values would impact the processes that evolve.

Another illustration of how and when heuristics develop comes from a reward rate study in which agents had to classify the source of a stimulus based on incoming streams of information (Kvam & Hintze, 2018). In this task, agents had a finite amount of time (1000 time steps in a lifetime) to correctly classify as many stimuli as they could. At each time step, agents received a single piece of information that indicated the correct or incorrect source, where the frequency of correct or incorrect information was manipulated. After each new piece of information, an agent could decide that the information came from source A or source B, or opt to defer the decision until later. The quality of the incoming information was varied by manipulating the relative proportion of correct information to noise (as in the study by Kvam et al., 2015) in order to adjust the average time needed to accumulate sufficient information for a decision. The relative magnitude of rewards and punishments that agents incurred for correct or incorrect decisions was also varied.

In this task, an optimally performing agent should gather information until the number of pieces of information favoring one option (A) minus the number of pieces of information favoring the other (B) is greater than a log-linear transformation of the ratio of punishment to reward magnitude. With higher punishments, an agent should be more careful, avoiding incorrect answers by setting a higher threshold for each new classification decision. The time to reach this threshold should also be affected by the quality of information: decisions take longer when agents receive conflicting information than when information consistently favors one of the options.

The results of this study are summarized in figure 15.4. Agents evolved different information-processing architectures depending on both the quality of the information and the relative magnitude of punishments and rewards: in cases where information quality was high or punishments were low relative to rewards, they approximated optimal behavior. However, in situations where punishments were high relative to rewards and information quality was low—the latter a hallmark of environments replete with

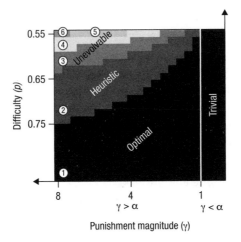

Figure 15.4
Overview of the findings from Kvam and Hintze (2018). The x-axis describes the relative magnitude of punishments for incorrect answers (γ) relative to rewards for correct answers (α). Note that optimal performance could be obtained in region 1, giving way to heuristic strategies in region 2 but high-difficulty conditions such as those in regions 4, 5, and 6 were too harsh for successful decision makers to evolve (recreated from Kvam & Hintze, 2018).

uncertainty—agents tended to look for specific strings of information that were especially unlikely to come from an incorrect source. For example, they could look for a series of inputs "[01], [01], [01]." This particular string is rare even from a [01] source; the likelihood that it would be generated by a [10] source is low enough that the agent can be assured of reasonable accuracy in deciding in favor of [01]. Because these strings were rare, agents using heuristics like these runs could be identified because they made decisions more slowly (less often) than optimal strategies while maintaining the same level of accuracy. In these cases, the harshness of the task environment led to diverging, qualitatively different strategies.

The boundaries around each of these strategies corresponded closely to the amount of information agents would need to integrate in order to make accurate decisions in the minimum amount of time (optimal) and how much information they would need to make accurate decisions in more than the minimal time (heuristic). For example, if the task required three pieces of information for optimal performance and two for heuristics, agents could often evolve to behave optimally. However, if the task required integrating four pieces to behave optimally and two for a heuristic process, then the agents tended to operate in the domain of heuristics unless they could somehow make the leap in processing capacity from two to four. And if the heuristic strategy required four or more pieces of information, agents frequently opted to never make decisions at all ("unevolvable").

These heuristics allowed agents to use fewer nodes for storing information, as they could just evaluate a recent subset of received information (e.g., two pieces/four bits) rather than the full set (e.g., four pieces/eight bits) of information that would be needed in order to execute the full optimal integration strategy. The heuristics, echoing the results from the German city analysis, also tended to change based on mutations that resulted in additional memory or enabled the use of more cues. This systematic change tended to happen in simpler conditions—agents first evolved heuristic strategies that utilized a reduced memory load and achieved the accuracy required for positive fitness, and later evolved larger memory that allowed their performance in terms of decision time to improve incrementally. In this way, the heuristic strategies can be thought of as an effective method of coping with agents' computational limitations as well as a stepping stone toward more advanced strategies.

Evolved information-processing architectures may support a combination of heuristic and optimal strategies contingent on computational capacities and the demands of the task environment. The resulting strategies can come from a vast space of heuristics that can be specified by a genome. As a result, evolved strategies are not exemplars of the fixed and clear-cut heuristic or optimal strategies proposed in decision theory. Even if they are not always predicted by evolutionary models, heuristics like those discussed in earlier chapters (e.g., chapters 2, 3, 4, and 5) can nevertheless often provide good descriptions of behavior. In some cases, a failure to generate a particular heuristic is the fault of the evolutionary modeler: the environmental conditions in the model do not perfectly match those experienced by real agents and so its conclusions diverge from observed behavior. At other times, behavior resembling heuristics may be the result of more proximate mechanisms like learning, rather than arising directly from differences in genetic codes. In such cases, evolution underlies the generation of the mechanisms that implement heuristic strategies rather than the heuristic itself. Such general-purpose mechanisms like working memory, kinship recognition, and sensory and motor processes have evolved in agents whose fitness is or was dependent on their performance on multiple tasks, providing "building blocks" for strategy construction (see chapter 1; as in the adaptive toolbox, see Gigerenzer et al., 1999). In turn, these existing mechanisms can be used to generate more complex behaviors for dealing with uncertainty.

15.5   How Evolution Struggles with Uncertainty

The artificial agents in computational evolution experiments experience manifold uncertainties. At minimum, this includes the stochastic information uncertainty imposed by the task environment; uncertainty about which internal states correspond to which outcomes (or even which behaviors); uncertainty about agents' own fitness and their fitness relative to competing agents; uncertainty about how this will map onto reproductive success; and uncertainty about the random mutations that may occur when agents produce offspring. Yet, as we have shown, evolution—using the three processes of variation, selection, and reproduction—represents a powerful agent of change that gives rise to organisms that successfully deal with all of these sources of uncertainty. The agents in our case studies went from producing random behavior to executing effective decision strategies ranging from simple to complex. This finding illustrates just how powerful the evolutionary process is, and how integral it can be in shaping the strategies humans use to cope with uncertainty. Of course, within-generation changes can also create vast diversity in a population. Yet the most dramatic variation in cognition that occurs across organisms was brought about long ago as a product of evolution.

To conclude, we have examined how evolution may shape decision making under uncertainty. The behaviors that evolve do not always line up with the conventional wisdom of normative or behavioral decision theory. Factors like information-processing constraints, multimodal fitness landscapes, or population-level traits can heavily influence the evolution of decision mechanisms and the strategies they produce. In some cases, these factors may still allow solutions that approximate the optimal solutions of the task to evolve; in others, they may lead to heuristics that feature shortcuts or workarounds that bypass some of the heavy task demands. In this sense, these case studies both illustrate how agents evolve ecological rationality and extend the understanding of what ecological rationality may be.

16 How the Adaptive Adolescent Mind Navigates Uncertainty

Wouter van den Bos, Corinna Laube, and Ralph Hertwig

16.1 The Turbulent Period of Adolescence

At a turning point in the classic coming-of-age movie *Rebel Without a Cause* (Weisbart & Ray, 1955), two teenagers stand at the edge of a cliff and gaze into the abyss. Buzz, the local bully, has just explained to Jim, the new kid on the block played by James Dean, the game of "chickie run." Each of them will race a stolen car toward the edge of the cliff, jumping out at the last minute. The game is a test of courage: whoever jumps first is a chicken. Before heading to their cars, Jim asks Buzz, "What are we doing this for?" Buzz seems puzzled by the question. After giving it some thought, he replies, "We got to do something. Don't we?" But that something goes wrong. Buzz's jacket sleeve gets caught on the door handle; he cannot escape in time. The car plunges over the cliff.

Colloquially, human adolescence means the teenage years. Scientifically, it covers a broader and somewhat more flexible period of development, starting with the onset of puberty (see box 16.1) at about 10 years of age and ending whenever a culture considers an individual to have become an adult. During this turbulent period, adolescents have to navigate a novel and inherently uncertain environment while at the same time learning to take on adult roles and responsibilities. As *Rebel Without a Cause* illustrates, adolescence is often portrayed as a period of wildly erratic behavior. The empirical data are consistent with this impression: mortality and morbidity caused by risky and impulsive behaviors increase in adolescence. In the United States, for example, nearly 75% of deaths in the second decade of life result from unintentional injuries incurred in circumstances such as car accidents, poisoning and drug overdose, drowning, and the discharge of firearms

Box 16.1
Pubertal hormones.

Adolescence starts in biology and ends in society. It begins with the onset of puberty, which is characterized by a rapid increase in gonadal hormone release. The sex hormones testosterone, estradiol, and dehydroepiandrosterone initiate development of secondary sexual characteristics, such as facial hair, and boost physical growth. Puberty is triggered by both internal and external cues providing information on the availability of resources required for successful reproduction. Internal cues include metabolic levels of insulin, glucose, and leptin, which indicate somatic growth and metabolic fuel availability. External cues include information on the harshness and unpredictability of the environment (e.g., availability of mates and scarcity of resources). In a stable environment with plenty of resources, puberty may start later because an individual can afford to grow big and healthy before investing all their energy in procreating. In a harsh environment characterized by periods of severe weather, food shortages, and unpredictable conditions, in contrast, puberty occurs earlier (Sapolsky, 1997), and individuals' risk propensity remains stable across the adult life span, attenuating the typical decline in risk-taking behavior associated with old age (see chapter 17). Research on which environmental aspects lead to early onset of puberty is currently scarce, but understanding these processes is of high societal relevance: early entry into puberty (relative to same-aged peers) is associated with psychosocial problems throughout adolescence (Copeland et al., 2010) and with vulnerability to a wide range of psychological disorders (Mendle & Ferrero, 2012).

(Mulye et al., 2009). Although 15- to 24-year-olds represent only a quarter of the sexually active population, nearly half of all sexually transmitted diseases (48%) occur in that age group (Satterwhite et al., 2013) and there is a dramatic rise in criminal behavior in adolescence, peaking at the age of 19 before declining again in young adulthood (the age–crime curve).

It is as if adolescents are magically drawn to the edge of the cliff. However, not all adolescents are inclined to act self-destructively or turn into criminals—most will never come into contact with the law. And, for the most part, they will emerge from the other side of adolescence: slightly more than 99.9% of North American teenagers, for instance, survive this tumultuous time (Willoughby, Tavernier, Hamza, Adachi, & Good, 2014). But there is converging evidence that the occurrence of adolescent typical behavior, in some form or another, is historically and culturally invariant (e.g., Schlegel & Barry, 1991). It is this higher propensity for risky, impulsive, and dysfunctional behavior that has led countless writers, researchers, and parents to believe that there is something fundamentally wrong with adolescents, who seem to be afflicted by some temporary form of irrationality. Yet adolescence as a distinct developmental period has roots not only in human history—it has also been described in numerous other animals, including mammals and birds. Taken together, this evidence suggests that adolescent behavioral characteristics, including increased impulsive and exploratory behavior, may have had adaptive functions across evolutionary history (Spear, 2000). Consequently, we take an evolutionary perspective on adolescent behavior under uncertainty. This approach offers a different view on the irrational adolescent and emphasizes the potential benefits of an ecological analysis for understanding adolescent behavior. Drawing on life-history theory (Kaplan & Gangestad, 2005; Stearns, 1992), we discuss two types of evolutionary mechanisms that may explain how adolescent behavior emerges in response to environmental properties, and review supporting evidence for each. Finally, we outline how an ecological analysis raises new research questions that could, if explored, help young people navigate their teenage years.

We should emphasize that an adaptive framework of adolescent behavior does not fall into the Panglossian trap of claiming that everything adolescents do is good or beneficial for them. For instance, there may be a mismatch between the *environment of evolutionary adaptedness* (Bowlby, 1969), specifically the developmental niche, and the current adolescent environment. As a result, evolved behavioral tendencies may not optimally contribute to the overall fitness of a 21st-century adolescent. A classic example of such a mismatch is the preference for fatty, sweet, and salty foods, which evolved in an environment where food, calories, and salt were scarce. These preferences are increasingly dysfunctional in today's obesogenic environment (see chapter 6).

16.1.1 The Ecological Rationality of Adolescent Behavior

In the decision sciences, the ecological rationality framework proposes an intimate fit between mind and environment (Simon, 1956; Todd, Gigerenzer, & the ABC Research Group, 2012). By exploring how minds fit environments, researchers studying ecological rationality aim to specify the structure of information-processing mechanisms, the structure of information available in the environment, and the way the two structures fit together. Mapping out particular aspects of the decision maker's environment allows researchers to ask specific questions regarding the mind. Whereas the environment may often seem more or less immutable from the decision maker's point of view, the capacities (including cognitive and behavioral strategies) of the cognitive system will be shaped—by evolution or development—to take advantage of the structure of the external environment (Todd & Brighton, 2016). From this perspective, adolescents' behavior results from the interaction of immediate environmental demands and affordances on the one hand, and the cognitive capacities and motivational states of the developing individual on the other. In addition, the observed cognitive capacities and motivational states are expected to drive patterns of behavior that have evolutionary advantages (i.e., promoting inclusive fitness). Thus, to fully understand adolescent behavior, researchers need to not only consider ontogenetic, or individual, development, but also to adopt a phylogenetic perspective that considers how recurrent properties of the ancestral environment shaped the adolescent mind.

Here we will discuss two such mechanisms. First, life history theory posits that developing organisms adopt different behavioral strategies in response to fitness-relevant properties of the environment and changes therein. Specifically, it suggests that *fast life history strategies*—including the increased risky and impulsive behavior so typical of adolescence—represent responses to higher levels of environmental uncertainty and harshness. Second, explanations based on *ontogenetic* and *deferred* adaptations do not postulate that the level of uncertainty per se is more pronounced for adolescents than it is for children or adults. Rather, they propose that adolescents show systematically different responses when confronted with the same level of uncertainty. Ontogenetic adaptations are behavioral patterns that are tuned to the specific environment of the organism's developmental stage; deferred adaptations prepare adolescents for later developmental stages (e.g., adulthood). All these possibilities highlight that the developmental changes in cognitive and affective capacities observed in adolescence are not immature stages of adult functioning but may represent specific responses to environmental properties and demands unique to that developmental stage.

16.2   Life History Theory: Live Fast, Die Young, or Live Long and Prosper?

According to the evolutionary perspective on human development, neurobiological mechanisms adaptively calibrate behavioral strategies across the life span, allowing the individual to navigate the current developmental niche and to anticipate future environments (Kaplan & Gangestad, 2005). Specifically, *conditional adaptations* are thought to respond to relevant environmental cues, altering developmental pathways in ways that are better adapted to the current or future environment. Life history theory, a framework with origins in developmental biology, suggests that behavior across the life span can be explained in terms of evolved strategies for distributing metabolic resources between the competing demands of growth, maintenance, and reproduction. These strategies are thought to lie on a continuum from "slow" to "fast," where "species on the fast end exhibit short gestation times, early reproduction, small body size, large litters, and high mortality rates, whereas species on the slow end have the opposite features" (Kaplan & Gangestad, 2005, p. 73). Humans are paradigmatic representatives of the "slow" track, whereas smaller mammals, such as rodents, are at the fast end of the continuum. The course of a life history strategy varies not only across species, but also across individuals within a species. It follows that ontogenetic differences in strategies are the result of individual differences in the experienced environment (Fabio, Tu, Loeber, & Cohen, 2011). Furthermore, different life history strategies may also arise from the environments experienced across the life span.

Life history theory identifies two environmental dimensions that drive the fast versus slow dynamic—namely, harshness and unpredictability (or uncertainty; Ellis, Figueredo, Brumbach, & Schlomer, 2009; Frankenhuis, Panchanathan, & Nettle, 2016; see figure 16.1). Harshness refers to conditions with a negative impact on fitness, caused by factors over which the individual has no control. For humans, poverty and low socioeconomic status (i.e., resource scarcity) can represent harsh conditions that not only lead to hunger and malnutrition, but are also associated with high crime rates and heightened vulnerability to disease. Uncertainty may be due either to variance in the level of harshness (what will happen) or to differences in the spatial or temporal location of outcomes (where and when things

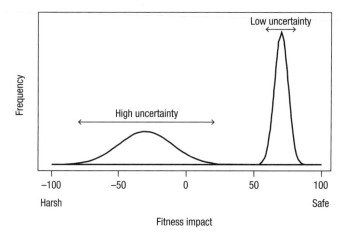

Figure 16.1
Two hypothetical frequency distributions of fitness-relevant events in the local environment. The distribution on the left has a negative mean and a large variance. It is both harsh and unpredictable. The distribution on the right represents a safe and predictable environment (see also Frankenhuis et al., 2016).

happen). More contemporary examples of environmental unpredictability include residential moves, job changes, and changes in the relationships of parents (e.g., separation, divorce, and new partners). These environmental changes often entail transitions to new social circles.

Both harshness and uncertainty push an organism to select "fast" strategies: the shorter one's expected reproductive life span, the greater the benefits of accelerating maturation and reproducing early, even if it compromises longevity (Kaplan & Gangestad, 2005). Research has shown that environmental uncertainty during early childhood predicts earlier onset of puberty and reproduction in humans; similar patterns have been observed in other animals (Ellis et al., 2009). Life history strategies may also be reflected in specific psychological mechanisms. For instance, present-orientation, that is, a preference for present over future rewards, may be adaptive in harsh and uncertain environments (Fawcett, McNamara, & Houston, 2012; see chapter 9). In these contexts, organisms are expected to prioritize the fitness benefits of immediately available rewards (e.g., by increasing access to mates) at the expense of future rewards, which are less likely to be received. Indeed, exposure to uncertain environments predicts present-orientation in diverse populations, including children and adolescents (Frankenhuis et al., 2016). For example, Mischel observed that 7- to 9-year-old children from single-parent households—burdened, all other things being equal, with increased uncertainty—were more likely to choose a small immediate reward over a larger one promised at some time in the future (Mischel, 1961; but see also Watts, Duncan, & Quan, 2018). By the same token, adult women who reported more early-life stress reported a shorter expected life span (e.g., higher future uncertainty) and a younger age of first sexual intercourse (Chisholm, 1999). Although harshness and uncertainty often go hand in hand, several studies have shown that the two dimensions can have unique effects on life history strategies (Doom, Vanzomeren-Dohm, & Simpson, 2016).

Thus, life history theory suggests that there is a universal mechanism that determines how environmental signals prompt organisms to choose adaptive life history strategies across the life span. Most of this work has focused on how early-life stress, in the first few years after birth, triggers a shift toward the fast end of the continuum that often becomes manifest in adolescence or young adulthood. However, early-life stress in itself does not explain the adolescent-specific pattern of a rise and fall in behaviors associated with fast life history strategies. Let us think back to the age–crime curve mentioned earlier. The rise in arrests in early adolescence may be partly explained by adolescents having more opportunities than children to break the law, as they are less subject to parental oversight. Given that this rise in crime is only caused by a subset of adolescents, one could hypothesize that those are the ones that experienced early-life stress. But even then, life history theory does not explain why there would be a decline in criminal behavior observed in late adolescence/young adulthood. In contrast, early-life stress is a good predictor of criminal behavior that persists beyond adolescence (Brumbach, Figueredo, & Ellis, 2009). Thus, there must be a different explanation for the adolescents who show an increase followed by a decrease in criminal behavior.

This pattern of adolescent behavior can be explained as a conditional adaptation within the life history theory framework only if two requirements are met. The first is a systematic shift in the uncertainty of the environment during adolescence—specifically, a sudden increase in uncertainty (and/or harshness) in early adolescence, followed by a decrease in mid/late

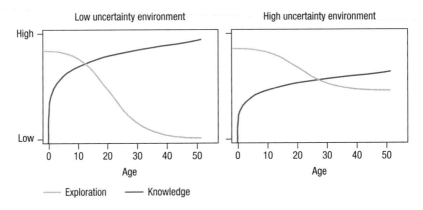

Figure 16.2
In a stable environment (left panel) there is a benefit of increased exploration which declines the more is learned about the environment. Thus, as knowledge is reaching a plateau, the need for exploration is going down. In contrast, in more volatile and unpredictable environments (right panel) the need to explore never truly declines and there is a limit to the knowledge one can ever have about the world (for similar ideas see Gopnik, Griffiths, & Lucas, 2015; Romer, Reyna, & Satterthwaite, 2017).

adolescence. For instance, the transition to high school and a new social group may create a volatile, uncertain environment that stabilizes over time. Note, however, that the level of uncertainty about the environment is also related to learning. For example, in a relatively stable environment, the overall level of uncertainty is likely to decline with age and experience (see figure 16.2). As a result, the need for exploratory behavior will decrease. Following this logic, a gradual decline in typical adolescent behavior toward the end of adolescence may be rendered possible by past behavior (e.g., exploration). In a relatively stable environment, risky explorative behavior becomes increasingly obsolete because the individual knows what to expect. The second requirement for explaining typical adolescent behavior as a conditional adaptation is that there is significant plasticity in the adjustment of life history strategies across adolescent development (speeding up or slowing down). It remains unclear whether these two conditions apply. There is evidence for increased neural plasticity during adolescence (see box 16.2), but little is known about the changing levels of uncertainty of the typical adolescent environment. We will address this question in section 16.2.1.

Box 16.2

Adolescent brain development.

Cerebral alterations in adolescence are characterized by early maturation of the subcortical motivational system, but slower development of the prefrontal top-down control mechanisms (Somerville & Casey, 2010). More generally, neurons, synapses, and receptors are overproduced during the transition from childhood to adulthood and undergo dramatic rearrangement with increasing age, resulting in reduction of gray matter through pruning (Luna, Paulsen, Padmanabhan, & Geier, 2013). Furthermore, white matter tracts—the links between neurons—develop across almost the whole brain throughout childhood and adolescence into adulthood (Luna et al., 2013). The constant refinement of the neural architecture during adolescence is also related to changes in cognitive abilities (e.g., working memory and problem solving) and social cognition (e.g., perspective taking). In view of these specific neural changes, it has been argued that this developmental period may be a sensitive period for the shaping of sociocognitive skills (Fuhrmann, Knoll, & Blakemore, 2015). Adolescence is already known to be a delicate period in terms of the effects of stress on mental health. Psychiatric disorders such as depression or schizophrenia have their onset in adolescence (Paus, Keshavan, & Giedd, 2008) and can be triggered by stress exposure. Taken together, the high level of neural plasticity during adolescence seems to coincide with the development of higher cognitive and social functioning. The flip side of this plasticity-related learning potential is that stress or other environmental deprivation may have pronounced and long-lasting effects.

With respect to the development of brain function, neuroimaging studies have shown that adolescents show higher subcortical activity than adults (see Silverman, Jedd, & Luciana, 2015 for a meta-analysis). For instance, the ventral striatum has been shown to be more responsive to rewards in adolescents than in children and adults. This increased level of activation has been linked to self-reported risk taking and sensation seeking and is even more exaggerated in the presence of peers (Albert, Chein, & Steinberg, 2013). Furthermore, the increased engagement of the valuation network is hypothesized to lead to an increase in social motivation (Crone & Dahl, 2012). Indeed, studies with both adult humans and rats have shown that striatum activity is associated with greater susceptibility to, and drive to learn from, social information (Klucharev, Hytönen, Rijpkema, Smidts, & Fernández, 2009).

Finally, pubertal hormones such as testosterone also impact the developing brain (Laube & van den Bos, 2016; Schulz & Sisk, 2016). It has been suggested that pubertal hormones are crucial in initiating a sensitive period for social and motivational processing in adolescence (Crone & Dahl, 2012). For instance, impatient behavior in boys is related to pubertal stage measured not in terms of chronological age, but in terms of testosterone levels (Laube, Suleiman, Johnson, Dahl, & van den Bos, 2017), and testosterone levels in adolescent girls predict sensitivity to social status (Cardoos et al., 2017).

16.2.1 Adolescence: An Age of Uncertainty?

"Who are you?" said the Caterpillar. Alice replied, rather shyly, "I—I hardly know, sir, just at present—at least I know who I was when I got up this morning, but I think I must have changed several times since then."

—Lewis Carroll, *Alice's Adventures in Wonderland*

The story of *Alice's Adventures in Wonderland* captures a great deal of the bewilderment of adolescence. Alice's body has taken on a will of its own, growing and shrinking. More generally, the world around her seems to be operating on the basis of a set of irrational rules, causing Alice to question her identity. Adolescence is indeed a period of major upheaval. On their path to independence, adolescents begin to separate from their parents and from other caregivers with whom they have spent most of their waking hours. They now have more autonomy to choose what to do, when to do it, and with whom. But the path to independence is fraught with uncertainty. The social world changes profoundly during adolescence, a time when teenagers often move to a new school and have to fit in with a new group of peers. As they reach sexual maturity (Suleiman, Galván, Harden, & Dahl, 2017), they enter into their first romantic relationships, and friendships take on more profound forms. During this period, adolescents become more aware of, and preoccupied by, the structure of the peer group and their place in it (Coleman, Herzberg, & Morris, 1977). The new peer group becomes a developing adolescent's main framework. Finding out how this new social world works, who they are, and where they fit in—that is, positioning themselves within the social hierarchy—is a major developmental task for adolescents. One's position in the social hierarchy is likely to impact one's future success and, in evolutionary terms, even their potential overall fitness (von Rueden, Gurven, & Kaplan, 2011). Yet researchers know relatively little about how uncertainty about the adolescent social world affects young people's behavior and development.

Along with their path to independence, an adolescent's future itself is also fraught with uncertainty. The promise of independence may seem appealing but it also brings many unknowns. What will I do after school? What job will I work in? How much money will I make? Who will be my partner? Uncertainty about these prospects may also contribute to adolescents adopting faster life history strategies. For instance, U.S. adolescents have been shown to overestimate their probability of dying in the next year by 18.6% (base rate: 0.1%; Bruine de Bruin, Parker, & Fischhoff, 2007). Mortality estimates were even higher for adolescents who reported having experienced personal threats (e.g., living in an unsafe neighborhood; Fischhoff, Bruine de Bruin, Parker, Millstein, & Halpern-Felsher, 2010). This finding suggests that there is meaningful variability in these overestimates, and that the degree of misjudgment is linked to environmental variables. Consistent with life history theory and the notion that future uncertainty promotes fast life history strategies, Bruine de Bruin and colleagues also found that the more teenagers overestimated their probability of dying, the more risky behaviors they reported (McDade et al., 2011). It is possible that similar effects will be observed for less dramatic—but still fitness-relevant—future uncertainties.

It would be premature to claim that adolescence represents a unique age of uncertainty in terms of sheer quantity. But the quality of uncertainty during adolescence may indeed be unique. A systematic investigation of adolescents' *Umwelt* (Uexküll, 1992)—that is, their subjective environment, which is a function of the cognitive and sensory machinery—would cast light on the kinds of uncertainties specific to adolescence, as well as their sources. One domain of adolescent life in which little is certain and much is to be discovered is the novel social world. Ecological analyses of this social environment would open several interesting avenues for further research (see section 16.4). But it is important not to overlook another important possibility. The Umwelt in which adolescents find themselves may be just as uncertain as the Umwelt of children or adults. The crucial difference may lie in adolescents' response to that same environmental uncertainty—the reason being that their learning objectives are different. We turn to this possibility in section 16.3.

16.3   Ontogenetic and Deferred Adaptations in Adolescence

A developmental niche is a period in an organism's life span characterized by unique demands and affordances. It is thus possible that some behaviors that are more pronounced in adolescence than in other developmental periods are *ontogenetic adaptations*: behaviors and mechanisms that adapt an organism to its current (as opposed to its future or past) developmental niche (Geary & Bjorklund, 2000). Ontogenetic adaptations are not immature forms of adult adaptations; they may even "disappear" when no longer necessary. For instance, it has been proposed that neonatal imitation of facial expressions (e.g., tongue protrusion) is an ontogenetic adaptation designed to foster infant–mother interaction at a moment in development at which infants have little intentional control over their behavior (Bjorklund, 1997). Another example of an ontogenetic adaptation in childhood is the tendency of children to overestimate their abilities, which enables them to keep motivated on difficult learning tasks (Bjorklund, 1997). Along the same lines, it is possible that typical adolescent behavioral patterns, such as risk taking and sensation seeking, have specific fitness benefits at this particular stage of life. *Deferred adaptations*, in contrast, are future-oriented adaptations to the extent that their benefits are delayed and occur in the future (e.g., the adult developmental niche). For instance, gender differences in rough-and-tumble play in childhood itself do not increase the direct chances of survival; in fact, survival chances may even decrease due to minor injuries. However, this type of play is thought to be an essential preparation for adult social life (Pellegrini & Bjorklund, 2004).

Consistent with these ideas, it has long been argued that typical adolescent risk and impulsivity attitudes have adaptive functions, giving adolescents the drive to learn the new skills needed to navigate the challenges of adult life (Csikszentmihalyi, Larson, & Prescott, 1977). Adolescent animals often have to leave the nest and explore novel, potentially dangerous, environments in the search for food and mates. They have to take risks when testing their strength against competitors (Bercovitch et al., 2003). Succeeding in these developmental tasks may directly contribute to their survival by providing increased access to food resources (ontogenetic adaptation). However, adolescent behavior may also have benefits that materialize only in the future (deferred adaptations)—in other words, the learning that occurs during adolescence pays off later in life. Phelps et al. (2007) also found evidence that high scores on risk and problem behaviors among adolescents are associated with positive developmental trajectories (e.g., increasing social competence, caring, confidence, and character).

Feeling less anxiety about the unknown may have adaptive functions for adolescents. Adolescence is about learning to become an independent agent (Sercombe, 2014). For the first time, learning new skills and discovering novel environments takes place largely without parental guidance and oversight. Exploring a novel environment may lead to the discovery of new niches and opportunities (e.g., food resources, social alliances, and reproductive partners). But it can also be dangerous—and a cause of anxiety—due to social and physical risks. Animal studies have shown that an increased exploratory drive in adolescent mammals is paralleled by a reduction in uncertainty-related anxiety. For instance, Macri, Adriani, Chiarotti, & Laviola (2002) compared the exploratory behavior of juvenile, adolescent, and adult mice in a radial maze with open and enclosed arms. Juvenile and adult mice strongly avoided the maze's open arms, whereas the adolescent mice spent equal time in the open and enclosed arms. They also showed less anxiety when out in the open than juvenile or adult mice. These findings suggest that temporary reduction in anxiety about the unknown may be an ontogenetic or deferred adaptation during adolescence, fostering a higher intensity of exploratory and risk-taking behavior. Unfortunately, data on these temporal dynamics are sparse and longitudinal studies of mice and humans are lacking.

16.3.1 Developmental Differences in Navigating Uncertainty: Empirical Evidence

Both ontogenetic and deferred adaptations can lead to an adolescent-specific pattern of behavior, but is there any evidence that adolescents are less averse to uncertainty than adults and children? There have been surprisingly few studies of adolescents' behavior under uncertainty. Instead, most experimental studies have presented adolescents with choice problems in which they are forced to make a selection between one of two options. Both are fully described in terms of the potential outcomes and associated probabilities (see figure 16.3a). In reality, such situations are rare; people seldom know everything there is to know about an upcoming decision. In this sense, common experimental designs are "strange situations" that fail to capture the environment or the choices adolescents actually face (Bronfenbrenner, 1979). It is therefore not surprising that this type of experimental study has regularly failed to reproduce the typically adolescent patterns of risk behavior that are so striking in the real world (I. N. Defoe, Dubas, Figner, & van Aken, 2015; Rosenbaum, Venkatraman, Steinberg, & Chein, 2018). When adolescents use drugs or engage in unprotected sex, they may have only a vague idea of the possible consequences of their actions because they lack personal experience. Van den Bos and Hertwig (2017) recently examined what happens when adolescents are given the opportunity to "look before they leap"—that is, when they are empowered to search for information

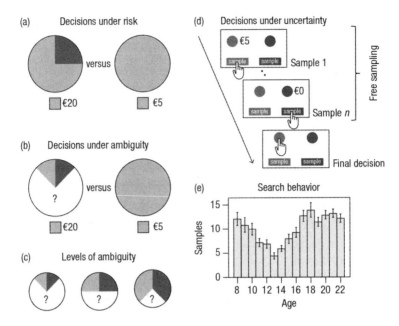

Figure 16.3
Experimental tasks. (a) Decisions under risk were represented by a wheel of fortune consisting of eight slices. If the spinner stopped on a dark gray slice, the player received nothing. If the spinner stopped on a light gray slice, the player won or lost a certain amount of money. (b) Decisions under ambiguity were represented in exactly the same way as the risky gambles, but this time occluders (here in white) on top of the wheels hid part of the information. (c) Three levels of ambiguity were implemented. (d) In the decisions under uncertainty task, participants were able to sample from two payoff distributions before making a final decision. Respondents sampled by pressing the sample button and chose by clicking on the corresponding circle. All experimental tasks were self-paced. (e) Age-related changes in the amount of search in the sampling paradigm. (Adapted from van den Bos & Hertwig, 2017.)

(e.g., by actively probing their peers' experience or observing what happens to others engaging in a risky activity), hence reducing the level of uncertainty, before embarking on an activity. Using a paradigm developed in research on *decisions from experience* (see chapters 1 and 7) to implement conditions more representative of the adolescent ecology, van den Bos and Hertwig asked 105 respondents, ranging in age from 8 to 22 years, to make decisions in three kinds of environments: risky, ambiguous, and uncertain (see figure 16.3).

Decisions under risk are the canonical way to study individuals' risk preference in psychology and economics. Here, full information about the options' possible outcomes and probabilities is provided for free. In *decisions under ambiguity*, the information available on probabilities is incomplete, as is often the case in the real world. Many experimental studies have found that adults tend to be ambiguity averse. In other words, they prefer *known* risks (e.g., an urn of 50 red and 50 green balls, with a reward for drawing a green ball) to *unknown* risks (e.g., an urn with 100 red and green balls in some unknown combination; Ellsberg, 1961; Tymula et al., 2012). In light of typical adolescent behavior, one might expect adolescents to be less ambiguity averse than adults or children. In the *decisions under uncertainty* task, respondents were presented with two options that they could explore as much as they wanted before choosing between them, with the outcome of this decision being incentivized. In this environment, the individual determined how much information to sample before making a final decision. One signature finding from the adult literature is that people tend to sample relatively little information before making a consequential decision (Hertwig & Erev, 2009; Wulff Mergenthaler-Canseco, & Hertwig, 2018; see chapter 7 for details). Given adolescents' propensity to act impulsively, one may expect them to explore less than adults and children—in other words, to be even more accepting of incomplete knowledge about the possible consequences of their actions than other age groups.

Echoing previous experimental results, children appeared to take more risks than adolescents in the canonical decisions under risk measure. For decisions under ambiguity, in contrast, things looked very different. Here, a nonlinear developmental trend emerged, with ambiguity tolerance peaking in adolescence. This result is in line with two previous studies that also found adolescents to be more tolerant of ambiguity than adults (Blankenstein, Crone, van den Bos, & van Duijvenvoorde, 2016; Tymula et al., 2012). A similar nonlinear developmental trajectory in search behavior also emerged for decisions under uncertainty: adolescents searched for markedly less information before making a consequential decision than either children or adults (see figure 16.3e). Here again, they were more tolerant of incomplete knowledge. Moreover, additional analyses (for details, see van den Bos & Hertwig, 2017) suggest that developmental changes in ambiguity and uncertainty attitudes are driven by developmental change in novelty seeking, the personality trait specifically associated with exploratory activity in response to novel stimulation (Arnett, 1994).

In sum, there is emerging evidence that adolescents respond to uncertainty in distinct ways. Their behaviors are consistent with the idea that they are more willing to accept incomplete knowledge and to engage with uncertain environments. However, only a handful of studies to date have examined these behavioral regularities (e.g., Rosenbaum et al., 2018). Furthermore, such a pattern in itself provides supporting evidence for both deferred and ontogenetic adaptations. Next, we set out a road map for further investigation of how adolescents navigate uncertainty.

16.4   Charting the Territory: Where Do We Go from Here?

Adolescent behavioral patterns may be adaptive responses to environmental demands and developmental tasks, such as practicing agency, independence, and autonomy. It is therefore imperative to study the adolescent environment and how the adolescent mind responds to it. Here, we identify two questions for future investigations. First, what is the structure and level of uncertainty in the environments that adolescents seek out? Second, why do adolescents respond differently, relative to other individuals in earlier or later developmental periods, when confronted with uncertainty? The first question requires a thorough ecological analysis of the adolescent environment to map out actual and perceived changes in levels of uncertainty. The second question relates to the motivational and cognitive capacities that may underlie the use of particular strategies for navigating uncertainty.

Eliciting probabilistic expectations would seem to be a promising method for mapping out perceived environmental uncertainty (Bruine de Bruin & Fischhoff, 2017). In this method, people are asked to estimate the probability that a specific event will occur in the near or far future. In combination with experimental and longitudinal data, it can provide insights into how uncertainty increases or decreases across adolescence, what kind of uncertainty is involved, and how these changes affect behavior. Eliciting probabilistic beliefs about single events (e.g., dying within the next five years) can provide a wealth of data. However, the methodology presented in chapter 3 on the *risk–reward heuristic* may offer a richer or at least complementary source of information. As observed in research on this heuristic, people appear sensitive to the structural relationship between risks and rewards in the real world.

Adults tend to rely on mental models of risk–reward structures when making judgments in novel uncertain situations. Building on this research, one could aim to reveal the perceived risk–reward structures of adolescents' environments. Although for adolescents, as for adults, the relationships between risks and rewards are likely to be negative—after all, there really is no such thing as a free lunch—there may be notable differences in the subjective functions describing these relationships. For instance, adolescents do not necessarily judge the probability of detrimental outcomes (e.g., the risk of getting cancer from smoking) more optimistically than adults (Cohn, Imai, Macfarlane, & Yanez, 1995). Instead, it seems that their behavior is driven by the perceived rewards of these risky behaviors (Siegel et al., 1994). These subjective measures are highly relevant given that they predict future engagement in those behaviors (Helfinstein, Mumford, & Poldrack, 2015).

Apart from the subjective perception of uncertainty, it is also worth studying the objective structures of adolescents' environments. Chapter 3 focused on the relation between risks and rewards; let us now consider risk and losses, taking driving behavior as an illustration. Motor vehicle crashes are the leading cause of death for U.S. teenagers. In the United States, six young people aged 16–19 died every day from motor vehicle injuries in 2015 (Centers for Disease Control and Prevention, 2017), and an adolescent is about 2.6 times more likely to be in a fatal accident (Tefft, 2017). However, the odds of being in a fatal accident are low—only about 8 in 100,000 (National Safety Council, 2018). A back-of-an-envelope calculation reveals that the chances of a fatal accident for an adolescent are still very small (23 in 100,000). In other words, a fatal car crash is, luckily, an extremely rare event, even for a teenager. Similar statistics are likely to apply in other risk domains (e.g., there is only a 1 in 33,000 chance of dying in a parachute jumping accident; British Parachute Association, 2018). It is therefore important to understand how adolescents respond to such statistical structures—how do they deal with events that are highly improbable but, if they occur, highly consequential or even deadly (Taleb, 2007)? Could it be that adolescents' behavior differs most strongly from adults' behavior in environments in which rarity and severity join in creating powerful but somewhat veiled risks?

The decisions under uncertainty environment (see figure 16.3d) involving sequential sampling is a valuable tool for uncovering how people respond to environments featuring rare events (Wulff et al., 2018). For instance, there is evidence that when people experience rare events in the sequence of sampled outcomes, they choose as if those events have less weight than they deserve in light of their objective probabilities (see chapters 7 and 8). It is possible that adolescents underweight rare events to an even greater extent than adults. One of the mechanisms behind this underweighting pattern is reliance on very small samples—in which rare events are, by definition, unlikely to occur. More generally, experience-based experimental paradigms (see Hertwig & Erev, 2009) offer novel ways to investigate adolescent behavior under uncertainty. Research on decisions from experience provides many examples of how adults adjust their search as a function of cognitive, emotional, strategic, and environmental variables (Wulff et al., 2018). For instance, adult decision makers increase their sample size (a) in the presence of negative events (Lejarraga, 2010; see chapter 7), (b) when they operate in a state of fear (Frey, Mata, & Hertwig, 2014), and (c) when the number of options increases (Noguchi & Hills, 2016). Furthermore, decisions from experience rely on learning and memory processes and therefore forge a bridge between research on behavioral decision making and neuroscience-based research on basic reinforcement learning processes. The latter has, for instance, observed significant changes in learning skills across adolescence (van den Bos, Cohen, Kahnt, & Crone, 2012).

When investigating adolescent environments, it is vital to consider what is perhaps the most important environment to teenagers: the peer group (van den Bos, 2013). Adolescents spend most of their time with peers, and most typical adolescent behavior occurs in the presence of peers. For many serious crimes, co-offending is more common than offending alone (Zimring & Laqueur, 2015), and car accidents are more likely to occur with peers on board (Chen, 2000). The social environment offers new sources of uncertainty and they are likely to impact adolescents' behavior. Take, for instance, explorative behavior in competitive social environments: the presence of competitors can significantly reduce search efforts, to the extent that people sample only minimally before making a final decision (see chapter 12). Adolescents might be even more willing to act in haste, rush to conclusions, and take risks in the presence of their peers (Albert et al., 2013).

To the extent that the social structure of the adolescent peer network is subject to competition, a hierarchical organization will emerge that may, in turn, also contribute to specific behavioral patterns. For instance, hierarchically organized social structures are often associated with a winner-takes-all

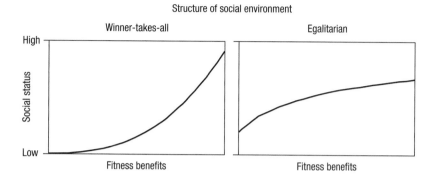

Figure 16.4

Relations between evolutionary fitness and status within a peer group. In hierarchical winner-takes-all environments, the typical alpha male will have preferential access to mates and resources. In this context, it may make sense to take large risks to increase one's social status. In a more egalitarian social structure, in contrast, the fitness benefits are more equally distributed and taking large risks to gain social status has little payoff in terms of fitness benefits. (Inspired by Kacelnik & Bateson, 1997.)

distribution of resources (Wolfe, Frank, & Cook, 1996). As a result, there may be a convex relationship between social status (place in hierarchy) and fitness benefits (see figure 16.4). Evolutionary models suggest that there is more risk-seeking behavior in environments with convex fitness curves than in those with concave fitness curves (Kacelnik & Bateson, 1997). Thus, in a developmental period in which the peer social network and the establishment of one's social status is of paramount importance, the network's structure itself may promote risk-taking behavior (van den Bos, Crone, Meuwese, & Güroğlu, 2018).

16.5   *Sturm und Drang*

A time-honored view of adolescence is that it is a period of pathological—but, thankfully, transient—trials and tribulations (*Sturm und Drang*) on the way to adulthood (Hall, 1904). It seems that raging hormones (Buchanan, Eccles, & Becker, 1992) or unfinished brains (Bell & McBride, 2010) are throwing a wrench in the works. From this perspective, adolescence is a nuisance for adolescents and everybody around them—but fortunately they grow out of it. An ecological perspective, as outlined here, offers a different view, emphasizing the key developmental tasks that adolescents face and arguing that typical adolescent behaviors may have an adaptive core. In addition, it adds nuance to classic models of development focusing on growth or improvement. These models implicitly assume that the function of development is to reach the adult phenotype; accordingly, they conceive of cognitive functions as a series of intermediate stages on the way to completion. The ecological approach—while acknowledging developmental growth and decline in cognition—instead emphasizes the need to understand the structure of the environment and the mind–environment interaction. Most investigations of adolescent behavior are implemented in the laboratory, often using experimental stimuli that do not accurately reflect the key structural elements of the adolescent world; these artificial settings do not offer the insight necessary for deciphering the logic of adolescents' observable behavior.

By drawing on research on decisions from experience (see chapter 7), we have illustrated how insights can be gained by designing experimental microworlds that are better proxies for the decisions adolescents face. In addition, we have identified avenues for exploring the perceived structure of uncertainty in the adolescent environment. In our view, what is required next are ecological analyses of the social and nonsocial environments that adolescents seek out and experience. Understanding the payoff structures, affordances, and constraints of these environments will give a more nuanced perspective than the pathological, or simple cognitive growth, views. Ultimately, an ecological view also promises to inform interventions to prevent the most negative consequences of adolescent behaviors. For instance, it may help us understand why the introduction of skate parks may have a positive influence on youth development, even though the skating scene itself is often (wrongly) associated with deviant behavior. Adolescents become adults by interacting with the environment; relatives, teachers, and society cannot lock teenagers in their rooms and wait until they emerge as well-behaved adults. Parents who often feel that their budding adult landed from another planet may find some comfort in taking an ecological view, which suggests that the adolescent world is indeed different in some ways, and it is impossible to fully understand adolescent behavior without understanding these worlds as well. Remembering that in some places, more than 99.9% of adolescents survive this turbulent period (Willoughby et al., 2014) might make it easier for parents, guardians, and mentors to keep a cool head. In the meantime, more research into Planet Adolescence is needed to eventually help teenagers navigate their world even better.

17   The Life-Span Development of Risk Preference

Rui Mata and Renato Frey

17.1   The Ebb and Flow of Life Risks

Throughout history, humans have led a precarious existence, exposed to risks of predation, starvation, infection, violence, and natural hazards. Risks are also an inextricable part of modern life. In fact, modern society has been described as a *risk society*, constantly dealing with the hazards and insecurities that modernization itself has produced (Beck, 1992). Although institutions such as health insurance, hospitals, medical alert systems, police and fire services, and international treaties buffer people from the worst consequences of risks, modernization has also brought new risks, such as deadly hospital germs, synthetic drugs (e.g., the opioid epidemic in the United States), climate change, and pollution. Just as the risks humans face have changed across history, the risks to which modern humans are exposed change across the life span. As illustrated in figure 17.1, boys are much more likely to die of drowning than in car or motorcycle crashes, which are in turn the leading causes of death for males in adolescence and young adulthood. As men age, they become more likely to die of drug use disorders, alcohol use disorders, or—in old age—of falls. These epidemiological patterns make it clear that exposure to risks is not a phenomenon restricted to a single phase of the life span; rather, different phases of the life span are associated with different challenges—probably due to the changing nature of the developmental tasks faced by individuals at various points in life (see chapter 16 for more on life history theory and developmental tasks).

In this chapter, we zoom in on what the behavioral sciences—particularly psychology and economics—see as one of the most important building blocks of human behavior, namely, risk preference. An individual's risk

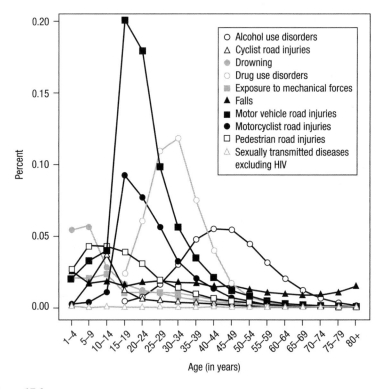

Figure 17.1
Cause-specific mortality in males for selected causes (GBD 2013 Mortality and Causes of Death Collaborators, 2015).

preference is reflected in their response to specific events and properties of the world (e.g., probability, uncertainty, outcome variance, expected value, losses, danger, threat). As a key component in the cognitive machinery, it is also thought to shape how people respond to life's vagaries. This means that any attempt to understand how people cope with uncertainty will be incomplete unless it also tries to come to grips with risk preference, which may, for instance, influence which heuristics people choose (e.g., one that seeks to avoid the worst or one that aims for the stars); how much information they search for or deliberately choose not to consult (see Gigerenzer & Garcia-Retamero, 2017; Hertwig & Engel, 2016) and whether they seek to share responsibility through collective decisions when uncertainty looms large. Here, we examine this important aspect of how the mind reckons with uncertainty and, in particular, explores the dynamic nature of risk preference across the life span. According to some researchers—such as Nobel laureates G. J. Stigler and Becker (1977)—risk preference does not have the power to explain age-dependent patterns in the causes of mortality (see figure 17.1) or other interindividual differences in how people respond to risk and uncertainty. For them, risk preferences are the same "across men and periods" (p. 76), and any changes observed in risky behavior can be understood as the product of changing reward structures and institutions rather than as a reflection of changes in a psychological trait or preference. This is an extreme position that we do not share. Instead, we seek to develop a coherent and empirically informed alternative view on how risk preference changes across the life span. We outline recent progress that has been made toward understanding the nature of risk preference and highlight the conceptual and methodological disagreements that need to be resolved in order to fully understand how individuals deal with risk and uncertainty across the life span.

17.2   Getting a Grip on Risk Taking and Risk Preference

Risk preference has been posited as a major explanatory construct, capable of accounting for individual differences in how people deal with risk and uncertainty (Frey, Pedroni, Mata, Rieskamp, & Hertwig, 2017; Mata, Frey, Richter, Schupp, & Hertwig, 2018). Here, we use the term "preference"—akin to the terms "attitude" and "behavioral syndrome" common in the psychological (E. U. Weber, 2010) and behavioral ecology literature (Sih & Del Giudice, 2012)—to mean a general tendency to appraise situations in terms of specific emotions, thoughts, and behavioral patterns. Risk preference has been invoked to explain how people make choices about many aspects of their lives, including whether to migrate, start a business, or buy insurance (e.g., Caliendo, Fossen, & Kritikos, 2009; Clark & Liwoski, 2017; Dohmen et al., 2011). A universally accepted understanding of what risk preference is has proven elusive. Some see risk preference as a personality construct with some degree of temporal stability, similar to psychological traits such as intelligence or the Big Five (Frey et al., 2017). Others argue that risk preference cannot be a psychological trait because evaluations of risk are constructed on the fly as a function of momentary cues and conditions (Slovic, 1995). Moreover, there has been considerable debate on whether risk preference is a unitary construct, a multidimensional construct that varies across life domains, or a combination of the two (Blais & Weber, 2006; Frey et al., 2017; Yechiam & Ert, 2011). Paralleling—and possibly fueling—this conceptual disagreement, there is a lack of consensus on how best to measure risk preference (see Frey et al., 2017; Hertwig, Wulff, & Mata, 2018). Two main approaches can be distinguished, echoing the distinction that Cronbach (1957) made between two major research streams in psychology, the *experimental* and the *correlational*. One approach assumes the concept of revealed preference and uses behavioral measures; the other assumes the concept of stated preference and uses self-report measures. These two approaches have progressed largely in parallel, with little overlap (Frey et al., 2017; Mamerow, Frey, & Mata, 2016). Although this disconnect is not specific to the study of risk preference (Tracy, Robins, & Sherman, 2009), it is particularly important in this domain, where the two traditions paint very different pictures of the nature of the construct and its life-span changes.

The *revealed preferences approach* has focused on developing and deploying behavioral paradigms involving risk and uncertainty to assess the role of situational or task variables on overt choices, such as decisions between monetary gambles (Harrison & Rutström, 2008). In these paradigms, individuals make decisions between options whose probabilities or outcomes (or both) differ, such as receiving €5 for sure or taking a gamble with a $p = .5$ chance of winning €10, otherwise nothing. There are many implementations of these paradigms—they may, for example, involve fully described versus experienced risks (Hertwig & Erev, 2009) or use game-like properties (e.g., card games, balloons) to engage participants (e.g., Lejuez et al., 2002; Pleskac, 2008). Researchers using such tasks can fully control the characteristics of the choice problems (e.g., the level of risk and uncertainty and the rewards and losses involved), allowing participants' actual choices to be assessed in well-controlled settings (Mata, Josef, Samanez-Larkin, & Hertwig, 2011, for an overview of tasks).

The *stated preferences approach* has used correlational designs to understand intraindividual consistency by means of "stated" self-reports (e.g., Blais & Weber, 2006). There is a long tradition in psychology of capturing individuals' personality characteristics by tapping their responses to hypothetical or real-world scenarios through questionnaires. For example, respondents may be asked to rate themselves on a scale from "not at all willing to take risks" to "very willing to take risks" or to gauge the likelihood that they will engage in specific risky behaviors (e.g., "How likely would you be to go white-water rafting at high water in the spring?"). A growing body of work on risk preference builds primarily on findings from single-item (e.g., Dohmen et al., 2011) or multiple-item self-report measures of risk preference (e.g., Blais & Weber, 2006; Dohmen, Falk, Golsteyn, Huffman, & Sunde, 2017). Self-report measures are now also included in several large representative panel studies, and these survey data have significantly advanced the understanding of individual and age-related differences in self-reported risk preference (Dohmen et al., 2017; Josef et al., 2016).

In the following sections, we review the insights that the revealed and the stated preference approaches, with their behavioral and stated measures of risk preference, respectively, have provided into the stability of risk preference across the life span. However, let us first unpack the term "stability," which is often used to mean different things in research on risk preference. For example, in a special journal issue addressing the nature of risky choice (van Schaik, Kusev, & Juliusson, 2011), a number of contributors used the term "stability" to discuss the extent to which different measures provide the same picture of individual risk taking (in other words, whether an individual's risk-taking level was stable across measures). Other contributors used it to mean the agreement of a single measure across time. We distinguish between these two meanings by referring to the former as "convergent validity" and the latter as "temporal stability."

17.3   Convergent Validity

When different measures of risk preference speak with one voice in describing individual differences in the appetite for risk, they are said to exhibit *convergent validity*. The literature on risk preference suggests a clear gap in findings emerging from the revealed and stated preference measurement approaches—that is, a lack of convergent validity. In a large study, Frey et al. (2017) implemented many different measures of risk preference from both approaches, including a wide set of behavioral tasks (e.g., monetary gambles in which risk was described or experienced, simulated driving) and self-report measures. The findings showed that the behavioral measures did not correlate strongly with each other or with self-report measures of risk preference (see also Pedroni et al., 2017). In contrast, there was a high degree of consistency across stated self-report measures of risk preference across situations and life domains. Indeed, a general risk preference factor emerged from different self-report measures, capturing 61% of the explained variance, with a variety of more specific facets accounting for the remaining variance (Frey et al, 2017; see also Highhouse, Nye, Zhang, & Rada, 2017).

These findings suggest that measures of risk preference cannot be used interchangeably, at least not across the different measurement approaches. This applies to behavioral measures in particular. Furthermore, the results from stated preference measures seem to dispel the rather simplistic notion of risk preference being either general or domain-specific (Blais & Weber, 2006; Jackson, Hourany, & Vidmar, 1972; Slovic, 1964). Instead, it may be helpful to conceptualize the construct as having *both* a general component that impacts many domains of life *and* a plethora of components that are specific to particular psychological and/or situational characteristics and demands (Frey et al., 2017; Mata et al., 2018).

17.4   Temporal Stability and Change in Risk Preference across the Life Span

Let us first distinguish between two types of temporal stability: *mean-level stability*, which refers to stability (or change) in the average of a population over time and *rank-order stability*, which refers to differences between individuals being preserved (or changing) over time (Caspi, Roberts, & Shiner, 2005). This distinction can be particularly helpful in clearing up misconceptions about the nature of stability and change—and in illustrating how certain constructs, including risk preference, may be seen as a stable individual characteristic (a trait) that is nonetheless subject to some change. For example, intelligence and personality traits show considerable test–retest stability in the form of rank-order stability, meaning that the rank order between individuals tends to be preserved across multiple measurement occasions (Anusic & Schimmack, 2016). At the same time, these constructs are subject to sizeable and systematic mean-level changes: individuals differ significantly from themselves over time and may do so in similar ways—for example, as knowledge increases systematically across the life span (Baltes, Staudinger, & Lindenberger, 1999). It follows that it may be essential to consider both stable differences *between* individuals and change *within* individuals when discussing life-span stability and change in risk preference.

Why would risk preference change reliably across the life span? The idea that individuals are endowed with stable psychological traits and behavioral tendencies (e.g., risk preference) suggests that such characteristics have an adaptive character. Generally, stable personality characteristics or behavioral tendencies can be regarded as different solutions to tackling the challenges posed by the environment (see chapter 15; Hintze, Olson, Adami, & Hertwig, 2015; Wolf, van Doorn, Leimar, & Weissing, 2007). For example, it has been proposed that variation in risk preference reflects different life or reproductive strategies for dealing with risk–reward trade-offs (see also chapter 3): individuals may have to opt between striving for large, but unlikely, rewards and settling for small, but likely, rewards (Sih & Del Giudice, 2012). But are such dispositions set for life or could they change as a function of contextual factors? The answer is not necessarily an either/ or response; both options may be available (Fraley & Roberts, 2005), as illustrated by the increase and the decline in risk taking during adolescence (see chapter 16).

On the one hand, because personality and behavioral dispositions are to some extent genetically determined and have implications for large portions of the life span, continuity across the life span could be expected. Indeed, there is some evidence that risk preference has a genetic basis, although heritability estimates vary widely (Benjamin et al., 2012; Cesarini, Johannesson, Magnusson, & Wallace, 2012; Day et al., 2016; Linnér et al., 2017; Wang, Zheng, Xuan, Chen, & Li, 2016). Persistent differences in risk preference may also arise in response to contextual influences early in life: life history theory (Ellis et al., 2012; Stearns, 1992) suggests that personality and behavioral tendencies represent an adaptive response to environmental conditions experienced in the early years. Crucially, such views suggest that domain-general personality traits can arise whenever the development of the basic physiological or cognitive makeup (e.g., brain structure) is shaped by the context early in life, with implications for the full life span (Dall, Houston, & McNamara, 2004; Sih & Del Giudice, 2012). For example, some researchers have suggested that stressful early life experiences may presage future environmental uncertainty and thus lead to risk taking throughout life. In harsh and uncertain environments, risk taking may be adaptive (Frankenhuis & de Weerth, 2013; Mata, Josef, & Hertwig, 2016; see also box 17.1 and chapter 16).

On the other hand, changes across the life span may themselves be adaptive and are not incompatible with persistent between-person differences. It may be adaptive to react to life circumstances and take risks in some

Box 17.1

Life-span differences in risk taking and hardship.

Are patterns of decline in risk taking across the life span universal? Mata et al. (2016) analyzed age patterns of self-reported risk taking across 77 countries and found systematic variation. The preference for taking risks in an everyday context decreased with age in most countries; however, countries in which people are exposed to greater hardships (e.g., high infant mortality, high homicide rates, low GDP) seemed to be characterized by flatter age–risk curves. In some countries—for example, Nigeria (NG; upper right corner of figure 17.B1)—the

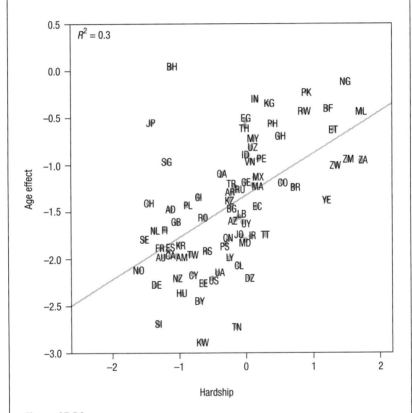

Figure 17.B1

Relationship between the hardship index and age-related decline in risk taking (0=no age differences in self-reported risk taking). The higher the hardship experienced in a country, the closer the age-effect coefficient was to 0, representing a flatter risk-taking propensity curve across the adult life span. See Mata et al. (2016) for details.

Box 17.1 (continued)

appetite for risk did not appear to decline across the life span. Ecologies with scarce resources and, in consequence, heightened competition seem to be associated with an increased propensity for risk taking, regardless of age. These findings are compatible with the idea that hardship may function as a cue that guides life history strategies (see also chapter 16). The rationale is that harsh environments are less predictable and lead individuals to bet on having a shorter life span.

contexts but not in others (Mishra, Barclay, & Sparks, 2016). For example, risk-sensitivity theory (Kacelnik & Bateson, 1997) suggests that individuals will take risks whenever low-risk options are unlikely to achieve their desired outcomes: when facing starvation, even a generally risk-averse animal should and will take the risk of being eaten by a predator if foraging offers a chance of satisfying its caloric needs. This kind of contextual, state-dependent departure from a baseline preference for risk does not contradict the idea that organisms may differ from each other in their *average* appetite for risk. In line with this idea of contextual change, there is evidence for momentary change in individual risk preference as a function of contextual changes and life events, such as finding a partner or having children (e.g., Schildberg-Hörisch, 2018).

In sum, there are plausible reasons to expect both continuity and change in risk preference across the life span. Against this background, it is important to understand the sources of short- and long-term change in risk preference. For example, aging is associated with changes in cognitive ability (Dohmen, Falk, Huffman, & Sunde, 2018) and motivation (Depping & Freund, 2011) that may affect decision making under risk and uncertainty. We now turn to reviewing empirical findings on these issues.

17.4.1 Mean-Level Change

The vast majority of work on age differences in risk preference has used self-report measures of risk taking to assess whether older and younger adults differ in their appetite for risk. These cross-sectional studies suggest that, overall, risk taking decreases with age (Bonem, Ellsworth, & Gonzalez, 2015; Dohmen et al., 2017; Mata et al., 2016; Roalf, Mitchell, Harbaugh, & Janowsky, 2012; Rolison, Hanoch, Wood, & Liu, 2014; Rosman, Garcia, Lee,

Butler, & Schwartz, 2013; Schwartz et al., 2013). Some of this research has investigated whether such age-related patterns generalize across domains (e.g., recreational, health, and social domains). The results suggest that the overall reduction in risk taking varies somewhat as a function of domain. For example, risk taking declines more steeply in recreational contexts than in the social or health domains (e.g., Rolison et al., 2014). Consistent with these cross-sectional findings, longitudinal research also points to a reduction in risk taking with age (Josef et al., 2016; see figure 17.2). Importantly, longitudinal findings also support the idea that age-related changes may be more or less pronounced across domains. The source of these differences remains unclear, however. One likely contributing factor is that opportunities for risk taking vary across the life span depending on the setting. For example, the scope for occupational risk taking varies across the life cycle of education–work–retirement. By contrast, the scope for risk taking in the social domain may be less subject to change over time, as a result of which the tendency for risk taking in this domain remains fairly stable across the life span (Josef et al., 2016).

The overall decline in risk taking across the life span described earlier in this section seems to be virtually universal, being observed in many countries and regions of the world (e.g., Mamerow et al., 2016; Mata et al., 2016; Dohmen et al., 2017). In line with theories positing that life experience can shape the life-course trajectory of risk preference and risk taking, some cross-country differences suggest that environmental characteristics play an important role in shaping levels of risk taking and the associated life-span patterns (see box 17.1).

All these findings on life-span patterns of risk taking have emerged from the stated preference approach. Do findings from the revealed risk preference approach yield similar patterns of mean-level differences? Studies in the revealed preference measurement traditions have examined age-related differences in risk preference almost exclusively by comparing groups of younger and older adults in cross-sectional studies. Results are mixed. Best and Charness (2015) conducted a meta-analysis of studies that used choices between gambles with positively or negatively described risks (i.e., setups in which reward/loss magnitudes and probabilities are known) to capture behavioral differences between younger and older adults. For positively framed items, they found a tendency for younger adults to choose the risky option more often than older adults in some scenarios (e.g., small monetary

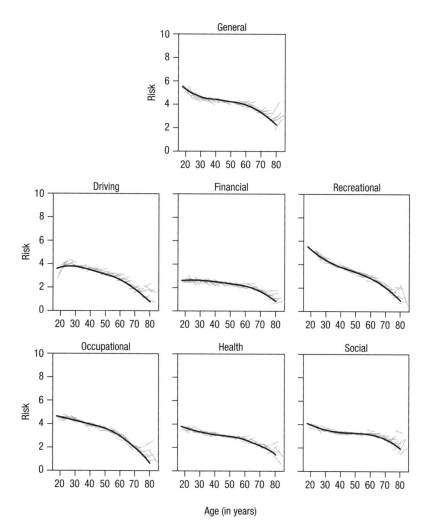

Figure 17.2

Mean-level changes in general and domain-specific risk taking across the life span, as captured by the German Socio-Economic Panel (SOEP; Josef et al., 2016). SOEP respondents were asked to rate their risk taking in general ("Are you generally a person who is willing to take risks or do you try to avoid taking risks?") and in specific domains ("How would you rate your willingness to take risks while driving/in financial matters/during leisure and sport/in business and professional matters/in health matters/when trusting other people?") on an 11-point scale over several years (e.g., 2004, 2009, 2014). Figure 17.2 shows average mean-level change (obtained from a Loess regression across the first measurement occasion) superimposed on spaghetti plots capturing two measurements 5 years apart for each age cohort from 18 to 80 years of age. See Josef et al. (2016) for details and extensive longitudinal analyses of the data.

amounts); for negatively framed items, in contrast, there was no overall age difference in risky decision making. Moreover, there is evidence that the direction of age differences in risk preference is influenced by whether or not the choice set includes a safe option (e.g., Mather et al., 2012). For instance, in choices between two positively framed risky gambles, Pachur, Mata, and Hertwig (2017; see also Kellen, Mata, & Davis-Stober, 2017) found a tendency for older adults to choose the more risky option more often than younger adults—the opposite pattern of what is usually found in choices between a gamble and a safe option (Mather et al., 2012; Rutledge et al., 2016).

In a previous meta-analysis comparing results from choices between described risks (e.g., gambles) and decisions from experience (e.g., paradigms that involved learning; see also chapter 7), Mata, Josef, et al. (2011) found considerable heterogeneity as a function of task characteristics. Notably, age-related differences varied considerably as a function of the learning requirements of the task. In decisions from experience, age-related differences in risk taking were a function of decreased learning performance: older adults were more risk-seeking than younger adults when learning implied a shift toward risk-avoidant behavior but were more risk-averse when learning implied a shift toward risk-seeking behavior. In decisions from description, younger and older adults showed similar risk-taking behavior in the majority of tasks, and there were no clear age-related differences as a function of gain/loss framing (but see also Best & Charness, 2015).

Moreover, studies investigating how younger and older individuals navigate uncertainty in decisions from experience have demonstrated the importance of the choice ecology and shown that age differences do not necessarily emerge across the board (Frey, Mata, & Hertwig, 2015): in problems where there were relatively few options for participants to explore, age differences were not pronounced. That is, although older adults experience a substantial decline in fluid cognitive intelligence (as a result of which their learning abilities are attenuated), they may recruit adaptive cognitive strategies that enable them to learn about uncertain choice options. Age differences emerged only when choice set sizes exceeded a certain threshold, requiring participants to keep track of the risks involved in several choice options (Frey et al. 2015; see figure 17.3). To conclude, these and other results suggest one possible reason for the differences between age-related patterns of risk preference observed in behavioral and self-report measures:

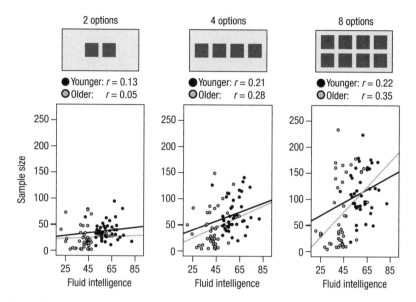

Figure 17.3
Relationship between fluid intelligence and search effort, separately for younger (M = 25 years old) and older (M = 71 years old) adults, as a function of increasingly complex choice environments (i.e., choice problems with two, four, or eight options). Fluid intelligence was measured using the digit–symbol substitution task. See Frey et al. (2015) for details.

behavioral measures enlist processes involving cognitive or learning abilities that are affected by aging, but that do not, per se, reflect changes in the appetite for risk.

17.4.2 Rank-Order Stability

We now turn to rank-order stability of risk preference. Rank-order stability means that the rank order between individuals tends to be preserved across multiple measurement occasions—over a few years or a decade, for example. The literature on temporal stability of risk-preference measures indicates that the rank-order stability of self-report measures is moderate to high over test–retest periods of up to 10 years (r ≈ .5). Importantly, this coefficient is only a little lower than for other major personality factors (Anusic & Schimmack, 2016) and considerably higher than for behavioral measures, such as choices between gambles (r ≤ .2). Note, however, that no studies currently exist that estimate the rank-order stability of behavioral measures for periods of over 5 years (Frey et al., 2017; Mata et al., 2018). For self-report measures, in contrast, there is evidence of an inverted U-shaped pattern in rank-order stability coefficients across the life span. Specifically, Josef et al. (2016) found that rank-order stability coefficients in risk-taking propensity increased from young to middle adulthood, before declining again in older age. This trajectory is consistent with the notion that developmental periods involving significant change and intrapersonal adaptation as a function of specific life events—i.e., young adulthood and old age—are characterized by lower stability. The same inverted U-shaped pattern of rank-order stability from young to old adulthood has been observed for major personality dimensions, such as the Big Five (Briley & Tucker-Drob, 2014).

Josef et al. (2016) also found that individuals differ significantly in how their risk-taking preferences change over time. Modeling risk-taking propensity across up to 10 years, they found that a significant portion of the variance in risk taking was due to individual differences in the rate of change. In other words, some people seem to have experienced stronger changes in their reported risk preference than others. These findings provide further support for the idea that idiosyncratic characteristics or life events have a differential impact across the life span.

17.5   An Emerging Life-Span Pattern and Future Directions

Self-reports of risk-taking behaviors suggest that there are systematic mean-level changes across the life span, with risk taking decreasing from young adulthood to old age, but that individual differences (rank ordering) largely persist over periods of up to a decade. Such patterns of simultaneous change and stability are similar to those observed for other personality characteristics, such as the Big Five (Roberts & DelVecchio, 2000; Roberts, Walton, & Viechtbauer, 2006). The pattern of age-related decline in risk taking throughout adulthood also appears to be a function of environmental characteristics, with harsh environments favoring flatter age-risk curves (e.g., Mata et al., 2016; see box 17.1).

So far, so good. However, studies using behavioral measures have yielded a much more mixed pattern of results on age differences in risk taking. The confounding role of learning and memory demands in influencing how older adults make decisions under risk in behavioral paradigms may be one key to this frustratingly ambiguous picture; another may be motivational changes with age, such as processing gains and losses (Best & Charness, 2015; Pachur, Mata, & Hertwig, 2017). Unfortunately, data on age differences in behavioral paradigms are scarce; in particular, there has been almost no longitudinal research on adult age differences in risk taking over time. Future work relying on behavioral measures of risk preference should strive to account for longitudinal changes while considering important confounds related to learning and memory abilities.

Beyond the question of whether self-report and behavioral measures of risk preference converge, two further issues relating to the sources of stability and change in risk preference across the life span need to be resolved—namely, the impact of environmental influences and person–environment interactions. Attributing age-related differences in behavior to psychological traits, such as risk preference, may come naturally to psychologists. As G. J. Stigler and Becker (1977) argued, however, it is also important to consider the role of the environment in both stability and change. After all, life-span changes in risk taking are likely to be influenced by the opportunities and incentives associated with risky behaviors. For example, new jobs, partners, or friends are all life events that could contribute to changes in risk-taking behavior without necessarily entailing a change in psychological makeup, although the two typically go hand in hand (Specht, Egloff, & Schumkle, 2011). Similarly, domain-specific patterns of age-related changes in risk taking—for example, a larger decrease in the recreational domain than in others in early adulthood (Josef et al., 2016)—could be attributable to reduced opportunities for risk taking in the recreational domain due to starting a family and pursuing a career.

Given that the opportunities to take risks and the incentives for doing so change across the life span, future research needs to focus on the critical events and situations that people face at different points in their lives (e.g., starting a job, marrying, having children) and to assess the role of each event, or combinations thereof, in determining individual differences in risk-taking behaviors. To date, there has been little investigation of such situations and how they can influence risk-taking profiles (Schildberg-Hörisch, 2018). More broadly, it is only recently that there has been a movement toward taking "situations" seriously in personality psychology (Funder, 2016). A truly ecological approach to risk taking that both provides a taxonomy of "risky" situations and identifies the psychological mechanisms and motivations that lead people to seek or avoid risk in such situations across the life span is still lacking. More research is needed to cast light on the role of the environment in determining individual and age differences in risk taking.

Interactions between person and environment characteristics are also to be expected. Current models of intellectual and personality development suggest that small individual differences early in life can be amplified over time through environmental effects. For example, people with slightly higher genetically endowed mental abilities select (and are selected into) environmental niches that lead to further increases in intellectual skills and performance (Dickens & Flynn, 2001). Similarly, individuals selected into a niche due to one ability may develop other abilities (e.g., students accepted into training programs due to high verbal skills may receive additional training in nonverbal skills as a result), leading to associations between traits that are not per se due to genetics (Bartholomew, Deary, & Lawn, 2009). Are similar processes at play in the context of risk preference and risk-taking behaviors? Future work should examine the interplay of genetics and the physical or social environment in determining how risk-taking propensity develops in different contexts and across the life span.

17.6 Conclusion

Findings from studies using self-report measures suggest that risk preference can be regarded as a moderately stable trait across the life span. People who are risk takers as young adults will also tend to take more risks than their peers later in life (rank-order stability). Overall, however, people tend to become less risk-taking with age (mean-level change), though there is considerable individual variation around this trend. In contrast, findings from studies using behavioral measures of risk taking are mixed and probably confounded by task characteristics, including demands on learning and memory. To date, research has focused on describing patterns of age differences in risk-taking propensity, but little is yet known about the causes of stability or change. There is a clear need to address the role of genetics, environment, and person–environment interactions in shaping risk preference across the life span.

VI Looking Back to Look Forward

18 Interpreting Uncertainty: A Brief History of Not Knowing

Anastasia Kozyreva, Timothy J. Pleskac, Thorsten Pachur, and Ralph Hertwig

18.1 Introduction

> I can live with doubt and uncertainty and not knowing. I think it's much more interesting to live not knowing than to have answers which might be wrong. I have approximate answers and possible beliefs and different degrees of uncertainty about different things, but I am not absolutely sure of anything and there are many things I don't know anything about, such as whether it means anything to ask why we're here ... I don't have to know an answer. I don't feel frightened not knowing things, by being lost in a mysterious universe without any purpose, which is the way it really is as far as I can tell.
>
> —Richard Feynman, *The Pleasure of Finding Things Out*

As a physicist, Richard Feynman had trained his mind to embrace the uncertainty that is inherent in the pursuit of scientific knowledge. His words in the epigraph, however, indicate something deeper—a view in which uncertainty touches on the existential state of not knowing that permeates all areas of human life and understanding. This book examines some of the uncertainties that people, both as individuals and in groups, encounter in a range of experiences. The specific focus is on how boundedly rational decision makers find their way despite limited knowledge and environmental complexity. In this final chapter, we turn to the philosophical origins of the concept of uncertainty and explore how its interpretation transformed with time, with each conceptualization of uncertainty being shaped by a different view of rationality.

Our historical survey focuses on a few milestones in the understanding of uncertainty. The first can be found in the philosophical skepticism of ancient Greek and Roman thought. Its main contribution to the topic was the recognition that human knowledge has limits—human existence is fundamentally intertwined with uncertainty and ignorance—and that the essence of wisdom and rationality consists in finding solutions to this human condition. The second milestone was reached with the emergence of probability and decision theory in the 17th century. These new concepts radically changed the understanding of rationality in Western thought, led to a differentiation between degrees and sources of uncertainty, and offered new tools to deal with the unknown. The next series of crucial developments took place in the 20th century, when a number of thinkers proposed formal normative theories of choice and introduced different interpretations of probability. Each interpretation gave rise to a unique conception of uncertainty in decision making, thereby exposing the limitations of approaches to the unknown based on probability theory. Highlighting these limits opened up space for what is perhaps the most recent milestone in the conceptual journey of uncertainty: the development of the approaches of bounded and ecological rationality. These developments put the focus on the role of heuristic mental tools in conditions of limited knowledge and on the mapping of those tools onto environmental structures. The aim is to describe how real people—as opposed to the idealized "rational men" or optimizing agents implicitly assumed in probability theory—make decisions under uncertainty. In so doing, the approaches of bounded and ecological rationality suggest a new view on uncertainty—a systemic one, in which the uncertain world and the cognitive tools of the human mind are intertwined.

18.2   Uncertainty and Philosophical Skepticism

> For in things uncertain there is nothing probable, but in things where there is probability the wise man will not be at a loss either what to do or what to answer. (Cicero, 45 BCE/1933, p. 609)

The idea that uncertainty is inherent to human life and knowledge has a long history. Roman stoic philosopher Seneca wrote in 49 CE that "all things that are still to come lie in uncertainty" (Seneca, 49 CE/1990, p. 313) and emphasized how dreadful it is to constantly worry about the unknown future (Seneca, ca. 65 CE/2000, p. 121). At least since the time of Socrates, awareness of one's ignorance has been seen as a sign—or even the essence—of wisdom; and the pursuit of truth and knowledge has been balanced against the recognition of people's epistemic limitations. Socrates himself embodied this balance, coupling a love of wisdom and self-reflective deliberation ("unexamined life is not worth living"; cited in Plato, 1966, 38a) with the acknowledgment of his own ignorance ("what I do not know I do not think I know"; cited in Plato, 1966, 21d).

Skeptical philosophers of the Academic and Pyrrhonist schools became the most devoted scholars of uncertainty in ancient Greek and Roman thought (ca. third century BCE–second century CE). Skepticism as a philosophical view or movement refers to the tradition of thought concerned with the possibility of knowledge and rational beliefs, and ancient skepticism was generally meant to describe "a way of life devoted to inquiry" (Vogt, 2010). Skeptical philosophers were consumed by the idea that neither the human senses nor reason could provide knowledge that is definitely true or false, and widely discussed how to navigate this human condition. Pyrrhonists valued the tranquility of the mind above all and believed it wise to suspend all judgment (*epoché*) and act undogmatically (adapting by default to society's customs; see Annas & Barnes, 2000). They held that uncertainty cannot be remedied by any rational means and should thus simply be accepted as an inevitable condition. Skeptics of the Academic school, by contrast, believed in a life rooted in reason and considered it rational to follow plausible opinions and adopt views that are likely to be true. The ideas of the Academic school on uncertainty are perhaps best captured by the Roman politician and scholar Cicero.[1] Following the Greek skeptic Carneades, he claimed that even if all things uncertain or hidden could not be fully comprehended, a wise person would be foolish not to rely on plausible opinions when it comes to practical matters and decisions (Cicero, 45 BCE/1933, p. 595). In fact, it was Cicero who introduced the terms "uncertain" and "probable" into Latin—and by extension European—philosophical vocabulary. He used *incertus* to translate the Greek term *ádēlos*, meaning not manifest or not evident (p. 535); and *probabilis* for the Greek *pithanós*, meaning "persuasive," "plausible," or "similar to the truth" (*veri simile*; p. 508).

---

1. In *Academica* (45 BCE/1933), his work on philosophical skepticism, Cicero discussed uncertainty and probability based mainly on the teachings of Carneades (214–129/8 BCE), an Academic skeptic who himself left no writings.

The significance of the skeptical approach was not limited to ancient Greek and Roman thought. After a long hiatus during the Middle Ages, skeptical philosophy experienced a powerful comeback in the late Renaissance and in early modern philosophy (16th and 17th centuries). Thanks in no small part to translations of Sextus Empiricus's *Outlines of Pyrrhonism* and the influential work of Michel de Montaigne in the 16th century, the specter of skepticism returned to haunt European philosophy and quickly became "the avant-garde view of the new intellectual era dawning in early seventeenth-century France" (Popkin, 2003, p. 79). As Popkin noted, the skeptical challenges in the philosophy of the time were so prominent that they encompassed three broad domains of thought: religion, humanism, and science (pp. 54–55). While the Reformation and Counter-Reformation triggered a theological crisis of faith, the crisis of humanistic knowledge was precipitated by the discovery of the New World and its novel cultural universe. The most consequential challenge for the understanding of rationality and uncertainty, however, was the crisis of scientific knowledge that stemmed from the growing realization that establishing a science in the Aristotelian sense of certain truths was impossible. This atmosphere of total skepticism in the 17th century was particularly important because it gave rise to two disparate variants of rationality, each with its own consequences for overcoming this crisis of thought.

One variant of rationality was Cartesian philosophy, with its method of proceeding from universal doubt to establish the absolute certainty of the thinking self (*ego cogito*). Pushed to the extreme, this method allowed Descartes to formulate one unshakable truth—the existence of the thinking being—that served as a first principle for his metaphysical system (Descartes, 1641/1996). From this perspective, the uncertainty of empirical knowledge was still contrasted with the ideal of scientific certainty and demonstrative reason. An alternative solution to the challenges posed by skepticism came from a source slightly more mundane than metaphysics— namely, practical matters such as gambling, legal disputes, and annuities. Contrary to Descartes, Pascal and his colleagues at Port Royal not only accepted uncertainty as an inevitable dimension of human knowledge, but also made use of it in the then-new mathematical calculus of probability (Arnauld & Nicole, 1662/1850; Pascal, 1670/2000). The invention of the calculus of probability marked the emergence of a probabilistic approach to the unknown. To this day, it remains the most influential contribution to the conceptual comprehension of uncertainty.

18.3 Uncertainty and Classical Probability

> Now when we work for tomorrow, and the uncertain, we are acting reasonably; for we ought to work for the uncertain according to the demonstrated rules of chance. (Pascal, 1670/2000, p. 758)

The skeptical philosophers realized that human cognition exists in an epistemic space between truth and ignorance and that reasonable people should seek methods to overcome the practical and moral difficulties associated with this condition. What separates approaches to uncertainty before and after the 17th century is, above all, a difference in these methods. While Cicero's *sapiens* ("wise man") had to navigate uncertainty according to what is likely and plausible, he had no formal rules for doing so at his disposal. The Enlightenment's own human species, the "reasonable man," could rely on a new mathematical tool: classical probability. From its very beginnings it aimed to assist people in finding better—or even rational—decisions and was generally regarded as a "reasonable calculus" for "reasonable men" (Daston, 1988/1995, p. 56). As Laplace, a key figure in the conceptualization of classical probability, famously put it: probability is simply "common sense reduced to calculus" (Laplace, 1814/1902, p. 196).

The development of this new type of pragmatic rationality was due to two closely connected conceptual events: the emergence of mathematical probability and the invention of decision theory. The first is usually associated with the correspondence between Blaise Pascal and Pierre de Fermat in 1654 that gave rise to the concept of mathematical expectation and the probability calculus (Edwards, 1982; Todhunter, 1865/2014). They were concerned with puzzles such as the "problem of points": two players stake 32 coins each on a three-point game of chance. The game is interrupted at a moment when one player has two points and the other player one point. How should the stakes be divided between the two players? (Pascal 1654/1998, p. 147). The two French mathematicians proposed solutions for this and other problems by determining the chances of uncertain events based on mathematical expectation (Pascal) and rules of combinatorics (de Fermat).

The second crucial event, the invention of decision theory, took place several years later, when Pascal (1670/2000) introduced the famous wager about God's existence in the passage *"Infini-rien"* of his *Pensées*. This step marked one in a series of many applications of mathematical probability to decision making. The question of whether it is rational to believe in God was introduced in the form of a bet: "A game is being played at the extremity of this infinite distance where heads or tails will turn up. What will you wager?" (Pascal, 1670/2000, p. 677). Unlike a typical betting game, the stakes in this "game of life" are infinitely high: if one acts as a believer and God exists, one wins eternal salvation; however, if one wagers against God and God exists, the loss brings eternal damnation. By contrast, if one chooses to live a pious life and God does not exist, one forgoes the finite but still valuable reward of having lived a life of worldly pleasures. What should a person do: act as a believer or as an atheist? Following Pascal's argument, one should reason according to the rules of probability and choose a pious life over a life of worldly pleasures because its expectation—derived on the crucial assumption of a nonzero chance of God's existence times infinite reward—is infinitely greater than that of a "cheerful party-going atheist" life strategy and its finite gratification (Hacking, 2001, pp. 121–122). The value of this argument lies not in any indisputable line of reasoning, but rather in its illustration of a new way of approaching decision problems: using the logic of probability.

A similar probabilistic argument can be found in *Port-Royal Logic*, whose last chapter explicitly examines the numerical measurement of probability. It considers a game where 10 people stake a crown (a French coin) and only one person can win the prize ("there are nine degrees of probability of losing a crown, and only one of gaining the nine"; Arnauld & Nicole, 1662/1850, p. 360). Arnauld and Nicole claimed that this logic for understanding the chances of winning can be applied to other matters, thus making "us more reasonable in our hopes and fears" (p. 361). For instance, the fear of death by thunderstorm, so the argument goes, should be proportionate not only to the magnitude of the possible damage but also to the chance of it occurring. Just as it would be unreasonable to stake too much on a gamble with a high potential payoff but merely a slight chance of winning, it would also be unreasonable to take extreme precautions against highly unlikely events such as death by thunderstorm.

This analogy reveals one of the most important aspects of the classical notion of probability: it combines degrees of subjective beliefs and rules of chance. The insight that the two can be combined lies at the heart of Hacking's view that the modern notion of probability is essentially dual, as it is related to both "the degree of belief warranted by evidence" (*epistemic* probability) and the stable relative frequencies produced by some chance devices, such as coins or dice (*aleatory* probability; Hacking, 1975/2006, p. 1). Hacking argued that the emergence of probability became possible only when Pascal explicitly linked epistemic and aleatory probabilities and applied them to reasoning about decision making.[2]

Before we move on to modern approaches to probability, let us highlight two key aspects of classical probability: the distinction between epistemic and aleatory uncertainty, and the measurement of uncertainty on a scale from complete knowledge to total ignorance. These aspects still underlie the two main ways of classifying uncertainty in the modern day: one is based on the *source of uncertainty* and the other on the *degree of uncertainty* in one's knowledge (figure 18.1). The sources of uncertainty are characterized as aleatory (objective) or epistemic (subjective), a distinction that stems from the duality of probability discussed above[3] and that has become deeply ingrained in treatments of uncertainty across domains (Budescu & Wallsten, 1987; Elvers, Jandrig, & Tannert, 2007; Fox & Ülkümen, 2011; Kahneman & Tversky, 1982; Thunnissen, 2003; W. E. Walker et al., 2003). In general, epistemic uncertainty refers to incompleteness of knowledge, whereas aleatory uncertainty stems from the statistical properties of the environment that exist independent of a person's knowledge.

---

2. Leibniz followed the same logic in applying the calculus of probability to legal reasoning, as did Jakob Bernoulli when he ordered different degrees of assurance as "ranging from total disbelief or doubt to greatest certainty" (Gigerenzer et al., 1989, p. 7).

3. This duality of epistemic and aleatory aspects of probability did not amount to different interpretations of probability in the classical period, which only became the case in the 20th century. The subjective and objective sides of probability initially enjoyed a rather unproblematic coexistence; the end of the classical interpretation was closely related to the emergence of the *clear-cut* differentiation around 1837–1843 (Daston, 1988/1995). This aspect of the classical approach to probability is in line with the fact that early theoreticians of probability—from Pascal to Laplace—generally committed to the deterministic view of the universe and therefore regarded uncertainty as belonging to people's epistemic limitations or ignorance. This view was famously expressed in Laplace's (1814/1902) *Philosophical Essay on Probabilities*, in which he claimed that a sufficiently vast intelligence (Laplace's demon) could calculate the entire future of the universe and eliminate all uncertainty inherent to the current state of human knowledge.

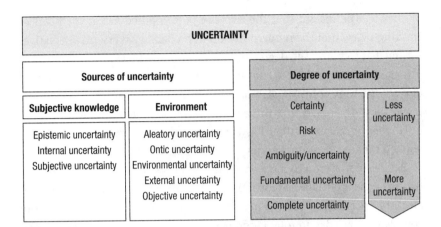

Figure 18.1
Variants of uncertainty. Uncertainty has frequently been classified in two fundamentally different ways, with one focusing on the person or the world as the source of uncertainty and the other focusing on degrees of uncertainty. The concepts listed represent an incomplete collection of terminology that has been used in the literature.

The aleatory–epistemic distinction has been shown to be psychologically meaningful as well. For instance, Fox and Ülkümen (2011) have argued that judgments under uncertainty comprise attributions to both epistemic and aleatory sources of uncertainty, which reflect different coping strategies and have distinct markers in natural language (p. 24). In this view, aleatory or environmental uncertainty is attributed to stochastic outcomes of external events and is expressed in likelihood statements (e.g., "I'd say there is a 90% chance," or "I think there is a high probability"); epistemic uncertainty, by contrast, is attributed to inadequate or missing information on the part of the subject and is expressed in confidence statements (e.g., "I am 80% sure," or "I am reasonably certain"; see also Ülkümen, Fox, & Malle, 2016). The distinction between epistemic and environmental uncertainty is addressed in various ways throughout this book (e.g., chapters 3, 7, 8, 12, and 16), showing that uncertainty can ensue either from an individual's epistemic constraints or from the properties of the world that an individual experiences. Sources of uncertainty become even more varied when one takes into account situations involving other people. For instance, strategic uncertainty associated with unknown actions and preferences of interacting agents can be an additional source of uncertainty in the social environment (see chapters 5, 12). Social uncertainty can also constitute the main source of uncertainty in collective decision making (see chapters 13, 14).

The second type of classification refers to the degree of uncertainty and its quantitative and qualitative measurement. Mapping uncertainty according to degrees of subjective knowledge predates quantitative probability theory, but it was the probabilistic approach that first made defining and measuring degrees of uncertainty possible. Modern decision sciences have arguably adopted more or less the same logic of measuring epistemic uncertainty as was outlined in the 17th century—namely, distinguishing between different uncertainty situations as a function of the amount and nature of information available to the individual. Although degrees of knowledge in human judgment can range from total ignorance to complete certainty, it has become customary to classify such degrees in terms of *certainty*, *risk*, and *uncertainty* (Luce & Raiffa, 1957), with the last often referred to as *ambiguity* in economics (Ellsberg, 1961; Trautmann & van de Kuilen, 2015). The scale of uncertainty further includes fundamental and severe uncertainty (see, e.g., Bradley & Steele, 2015; Mousavi & Gigerenzer, 2014), as well as the extreme state of complete uncertainty and total ignorance.

Distinguishing between degrees of uncertainty has become equally relevant in behavioral decision theory. Ward Edwards's seminal paper "The Theory of Decision Making" (1954) introduced the distinction between risk and uncertainty to behavioral research. At the time, decision scientists were primarily focused on studies of risky choice, as exemplified in experiments using fully described monetary gambles—a line of research that culminated in the development of prospect theory (Kahneman & Tversky, 1979; see chapter 8). Expanding decision research to areas beyond risky choice led to the discovery of distinct patterns of behavior in decisions under risk (description) and uncertainty (experience), known as the description–experience gap (see Hertwig & Erev, 2009). As shown in chapters 7 and 8, research on decisions from experience demonstrated the empirical value of this distinction by revealing systematic behavioral differences between description-based and experience-based choice (see also chapter 10).

The integration of these classical distinctions between different sources and degrees of uncertainty into research in cognitive science shows that they are not merely philosophically meaningful—they also represent relevant psychological categories that describe how people distinguish between different sources or degrees of uncertainty. However, in order to understand the conceptual origins of uncertainty in decision research, it is important to look into the developments that probabilistic interpretations of uncertainty underwent in the 20th century. These developments highlighted the limits of quantitative approaches to uncertainty based on probability theory.

18.4   Uncertainty and Modern Interpretations of Probability

The value of classical probability consisted in its applicability to practical problems, ranging from gambling, legal disputes, and matters of insurance to questions of moral conduct and religious commitment. In the 20th century, the scope of probability theory and statistical thinking extended to include the natural and social sciences, as well as parts of law, medicine, and industry (Gigerenzer et al., 1989, p. 271). At the same time, several crucial developments occurred in both basic mathematical theory and its philosophical interpretation. One turning point was Kolmogorov's (1933) axiomatization of probability theory, which elevated the theory to the status of a legitimate branch of mathematics. The other development was more philosophical in nature: as distinct interpretations of probability unfolded, the question arose of what probability was supposed to measure. The three most prominent philosophical interpretations of probability advanced in the 20th century were objective, subjective, and logical (Gillies, 2000). Importantly, these delineations did not concern the mathematical calculus of probability, but only the interpretation of its extramathematical and philosophical properties. Whereas objectivists maintained that probability represents the physical frequencies (von Mises, 1928/1961) or propensities (Popper, 1959) of external events, subjectivists held that if reflects degrees of personal confidence (De Finetti, 1931/1989, 1937; Ramsey, 1926). According to the logical interpretation, probability is neither purely objective nor subjective, but rather relational, because it expresses degrees of certainty given the available evidence (Carnap, 1950; Keynes, 1921/1973b).

These three interpretations of probability played a major role in the theories of uncertainty developed in the 20th century, arguably accounting for three different ways of explaining relations between uncertainty and probability. Knight's objective interpretation limited probabilistic calculations to risk (i.e., measurable uncertainty) and liberated true uncertainty from calculations altogether (Knight, 1921/2002). Keynes, as one of the main proponents of a logical interpretation, offered an account of unmeasurable uncertainty that reflected cases with missing evidence or with "probability-relation," as he called it (Keynes, 1921/1973b; see section 18.4.2). Finally, the subjective interpretation of probability in Savage's work placed uncertainty in the realm of measurable probability, thus including personal beliefs as something that could be assigned a probability (Savage, 1954). The resulting concepts of true and unmeasurable uncertainty proposed by Knight and Keynes, as well as the incorporation of the Knightian distinction between risk and uncertainty in modern decision theory, remain among the century's most impactful legacies for understanding uncertainty in decision making.

18.4.1   Knightian Uncertainty

In his book *Risk, Uncertainty, and Profit* (1921/2002), economist Frank Knight introduced the distinction between risk and uncertainty. Whereas risk applies to situations of measurable probability, uncertainty applies to situations where such measurement is not possible, causing people to rely on "estimates," a concept to which we will return shortly. The distinction between risk and uncertainty reflects Knight's objective interpretation of probability, which he considered to be a property of the real external world. Knight further distinguished three "probability situations," each representing a distinct type of judgment about uncertain events: a priori probability, statistical probability, and estimates (Knight, 1921/2002, pp. 224–225). In *a priori probability*, the chances of random events occurring can be computed based on general mathematical principles. Examples can be found primarily in games of chance (e.g., the throw of a die), but are rare in real life. *Statistical probability* refers to the chances of events occurring that can be determined empirically by applying statistical methods to experiential data. Examples include an insurance company determining whether a building will burn, or a champagne producer quantifying the risk of bottles bursting. Finally, *estimates* describe situations of unmeasurable uncertainty, which concern unique or unprecedented events and situations. These singular events require practical judgments or decisions to be made in the absence of a "*valid basis of any kind* for classifying instances" (p. 225), and are therefore not amenable to objective probabilistic or statistical calculations. In Knight's view, "most of conduct" (p. 226) as well as typical business decisions (e.g., a substantial investment to increase a manufacturer's capacity) rest on an estimate of the probable outcome of the considered course of action. Here, uncertainty is a matter of degree—not quantitative in a mathematical or statistical sense, but subjective, as a degree of confidence—which is, in Knight's view, itself of practical significance. As Knight supported an objective interpretation of probability, he lamented that the term "probability" was applied to estimates ("the usage is so well established that there is no hope of getting away from it," p. 224) and proposed that these estimates should at least be treated as a distinct type of judgment.

18.4.2 Keynesian Uncertainty

Like Knight, John Maynard Keynes also placed uncertainty at the heart of his economic theory. However, he proposed a different interpretation of probability, viewing it in terms of a logical relation between a hypothesis and the supporting evidence (Keynes, 1921/1973b). This relational approach imposes certain restrictions on what can be expressed by probability. More specifically, Keynes discussed cases when a probability relation is unknown or numerically immeasurable, as, for instance, when relevant evidence is missing or cannot be meaningfully used to support a proposition (Keynes, 1921/1973b; see also Lawson, 1985). In this view, fundamentally uncertain situations—such as those referring to the distant future—might lie beyond the numerical probability relation and allow for only very weak confidence. Consistent with this interpretation of probability, in *The General Theory of Employment, Interest, and Money* (1936/1973a; see also 1937), Keynes characterized uncertainty as strongly linked to the future and long-term expectations.[4] From this perspective, uncertainty is more or less equivalent to unpredictability, which carries the implication that statistical analyses and the theory of probability are useless for calculating the chances of some future events, because there is no data or evidence that could be used to do

---

4. Not to be confused with the notion of mathematical expectation, Keynesian expectation has a psychological meaning that designates subjective beliefs and predictions about the future. For example, long-term expectations might concern predictions about future returns on investments, while short-term expectations might designate a producer's estimates of profit from a finished product.

so. Even though there are situations in which it may be possible to make informed and principled forecasts, they should be carefully distinguished from situations that are fundamentally unpredictable. Here, Keynes's examples are similar to Knight's: he also mentions games of chance and insurance cases, in which probability calculations are admissible or even necessary. For other situations, however—such as the prospect of a war, the long-term prices of assets and commodities, or the future of inventions and major technological changes—"there is no scientific basis on which to form any calculable probability whatever. We simply do not know" (Keynes, 1937, p. 214). In sum, Knight and Keynes entertained distinct conceptions of unmeasurable uncertainty, which largely ensued from their different theoretical views of probability. It was, however, a third major interpretation of probability—subjective, or Bayesian—that proved to have the most impact on how modern decision theory conceptualizes uncertainty and, by extension, on the psychology of decision making.

18.4.3   Uncertainty in Bayesian Decision Theory

A key characteristic of modern decision theory is that it has axiomatized principles of rational decision making under uncertainty (Peterson, 2009, p. 13). In his essay "Truth and Probability," Ramsey (1926/1990) proposed axioms for the consistent treatment of subjective probabilities in rational choice under uncertainty. In their groundbreaking book *Theory of Games and Economic Behavior,* von Neumann and Morgenstern (1944/2007) put decision rules and Bernoulli's expected utility theory on axiomatic grounds and established the maximization of expected utility as the dominant rational choice strategy. Although the latter approach was not tied to any particular interpretation of probability, the further development of decision theory took a distinctively subjectivist turn.[5] Notably, in his book *The Foundations of Statistics*, Savage (1954) presented another influential

---

5. Another important adjustment of the expected utility framework for decision making in Savage's work concerned the normative interpretation of utility theory. Savage himself underlined that his approach followed from the von Neumann–Morgenstern theory of utility, but that "one idea held by me that I think von Neumann and Morgenstern do not explicitly support, and that so far as I know they might not wish to have attributed to them, is the normative interpretation of the theory" (Savage, 1954, p. 97).

axiomatic approach to decision making and the maximization of expected utility; he used the subjective interpretation of probability to extend expected utility to situations with unknown objective probabilities. Savage's subjective expected utility framework incorporates two concepts: a personal utility function capturing the subjective value of the possible outcomes and a personal probability distribution over future states of the world capturing subjective beliefs about the likelihood of those states to be realized. Savage argued that a rational decision maker should comply with the axioms of internal coherence and choose the option with the highest expected utility, taking into account both subjective probability and the desirability of the option relative to all other options.

Luce and Raiffa (1957) made what may be the clearest contribution of Bayesian decision theory to the conceptual shaping of uncertainty when they distinguished between certainty, risk, and uncertainty. In *Games and Decisions*, the authors proposed that in situations involving certainty, decision makers know that their actions invariably lead to specific outcomes. In decision making under risk, "each action leads to one of a set of possible specific outcomes, each outcome occurring with a known probability. The probabilities are assumed to be known to the decision maker" (Luce & Raiffa, 1957, p. 13). In contrast, the realm of decision making under uncertainty encompasses situations in which "either action or both has as its consequence a set of possible specific outcomes, but where the probabilities of these outcomes are completely unknown or are not even meaningful" (Luce & Raiffa, 1957, p. 13).

The main application of expected utility theory is in decision making under risk (i.e., decisions involving outcomes with known probabilities). Nevertheless, in the form of subjective expected utility theory, it is similarly applicable to decisions under uncertainty (i.e., decisions involving outcomes with unknown probabilities). Moreover, assuming a subjective interpretation of probability, situations of uncertainty and ambiguity can be reduced to risk by assigning probabilities to possible outcomes based on the individual's subjective degrees of belief. This point is important: in the framework of Bayesian decision theory, uncertainty is probabilistically unmeasurable only in the sense that it cannot be assigned objectively known probabilities. Yet, as long as one can form subjective distributions of probability that are consistent and add up to 1, uncertainty can be treated in a way similar to risk. According to Ellsberg's (1961) critical portrayal of this subjectivist spirit: "for a 'rational' man—*all* uncertainty can be reduced to *risks*" (p. 645).

In this regard, the Bayesian decision-theoretical interpretation of uncertainty differs considerably from Knight's and Keynes's notions of unmeasurable uncertainty. Whereas Knight's understanding of uncertainty was motivated by an objective approach to probability, and Keynesian uncertainty hinged on Keynes's logical interpretation, Luce and Raiffa (1957) used Savage's subjective expected utility theory as their theoretical framework. This framework largely motivated their succinct "certainty–risk–uncertainty" classification based on clear criteria of actions, outcomes, and the associated probabilities of these outcomes. The resulting classification continues to underlie most contemporary views on uncertainty in decision making.

The limitations of this framework did not escape the attention of decision theorists. Ellsberg (1961) showed that people violate Savage's axioms when presented with gambles that involve risk (i.e., known probabilities of the outcomes) and ambiguity (i.e., unknown probabilities of the outcomes). In his 1955 paper "A Behavioral Model of Rational Choice," Simon attacked the normative approach to rationality provided by subjective expected utility theory, highlighting that the rules and choice criteria it imposes on the human mind are unrealistic (Simon, 1955). Savage himself was well aware that he was presenting "a certain abstract theory of the behavior of a highly idealized person faced with uncertainty" (Savage, 1954, p. 5). Notably, his distinction between small and large worlds shows that Savage supported the application of his axiomatic approach and, by extension, Bayesian decision theory, mainly to the limited realm of small-world choice problems. Under small-world situations, all possible actions and their consequences can be anticipated, enumerated, and ordered according to subjective preferences. In Savage's words, you have enough information about your decision situation and can "look before you leap" (1954, p. 16). There is no possibility of surprises, pleasant or unpleasant. In large worlds, however, you must "cross th[e] bridge when you come to it" (Savage, 1954, p. 16)—that is, you must make a decision without being able to fully anticipate all decision variables in the present and in the future (partial or complete ignorance). In these worlds, "knee-jerk consistency is then no virtue" (Binmore, 2009, p. 117). Binmore emphasized that Savage restricted the sensible application of his theory to small worlds and in fact devoted the latter half of *The Foundations of*

Statistics to understanding decision making under complete ignorance—by invoking *heuristic principles*.

Notwithstanding these issues, the probabilistic approach to uncertainty remains to this day the default in rational and behavioral theories of choice. The Bayesian decision theorist Lindley (2014) went so far as to claim that "if you have a situation in which uncertainty plays a role, then probability is the tool you have to use" (Lindley, 2014, p. 376). It is undoubtedly a valuable tool that can substantially facilitate how people deal with uncertainty, and as a research methodology it is indispensable. However, when viewed from a historical perspective, the relation between uncertainty and probability turns out to be less harmonious than one might think. The realization that the probabilistic framework is hardly a "one size fits all" approach, and that it cannot account for unmeasurable uncertainty opened up the possibility that other tools are at work in taming the unknown. This brings us to what we consider to be the most recent milestone in the conceptual history of uncertainty: the adaptive and ecological approach to human rationality taken in this book.

18.5   Uncertainty in Bounded and Ecological Rationality

> Bounded rationality [is] the key to understanding how actual people make decisions without utilities and probabilities. (Gigerenzer & Selten, 2001, p. i)

The probabilistic revolution of the 17th century was a revolution in both methods and theoretical views of rationality. It turned uncertainty into a measurable notion and provided consistent rules for rational behavior under conditions of incomplete knowledge. As probability theory developed, diverse interpretations of probability revealed the limits of quantitative approaches to the unknown and further refined the conceptual meaning of uncertainty. Partly as a response to these developments and partly due to progress in cognitive science in the second half of the 20th century, approaches to rationality and uncertainty experienced another revolution. This revolution was inspired by both advances in behavioral research on decision making (e.g., Edwards, 1954) and theoretical developments in normative theories of choice. Simon's notion of bounded rationality stood at the intersection of these advances. His goal was to formulate a psychologically realistic theory of rational choice that would offer insight into how real people make decisions and how they can achieve their goals under the unmeasurable uncertainty and constraints of the real world (Simon, 1955, 1956).

Simon's main concern with the dominant normative models of choice (e.g., the subjective expected utility theory built upon the Bayesian interpretation of probability and Bernoulli's expected utility theory) was that their norms and postulates were inappropriate as descriptive accounts of behavior in real-world environments (see chapter 2). He called these theories "Olympian models" to reflect their idealistic assumption that decision makers are omniscient, with unlimited cognitive resources (Simon, 1983). He argued that the more successful tools of human rationality would need to differ considerably from the tools offered by the existing normative approaches. When faced with a choice where the computational costs of finding an optimal solution are too high or where such a solution is not available, the decision maker may look for an approximate and "good enough" solution instead of an optimal one (Simon, 1982, p. 295). Simon's ideas of satisficing and bounded rationality set in motion psychological research on boundedly rational heuristics—simple, adaptive tools—that, based on a modest amount of effort and computation, can render good performance possible (Gigerenzer, Hertwig, & Pachur, 2011; Gigerenzer, Todd, & the ABC Research Group, 1999; Hertwig, Hoffrage, & the ABC Research Group, 2013; Todd, Gigerenzer, & the ABC Research Group, 2012).

We should note there is also a somewhat different and influential view of heuristics in psychology. In their heuristics-and-biases research program, Kahneman and Tversky mapped the impact of cognitive limitations on people's judgments and decisions and documented a large catalog of systematic deviations from norms of rationality, drawn from probability theory, statistics, and axioms of rational choice (Kahneman, Slovic, & Tversky, 1982; Tversky & Kahneman, 1974). From this perspective, bounded rationality was interpreted in terms of behavior that diverges from such norms and, by extension, optimality. In this spirit, Kahneman (2003a) concluded: "Our research attempted to obtain a map of bounded rationality, by exploring the systematic biases that separate the beliefs that people have and the choices they make from the optimal beliefs and choices assumed in rational-agent models" (p. 1449).

By contrast, our view is that heuristics and the other tools of the adaptive toolbox (see chapter 1) offer a different way to deal with the type of uncertainty that people—as well as perhaps other species—commonly encounter in their daily lives. Far from optimizing tools provided by the calculus of probability and axioms of Bayesian decision theory, heuristics are "approximate methods" adapted to particular environments (Simon, 1990, p. 6). This last characteristic is of particular note: the efficiency and the success of decision strategies ultimately depend on how well they fit specific choice conditions. In this view, the essence of rational behavior consists in how an organism can adapt in order to achieve its goals under the constraints posed by both the environment and its own cognitive limitations. Here, rationality is defined in terms of correspondence rather than the content-free norms of coherence (Hammond, 2000).

In the concept of ecological rationality, the importance of the environment is emphasized even further. Rather than considering the organism and the environment as two independent but related systems (Brunswik, 1957/2001), this perspective views the organism and the environment as part of one shared system. The environment is not divorced from the agent; instead, it represents the "subjective ecology of the organism that emerges through the interaction of its mind, body, and sensory organs with its physical environment" (Todd & Gigerenzer, 2012, p. 18).

Viewing the organism and the environment as interdependent components of one system changes the conception of uncertainty. The contribution of the ecological approach consists in replacing the dualistic view invoked by distinguishing two major sources of uncertainty with a synthesis of aleatory and epistemic uncertainty. Uncertainty is thus no longer to be blamed solely on the actor or the environment but instead emerges as a property of the mind–environment system (Todd & Gigerenzer, 2012, p. 18). This suggests a *systemic* view in which uncertainty comprises both environmental unpredictability and uncertainties that stem from the mind's boundaries (e.g., limits in available knowledge and cognitive capabilities). As a consequence of the interdependence of mind and environment, domain-specific rather than domain-general methods are required to make decisions in the face of uncertainty (see also Arkes, Gigerenzer, & Hertwig, 2016). Different environments represent different statistical structures and affordances, which can arise naturally or through design from a variety of environmental considerations—including physical, biological, social, and cultural factors. Ecological rationality means that specific decision-making strategies fit to particular environmental structures but not to others. It suggests that there cannot be a single universal and domain-general tool—whether Bayesian decision theory, expected utility theory, or game theory—for making decisions. Rather, the concept of ecological rationality is linked to that of the adaptive toolbox (see chapter 1). The toolbox has often been thought to include a wide range of heuristics for games against nature and social games (Gigerenzer et al., 2011; Hertwig et al., 2013). This book proposes a more encompassing conception of the adaptive toolbox. Heuristics—as important as they are—are not the only tools at a person's disposal. They are complemented by tools such as learning through experience, social intelligence, aggregation of information, and others not contained within these pages (e.g., deliberate ignorance; see Hertwig & Engel, 2016). This rich repertoire helps people, both as individuals and as groups, to navigate different regions of uncertainty across the mind's lifelong development.

Taming Uncertainty focuses on several aspects of this systemic view of uncertainty. The first is that the tools people use to handle uncertainty cannot be understood separately from the structure of their environment. Part II, "The Heuristic Mind," zooms in on this very topic, analyzing simple cognitive strategies that embody strong but successful assumptions about the environment. A second aspect, the focus of Part III, "The Exploring Mind," is that in order to understand how the mind copes with uncertainty one must understand how the mind and the environment intersect—in particular, how the mind searches for and learns from information in the world. Part IV, "The Social Mind," highlights a third aspect—namely, that uncertainty looms large in environments shared with others—and examines the tools people enlist to deal with this source of unpredictability and how they turn the collective mind itself into a tool. Finally, taking a systemic view of uncertainty highlighted a new issue: the mind–environment interface is not stationary because its components are subject to change. Recognizing this, Part V, "The Unfinished Mind," turns to the ontogenetic and phylogenetic changes of the human mind and ever-changing environmental demands.

18.6 Optimism in the Face of Uncertainty

In this concluding chapter, we have presented a brief conceptual history of uncertainty as seen through the lenses of different approaches to human rationality: starting with skeptical philosophy, discussing in detail the time-honored probabilistic approach, and concluding with an ecological perspective. This look back across the larger conceptual map of uncertainty allows us to see that different theories of rationality offer different *interpretations* of uncertainty and different *tools* for dealing with it. In particular, the ecological perspective on uncertainty espoused in this book suggests that the human mind has developed various mental tools to adapt to its environment and navigate the numerous ways in which the unknown takes shape.

After looking at the past and the present, it is natural to turn to the future. But predicting the future is difficult—remember Günter Schabowski and the fall of the Berlin Wall (see chapter 1). There are many factors that seem to accentuate this difficulty today. The simultaneous developments of digitalization, automation, and globalization, compounded with challenges such as social inequality, climate change, exploding health care costs, migration, aging societies, terrorism, and the rise of authoritarian nationalism and demagogic populism—to name just a few—are sources of a soaring sense of uncertainty that evokes strong emotional reactions. The world, however, has always been uncertain; living with uncertainty has been and will continue to be a part of the human condition. Modern human societies are also seeing cumulative progress on many fronts—including better medicine, sanitation, rising IQ and life expectancy, and less violence and poverty than ever before. Pessimism has its place: it encourages individuals and collectives to be cautious and can even foster progress by preparing the ground for necessary change. But human progress needs more than pessimism and caution. The authors of this book remain optimistic. Throughout the history of thought, humankind has developed an ever-better understanding of how to cope with uncertainty. What this book aims to contribute is a deeper insight into how real people act, decide, and grapple with uncertainty. This means replacing omniscience with a limited search for information; substituting complex calculations by simple, tractable, robust solutions; and moving away from optimizing and toward satisficing and exploiting the mind's environment. A better grasp of the rationality of mere mortals will help people—both individually and collectively—to conceive new and humane ways of confronting the inescapable uncertainties of the future.

VII Accompanying Material

Glossary of Key Concepts

Anastasia Kozyreva and Philipp Gerlach

Accuracy–effort trade-off: Strategy selection dilemma in which the time and cognitive effort associated with the use of a cognitive strategy (e.g., procuring and evaluating information, computation) are balanced against its anticipated accuracy or other benchmarks of quality. It is typically assumed that more time and/or more cognitive effort lead to more accurate decisions. See also: *bias–variance dilemma*.

Adaptation: The process or product of change by which the organism becomes better adjusted to the challenges and affordances of the *environment*. It includes evolutionary, individual, and cultural learning. In evolutionary biology, adaptation refers to the properties and mechanisms of an organism that have developed as a consequence of differential reproductive success. In the context of *ecological rationality*, the term "adaptive" means that a strategy fits the informational structures of the environment. See also: *fitness*.

Adaptive toolbox: A collection of different types of cognitive *strategies* (e.g., *heuristics*, exploration strategies, and strategies to integrate collectively distributed information) that can be used to cope with *uncertainty*. The toolbox also includes the building blocks for these strategies (e.g., rules for search, stopping, information integration, and decision) and the core cognitive capacities they exploit.

Ambiguity aversion: A *preference* for options that have outcomes with known probabilities (i.e., *risk*) over options that have outcomes with unknown probabilities (i.e., *uncertainty*, ambiguity). See also: *risk aversion*.

Bias–variance dilemma: In prediction models, a trade-off between two sources of error: bias and variance. Bias is the systematic difference between the prediction of a model and the correct value. Variance is the variability of a model's predictions that is caused, for example, by model parameters being estimated on the basis of samples of data. Typically, reducing variance (e.g., making the model less flexible by reducing the number of adjustable parameters) amplifies bias, and increasing variance mitigates bias. See also: *accuracy–effort trade-off*.

Boosting: Fostering decision-making competencies (e.g., skills, use of efficient and simple heuristics, risk literacy) and motivational competencies (e.g., the ability to control one's impulses) with the goal of empowering people to exercise their own agency and thus to make better decisions. See also: *nudging.*

Compensatory environments: *Environments* in which any *cue* used to predict a criterion can be outweighed by a combination of other cues (e.g., environments in which cue weights are uniformly distributed). Compensatory *strategies* integrate cue values (e.g., linear weighting and adding strategy; tallying heuristic). See also: *noncompensatory environments.*

Cue: A piece of information (e.g., a symptom, a test result, an attribute of an object) that is used to make *inferences* about an unavailable or unknown criterion (e.g., medical condition). Cues can differ in the degree to which they help make a correct *inference* (i.e., in their cue validity or predictive value). See also: *compensatory environments; noncompensatory environments.*

Decision making under risk: The act or process of choosing between options in situations with known outcomes and probabilities. See also: *decision making under uncertainty; risk.*

Decision making under uncertainty: The act or process of choosing between options in situations where knowledge of the outcome space and/or the outcomes' probabilities is missing or incomplete. See also: *decision making under risk; uncertainty.*

Decisions from description: Choices between options whose properties are learned via stated (e.g., written) symbols. A typical example of such decisions is a gamble with explicitly stated outcomes and probabilities. See also: *decisions from experience; description–experience gap.*

Decisions from experience: Choices between options whose outcomes and probabilities are initially unknown, and whose properties are learned via sampling from the outcome distribution. See also: *decisions from description; description–experience gap.*

Decision theory: A broad class of normative, descriptive, and prescriptive theories of *decision making under risk* and *uncertainty,* including *expected value theory, (subjective) expected utility theory, prospect theory,* and *game theory.*

Description–experience gap: Systematic difference in choice behavior between *decisions from experience* and *decisions from description.* For instance, people making decisions from experience may behave as if rare events have less impact than they deserve according to their objective *probabilities,* whereas people making decisions from description may behave as if rare events have more impact than they deserve. Description–experience gaps have been demonstrated not only in *decision making under risk,* but also in contexts such as Bayesian reasoning, causal reasoning, and *intertemporal choice.*

Ecological rationality: A theoretical view of *rationality* that evaluates the reasonableness and success of behavior and decision making based on the fit of the employed *strategies* to the structures of the *environment*. Used as an attribute (e.g., an ecologically rational heuristic), ecological rationality indicates the fit of a *strategy* to the structure of an *environment*.

Environment (ecology): The external surroundings of the organism shaped by physical, biological, and social factors. The term "structures of the environment" refers to statistical and other descriptive properties that reflect patterns of information distribution in a given environment. See also: *adaptation; ecological rationality.*

Environmental uncertainty: *Uncertainty* associated with inherent unpredictability in the *environment* (e.g., high variance in outcomes and probability distributions). This type of uncertainty is related to similar concepts such as aleatory, ontic, and objective uncertainty. See also: *uncertainty.*

Epistemic uncertainty: *Uncertainty* associated with the state of ignorance or incomplete individual knowledge. This type of uncertainty is related to similar concepts such as subjective uncertainty. See also: *uncertainty.*

Expected utility theory: A modification of *expected value theory* in which objective values are replaced by utilities. Utilities represent subjective evaluations of objective outcomes (e.g., the utility of additional earnings may diminish with increasing wealth). Expected utility theory postulates that decision makers choose the option that maximizes their expected utility, defined as the sum of subjective utilities ($u[x]$) multiplied by their objective probability of occurrence (p): $EU = \Sigma p_i u(x_i)$. See also: *subjective expected utility theory.*

Expected value theory: A theory of choice that postulates that people choose the option that maximizes the sum of potential outcomes (x) multiplied by their probability of occurrence (p): $EV = \Sigma p_i x_i$. See also: *expected utility theory; subjective expected utility theory.*

Exploration–exploitation trade-off: The dilemma between searching for new options, opportunities, or more information about them (exploration) and obtaining the rewards from the known options (exploitation).

Fitness: In evolutionary theory, refers to the efficiency of the organism's *adaptation* to a certain environmental niche, measured in terms of its differential reproductive success. Fitness can be defined with respect to either a genotype (the organism's genetic makeup) or a phenotype (the organism's observable traits) in a given environment.

Game theory: A formal *decision theory* for strategic interactions between agents (e.g., people, companies), where the outcomes depend on the others' decisions. Strategic interactions can include cooperation, coordination, or conflict. See also: *Nash equilibrium, strategic uncertainty.*

Heuristic: A simple *strategy* for problem solving and decision making. Different schools of thought have emphasized different properties of heuristics. For instance, the term has been used to refer to strategies that lead to suboptimal solutions. It has also been used to refer to strategies that ignore part of the available information or search for only a subset of all possible solutions. Such strategies do not necessarily imply suboptimality but can perform better than computationally and information-ally more complex strategies due to factors such as the *bias–variance dilemma*. See also: *adaptive toolbox; ecological rationality*.

Inference: An act of drawing conclusions about an unknown (e.g., future) criterion from the available information. For example, inference may refer to the process of identifying a cause (e.g., of a disease) based on the observable data (e.g., symptoms, test results). See also: *preference*.

Intertemporal choice: Decisions between options whose outcomes materialize at different times. Such decisions can involve a trade-off between costs and benefits—for instance, when an option offering a sooner, smaller payoff is compared with an option offering a later, larger payoff (e.g., spending money on a beach vacation versus saving it for retirement).

Loss aversion: Asymmetry in evaluating gains and losses, such that the impact on *preferences* of losses is greater than that of equivalent gains (e.g., losing €10 produces more dissatisfaction than winning €10 produces satisfaction). Loss aversion is a central concept of *prospect theory*.

Nash equilibrium: In *game theory*, the Nash equilibrium is a set of *strategies* for all interacting players in which no player can obtain a better outcome by unilaterally changing their strategy (given the strategies of the others).

Noncompensatory environments: *Environments* in which a more valid *cue* used to predict a criterion cannot be outweighed (compensated) by any combination of less valid cues (e.g., environments in which the weights of cues decrease exponentially). Noncompensatory *strategies* are nonintegrative and instead rely on one or several cues, typically those with the highest predictive value (e.g., lexicographic heuristics). See also: *compensatory environments*.

Nudging: Systematically intervening in the *environment* ("choice architecture") to alter behavior in a predictable manner, with the goal of helping people make better decisions. Nudging does not involve coercion, limiting available options, or signifi-cantly changing economic incentives. See also: *boosting*.

Preference: An ordered relation between two or more options in terms of their subjective value. See also: *inference*.

Probability: A numerical measure of the degree of certainty about an event's occur-rence on a scale from 0 to 1, where 0 indicates impossibility and 1 certainty. Objec-tive probability refers to the frequencies or propensities attributed to external events within a specified reference class. Subjective probability refers to degrees of individual beliefs or personal certainty.

Probability weighting: Transformation of objective or subjective *probabilities* to determine the attractiveness of *risky* or *uncertain* options. The probability weighting function reflects the relationship between the probability of an outcome and how much weight the outcome receives in a judgment or a decision. See also: *prospect theory*.

Prospect theory: A theory of *decision making under risk* and *decision making under uncertainty* according to which the attractiveness of an option is a multiplicative function of its possible outcomes and the *probability* of those outcomes occurring. As a modification of *expected utility theory*, prospect theory treats expected utilities in the gain domain differently from expected utilities in the loss domain (see: *loss aversion*). In addition, prospect theory relies on the notion of *probability weighting*, arguing that people decide as if they are overweighting small probabilities and underweighting large probabilities.

Rationality: Quality or characteristic of a judgment, decision, or behavior that follows criteria of reasonableness. These criteria depend on the underlying theoretical approach. For example, rationality can be evaluated in terms of coherence (e.g., conformity to the axioms of *expected utility theory*) or correspondence (e.g., accuracy and adaptivity of judgments and decisions in relation to the *environment*). See also: *decision theory*; *ecological rationality*.

Risk: A concept that has different meanings in different disciplines. Risk can describe (a) the statistical *probability* of a hazardous event (e.g., the probability of dying from measles); (b) a condition of decision making in which the probabilities of possible outcomes are known to the decision maker (risk as opposed to *uncertainty*; see also *ambiguity aversion*; *decisions under risk*); (c) variability in outcomes (risk as opposed to sure events; see also *risk aversion*); (d) hazardous events that have dimensions other than probabilities and outcomes, such as controllability, voluntariness, and catastrophic potential (e.g., the risk of a nuclear disaster or a motorcycle accident).

Risk aversion: A *preference* for options with less variability in outcomes over options with more variability in outcomes. A typical example of risk aversion is a preference for a sure gain (e.g., €10 guaranteed) over a risky gamble (e.g., a 10% chance of winning €100). See also: *ambiguity aversion*.

Strategic uncertainty: *Uncertainty* about the actions of others in interactive situations. Sources of strategic uncertainty include the *preferences*, beliefs, and knowledge of the interacting others. This type of uncertainty is related to similar concepts such as social uncertainty. See also: *uncertainty*.

Strategy: A method for judgment and decision making that may include rules for search, evaluation, and integration of information. In *game theory*, a strategy defines a set of actions that respond to the potential actions of other agents. Strategy selection refers to the process of choosing among multiple cognitive or behavioral strategies applicable in a given situation (e.g., which *heuristic* or crowd rule to use).

Subjective expected utility theory: A variety of *expected utility theory* that relies on a personal probability distribution, traditionally associated with a Bayesian (subjective) interpretation of *probability*.

Uncertainty: A state or condition of incomplete knowledge that may be due to (a) inherent unpredictability in the environment (*environmental uncertainty*); (b) cognitive and epistemic limitations (*epistemic uncertainty*); (c) other people's actions and intentions (*strategic uncertainty*). In *decision theory*, uncertainty describes situations in which the probabilities of the possible outcomes are unknown (as opposed to *risk*, in which they are known). In situations of fundamental uncertainty, knowledge about the options, their outcomes, and probabilities may be incomplete or missing entirely.

Wisdom of crowds: The effect that aggregating the judgments of different individuals outperforms a randomly selected individual judgment and can outperform the best individual judgment. The wisdom of crowds is a part of the broader phenomenon of collective intelligence.

References

A 120-year lease on life outlasts apartment heir (1995, December 29). *The New York Times*. Retrieved from https://www.nytimes.com/1995/12/29/world/a-120-year-lease-on-life-outlasts-apartment-heir.html

Abarca-Gómez, L., Abdeen, Z. A., Hamid, Z. A., Abu-Rmeileh, N. M., Acosta-Cazares, B., Acuin, C., ... Agyemang, C. (2017). Worldwide trends in body-mass index, underweight, overweight, and obesity from 1975 to 2016: A pooled analysis of 2416 population-based measurement studies in 128.9 million children, adolescents, and adults. *The Lancet, 390*, 2627–2642.

Abdellaoui, M., l'Haridon, O., & Paraschiv, C. (2011). Experienced versus described uncertainty: Do we need two prospect theory specifications? *Management Science, 57*, 1879–1895.

Adami, C., & Hintze, A. (2013). Evolutionary instability of zero-determinant strategies demonstrates that winning is not everything. *Nature Communications, 4*, 21–93.

Addessi, E., Galloway, A. T., Visalberghi, E., & Birch, L. L. (2005). Specific social influences on the acceptance of novel foods in 2–5-year-old children. *Appetite, 45*, 264–271.

Aiello, L. C., & Dunbar, R. I. M. (1993). Neocortex size, group size, and the evolution of language. *Current Anthropology, 34*, 184–193.

Ainslie, G. (1975). Specious reward: A behavioral theory of impulsiveness and impulse control. *Psychological Bulletin, 82*, 463–496.

Akbaraly, T. N., Ferrie, J. E., Berr, C., Brunner, E. J., Head, J., Marmot, M. G., ... Kivimaki, M. (2011). Alternative healthy eating index and mortality over 18y of follow-up: Results from the Whitehall II cohort. *The American Journal of Clinical Nutrition, 94*, 247–253.

Albert, D., Chein, J., & Steinberg, L. (2013). The teenage brain: Peer influences on adolescent decision making. *Current Directions in Psychological Science, 22*, 114–120.

Aldridge, V., Dovey, T. M., & Halford, J. C. G. (2009). The role of familiarity in dietary development. *Developmental Review, 29*, 32–44.

Alemanno, A., & Sibony, A. (2015). *Nudge and the law: A European perspective*. Oxford, United Kingdom: Hart.

Allais, M. (1953). L'extension des théories de l'équilibre économique général et du rendement social au cas du risque [Extension of the theories of general economic equilibrium and social output to the case of risk]. *Econometrica, 21*, 503–546.

Ambady, N., & Rosenthal, R. (1992). Thin slices of expressive behavior as predictors of interpersonal consequences: A meta-analysis. *Psychological Bulletin, 111*, 256–274.

American Diabetes Association. (2009). Diagnosis and classification of diabetes mellitus. *Diabetes Care, 33*, 62–69.

Analytis, P. P., Barkoczi, D., & Herzog, S. M. (2018). Social learning strategies for matters of taste. *Nature Human Behaviour, 2*, 415–424.

Anderson, J. R. (1990). *The adaptive character of thought*. Hillsdale, NJ: Lawrence Erlbaum Associates.

Andrade, A. M., Kresge, D. L., Teixeira, P. J., Baptista, F., & Melanson, K. J. (2012). Does eating slowly influence appetite and energy intake when water intake is controlled? *International Journal of Behavioral Nutrition and Physical Activity, 9*, 135.

Annas, J., & Barnes, J. (Eds.). (2000). *Sextus Empiricus: Outlines of scepticism*. Cambridge, United Kingdom: Cambridge University Press.

Anusic, I., & Schimmack, U. (2016). Stability and change of personality traits, self-esteem, and well-being: Introducing the meta-analytic stability and change model of retest correlations. *Journal of Personality and Social Psychology, 110*, 766–781.

Archer, E., Hand, G. A., & Blair, S. N. (2013). Validity of US nutritional surveillance: National Health and Nutrition Examination Survey caloric energy intake data, 1971–2010. *PLOS ONE, 8*, e76632.

Arendt, H. (2013). *The human condition*. Chicago, IL: University of Chicago Press. (Original work published 1958)

Arkes, H. R. (2001). Overconfidence in judgmental forecasting. In J. S. Armstrong (Ed.), *Principles of forecasting: A handbook for researchers and practitioners* (pp. 495–515). Norwell, MA: Kluwer Academic.

Arkes, H. R., Gigerenzer, G., & Hertwig, R. (2016). How bad is incoherence? *Decision, 3*, 20–39.

Armstrong, B., & Spaniol, J. (2017). Experienced probabilities increase understanding of diagnostic test results in younger and older adults. *Medical Decision Making, 37*, 670–679.

Armstrong, J. S. (2001). Combining forecasts. In J. S. Armstrong (Ed.), *Principles of forecasting: A handbook for researchers and practitioners* (pp. 417–439). Norwell, MA: Kluwer Academic Publishers.

Arnauld, A., & Nicole, P. (1850). *Logic, or, the art of thinking: Being the Port-Royal logic* (T. S. Baynes, Trans.). Edinburgh, United Kingdom: Sutherland and Knox. (Original work published 1662)

Arnett, J. (1994). Sensation seeking: A new conceptualization and a new scale. *Personality and Individual Differences, 16*, 289–296.

Arrow, K. (1951). Alternative approaches to the theory of choice in risk-taking situations. *Econometrica, 19*, 404–437.

Ashby, N. J., & Rakow, T. (2014). Forgetting the past: Individual differences in recency in subjective valuations from experience. *Journal of Experimental Psychology: Learning, Memory, and Cognition, 40*, 1153–1162.

Asimov, I. (1994). *I, Asimov: A memoir*. New York, NY: Doubleday.

Atkinson, A. B., & Piketty, T. (Eds.). (2010). *Top incomes: A global perspective*. Oxford, United Kingdom: Oxford University Press.

Attaran, A. (2016, May). Off the podium: Why public health concerns for global spread of Zika virus means that Rio de Janeiro's 2016 Olympic Games must not proceed. *Harvard Public Health Review, 8*. Retrieved from http://harvardpublichealthreview.org /off-the-podium-why-rios-2016-olympic-games-must-not-proceed/

Baltes, P. B., Staudinger, U. M., & Lindenberger, U. (1999). Lifespan psychology: Theory and application to intellectual functioning. *Annual Review of Psychology, 50*, 471–507.

Bang, D., & Frith, C. D. (2017). Making better decisions in groups. *Open Science, 4*, 170–193.

Bang, D., Fusaroli, R., Tylén, K., Olsen, K., Latham, P. E., Lau, J. Y. F., … Bahrami, B. (2014). Does interaction matter? Testing whether a confidence heuristic can replace interaction in collective decision-making. *Consciousness and Cognition, 26*, 13–23.

Barclay, E. (2015, March 2). Your grandparents spent more of their money on food than you do. *npr*. Retrieved from https://www.npr.org/sections/thesalt/2015/03/02 /389578089/your-grandparents-spent-more-of-their-money-on-food-than-you-do

Barkow, J. H., Cosmides, L., & Tooby, J. (Eds.). (1995). *The adapted mind: Evolutionary psychology and the generation of culture*. Oxford, United Kingdom: Oxford University Press.

Baron, R. S. (2005). So right it's wrong: Groupthink and the ubiquitous nature of polarized group decision making. In M. P. Zanna (Ed.), *Advances in Experimental Social Psychology* (pp. 219–253). San Diego, CA: Elsevier Academic Press.

Barrett, H. C. (2005). Enzymatic computation and cognitive modularity. *Mind & Language, 20,* 259–287.

Barrett, H. C., & Kurzban, R. (2006). Modularity in cognition: Framing the debate. *Psychological Review, 113,* 628–647.

Barron, G., & Erev, I. (2003). Small feedback-based decisions and their limited correspondence to description-based decisions. *Journal of Behavioral Decision Making, 16,* 215–233.

Bartholomew, D. J., Deary, I. J., & Lawn, M. (2009). A new lease of life for Thomson's bonds model of intelligence. *Psychological Review, 116,* 567–579.

Bartlema, A., Lee, M., Wetzels, R., & Vanpaemel, W. (2014). A Bayesian hierarchical mixture approach to individual differences: Case studies in selective attention and representation in category learning. *Journal of Mathematical Psychology, 59,* 132–150.

Batchelor, R., & Dua, P. (1995). Forecaster diversity and the benefits of combining forecasts. *Management Science, 41,* 68–75.

Beck, U. (1992). *Risk society: Towards a new modernity.* London, United Kingdom: Sage.

Beglinger, B., Rohacek, M., Ackermann, S., Hertwig, R., Karakoumis-Ilsemann, J., Boutellier, S., ... Bingisser, R. (2015). Physician's first clinical impression of emergency department patients with nonspecific complaints is associated with morbidity and mortality. *Medicine, 94,* e374.

Bell, C. C., & McBride, D. F. (2010). Affect regulation and prevention of risky behaviors. *JAMA, 304,* 565–566.

Bellisle, F. D., & Slama, G. (2004). Non food-related environmental stimuli induce increased meal intake in healthy women: Comparison of television viewing versus listening to a recorded story in laboratory settings. *Appetite, 43,* 175–180.

Benartzi, S., & Thaler, R. H. (2001). Naive diversification strategies in defined contribution saving plans. *American Economic Review, 91,* 79–98.

Benjamin, D. K., Cesarini, D., van der Loos, M. J., Dawes, C. T., Koellinger, P. D., Magnusson, P. K., ... Visscher, P. M. (2012). The genetic architecture of economic and political preferences. *Proceedings of the National Academy of Sciences, 109,* 8026–8031.

Benjamin, D. K., & Dougan, W. R. (1997). Individuals' estimates of the risks of death: Part I—A reassessment of the previous evidence. *Journal of Risk and Uncertainty, 15,* 115–133.

Benzion, U., Rapoport, A., & Yagil, J. (1989). Discount rates inferred from decisions: An experimental study. *Management Science, 35,* 270–284.

Bercovitch, F. B., Widdig, A., Trefilov, A., Kessler, M. J., Berard, J. D., Schmidtke, J., ... Krawczak, M. (2003). A longitudinal study of age-specific reproductive output and body condition among male rhesus macaques, Macaca mulatta. *Naturwissenschaften, 90*, 309–312.

Bergert, F. B., & Nosofsky, R. M. (2007). A response-time approach to comparing generalized rational and take-the-best models of decision making. *Journal of Experimental Psychology: Learning, Memory, and Cognition, 33*, 107–129.

Berkowitz, R. I., Moore, R. H., Faith, M. S., Stallings, V. A., Kral, T. V., & Stunkard, A. J. (2010). Identification of an obese eating style in 4-year-old children born at high and low risk for obesity. *Obesity, 18*, 505–512.

Berlin, L. (2008, November 21). Lessons of survival, from the dot-com attic. *The New York Times*. Retrieved from https://www.nytimes.com/2008/11/23/business/23proto.html

Berner, E. S., & Graber, M. L. (2008). Overconfidence as a cause of diagnostic error in medicine. *The American Journal of Medicine, 121*, 2–23.

Bernoulli, D. (1954). Exposition of a new theory on the measurement of risk (L. Sommer, Trans.). *Econometrica, 22*, 23–36. (Original work published 1738)

Beshears, J., Choi, J. J., Laibson, D., & Madrian, B. C. (2010). The impact of employer matching on savings plan participation under automatic enrollment. In D. A. Rise (Ed.), *Research findings in the economics of aging* (pp. 311–327). Chicago, IL: University of Chicago Press.

Best, R., & Charness, N. (2015). Age differences in the effect of framing on risky choice: A meta-analysis. *Psychology and Aging, 30*, 688–698.

Betsch, T., & Pohl, D. (2002). Tversky and Kahneman's availability approach to frequency judgement: A critical analysis. In P. Sedlmeier & T. Betsch (Eds.), *Etc: Frequency processing and cognition* (pp. 109–119). Oxford, United Kingdom: Oxford University Press.

Betts, R. K. (1978). Analysis, war, and decision: Why intelligence failures are inevitable. *World Politics, 31*, 61–89.

Biener, A., Cawley, J., & Meyerhoefer, C. (2017). The impact of obesity on medical care costs and labor market outcomes in the US. *Clinical Chemistry, 64*, 108–117.

Binmore, K. (2007). Rational decisions in large worlds. *Annales d'Economie et de Statistique, 86*, 25–41.

Binmore, K. (2009). *Rational decisions*. Princeton, NJ: Princeton University Press.

Binmore, K., Swierzbinski, J., & Proulx, C. (2001). Does minimax work? An experimental study. *Economic Journal, 111*, 445–464.

Birch, L. L. (1989). Effects of experience on the modification of food acceptance patterns. *Annals of the New York Academy of Sciences, 561*, 209–216.

Birnbaum, M. H., & Chavez, A. (1997). Tests of theories of decision making: Violations of branch independence and distribution independence. *Organizational Behavior and Human Decision Processes, 71*, 161–194.

Bjorklund, D. F. (1997). The role of immaturity in human development. *Psychological Bulletin, 122*, 153–169.

Blais, A.-R., & Weber, E. U. (2006). A domain-specific risk-taking (DOSPERT) scale for adult populations. *Judgment and Decision Making, 1*, 33–47.

Blankenstein, N. E., Crone, E. A., van den Bos, W., & van Duijvenvoorde, A. C. K. (2016). Dealing with uncertainty: Testing risk- and ambiguity-attitude across adolescence. *Developmental Neuropsychology, 5631*, 77–92.

Blass, E. M. A., Kirkorian, H. L., Pempek, T. A., Price, I., & Koleini, M. F. (2006). On the road to obesity: Television viewing increases intake of high-density foods. *Physiology & Behavior, 86*, 347–358.

Blavatskyy, P. R. (2005). Back to the St. Petersburg paradox? *Management Science, 51*, 677–678.

Bode, N. W. F., & Codling, E. (2013). Human exit route choice in virtual crowd evacuations. *Animal Behaviour, 86*, 347–358.

Bogacz, R., Brown, E., Moehlis, J., Holmes, P., & Cohen, J. D. (2006). The physics of optimal decision making: A formal analysis of models of performance in two-alternative forced-choice tasks. *Psychological Review, 113*, 700–765.

Boland, P. J. (1989). Majority systems and the Condorcet jury theorem. *The Statistician, 38*, 181–189.

Bonaccio, S., & Dalal, R. S. (2006). Advice taking and decision-making: An integrative literature review, and implications for the organizational sciences. *Organizational Behavior and Human Decision Processes, 101*, 127–151.

Bond, C. F., Jones, R. L., & Weintraub, D. L. (1985). On the unconstrained recall of acquaintances: A sampling-traversal model. *Journal of Personality and Social Psychology, 49*, 327–337.

Bonem, E. M., Ellsworth, P. C., & Gonzalez, R. (2015). Age differences in risk: Perceptions, intentions and domains. *Journal of Behavioral Decision Making, 28*, 317–330.

Bordalo, P., Gennaioli, N., & Shleifer, A. (2012). Salience theory of choice under risk. *Quarterly Journal of Economics, 127*, 1243–1285.

Bornstein, G., Kugler, T., & Ziegelmeyer, A. (2004). Individual and group decisions in the centipede game: Are groups more "rational" players? *Journal of Experimental Social Psychology, 40*, 599–605.

Bowlby, J. (1969). *Attachment and loss: Vol. 1. Attachment*. New York, NY: Basic Books.

Boyd, R., & Richerson, P. J. (1988). *Culture and the evolutionary process.* Chicago, IL: University of Chicago Press.

Bradbury, M. A., Hens, T., & Zeisberger, S. (2014). Improving investment decisions with simulated experience. *Review of Finance, 19,* 1019–1052.

Bradley, R., & Steele, K. (2015). Making climate decisions. *Philosophy Compass, 10,* 799–810.

Brandenburger, A. (1996). Strategic and structural uncertainty in games. In R. Zeckhauser, R. Keeney, & J. Sebenius (Eds.), *Wise choices: Decisions, games, and negotiations* (pp. 221–232). Boston, MA: Harvard Business School Press.

Brandstätter, E., Gigerenzer, G., & Hertwig, R. (2006). The priority heuristic: Making choices without trade-offs. *Psychological Review, 113,* 409–432.

Breaugh, J. A. (2008). Employee recruitment: Current knowledge and important areas for future research. *Human Resource Management Review, 18,* 103–118.

Brehmer, B. (1980). In one word: Not from experience. *Acta Psychologica, 45,* 223–241.

Brezzi, M., & Lai, T. L. (2002). Optimal learning and experimentation in bandit problems. *Journal of Economic Dynamics and Control, 27,* 87–108.

Brighton, H., & Gigerenzer, G. (2015). The bias bias. *Journal of Business Research, 68,* 1772–1784.

Briley, D. A., & Tucker-Drob, E. M. (2014). Genetic and environmental continuity in personality development: A meta-analysis. *Psychological Bulletin, 140,* 1303–1331.

British Parachute Association. (2018). How safe? Retrieved from http://www.bpa.org.uk/staysafe/how-safe/

Bröder, A. (2000). Assessing the empirical validity of the "take-the-best" heuristic as a model of human probabilistic inference. *Journal of Experimental Psychology: Learning, Memory, and Cognition, 26,* 1332–1346.

Bröder, A. (2011). The quest for take-the-best: Insights and outlooks from experimental research. In G. Gigerenzer, R. Hertwig, & T. Pachur (Eds.), *Heuristics: The foundations of adaptive behavior* (pp. 364–380). New York, NY: Oxford University Press.

Brody, R. (2011, February 24). My Oscar picks. *The New Yorker.* Retrieved from https://www.newyorker.com/culture/richard-brody/my-oscar-picks#ixzz1FCt1d1Mw

Bronfenbrenner, U. (1979). Contexts of child rearing: Problems and prospects. *American Psychologist, 34,* 844–850.

Broomell, S. B., & Bhatia, S. (2014). Parameter recovery for decision modeling using choice data. *Decision, 1,* 252–274.

Brown, G., Wyatt, J., Harris, R., & Yao, X. (2005). Diversity creation methods: A survey and categorisation. *Information Fusion, 6*, 5–20.

Bruine de Bruin, W., & Fischhoff, B. (2017). Eliciting probabilistic expectations: Collaborations between psychologists and economists. *Proceedings of the National Academy of Sciences, 114*, 3297–3304.

Bruine de Bruin, W., Parker, A. M., & Fischhoff, B. (2007). Can adolescents predict significant life events? *Journal of Adolescent Health Care, 41*, 208–210.

Brumbach, B. H., Figueredo, A. J., & Ellis, B. J. (2009). Effects of harsh and unpredictable environments in adolescence on development of life history strategies: A longitudinal test of an evolutionary model. *Human Nature, 20*, 25–51.

Brunswik, E. (1952). The conceptual framework of psychology. In O. Neurath, N. Bohr, J. Dewey, B. Russell, R. Carnap, & W. Charles (Eds.), *International encyclopedia of unified science* (Vol. 1, pp. 656–760). Chicago, IL: University of Chicago Press.

Brunswik, E. (1955). Representative design and probabilistic theory in a functional psychology. *Psychological Review, 62*, 193–217.

Brunswik, E. (2001). Scope and aspects of the cognitive problem. In K. R. Hammond & T. R. Stewart (Eds.), *The essential Brunswik: Beginnings, explications, applications* (pp. 300–312). Oxford, United Kingdom: Oxford University Press. (Original work published 1957)

Buchanan, C. M., Eccles, J. S., & Becker, J. B. (1992). Are adolescents the victims of raging hormones? Evidence for activational effects of hormones on moods and behavior at adolescence. *Psychological Bulletin, 111*, 62–107.

Buchner, F. L., Bueno-de-Mesquita, H. B., Linseisen, J., Boshuizen, H. C., Kiemeney, L. A., Ros, M. M., … Riboli, E. (2010). Fruits and vegetables consumption and the risk of histological subtypes of lung cancer in the European Prospective Investigation into Cancer and Nutrition (EPIC). *Cancer Causes & Control, 21*, 357–371.

Budescu, D. V., & Chen, E. (2014). Identifying expertise to extract the wisdom of crowds. *Management Science, 61*, 267–280.

Budescu, D. V., & Wallsten, T. S. (1987). Subjective estimation of precise and vague uncertainties. In G. Wright & P. Ayton (Eds.), *Judgmental forecasting* (pp. 63–82). New York, NY: Wiley & Sons.

Buffon, G. L. L. (1777). *Essai d'arithmétique morale* [Essay on moral arithmetic] (Vol. 4). Paris, France: Imprimerie Royale.

Busemeyer, J. R. (1982). Choice behavior in a sequential decision-making task. *Organizational Behavior and Human Performance, 29*, 175–207.

Busemeyer, J. R., & Bruza, P. D. (2012). *Quantum models of cognition and decision*. Cambridge, United Kingdom: Cambridge University Press.

Busemeyer, J. R., & Pleskac, T. J. (2009). Theoretical tools for understanding and aiding dynamic decision making. *Journal of Mathematical Psychology, 53*, 126–138.

Busemeyer, J. R., & Townsend, J. T. (1993). Decision field theory: A dynamic-cognitive approach to decision making in an uncertain environment. *Psychological Review, 100*, 432–459.

Buss, D. M., & Conroy-Beam, D. (2016). How are mate preferences linked with actual mate selection? Tests of mate preference integration algorithms using computer simulations and actual mating couples. *PLOS ONE, 11*, e0156078.

Caliendo, M., Fossen, F., & Kritikos, A. (2009). Risk attitudes of nascent entrepreneurs: New evidence from an experimentally-validated survey. *Small Business Economics, 32*, 153–167.

Camazine, S. (2003). *Self-organization in biological systems*. Princeton, NJ: Princeton University Press.

Camerer, C. (2003). *Behavioral game theory: Experiments in strategic interaction*. New Jersey, NJ: Princeton University Press.

Camerer, C., & Ho, T.-H. (1994). Violations of the betweenness axiom and nonlinearity in probability. *Journal of Risk and Uncertainty, 8*, 167–196.

Camerer, C., Ho, T.-H., & Chong, J. K. (2004). A cognitive hierarchy model of games. *The Quarterly Journal of Economics, 119*, 861–898.

Camerer, C., & Weber, M. (1992). Recent developments in modeling preferences: Uncertainty and ambiguity. *Journal of Risk and Uncertainty, 5*, 325–370.

Camilleri, A. R., & Newell, B. R. (2011a). Description- and experience-based choice: Does equivalent information equal equivalent choice? *Acta Psychologica, 136*, 276–284.

Camilleri, A. R., & Newell, B. R. (2011b). When and why rare events are underweighted: A direct comparison of the sampling, partial feedback, full feedback and description choice paradigms. *Psychonomic Bulletin & Review, 18*, 377–384.

Cardoos, S. L., Ballonoff Suleiman, A., Johnson, M., van den Bos, W., Hinshaw, S. P., & Dahl, R. E. (2017). Social status strategy in early adolescent girls: Testosterone and value-based decision making. *Psychoneuroendocrinology, 81*, 14–21.

Carnap, R. (1950). *Logical foundations of probability*. Chicago, IL: University of Chicago Press.

Carney, P. A., Bogart, T. A., Geller, B. M., Haneuse, S., Kerlikowske, K., Buist, D. S., … Onega, T. (2012). Association between time spent interpreting, level of confidence, and accuracy of screening mammography. *American Journal of Roentgenology, 198*, 970–978.

Caspi, A., Roberts, B. W., & Shiner, R. L. (2005). Personality development: Stability and change. *Annual Review of Psychology, 56*, 453–484.

Cavalli-Sforza, L. L., & Feldman, M. W. (1981). *Cultural transmission and evolution: A quantitative approach.* Princeton, NJ: Princeton University Press.

Centers for Disease Control and Prevention. (2017). Teen drivers: Get the facts. Retrieved from https://www.cdc.gov/motorvehiclesafety/teen_drivers/teendrivers_fact sheet.html

Cesarini, D., Johannesson, M., Magnusson, P. K., & Wallace, B. (2012). The behavioral genetics of behavioral anomalies. *Management Science, 58*, 21–34.

Chapman, G. B. (1996). Temporal discounting and utility for health and money. *Journal of Experimental Psychology: Learning, Memory, and Cognition, 22*, 771–791.

Chen, E., Budescu, D. V., Lakshmikanth, S. K., Mellers, B. A., & Tetlock, P. E. (2016). Validating the contribution-weighted model: Robustness and cost–benefit analyses. *Decision Analysis, 13*, 128–152.

Chen, L. H. (2000). Carrying passengers as a risk factor for crashes fatal to 16- and 17-year-old drivers. *JAMA, 283*, 1578–1582.

Chen, S. E., Moeser, A., & Nayga, R. M., Jr. (2015). Too busy to eat with the kids? Parental work and children's eating. *Applied Economic Perspectives and Policy, 37*, 347–377.

Chisholm, J. S. (1999). Attachment and time preference relations between early stress and sexual behavior in a sample of American university women. *Human Nature, 10*, 51–83.

Chong, J. K., Ho, T. H., & Camerer, C. (2016). A generalized cognitive hierarchy model of games. *Games and Economic Behavior, 99*, 257–274.

Cicero, M. T. (45 BCE/1933). Academica (H. Rackham, Trans.). In H. Rackham (Ed.), *Cicero in twenty-eight volumes* (Vol. XIX). Cambridge, MA: Harvard University Press.

Clancy, T. (1984). *The hunt for Red October.* Annapolis, MD: Naval Institute Press.

Clark, W. A. (2016). *Surfing uncertainty: Prediction, action, and the embodied mind.* New York, NY: Oxford University Press.

Clark, W. A., & Liwoski, W. (2017). Prospect theory and the decision to move or stay. *Proceedings of the National Academy of Sciences, 114*, 7432–7440.

Clauset, A., Shalizi, C. R., & Newman, M. E. J. (2009). Power-law distributions in empirical data. *Society of Industrial and Applied Mathematics, 51*, 661–703.

Clemen, R. T. (1989). Combining forecasts: A review and annotated bibliography. *International Journal of Forecasting, 5*, 559–583.

Coatney, M. (1997, August 4). The oldest woman in the world: Jeanne Calment, dead at 122. *Time*. Retrieved from http://content.time.com/time/magazine/article /0,9171,8599,00.html

Cohen, J. D., McClure, S. M., & Yu, A. J. (2007). Should I stay or should I go? How the human brain manages the trade-off between exploitation and exploration. *Philosophical Transactions of the Royal Society B: Biological Sciences, 362*, 933–942.

Cohn, L., Imai, W., Macfarlane, S., & Yanez, C. (1995). Risk-perception: Differences between adolescents and adults. *Health Psychology, 14*, 217–222.

Coleman, J., Herzberg, J., & Morris, M. (1977). Identity in adolescence: Present and future self-concepts. *Journal of Youth and Adolescence, 6*, 63–75.

Combs, B., & Slovic, P. (1979). Newspaper coverage of causes of death. *Journalism & Mass Communication Quarterly, 56*, 837–849.

Condorcet, M. (1785). Essay on the application of analysis to the probability of majority decisions. *Encyclopaedia Britannica*. Retrieved from https://www.britan nica.com/topic/Essay-on-the-Application-of-Analysis-to-the-Probability-of-Major ity-Decisions

Copeland, W., Shanahan, L., Miller, S., Costello, E. J., Angold, A., & Maughan, B. (2010). Outcomes of early pubertal timing in young women: A prospective population-based study. *The American Journal of Psychiatry, 167*, 1218–1225.

Costa-Gomes, M. A., Crawford, V. P., & Broseta, B. (2001). Cognition and behavior in normal-form games: An experimental study. *Econometrica, 69*, 1193–1235.

Costa-Gomes, M. A., & Weizsäcker, G. (2008). Stated beliefs and play in normal-form games. *The Review of Economic Studies, 75*, 729–762.

Couzin, I. (2009). Collective cognition in animal groups. *Trends in Cognitive Science, 13*, 36–43.

Couzin, I., & Franks, N. (2003). Self-organized lane formation and optimized traffic flow in army ants. *Proceedings of the Royal Society B: Biological Sciences, 270*, 139–146.

Cover, T. M., & Thomas, J. A. (2012). *Elements of information theory*. Hoboken, NJ: John Wiley & Sons.

Cronbach, L. J. (1957). The two disciplines of scientific psychology. *American Psychologist, 12*, 671–684.

Crone, E., & Dahl, R. E. (2012). Understanding adolescence as a period of social–affective engagement and goal flexibility. *Nature Reviews Neuroscience, 13*, 636–650.

Cross, G. S., & Proctor, R. N. (2014). *Packaged pleasures: How technology and marketing revolutionized desire*. Chicago, IL: The University of Chicago Press.

Csikszentmihalyi, M., Larson, R., & Prescott, S. (1977). The ecology of adolescent activity and experience. *Journal of Youth and Adolescence, 6*, 281–294.

Dai, J., Pachur, T., Pleskac, T. J., & Hertwig, R. (2018). What the future holds and when: A description–experience gap in intertemporal choice. Retrieved from https://psyarxiv.com/grwye/

Dall, S. R. X., Houston, A. I., & McNamara, J. M. (2004). The behavioural ecology of personality: Consistent individual differences from an adaptive perspective. *Ecology Letters, 7*, 734–739.

Dallacker, M., Hertwig, R., & Mata, J. (2018a). Building blocks of healthy family meals: A meta-analysis. Retrieved from https://psyarxiv.com/cytek/

Dallacker, M., Hertwig, R., & Mata, J. (2018b). The frequency of family meals and nutritional health in children: A meta-analysis. *Obesity Reviews, 19*, 638–653.

Dallacker, M., Hertwig, R., & Mata, J. (2018c). Parents' considerable underestimation of sugar and their child's risk of overweight. *International Journal of Obesity, 42*, 1097–1100.

Dana, J., & Dawes, R. M. (2004). The superiority of simple alternatives to regression for social science predictions. *Journal of Educational and Behavioral Statistics, 29*, 317–331.

Danchin, E., Giraldeau, L.-A., Valone, T. J., & Wagner, R. H. (2004). Public information: From nosy neighbors to cultural evolution. *Science, 305*, 487–491.

Darwin, C. (1859). *On the origin of species*. London, United Kingdom: Murray.

Daston, L. (1995). *Classical probability in the enlightenment*. Princeton, NJ: Princeton University Press. (Original work published 1988)

Davidson, D. (1991). Children's decision-making examined with an information-board procedure. *Cognitive Development, 6*, 77–90.

Davies, N. B., Krebs, J. R., & West, S. A. (2012). *An introduction to behavioural ecology* (Vol. 4). Oxford, United Kingdom: Wiley-Blackwell.

Davis, J. H. (1973). Group decision and social interaction: A theory of social decision schemes. *Psychological Review, 80*, 97–125.

Davis-Stober, C. P. (2011). A geometric analysis of when fixed weighting schemes will outperform ordinary least squares. *Psychometrika, 76*, 650–669.

Davis-Stober, C. P., Budescu, D. V., & Broomell, S. B. (2015). The composition of optimally wise crowds. *Decision Analysis, 12*, 130–143.

Davis-Stober, C. P., Budescu, D. V., Dana, J., & Broomell, S. B. (2014). When is a crowd wise? *Decision, 1*, 79–101.

Davis-Stober, C. P., Dana, J., & Budescu, D. V. (2010). A constrained linear estimator for multiple regression. *Psychometrika, 75*, 521–541.

Dawes, R. M. (1979). The robust beauty of improper linear models in decision making. *American Psychologist, 34*, 571–582.

Day, F. R., Helgason, H., Chasman, D. I., Rose, L. M., Loh, P. R., Scott, R. A., … Gudbjartsson, D. (2016). Physical and neurobehavioral determinants of reproductive onset and success. *Nature Genetics, 48*, 617–623.

Dayan, P., & Daw, N. D. (2008). Decision theory, reinforcement learning, and the brain. *Cognitive, Affective, & Behavioral Neuroscience, 8*, 429–453.

De Finetti, B. (1989). Probabilism. *Erkenntnis, 31*, 169–223. (Original work published 1931)

De Finetti, B. (1937). La prévision: Ses lois logiques, ses sources subjectives [Foresight: Its logical laws, its subjective sources]. *Annales de l'institut Henri Poincaré, 7*, 1–68.

De Finetti, B. (1981). The role of Dutch books and of proper scoring rules. *British Journal for the Philosophy of Science, 32*, 55–56.

de Zoete, A., Assendelft, W. J., Algra, P. R., Oberman, W. R., Vanderschueren, G. M., & Bezemer, P. D. (2002). Reliability and validity of lumbosacral spine radiograph reading by chiropractors, chiropractic radiologists, and medical radiologists. *Spine, 27*, 1926–1933.

Defoe, D. (1980). Robinson Crusoe. Harmondsworth, United Kingdom: Penguin. (Original work published 1719)

Defoe, I. N., Dubas, J. S., Figner, B., & van Aken, M. A. G. (2015). A meta-analysis on age differences in risky decision making: Adolescents versus children and adults. *Psychological Bulletin, 141*, 48–84.

DeLosh, E. L., Busemeyer, J. R., & McDaniel, M. A. (1997). Extrapolation: The sine qua non for abstraction in function learning. *Journal of Experimental Psychology: Learning, Memory, and Cognition, 23*, 968–986.

DeMiguel, V., Garlappi, L., & Uppal, R. (2009). Optimal versus naive diversification: How inefficient is the 1/N portfolio strategy? *Review of Financial Studies, 22*, 1915–1953.

Dennett, D. C. (1995). Darwin's dangerous idea. *The Sciences, 35*, 34–40.

Denrell, J. (2005). Why most people disapprove of me: Experience sampling in impression formation. *Psychological Review, 112*, 951–978.

Denrell, J. (2007). Adaptive learning and risk taking. *Psychological Review, 114*, 177–187.

Denrell, J., & March, J. G. (2001). Adaption as information restriction: The hot stove effect. *Organization Science, 12*, 523–538.

Depping, M. K., & Freund, A. M. (2011). Normal aging and decision making: The role of motivation. *Human Development, 54*, 349–367.

Derex, M., & Boyd, R. (2015). The foundations of the human cultural niche. *Nature Communications, 6*, 83–98.

Descartes, R. (1996). *Meditations on first philosophy.* Cambridge, United Kingdom: Cambridge University Press. (Original work published 1641)

Devetag, G. M., Di Guida, S., & Polonio, L. (2016). An eye-tracking study of feature-based choice in one-shot games. *Experimental Economics, 19*, 177–201.

Dhami, M. K., Hertwig, R., & Hoffrage, U. (2004). The role of representative design in an ecological approach to cognition. *Psychological Bulletin, 130*, 959–988.

Dickens, W. T., & Flynn, J. R. (2001). Heritability estimates versus large environmental effects: The IQ paradox resolved. *Psychological Review, 108*, 346–389.

Dohmen, T., Falk, A., Golsteyn, B., Huffman, D., & Sunde, U. (2017). Risk attitudes across the life course. *The Economic Journal, 127*, 95–116.

Dohmen, T., Falk, A., Huffman, D., & Sunde, U. (2018). On the relationship between cognitive ability and risk preference. *Journal of Economic Perspectives, 32*, 115–134.

Dohmen, T., Falk, A., Huffman, D., Sunde, U., Schupp, J., & Wagner, G. G. (2011). Individual risk attitudes: Measurement, determinants, and behavioral consequences. *Journal of the European Economic Association, 9*, 522–550.

Doom, J. R., Vanzomeren-Dohm, A. A., & Simpson, J. A. (2016). Early unpredictability predicts increased adolescent externalizing behaviors and substance use: A life history perspective. *Development and Psychopathology, 28*, 1505–1516.

Dougherty, M. R. P., Gettys, C. F., & Ogden, E. E. (1999). MINERVA-DM: A memory processes model for judgments of likelihood. *Psychological Review, 106*, 180–209.

Downs, J. S., Loewenstein, G., & Wisdom, J. (2009). Strategies for promoting healthier food choices. *American Economic Review, 99*, 159–164.

Dudai, Y., & Carruthers, M. (2005). The Janus face of mnemosyne. *Nature, 434*, 567.

Dunbar, R. I. M. (1998). The social brain hypothesis. *Brain, 9*, 178–190.

Dunlap, A. S., & Stephens, D. W. (2014). Experimental evolution of prepared learning. *Proceedings of the National Academy of Sciences, 111*, 11750–11755.

Dutka, J. (1988). On the St. Petersburg paradox. *Archive for History of Exact Sciences, 39*, 13–39.

Edwards, W. (1954). The theory of decision making. *Psychological Bulletin, 51,* 380–417.

Edwards, W. (1955). The prediction of decisions among bets. *Journal of Experimental Psychology, 50,* 201–214.

Edwards, W. (1956). Reward probability, amount, and information as determiners of sequential two-alternative decisions. *Journal of Experimental Psychology, 52,* 177–188.

Edwards, W. (1961). Behavioral decision theory. *Annual Review of Psychology, 12,* 473–498.

Edwards, W. (1962a). Dynamic decision theory and probabilistic information processing. *Human Factors, 4,* 59–74.

Edwards, W. (1962b). Subjective probabilities inferred from decisions. *Psychological Review, 69,* 109–135.

Edwards, W. (1965). Optimal strategies for seeking information: Models for statistics, choice reaction times, and human information processing. *Journal of Mathematical Psychology, 2,* 312–329.

Edwards, W. (1982). Pascal and the problem of points. *International Statistical Review/ Revue Internationale de Statistique, 50,* 259–266.

Elliott, L., & Milner, M. (2001, July 10). Age of anxiety. *The Guardian.* Retrieved from https://www.theguardian.com/business/2001/jul/10/globalrecession

Ellis, B. J., Del Giudice, M., Dishion, T. J., Figueredo, A. J., Gray, P., Griskevicius, V., & Wilson, D. S. (2012). The evolutionary basis of risky adolescent behavior: Implications for science, policy, and practice. *Developmental Psychology, 48,* 598–623.

Ellis, B. J., Figueredo, A. J., Brumbach, B. H., & Schlomer, G. L. (2009). Fundamental dimensions of environmental risk: The impact of harsh versus unpredictable environments on the evolution and development of life history strategies. *Human Nature, 20,* 204–268.

Ellsberg, D. (1961). Risk, ambiguity, and the Savage axioms. *Quarterly Journal of Economics, 75,* 643–669.

Elvers, H.-D., Jandrig, B., & Tannert, C. (2007). The ethics of uncertainty. *EMBO Reports, 8,* 892–896.

Endler, J. A. (1986). *Natural selection in the wild* (Vol. 21). Princeton, NJ: Princeton University Press.

Epstein, J. M. (2001). Learning to be thoughtless: Social norms and individual computation. *Computational Economics, 18,* 9–24.

Erev, I., Ert, E., Plonsky, O., Cohen, D., & Cohen, O. (2017). From anomalies to forecasts: Toward a descriptive model of decisions under risk, and from experience. *Psychological Review, 124*, 369–409.

Erev, I., Ert, E., Roth, A. E., Haruvy, E., Herzog, S. M., Hau, R., ... Lebiere, C. (2010). A choice prediction competition: Choices from experience and from description. *Journal of Behavioral Decision Making, 23*, 15–47.

Erev, I., & Roth, A. E. (1998). Predicting how people play games: Reinforcement learning in experimental games with unique, mixed strategy equilibria. *American Economic Review, 88*, 848–881.

Erev, I., Wallsten, T. S., & Budescu, D. V. (1994). Simultaneous over-and underconfidence: The role of error in judgment processes. *Psychological Review, 101*, 519–527.

Erickson, M. A., & Kruschke, J. K. (1998). Rules and exemplars in category learning. *Journal of Experimental Psychology: General, 127*, 107–140.

Ervin, R. B., Kit, B. K., Carroll, M. D., & Ogden, C. L. (2012). Consumption of added sugar among US children and adolescents, 2005–2008. *NCHS Data Brief, 87*, 1–8.

Estes, W. K. (1959). Component and pattern models with Markovian interpretations. In R. R. Bush & W. K. Estes (Eds.), *Studies in mathematical learning theory* (pp. 9–52). Stanford, CA: Stanford University Press.

Estes, W. K., & Maddox, W. T. (2005). Risks of drawing inferences about cognitive processes from model fits to individual versus average performance. *Psychonomic Bulletin & Review, 12*, 403–408.

European Parliament and European Council. (2004, April 21). *Markets in financial instruments directive.* Directive 2004/39/EC. Retrieved from https://eur-lex.europa.eu/legal-content/EN/TXT/PDF/?uri=CELEX:32004L0039&from=EN

Fabio, A., Tu, L.-C., Loeber, R., & Cohen, J. (2011). Neighborhood socioeconomic disadvantage and the shape of the age–crime curve. *American Journal of Public Health, 101*, 325–332.

Fama, E. F. (1965). The behavior of stock-market prices. *Journal of Business, 38*, 34–105.

Fawcett, T. W., Fallenstein, B., Higginson, A. D., Houston, A. I., Mallpress, D. E., Trimmer, P. C., & McNamara, J. M. (2014). The evolution of decision rules in complex environments. *Trends in Cognitive Sciences, 18*, 153–161.

Fawcett, T. W., McNamara, J. M., & Houston, A. I. (2012). When is it adaptive to be patient? A general framework for evaluating delayed rewards. *Behavioural Processes, 89*, 128–136.

Fechner, H. B., Schooler, L. J., & Pachur, T. (2018). Cognitive costs of decision-making strategies: A resource demand decomposition with a cognitive architecture. *Cognition, 170*, 102–122.

Fehr, E., & Fischbacher, U. (2004). Social norms and human cooperation. *Trends in Cognitive Sciences, 8,* 185–190.

Fehr, E., & Schmidt, K. M. (1999). A theory of fairness, competition, and cooperation. *Quarterly Journal of Economics, 114,* 817–868.

Fennell, J., & Baddeley, R. (2012). Uncertainty plus prior equals rational bias: An intuitive Bayesian probability weighting function. *Psychological Review, 119,* 878–887.

Fernández-Delgado, M., Cernadas, E., Barro, S., & Amorim, D. (2014). Do we need hundreds of classifiers to solve real world classification problems? *Journal of Machine Learning Research, 15,* 3133–3181.

Fey, M., McKelvey, R. D., & Palfrey, T. R. (1996). An experimental study of constant-sum centipede games. *International Journal of Game Theory, 25,* 269–287.

Feynman, R. P. (2005). *The pleasure of finding things out: The best short works of Richard P. Feynman.* Cambridge, MA: Helix Books.

Fiedler, K. (2000). Beware of samples! A cognitive–ecological sampling approach to judgment biases. *Psychological Review, 107,* 659–676.

Fiedler, K., & Armbruster, T. (1994). Two halfs may be more than one whole: Category-split effects on frequency illusions. *Journal of Personality and Social Psychology, 66,* 633–645.

Fiedler, K., & Juslin, P. (2006). Taking the interface between mind and environment seriously. In K. Fiedler & P. Juslin (Eds.), *Information sampling and adaptive cognition* (pp. 3–29). New York, NY: Cambridge University Press.

Fiese, B. H., Jones, B. L., & Jarick, J. M. (2015). Family mealtime dynamics and food consumption: An experimental approach to understanding distractions. *Couple and Family Psychology: Research and Routine, 4,* 199–211.

Fildes, A., Charlton, J., Rudisill, C., Littlejohns, P., Prevost, A. T., & Gulliford, M. C. (2015). Probability of an obese person attaining normal body weight: Cohort study using electronic health records. *American Journal of Public Health, 105,* e54–59.

Finucane, M. M., Stevens, G. A., Cowan, M. J., Danaei, G., Lin, J. K., Paciorek, C. J., … Ezzati, M. (2011). National, regional, and global trends in body-mass index since 1980: Systematic analysis of health examination surveys and epidemiological studies with 960 country-years and 9.1 million participants. *The Lancet, 377,* 557–567.

Fischhoff, B., Bruine de Bruin, W., Parker, A. M., Millstein, S. G., & Halpern-Felsher, B. L. (2010). Adolescents' perceived risk of dying. *Journal of Adolescent Health, 46,* 265–269.

Fisher, I. (1930). *The theory of interests.* New York, NY: Macmillan.

Fiske, A. P. (1995). Social schemata for remembering people: Relationships and person attributes in free recall of acquaintances. *Journal of Quantitative Anthropology, 5*, 305–324.

Fleischhut, N., Artinger, F., Olschewski, S., Volz, K. G., & Hertwig, R. (2018). *Not all uncertainty is treated equally: Information search in social and nonsocial environments.* Retrieved from https://psyarxiv.com/c7ht2/

Fox, C. R., & Hadar, L. (2006). "Decisions from experience" = sampling error + prospect theory: Reconsidering Hertwig, Barron, Weber & Erev (2004). *Judgment and Decision Making, 1*, 159–161.

Fox, C. R., & Tversky, A. (1995). Ambiguity aversion and comparative ignorance. *The Quarterly Journal of Economics, 110*, 585–603.

Fox, C. R., & Ülkümen, G. (2011). Distinguishing two dimensions of uncertainty. In W. Brun, G. Keren, G. Kirkebøen, & H. Montgomery (Eds.), *Perspectives on thinking, judging, and decision making: A tribute to Karl Halvor Teigen* (pp. 1–14). Oslo, Norway: Universitetsforlaget.

Fraley, R. C., & Roberts, B. W. (2005). Patterns of continuity: A dynamic model for conceptualizing the stability of individual differences in psychological constructs across the life course. *Psychological Review, 112*, 60–74.

Frankenhuis, W. E., Panchanathan, K., & Nettle, D. (2016). Cognition in harsh and unpredictable environments. *Current Opinion in Psychology, 7*, 76–80.

Frankenhuis, W. E., & de Weerth, C. (2013). Does early-life exposure to stress shape or impair cognition? *Current Directions in Psychological Science, 22*, 407–412.

Fraundorf, S. H., & Benjamin, A. S. (2014). Knowing the crowd within: Metacognitive limits on combining multiple judgments. *Journal of Memory and Language, 71*, 17–38.

Frederick, S., Loewenstein, G., & O'Donoghue, T. (2002). Time discounting and time preference: A critical review. *Journal of Economic Literature, 40*, 351–401.

Fretwell, S. D., & Lucas, H. L. (1969). On territorial behavior and other factors influencing habitat distribution in birds. *Acta Biotheoretica, 19*, 16–36.

Frey, R., Hertwig, R., & Rieskamp, J. (2014). Fear shapes information acquisition in decisions from experience. *Cognition, 132*, 90–99.

Frey, R., Mata, R., & Hertwig, R. (2015). The role of cognitive abilities in decisions from experience: Age differences emerge as a function of choice set size. *Cognition, 142*, 60–80.

Frey, R., Pedroni, A., Mata, R., Rieskamp, J., & Hertwig, R. (2017). Risk preference shares the psychometric structure of major psychological traits. *Science Advances, 3*, 60–80.

Friedman, D., Isaac, R. M., James, D., & Sunder, S. (2014). *Risky curves: On the empirical failure of expected utility*. London, United Kingdom: Routledge.

Frisch, D., & Baron, J. (1988). Ambiguity and rationality. *Journal of Behavioral Decision Making, 1*, 149–157.

Fu, W. T., & Gray, W. D. (2006). Suboptimal tradeoffs in information seeking. *Cognitive Psychology, 52*, 195–242.

Fudenberg, D., & Levine, D. K. (2016). Whither game theory? Towards a theory of learning in games. *The Journal of Economic Perspectives, 30*, 151–169.

Fuhrmann, D., Knoll, L. J., & Blakemore, S.-J. (2015). Adolescence as a sensitive period of brain development. *Trends in Cognitive Sciences, 19*, 558–566.

Funder, D. C. (2016). Taking situations seriously: The situation construal model and the riverside situational Q-sort. *Current Directions in Psychological Science, 25*, 203–208.

Funk, S. G., Rapoport, A., & Jones, L. V. (1979). Investing capital on safe and risky alternatives: An experimental study. *Journal of Experimental Psychology: General, 108*, 415–440.

Gächter, S. (2004). Behavioral game theory. In D. J. Koehler & N. Harvey (Eds.), *Blackwell handbook of judgment and decision making* (pp. 485–503). Oxford, United Kingdom: Blackwell.

Galesic, M., Olsson, H., & Rieskamp, J. (2012). Social sampling explains apparent biases in judgments of social environments. *Psychological Science, 23*, 1515–1523.

Galesic, M., Olsson, H., & Rieskamp, J. (2018). A sampling model of social judgment. *Psychological Review, 125*, 363–390.

Galton, F. (1907). Vox populi (the wisdom of crowds). *Nature, 75*, 450–451.

GBD 2013 Mortality and Causes of Death Collaborators. (2015). Global, regional, and national age-sex specific all-cause and cause-specific mortality for 240 causes of death, 1990–2013: A systematic analysis for the Global Burden of Disease Study 2013. *Lancet, 385*, 117–171.

Geary, D. C., & Bjorklund, D. F. (2000). Evolutionary developmental psychology. *Child Development, 71*, 57–65.

Geisler, W. S., & Diehl, R. L. (2003). A Bayesian approach to the evolution of perceptual and cognitive systems. *Cognitive Science, 27*, 379–402.

Geman, S., Bienenstock, E., & Doursat, R. (1992). Neural networks and the bias/variance dilemma. *Neural Computation, 4*, 1–58.

Gershman, S. J., & Daw, N. D. (2017). Reinforcement learning and episodic memory in humans and animals: An integrative framework. *Annual Review of Psychology, 68*, 101–128.

Gershman, S. J., Horvitz, E. J., & Tenenbaum, J. B. (2015). Computational rationality: A converging paradigm for intelligence in brains, minds, and machines. *Science, 349*, 273–278.

Gibson, J. J. (1958). Visually controlled locomotion and visual orientation in animals. *British Journal of Psychology, 49*, 182–194.

Gibson, J. J. (1979). *The ecological approach to visual perception: Classic edition*. Routledge, United Kingdom: Psychology Press.

Gigerenzer, G., & Brighton, H. (2009). Homo heuristicus: Why biased minds make better inferences. *Topics in Cognitive Science, 1*, 107–143.

Gigerenzer, G., & Gaissmaier, W. (2011). Heuristic decision making. *Annual Review of Psychology, 62*, 451–482.

Gigerenzer, G., & Garcia-Retamero, R. (2017). Cassandra's regret: The psychology of not wanting to know. *Psychological Review, 124*, 179–196.

Gigerenzer, G., & Goldstein, D. G. (1996). Reasoning the fast and frugal way: Models of bounded rationality. *Psychological Review, 103*, 650–669.

Gigerenzer, G., Hertwig, R., & Pachur, T. (Eds.). (2011). *Heuristics: The foundations of adaptive behavior*. New York, NY: Oxford University Press.

Gigerenzer, G., & Selten, R. (Eds.). (2001). *Bounded rationality: The adaptive toolbox*. Cambridge, MA: Cambridge University Press.

Gigerenzer, G., Switjtink, Z., Porter, T., Daston, L., Beatty, J., & Krüger, L. (1989). *The empire of chance: How probability changed science and everyday life*. Cambridge, MA: Cambridge University Press.

Gigerenzer, G., Todd, P. M., & the ABC Research Group. (1999). *Simple heuristics that make us smart*. New York, NY: Oxford University Press.

Gigone, D., & Hastie, R. (1997). Proper analysis of the accuracy of group judgments. *Psychological Bulletin, 121*, 149–167.

Gillies, D. (2000). *Philosophical theories of probability*. London, United Kingdom: Routledge.

Gilovich, T., Griffin, D., & Kahneman, D. (Eds.). (2002). *Heuristics and biases: The psychology of intuitive judgment*. Cambridge, United Kingdom: Cambridge University Press.

Gittins, J. C. (1979). Bandit processes and dynamic allocation indices. *Journal of the Royal Statistical Society: Series B (Methodological), 41*, 148–177.

Gittins, J. C., Glazebrook, K., & Weber, R. (2011). *Multi-armed bandit allocation indices*. New York, NY: Wiley and Sons.

Glöckner, A., Hilbig, B. E., Henninger, F., & Fiedler, S. (2016). The reversed description–experience gap: Disentangling sources of presentation format effects in risky choice. *Journal of Experimental Psychology: General, 145*, 486–508.

Glöckner, A., & Pachur, T. (2012). Cognitive models of risky choice: Parameter stability and predictive accuracy of prospect theory. *Cognition, 123*, 21–32.

Goldstein, D. G., & Gigerenzer, G. (2002). Models of ecological rationality: The recognition heuristic. *Psychological Review, 109*, 75–90.

Goldstein, D. G., McAfee, R. P., & Suri, S. (2014). The wisdom of smaller, smarter crowds. In M. Babaioff, *Proceedings of the 15th ACM conference on economics and computation* (pp. 471–488). Retrieved from https://dl.acm.org/citation.cfm?id=2602886

Goldstein, W. M., & Einhorn, H. J. (1987). Expression theory and the preference reversal phenomena. *Psychological Review, 94*, 236–254.

Goldstone, R. L., Ashpole, B. C., & Roberts, M. E. (2005). Knowledge of resources and competitors in human foraging. *Psychonomic Bulletin & Review, 12*, 81–87.

Gonzalez, C., & Dutt, V. (2011). Instance-based learning: Integrating sampling and repeated decisions from experience. *Psychological Review, 118*, 523–551.

Gonzalez, R., & Wu, G. (1999). On the shape of the probability weighting function. *Cognitive Psychology, 38*, 129–166.

Gopnik, A., Griffiths, T. L., & Lucas, C. G. (2015). When younger learners can be better (or at least more open-minded) than older ones. *Current Directions in Psychological Science, 24*, 87–92.

Gordon, M. J., Paradis, G. E., & Rorke, C. H. (1972). Experimental evidence on alternative portfolio decision rules. *The American Economic Review, 62*, 107–108.

Gorn, G. J., & Goldberg, M. E. (1982). Behavioral evidence of the effects of televised food messages on children. *Journal of Consumer Research, 9*, 200–205.

Green, L., Fristoe, N., & Myerson, J. (1994). Temporal discounting and preference reversals in choice between delayed outcomes. *Psychonomic Bulletin & Review, 1*, 383–389.

Green, L., Fry, A. F., & Myerson, J. (1994). Discounting of delayed rewards: A lifespan comparison. *Psychological Science, 5*, 33–36.

Green, L., & Myerson, J. (1996). Exponential versus hyperbolic discounting of delayed outcomes: Risk and waiting time. *American Zoologist, 36*, 496–505.

Gregory, A., Harris, R. D., & Michou, M. (2001). An analysis of contrarian investment strategies in the UK. *Journal of Business Finance & Accounting, 28*, 1192–1228.

Griffin, D., & Brenner, L. A. (2004). Perspectives on probability judgment calibration. In D. J. Koehler & N. Harvey (Eds.), *Blackwell handbook of judgment and decision making* (pp. 177–199). Oxford, United Kingdom: Blackwell.

Griffiths, T. L., Chater, N., Kemp, C., Perfors, A., & Tenenbaum, J. B. (2010). Probabilistic models of cognition: Exploring representations and inductive biases. *Trends in Cognitive Sciences, 14*, 357–364.

Grigsby-Toussaint, D. S., Moise, I. K., & Geiger, S. D. (2011). Observations of marketing on food packaging targeted to youth in retail food stores. *Obesity, 19*, 1898–1900.

Grinblatt, M., Titman, S., & Wermers, R. (1995). Momentum investment strategies, portfolio performance, and herding: A study of mutual fund behavior. *The American Economic Review, 5*, 1088–1105.

Griskevicius, V., Ackerman, J. M., Cantú, S. M., Delton, A. W., Robertson, T. E., Simpson, J. A., & Tybur, J. M. (2013). When the economy falters, do people spend or save? Responses to resource scarcity depend on childhood environments. *Psychological Science, 24*, 197–205.

Grofman, B., Feld, S. L., & Owen, G. (1984). Group size and the performance of a composite group majority: Statistical truths and empirical results. *Organizational Behavior and Human Performance, 33*, 350–359.

Grofman, B., Owen, G., & Feld, S. L. (1983). Thirteen theorems in search of the truth. *Theory and Decision, 15*, 261–278.

Grüne-Yanoff, T., & Hertwig, R. (2016). Nudge versus boost: How coherent are policy and theory? *Minds and Machines, 26*, 149–183.

Grunert, K. G., Wills, J. M., & Fernandez-Celemin, L. (2010). Nutrition knowledge, and use and understanding of nutrition information on food labels among consumers in the UK. *Appetite, 55*, 177–189.

Hacking, I. (2001). *An introduction to probability and inductive logic.* Cambridge, United Kingdom: Cambridge University Press.

Hacking, I. (2006). *The emergence of probability: A philosophical study of early ideas about probability, induction and statistical inference.* Bristol, United Kingdom: Cambridge University Press. (Original work published 1975)

Hall, S. (1904). Adolescence: Its psychology and its relations to physiology, anthropology, sociology, sex, crime, religion and education. *Science, 20*, 142–145.

Halpern, D. (2015). *Inside the nudge unit: How small changes can make a big difference.* New York, NY: Random House.

Hamlin, R. P. (2017). "The gaze heuristic": Biography of an adaptively rational decision process. *Topics in Cognitive Science, 9*, 264–288.

Hammerstein, P., & Selten, R. (1994). Game theory and evolutionary biology. In R. J. Aumann & S. Hart (Eds.), *Handbook of game theory with economic applications* (Vol. 2, pp. 929–993). Amsterdam, Netherlands: Elsevier.

Hammond, K. R. (1955). Probabilistic functioning and the clinical method. *Psychological Review, 62*, 255–262.

Hammond, K. R. (2000). Coherence and correspondence theories in judgment and decision making. In T. Connolly, H. A. Arkes, & K. R. Hammond (Eds.), *Judgment and decision making: An interdisciplinary reader* (pp. 53–65). Cambridge, United Kingdom: Cambridge University Press.

Hardin, G. (1968). The tragedy of the commons. *Science, 13*, 1243–1248.

Harris, J. L., Brownell, K. D., & Bargh, J. A. (2009). The food marketing defense model: Integrating psychological research to protect youth and inform public policy. *Social Issues and Policy Review, 3*, 211–271.

Harrison, G. W., & Rutström, E. E. (2008). Risk aversion in the laboratory. In J. C. Cox & G. W. Harrison (Eds.), *Risk aversion in experiments* (pp. 41–196). Bingley, United Kingdom: Emerald Group Publishing.

Harsanyi, J. C. (1968). Games with incomplete information played by "Bayesian" players, part III: The basic probability distribution of the game. *Management Science, 14*, 486–502.

Harsanyi, J. C., & Selten, R. (1988). *A general theory of equilibrium selection in games.* Cambridge, MA: MIT Press.

Harvard School of Public Health. (2018). Healthy eating plate vs. USDA's MyPlate. Retrieved from https://www.hsph.harvard.edu/nutritionsource/healthy-eating-plate-vs-usda-myplate/

Hasher, L., & Zacks, R. T. (1979). Automatic and effortful processes in memory. *Journal of Experimental Psychology: General, 108*, 356–388.

Hasher, L., & Zacks, R. T. (1984). Automatic processing of fundamental information: The case of frequency of occurrence. *American Psychologist, 39*, 1372–1388.

Hastie, R., & Kameda, T. (2005). The robust beauty of majority rules in group decisions. *Psychological Review, 112*, 494–508.

Hastie, T., Tibshirani, R., & Friedman, J. (2001). *The elements of statistical learning.* New York, NY: Springer.

Hastie, T., Tibshirani, R., & Friedman, J. (2009). *The elements of statistical learning: Data mining, inference, and prediction* (2nd ed.). New York, NY: Springer.

Hau, R., Pleskac, T. J., & Hertwig, R. (2010). Decisions from experience and statistical probabilities: Why they trigger different choices than a priori probabilities. *Journal of Behavioral Decision Making, 23*, 48–68.

Hau, R., Pleskac, T. J., Kiefer, J., & Hertwig, R. (2008). The description–experience gap in risky choice: The role of sample size and experienced probabilities. *Journal of Behavioral Decision Making, 21*, 493–518.

Hawkes, C. (2004). *Nutrition labels and health claims: The global regulatory environment around nutrition labelling.* Geneva, Switzerland: World Health Organization.

Hawkins, G., Camilleri, A., Heathcote, A., Newell, B., & Brown, S. (2014). Modeling probability knowledge and choice in decisions from experience. In P. Bello, M. Guarini, M. McShane, & B. Scassellati (Eds.), *Proceedings of the 36th Annual Meeting of the Cognitive Science Society* (pp. 595–600). Quebec City, Canada: Cognitive Science Society.

Hayden, B. Y., & Platt, M. L. (2009). The mean, the median, and the St. Petersburg Paradox. *Judgment and Decision Making, 4*, 256–273.

Helbing, D. (1991). A mathematical model for the behavior of pedestrians. *System Research and Behavioral Science, 36*, 298–310.

Helbing, D., Brockmann, D., Chadefaux, T., Donnay, K., Blanke, U., Woolley-Meza, O., … Perc, M. (2014). Saving human lives: What complexity science and information systems can contribute. *Journal of Statistical Physics, 158*, 735–781.

Helbing, D., Buzna, L., Johansson, A., & Werner, T. (2005). Self-organized pedestrian crowd dynamics: Experiments, simulations, and design solutions. *Transportation Science, 39*, 1–24.

Helbing, D., Johansson, A., & Al-Abideen, H. (2007). The dynamics of crowd disasters: An empirical study. *Physical Review E, 75*, 46–109.

Helbing, D., Johansson, A., Mathiesen, J., Jensen, M., & Hansen, A. (2006). Analytical approach to continuous and intermittent bottleneck flows. *Physical Review Letters, 97*, 168–172.

Helbing, D., & Molnár, P. (1995). Social force model for pedestrian dynamics. *Physical Review E, 51*, 4282–4286.

Helbing, D., Molnár, P., Farkas, I. J., & Bolay, K. (2001). Self-organizing pedestrian movement. *Environment and Planning B: Planning and Design, 28*, 361–383.

Helbing, D., & Mukerji, P. (2012). Crowd disasters as systemic failures: Analysis of the Love Parade disaster. *EPJ Data Science, 1*, 7–40.

Helfinstein, S. M., Mumford, J. A., & Poldrack, R. A. (2015). If all your friends jumped off a bridge: The effect of others' actions on engagement in and recommendation of risky behaviors. *Journal of Experimental Psychology: General, 144*, 12–17.

Henderson, L. (1974). On the fluid mechanics of human crowd motion. *Transportation Research, 8*, 509–515.

Hendy, H. M., & Raudenbush, B. (2000). Effectiveness of teacher modeling to encourage food acceptance in preschool children. *Appetite, 34*, 61–76.

Hertle, H. H. (2001). The fall of the wall: The unintended self-dissolution of East Germany's ruling regime. *Cold War International History Project Bulletin, 12*, 131–164.

Hertwig, R. (2012a). The psychology and rationality of decisions from experience. *Synthese, 187*, 269–292.

Hertwig, R. (2012b). Tapping into the wisdom of the crowd—with confidence. *Science, 336*, 303–304.

Hertwig, R. (2015). Decisions from experience. In G. Keren & G. Wu (Eds.), *The Wiley Blackwell handbook of judgment and decision making* (Vol. 1, pp. 239–267). Chichester, United Kingdom: Wiley Blackwell.

Hertwig, R. (2017). When to consider boosting: Some rules for policy-makers. *Behavioural Public Policy, 1*, 143–161.

Hertwig, R., Barron, G., Weber, E. U., & Erev, I. (2004). Decisions from experience and the effect of rare events in risky choice. *Psychological Science, 15*, 534–539.

Hertwig, R., Barron, G., Weber, E. U., & Erev, I. (2006). The role of information sampling in risky choice. In K. Fiedler & P. Juslin (Eds.), *Information sampling and adaptive cognition* (pp. 72–91). New York, NY: Cambridge University Press.

Hertwig, R., Davis, J. N., & Sulloway, F. J. (2002). Parental investment: How an equity motive can produce inequality. *Psychological Bulletin, 128*, 728–745.

Hertwig, R., & Engel, C. (2016). The homo ignorans: Deliberately choosing not to know. *Perspectives on Psychological Science, 11*, 359–372.

Hertwig, R., & Erev, I. (2009). The description–experience gap in risky choice. *Trends in Cognitive Sciences, 13*, 517–523.

Hertwig, R., & Grüne-Yanoff, T. (2017). Nudging and boosting: Steering or empowering good decisions. *Perspectives on Psychological Science, 12*, 973–986.

Hertwig, R., & Herzog, S. M. (2009). Fast and frugal heuristics: Tools of social rationality. *Social Cognition, 27*, 661–698.

Hertwig, R., & Hoffrage, U. (2013). Simple heuristics in a simple world. In R. Hertwig, U. Hoffrage, & the ABC Research Group, *Simple heuristics in a social world*. New York, NY: Oxford University Press.

Hertwig, R., Hoffrage, U., & the ABC Research Group. (2013). *Simple heuristics in a social world*. New York, NY: Oxford University Press.

Hertwig, R., Hogarth, R. M., & Lejarraga, T. (2018). Experience and description: Exploring two paths to knowledge. *Current Directions in Psychological Science, 27*, 123–128.

Hertwig, R., Pachur, T., & Kurzenhäuser, S. (2005). Judgments of risk frequencies: Tests of possible cognitive mechanisms. *Journal of Experimental Psychology: Learning, Memory, and Cognition, 31*, 621–642.

Hertwig, R., & Pleskac, T. J. (2008). The game of life: How small samples render choice simpler. In N. Chater & M. Oaksford (Eds.), *The probabilistic mind: Prospects for Bayesian cognitive science* (pp. 209–235). New York, NY: Oxford University Press.

Hertwig, R., & Pleskac, T. J. (2010). Decisions from experience: Why small samples? *Cognition, 115*, 225–237.

Hertwig, R., & Pleskac, T. J. (2018). The construct–behavior gap and the description–experience gap: Comment on Regenwetter and Robinson (2017). *Psychological Review, 125*, 844–849.

Hertwig, R., & Todd, P. M. (2003). More is not always better: The benefits of cognitive limits. In D. Hardman & L. Macchi (Eds.), *Thinking: Psychological perspectives on reasoning, judgment and decision making* (pp. 213–231). Chichester, United Kingdom: Wiley.

Hertwig, R., Wulff, D. U., & Mata, R. (2018). Three gaps and what they may mean for risk preference. *Philosophical Transactions of the Royal Society B: Biological Sciences, 374*, 20180140.

Herzog, S. M., & Hertwig, R. (2009). The wisdom of many in one mind: Improving individual judgments with dialectical bootstrapping. *Psychological Science, 20*, 231–237.

Herzog, S. M., & Hertwig, R. (2014a). Harnessing the wisdom of the inner crowd. *Trends in Cognitive Sciences, 18*, 504–506.

Herzog, S. M., & Hertwig, R. (2014b). Think twice and then: Combining or choosing in dialectical bootstrapping? *Journal of Experimental Psychology: Learning, Memory, and Cognition, 40*, 218–232.

Herzog, S. M., & von Helversen, B. (2018). Strategy selection versus strategy blending: A predictive perspective on single- and multi-strategy accounts in multiple-cue estimation. *Journal of Behavioral Decision Making, 31*, 233–249.

Hibon, M., & Evgeniou, T. (2005). To combine or not to combine: Selecting among forecasts and their combinations. *International Journal of Forecasting, 21*, 15–24.

Highhouse, S., Nye, C. D., Zhang, D. C., & Rada, T. B. (2017). Structure of the DOSPERT: Is there evidence for a general risk factor? *Journal of Behavioral Decision Making, 30*, 400–406.

Hill, L., Casswell, S., Maskill, C., Jones, S., & Wyllie, A. (1998). Fruit and vegetables as adolescent food choices in New Zealand. *Health Promotion International, 13*, 55–65.

Hill, R. A., & Dunbar, R. I. M. (2003). Social network size in humans. *Human Nature, 14*, 53–72.

Hills, T. T., & Hertwig, R. (2010). Information search in decisions from experience: Do our patterns of sampling foreshadow our decisions? *Psychological Science, 21*, 1787–1792.

Hills, T. T., Jones, M. N., & Todd, P. M. (2012). Optimal foraging in semantic memory. *Psychological Review, 119*, 431–440.

Hills, T. T., Noguchi, T., & Gibbert, M. (2013). Information overload or search-amplified risk? Set size and order effects on decisions from experience. *Psychonomic Bulletin & Review, 20*, 1023–1031.

Hills, T. T., & Pachur, T. (2012). Dynamic search and working memory in social recall. *Journal of Experimental Psychology: Learning, Memory, and Cognition, 38*, 218–228.

Hintze, A., Edlund, J. A., Olson, R. S., Knoester, D. B., Schossau, J., Albantakis, L., … Goldsby, H. (2017). *Markov brains: A technical introduction*. Retrieved from https://arxiv.org/abs/1709.05601

Hintze, A., Olson, R. S., Adami, C., & Hertwig, R. (2015). Risk sensitivity as an evolutionary adaptation. *Scientific Reports, 4*, 42–82.

Hintze, A., Phillips, N., & Hertwig, R. (2015). The Janus face of Darwinian competition. *Scientific Reports, 5*, 13662.

Hoffmann, J. A., von Helversen, B., & Rieskamp, J. (2013). Deliberation's blindsight: How cognitive load can improve judgments. *Psychological Science, 24*, 869–879.

Hoffmann, J. A., von Helversen, B., & Rieskamp, J. (2014). Pillars of judgment: How memory abilities affect performance in rule-based and exemplar-based judgments. *Journal of Experimental Psychology: General, 143*, 2242–2261.

Hoffmann, J. A., von Helversen, B., & Rieskamp, J. (2016). Similar task features shape judgment and categorization processes. *Journal of Experimental Psychology: Learning, Memory, and Cognition, 42*, 1193–1217.

Hogarth, R. M., & Einhorn, H. J. (1990). Venture theory: A model of decision weights. *Management Science, 36*, 780–803.

Hogarth, R. M., & Karelaia, N. (2006). Regions of rationality: Maps for bounded agents. *Decision Analysis, 3*, 124–144.

Hogarth, R. M., Lejarraga, T., & Soyer, E. (2015). The two settings of kind and wicked learning environments. *Current Directions in Psychological Science, 24*, 379–385.

Hollands, G. J., Shemilt, I., Marteau, T. M., Jebb, S. A., Kelly, M. P., Nakamura, R., … Ogilvie, D. (2013). Altering micro-environments to change population health behaviour: Towards an evidence base for choice architecture interventions. *BMC Public Health, 13,* 1218.

Horn, S. S., Ruggeri, A., & Pachur, T. (2016). The development of adaptive decision making: Recognition-based inference in children and adolescents. *Developmental Psychology, 52,* 1470–1485.

Houston, A. I., Kacelnik, A., & McNamara, J. M. (1982). Some learning rules for acquiring information. In D. McFarland (Ed.), *Functional ontogeny* (pp. 140–191). London, United Kingdom: Pitman.

Humphrey, N. K. (1976). The social function of intellect. In P. P. G. Bateson & R. A. Hinde (Eds.), *Growing points in ethology* (pp. 303–317). Cambridge, United Kingdom: CUP Archive.

Humphrey, N. K. (1988). The social function of intellect. In R. W. Byrne & A. Whiten (Eds.), *Machiavellian intelligence: Social expertise and the evolution of intellect in monkeys, apes and humans* (pp. 13–33). Oxford, United Kingdom: Clarendon Press.

Hung, H. C., Joshipura, K. J., Jiang, R., Hu, F. B., Hunter, D., Smith-Warner, S. A., … Willett, W. C. (2004). Fruit and vegetable intake and risk of major chronic disease. *Journal of the National Cancer Institute, 96,* 1577–1584.

Hutchinson, J. M., & Gigerenzer, G. (2005). Simple heuristics and rules of thumb: Where psychologists and behavioural biologists might meet. *Behavioural Processes, 69,* 97–124.

Ioannidis, J. P. (2013). Implausible results in human nutrition research. *BMJ, 347,* f6698.

Jackson, D. N., Hourany, L., & Vidmar, N. J. (1972). A four-dimensional interpretation of risk taking. *Journal of Personality, 40,* 483–501.

Jacobs, H., Müller, S., & Weber, M. (2014). How should individual investors diversify? An empirical evaluation of alternative asset allocation policies. *Journal of Financial Markets, 19,* 62–85.

Janis, I. L. (1972). *Victims of groupthink: A psychological study of foreign-policy decisions and fiascoes.* Oxford, United Kingdom: Houghton Mifflin.

Jarvstad, A., Hahn, U., Rushton, S. K., & Warren, P. A. (2013). Perceptuomotor, cognitive, and description-based decision-making seem equally good. *Proceedings of the National Academy of Sciences, 110,* 16271–16276.

Jefferson, T., & Johnston, R. H. (1903). *The writings of Thomas Jefferson* (Vol. 20). Washington, WA: Issued under the auspices of the Thomas Jefferson Memorial Association of the United States.

Jeffery, R. W., Drewnowski, A., Epstein, L. H., Stunkard, A. J., Wilson, G. T., Wing, R. R., & Hill, D. R. (2000). Long-term maintenance of weight loss: Current status. *Health Psychology, 19*, 5–16.

Jimura, K., Myerson, J., Hilgard, J., Braver, T. S., & Green, L. (2009). Are people really more patient than other animals? Evidence from human discounting of real liquid rewards. *Psychonomic Bulletin & Review, 16*, 1071–1075.

Johansson, A. (2009). Constant-net-time headway as a key mechanism behind pedestrian flow dynamics. *Physical Review E, 80*, 26120.

Johansson, A., Helbing, D., Al-Abideen, H. Z., & Al-Bosta, S. (2008). From crowd dynamics to crowd safety: A video-based analysis. *Advances in Complex Systems, 11*, 479–527.

Johnson, J. J., & Busemeyer, J. R. (2016). A computational model of the attention process in risky choice. *Decision, 3*, 254–280.

Jones, M., & Love, B. C. (2011). Bayesian fundamentalism or enlightenment? On the explanatory status and theoretical contributions of Bayesian models of cognition. *Behavioral and Brain Sciences, 34*, 169–188.

Jorland, G. (1987). The Saint Petersburg paradox 1713–1937. In L. Krüger, L. J. Daston, & M. Heidelberger (Eds.), *The probabilistic revolution* (Vol. 1, pp. 157–190). Cambridge, MA: MIT Press.

Josef, A., Richter, D., Samanez-Larkin, G. R., Wagner, G., Hertwig, R., & Mata, R. (2016). Stability and change in risk-taking propensity across the adult lifespan. *Journal of Personality and Social Psychology, 111*, 430–450.

Joshipura, K. J., Hu, F. B., Manson, J. E., Stampfer, M. J., Rimm, E. B., Speizer, F. E., … Willett, W. C. (2001). The effect of fruit and vegetable intake on risk for coronary heart disease. *Annals of Internal Medicine, 134*, 1106-1114.

Juni, M. Z., & Eckstein, M. P. (2017). The wisdom of crowds for visual search. *Proceedings of the National Academy of Sciences, 114*, 4306–4315.

Juslin, P., Karlsson, L., & Olsson, H. (2008). Information integration in multiple cue judgment: A division of labor hypothesis. *Cognition, 106*, 259–298.

Juslin, P., Nilsson, H., & Winman, A. (2009). Probability theory, not the very guide of life. *Psychological Review, 116*, 856–874.

Juslin, P., Olsson, H., & Olsson, A.-C. (2003). Exemplar effects in categorization and multiple-cue judgment. *Journal of Experimental Psychology: General, 132*, 133–156.

Kacelnik, A., & Bateson, M. (1997). Risk-sensitivity: Crossroads for theories of decision-making. *Trends in Cognitive Sciences, 1*, 304–309.

Kagel, J. H., Green, L., & Caraco, T. (1986). When foragers discount the future: Constraint or adaptation? *Animal Behaviour, 34,* 271–283.

Kahneman, D. (2003a). Maps of bounded rationality: Psychology for behavioral economics. *American Economic Review, 93,* 1449–1475.

Kahneman, D. (2003b). A perspective on judgment and choice: Mapping bounded rationality. *American Psychologist, 58,* 697–698.

Kahneman, D. (2011). *Thinking, fast and slow.* Basingstoke, United Kingdom: Macmillan.

Kahneman, D., Slovic, P., & Tversky, A. (Eds.). (1982). *Judgment under uncertainty: Heuristics and biases.* New York, NY: Cambridge University Press.

Kahneman, D., & Thaler, R. H. (2006). Anomalies: Utility maximization and experienced utility. *Journal of Economic Perspectives, 20,* 221–234.

Kahneman, D., & Tversky, A. (1973). On the psychology of prediction. *Psychological Review, 80,* 237–251.

Kahneman, D., & Tversky, A. (1979). Prospect theory: An analysis of decision under risk. *Econometrica, 47,* 263–291.

Kahneman, D., & Tversky, A. (1982). Variants of uncertainty. *Cognition, 11,* 143–157.

Kämmer, J. E., Hautz, W. E., Herzog, S. M., Kunina-Habenicht, O., & Kurvers, R. H. J. M. (2017). The potential of collective intelligence in emergency medicine: Pooling medical students' independent decisions improves diagnostic performance. *Medical Decision Making, 37,* 715–724.

Kandori, M., Mailath, G. J., & Rob, R. (1993). Learning, mutation, and long run equilibria in games. *Econometrica, 61,* 29–56.

Kaplan, H. S., & Gangestad, S. W. (2005). Life history theory and evolutionary psychology. In D. M. Buss, *The handbook of evolutionary psychology* (pp. 68–95). Hoboken, NJ: Wiley & Sons.

Kareev, Y. (1995). Through a narrow window: Working memory capacity and the detection of covariation. *Cognition, 56,* 263–269.

Karlsson, L., Juslin, P., & Olsson, H. (2007). Adaptive changes between cue abstraction and exemplar memory in a multiple-cue judgment task with continuous cues. *Psychonomic Bulletin & Review, 14,* 1140–1146.

Katsikopoulos, K. V., & Gigerenzer, G. (2008). One-reason decision-making: Modeling violations of expected utility theory. *Journal of Risk and Uncertainty, 37,* 35–56.

Katsikopoulos, K. V., Schooler, L. J., & Hertwig, R. (2010). The robust beauty of ordinary information. *Psychological Review, 117,* 1259–1266.

Kaufmann, C., Weber, M., & Haisley, E. (2013). The role of experience sampling and graphical displays on one's investment risk appetite. *Management Science, 59,* 323–340.

Kaunitz, L., Zhong, S., & Kreiner, J. (2017). Beating the bookies with their own numbers—and how the online sports betting market is rigged. Retrieved from https://arxiv.org/abs/1710.02824

Kearns, C. E., Schmidt, L. A., & Glantz, S. A. (2016). Sugar industry and coronary heart disease research: A historical analysis of internal industry documents. *JAMA Internal Medicine, 176,* 1680–1685.

Keats, J. (Ed.). (1891). *The letters of John Keats to his family and friends.* London, United Kingdom: Macmillan.

Kellen, D., Mata, R., & Davis-Stober, C. P. (2017). Individual classification of strong risk attitudes: An application across lottery types and age groups. *Psychonomic Bulletin & Review, 24,* 1341–1349.

Kellen, D., Pachur, T., & Hertwig, R. (2016). How (in)variant are subjective representations of described and experienced risk and rewards? *Cognition, 157,* 126–138.

Kemel, E., & Travers, M. (2016). Comparing attitudes toward time and toward money in experience-based decisions. *Theory and Decision, 80,* 71–100.

Keren, G., & Roelofsma, P. (1995). Immediacy and certainty in intertemporal choice. *Organizational Behavior and Human Decision Processes, 63,* 287–297.

Kerr, N. L., & Tindale, R. S. (2004). Group performance and decision making. *Annual Review of Psychology, 55,* 623–655.

Keynes, J. M. (1937). The general theory of employment. *The Quarterly Journal of Economics, 51,* 209–223.

Keynes, J. M. (1973a). *The general theory of employment, interest, and money.* The collected writings of John Maynard Keynes (Vol. 7). London, United Kingdom: Macmillan. (Original work published 1936)

Keynes, J. M. (1973b). *A treatise on probability.* The collected writings of John Maynard Keynes (Vol. 8). London, United Kingdom: Macmillan. (Original work published 1921)

Khader, P. H., Pachur, T., Meier, S., Bien, S., Jost, K., & Rösler, F. (2011). Memory-based decision-making with heuristics: Evidence for a controlled activation of memory representations. *Journal of Cognitive Neuroscience, 23,* 3540–3554.

Khomami, N. (2017, July 27). Firefighters describe their battle with Grenfell Tower blaze. *The Guardian.* Retrieved from https://www.theguardian.com/uk-news/2017/jul/27/firefighters-describe-their-battle-with-grenfell-tower-blaze

Kidd, C., Palmeri, H., & Aslin, R. N. (2013). Rational snacking: Young children's decision-making on the marshmallow task is moderated by beliefs about environmental reliability. *Cognition, 126,* 109–114.

Klein, G. (1999). *Sources of power: How people make decisions.* Cambridge, MA: MIT Press.

Klein, G., Calderwood, R., & Clinton-Cirocco, A. (2010). Rapid decision making on the fire ground: The original study plus a postscript. *Journal of Cognitive Engineering and Decision Making, 4,* 186–209.

Klucharev, V., Hytönen, K., Rijpkema, M., Smidts, A., & Fernández, G. (2009). Reinforcement learning signal predicts social conformity. *Neuron, 61,* 140–151.

Knight, F. H. (2002). *Risk, uncertainty and profit.* Washington, DC: Beard Books. (Original work published 1921)

Kolmogorov, A. N. (1933). *Grundbegriffe der Wahrscheinlichkeitsrechnung* [Foundations of the theory of probability]. Berlin, Germany: Springer.

Koriat, A. (2012a). The self-consistency model of subjective confidence. *Psychological Review, 119,* 80–113.

Koriat, A. (2012b). When are two heads better than one and why? *Science, 336,* 360–362.

Koriat, A. (2015). When two heads are better than one and when they can be worse: The amplification hypothesis. *Journal of Experimental Psychology, 144,* 934–950.

Krause, J., Ruxton, G. D., & Krause, S. (2010). Swarm intelligence in animals and humans. *Trends in Ecology & Evolution, 25,* 28–34.

Krizan, Z., & Windschitl, P. D. (2007). The influence of outcome desirability on optimism. *Psychological Bulletin, 133,* 95–121.

Krockow, E. M., Pulford, B. D., & Colman, A. M. (2015). Competitive centipede games: Zero-end payoffs and payoff inequality deter reciprocal cooperation. *Games, 6,* 262–272.

Kroll, Y., Levy, H., & Rapoport, A. (1988). Experimental tests of the mean-variance model for portfolio selection. *Organizational Behavior and Human Decision Processes, 42,* 388–410.

Kühberger, A., & Perner, J. (2003). The role of competition and knowledge in the Ellsberg task. *Journal of Behavioral Decision Making, 16,* 181–191.

Kuhn, M., & Johnson, K. (2013). *Applied predictive modeling.* New York, NY: Springer.

Kuncheva, L. (2004). *Combining pattern classifiers: Methods and algorithms.* Hoboken, NJ: Wiley & Sons.

Kurvers, R. H. J. M., de Zoete, A., Bachman, S. L., Algra, P. R., & Ostelo, R. (2018). Combining independent decisions increases diagnostic accuracy of reading lumbosacral radiographs and magnetic resonance imaging. *PLOS ONE, 13*, e0194128.

Kurvers, R. H. J. M., Herzog, S. M., Hertwig, R., Krause, J., Carney, P. A., Bogart, A., … Wolf, M. (2016). Boosting medical diagnostics by pooling independent judgments. *Proceedings of the National Academy of Sciences, 113*, 8777–8782.

Kurvers, R. H. J. M., Krause, J., Argenziano, G., Zalaudek, I., & Wolf, M. (2015). Detection accuracy of collective intelligence assessments for skin cancer diagnosis. *JAMA Dermatology, 151*, 1346–1353.

Kvam, P. D., Cesario, J., Schossau, J., Eisthen, H., & Hintze, A. (2015). Computational evolution of decision-making strategies. In D. C. Noelle, R. Dale, A. S. Warlaumont, J. Yoshimi, T. Matlock, C. D. Jennings, & P. P. Maglio (Eds.), *Proceedings of the 37th Annual Meeting of the Cognitive Science Society* (pp. 1225–1230). Austin, TX: Cognitive Science Society.

Kvam, P. D., & Hintze, A. (2018). Risks, rewards, and reaching the right strategy: Evolutionary paths from heuristic to optimal strategies. *Evolutionary Behavioral Sciences, 12*, 177–190.

Kvam, P. D., Pleskac, T. J., Yu, S., & Busemeyer, J. R. (2015). Interference effects of choice on confidence: Quantum characteristics of evidence accumulation. *Proceedings of the National Academy of Sciences, 112*, 10645–10650.

Laan, A., Madirolas, G., & De Polavieja, G. G. (2017). Rescuing collective wisdom when the average group opinion is wrong. *Frontiers in Robotics and AI, 4*, 358–366.

Ladha, K. K. (1992). The Condorcet jury theorem, free speech, and correlated votes. *American Journal of Political Science, 36*, 617–634.

Ladha, K. K. (1995). Information pooling through majority-rule voting: Condorcet's jury theorem with correlated votes. *Journal of Economic Behavior & Organization, 26*, 353–372.

Laming, D. R. J. (1968). *Information theory of choice-reaction times*. London, United Kingdom: Academic Press.

Laplace, P.-S. (1776). Recherches sur l'intégration des équations différentielles aux différences finies et leur usage dans la théorie des hasards [Research on the integration of differential equations with finite differences and their use in the theory of randomness]. *Mémoire de l'Académie Royale des Sciences de Paris (savants étrangers), 7*.

Laplace, P.-S. (1902). *A philosophical essay on probabilities*. New York, NY: Wiley and Sons. (Original work published 1814)

Larrick, R. P., Mannes, A. E., & Soll, J. B. (2012). The social psychology of the wisdom of crowds. In J. I. Krueger (Ed.), *Frontiers in social psychology: Social judgment and decision making* (pp. 227–242). New York, NY: Psychology Press.

Larrick, R. P., & Soll, J. B. (2006). Intuitions about combining opinions: Misappreciation of the averaging principle. *Management Science, 52*, 111–127.

Laube, C., Suleiman, A. B., Johnson, M., Dahl, R. E., & van den Bos, W. (2017). Dissociable effects of age and testosterone on adolescent impatience. *Psychoneuroendocrinology, 80*, 162–169.

Laube, C., & van den Bos, W. (2016). Hormones and affect in adolescent decision making. In S. Kim, J. M. Reeve, & M. Bong (Eds.), *Recent developments in neuroscience research on human motivation* (pp. 259–281). Bingley, United Kingdom: Emerald Group Publishing.

Lawson, T. (1985). Uncertainty and economic analysis. *The Economic Journal, 95*, 909–927.

Lebon, G. (2007). *The crowd: A study of the popular mind.* New York, NY: Classic Books Library.

Lejarraga, T. (2010). When experience is better than description: Time delays and complexity. *Journal of Behavioral Decision Making, 23*, 100–116.

Lejarraga, T., Hertwig, R., & Gonzalez, C. (2012). How choice ecology influences search in decisions from experience. *Cognition, 124*, 334–342.

Lejarraga, T., Pachur, T., Frey, R., & Hertwig, R. (2016). Decisions from experience: From monetary to medical gambles. *Journal of Behavioral Decision Making, 29*, 67–77.

Lejarraga, T., Woike, J. K., & Hertwig, R. (2016). Description and experience: How experimental investors learn about booms and busts affects their financial risk taking. *Cognition, 157*, 365–383.

Lejuez, C. W., Read, J. P., Kahler, C. W., Richards, J. B., Ramsey, S. E., Strong, D., … Brown, R. A. (2002). Evaluation of a behavioral measure of risk taking: The Balloon Analogue Risk Task (BART). *Journal of Experimental Psychology: Applied, 8*, 75–84.

Lenski, R. E. (2017). Convergence and divergence in a long-term experiment with bacteria. *The American Naturalist, 190*, 57–68.

Leonard, R. J. (1995). From parlor games to social science: von Neumann, Morgenstern, and the creation of game theory. *Journal of Economic Literature, 33*, 730–761.

Leuker, C., Pachur, T., Hertwig, R., & Pleskac, T. J. (2018). Exploiting risk–reward structures in decision making under uncertainty. *Cognition, 175*, 186–200.

Leuker, C., Pachur, T., Hertwig, R., & Pleskac, T. J. (in press). Too good to be true? Psychological responses to uncommon options in risk–reward environments. *Journal of Behavioral Decision Making.*

Li, S.-C., Lindenberger, U., & Sikström, S. (2001). Aging cognition: From neuromodulation to representation. *Trends in Cognitive Sciences, 5*, 479–486.

Lichtenberg, J. M., & Şimşek, Ö. (2017). Simple regression models. *Proceedings of Machine Learning Research, 58,* 13–25. Retrieved from http://proceedings.mlr.press /v58/lichtenberg17a.html

Lichtenstein, S., Slovic, P., Fischhoff, B., Layman, M., & Combs, B. (1978). Judged frequency of lethal events. *Journal of Experimental Psychology: Human Learning and Memory, 4,* 551–578.

Lindley, D. (2014). *Understanding uncertainty.* Hoboken, NJ: Wiley and Sons.

Linnér, R. K., Marioni, R. E., Rietveld, C. A., Simpkin, A. J., Davies, N. M., Watanabe, K., & Benjamin, D. J. (2017). An epigenome-wide association study meta-analysis of educational attainment. *Molecular Psychiatry, 22,* 1680–1690.

Little, K. (2018). Understanding risk: Risk and reward are part of investing. Retrieved from https://www.thebalance.com/understanding-risk-3141268

Lo, A. W., & Mueller, M. (2010). Warning: Physics envy may be hazardous to your wealth. *Journal of Investment Management, 8,* 13–63.

Loftus, E. F. (1993). The reality of repressed memories. *American Psychologist, 48,* 518–537.

Loomes, G., Orr, S., & Sugden, R. (2009). Taste uncertainty and status quo effects in consumer choice. *Journal of Risk and Uncertainty, 39,* 113–135.

Lopes, L. L. (1983). Some thoughts on the psychological concept of risk. *Journal of Experimental Psychology: Human Perception and Performance, 9,* 137–144.

Lopes, L. L. (1995). Algebra and process in the modeling of risky choice. In J. R. Busemeyer, R. Hastie, & D. Medin (Eds.), *Decision making from the perspective of cognitive psychology* (pp. 177–220). New York, NY: Academic Press.

Lopes, L. L., & Oden, G. C. (1999). The role of aspiration level in risky choice: A comparison of cumulative prospect theory and SP/A theory. *Journal of Mathematical Psychology, 43,* 286–313.

Lotka, A. J. (1932). The growth of mixed populations: Two species competing for a common food supply. *Journal of the Washington Academy of Sciences, 22,* 461–469.

Lourenso, J. S., Ciriolo, E., Almeida, S. R., & Troussard, X. (2016). *Behavioural insights applied to policy: European report 2016 (EUR 27726 EN).* Brussels, Belgium: Publication Office of the European Union.

Luan, S., Katsikopoulos, K. V., & Reimer, T. (2012). When does diversity trump ability (and vice versa) in group decision making? A simulation study. *PLOS ONE, 7,* e31043.

Luce, D. (2000). *Utility of gains and losses.* Mahwah, NJ: Erlbaum.

Luce, R. D., & Raiffa, H. (1957). *Games and decisions: Introduction and critical survey.* New York, NY: Dover Publications.

Ludvig, E. A., Madan, C. R., & Spetch, M. L. (2014). Extreme outcomes sway risky decisions from experience. *Journal of Behavioral Decision Making, 27*, 146–156.

Ludwig, D. S. (2016). Lifespan weighed down by diet. *JAMA, 315*, 2269–2270.

Luna, B., Paulsen, D. J., Padmanabhan, A., & Geier, C. (2013). The teenage brain: Cognitive control and motivation. *Current Directions in Psychological Science, 22*, 94–100.

Macri, S., Adriani, W., Chiarotti, F., & Laviola, G. (2002). Risk taking during exploration of a plus-maze is greater in adolescent than in juvenile or adult mice. *Animal Behaviour, 64*, 541–546.

Makridakis, S., Hogarth, R. M., & Gaba, A. (2009). *Dance with chance: Making luck work for you*. Oxford, United Kingdom: Oneworld Publications.

Malmendier, U., & Nagel, S. (2011). Depression babies: Do macroeconomic experiences affect risk taking? *The Quarterly Journal of Economics, 126*, 373–416.

Malone, T. W., & Bernstein, M. S. (2015). *Handbook of collective intelligence*. Cambridge, MA: MIT Press.

Mamerow, L., Frey, R., & Mata, R. (2016). Risk taking across the life span: A comparison of self-report and behavioral measures of risk taking. *Psychology and Aging, 31*, 711–723.

Mannes, A. E., Soll, J. B., & Larrick, R. P. (2014). The wisdom of select crowds. *Journal of Personality and Social Psychology, 107*, 276–299.

March, J. G. (1996). Learning to be risk averse. *Psychological Review, 103*, 309–319.

March, J. G. (2010). *The ambiguities of experience*. Ithaca, NY: Cornell University Press.

Marewski, J. N., & Link, D. (2014). Strategy selection: An introduction to the modeling challenge. *WIREs Cognitive Science, 5*, 39–59.

Marewski, J. N., & Schooler, L. J. (2011). Cognitive niches: An ecological model of strategy selection. *Psychological Review, 118*, 393–437.

Markant, D. B., & Gureckis, T. M. (2014). Is it better to select or to receive? Learning via active and passive hypothesis testing. *Journal of Experimental Psychology: General, 143*, 94–122.

Markant, D. B., Phillips, N. D., Kareev, Y., Avrahami, J., & Hertwig, R. (2018). To act fast or bide time? Adaptive exploration under competitive pressure. Retrieved from https://psyarxiv.com/3jwtq/

Markant, D. B., Pleskac, T. J., Diederich, A., Pachur, T., & Hertwig, R. (2015). Modeling choice and search in decisions from experience: A sequential sampling approach. In D. C. Noelle, R. Dale, A. S. Warlaumont, J. Yoshimi, T. Matlock, C. D. Jennings,

& P. P. Maglio (Eds.), *Proceedings of the 37th Annual Meeting of the Cognitive Science Society* (pp. 1512–1517). Austin, TX: Cognitive Science Society.

Markowitz, H. M. (1952). Portfolio selection. *Journal of Finance, 7*, 77–91.

Marr, D. (1982). *Vision: A computational investigation into the human representation and processing of visual information*. San Francisco, CA: W. H. Freeman.

Martignon, L., & Hoffrage, U. (1999). Why does one-reason decision making work. In G. Gigerenzer, P. M. Todd, & the ABC Research Group, *Simple heuristics that make us smart* (pp. 119–140). New York, NY: Oxford University Press.

Martignon, L., & Hoffrage, U. (2002). Fast, frugal, and fit: Simple heuristics for paired comparison. *Theory and Decision, 52*, 29–71.

Mata, J., Dallacker, M., & Hertwig, R. (2017). Social nature of eating could explain missing link between food insecurity and childhood obesity. *Behavioral and Brain Sciences, 40*, e122.

Mata, R., Frey, R., Richter, D., Schupp, J., & Hertwig, R. (2018). Risk preference: A view from psychology. *Journal of Economic Perspectives, 32*, 105–110.

Mata, R., Josef, A. K., & Hertwig, R. (2016). Propensity for risk taking across the life span and around the globe. *Psychological Science, 27*, 231–243.

Mata, R., Josef, A. K., Samanez-Larkin, G. R., & Hertwig, R. (2011). Age differences in risky choice: A meta-analysis. *Annals of the New York Academy of Sciences, 1235*, 18–29.

Mata, R., & von Helversen, B. (2015). Search and the aging mind: The promise and limits of the cognitive control hypothesis of age differences in search. *Topics in Cognitive Science, 7*, 416–427.

Mata, R., von Helversen, B., & Rieskamp, J. (2011). When easy comes hard: The development of adaptive strategy selection. *Child Development, 82*, 687–700.

Mather, M., Mazar, N., Gorlick, M. A., Lighthall, N. R., Burgeno, J., Schoeke, A., & Ariely, D. (2012). Risk preferences and aging: The "certainty effect" in older adults' decision making. *Psychological Aging, 27*, 801–816.

Mazur, J. E. (1987). An adjusting procedure for studying delayed reinforcement. In M. L. Commons, J. E. Mazur, J. A. Nevin, & H. Rachlin (Eds.), *Quantitative analyses of behavior: Vol. 5. The effect of delay and of intervening events on reinforcement value* (pp. 55–73). Mahwah, NJ: Erlbaum.

McClelland, J. L., Botvinick, M. M., Noelle, D. C., Plaut, D. C., Rogers, T. T., Seidenberg, M. S., & Smith, L. B. (2010). Letting structure emerge: Connectionist and dynamical systems approaches to cognition. *Trends in Cognitive Sciences, 14*, 348–356.

McDade, T. W., Chyu, L., Duncan, G. J., Hoyt, L. T., Doane, L. D., & Adam, E. K. (2011). Adolescents' expectations for the future predict health behaviors in early adulthood. *Social Science & Medicine, 73,* 391–398.

McElreath, R., & Boyd, R. (2008). *Mathematical models of social evolution: A guide for the perplexed.* Chicago, IL: University of Chicago Press.

McGuire, J. T., & Kable, J. W. (2012). Decision makers calibrate behavioral persistence on the basis of time-interval experience. *Cognition, 124,* 216–226.

McGuire, J. T., & Kable, J. W. (2013). Rational temporal predictions can underlie apparent failures to delay gratification. *Psychological Review, 120,* 395–410.

McKelvey, R. D., & Palfrey, T. R. (1992). An experimental study of the centipede game. *Econometrica, 60,* 803–836.

McKenzie, C. R. M., & Nelson, J. D. (2003). What a speaker's choice of frame reveals: Reference points, frame selection, and framing effects. *Psychonomic Bulletin & Review, 10,* 596–602.

McPherson, M., Smith-Lovin, L., & Cook, J. M. (2001). Birds of a feather: Homophily in social networks. *Annual Review of Sociology, 27,* 415–444.

Medin, D. L., & Schaffer, M. M. (1978). Context theory of classification learning. *Psychological Review, 85,* 207–238.

Mellers, B. A., Ungar, L. H., Baron, J., Ramos, J., Gurcay, B., Fincher, K., … Swift, S. A. (2014). Psychological strategies for winning a geopolitical forecasting tournament. *Psychological Science, 25,* 1106–1115.

Mendle, J., & Ferrero, J. (2012). Detrimental psychological outcomes associated with pubertal timing in adolescent boys. *Developmental Review, 32,* 49–66.

Menger, K. (1934). Das Unsicherheitsmoment in der Wertlehre [The role of uncertainty in economics]. *Zeitschrift für Nationalökonomie, 5,* 459–485.

Meyer, M. (2015, November 6). Günter Schabowski, the man who opened the wall. *The New York Times.* Retrieved from https://www.nytimes.com/2015/11/07/opinion/gnter-schabowski-the-man-who-opened-the-wall.html

Milam, G. (2016, May 16). Rio mayor: Zika "not a big issue" for Olympics. *Sky News.* Retrieved from http://news.sky.com/story/rio-mayor-zika-not-a-big-issue-for-olympics-10284145

Milardo, R. M. (1992). Comparative methods for delineating social networks. *Journal of Social and Personal Relationships, 9,* 447–461.

Mintz, A. (1951). Non-adaptive group behavior. *Journal of Abnormal and Social Psychology, 46,* 150–159.

Mischel, W. (1961). Father-absence and delay of gratification. *The Journal of Abnormal and Social Psychology, 63*, 116–124.

Mischel, W. (2014). *The marshmallow test: Understanding self-control and how to master it.* London, United Kingdom: Transworld Publishers.

Mischel, W., & Ebbesen, E. B. (1970). Attention in delay of gratification. *Journal of Personality and Social Psychology, 16*, 329–337.

Mischel, W., & Grusec, J. (1967). Waiting for rewards and punishments: Effects of time and probability on choice. *Journal of Personality and Social Psychology, 5*, 24–31.

Mishra, S., Barclay, P., & Sparks, A. (2016). The relative state model: Integrating need-based and ability-based pathways to risk-taking. *Personality and Social Psychology Review, 21*, 176–198.

Mousavi, S., & Gigerenzer, G. (2014). Risk, uncertainty, and heuristics. *Journal of Business Research, 67*, 1671–1678.

Moussaïd, M., Brighton, H., & Gaissmaier, W. (2015). The amplification of risk in experimental diffusion chains. *Proceedings of the National Academy of Sciences, 112*, 5631–5636.

Moussaïd, M., Guillot, E. G., Moreau, M., Fehrenbach, J., Chabiron, O., Lemercier, S., ... Theraulaz, G. (2012). Traffic instabilities in self-organized pedestrian crowds. *PLOS Computational Biology, 8*, e1002442.

Moussaïd, M., Helbing, D., Garnier, S., Johansson, A., Combe, M., & Theraulaz, G. (2009). Experimental study of the behavioural mechanisms underlying self-organization in human crowds. *Proceedings of the Royal Society B: Biological Sciences, 276*, 2755–2762.

Moussaïd, M., Helbing, D., & Theraulaz, G. (2011). How simple rules determine pedestrian behavior and crowd disasters. *Proceedings of the National Academy of Sciences, 108*, 6884–6888.

Moussaïd, M., Kapadia, M., Thrash, T., Sumner, R. W., Gross, M., Helbing, D., & Hölscher, C. (2016). Crowd behaviour during high-stress evacuations in an immersive virtual environment. *Journal of the Royal Society Interface, 13*, 20160414.

Mullett, T. L., & Stewart, N. (2016). Implications of visual attention phenomena for models of preferential choice. *Decision, 3*, 231–253.

Mulye, T. P., Park, M. J., Nelson, C. D., Adams, S. H., Irwin, C. E., & Brindis, C. D. (2009). Trends in adolescent and young adult health in the United States. *Journal of Adolescent Health, 45*, 8–24.

Murphy, A. H. (1973). A new vector partition of the probability score. *Journal of Applied Meteorology, 12*, 595–600.

Nagel, R. (1995). Unraveling in guessing games: An experimental study. *American Economic Review, 85*, 1313–1326.

Nagel, R., & Tang, F. F. (1998). Experimental results on the centipede game in normal form: An investigation on learning. *Journal of Mathematical Psychology, 42*, 356–384.

National Safety Council. (2018). What are the odds of dying from ... Retrieved from https://www.nsc.org/work-safety/tools-resources/injury-facts/chart

Navarro, D. J., Newell, B. R., & Schulze, C. (2016). Learning and choosing in an uncertain world: An investigation of the explore–exploit dilemma in static and dynamic environments. *Cognitive Psychology, 85*, 43–77.

NCD Risk Factor Collaboration. (2016). Worldwide trends in diabetes since 1980: A pooled analysis of 751 population-based studies with 4.4 million participants. *The Lancet, 387*, 1513–1530.

Nettle, D., Andrews, C., & Bateson, M. (2017). Food insecurity as a driver of obesity in humans: The insurance hypothesis. *Behavioral and Brain Sciences, 40*, 1–53.

Neufeld, M. (Producer), & McTiernan, J. (Director). (1990). *The hunt for Red October* [Motion picture]. United States: Paramount Pictures.

Newell, B. R., Lagnado, D. A., & Shanks, D. R. (2015). *Straight choices: The psychology of decision making.* London, United Kingdom: Psychology Press.

Newell, B. R., Rakow, T., Weston, N. J., & Shanks, D. R. (2004). Search strategies in decision making: The success of "success." *Journal of Behavioral Decision Making, 17*, 117–137.

Newman, M. E. J. (2005). Power laws, Pareto distributions and Zipf's law. *Contemporary Physics, 46*, 323–351.

Nielsen, S. J., & Popkin, B. M. (2002). Trends in food locations and sources among adolescents and young adults. *Preventive Medicine, 35*, 107–113.

Nisbett, R. E., & Kunda, Z. (1985). Perception of social distributions. *Journal of Personality and Social Psychology, 48*, 297–311.

Noelle-Neumann, E. (1974). The spiral of silence: A theory of public opinion. *Journal of Communication, 24*, 43–51.

Noguchi, T., & Hills, T. T. (2016). Experience-based decisions favor riskier alternatives in large sets. *Journal of Behavioral Decision Making, 29*, 489–498.

Norton, M. I., Mochon, D., & Ariely, D. (2012). The IKEA effect: When labor leads to love. *Journal of Consumer Psychology, 22*, 453–460.

Nosofsky, R. M. (1984). Choice, similarity, and the context theory of classification. *Journal of Experimental Psychology: Learning, Memory, and Cognition, 10*, 104–114.

Nosofsky, R. M., & Bergert, B. F. (2007). Limitations of exemplar models of multiattribute probabilistic inference. *Journal of Experimental Psychology: Learning, Memory, and Cognition, 33*, 999–1019.

Oaksford, M., & Chater, N. (2007). *Bayesian rationality: The probabilistic approach to human reasoning*. Oxford, United Kingdom: Oxford University Press.

Ochs, J. (1995). Games with unique, mixed strategy equilibria: An experimental study. *Games and Economic Behavior, 10*, 202–217.

Olshansky, S. J., Passaro, D. J., Hershow, R. C., Layden, J., Carnes, B. A., Brody, J., ... Ludwig, D. S. (2005). A potential decline in life expectancy in the United States in the 21st century. *New England Journal of Medicine, 352*, 1138–1145.

Olsson, A. C., Enkvist, T., & Juslin, P. (2006). Go with the flow: How to master a nonlinear multiple-cue judgment task. *Journal of Experimental Psychology: Learning, Memory, and Cognition, 32*, 1371–1384.

Olsson, H. (2014). Measuring overconfidence: Methodological problems and statistical artifacts. *Journal of Business Research, 67*, 1766–1770.

Olsson, H., & Loveday, J. (2015). A comparison of small crowd selection methods. In D. C. Noelle, R. Dale, A. S. Warlaumont, J. Yoshimi, T. Matlock, C. D. Jennings, & P. P. Maglio (Eds.), *Proceedings of the 37th Annual Meeting of the Cognitive Science Society* (pp. 1769–1774). Austin, TX: Cognitive Science Society.

Olsson, H., & Poom, L. (2005). The noisy cue abstraction model is equivalent to the multiplicative prototype model. *Perceptual and Motor Skills, 100*, 819–820.

Onay, S., La-Ornual, D., & Öncüler, A. (2013). The effect of temporal distance on attitudes toward imprecise probabilities and imprecise outcomes. *Journal of Behavioral Decision Making, 26*, 362–374.

Onay, S., & Öncüler, A. (2007). Intertemporal choice under timing risk: An experimental approach. *Journal of Risk and Uncertainty, 34*, 99–121.

Oppenheimer, D. M. (2004). Spontaneous discounting of availability in frequency judgment tasks. *Psychological Science, 15*, 100–105.

Organisation for Economic Co-operation and Development. (2017). *Behavioural insights and public policy: Lessons from around the world*. Paris, France: OECD Publishing.

Ostwald, D., Starke, L., & Hertwig, R. (2015). A normative inference approach for optimal sample sizes in decisions from experience. *Frontiers in Psychology, 6*, 1342.

Pachur, T. (2010). Recognition-based inference: When is less more in the real world? *Psychonomic Bulletin & Review, 17*, 589–598.

Pachur, T., & Hertwig, R. (2006). On the psychology of the recognition heuristic: Retrieval primacy as a key determinant of its use. *Journal of Experimental Psychology: Learning, Memory, and Cognition, 32,* 983–1002.

Pachur, T., Hertwig, R., Gigerenzer, G., & Brandstätter, E. (2013). Testing process predictions of models of risky choice: A quantitative model comparison approach. *Frontiers in Psychology, 4,* 646.

Pachur, T., Hertwig, R., & Rieskamp, J. (2013a). Intuitive judgments of social statistics: How exhaustive does sampling need to be? *Journal of Experimental Social Psychology, 49,* 1059–1077.

Pachur, T., Hertwig, R., & Rieskamp, J. (2013b). The mind as an intuitive pollster: Frugal search in social spaces. In R. Hertwig, U. Hoffrage, & the ABC Research Group, *Simple heuristics in a social world* (pp. 261–291). New York, NY: Oxford University Press.

Pachur, T., Hertwig, R., & Steinmann, F. (2012). How do people judge risks: Availability heuristic, affect heuristic, or both? *Journal of Experimental Psychology: Applied, 18,* 314–330.

Pachur, T., & Marinello, G. (2013). Expert intuitions: How to model the decision strategies of airport customs officers? *Acta Psychologica, 144,* 97–103.

Pachur, T., Mata, R., & Hertwig, R. (2017). Who dares, who errs? Disentangling cognitive and motivational roots of age differences in decisions under risk. *Psychological Science, 28,* 504–518.

Pachur, T., & Olsson, H. (2012). Type of learning task impacts performance and strategy selection in decision making. *Cognitive Psychology, 65,* 207–240.

Pachur, T., & Scheibehenne, B. (2012). Constructing preference from experience: The endowment effect reflected in external information search. *Journal of Experimental Psychology: Learning, Memory, and Cognition, 38,* 1108–1116.

Pachur, T., Schulte-Mecklenbeck, M., Murphy, R. O., & Hertwig, R. (2018). Prospect theory reflects selective allocation of attention. *Journal of Experimental Psychology: General, 147,* 147–169.

Pachur, T., Suter, R. S., & Hertwig, R. (2017). How the twain can meet: Prospect theory and models of heuristics in risky choice. *Cognitive Psychology, 93,* 44–73.

Page, S. E. (2007a). *The difference: How the power of diversity creates better groups, firms, schools, and societies.* Princeton, NJ: Princeton University Press.

Page, S. E. (2007b). Making the difference: Applying a logic of diversity. *The Academy of Management Perspectives, 21,* 6–20.

Palacios-Huerta, I., & Volij, O. (2009). Field centipedes. *The American Economic Review, 99,* 1619–1635.

Parco, J. E., Rapoport, A., & Stein, W. E. (2002). Effects of financial incentives on the breakdown of mutual trust. *Psychological Science, 13*, 292–297.

Pascal, B. (1998). Correspondance avec Fermat sur la règle des partis [Correspondence with Fermat on the problem of points]. In Michel Le Guern (Ed.), *Oeuvres complètes* (Vol. 1). Paris, France: Gallimard. (Original work published 1654)

Pascal, B. (2000). Pensées [Thoughts]. In Michel Le Guern (Ed.), *Oeuvres complètes* (Vol. 2). Paris, France: Gallimard. (Original work published 1670)

Paus, T., Keshavan, M., & Giedd, J. N. (2008). Why do many psychiatric disorders emerge during adolescence? *Nature Reviews Neuroscience, 9*, 947–957.

Payne, J. W., Bettman, J. R., & Johnson, E. J. (1988). Adaptive strategy selection in decision making. *Journal of Experimental Psychology: Learning, Memory, and Cognition, 14*, 534–552.

Payne, J. W., Bettman, J. R., & Johnson, E. J. (1993). *The adaptive decision maker*. Cambridge, United Kingdom: Cambridge University Press.

Payne, J. W., Bettman, J. R., & Luce, M. F. (1996). When time is money: Decision behavior under opportunity-cost time pressure. *Organizational Behavior and Human Decision Processes, 66*, 131–152.

Payne, M. (2016, September 3). No new cases of Zika connected to the Olympics, WHO says. *The Washington Post*. Retrieved from https://www.washingtonpost.com/news/early-lead/wp/2016/09/03/no-new-cases-of-zika-connected-to-the-olympics-who-says/

Pedroni, A., Frey, R., Bruhin, A., Dutilh, G., Hertwig, R., & Rieskamp, J. (2017). The risk elicitation puzzle. *Nature Human Behaviour, 1*, 803–809.

Pellegrini, A. D., & Bjorklund, D. F. (2004). The ontogeny and phylogeny of children's object and fantasy play. *Human Nature, 15*, 23–43.

Pennock, R. T. (2007). Models, simulations, instantiations, and evidence: The case of digital evolution. *Journal of Experimental & Theoretical Artificial Intelligence, 19*, 29–42.

Perlich, C., Provost, F., & Simonoff, J. S. (2003). Tree induction vs. logistic regression: A learning-curve analysis. *Journal of Machine Learning Research, 4*, 211–255.

Peterson, M. (2009). *An introduction to decision theory*. Cambridge, United Kingdom: Cambridge University Press.

Phelps, E., Balsano, A. B., Fay, K., Peltz, J. S., Zimmerman, S. M., Lerner, R. M., & Lerner, J. V. (2007). Nuances in early adolescent developmental trajectories of positive and problematic/risk behaviors: Findings from the 4-H study of positive youth development. *Child and Adolescent Psychiatric Clinics of North America, 16*, 473–496.

Phillips, N. D., Hertwig, R., Kareev, Y., & Avrahami, J. (2014). Rivals in the dark: How competition influences search in decisions under uncertainty. *Cognition, 133*, 104–119.

Pinard, C. A., Yaroch, A. L., Hart, M. H., Serrano, E. L., McFerren, M. M., & Esta-brooks, P. A. (2012). Measures of the home environment related to childhood obesity: A systematic review. *Public Health Nutrition, 15*, 97–109.

Pitt, M. A., Myung, I. J., & Zhang, S. (2002). Toward a method of selecting among computational models of cognition. *Psychological Review, 109*, 472–491.

Plato. (1966). *Plato in twelve volumes: Vol. 1. Euthpyhro, Apology, Crito, Phaedo, Phaedrus*. Cambridge, MA: Harvard University Press.

Pleskac, T. J. (2007). A signal detection analysis of the recognition heuristic. *Psychonomic Bulletin & Review, 14*, 379–391.

Pleskac, T. J. (2008). Decision making and learning while taking sequential risks. *Journal of Experimental Psychology: Learning Memory and Cognition, 34*, 167–185.

Pleskac, T. J. (2015). Learning models in decision making. In G. Keren & G. Wu (Eds.), *The Wiley Blackwell handbook of judgment and decision making* (Vol. 2, pp. 629–657). Chichester, United Kingdom: Wiley Blackwell.

Pleskac, T. J., & Busemeyer, J. R. (2010). Two-stage dynamic signal detection: A theory of choice, decision time, and confidence. *Psychological Review, 117*, 864–901.

Pleskac, T. J., Conradt, L., Leuker, C., & Hertwig, R. (2018). *The ecology of competition: A linchpin for the risk–reward structure*. Retrieved from https://psyarxiv.com/ewzcb/

Pleskac, T. J., Diederich, A., & Wallsten, T. S. (2015). Models of decision making under risk and uncertainty. In J. R. Busemeyer, J. T. Townsend, Z. J. Wang, & A. Eidels (Eds.), *Oxford handbook of computational and mathematical psychology* (pp. 209–231). New York, NY: Oxford University Press.

Pleskac, T. J., & Hertwig, R. (2014). Ecologically rational choice and the structure of the environment. *Journal of Experimental Psychology: General, 143*, 2000–2019.

Pleskac, T. J., Yu, S., Hopwood, C., & Liu, T. (2019). Mechanisms of deliberation during preferential choice: Perspectives from computational modeling and individual differences. *Decision, 6*, 77–107.

Plonsky, O., Teodorescu, K., & Erev, I. (2015). Reliance on small samples, the wavy recency effect, and similarity-based learning. *Psychological Review, 122*, 621–647.

Pollan, M. (2009). *Food rules: An eater's manual*. London, United Kingdom: Penguin Books.

Polonio, L., & Coricelli, G. (2015). Testing the level of consistency between choices and beliefs in games using eye-tracking. *International Journal of Game Theory, 182*, 1–40.

Popkin, R. H. (2003). *The history of scepticism: From Savonarola to Bayle*. Oxford, United Kingdom: Oxford University Press.

Popper, K. R. (1959). The propensity interpretation of probability. *The British Journal for the Philosophy of Science, 10*, 25–42.

Poti, J. M., & Popkin, B. M. (2011). Trends in energy intake among US children by eating location and food source, 1977–2006. *Journal of American Diet Association, 111*, 1156–1164.

Prelec, D. (1998). The probability weighting function. *Econometrica, 66*, 497–527.

Prelec, D., Seung, H. S., & McCoy, J. (2017). A solution to the single-question crowd wisdom problem. *Nature, 541*, 532–535.

Preston, M. G., & Baratta, P. (1948). An experimental study of the auction-value of an uncertain outcome. *American Journal of Psychology, 61*, 183–193.

Quervain, D. J. F., Fischbacher, U., Treyer, V., Schellhammer, M., Schnyder, U., Buck, A., & Fehr, E. (2004). The neural basis of altruistic punishment. *Science, 305*, 1254–1258.

Quetelet, L. A. J. (2013). *A treatise on man and the development of his faculties.* New York, NY: Cambridge University Press. (Original work published 1842)

Quiggin, J. (1982). A theory of anticipated utility. *Journal of Economic Behavior and Organization, 3*, 323–343.

Rabin, M. (1993). Incorporating fairness into game-theory and economics. *American Economic Review, 83*, 1281–1302.

Rachlin, H. (2006). Notes on discounting. *Journal of the Experimental Analysis of Behavior, 85*, 425–435.

Rakow, T., Demes, K. A., & Newell, B. R. (2008). Biased samples not mode of presentation: Re-examining the apparent underweighting of rare events in experience-based choice. *Organizational Behavior and Human Decision Processes, 106*, 168–179.

Rakow, T., & Newell, B. R. (2010). Degrees of uncertainty: An overview and framework for future research on experience-based choice. *Journal of Behavioral Decision Making, 23*, 1–14.

Ramsey, F. P. (1990). Truth and probability. In D. H. Mellor (Ed.), *Philosophical papers of F. P. Ramsey* (pp. 52–94). Cambridge, United Kingdom: Cambridge University Press. (Original work published 1926)

Rangel, J., Griffin, S. R., & Seeley, T. D. (2010). Nest-site defense by competing honey bee swarms during house-hunting. *Ethology, 116*, 608–618.

Rapoport, A. (1964). Sequential decision-making in a computer-controlled task. *Journal of Mathematical Psychology, 1*, 351–374.

Rapoport, A. (1984). Effects of wealth on portfolios under various investment conditions. *Acta Psychologica, 55*, 31–51.

Rapoport, A. (2003). Games: Centipede. In L. Nadel (Ed.), *Encyclopedia of cognitive science* (Vol. 2, pp. 196–203). London, United Kingdom: Nature Publishing Group.

Rapoport, A., Guyer, M., & Gordon, D. G. (1976). *The 2×2 game.* Michigan, MI: University of Michigan Press.

Rapoport, A., Stein, W. E., Parco, J. E., & Nicholas, T. E. (2003). Equilibrium play and adaptive learning in a three-person centipede game. *Games and Economic Behavior, 43,* 239–265.

Ratcliff, R., & Smith, P. L. (2004). A comparison of sequential sampling models for two-choice reaction time. *Psychological Review, 111,* 333–367.

Reber, R. (2017). Availability. In R. F. Pohl (Ed.), *Cognitive illusions: Intriguing phenomena in thinking, judgement and memory* (2nd ed., pp. 185–203). New York, NY: Routledge.

Rebonato, R. (2012). *Taking liberties: A critical examination of libertarian paternalism.* New York, NY: Palgrave Macmillan.

Regenwetter, M., & Robinson, M. M. (2017). The construct–behavior gap in behavioral decision research: A challenge beyond replicability. *Psychological Review, 124,* 533–550.

Rehder, B., & Waldmann, M. R. (2017). Failures of explaining away and screening off in described versus experienced causal learning scenarios. *Memory & Cognition, 45,* 245–260.

Rieskamp, J. (2008). The probabilistic nature of preferential choice. *Journal of Experimental Psychology: Learning, Memory, and Cognition, 34,* 1446–1465.

Rieskamp, J., & Otto, P. E. (2006). SSL: A theory of how people learn to select strategies. *Journal of Experimental Psychology: General, 135,* 207–236.

Roalf, D. R., Mitchell, S. H., Harbaugh, W. T., & Janowsky, J. S. (2012). Risk, reward, and economic decision making in aging. *The Journals of Gerontology. Series B. Psychological Sciences and Social Sciences, 67,* 289–298.

Roberts, B. W., & DelVecchio, W. F. (2000). The rank-order consistency of personality traits from childhood to old age: A quantitative review of longitudinal studies. *Psychological Bulletin, 126,* 3–25.

Roberts, B. W., Walton, K. E., & Viechtbauer, W. (2006). Patterns of mean-level change in personality traits across the life course: A meta-analysis of longitudinal studies. *Psychological Bulletin, 132,* 1–25.

Rode, C., Cosmides, L., Hell, W., & Tooby, J. (1999). When and why do people avoid unknown probabilities in decisions under uncertainty? Testing some predictions from optimal foraging theory. *Cognition, 72,* 269–304.

Rokach, L. (2010). Ensemble-based classifiers. *Artificial Intelligence Review, 33*, 1–39.

Rokach, L. (2016). Decision forest: Twenty years of research. *Information Fusion, 27*, 111–125.

Rolison, J. J., Hanoch, Y., Wood, S., & Liu, P. J. (2014). Risk-taking differences across the adult life span: A question of age and domain. *The Journals of Gerontology. Series B. Psychological Sciences and Social Sciences, 69*, 870–880.

Romer, D., Reyna, V. F., & Satterthwaite, T. D. (2017). Beyond stereotypes of adolescent risk taking: Placing the adolescent brain in developmental context. *Developmental Cognitive Neuroscience, 12*, 19–34.

Rong, Y., Chen, L., Zhu, T., Song, Y., Yu, M., Shan, Z., ... Liu, L. (2013). Egg consumption and risk of coronary heart disease and stroke: Dose-response meta-analysis of prospective cohort studies. *BMJ, 346*, 2–13.

Rosenbaum, G. M., Venkatraman, V., Steinberg, L., & Chein, J. M. (2018). The influences of described and experienced information on adolescent risky decision making. *Developmental Review, 47*, 148–158.

Rosenthal, R. W. (1981). Games of perfect information, predatory pricing and the chain-store paradox. *Journal of Economic Theory, 25*, 92–100.

Rosman, A., Garcia, M., Lee, S., Butler, S., & Schwartz, A. (2013). DOSPERT+M: A survey of medical risk attitudes in the United States. *Judgment and Decision Making, 8*, 470–481.

Ross, L., Greene, D., & House, P. (1977). The "false consensus effect": An egocentric bias in social perception and attribution processes. *Journal of Experimental Social Psychology, 13*, 279–301.

Roth, A. E., & Erev, I. (1995). Learning in extensive-form games: Experimental data and simple dynamic models in the intermediate term. *Games and Economic Behavior, 8*, 164–212.

Rotjan, R. D., Chabot, J. R., & Lewis, S. M. (2010). Social context of shell acquisition in Coenobita clypeatus hermit crabs. *Behavioral Ecology, 21*, 639–646.

Rumelhart, D. E., McClelland, J. L., & the PDP research group. (1986). *Parallel distributed processing: Explorations in the microstructure of cognition* (Vol. 1 & 2). Cambridge, MA: MIT Press.

Russolillo, S. (2014, May 29). Chart of the day: Millennials are really risk averse. *The Wall Street Journal*. Retrieved from https://blogs.wsj.com/moneybeat/2014/05/29/chart-of-the-day-millennials-are-really-risk-averse/

Rutledge, R. B., Smittenaar, P., Zeidman, P., Brown, H. R., Adams, R. A., Lindenberger, U., ... Dolan, R. J. (2016). Risk taking for potential rewards decreases across the lifespan. *Current Biology, 26*, 1–6.

Salali, G. D., Chaudhary, N., Thompson, J., Grace, O. M., van der Burgt, X. M., Dyble, M., ... Migliano, A. B. (2016). Knowledge-sharing networks in hunter-gatherers and the evolution of cumulative culture. *Current Biology, 26*, 2516–2521.

Samuelson, L. (1937). A note on measurement of utility. *The Review of Economic Studies, 4*, 155–161.

Sapolsky, R. M. (1997). *The trouble with testosterone*. New York, NY: Scribner.

Sargent, T. J. (1993). *Bounded rationality in macroeconomics*. Oxford, United Kingdom: Oxford University Press.

Sartre, J. P. (1944). *In camera and other plays* (S. Gilbert, Trans.). Harmondsworth, United Kingdom: Penguin.

Satterwhite, C. L., Torrone, E., Meites, E., Dunne, E. F., Mahajan, R., Ocfemia, M. C., ... Weinstock, H. (2013). Sexually transmitted infections among US women and men: Prevalence and incidence estimates, 2008. *Sexually Transmitted Diseases, 40*, 187–193.

Savage, L. J. (1954). *The foundations of statistics*. New York, NY: Wiley and Sons.

Schacter, D. L. (1999). The seven sins of memory: Insights from psychology and cognitive neuroscience. *American Psychologist, 54*, 182–202.

Schadschneider, A., Klingsch, W., Klüpfel, H., Kretz, T., Rogsch, C., & Seyfried, A. (2009). Evacuation dynamics: Empirical results, modeling and applications. In R. A. Meyers (Ed.), *Extreme environmental events* (pp. 3142–3176). New York, NY: Springer.

Schelling, T. C. (1978). *Micromotives and macrobehavior*. New York, NY: W. W. Norton & Company.

Schildberg-Hörisch, H. (2018). Are risk preferences stable? *Journal of Economic Perspectives, 32*, 135–154.

Schlegel, A., & Barry, H. I. (1991). *Adolescence: An anthropological inquiry*. New York, NY: Free Press.

Schmandt-Besserat, D. (1996). Writing. In B. M. Fagan (Ed.), *The Oxford companion to archaeology* (pp. 761–763). New York, NY: Oxford University Press.

Schoenfeld, J. D., & Ioannidis, J. P. (2013). Is everything we eat associated with cancer? A systematic cookbook review. *The American Journal of Clinical Nutrition, 97*, 127–134.

Schulz, K. M., & Sisk, C. L. (2016). The organizing actions of adolescent gonadal steroid hormones on brain and behavioral development. *Neuroscience and Biobehavioral Reviews, 70*, 148–158.

Schulze, C., Pachur, T., & Hertwig, R. (2017). How does instance-based inference about event frequencies develop? An analysis with a computational process model.

In G. Gunzelmann, A. Howes, T. Tenbrink, & E. Davelaar (Eds.), *Proceedings of the 39th Annual Meeting of the Cognitive Science Society* (pp. 1053–1058). London, United Kingdom: Cognitive Science Society.

Schurz, G., & Thorn, P. D. (2016). The revenge of ecological rationality: Strategy-selection by meta-induction within changing environments. *Minds and Machines, 26*, 31–59.

Schwartz, H. A., Eichstaedt, J. C., Kern, M. L., Dziurzynski, L., Ramones, S. M., Agrawal, M., & Ungar, L. H. (2013). Personality, gender, and age in the language of social media: The open-vocabulary approach. *PLOS ONE, 8*, e73791.

Sedlmeier, P., Hertwig, R., & Gigerenzer, G. (1998). Are judgments of the positional frequencies of letters systematically biased due to availability? *Journal of Experimental Psychology: Learning, Memory, and Cognition, 24*, 754–770.

Seeley, T. D., Visscher, P. K., & Passino, K. M. (2006). Group decision making in honey bee swarms. *American Scientist, 94*, 220–229.

Seitz, M. J., Bode, N. W. F., & Köster, G. (2016). How cognitive heuristics can explain social interactions in spatial movement. *Journal of the Royal Society Interface, 13*, 20160439.

Selten, R. (1975). Reexamination of the perfectness concept for equilibrium points in extensive games. *International Journal of Game Theory, 4*, 25–55.

Seneca, L. A. (1990). *Moral essays* (Vol. 2). Cambridge, MA: Harvard University Press. (Original work ca. 49 CE)

Seneca, L. A. (2000). *Epistles* (Vol. 3). Cambridge, MA: Harvard University Press. (Original work ca. 65 CE)

Sercombe, H. (2014). Risk, adaptation and the functional teenage brain. *Brain and Cognition, 89*, 61–69.

Seyfried, A., Steffen, B., Klingsch, W., & Boltes, M. (2005). The fundamental diagram of pedestrian movement revisited. *Journal of Statistical Mechanics: Theory and Experiment, 10*, 13–26.

Seymour, B., & Dolan, R. (2008). Emotion, decision making, and the amygdala. *Neuron, 58*, 662–671.

Shah, A. K., & Oppenheimer, D. M. (2008). Heuristics made easy: An effort-reduction framework. *Psychological Bulletin, 134*, 207–222.

Shannon, C. E., & Weaver, W. (1949). *The mathematical theory of communication.* Champaign, IL: University of Illinois Press.

Shepard, R. N. (1987). Toward a universal law of generalization for psychological science. *Science, 237*, 1317–1323.

Sher, S., & McKenzie, C. R. M. (2006). Information leakage from logically equivalent frames. *Cognition, 101,* 467–494.

Shimojo, S., Simion, C., Shimojo, E., & Scheier, C. (2003). Gaze bias both reflects and influences preference. *Nature Neuroscience, 6,* 1317–1322.

Shulman, S. T., & Lustig, R. H. (2013). A conversation with Robert H. Lustig, MD, MSL. *Pediatric Annals, 42,* 296–297.

Siegel, A. W., Cousins, J. H., Rubovits, D. S., Parsons, J. T., Lavery, B., & Crowley, C. L. (1994). Adolescents' perceptions of the benefits and risks of their own risk taking. *Journal of Emotional and Behavioral Disorders, 2,* 89–98.

Sih, A., & Del Giudice, M. (2012). Linking behavioural syndromes and cognition: A behavioural ecology perspective. *Philosophical Transactions of the Royal Society B: Biological Sciences, 367,* 2762–2772.

Silverman, M. H., Jedd, K., & Luciana, M. (2015). Neural networks involved in adolescent reward processing: An activation likelihood estimation meta-analysis of functional neuroimaging studies. *NeuroImage, 122,* 427–439.

Simon, H. A. (1945). Theory of Games and Economic Behavior by John Von Neumann and Oskar Morgenstern [Review]. *American Journal of Sociology, 50,* 558–560.

Simon, H. A. (1955). A behavioral model of rational choice. *The Quarterly Journal of Economics, 69,* 99–118.

Simon, H. A. (1956). Rational choice and the structure of the environment. *Psychological Review, 63,* 129–138.

Simon, H. A. (1982). *Models of bounded rationality: Vol. 3. Empirically grounded economic reason.* Cambridge, MA: MIT Press.

Simon, H. A. (1983). *Reason in human affairs.* Stanford, CA: Stanford University Press.

Simon, H. A. (1990). Invariants of human behavior. *Annual Review of Psychology, 41,* 1–20.

Şimşek, Ö. (2001). Linear decision rule as aspiration for simple decision heuristics. In M. I. Jordan, Y. LeCun, & S. A. Solla (Eds.), *Advances in neural information processing systems* (pp. 2904–2912). Cambridge, MA: MIT Press.

Şimşek, Ö., & Buckmann, M. (2015). Learning from small samples: An analysis of simple decision heuristics. In C. Cortes, N. Lawrence, D. D. Lee, M. Sugiyama, & R. Garnett (Eds.), *Advances in Neural Information Processing Systems 28 (NIPS 2015)* (pp. 3159–3167). Red Hook, NY: Curran.

Singh, M. (2014). Mood, food, and obesity. *Frontiers in Psychology, 5,* 925–928.

Slavin, J. L., & Lloyd, B. (2012). Health benefits of fruits and vegetables. *Advances in Nutrition, 3,* 506–516.

Slovic, P. (1964). Assessment of risk taking behavior. *Psychological Bulletin, 61*, 220–233.

Slovic, P. (1995). The construction of preference. *American Psychologist, 50*, 364–371.

Slovic, P., Finucane, M. L., Peters, E., & MacGregor, D. G. (2002). The affect heuristic. In T. Gilovich, D. Griffin, & D. Kahneman (Eds.), *Heuristics and biases: The psychology of intuitive judgment* (pp. 397–420). New York, NY: Cambridge University Press.

Slovic, P., Fischhoff, B., & Lichtenstein, S. (1982). Facts versus fears: Understanding perceived risk. In D. Kahneman, P. Slovic, & A. Tversky (Eds.), *Judgment under uncertainty: Heuristics and biases* (pp. 463–489). Cambridge, United Kingdom: Cambridge University Press.

Smedslund, J. (1955). *Multiple-probability learning; an inquiry into the origins of perception*. Oxford, United Kingdom: Akademisk.

Smith, A. (2008). *An inquiry into the nature and causes of the wealth of nations*. Oxford, United Kingdom: Clarendon Press. (Original work published 1776)

Smith, E. A., & Winterhalder, B. (Eds.). (1992). *Evolutionary ecology and human behavior*. New York, NY: Walter de Gruyter.

Sofi, F., Macchi, C., Abbate, R., Gensini, G. F., & Casini, A. (2014). Mediterranean diet and health status: An updated meta-analysis and a proposal for a literature-based adherence score. *Public Health Nutrition, 17*, 2769–2782.

Soll, J. B. (1999). Intuitive theories of information: Beliefs about the value of redundancy. *Cognitive Psychology, 38*, 317–346.

Somerville, L. H., & Casey, B. J. (2010). Developmental neurobiology of cognitive control and motivational systems. *Current Opinion in Neurobiology, 20*, 236–241.

Sorkin, R. D., Hays, C. J., & West, R. (2001). Signal-detection analysis of group decision making. *Psychological Review, 108*, 183–203.

Sozou, P. D. (1998). On hyperbolic discounting and uncertain hazard rates. *Proceedings of the Royal Society B: Biological Sciences, 265*, 2015–2020.

Spear, L. P. (2000). The adolescent brain and age-related behavioral manifestations. *Neuroscience and Biobehavioral Reviews, 24*, 417–463.

Specht, J., Egloff, B., & Schumkle, S. C. (2011). Stability and change of personality across the life course: The impact of age and major life events on mean-level and rank-order stability of the Big Five. *Journal of Personality and Social Psychology, 101*, 862–882.

Spiliopoulos, L., & Hertwig, R. (2018). *Heuristics can withstand environmental and strategic uncertainty*. Retrieved from https://papers.ssrn.com/sol3/papers.cfm?abstract_id=3263292

Spiliopoulos, L., Ortmann, A., & Zhang, L. (2018). Complexity, attention and choice in games under time constraints: A process analysis. *Journal of Experimental Psychology: Learning, Memory, and Cognition, 44*(10), 1609–1640.

Stahl, D. O. (1996). Boundedly rational rule learning in a guessing game. *Games and Economic Behavior, 16*, 303–330.

Stahl, D. O., & Wilson, P. W. (1994). Experimental evidence on players' models of other players. *Journal of Economic Behavior & Organization, 25*, 309–327.

Stahl, D. O., & Wilson, P. W. (1995). On players' models of other players: Theory and experimental evidence. *Games and Economic Behavior, 10*, 218–254.

Statistisches Bundesamt. (2011). *Statistisches Jahrbuch 2011 für die Bundesrepublik Deutschland* [Statistical yearbook 2011 for the Federal Republic of Germany]. Wiesbaden, Germany: Author.

Stearns, S. C. (1992). *The evolution of life histories.* Oxford, United Kingdom: Oxford University Press.

Steinbeck, J. (2014). *The grapes of wrath.* London, United Kingdom: Penguin Modern Classics. (Original work published 1939)

Stephens, D. W. (2002). Discrimination, discounting and impulsivity: A role for an informational constraint. *Philosophical Transactions of the Royal Society B: Biological Sciences, 357*, 1527–1537.

Sterelny, K. (2003). *Thought in a hostile world: The evolution of human cognition.* New York, NY: Wiley and Sons.

Stevens, J. R. (2010). Intertemporal choice. In M. C. Breed & J. Moore (Eds.), *Encyclopedia of animal behavior* (Vol. 2, pp. 203–208). Amsterdam, Netherlands: Elsevier.

Stevenson, M. K. (1986). A discounting model for decisions with delayed positive or negative outcomes. *Journal of Experimental Psychology: General, 115*, 131–154.

Steyvers, M., & Miller, B. (2015). Cognition and collective intelligence. In T. Malone & M. S. Bernstein (Eds.), *Handbook of Collective Intelligence* (pp. 119–125). Cambridge, MA: MIT Press.

Steyvers, M., Wallsten, T. S., Merkle, E. C., & Turner, B. M. (2014). Evaluating probabilistic forecasts with Bayesian signal detection models. *Risk Analysis, 34*, 435–452.

Stigler, G. J., & Becker, G. S. (1977). De gustibus non est disputandum. *The American Economic Review, 67*, 76–90.

Stigler, S. M. (1980). Stigler's law of eponymy. *Transactions of the New York Academy of Sciences, 39*, 147–157.

Stigler, S. M. (1991). Statistical simulation in the nineteenth century. *Statistical Science, 6*, 89–97.

Story, M., & French, S. (2004). Food advertising and marketing directed at children and adolescents in the US. *International Journal of Behavioral Nutrition Physical Activity, 1*, 3.

Stott, H. P. (2006). Cumulative prospect theory's functional menagerie. *Journal of Risk and Uncertainty, 32*, 101–130.

Stroop, J. (1932). Is the judgment of the group better than that of the average member of the group? *Journal of Experimental Psychology, 15*, 550–562.

Strotz, R. H. (1955). Myopia and inconsistency in dynamic utility maximization. *The Review of Economic Studies, 23*, 165–180.

Suleiman, A. B., Galván, A., Harden, K. P., & Dahl, R. E. (2017). Becoming a sexual being: The "elephant in the room" of adolescent brain development. *Developmental Cognitive Neuroscience, 25*, 209–220.

Sumpter, D. J. T. (2006). The principles of collective animal behaviour. *Philosophical Transactions of the Royal Society B: Biological Sciences, 361*, 5–22.

Sumpter, D. J. T., & Pratt, S. C. (2009). Quorum responses and consensus decision making. *Philosophical Transactions of the Royal Society B: Biological Sciences, 364*, 743–753.

Sun, L. H. (2016, May 27). 150 experts say Olympics must be moved or postponed because of Zika. *The Washington Post*. Retrieved from https://www.washingtonpost.com/news/to-your-health/wp/2016/05/27/125-experts-say-olympics-must-be-moved-or-postponed-because-of-zika/

Sunstein, C. R. (2015). *Why nudge? The politics of libertarian paternalism*. New Haven, CT: Yale University Press.

Sunstein, C. R., & Hastie, R. (2015). *Wiser: Getting beyond groupthink to make groups smarter*. New York, NY: Harvard Business Press.

Surowiecki, J. (2004). *The wisdom of crowds: Why the many are smarter than the few and how collective wisdom shapes business, economies, societies and nations*. Garden City, NY: Doubleday.

Suter, R. S., Pachur, T., & Hertwig, R. (2016). How affect shapes risky choice: Distorted probability weighting versus probability neglect. *Journal of Behavioral Decision Making, 29*, 437–449.

Sutton, R. S., & Barto, A. G. (1998). *Introduction to reinforcement learning*. Cambridge, MA: MIT Press Cambridge.

Taleb, N. N. (2007). *The black swan: The impact of the highly improbable*. London, United Kingdom: Penguin Books.

Tefft, B. C. (2017). Rates of motor vehicle crashes, injuries, and deaths in relation to driver age, United States, 2014–2015. Retrieved from http://aaafoundation.org/rates-motor-vehicle-crashes-injuries-deaths-relation-driver-age-united-states-2014-2015/

Thaler, R. H. (1981). Some empirical evidence on dynamic inconsistency. *Economic Letters, 8*, 201–207.

Thaler, R. H., & Sunstein, C. R. (2008). *Nudge: Improving decisions about health, wealth and happiness.* New York, NY: Simon & Schuster.

Thompson, H. S. (1955). *Proud highway: Saga of a desperate Southern gentleman, 1955–1967.* New York, NY: Ballantine Books.

Thorndike, A. N., Bright, O. J. M., Dimond, M. A., Fishman, R., & Levy, D. E. (2017). Choice architecture to promote fruit and vegetable purchases by families participating in the Special Supplemental Program for Women, Infants, and Children (WIC): Randomized corner store pilot study. *Public Health Nutrition, 20*, 1297–1305.

Thorngate, W. (1980). Efficient decision heuristics. *Behavioral Science, 25*, 219–225.

Thunnissen, D. P. (2003). *Uncertainty classification for the design and development of complex systems.* Paper presented at the 3rd Annual Predictive Methods Conference, Santa Ana, CA.

Timmermann, A. G. (2006). Forecast combinations. In G. Elliott, C. W. J. Granger, & A. G. Timmermann (Eds.), *Handbook of economic forecasting* (pp. 135–196). Amsterdam, Netherlands: North-Holland.

Todd, P. M., & Brighton, H. (2016). Building the theory of ecological rationality. *Minds and Machines, 26*, 9–30.

Todd, P. M., & Gigerenzer, G. (2012). What is ecological rationality. In P. M. Todd, G. Gigerenzer, & the ABC Research Group, *Ecological rationality: Intelligence in the world* (pp. 3–30). New York, NY: Oxford University Press.

Todd, P. M., Gigerenzer, G., & the ABC Research Group. (2012). *Ecological rationality: Intelligence in the world.* New York, NY: Oxford University Press.

Todd, P. M., Hills, T. T., & Robbins, T. W. (Eds.). (2012). *Cognitive search: Evolution, algorithms, and the brain.* Cambridge, MA: MIT Press.

Todhunter, I. (2014). *A history of the mathematical theory of probability.* London, United Kingdom: Cambridge University Press. (Original work published 1865)

Tracy, J. L., Robins, R. W., & Sherman, J. W. (2009). The practice of psychological science: Searching for Cronbach's two streams in social–personality psychology. *Journal of Personality and Social Psychology, 96*, 1206–1225.

Trautman, P., & Krause, A. (2010). *Unfreezing the robot: Navigation in dense, interacting crowds.* Paper presented at the 2010 IEEE/RSJ International Conference on Intelligent

Robots and Systems, Taipei, Taiwan. Retrieved from http://ieeexplore.ieee.org/docu ment/5654369/

Trautmann, S. T., & van de Kuilen, G. (2015). Ambiguity attitudes. *The Wiley Blackwell handbook of judgment and decision making* (Vol. 1, pp. 89–116). Chichester, United Kingdom: Wiley Blackwell.

Trippas, D., & Pachur, T. (in press). Nothing compares: Unraveling learning task effects in categorization and judgment. *Journal of Experimental Psychology: Learning, Memory, & Cognition.*

Tsetsos, K., Chater, N., & Usher, M. (2012). Salience driven value integration explains decision biases and preference reversal. *Proceedings of the National Academy of Sciences, 109*, 9659–9664.

Tu, J., & Zhou, G. (2011). Markowitz meets Talmud: A combination of sophisticated and naive diversification strategies. *Journal of Financial Economics, 99*, 204–215.

Tump, A. N., Wolf, M., Krause, J., & Kurvers, R. H. J. M. (2018). Individuals fail to reap the collective benefits of diversity because of over-reliance on personal information. *Journal of the Royal Society Interface, 15*, 20180155.

Turner, A., & Penn, A. (2002). Encoding natural movement as an agent-based system: An investigation into human pedestrian behaviour in the built environment. *Environment and Planning B: Planning & Design, 29*, 473–90.

Tversky, A. (1967). Utility theory and additivity analysis of risky choices. *Journal of Experimental Psychology, 75*, 27–36.

Tversky, A. (1969). Intransitivity of preferences. *Psychological Review, 76*, 31–48.

Tversky, A. (1972). Elimination by aspects: A theory of choice. *Psychological Review, 79*, 281–299.

Tversky, A., & Edwards, W. (1966). Information versus reward in binary choices. *Journal of Experimental Psychology, 71*, 680–683.

Tversky, A., & Fox, C. R. (1995). Weighing risk and uncertainty. *Psychological Review, 102*, 269–283.

Tversky, A., & Kahneman, D. (1973). Availability: A heuristic for judging frequency and probability. *Cognitive Psychology, 5*, 207–232.

Tversky, A., & Kahneman, D. (1974). Judgment under uncertainty: Heuristics and biases. *Science, 185*, 1124–1131.

Tversky, A., & Kahneman, D. (1992). Advances in prospect theory: Cumulative representation of uncertainty. *Journal of Risk and Uncertainty, 5*, 297–323.

Tversky, A., & Wakker, P. P. (1995). Risk attitudes and decision weights. *Econometrica, 63*, 1255–1280.

Twain, M. (2004). *Pudd'nhead Wilson*. London, United Kingdom: Penguin Classics. (Original work published 1894)

Tymula, A., Rosenberg Belmaker, L. A., Roy, A. K., Ruderman, L., Manson, K., Glimcher, P. W., & Levy, I. (2012). Adolescents' risk-taking behavior is driven by tolerance to ambiguity. *Proceedings of the National Academy of Sciences, 109*, 17135–17140.

Uexküll, J. J. (1992). A stroll through the worlds of animals and men: A picture book of invisible worlds. *Semiotica, 89*, 319–391.

Ülkümen, G., Fox, C. R., & Malle, B. F. (2016). Two dimensions of subjective uncertainty: Clues from natural language. *Journal of Experimental Psychology: General, 145*, 1280–1297.

Ungemach, C., Chater, N., & Stewart, N. (2009). Are probabilities overweighted or underweighted when rare outcomes are experienced (rarely)? *Psychological Science, 20*, 473–479.

United States Department of Agriculture. (2015). MyPlate. Retrieved from https://www.fns.usda.gov/tn/myplate

Urminsky, O., & Zauberman, G. (2015). The psychology of intertemporal preferences. In G. Keren & G. Wu (Eds.), *The Wiley Blackwell handbook of judgment and decision making* (Vol. 1, pp. 141–181). Chichester, United Kingdom: Wiley Blackwell.

Valone, T. J., & Templeton, J. J. (2002). Public information for the assessment of quality: A widespread social phenomenon. *Philosophical Transactions of the Royal Society B: Biological Sciences, 357*, 1549–1557.

van de Kuilen, G., & Wakker, P. P. (2011). The midweight method to measure attitudes toward risk and ambiguity. *Management Science, 57*, 582–598.

van den Bos, W. (2013). Neural mechanisms of social reorientation across adolescence. *The Journal of Neuroscience, 33*, 13581–13601.

van den Bos, W., Cohen, M. X., Kahnt, T., & Crone, E. (2012). Striatum-medial prefrontal cortex connectivity predicts developmental changes in reinforcement learning. *Cerebral Cortex, 22*, 1247–1255.

van den Bos, W., Crone, E. A., Meuwese, R., & Güroğlu, B. (2018). Social network cohesion in school classes promotes prosocial behavior. *PLOS ONE, 13*, e0194656.

van den Bos, W., & Hertwig, R. (2017). Adolescents display distinctive tolerance to ambiguity and to uncertainty during risky decision making. *Scientific Reports, 7*, 40962.

van der Waerden, B. L. (Ed.). (1975). *Die Werke von Jakob Bernoulli* [The works of Jacob Bernoulli] (Vol. 2). Basel, Switzerland: Birkhäuser.

van Dolder, D., & van den Assem, M. J. (2018). The wisdom of the inner crowd in three large natural experiments. *Nature Human Behaviour, 2*, 21–26.

van Schaik, P., Kusev, P., & Juliusson, A. (2011). Human preferences and risky choices. *Frontiers in Psychology, 2*, 333.

van Trijp, H. C. (2009). Consumer understanding and nutritional communication: Key issues in the context of the new EU legislation. *European Journal of Nutrition, 48*, 41–48.

Vogt, K. (2010). Ancient skepticism. In E. N. Zalta (Ed.), *The Stanford encyclopedia of philosophy*. Retrieved from https://plato.stanford.edu/entries/skepticism-ancient/

Volterra, V. (1928). Variations and fluctuations of the number of individuals in animal species living together. *ICES Journal of Marine Science, 3*, 3–51.

von Mises, R. (1961). *Probability, statistics, and truth*. New York, NY: Dover Publications. (Original work published 1928)

von Neumann, J., & Morgenstern, O. (2007). *Theory of games and economic behavior*. Princeton, NJ: Princeton University Press. (Original work published 1944)

von Rueden, C., Gurven, M., & Kaplan, H. (2011). Why do men seek status? Fitness payoffs to dominance and prestige. *Proceedings of the Royal Society B: Biological Sciences, 278*, 2223–2232.

Vul, E., Goodman, N., Griffiths, T. L., & Tenenbaum, J. B. (2014). One and done? Optimal decisions from very few samples. *Cognitive Science, 38*, 599–637.

Vul, E., & Pashler, H. (2008). Measuring the crowd within: Probabilistic representations within individuals. *Psychological Science, 19*, 645–647.

Wakker, P. P. (2010). *Prospect theory for risk and ambiguity*. Cambridge, United Kingdom: Cambridge University Press.

Wald, A. (1945). Statistical decision functions which minimize the maximum risk. *The Annals of Mathematics, 46*, 265–280.

Wald, A. (1947). *Sequential analysis*. New York, NY: Wiley and Sons.

Walker, A., & Smith, S. (1987). Mitochondrial DNA and human evolution. *Nature, 325*, 1–5.

Walker, W. E., Harremoës, P., Rotmans, J., van der Sluijs, J. P., van Asselt, M. B., Janssen, P., & Krayer von Krauss, M. P. (2003). Defining uncertainty: A conceptual basis for uncertainty management in model-based decision support. *Integrated Assessment, 4*, 5–17.

Wang, X. T., Zheng, R., Xuan, Y.-H., Chen, J., & Li, S. (2016). Not all risks are created equal: A twin study and meta-analyses of risk taking across seven domains. *Journal of Experimental Psychology: General, 145*, 1548–1560.

Watts, T. W., Duncan, G. J., & Quan, H. (2018). Revisiting the marshmallow test: A conceptual replication investigating links between early delay of gratification and later outcomes. *Psychological Science, 29*, 1159–1177.

Weber, B. J., & Chapman, G. B. (2007). The combined effects of risk and time on choice: Does uncertainty eliminate the immediacy effect? Does delay eliminate the certainty effect? *Organizational Behavior and Human Decision Processes, 96*, 104–108.

Weber, E. U. (2010). Risk attitude and preference. *Wiley Interdisciplinary Reviews: Cognitive Science, 1*, 79–88.

Weber, E. U., Shafir, S., & Blais, A. R. (2004). Predicting risk sensitivity in humans and lower animals: Risk as variance or coefficient of variation. *Psychological Review, 111*, 430–445.

Weisbart, D. (Producer), & Ray, N. (Director). (1955). *Rebel without a cause* [Motion picture]. United States: Warner Bros. Entertainment.

Wendt, S., & Czaczkes, T. J. (2017). Individual ant workers show self-control. *Biology Letters, 13*, 96–100.

Wertz, A. E., & Wynn, K. (2014a). Selective social learning of plant edibility in 6- and 18-month-old infants. *Psychological Science, 25*, 874–882.

Wertz, A. E., & Wynn, K. (2014b). Thyme to touch: Infants possess strategies that protect them from dangers posed by plants. *Cognition, 130*, 44–49.

Whiten, A., & Byrne, R. W. (1988). Tactical deception in primates. *Behavioral and Brain Sciences, 11*, 233–244.

Whiten, A., & Byrne, R. W. (1997). *Machiavellian intelligence II: Extensions and evaluations* (Vol. 2). Cambridge, United Kingdom: Cambridge University Press.

Wilke, C. O. (2001). Selection for fitness versus selection for robustness in RNA secondary structure folding. *Evolution, 55*, 2412–2420.

Willoughby, T., Tavernier, R., Hamza, C., Adachi, P. J., & Good, M. (2014). The triadic systems model perspective and adolescent risk taking. *Brain and Cognition, 89*, 114–115.

Wilson, M., & Daly, M. (1997). Life expectancy, economic inequality, homicide, and reproductive timing in Chicago neighbourhoods. *BMJ, 314*, 1271–1274.

Wilson, T. D., & Gilbert, D. T. (2003). Affective forecasting. *Advances in Experimental Social Psychology, 35*, 345–411.

Wimsatt, W. C. (2007). *Re-engineering philosophy for limited beings: Piecewise approximations to reality*. Cambridge, MA: Harvard University Press.

Wing, R. R., & Phelan, S. (2005). Long-term weight loss maintenance. *The American Journal of Clinical Nutrition, 82*, 222–225.

Winterfeldt, D. V., & Edwards, W. (1986). *Decision analysis and behavioral research*. Cambridge, United Kingdom: Cambridge University Press.

Wixted, J. T., & Wells, G. L. (2017). The relationship between eyewitness confidence and identification accuracy: A new synthesis. *Psychological Science in the Public Interest, 18,* 10–65.

Wolf, M., Krause, J., Carney, P. A., Bogart, A., & Kurvers, R. H. J. M. (2015). Collective intelligence meets medical decision-making: The collective outperforms the best radiologist. *PLOS ONE, 10,* e0134269.

Wolf, M., van Doorn, G. S., Leimar, O., & Weissing, F. J. (2007). Life-history trade-offs favour the evolution of animal personalities. *Nature, 447,* 581–584.

Wolfe, A., Frank, R. H., & Cook, P. J. (1996). The winner-take-all society: How more and more Americans compete for ever fewer and bigger prizes, encouraging economic waste, income inequality, and an impoverished cultural life. *Contemporary Sociology, 25,* 539–541.

Woolley, A. W., Chabris, C. F., Pentland, A., Hashmi, N., & Malone, T. W. (2010). Evidence for a collective intelligence factor in the performance of human groups. *Science, 330,* 686–688.

World Bank. (2015). *World development report 2015: Mind, society and behaviour.* Washington, DC: Author.

World Food Programme. (2016). The year in review 2016. Retrieved from http://documents.wfp.org/stellent/groups/public/documents/eb/wfp291465.pdf

World Health Organization. (2018). Fact sheet N°311: Obesity and overweight. Retrieved from http://www.who.int/news-room/fact-sheets/detail/obesity-and-overweight

Wu, G., & Gonzalez, R. (1996). Curvature of the probability weighting function. *Management Science, 42,* 1676–1690.

Wulff, D. U., Hills, T. T., & Hertwig, R. (2015a). How short-and long-run aspirations impact search and choice in decisions from experience. *Cognition, 144,* 29–37.

Wulff, D. U., Hills, T. T., & Hertwig, R. (2015b). Online product reviews and the description–experience gap. *Journal of Behavioral Decision Making, 28,* 214–223.

Wulff, D. U., Mergenthaler-Canseco, M., & Hertwig, R. (2018). A meta-analytic review of two modes of learning and the description–experience gap. *Psychological Bulletin, 144,* 140–176.

Wulff, D. U., & Pachur, T. (2016). Modeling valuations from experience: A comment on Ashby and Rakow (2014). *Journal of Experimental Psychology: Learning, Memory, and Cognition, 42,* 158–166.

Yaniv, I. (1997). Weighting and trimming: Heuristics for aggregating judgments under uncertainty. *Organizational Behavior and Human Decision Processes, 69,* 237–249.

Yaniv, I., & Foster, D. (1997). Precision and accuracy of judgmental estimation. *Journal of Behavioral Decision Making, 10*, 21–32.

Yates, J. F. (1990). *Judgment and decision making.* Upper Saddle River, NJ: Prentice-Hall.

Yates, J. F., & Zukowsky, L. G. (1976). Characterization of ambiguity in decision making. *Behavioral Science, 21*, 19–25.

Yechiam, E., & Ert, E. (2011). Risk attitude in decision making: In search of trait-like constructs. *Topics in Cognitive Science, 3*, 166–186.

Yetton, P. W., & Bottger, P. C. (1982). Individual versus group problem solving: An empirical test of a best-member strategy. *Organizational Behavior and Human Performance, 29*, 307–321.

Zacks, R. T., & Hasher, L. (2002). Frequency processing: A twenty-five-year perspective. In P. Sedlmeier & T. Betsch (Eds.), *Etc: Frequency processing and cognition* (pp. 21–36). Oxford, United Kingdom: Oxford University Press.

Zalaudek, I., Argenziano, G., Soyer, H. P., Corona, R., Sera, F., Blum, A., ... Kopf, A. W. (2006). Three-point checklist of dermoscopy: An open internet study. *British Journal of Dermatology, 154*, 431–437.

Zeigenfuse, M. D., Pleskac, T. J., & Liu, T. (2014). Rapid decisions from experience. *Cognition, 131*, 181–194.

Zick, C. D., & Stevens, R. B. (2011). Time spent eating and its implications for Americans' energy balance. *Social Indicators Research, 101*, 267–273.

Zimring, F. E., & Laqueur, H. (2015). Kids, groups, and crime: In defense of conventional wisdom. *Journal of Research in Crime and Delinquency, 52*, 403–413.

Name Index

Abarca-Gómez, L., 112
Abbate, R., 114
Abdellaoui, M., 138, 163, 166
Adachi, P. J., 306
Adami, C., 287, 289, 331
Addessi, E., 123
Adriani, W., 317
Aiello, L. C., 291
Ainslie, G., 177
Akbaraly, T. N., 117
Al-Abideen, H., 275, 282
Albert, D., 313, 322
Al-Bosta, S., 282
Aldridge, V., 123
Alemanno, A., 119
Algra, P. R., 246
Allais, M., 30, 47
Almeida, S. R., 118
Ambady, N., 73
Amorim, D., 261
Analytis, P. P., 259, 262
Anderson, J. R., 286
Andrade, A. M., 124
Andrews, C., 127
Annas, J., 345
Anusic, I., 330, 337
Archer, E., 114
Arendt, H., 4
Argenziano, G., 246
Ariely, D., 124
Arkes, H. R., 7, 256, 360

Armbruster, T., 74
Armstrong, B., 16
Armstrong, J. S., 252, 261
Arnauld, A., 346, 348
Arnett, J., 320
Arrow, K., 7, 46
Artinger, F., 141, 240
Ashby, N. J., 164
Ashpole, B. C., 241
Asimov, I., 191, 205
Aslin, R. N., 179, 243
Atkinson, A. B., 82
Attaran, A., 71
Avrahami, J., 134, 234, 237

Bachman, S. L., 246
Baddeley, R., 168, 169, 170
Baker, J., 4
Baltes, P. B., 330
Bang, D., 245, 255
Baptista, F., 124
Baratta, P., 156, 157, 158, 159
Barclay, E., 113
Barclay, P., 333
Bargh, J. A., 122
Barkoczi, D., 259
Barkow, J. H., 285, 289
Barnes, J., 345
Baron, J., 67
Baron, R. S., 15, 248
Barrett, H. C., 7

Barro, S., 261

Barron, G., 15, 133, 134, 135, 137, 156, 162, 163, 233

Barry, H. I., 307

Bartholomew, D. J., 340

Bartlema, A., 80

Barto, A. G., 144

Batchelor, R., 249

Bateson, M., 127, 323, 333

Beck, U., 325

Becker, G. S., 327, 339

Becker, J. B., 323

Beglinger, B., 73

Bell, C. C., 323

Bellisle, F. D., 122

Benartzi, S., 199, 201

Benjamin, A. S., 258

Benjamin, D. K., 87, 331

Benzion, U., 176, 177

Bercovitch, F. B., 316

Bergert, F. B., 78, 217

Berkowitz, R. I., 124

Berner, E. S., 255

Bernoulli, D., 29, 47, 153, 154, 155, 156, 157

Bernoulli, J., 349

Bernoulli, N., 153, 154, 155, 159, 174

Bernstein, M. S., 245, 248

Beshears, J., 119

Best, R., 334, 336, 339

Betsch, T., 75

Bettman, J. R., 5, 31, 100, 146, 257

Betts, R. K., 255

Bhatia, S., 164

Bienenstock, E., 37, 259

Bierner, A., 118

Binmore, K., 67, 92, 357

Birch, L. L., 122, 123

Birnbaum, M. H., 155, 157

Bjorklund, D. F., 315, 316

Blair, S. N., 114

Blais, A. R., 14, 132, 133, 135, 162, 328, 329, 330

Blakemore, S.-J., 313

Blankenstein, N. E., 319

Blass, E. M. A., 122

Blavatskyy, P. R., 159

Bode, N. W. F., 270, 276

Bogacz, R., 146

Bogart, A., 246

Bohr, Niels, 4

Boland, P. J., 249

Bolay, K., 269

Boltes, M., 273

Bonaccio, S., 74

Bond, C. F., 77

Bonem, E. M., 333

Bordalo, P., 172

Bornstein, G., 230

Bottger, P. C., 247, 248, 252

Bowlby, J., 307

Boyd, R., 248, 268, 286

Bradbury, M. A., 204

Bradley, R., 351

Brandenburger, A., 226

Brandstätter, E., 10, 49

Braver, T. S., 189

Breaugh, J. A., 121

Brehmer, B., 214

Brenner, L. A., 256

Brezzi, M., 18

Bright, O. J. M., 119

Brighton, H., 9, 23, 37, 48, 74, 90, 259, 262, 294, 298, 308, 310

Briley, D. A., 338

Bröder, A., 49, 216

Brody, R., 87

Bronfenbrenner, U., 317

Broomell, S. B., 164, 249, 253

Broseta, B., 97

Brown, E., 146

Brown, G., 259

Brown, S., 144

Brownell, K. D., 122

Bruine de Bruin, W., 315, 320

Brumbach, B. H., 309, 311

Brunswik, E., 9, 11, 16, 96, 245, 289, 360
Bruza, P. D., 8
Buchanan, C. M., 323
Buchner, F. L., 117
Buckmann, M., 11, 210
Budescu, D. V., 61, 249, 253, 255, 259, 261, 349
Buffon, G. L. L., 155, 156, 159, 174
Busemeyer, J. R., 8, 14, 133, 134, 144, 172, 214, 256
Buss, D. M., 285, 286
Butler, S., 334
Buzna, L., 269
Byrne, R. W., 110, 242

Calderwood, R., 208, 212
Caliendo, M., 327
Camazine, S., 272
Camerer, C., 15, 66, 97, 159, 228
Camilleri, A. R., 137, 144, 165, 166
Caraco, T., 176
Cardoos, S. L., 313
Carnap, R., 352
Carneades, 345
Carney, P. A., 246
Carroll, L., 314
Carroll, M. D., 126
Carruthers, M., 13
Casey, B. J., 313
Casini, A., 114
Caspi, A., 330
Casswell, S., 124
Cavalli-Sforza, L. L., 268
Cawley, J., 118
Cernadas, E., 261
Cesarini, D., 331
Cesario, J., 292
Chabot, J. R., 18, 225
Chabris, C. F., 20
Chapman, G. B., 176, 177
Charness, N., 334, 336, 339
Chater, N., 8, 135, 137, 163, 286
Chavez, A., 155, 157

Chein, J. M., 313, 317
Chen, E., 255, 322
Chen, J., 331
Chen, S. E., 121
Chiarotti, F., 317
Chisholm, J. S., 311
Choi, J. J., 119
Chong, J. K., 97
Cicero, 344, 345, 347
Ciriolo, E., 118
Clancy, T., 89
Clark, W. A., 5, 8, 23, 327
Clauset, A., 82
Clemen, R. T., 252
Clinton-Cirocco, A., 208, 212
Coatney, M., 177
Codling, E., 276
Cohen, D., 162
Cohen, J., 309
Cohen, J. D., 18, 146
Cohen, M. X., 322
Cohen, O., 162
Cohn, L., 321
Coleman, J., 314
Colman, A. M., 230
Combs, B., 72, 77
Condorcet, M., 249
Conradt, L., 12, 58
Conroy-Beam, D., 285, 286
Cook, J. M., 83
Cook, P. J., 323
Copeland, W., 306
Coricelli, G., 97, 101
Cosmides, L., 67, 285
Costa-Gomes, M. A., 97, 101
Couzin, I., 20, 272
Cover, T. M., 300
Crawford, V. P., 97
Cronbach, L. J., 328
Crone, E., 313, 319, 322
Cross, G. S., 115, 126
Csikszentmihalyi, M., 316
Czaczkes, T. J., 179

Dahl, R. E., 313, 314
Dai, J., 187, 188
Dalal, R. S., 74
Dall, S. R. X., 331
Dallacker, M., 115, 120, 121, 122, 123, 125, 127
Daly, M., 179
Dana, J., 249, 259, 261
Danchin, E., 241
Darwin, C., 113
Daston, L., 69, 347, 349
Davidson, D., 81
Davies, N. B., 285
Davis, J. H., 248
Davis, J. N., 19
Davis-Stober, C. P., 248, 249, 253, 256, 259, 260, 261, 336
Daw, N. D., 134, 135, 288
Dawes, R. M., 32, 101, 108, 259
Day, F. R., 331
Dayan, P., 288
Deary, I. J., 340
De Finetti, B., 68, 352
Defoe, D., 13, 17
Defoe, I. N., 317
Del Giudice, M., 327, 331
DeLosh, E. L, 214
DelVecchio, W. F., 338
Demes, K. A., 137
DeMiguel, V., 199
de Montaigne, M., 346
Dennett, D. C., 287
Denrell, J., 142, 193
De Polavieja, G. G., 245
Depping, M. K., 333
Derex, M., 248
Descartes, René, 346
Devetag, G. M., 97, 101
de Weerth, C., 331
de Zoete, A., 246
Dhami, M. K., 96
Dickens, W. T., 340
Diederich, A., 10, 144, 166

Diehl, R. L., 289
Di Guida, S., 97
Dimond, M. A., 119
Dohmen, T., 327, 328, 329, 333, 334
Dolan, R., 110
Doom, J. R., 311
Dougan, W. R., 87
Dougherty, M. R. P., 74
Doursat, R., 37, 259
Dovey, T. M., 123
Downs, J. S., 127
Dua, P., 249
Dubas, J. S., 317
Dudai, Y., 13
Dunbar, R. I. M., 73, 78, 242, 291
Duncan, G. J., 311
Dunlap, A. S., 286
Dutka, J., 155
Dutt, V., 15, 144, 152

Ebbesen, E. B., 175
Eccles, J. S., 323
Eckstein, M. P., 252
Edwards, W., 14, 67, 68, 133, 134, 147, 151, 155, 157, 159, 288, 347, 351, 358
Egloff, B., 339
Einhorn, H. J., 160, 172
Eisthen, H., 292
Elliott, L., 192
Ellis, B. J., 309, 310, 311, 331
Ellsberg, D., 66, 182, 319, 351, 357
Ellsworth, P. C., 333
Elvers, H.-D., 349
Endler, J. A., 286
Engel, C., 326, 361
Enkvist, T., 216
Epstein, J. M., 72
Erev, I., 15, 16, 49, 61, 92, 133, 134, 135, 137, 152, 156, 162, 163, 187, 221, 232, 233, 319, 322, 328, 351
Erickson, M. A., 16, 214
Ert, E., 162, 328

Ervin, R. B., 126
Estes, W. K., 134, 164
Evgeniou, T., 261

Fabio, A., 309
Falk, A., 329, 333
Fama, E. F., 51
Farkas, I. J., 269
Fawcett, T. W., 10, 310
Fechner, H. B., 86, 100
Fehr, E., 58, 240
Feld, S. L., 247, 249
Feldman, M. W., 268
Fennell, J., 168, 169, 170
Fermat, P., 347
Fernández, G., 313
Fernandez-Celemin, L., 115
Fernández-Delgado, M., 261
Ferrero, J., 306
Fey, M., 230, 231
Feynman, R., 343
Fiedler, K., 74, 86
Fiedler, S., 144, 156
Fiese, B. H., 124
Figner, B., 317
Figueredo, A. J., 309, 311
Fildes, A., 121
Finucane, M. M., 74, 112
Fischbacher, U., 240
Fischhoff, B., 72, 75, 315, 320
Fisher, I., 177
Fishman, R., 119
Fiske, A. P., 77
Fleischhut, N., 240
Flynn, J. R., 340
Fossen, F., 327
Foster, D., 255
Fox, C. R., 15, 61, 67, 135, 137, 144,
    155, 161, 162, 167, 349, 350
Fraley, R. C., 331
Frank, R. H., 323
Frankenhuis, W. E., 242, 309, 310, 311,
    331

Franks, N., 272
Fraundorf, S. H., 258
Frederick, S., 175, 176
French, S., 122
Fretwell, S. D., 58
Freund, A. M., 333
Frey, R., 139, 141, 146, 149, 150, 163, 165,
    322, 327, 328, 329, 330, 336, 337, 338
Friedman, D., 290
Friedman, J., 37, 260
Frisch, D., 67
Fristoe, N., 177
Frith, C. D., 245
Fry, A. F., 180
Fu, W. T., 146
Fudenberg, D., 232
Fuhrmann, D., 313
Funder, D. C., 339
Funk, S. G., 198

Gaba, A., 199
Gächter, S., 228
Gaissmaier, W., 8, 32, 74
Galesic, M., 71, 74, 77, 86, 87
Galloway, A. T., 123
Galton, F., 247, 251
Galván, A., 314
Gangestad, S. W., 307, 309
Garcia, M., 333
Garcia-Retamero, R., 326
Garlappi, L., 199
Geary, D. C., 315
Geier, C., 313
Geiger, S. D., 127
Geisler, W. S., 289
Geman, S., 37, 259
Gennaioli, N., 172
Gensini, G. F., 114
Gershman, S. J., 8, 134
Gershman, S. K., 134
Gettys, C. F., 74
Gibbert, M., 139
Gibson, J. J., 273, 289

Giedd, J. N., 313

Gigerenzer, G., 5, 7, 8, 9, 10, 11, 21, 23, 32, 37, 48, 49, 73, 75, 79, 82, 90, 93, 108, 170, 236, 259, 262, 267, 294, 297, 298, 304, 307, 326, 349, 351, 352, 358, 359, 360, 361

Gigone, D., 251

Gilbert, D. T., 183

Gillies, D., 352

Gilovich, T., 9

Giraldeau, L.-A., 241

Gittins, J. C., 18

Glantz, S. A., 114

Glazebrook, K., 18

Glöckner, A., 49, 144, 156, 163, 165, 167, 168

Goldberg, M. E., 122

Goldstein, D. G., 8, 11, 21, 255, 297, 298

Goldstein, M. W., 160

Goldstone, R. L., 241

Golsteyn, B., 329, 333

Gonzalez, C., 15, 139, 144, 152

Gonzalez, R., 159, 160, 333

Good, M., 306

Goodman, N., 14, 139, 291

Gopnik, A., 312

Gorbachev, Mikhail, 4

Gordon, D. G., 95

Gordon, M. J., 198

Gorn, G. J., 122

Goulbourne, P., 207

Graber, M. L., 255

Gray, W. D., 146

Green, L., 176, 177, 179, 180, 189

Greene, D., 77

Gregory, A., 202

Griffin, D., 9, 256

Griffin, S. R., 226

Griffiths, T. L., 8, 14, 139, 286, 291, 312

Grigsby-Toussaint, D. S., 127

Grinblatt, M., 202

Griskevicius, V., 243

Grofman, B., 247, 248, 249, 251, 254

Grunert, K. G., 115

Grüne-Yanoff, T., 120

Grusec, J., 176

Gureckis, T. M., 16

Gurven, M., 314

Guyer, M., 95

Hacking, I., 22, 31, 61, 348, 349

Hadar, L., 15, 137, 143, 144

Hahn, U., 166

Haisley, E., 203

Halford, J. C. G., 123

Hall, S., 323

Halpern, D., 119

Halpern-Felsher, B. L., 315

Hamlin, R. P., 265

Hammerstein, P., 286

Hammond, K. R., 208, 360

Hamza, C., 306

Hand, G. A., 114

Hanoch, Y., 333

Hansen, A., 273

Harbaugh, W. T., 333

Harden, K. P., 314

Hardin, G., 272

Harris, J. L., 122

Harris, R., 259

Harris, R. D., 202

Harrison, G. W., 328

Harsanyi, J. C., 91, 92

Hasher, L., 86

Hashmi, N., 20

Hastie, R., 20, 249, 251

Hastie, T., 37, 260

Hau, R., 15, 49, 137, 146, 163, 165

Hautz, W. E., 255

Hawkes, C., 115

Hawkins, G., 144

Hayden, B. Y., 154, 155

Hays, C. J., 252

Heathcote, A., 144

Helbing, D., 19, 265, 266, 269, 270, 273, 275, 282

Helfinstein, S. M., 321
Hell, W., 67
Henderson, L., 265
Hendy, H. M., 125
Henninger, F., 144, 156
Hens, T., 204
Hertle, H. H., 3, 4
Hertwig, R., 5, 7, 8, 9, 10, 12, 14, 15,
    16, 17, 19, 24, 31, 37, 39, 47, 48, 49,
    51, 53, 54, 56, 58, 60, 63, 67, 69, 71,
    72, 73, 74, 75, 78, 84, 93, 95, 96, 97,
    108, 109, 115, 119–120, 120, 122,
    127, 133, 134, 135, 137, 138, 139,
    141, 144, 156, 162, 163, 164, 165,
    166, 167, 170, 171, 173, 174, 187,
    193, 204, 221, 226, 227, 233, 234,
    236, 237, 240, 242, 246, 249, 257,
    258, 289, 291, 294, 317, 318, 319,
    322, 326, 327, 328, 331, 336, 339,
    351, 359, 360, 361
Herzberg, J., 314
Herzog, S. M., 12, 249, 255, 256, 257,
    258, 259
Hibon, M., 261
Highhouse, S., 330
Hilbig, B. E., 144, 156
Hilgard, J., 189
Hill, L., 124
Hill, R. A., 73, 78
Hills, T. T., 14, 72, 77, 138, 139, 141,
    322
Hintze, A., 242, 287, 289, 292, 293, 294,
    301, 302, 331
Ho, T.-H., 97, 159
Hoffmann, J. A., 216, 217
Hoffrage, U., 5, 10, 12, 93, 96, 226, 242,
    301, 359
Hogarth, R. M., 10, 17, 93, 172, 199, 204
Hollands, G. J., 119
Holmes, P., 146
Hopwood, C., 135
Horn, S. S., 21, 86
Horvitz, E. J., 8

Hourany, L., 330
House, P., 77
Houston, A. I., 178, 310, 331
Huffman, D., 329, 333
Humphrey, N. K., 110
Hung, H. C., 117
Hutchinson, J. M., 48, 297
Hytönen, K., 313

Imai, W., 321
Ioannidis, J. P., 114
Isaac, R. M., 290

Jackson, D. N., 330
Jacobs, H., 200
James, D., 290
Jandrig, B., 349
Janis, I. L., 248
Janowsky, J. S., 333
Jarick, J. M., 124
Jarvstad, A., 166
Jedd, K., 313
Jefferson, T., 119
Jeffery, R. W., 121
Jensen, M., 273
Jimura, K., 189
Johannesson, M., 331
Johansson, A., 269, 270, 273, 275, 282
Johnson, E. J., 5, 31, 100, 257
Johnson, J. J., 172
Johnson, K., 260
Johnson, M., 313
Johnston, R. H., 119
Jones, B. C., 8
Jones, B. L., 124
Jones, L. V., 198
Jones, M. N., 14
Jones, R. L., 77
Jones, S., 124
Jorland, G., 155
Josef, A., 328, 329, 331, 334, 335, 336,
    338, 339
Joshipura, K. J., 117

Juliusson, A., 329
Juni, M. Z., 252
Juslin, P., 38, 86, 209, 210, 212, 214, 215, 216, 217, 218, 221

Kable, J. W., 183, 185, 186
Kacelnik, A., 178, 323, 333
Kael, P., 87
Kagel, J. H., 176
Kahneman, D., 9, 14, 32, 47, 49, 62, 71, 74, 75, 93, 131, 132, 135, 136, 143, 155, 157, 159, 160, 161, 163, 183, 187, 349, 351, 359
Kahnt, T., 322
Kameda, T., 249
Kämmer, J. E., 255, 256
Kandori, M., 92
Kaplan, H. S., 307, 309, 310, 314
Kareev, Y., 73, 85, 134, 234, 237, 291
Karelaia, N., 10, 93
Karlsson, L., 214, 216
Katsikopoulos, K. V., 9, 10, 14, 37, 257
Kaufmann, C., 203, 204
Kaunitz, L., 68, 69
Kearns, C. E., 114
Kellen, D., 137, 144, 156, 163, 164, 166, 167, 168, 170, 336
Kemel, E., 166
Kemp, C., 8, 286
Keren, G., 176
Kerr, N. L., 248
Keshavan, M., 313
Keynes, J. M., 32, 61, 66, 352, 353, 354–355, 357
Khader, P. H., 86
Khomami, N., 207
Kidd, C., 179, 243
Kiefer, J., 15, 49, 137, 163
Kirkorian, H. L., 122
Kit, B. K., 126
Klein, G., 207, 208, 212
Klingsch, W., 273
Klucharev, V., 313

Knight, F. H., 22, 29, 47, 352–354, 355, 357
Knoll, L. J., 313
Koleini, M. F., 122
Kolmogorov, A. N., 352
Koriat, A., 247, 248, 255, 256
Köster, G., 270
Krause, A., 263
Krause, J., 20, 246, 248, 252
Krause, S., 20, 248
Krebs, J. R., 285
Kreiner, J., 68, 69
Kresge, D. L., 124
Kritikos, A., 327
Krizan, Z., 61
Krockow, E. M., 230
Kroll, Y., 198
Kruschke, J. K., 16, 214
Kugler, T., 230
Kühberger, A., 67
Kuhn, M., 260
Kuncheva, L., 248, 261
Kunda, Z., 86
Kunina-Habenicht, O., 255
Kurvers, R. H. J. M., 246, 247, 252, 254, 255, 256
Kurzban, R., 7
Kurzenhäuser, S., 71
Kusev, P., 329
Kvam, P. D., 8, 292, 301, 302

Laan, A., 245, 248, 249
Ladha, K. K., 249, 252
Lagnado, D. A., 68
Lai, T. L., 18
Laibson, D., 119
Lakshmikanth, S. K., 255
Laming, D. R. J., 144
La-Ornual, D., 183
Laplace, P.-S., 61, 69, 347, 349
Laqueur, H., 322
Larrick, R. P., 245, 247, 248, 249, 251, 252, 253

Larson, R., 316
Laube, C., 313
Laviola, G., 317
Lawn, M., 340
Lawson, T., 354
Layman, L., 72
Lebon, G., 278
Lee, M., 80
Lee, S., 333
Leibniz, G. W., 153, 349
Leimar, O., 331
Lejarraga, T., 17, 139, 141, 147, 163,
    165, 167, 193, 195, 198, 204, 322
Lejuez, C. W., 328
Lenski, R. E., 286
Leonard, R. J., 29
Leuker, C., 12, 58, 63, 64, 69, 221
Levine, D. K., 232
Levy, D. E., 119
Levy, H., 198
Lewis, S. M., 18, 225
L'Haridon, O., 138, 163
Li, S., 331
Li, S.-C., 20
Lichtenberg, J. M., 259
Lichtenstein, S., 72, 75
Lindenberger, U., 20, 330
Lindley, D., 358
Link, D., 257
Linnér, R. K., 331
Little, K., 52
Liu, P. J., 333
Liu, T., 135, 166
Liwoski, W., 327
Lloyd, B., 114
Lo, A. W., 5
Loeber, R., 309
Loewenstein, G., 127, 175
Loftus, E. F., 4
Loomes, G., 183
Lopes, L. L., 67, 151, 155, 157, 160, 172
Lotka, A. J., 294
Lourenso, J. S., 118

Love, B. C., 8
Loveday, J., 255
Luan, S., 257
Lucas, C. G., 312
Lucas, H. L., 58
Luce, D., 155
Luce, M. F., 146
Luce, R. D., 10, 29, 32, 47, 52, 103, 228,
    351, 356, 357
Luciana, M., 313
Ludvig, E. A., 144
Ludwig, D. S., 113
Luna, B., 313
Lustig, R. H., 115

Macchi, C., 114
Macfarlane, S., 321
MacGregor, D. G., 74
Machiavelli, N., 52
Macri, S., 317
Madan, C. R., 144
Maddox, W. T., 164
Madirolas, G., 245
Madrian, B. C., 119
Magnusson, P. K., 331
Mailath, G. J., 92
Makridakis, S., 199
Malle, B. F., 350
Malmendier, U., 191, 197, 243
Malone, T. W., 20, 245, 248
Mamerow, L., 328, 334
Mannes, A. E., 245, 247, 248, 254, 255,
    257, 261
March, J. G., 17, 142, 193
Marewski, J. N., 11, 24, 257
Marinello, G., 48, 49
Markant, D. B., 16, 134, 144, 166, 237,
    238, 239, 243
Markowitz, H. M., 199
Marr, D., 289
Martignon, L., 10, 301
Maskill, C., 124
Mata, J., 115, 120, 122, 127

Mata, R., 49, 81, 86, 134, 141, 165, 322,
  327, 328, 330, 331, 332, 333, 334,
  336, 338, 339
Mather, M., 336
Mathiesen, J., 273
Mazur, J. E., 177, 180
McAfee, R. P., 255
McBride, D. F., 323
McClelland, J. L., 8
McClure, S. M., 18
McCoy, J., 248
McDade, T. W., 315
McDaniel, M. A., 214
McElreath, R., 286
McGuire, J. T., 183, 185, 186
McKelvey, R. D., 228, 229, 230, 231
McKenzie, C. R. M., 68
McNamara, J. M., 178, 310, 331
McPherson, M., 83, 86
McTiernan, J., 89
Medin, D. L., 208
Melanson, K. J., 124
Mellers, B. A., 255
Mendle, J., 306
Menger, K., 154, 155, 159
Mergenthaler-Canseco, M., 49, 162,
  291, 319
Merkle, E. C., 252
Meyer, M., 4
Meyerhoefer, C., 118
Michou, M., 202
Milam, G., 71
Milardo, R. M., 73
Miller, B., 248
Millstein, S. G., 315
Milner, M., 192
Mintz, A., 280
Mischel, W., 175, 176, 311
Mishra, S., 333
Mitchell, S. H., 333
Mitterrand, F., 4
Mochon, D., 124
Moehlis, J., 146
Moeser, A., 121

Moise, I. K., 127
Molnár, P., 265, 269
Morgenstern, O., 29, 30, 50, 228, 288,
  290, 355
Morgenthaler-Canseco, M., 133
Morris, M., 314
Mousavi, S., 351
Moussaïd, M., 19, 74, 266, 269, 270,
  271, 272, 273, 275, 277
Mueller, M., 5
Mukerji, P., 275, 282
Müller, S., 200
Mullett, T. L., 142
Mulye, T. P., 306
Mumford, J. A., 321
Murphy, A. H., 256
Murphy, R. O., 174
Myerson, J., 177, 179, 180, 189
Myung, I. J., 38

Nagel, R., 97, 230
Nagel, S., 191, 197, 243
Navarro, D. J., 134
Nayga, R. M., Jr., 121
Nelson, J. D., 68
Nettle, D., 127, 243, 309
Neufeld, M., 89
Newell, B. R., 68, 78, 134, 137, 144, 165,
  166, 301
Newman, M. E. J., 82
Nicholas, T. E., 230
Nicole, P., 346, 348
Nielsen, S. J., 122
Nilsson, H., 38
Nisbett, R. E., 86
Noelle-Neumann, E., 72, 87
Noguchi, T., 139, 141, 322
Norton, M. I., 124
Nosofsky, R. M., 78, 208, 211, 217
Nye, C. D., 330

Oaksford, M., 286
Ochs, J., 92
Oden, G. C., 155, 157

O'Donoghue, T., 175
Ogden, C. L., 126
Ogden, E. E., 74
Olschewski, S., 141, 240
Olshansky, S. J., 113
Olson, R. S., 289, 331
Olsson, A. C., 216
Olsson, H., 71, 77, 208, 209, 214, 216,
     217, 218, 220, 221, 255, 256
Onay, S., 183, 186, 187
Öncüler, A., 183, 186, 187
Oppenheimer, D. M., 8, 78, 86
Orr, S., 183
Ortmann, A., 97
Ostelo, R., 246
Ostwald, D., 139
Otto, P. E., 48, 257
Owen, G., 247, 249

Pachur, T., 5, 8, 10, 14, 21, 24, 48, 49,
     63, 64, 69, 71, 72, 73, 74, 76, 77, 78,
     79, 80, 82, 83, 84, 86, 100, 108, 137,
     142, 144, 147, 156, 163, 164, 166,
     170, 171, 173, 174, 187, 217, 218,
     220, 221, 236, 336, 339, 359
Padmanabhan, A., 313
Paes, E., 71, 87
Page, S. E., 245, 248, 249
Palacios-Huerta, L., 231, 232
Palfrey, T. R., 228, 229, 230, 231
Palmeri, H., 179, 243
Panchanathan, K., 242, 309
Paradis, G. E., 198
Paraschiv, C., 138, 163
Parco, J. E., 230
Parker, A. M., 315
Pascal, B., 346, 347, 348, 349
Pashler, H., 257
Passino, K. M., 225
Paulsen, D. J., 313
Paus, T., 313
Payne, J. W., 5, 9, 10, 31, 35–36, 39, 40,
     43, 46, 47, 49, 100, 146, 257
Payne, M., 71

Pedroni, A., 327, 329
Pellegrini, A. D., 316
Pempek, T. A., 122
Penn, A., 270
Pennock, R. T., 287
Pentland, A., 20
Perfors, A., 8, 286
Perlich, C., 260
Perner, J., 67
Peters, E., 74
Peterson, M., 355
Phelan, S., 121
Phelps, E., 316
Phillips, N. D., 134, 139, 141, 146, 234,
     235, 236, 237, 239, 242, 294
Piketty, T., 82
Pinard, C. A., 121
Pitt, M. A., 38
Plato, 345
Platt, M. L., 154, 155
Pleskac, T. J., 8, 10, 12, 14, 15, 39, 49,
     51, 53, 54, 56, 58, 60, 61, 63, 64, 67,
     69, 73, 74, 84, 95, 134, 135, 137,
     138, 139, 142, 144, 149, 163, 164,
     166, 187, 221, 256, 291, 328
Plonsky, O., 16, 134, 162, 221
Pohl, D., 75
Poldrack, R. A., 321
Pollan, M., 111, 126
Polonio, L., 97, 101
Poom, L., 208
Popkin, B. M., 121, 122
Popkin, R. H., 346
Popper, K. R., 352
Poti, J. M., 121
Pratt, S. C., 249
Prelec, D., 155, 160, 248
Prescott, S., 316
Preston, M. G., 156, 157, 158, 159
Prevost, F., 260
Price, I., 122
Proctor, R. N., 115, 126
Proulx, C., 92
Pulford, B. D., 230

Quan, H., 311
Quervain, D. J. F., 58
Quetelet, L. A. J., 72
Quiggin, J., 157

Rabin, M., 58
Rachlin, H., 180
Rada, T. B., 330
Raffrey, A.-F., 177
Raiffa, H., 10, 29, 32, 47, 52, 103, 228,
    351, 356, 357
Rakow, T., 78, 137, 141, 164, 301
Ramsey, F. P., 68, 352, 355
Rangel, J., 226
Rapoport, A., 95, 134, 176, 198, 228,
    230, 231, 232, 239
Ratcliff, R., 144, 146
Raudenbush, B., 125
Ray, N., 305
Reagan, R., 4
Rebonato, R., 119
Regenwetter, M., 135, 144, 156, 163,
    164, 167
Rehder, B., 16
Reimer, T., 257
Rémont de Montmort, P., 153
Reyna, V. F., 312
Richerson, P. J., 248, 268
Richter, D., 327
Rieskamp, J., 10, 48, 71, 73, 77, 81, 139,
    216, 217, 257, 327
Rijpkema, M., 313
Roalf, D. R., 333
Rob, R., 92
Robbins, T. W., 72
Roberts, B. W., 330, 331, 338
Roberts, M. E., 241
Robins, R. W., 328
Robinson, M. M., 135, 144, 156, 163,
    164, 167
Rode, C., 67
Roelofsma, P., 176
Rokach, L., 248, 261

Rolison, J. J., 333, 334
Romer, D., 312
Rong, Y., 117
Rorke, C. H., 198
Rosenbaum, G. M., 317, 320
Rosenthal, R., 73
Rosenthal, R. W., 228, 230
Rosman, A., 333
Ross, L., 77, 86
Roth, A. E., 92, 232
Rotjan, R. D., 18, 225
Ruggeri, A., 21, 86
Rumelhart, D. E., 8
Rushton, S. K., 166
Russolillo, S., 192
Rutledge, R. B., 336
Rutström, E. E., 328
Ruxton, G. D., 20, 248

Salali, G. D., 121
Samanez-Larkin, G. R., 328
Samuelson, L., 180
Sapolsky, R. M., 306
Sargent, T. J., 93
Sartre, J.-P., 275
Satterthwaite, T. D., 312
Savage, L. J., 5, 10, 29, 30–31, 47,
    50, 66, 103, 155, 170, 288, 353,
    355–356, 357
Schabowski, G., 3, 24, 362
Schacter, D. L., 4
Schadschneider, A., 280
Schaffer, M. M., 208
Scheibehenne, B., 147
Scheier, C., 142
Schelling, T. C., 267
Schildberg-Hörisch, H., 333, 339
Schimmack, U., 330, 337
Schlegel, A., 307
Schlomer, G. L., 309
Schmandt-Besserat, D., 193
Schmidt, K. M., 58
Schmidt, L. A., 114

Schoenfeld, J. D., 114
Schooler, L. J., 9, 11, 24, 37, 86, 100
Schossau, J., 292
Schulte-Mecklenbeck, M., 174
Schulz, K. M., 313
Schulze, C., 16, 78, 81, 134
Schumkle, S. C., 339
Schupp, J., 327
Schurz, G., 48
Schwartz, A., 334
Sedlmeier, P., 75
Seeley, T. D., 225, 226
Seitz, M. J., 270
Selten, R., 92, 286, 358
Seneca, 344
Sercombe, H., 316
Seung, H. S., 248
Sextus Empiricus, 346
Seyfried, A., 273
Seymour, B., 110
Shafir, S., 14, 132, 133, 135, 162
Shah, A. K., 8
Shalizi, C. R., 82
Shanks, D. R., 68, 78, 301
Shannon, C. E., 300
Shepard, R. N., 289
Sher, S., 68
Sherman, J. W., 328
Shimojo, E., 142
Shimojo, S., 142
Shiner, R. L., 330
Shleifer, A., 172
Shulman, S. T., 115
Sibony, A., 119
Siegel, A. W., 321
Sih, A., 327, 331
Sikström, S., 20
Silverman, M. H., 313
Simion, C., 142
Simon, H. A., 5, 10, 11, 23, 30, 31, 43,
     46, 50, 94, 156, 265, 289, 307, 357,
     359, 360
Simonoff, J. S., 260

Simpson, J. A., 311
Simsek, Ö., 11, 210, 259
Singh, M., 123
Sisk, C. L., 313
Slama, G., 122
Slavin, J. L., 114
Slovic, P., 9, 32, 72, 74, 77, 80, 327, 330,
     359
Smedslund, J., 208
Smidts, A., 313
Smith, A., 270
Smith, E. A., 285
Smith, P. L., 144, 146
Smith, S., 291
Smith-Lovin, L., 83
Socrates, 344, 345
Sofi, F., 114
Soll, J. B., 245, 247, 249, 252, 253
Somerville, L. H., 313
Sorkin, R. D., 252
Sozou, P. D., 180
Spaniol, J., 16
Sparks, A., 333
Spear, L. P., 307
Specht, J., 339
Spetch, M. L., 144
Spiliopoulos, L., 97, 100, 109
Stahl, D. O., 97, 101
Starke, L., 139
Staudinger, U. M., 330
Stearns, S. C., 307, 331
Steele, K., 351
Steffen, B., 273
Stein, W. E., 230
Steinbeck, J., 193
Steinberg, L., 313, 317
Steinmann, F., 71
Stephens, D. W., 179, 286
Sterelny, K., 12, 90, 108
Stevens, J. R., 179
Stevens, R. B., 122
Stevenson, M. K., 176
Stewart, N., 137, 142, 163

Steyvers, M., 248, 252
Stigler, G. J., 327, 339
Stigler, S. M., 4, 155
Story, M., 122
Stott, H. P., 160
Stroop, J., 258
Strotz, R. H., 180
Sudgen, R., 183
Suleiman, A. B., 313, 314
Sulloway, F. J., 19
Sumpter, D. J. T., 249, 272
Sun, L. H., 71
Sunde, U., 329, 333
Sunder, S., 290
Sunstein, C. R., 20, 118, 119, 120
Suri, S., 255
Surowiecki, J., 245, 248
Suter, R. S., 170, 171, 173, 174
Sutton, R. S., 144
Swierzbinski, J., 92

Taleb, N. N., 192, 199, 321
Tang, F. F., 230
Tannert, C., 349
Tavernier, R., 306
Tefft, B. C., 321
Teixeira, P. J., 124
Templeton, J. J., 241
Tenenbaum, J. B., 8, 14, 139, 286, 291
Teodorescu, K., 16, 134, 221
Tetlock, P. E., 255
Thaler, R. H., 118, 119, 120, 177, 183, 199, 201
Theraulaz, G., 19, 266
Thomas, J. A., 300
Thompson, H. S., 52
Thorn, P. D., 48
Thorndike, A. N., 119
Thorngate, W., 31, 32, 34, 35, 36, 38, 39, 40, 41, 42, 47, 49
Thunnissen, D. P., 349
Tibshirani, R., 37, 260
Timmermann, A. G., 261
Tindale, R. S., 248

Titman, S., 202
Todd, P. M., 5, 7, 8, 9, 10, 11, 14, 72, 73, 82, 93, 236, 259, 267, 297, 298, 307, 308, 359, 360
Todhunter, I., 347
Tooby, J., 67, 285
Townsend, J. T., 144
Tracy, J. L., 328
Trautman, P., 263
Trautmann, S. T., 351
Travers, M., 166
Trippas, D., 218, 220, 221
Troussard, X., 118
Tsetsos, K., 135
Tu, J., 200
Tu, L.-C., 309
Tucker-Drob, E. M., 338
Tump, A. N., 252
Turner, A., 270
Turner, B. M., 252
Tversky, A., 9, 10, 14, 32, 47, 49, 61, 62, 67, 71, 74, 75, 131, 134, 135, 136, 143, 155, 157, 159, 160, 161, 162, 163, 167, 187, 349, 351, 359
Twain, M., 193
Tymula, A., 319

Uexküll, J. J., 315
Ülkümen, G., 349, 350
Ungemach, C., 137, 163, 164, 165
Uppal, R., 199
Urminsky, O., 176
Usher, M., 135

Valone, T. J., 241
van Aken, M. A. G., 317
van de Kuilen, G., 136, 351
van den Assem, M. J., 258
van den Bos, W., 313, 317, 318, 319, 322
van der Waerden, B. L., 155, 174
van Dolder, D., 258
van Doorn, G. S., 331
van Duijvenvoorde, A. C. K., 319
Vanpaemel, W., 80

van Schaik, P., 329
van Trijp, H. C., 116
Vanzomeren-Dohm, A. A., 311
Venkatramen, V., 317
Vidmar, N. J., 330
Viechtbauer, W., 338
Visalberghi, E., 123
Visscher, P. K., 225
Vogt, K., 345
Volij, O., 231, 232
Volterra, V., 294
Volz, K. G., 240
von Helversen, B., 81, 86, 134, 216, 217, 256, 258
von Mises, R., 352
von Neumann, J., 29, 30, 50, 228, 288, 290, 355
von Rueden, C., 314
Vul, E., 14, 139, 257, 258, 291

Wagner, R. H., 241
Wakker, P. P., 14, 136, 160, 161
Wald, A., 72, 104, 144
Waldmann, M. R, 16
Walker, A., 291
Walker, W. E., 349
Wallace, B., 331
Wallsten, T. S., 10, 61, 252, 349
Walton, K. E., 338
Wang, X. T., 331
Warren, P. A., 166
Washington, G., 119
Watts, T. W., 311
Weaver, W., 300
Weber, B. J., 176
Weber, E. U., 14, 15, 16, 132, 133, 135, 137, 156, 162, 163, 233, 327, 328, 329, 330
Weber, M., 15, 66, 200, 203
Weber, R., 18
Weintraub, D. L., 77
Weisbart, D., 305
Weissing, F. J., 331
Weiszäcker, G., 97, 101

Wells, G. L., 255
Wendt, S., 179
Wermers, R., 202
Werner, T., 269
Wertz, A. E., 291, 292
West, R., 252
West, S. A., 285
Weston, N. J., 78, 301
Wetzels, R., 80
Whiten, A., 110, 242
Wilke, C. O., 289
Willoughby, T., 306, 324
Wills, J. M., 115
Wilson, M., 179
Wilson, P. W., 97, 101
Wilson, T. D., 183
Wimsatt, W. C., 23
Windschitl, P. D., 61
Wing, R. R., 121
Winman, A., 38
Winterfeldt, D. V., 68
Winterhalder, B., 285
Wisdom, J., 127
Wixted, J. T., 255
Woike, J. K., 141, 193
Wolf, M., 246, 252, 331
Wolfe, A., 323
Wood, S., 333
Woolley, A. W., 20
Wu, G., 159, 160
Wulff, D. U., 49, 133, 134, 135, 136, 137, 139, 141, 142, 143, 146, 147, 162, 164, 165, 168, 291, 319, 321, 322, 328
Wyatt, J., 259
Wyllie, A., 124
Wynn, K., 291, 292

Xuan, Y.-H., 331

Yagil, J., 176
Yanez, C., 321
Yaniv, I., 255
Yao, X., 259
Yates, J. F., 67, 256

Yechiam, E., 328
Yetton, P. W., 247, 248, 252
Yu, A. J., 18
Yu, S., 8, 135

Zacks, R. T., 86
Zalaudek, I., 246
Zauberman, G., 176
Zeigenfuse, M. D., 135, 144, 166
Zeisberger, S., 204
Zhang, D. C., 330
Zhang, L., 97
Zhang, S., 38
Zheng, R., 331
Zhong, S., 68, 69
Zhou, G., 200
Zick, C. D., 122
Ziegelmeyer, A., 230
Zimring, F. E., 322
Zukowsky, L. G., 67

Subject Index

Note: Page numbers in **boldface** indicate glossary entries.

Academica (Cicero), 345n1
Academic school, 345
Accuracy
  confidence and, 255–256
  estimating individual, 257–259
Accuracy–effort trade-off, 109, **365**
  bounded rationality and, 46–47
  in choice, 35–37
  heuristics and, 9, 12
Adaptation, **365**. *See also* Deferred
    adaptation; Ontogenetic adaptation
  conditional, 309
Adaptive cognition, 13
  preferential decision process and,
    288–289
Adaptive decision maker, 31–32, 35–37
Adaptive exploration, 138–143
  adaptive explorer hypothesis, 131–132
  Choice from Accumulated Samples of
    Experience (CHASE), 132, 144–151,
    152
  description–experience gap, 135–138
  distinguishing decisions under
    uncertainty from decisions under
    risk, 151–152
  modeling search and choice in
    decisions from experience, 143–144
  moderators of exploration, 139
  sampling paradigm, 133–135

  small samples and, 138–139
  terminating search routes, 139–143
Adaptive response, 156, 176, 179, 183,
    186, 320, 331
Adaptive strategy selection, 209
  boosting, 219–220
  cognitive load and, 217
Adaptive toolbox, 4–8, 361, **365**
  advantages of, 24–25
  human decision making and, 7
  unfinished nature of, 20–22
Adolescence
  defined, 305
  puberty, 305, 306, 310, 313
Adolescent mind, 305–324
  adolescence as age of uncertainty,
    314–315
  adolescent brain development, 313
  adolescent driving behavior,
    321–322
  ambiguity, adolescent tolerance for,
    319–320
  conditional adaptation, 311–312
  ecological rationality of adolescent
    behavior, 307–308
  life history theory and, 308,
    309–315
  ontogenetic and deferred adaptations
    in adolescence, 315–320

Adolescent mind (cont.)
   peer group and, 322–323
   probabilistic expectations and,
      320–321
   risk and losses and, 321–322
   Sturm und Drang and, 323–324
   turbulent period of adolescence,
      305–308
   weighting of rare events and, 322
Age, use of recognition heuristic
   and, 21
Age–crime curve, 306, 311
Age-related changes in risk preference
   learning and memory and, 338–339
   mean-level change and, 333–337
   rank-order stability of, 337–338, 340
Age-related decline in risk taking, 306,
   311, 332–337
Aggregation, 260–261
Aggregation rules, 6–7
Aleatory probability, 349–350
Aleatory uncertainty, 7, 22–23, 360.
   See also Uncertainty
Alice's Adventures in Wonderland
   (Carroll), 314
Alternative Healthy Eating Index, 117
Ambiguity aversion, **365**
   risk–reward heuristic and, 66–67
Ambiguity (economic), 351
Ancient Greeks and Romans, concept of
   uncertainty and, 343–346
A priori probability, 353
Army ants, collective behavior of, 272
Artificial insemination, relationship
   between payoffs and probabilities
   in, 56–57
Availability-by-recall, 75–77, 79, 80, 81,
   82, 83, 84
Availability heuristic, 75. *See also*
   Heuristics
Averaging rule, 247, 248, 251–252
Axiomatized expected utility, 50
Axiomatized utility theory, 29–30

Backwards induction strategy, in
   centipede game, 230, 232
Bayesian approach for probability
   weighting, 169
Bayesian decision theory, 29–30
   uncertainty in, 355–358
Bayesian deep learning, 8
Bayesian Nash equilibrium
   properties of the environment
      and, 96
   in strategic games, 91–92
Bayesian reasoning, decision making
   under risk and, 17
Bayesian statistics, 23
Bayes' rule, uncertainty in hazard rate
   and, 180
Behavioral decision theory, degrees of
   uncertainty and, 351
Behavioral game theory, tension
   between environmental and strategic
   uncertainty in, 227–233
Behavioral measures of risk preference,
   328
Berlin Wall, fall of, 3–4
Best-member rule, 247, 248, 252–254,
   255, 259, 260, 261
Bets
   fair, 54–55
   risk–reward heuristic and, 68–69
Bias
   defined, 37
   error cancellation and, 253
Bias–variance dilemma, 257–259, **365**
Bias–variance framework, 37–38
"Black swans," 199n1
Boom babies, 204
Boosting, 119–120, **366**. *See also*
   Adaptive strategy selection
   for parents as architects of the family
      meal, 120, 121–125
Bottleneck events, evolution and, 291
Bottlenecks, collective pedestrian
   behavior and, 282

Bounded rationality, 5, 11, 46, 91, 93, 94, 344
  accuracy–effort trade-off and, 46–47
  choice environments and, 11–12
  heuristics and, 5, 170, 172
  uncertainty in, 358–361
Bracketing
  error cancellation and, 252, 253
  estimation tasks and, 254–255
Brain, adolescent brain development, 313

Cancer diagnosis, 245–247
Cartesian philosophy, uncertainty and, 346
Categorization, 16–17, 211, 217–218, 351
Cauchy distribution, 40, 45
Causal reasoning, 17
Centers for Disease Control and Prevention, 113
Centipede game, 228–233, 235n1, 239
Certainty, risk, uncertainty, and, 356, 357
Chance, probability and rules of, 348–349
Children. See also Adolescent mind
  family meals and nutritional health of, 121–125
  involvement in meal preparation, 123–124
  risks in decision making and, 319
  search strategies used by, 81
Choice
  modeling in decisions from experience, 143–144
  normative theories of, 344
  sample size and, 146, 147
  search and, 15–16
Choice from Accumulated Samples of Experience (CHASE), 132, 144–151, 152
  adapting to costs and benefits, 145–146

  adapting to environmental uncertainty, 147
  explaining the description–experience gap using, 147–148
  moderators of search and their representation in, 140–141
  predictions of, 136
  understanding the weight of experience through, 148–151
Choice problems, probability weighting of, 168
Classical probability, 346–352
Cognition
  adaptive, 13
  environment and, 9–10, 11–12
  managing uncertainty and, 5
Cognitive abilities
  evolution of, 295
  strategic interaction as evolutionary driver of, 242
Cognitive architecture, 100
Cognitive constraints, competition and frugal sampling and, 291–296
Cognitive control, selection of cognitive tools and, 6
Cognitive development, decision-making tools and life-span trajectory of, 20–22
Cognitive hierarchy theory, 97
Cognitive load, adaptive strategy selection and, 217
Cognitive niches, 24
Cognitive simplicity in choice under uncertainty, 38–46
  competitors, 39
  environmental allies and, 43–46
  environments, 39–40
  learning by sampling, 40–41
  performance gap, 42–43
  performance of heuristics under uncertainty, 41–42
Cognitive tools, developmental change and, 6, 7

Coherence criteria of rationality, 10
Coin toss, St. Petersburg paradox and,
    153
Collective behavior, 19
  collective dynamics, 267–268
  collective intelligence, reducing
    uncertainty and tapping, 6
Combinatorics, rules of, 347
Comparison, learning by, 217–218
Compensatory environments, **366**
Compensatory strategy, 298
Competences
  boosts and, 119–120
  food choice, 111, 121–127
Competition
  adolescent peer network and, 322–323
  combining strategic and
    environmental uncertainty and,
    233–241
  environmental and strategic
    uncertainty and, 226–228
  frugal sampling and, 291–296
  learning to compete, 241–243
  search and challenges of, 18–19
  social norms and learning and,
    240–241
  strategic uncertainty and range of
    competitive pressures, 242–243
Competition for limited resources, risk–
    reward relationship and, 58–59
Competitive environments, heuristics
    and, 12–13
Competitors, strategic uncertainty and,
    228–233
Complexity, 100, 108, 109, 110
Computational evolution
  computer simulations of evolution, 286
  described, 287
  rational analysis, 286, 288
Condorcet's jury theorem, 249
Confidence rule, 247, 248, 255–257,
    261
  wicked cases and, 256

Confidence statements, epistemic
    uncertainty and, 350
Constant-target investment strategy,
    201, 203
Contextual influences, on risk
    preference, 331, 333
Contrarian investment strategies,
    202–203
Convergent validity, risk preference
    and, 329–330
Cooperation, crowd movement
    and, 19
Correspondence criteria of rationality,
    360
Costs, CHASE and adapting to, 145–146
Crime
  age–crime curve, 306, 311
  early-life stress and, 311
Criterion
  cues and, 220
  medical diagnoses and, 245
Crowd aggregation rules, 6, 7, 249–252,
    258, 260–261
Crowd disasters, mechanics of, 273–275
Crowd managers, 282
Crowd modeling
  historical perspective on, 265
  physics-based and heuristic-based,
    266–267
Crowd movement, cooperation and, 19
Crowd panics, 277
Crowd rules, 247
  ecological rationality of, 247–257
  estimating individual accuracy and
    bias–variance dilemma, 257–259
  increasing safety and, 281–282
  principles for selecting without benefit
    of omniscience, 260–262
  selecting in practice, 260
  selecting without benefit of
    omniscience, 257–262
  statistical structure of environment
    and, 256–257

Crowds. *See also* Pedestrian behavior, collective
  blending judgments of whole crowd, 248, 249–252
  density and collective pedestrian behavior, 271–272, 273–275, 281–282
  emergency evacuations, 278–280
  flocks, swarms, and, 272
  inner crowd, 258
  relying on best individual, 252–254, 255
  relying on most confident individual, 255–257
  using select, 254–255
  wisdom of, 19–20, 245–247
  wisdom of the inner crowd, 258
Crowd turbulence, 19, 275, 280–281
Crystallized intelligence, 20–21
Cue-based inference, 78, 79–80, 93
Cues, 209–210, **366**
  confidence rule and, 256
  criterion and, 220
  for Germany city environment, 298–301
  medical diagnoses and, 245–246
  validity of, 297
Cultural evolution, 248n1

Decision architecture, 297–298
Decision making
  heuristics and, 5–6, 8–13
  interpretation of uncertainty in, 344
  prediction and, 24
  under risk, 16–17, **366**
  taxonomy of dynamic, 134–135
  under uncertainty, 10, **366**
Decision policies, 90
  measuring performance of, 103–105
  performance measured by Indifference criterion, 105–107
  in strategic games, 95

Decisions from description, 14–15, 131–132, **366**
  divergence from decisions from experience, 142–143
  probability weighting and, 156
  steering investment behavior, 194–198
Decisions from experience, 15–16, 131–132, **366**. *See also* Choice from Accumulated Samples of Experience (CHASE)
  adaptive exploration and, 152
  adolescents and, 318–319, 322
  age-related differences in risk taking and, 336, 338–339
  as class of dynamic decision making, 134–135
  divergence from decisions from description, 142–143
  modeling search and choice in, 143–144
  probability weighting and, 155–156
  sampling more toward end of sampling sequence and, 142, 143
  sampling paradigm and, 133–135
Decisions under ambiguity, 318, 319–320
Decisions under risk
  adaptive exploration and, 151–152
  adolescents and, 319
  rule-based and exemplar-based strategies in, 220–222
Decisions under uncertainty, 52
  adaptive exploration and, 151–152
  adolescents and, 319, 321–322
  experience and, 207–208 (*see also* Exemplar–based strategies; Rule–based strategies)
Decision theory, **366**
  rationality and invention of, 347–348
  uncertainty in Bayesian, 355–358
Decision threshold, in CHASE, 145–146, 147–148
Deep learning, 8

Default rules, as nudges, 119
Deferred adaptation, 308
  in adolescence, 315–320
Delay discount function, 179–180
Delay discounting, 178–182
  exponential or hyperbolic, 181–182
  outcome uncertainty and, 179
Depression baby effect, 191, 197
Description
  decisions from (*see* Decisions from
    description)
  description–experience gap, 15, 16,
    135–138, 351, **366**
  CHASE and, 146, 147–148
  financial shocks and, 197–198
  temporal uncertainty and, 186–188
Description of financial shock,
  experience of *vs.*, 193–194
Desirability bias, 61, 62
Developmental change, cognitive
  abilities and, 20–22, 313
Development niche, 307, 315
Dialectical bootstrapping, 258
Dietary patterns, 114
Direct competition, frugal sampling
  and, 295
Direct criterion learning, 217–218
Discounted utility model, 180, 186
Discount functions, 177, 178
Domain-specific rationality, 7
Dominance, strategic, 102–103
Dominance-1 (D1) heuristic, 98, 99.
  See also Heuristics
  performance of as measured by the
    Indifference criterion, 105,
    106, 107
  simplicity and, 107–108
  simplification of, 101
Dynamic decision making, 134–135

Early-life stress, criminal behavior and,
  311
East German travel law, 3–4

Eating rules, 111–127
  beyond simple heuristic rules,
    126–127
  boosting interventions, 119–120
  boosting parents' competence as
    architects of family meal, 121–125
  food labeling and, 114–116
  nudging interventions, 118–119
  nutritional health and the
    uncertainties of the obesogenic
    environment, 127
  nutritional sciences and, 113–114
  obesogenic and complex food
    environment, 113–113
  policy makers and regulators as
    producers of uncertainty, 116–118
  sources and producers of food-related
    uncertainty, 113–118
  uncertainty and, 112–113
Ecological analysis
  of adolescent environment, 320, 324
  of relationship between risk and
    reward, 52–59
Ecologically rational decision making,
    computational evolution and,
    285–304
  centrality of evolution to ecological
    rationality, 285–288
  cognitive constraints and competition
    and frugal sampling, 291–296
  evolution struggling with uncertainty,
    304
  heuristics exploiting information
    structure of task environments,
    297–304
  tuning preferential decision processes
    to environment, 288–291
Ecologically rational heuristics, 297
Ecological rationality, 7, 9, 93, 344, **367**
  of adolescent behavior, 307–308
  of crowd rules, 247–257
  dualistic view of uncertainty and,
    23–24

of pedestrian heuristics, 280–282
of rule-based and exemplar-based
    strategies, 209–215
uncertainty in, 360–361
of the wisdom of crowds (*see* Crowds)
Ecological rationality of crowds
    kind cases, 249, 250, 251, 256
    kind environment, 248, 249n2
    wicked cases, 249, 250, 251
    wicked environment, 249n2
Ecological rationality of limited social
    sampling, 82–88
    environmental properties impacting
        success of limited search, 82–86
    limitations and benefits of social
        sampling from proximate
        environments, 86–88
Ecological structure, recognition
    heuristic and, 11–12
Ecological validities, for German city
    environment, 298–301
Economic crisis of 2008, risk aversion
    and, 192
Economic shocks. *See also* Financial
    shocks; Financial uncertainty
    effects of experience of, 191–192
Efficient market hypothesis, 51–52
Emergency evacuations, 277–280
Emotional eating, 123
Environment, **367**
    adaptive exploration and, 139
    ambiguity aversion and, 67
    cognition and, 9–10, 11–12
    collective pedestrian behavior and,
        264–267
    crowd rules and statistical structure of,
        256–257
    ecological rationality of rule-based
        and exemplar-based strategies and,
        209–215, 220–221
    fit with heuristic, 23–24
    heuristic performance under
        uncertainty and, 39–40

heuristics exploiting information
    structure of task, 297–304
influence on development of risk
    preference across the life span,
    339–340
noncompensatory, **368**
obesogenic, 112–113, 127
risk–reward, adaptation to, 63–66
selection of rule-based and exemplar-
    based strategies and, 215–217
statistical structure of decision and,
    219–220
tuning preferential decision processes
    to, 288–291
using experience to adapt to,
    261–262
variance in probabilities as
    environmental property, 45–46
Environmental factors, evolution of risk
    aversion and, 289–291
Environmental properties, impacting
    success of limited search, 82–86
Environmental structures
    adaptive decision maker and, 35–37
    bounded rationality and, 94
    match of choice heuristics to, 46
Environmental uncertainty, 5, 89–91,
    225–228, 349–350, **367**. *See also*
    Uncertainty
    adolescents and, 320–323
    centipede game and, 229
    CHASE and adapting to, 147
    combining with strategic uncertainty,
        233–241
    heuristics' performance as function
        of, 107
    need to know *vs.* need for speed and,
        226–228
Environment of evolutionary
    adaptiveness, adolescence and, 307
Episodic memory, exemplar-based
    strategies and, 216–217
Epistemic probability, 349–350

Epistemic uncertainty, 7, 22–23, 360.
  See also Uncertainty
Equality (Eq) heuristic, 98, 99. *See also*
  Heuristics
  performance of as measured by the
    Indifference criterion, 106
  simplification of, 100–101
Equal weighting, 101, 105, 108
Equilibria, game theoretic analysis and
  identification of, 228
Equilibrium strategy, centipede game
  and, 230–231
Equiprobable heuristic (equal-weight
  heuristic), 32, 33, 34. *See also*
  Heuristics
  accuracy–effort trade-off and, 35–36
  actual use of, 49
  performance under uncertainty, 39,
    41–42, 43, 44–46
Error, variance as source of, 38
Error cancellation in estimation tasks,
  251–252, 253
Error diversity, majority rule and,
  249–251
Error portfolio, 261
Estimation tasks
  error cancellation in, 251–252, 253
  select crowd rule and, 254–255
European Commission, 118
European Council Directive 2004/39/
  EC, 205
Evidence accumulation, 151, 292
Evolution. *See* Ecologically rational
  decision making, computational
  evolution and
Evolutionary adaptiveness, adolescence
  and environment of, 307
Evolutionary game theory, 286
Evolutionary selection, 92
Exemplar-based strategies, 208–209
  boosting adaptive strategy selection,
    219–220
  in decisions under risk, 220–222

  ecological rationality of, 209–215
  formal description of, 210–211
  learning task design and influence on
    selection of, 219
  limitation in adaptive selection of,
    215–217
Exhaustive search strategies, advantages
  of, 86
Expectation
  Keynesian, 354, 354n5
  mathematical, 354n5
Expectation models, 221
Expected utility maximization, 23
Expected utility theory, 5, 14, 29, 50,
  154, **367**
  decision making under risk and,
    355–356, 359
Expected value maximization,
  objectives beyond, 48–49
Expected value theory, 38, **367**
  heuristic performance and, 34
  performance of heuristics under
    uncertainty and, 41
  St. Petersburg paradox and, 153–154
Experience. *See also under* Learning
  decisions from (*see* Decisions from
    experience)
  influence of recent *vs.* less recent on
    uncertainty avoidance, 198
  navigating financial uncertainty and,
    203–205
  reduction of strategic uncertainty and,
    231–233
  simulated, 203–205
  steering investment behavior,
    194–198
Experience of financial shock,
  description of *vs.*, 193–194
Experimental outcomes, 101, 110
Exploration
  adapting to competitive pressure,
    236–239
  during adolescence, 311–312

Exploration–exploitation trade-off, 18–19, 227, **367**

Exponential discount function, 180, 181–182

Exponential distribution, 40
probability distributions combined with, 44–45

Extrapolation, rule-based and exemplar-based strategies and, 213, 214

Extreme competition, frugal sampling and, 295

Fair bets, 54–55

False consensus effect, social sampling and, 86

Family meal
building blocks of, 122–124, 125
dynamics of family mealtime, 124–125
healthy eating behavior and, 120, 121–125
rules for, 126–127

Faster-is-slower effect, in collective pedestrian behavior, 280

Fast life history strategies, 308, 309–315

Feedback
dynamic decision making and, 134
learning task design and, 218–219

Financial shocks
description–experience gap and, 197–198
experience of, 191–192
experience of *vs.* description of, 193–194

Financial uncertainty, 191–205. *See also* Uncertainty
descriptions and experience and investors' behavior, 194–198
description *vs.* experience of financial shock, 193–194
experience of economic shocks and, 191–192

harnessing experience to help navigate, 203–205

influence of recent *vs.* less recent experiences, 198

navigating, 199–205

strategies reactive to fluctuations in stock price, 202–203

strategies unreactive to fluctuations in stock price, 201–202

Firefighters, decision-making strategies of, 207–208, 208n1, 219–220

Fitness, **367**
environment and, 295
evolution of risk aversion and, 289–291
harshness and, 309, 310
status within peer group and, 323
trade-off against mutational robustness, 289

Flocks, 272

Fluid dynamics, crowd dynamics and, 19

Fluid intelligence, 20–22
aging and changes in risk preference and, 336–337, 338–339

Follow-the-flow heuristic, 270, 275–277. *See also* Heuristics

Follow-the-leader heuristic, 270. *See also* Heuristics

Food advertising, 122

Food decisions, complex food environment and, 113. *See also* Eating rules

Food labeling
effectiveness of, 115–116
as source of food-related uncertainty, 114–116

Food pyramids, competing, 116–117

Food-related uncertainty, 114–116, 127. *See also* Uncertainty

Food rules, 111, 126–127

Food Rules: An Eater's Manual (Pollan), 126

Fooled by Randomness (Taleb), 199n1
Foraging in a group, 241
Forecasting future, difficulty of, 4
The Foundations of Statistics (Savage),
    355, 357–358
Fourfold pattern of risk attitudes, 134,
    135–137, 149, 151
Frugal exploration, description–
    experience gap and, 137
Frugal sampling
    cognitive constraints and competition
        and, 291–296
    competition and, 294–296
Fundamental diagram of traffic flow,
    273–274

"Games against nature," 226
Games and Decisions (Luce & Raiffa), 356
Game theory, 29, **367**
    environmental and strategic
        uncertainty and, 227–233
    evolutionary, 286
    one-shot game, 90
Gaze cascade effect, 141–142
    CHASE and, 145
Gaze heuristic, 265n1. *See also*
    Heuristics
*The General Theory of Employment,
    Interest, and Money* (Keynes), 354
Genetics, risk preference and, 331
German city problem, cues, ecological
    validities, discrimination rates, and
    mutual information for, 298–301
German Socio-Economic Panel (SOEP),
    335
Goals
    achievement of under environmental
        and cognitive constraints, 359–360
    adjusting decision threshold based
        on, 145
    behaviors consistent with, 119
    pedestrian behavior and, 268, 277
    searches adjusted based on, 132, 152

social dilemmas and, 268
stopping sampling and, 139, 141
uncertainty about competitors', 227,
    240
The Grapes of Wrath (Steinbeck), 193,
    194
Great Depression
    effects on generation experiencing,
        191–192
    learning about, 193
Grenfell Tower fire, 207, 219
Group decision making, 248n1
"Groupthink," 248n1
Guessing, 79–80

Habitat selection strategies, 225–226,
    233
Hardship, life-span differences in risk
    taking and, 332–333, 338
Harshness, fast *vs.* slow life history
    strategies and, 309–311
Hazard rate, 180
Herding, emergency evacuations and,
    279–280
Hermit crabs
    exploration–exploitation trade-off
        and, 18–19
    habitat selection strategy, 225
Heuristic-based crowd modeling,
    266–267
Heuristic mind, 8–13
Heuristics, **368**
    axiomatized utility theory and, 29–30
    bias–variance dilemma and, 37–38
    boundedly rational, 359
    cognitive simplicity in choice under
        uncertainty and, 38–46
    complementary tools for, 361
    decision making and, 5–6
    exploiting information structure of
        task environment, 297–304
    falling short of ideal of maximization,
        31–37, 49–50

fit with environment, 9–10, 23
objectives beyond expected value
    maximization, 48–49
performance of, 9
preferential choice, 10
probability weights as reflections of,
    170–174
strategic complexity and success of,
    12–13
strategy selection problem and
    uncertainty and, 47–48
systematic bias and, 32
testing in strategic games, 94–105
theoretical realism and imperfect
    knowledge and, 46–47
use of simplification policies, 49
view of in psychology, 359
Heuristics in strategic games, 94–105
classification of their paths to
    simplification, 100–101
decision policies' performance as
    measured by Indifference criterion,
    105–107
measuring competing decision
    policies' performance, 103–105
role of strategic dominance, 102–103
Hierarchical latent-mixture modeling,
    80n1, 81
Highway formation, collective
    pedestrian behavior and, 270,
    271–272
Homo heuristicus, 10, 90
probability weighting and, 170, 174
Homophily, 83
Honey bees, habitat selection strategy,
    225–226
Hormones, pubertal, 306, 313
Horse track
relationship between payoffs and
    probabilities, 54
risk–reward probabilities, 55
Human mind, bounded rationality and
    limitations of, 94

The Hunt for Red October (movie), 89–90
Hyperbolic discount function, 177, 178,
    180–182
Hyperbolic discounting model, 186

Ideal free distribution (IFD) theory,
    58–59
Ignorance prior, 169
"IKEA effect," 124
Immeasurable uncertainty, 22. *See also*
    Uncertainty
Imperfect knowledge, theoretical
    realism and, 46–47
Impulsivity, 316
Indifference, principle of, 61, 69–70
Indifference criterion, 103, 104
decision policies' performance
    measured by, 105–107
Indirect competition, frugal sampling
    and, 295
Individual
estimating individual accuracy,
    257–259
wisdom of crowds and relying on
    most confident, 255–257
wisdom of crowds and relying on best,
    252–254, 255
Inference, **368**
ecologically rational heuristics
    and, 10
instance-based, 71–73, 74
recognition and, 11
Inference domain
accuracy–effort trade-off and, 48
use of equiprobable and lexicographic
    heuristics, 49
Inference prior, 169
Inferential accuracy, influence of
    environmental structure on, 83–85
Inferential decisions, cognitive
    constraints and, 291–292
Inferential heuristic, risk–reward
    heuristic as, 62

Information
dynamic decision making and source of, 134
gambles leaking, 68
incomplete (*see* Strategic uncertainty)
Markov brains and, 293–294
sampling, 291–292
Information processing, 5, 8, 35, 286–287
Information-processing architecture, 35, 286, 294, 296, 301, 303
Information structure of task environment, heuristics exploiting, 297–304
Instance-based inference, 71–73, 74
Instance-based memory models, 144
Instance-based strategy, judgment of event frequencies and, 80
Interpretations of probability, 344, 349n3, 352–358
Intertemporal choice, 175–189, **368**
delay discounting and, 177–182
delays and reduction of uncertainty and, 188–189
intertemporal decisions under temporal uncertainty, 186–188
pervasiveness of uncertainty in, 175–177
shades of uncertainty in, 177–186
size of future outcome and, 182–183
temporal uncertainty and, 183–186
types of uncertainty, 175–176
utility uncertainty and, 183
Investment decisions, 196, 199
Investment strategies
definition of, 201
reactive to fluctuations in stock price, 202–203
unreactive to fluctuations in stock price, 201–202, 203
Investors
descriptions and experiences steering investment behavior, 194–198

experimental market and investment decisions, 196
risk attitudes, 192

Judgment, 216, 220, 245
Judgments of crowd
blending, 248, 249–252
when in doubt, aggregate more rather than fewer judgments, 260–262

Keynesian uncertainty, 354–355. *See also* Uncertainty
Knightian uncertainty, 353–354. *See also* Uncertainty
Knowledge
crisis of humanistic and scientific, 346
selection of cognitive tools and, 6
subjective, 348–349, 350
Knowledge gap, search strategies to reduce, 13–17

Lane formation, collective pedestrian behavior and, 270
Large worlds, 103, 357
Learning. *See also* Experience
Bayesian deep, 8
to compete, 241–243
competition and, 240–241
by probability distribution, 44–45
by sampling, 40–41
significance of, 16–17
Learning by comparison, 217–218
Learning curves, selecting crowd rule in practice and, 260
Learning from experience, 207–222
boosting adaptive strategy selection, 219–220
ecological rationality of rule-based and exemplar-based strategies, 209–215
influencing strategy selection through learning task design, 217–218
learning from description *vs.*, 193–194

limitations in adaptive selection of rule-based and exemplar-based strategies, 215–217
rule-based and exemplar-based strategies in decisions under risk, 220–222
rules and exemplars, 207–209
Learning task design, influence on strategy selection, 217–218, 220
Learning through repeated interaction, reduction of strategic uncertainty and, 231–233
Least-likely heuristic, 32, 33, 34. *See also* Heuristics
performance of, 48
performance under uncertainty, 39, 41–42, 43
probability weighting and, 170–173
Level-*k* heuristics, 97–98. *See also* Heuristics
execution errors and, 109
Nash equilibrium and, 103n3
performance of, 109–110
Level-1 (L1) heuristic, 98, 99. *See also* Heuristics
performance of as measured by the Indifference criterion, 105, 106, 107
simplicity and, 107, 108
simplification of, 101
Level-2 (L2) heuristic, 98, 99–100. *See also* Heuristics
performance of as measured by the Indifference criterion, 105, 106, 107
simplicity and, 107–108
Level-3 (L3) heuristic, 98, 100. *See also* Heuristics
performance of as measured by the Indifference criterion, 106, 107
simplicity and, 108
Lexicographic (LEX) heuristic, 62. *See also* Heuristics
accuracy–effort trade-off and, 36
actual use of, 49

performance under uncertainty, 39, 41, 42, 43, 44–46
probability weighting and, 170
Life expectancy, declines in, 113
Life history theory, 308, 309–315
risk preference and, 331
Life insurance policies
relationship between payoffs and probabilities, 54
risk–reward probabilities, 55
Life-span development of risk preference. *See* Risk preference, life-span development of
Likelihood statements, aleatory uncertainty and, 350
Limited search, 14, 16, 362
environmental properties affecting success of, 82–86
in social circles, 74, 76, 77–78, 80–81, 82
Linear environments, rule-based *vs.* exemplar-based strategies and, 212–215, 221–222
Lognormal distribution, 40
Loss aversion, **368**
Lottery
probability weighting and, 156–157
timing, 186–187
Love Parade tragedy, 275

Madness of crowds, 277, 280–281
Majority rule, 237, 238, 249–250
Majority voting, role of error diversity in, 250–251
Males, cause-specific mortality for, 325, 326, 327
Manuscript submission, risk–reward probabilities and, 56, 57, 63
Marketplace forces, risk–reward relationship and, 54–55, 57
Markov brains, 292
Germany city environment problem and, 298–299

Markov brains (cont.)
  mapping in, 293
  mutations in, 293, 294
  overview, 293
Marshmallow Test, 175, 179, 185–186
Mathematical expectation, 347, 354n5
Maximax (MaxMax) heuristic, 98, 99.
    See also Heuristics
  performance of as measured by the
    Indifference criterion, 106, 107
  probability weighting and, 170–173
  simplicity and, 107
  simplification of, 101
Maximin (MaxMin) heuristic, 98, 99.
    See also Heuristics
  performance of as measured by the
    Indifference criterion, 106, 107
  simplification of, 101
Maximization
  heuristic performance falling short of,
    49–50
  objectives beyond expected value and,
    48–49
  risky choice heuristics and, 31–37
Mean-level change, risk preference
    across the life span and, 333–337
Mean-level stability, 330
Mean-variance optimization
    model, 199
Measurable uncertainty, 22. *See also*
    Uncertainty
Mecca stampede, 275
Medical diagnoses, wisdom of the
    crowd and, 245–247
Mediterranean diet, 114
Memory
  age-related changes in risk preference
    and, 338–339
  episodic, 216–217
  working, 216–217
Minimax heuristic, probability
    weighting and, 170–173
Mini-ultimatum game, 240

Modernization, new risks brought by,
    325
Momentum-diversified strategies, 202,
    203
Momentum investment strategies, 202,
    203
Momentum-nondiversified strategies,
    202, 203
Momentum-risky investment strategies,
    202, 203
Momentum-safe investment strategies,
    202, 203
Monetary gambles, 31
  ecological analysis of risks and rewards
    in, 53–54
  fair bets, 54–55
  risk–reward heuristic and, 60
  three risk–reward environments with,
    63–68
Money, risk–reward heuristic and
    making, 68–69
Morbidity, adolescent, 305–306
Mortality
  adolescent, 305–306, 314–315, 325, 326
  cause-specific, for males, 325, 326, 327
Most-likely heuristic, probability
    weighting and, 170–173
Mutational robustness, trade-off against
    fitness, 289
Mutation load, 294
Mutations
  change in heuristics and, 303
  limiting complexity of situations and,
    293–294
  Markov brains and, 293, 294
Mutual information, German city
    problem and, 298, 300–301
MyPlate, 116–117

Naive diversification heuristic, 199–200,
    201, 203. *See also* Heuristics
Nash equilibrium, 90, 100, **368**
  execution errors and, 109

finite-player, finite-action games and, 97n1

level-*k* heuristic and, 103n3

performance of, 107–108

performance of as measured by the Indifference criterion, 105, 106, 107

strategic dominance and, 94

in strategic games, 91–93, 97, 98

National Health and Nutrition Examination Survey, 114

Natural-mean heuristic, 33. *See also* Heuristics

actual use of, 49

performance under uncertainty, 39, 41–42, 43

Navigation heuristics, 264–267

Need to know, uncertainty and, 226–228

Neural networks, 23

Nigeria, age-risk curve, 332–333

Noncompensatory heuristics, 46

Noncompensatory strategy, 36

Nondiversified investment strategy, 202, 203

Nonlinear environments, rule-based *vs.* exemplar-based strategies and, 212–215

Normal distribution, 40

Normative solution in strategic games, 91–92

Normative theories of choice, 344

Nudging, 118–119, **368**

Nutritional health, 120, 127

family meal and, 121–125

Nutritional recommendations, conflicting, 116

Nutritional science, as producer of food-related uncertainty, 113–114

Nutrition Labeling and Education Act of 1990, 116

Obesity

as global endemic, 112–113, 127

prevention of, 121, 127

Obesogenic environment, 112–113

nutritional health and uncertainties of, 127

Objective information, 14

Objective probabilities, 29, 50

Objectives beyond expected value maximization, 48–49

Old age, use of heuristics in, 22

Olympian models, 30–31, 50, 359

Omniscient expected value model, 38, 41

1/*N* heuristic (naive diversification), 199–200, 201. *See also* Heuristics

One-shot game, 90

Ontogenetic adaptation, 308

in adolescence, 315–320

Ontogenetic change, 6

Opponent-dominance, 102

Optimal solutions, 286, 288, 298–300, 304

Optimal strategies, 288, 289, 292–293, 302, 303

Optimization, 23, 90, 199

Optional stopping rule

CHASE and, 145n2

for terminating search, 138–141, 142

Organisation for Economic Co-operation and Development, 118

Outcome uncertainty, 175, 176. *See also* Uncertainty

in materialization of future, 176, 177–182

in size of future, 176, 182–183

Outlines of Pyrronism (Sextus Empiricus), 346

Overweighting. *See also* Prospect theory

cumulative prospective theory and, 158, 160–161

of low-probability events, 46

of rare events, 136, 160, 161, 163, 164, 165–166, 167–168

Pascal's wager, 348

Payoff-based simplification, 101

Payoffs
  ambiguity aversion and, 67
  Bayesian Nash equilibrium and, 91, 96
  ignoring opponent's, 90, 108
  Nash equilibrium and, 92, 94
  relationship between probabilities
    and, 53–54
Payoff uncertainty, 105, 107. *See also*
  Uncertainty
Payoff- *vs.* risk-dominance equilibrium, 92
Pay-to-play structure, risk–reward
  heuristic and, 60
Pedestrian behavior, collective, 248n1,
  263–282
  ecological rationality of pedestrian
    heuristics, 280–282
  emergence of collective patterns,
    267–268
  emergency evacuations, 277–280
  side preference heuristic, 268–273
  slowing down, pushing, and crowd
    disaster mechanics, 273–275
  uncertainty about behavior of others,
    268–275
  uncertainty about physical
    environments and, 275–277
  uncertainty in times of adversity,
    277–280
  walking together, 263–268
Pedestrian heuristics. *See also* Heuristics
  ecological rationality of, 280–282
  summary of, 270
Peer group, adolescents and, 314,
  322–323
Pensées (Pascal), 348
Performance of decision policies,
  103–104, 105
  competing decision policies, 103–105
  measured by the Indifference
    criterion, 105–107
Personality characteristic
  change and stability in, 338
  risk preference as, 327, 328, 331

Person–environment interactions, life-
  span development of risk preference
  and, 339–340
P-generators, 40, 44, 45
Philosophical Essay on Probabilities
  (Laplace), 349
Philosophical skepticism, uncertainty
  and, 344–347
Phylogenetic change, 6
Physical environment, collective
  pedestrian behavior and uncertainty
  about, 275–277
Physics-based crowd modeling,
  266–267
Planned stopping rule, for terminating
  search, 138–141
Policy makers, as producers of food-
  related uncertainty, 116–118
Port-Royal Logic (Arnauld & Nicole), 348
Power function, 221
Predictability, uncertainty and, 199
Predictions
  accuracy of, 5
  decision making and, 24
  difficulties in making, 4
Preference, **368**
  formation of, 132, 144
  relativity of, 144–145
  subjective valence and formation of,
    144
Preferential choice heuristics, 10,
  12–13
Preferential decisions, tuning to
  environment, 288–291
Present-orientation, harsh
  environments and, 310
Principle of indifference, 32, 61, 69–70,
  103
Principle of insufficient reasoning, 103
Priority heuristic, probability weighting
  and, 170–173
Prior knowledge, strategic uncertainty
  and, 231

Probabilistic expectations,
    environmental uncertainty mapping
    and, 320–321
Probability, **368**
    a priori, 353
    estimates, 353–354
    numerical measurement of, 348
    relationship between payoffs and,
        53–54
    risk–reward, 54–58
    risk–reward heuristic and, 52
    statistical, 353
    uncertainty and emergence of
        classical, 346–352
    uncertainty and modern
        interpretations of, 352–358
    variance in, 40
Probability-based simplification, 101
Probability information, variance in,
    43–46
Probability weighting, 153–174, **369**.
    See also Prospect theory
    in decisions under uncertainty, 161–168
    as framework for measuring response
        to uncertainty, 155–156
    history of, 156–161
    nonlinear, 168–170
    of rare experiences, 162–168
    as reflections of heuristics, 170–174
    regressive, 168–170
    St. Petersburg paradox, 153–156, 174
Probability weighting function,
    157–161
    curvature and elevation of, 159, 161,
        172–174
Probability weights, as reflections of
    heuristics, 170–174
Probable heuristic, 32, 33, 34. *See also*
    Heuristics
    performance under uncertainty, 39,
        41, 42, 43
Prospect theory, 14, 62, 351, **369**
    cumulative prospect theory, 47–49

cumulative prospect theory and
    weighting function, 157–161
differential probability weighting, 138
Proximate environments, limitations
    and benefits of social sampling from,
        86–88
Proximate social spaces, exhaustive
    search in, 75–77
Psychological probability, 157
Puberty, 305, 306, 310
    pubertal hormones and brain
        development, 306, 313
Public information, use of, 241
Public policies
    boosts and, 119–120
    nudges and, 118–119
    to prevent obesity, 127
Pushing
    collective pedestrian behavior and,
        273–275, 277
    emergency evacuations and, 278,
        279–280
Pyrrhonist school, 345

Quantum information processing, 8

Rank-dependent expected utility, 149, 160
Rank-order stability, 330
    life-span differences in risk preferences
        and, 337–338
Rare events. *See also* Prospect theory
    adolescents' underweighting, 322
    uncertainty of, 199
    weighting of, 164–168
    weighting of in decisions from
        experience, 162–164
Rare outcomes
    equiprobable heuristic and, 45
    lexicographic heuristic and, 45
Rational analysis, 286, 288
Rational choice
    axiomatizing, 29–30
    under uncertainty, 355–356

Rationality, **369**
  adaptive toolbox and environment
    and, 6–7
  bounded (*see* Bounded rationality)
  classical probability theory and, 347
  defined as adaptation under
    constraints, 360
  domain-specific, 7
  ecological (*see* Ecological rationality)
  interpretations of uncertainty and
    different theories of, 362
  probability and decision theory and
    understanding of, 344
Realism, imperfect knowledge and
    imperfect, 46–47
Rebel Without a Cause (movie), 305
Recalled instances to judge event
    frequency, 74
Recognition heuristics
  age and use of, 21
  inference and, 11
Recreational domain risk, age and, 335,
    339
Rectangular outcome distribution, 40
  probability distributions combined
    with, 44–45
Regressive probability weighting, 168–170
Regulators, as producers of food-related
    uncertainty, 116–118
Reinforcement learning models, 144
Resources, risk–reward relationship and
    finite, 58–59
Revealed preference approach to risk
    preference, 328
  age-related decline in risk taking and,
    334–335
Reward rate study, 301–302
Rewards
  competing for uncertain, 234–236
  decision making under risk and,
    221–222
  ecological analysis of relationship
    between risk and, 52–59

Risk, **369**
  adolescent decision making and, 319
  certainty, uncertainty, and, 356, 357
  choice heuristics in preference domain
    and, 10
  decision making under, 16–17,
    221–222
  ecological analysis of relationship
    between reward and, 52–59
  rewards and decision making under
    risk, 221–222
  uncertainty *vs.*, 151–152, 353
Risk, Uncertainty, and Profit (Knight),
    353
Risk attitudes
  fourfold pattern of, 135–137
  investors and, 192
Risk aversion, **369**
  evolution of, 289–291
Risk preference, life-span development
    of, 325–340
  convergent validity, 329–330
  ebb and flow of life risks, 325–327
  emerging life-span pattern, 338–340
  risk taking and risk preference,
    327–329
  temporal stability and change in,
    330–338
Risk–reward heuristic, 60. *See also*
    Heuristics
  actual use of, 60–63
  ambiguity aversion and, 66–67
  bets leak information, 68
  implications of, 66–69
  making money with, 68–69
Risk–reward relationship, 11
  competition for limited resources
    creating, 58–59
Risk–reward structures, 51–70
  adaptation to different risk–reward
    environments, 63–66
  of adolescents' environments,
    321–322

ecological analysis of relationship between risk and reward, 52–59

implications of risk–reward heuristic, 66–69

risk–reward heuristic, 51–52, 60

risk–reward hypothesis, 51–52

use of risk–reward heuristic, 60–63

Risk–reward trade-offs, variation in risk preference and, 331

Risk-sensitivity theory, 333

Risk society, 325

Risk taking, 327–329

age-related decline in, 332–337

Risky behavior, adolescents and, 305–307, 315

Risky choice, 177, 187, 329

Rivals-in-the-dark game, 234–236, 240, 243, 294

Roulette

relationship between payoffs and probabilities, 53–54

risk–reward probabilities, 55

Rule-based strategies, 208–209

boosting adaptive strategy selection, 219–220

in decisions under risk, 220–222

ecological rationality of, 209–215

formal description of, 210–211

learning task design and influence on selection of, 219

limitation in adaptive selection of, 215–217

Rules

collective behaviors arising from, 19

food, 111, 126–127

select-crowd, 247, 248, 254–255, 260, 261

Sample size

adaptive exploration and, 138–139, 140–141

description–experience gap and, 137–138

payoffs from in rivals game, 236–237

proportion of choices and, 146, 147

Sampling

frugal, 291–296

learning by, 40–41

with replacement, 39, 135

Sampling error, description–experience gap and, 137

Sampling information, 13–14

Sampling paradigm, 133–135, 145, 233

social norms and, 240

Satisficing, 359. See also Bounded rationality

Schools, architecture of mealtimes in, 125, 127

Search. See also Adaptive exploration

challenges of competition and, 18–19

choice and, 15–16

modeling in decisions from experience, 143–144

significance of, 16–17

social structures and (see Social structures and search)

terminating, 138–143

Search strategies, 7

reducing knowledge gap and, 13–17

reducing uncertainty via, 6

Secondary eating, 122

Seek empty spaces heuristic, 270. See also Heuristics

Select-crowd rule, 247, 248, 254–255, 260, 261

Self-consistency model, 256

Self-dominance, 94, 102

Self-dominance principle, 107, 108

Self-report measures of risk preference, 328–323

age-related decline in risk taking, 333–334

Sequential analysis, 72

Sequential sampling, decisions under uncertainty and, 321–322

Sharpe ratio, 200

Side preference heuristic, 268–273. *See also* Heuristics

Sidestep heuristic, 267, 270. *See also* Heuristics

Simplicity, robustness of, 107–108

Simplification
limits of, 108
payoff-based, 101
probability-based, 101

Simulated experience, 203–205

Skepticism, uncertainty and, 344–347

Skewed distribution
limited search and, 82, 83, 85
probability distributions combined with, 44–45

Slowing down, collective pedestrian behavior and, 273–275

Slow life history strategies, 309–315

Small samples, adaptive exploration and, 138–139

Small worlds
choice strategies and, 30–31
decision making in, 357–358
heuristic performance and, 47, 48

Social-circle heuristic, 75, 76, 77–78, 79–81, 82, 83, 85. *See also* Heuristics

Social circles, 73
exhaustive search in proximate social spaces, 75–77
sampling from, 75–78
sequentially ordered and limited search in, 77–78

Social dilemmas, collective pedestrian behavior and, 268

Social environments
collective pedestrian behavior and, 264–267
performance of simple heuristics in, 93

Social force model, 19, 265, 266

Social hierarchy, adolescents' position in, 314, 322–323

Social learning, side preference heuristic and, 269

Social maximum (SocMax) heuristic, 98, 99. *See also* Heuristics
performance of as measured by the Indifference criterion, 105, 106
simplicity and, 108
simplification of, 101

Social memory, limited search and, 85

Social mind, 17–20
complex collective behaviors from simple rules, 19
search and challenges of competition, 18–19
wisdom of the crowd, 19–20

Social networks, hierarchical structure of, 73

Social norms, competition, 240–241

Social physics, 72

Social pressure, frugal sampling and, 294–296

Social sampling, 72–75
ecological rationality of limited, 82–88
limits of, 86–88
reliance on, 79–81

Social sampling model, 77

Social structures and search, 71–88
ecological rationality of limited social sampling, 82–88
exhaustive search in proximate social spaces, 75–77
instance-based inference, 71–73, 74
reliance on social sampling strategies, 79–81
sequentially ordered and limited search in social circles, 77–78
social sampling strategies, 72–75

Social tools, facing uncertainty and, 6

Spanish stock market index (IBEX 35), 193–194

Spatial clustering of instances, limited search and, 83, 85

Speed
collective pedestrian behavior and, 273–275

emergency evacuations and, 280
  uncertainty and need for, 226–228
Speed–accuracy trade-off, decision
  threshold and, 146
Speed adaptation heuristic, 270, 273.
  See also Heuristics
Spiral of silence, 87
Stability of individual risk taking, 329
Stated preference approach to risk
  preference, 328–329
  self-reported age-related decline in risk
  taking, 333–334
Static decision task, 14–15
Statistical probability, 353
Step or wait heuristic, 270. *See also*
  Heuristics
Stochastic information uncertainty,
  304. *See also* Uncertainty
Stock market, experience of financial
  shock and investment in, 192
Stock price
  investment strategies reactive to,
  202–203
  investment strategies unreactive to,
  201–202
Stop-and-go waves in collective
  pedestrian behavior, 273–274,
  282
Stopping, collective pedestrian behavior
  and, 268, 274
Stopping a search, 15, 77, 78, 81,
  139–143, 147
Stopping rule, 139, 141–142, 144,
  145n2, 147
  optional, 138–141, 142, 145n2
  planned, 138–141
Storm Frederike, 199
St. Petersburg paradox, 153–156, 159,
  174
Strategic complexity, success of
  heuristics and, 12–13
Strategic dominance, heuristics and,
  102–103

Strategic games, testing heuristics in,
  94–105
  classification of heuristics' paths to
  simplification, 100–101
  competing decision policies, 97–100
  measuring competing decision
  policies' performance, 103–105
  properties of the environment,
  96–97
  role of strategic dominance, 102–103
Strategic uncertainty, 5, 89–110,
  225–228, 350–351, **369**. *See also*
  Uncertainty
  action of competitors and, 228–233
  collective pedestrian behavior and,
  264
  combining with environmental
  uncertainty, 233–241
  decision policies' performance as
  measured by Indifference criterion,
  105–107
  defined, 89
  learning to compete and, 241–243
  need to know *vs.* need for speed,
  226–228
  normative solution in strategic games,
  91–92
  overview, 89–91
  reasons people resort to simple
  heuristics in strategic games,
  92–93
  robustness of simplicity, 107–108
  Sterelny's error, 108–109
  testing heuristics in strategic games,
  94–105
Strategy, **369**
Strategy selection. *See also* Adaptive
  strategy selection
  uncertainty and, 47–48
Strategy tournament, 31–35
Sturm und Drang, adolescence and,
  323–324
Subadditivity of decision weights, 162

Subjective expected utility theory, 5, 10, 14, 29–30, 50, **370**
decision making under risk and, 356–357, 359
Subjective knowledge, in classical probability, 348–349, 350
Subjective valence, 144
Subjective weighting of outcomes, 148–149
Sugar consumption, eating rules and, 115, 126
Sure-timing option, 186, 187–188
Survey of Consumer Finances, 191–192
Swarm intelligence, 248n1
Swarms, 272
Systematic bias, heuristics and, 32
Systemic view of uncertainty, 7, 22–24, 361

Take-the-best heuristic, 297–300. *See also* Heuristics
Tallying heuristic, 298–300. *See also* Heuristics
Tallying strategies, 137–138
Tangential evasion heuristic, 270. *See also* Heuristics
Television, turning off during meals, 122, 124, 125
Temporal stability, change in risk preference across life span and, 330–338
Temporal uncertainty, 175, 176, 183–186. *See also* Uncertainty
intertemporal decisions under, 186–188
Testosterone, 306, 313
Theory of Games and Economic Behavior (von Neumann & Morgenstern), 29, 355
Thinking being, existence of, 346
3×3 normal-form game, 95
Timing lottery, 186–187
Timing risk, 186, 187–188

Timing uncertainty, 187. *See also* Uncertainty
Top-*k* approach, 254, 261
Traffic flow, fundamental diagram of, 273–274
Trembling-hand equilibrium, 92
2×2 (ordinal) games, 95
Two-stage prospect theory, 143–144

Ultimatum game, risk–reward probabilities, 56, 57–58
Umwelt, adolescents', 315
Uncertainty, **370**. *See also also* Environmental uncertainty; Strategic uncertainty
adaptive toolbox to address, 4–8
adolescence as time of, 314–315
aleatory, 7, 22–23, 349–350, 360
in Bayesian decision theory, 355–358
in bounded rationality, 358–361
classical probability and, 346–352
coconut uncertainty, 199n1
degree of, 349–350, 351
developmental differences in navigating, 317–320
eating rules and food-related, 112–113 (*see also* Eating rules)
in ecological rationality, 358–361
epistemic, 7, 22–23, 349–350, 360
evolution and, 304
fast *vs.* slow life history strategies and, 309–311
intertemporal choice and (*see* Intertemporal choice)
Keynesian, 354–355
Knightian, 353–354
measurable *vs.* immeasurable, 22
measurement of, 351
modern interpretations of probability and, 352–358
nonlinear probability weighting as rational response to, 168–170
optimism in face of, 361–362

performance of heuristics under, 41–42
philosophical origins of concept of, 343–347
philosophical skepticism and, 344–347
predictability in, 199
preferential choice heuristics and, 10
probability weighting in decisions under, 161–168
properties of, 4
quantitative measurement of, 349
risk, certainty, and, 356, 357
risk *vs.*, 151–152, 353
social sampling and, 74
sources of, 349–350
strategy selection problem and, 47–48
subway uncertainty, 199n1
systemic view of, 7, 22–24
Underweighting, 16. *See also* Prospect theory
of common events, 160, 161
cumulative prospect theory and, 158–161
of rare events, 137, 147, 164, 165–166, 167–168, 322
Unpredictability, fast *vs.* slow life history strategies and, 309–311
U.S. Department of Agriculture nutritional recommendations, 116–117, 118
U-shaped distribution, probability distributions combined with, 44–45
Utility theory, 355n6
Utility uncertainty, 176. *See also* Uncertainty
intertemporal choice and, 183

Validity, cue, 297
Value processing, selection of cognitive tools and, 6
Variance
bias–variance framework, 37–38
defined, 37
in probability information, 43–46

Waiting times, collective pedestrian behavior and, 282
The Wealth of Nations (Smith), 270–271
Weber–Fechner function, 154
Weight, awarded to sampled outcomes, 148–149
Weighting. *See also* Overweighting; Prospect theory; Underweighting
heuristic policies forgoing, 47
performance of decision policies as measured by the Indifference criterion and, 105, 108
of rare events, 322
success of equal, 108
Western diet, 114
"What you see is all there is" principle, 131, 132n1
Whole-crowd rule, 260
Wisdom of crowds, 19–20, 280–281, **370**. *See also* Crowds
Wisdom-of-the-crowd effect, 245–247
Working memory
rule-based strategies and, 216–217
selection of cognitive tools and capacity of, 6
use of heuristics and, 22
World Bank, 118
World Health Organization, 118

Zika virus, threat of, 71